MANAGEMENT OF FINANCIAL SERVICES, MARKETS AND INSTITUTIONS

(For Students of Management Studies)

AF731603

O.P. AGARWAL
M.Com., LL.B. (Hons.), CAIIB, CAIB (London),
Diplomas in Cooperation/Industrial Finance,
(Retired) Chief Manager, Bank of Maharashtra,
General Manager's Office, Mumbai.

First Edition : 2012

HPH

Himalaya Publishing House

MUMBAI • DELHI • NAGPUR • BENGALURU • HYDERABAD •
BHUBANESWAR • CHENNAI • PUNE • INDORE • AHMEDABAD
LUCKNOW • ERNAKULAM • KOLKATA • GUWAHATI

FIRST EDITION : 2012

PUBLISHED BY : Mrs. Meena Pandey
for **HIMALAYA PUBLISHING HOUSE PVT. LTD.**
"Ramdoot", Dr. Bhalerao Marg, Girgaon, **Mumbai-400 004**
☎ 23860170 • 23863863 • Fax: 022-23877178
Email: himpub@vsnl.com
Website: www.himpub.com

BRANCH OFFICES

New Delhi : "Pooja Apartments", 4-B, Murari Lal Street, Ansari Road, Darya Ganj, **New Delhi-110 002**. ☎ 011-23270392 • 23278631 • Fax: 011-23256286

Nagpur : Kundanlal Chandak Industrial Estate, Ghat Road, **Nagpur-440 018** ☎ 0712-2738731 • 3296733 • Telefax: 0712-2721215

Bengaluru : No. 16/1 (Old 12/1), 1st Floor, Next to Hotel Highlands, Madhava Nagar, Race Course Road, **Bangalore-560 001.** ☎ 080-22281541 • 22385461 • Fax: 080-22286611

Hyderabad : No. 3-4-184, Lingampally, Beside Raghavendra Swamy Matham, Kachiguda, **Hyderabad-500 027.** ☎ 040-27560041 • 27550139 • 09848130433

Chennai : No. 85/50, Bazullah Road, T-Nagar, **Chennai-600 017.** ☎ 044-28144004 • 28144005

Pune : No. 527, "Laksha Apartment", 1st Floor, Mehunpura, Shaniwarpeth, Near Prabhat Theatre, **Pune-411 030** ☎ 020-24496323 • 24496333

Lucknow : Jai Baba Bhavan, Near Manas Complex and Dr. Sanjiv Awasthi Clinic, Church Road, Aliganj, **Lucknow-226 024** ☎ 0522-2339329 • 4068914 9305302158 • 9415349385 • 9389593752

Ahmedabad : 114, Shail, 1st Floor, Opp. Madhusudan House, C.G. Road, Navrangpura, **Ahmedabad-380 009.** ☎ 079-26560126 • 09327324149 • 09314679413

Ernakulam : No. 39/104A, Laxmi Apt., Karikkamuri Cross Road, Ernakulam, **Cochin-622 011.** ☎ 0484-2378012 • 2378016. 09344199799

Bhubaneswar : 5, Station Square, Bhubaneshwar, Odisha - 751001. 9861046007.

Indore : Kesardeep Avenue Extension, 73, Narayan Bagh, Flat No. 302, IIIrd Floor, Near Humpty Dumpty School, Narayan Bagh, **Indore (M.P.)** 09301386468

Kolkata : 108/4, Beliaghata Main Road, Near ID Hospital, Opp. SBI Bank, **Kolkata-700 010,** 09910440956

Guwahati : House No. 15, Behind Pragjyotish College, Near Sharma Printing Press, P.O. Bharalumukh, Guwahati - 781 009. (Assam) 09883055590, 09883055536

DTP by : Sudhakar Shetty (HPH Pvt. Ltd., Mumbai)

Printed at : Geetanjali Press Pvt. Ltd. Nagpur.

Fold the Hands and Pray to God Ganesh

for

WISDOM

— Author

PREFACE TO FIRST EDITION

Students studying Financial Services, Markets and Institutions either in MBA (MMS), M.Com. and B.Com. (Hons.), find it very difficult to have all material at one place or enveloped in a book, so they do not waste their time and labour in searching the necessary requirements of their syllabus. I have endeavoured here to assimilate all the topics as are needed for students' compact study.

This book, *"Management of Financial Services, Markets and Institutions"* has been written not only for students of MBA and M.Com.'s but also for the students of B.Com. (Hons.) Degree course, which covers the entire syllabus of Mumbai and Delhi Universities. The material coverage is written in detail, length and width. Though there are only ten chapters in this book but extensively dealt on the topics as non-depository institutions like Life and Non-life Insurance/Mutual Funds/NBFCs and Financial Services like Merchant Banking/Lease Financing/Hire Purchase/Factoring/Securitisation/Venture Capital/Plastic Cards and Treasury Management by Banks.

Adequate coverage and up to date details have been incorporated in order to make the readers/students and professors with full and complete knowledgeable informations. I trust that my this effort would make the students/readers as happy readers.

I wish to acknowledge my indebtedness and gratitude to the persons who helped in completion of this book. First of such name is Sau. Veena Agarwal, M.A. (Eco.); my wife who allowed me to spare lot of time in completion of this book. I also thank my daughter, Professor Sau Shubha Shrikant Govil M.Sc. (Microbiology) who inspired and assisted me in collecting materials. Last but not the least, I acknowledge thanks to my publisher M/s. Himalaya Publishing House Pvt. Ltd., Mumbai, in publishing this book.

Suggestions from readers, as usual, are invited at all times, for further improvements.

I am grateful to the learned professors/students and readers community for their overwhelming support extended to my other 35 books already with them for various courses. This book would serve the purpose of students pursuing advanced career in Financial Services, Markets and Institutions.

O.P. AGARWAL
704/11-D, Springleaf Project,
Lokhandwala Complex,
Kandivali (East), Mumbai-400 101.

SYLLABUS

M.Com., Mumbai University

Paper-II: Financial Service

Overview of Indian Financial Services — Growth, Structure and Types

Lease Financing: Various Aspects of Lease Finance — Evaluation of Lease and Lease Agreement. Funding of Lease — Tax, Regulatory and Accounting Aspects of Lease. Qualitative Factor in Lease.

Merchant Banking: Facets of Merchant Banking — Merchant Banking Functions — Issue Management — Arranging International Finance including Loan Syndication — Global Merchant Banking Developments, Regulation Relating to Merchant Banking.

Treasury Management Services: Concept of Treasury Management — Functions of Treasury Management. Portfolio Management — Investment Management.

Other Financial Services: Hire Purchase — Factoring — Forfaiting. Consumer Finance — Securitisation — Corporate Advisory Services — Innovation in Financial Services.

Regulatory Mechanism: RBI Control and Supervision — Role and Functions of SEBI Self-regulation.

SYLLABUS OF MANAGEMENT STUDIES, UNIVERSITY OF DELHI

MANAGEMENT OF FINANCIAL SERVICES

Objectives

The main objective of this course is to help the students to learn the various financial services and their role in the overall financial system.

Course Contents

Financial System and Markets; Concept, Nature and Scope of Financial Services; Regulatory Framework for Financial Services; Management of Risk in Financial Services; Stock Exchange Operations; Mutual Funds; Merchant Banking Services; Leasing and Hire Purchase; Debt Securitization, Housing Finance; Credit Rating; Credit Cards; Banking and Insurance; Venture Capital, Factoring Forfaiting and Bill Discounting, Insurance; The Tax Environment and Financial Services; Pricing Financial Services.

SYLLABUS OF M.COM. UNIVERSITY OF DELHI

Financial Markets and Institutions

The objective of the course is to provide a sound information and knowledge of broad framework of Financial System and its constituents. The course will provide the students an understanding of the inter-linkages and regulatory framework within which the system operates in India.

Course Outline:

1 Financial Markets, Nature, Function and Efficiency; Financial System and Economic Development, Flow of Funds in Indian Economy; Indian Financial System — an Overview.

2. Construction and Uses of Flow of Fund Matrix. Analysis of Supply and Demand for funds, Sectoral and Inter-sectoral flows.

3. **Financial Markets:** Money market, organisation; instruments, functioning and its regulation, Capital Market, Primary and Secondary Markets and their Organisation. SEBI and its Role as Regulator.

4. **Interest Rate:** Level, Maturity and Structure of Interest Rate. Term Structure of Interest Rates. Financial Repression and Interest Rates. The Yield-curve.

5. **Financial Intermediation:** Depository Institutions: Commercial Banks and Industrial Finances. Bank Credit: Working Capital and Bank Funds; Term Lending, Developing a Credit Information System, Performance of Indian Banking, Regulatory Aspect of Banking.

6. **Non-depository Institutions:** Mutual Funds: Measuring Performance of Mutual Funds, Chit Funds Organisation, Functioning and Regulatory Aspects; UTI and Private Sector Mutual Funds; and Insurance Public and Private Organisation; Life and Non-life Insurance Companies; LIC and GICs Working and Regulatory Framework; Pension Funds; Organisation and Working of Pension Funds.

7. **Financial Instruments:** Equity Shares; New Issue Market and Secondary Market — the Allocative and Operational Efficiency, Preference Shares, Private Placement Channels, Debentures and other Fixed Income Securities, Engineered Financial and Monetary Instruments.

8. **Foreign Capital:** Foreign Capital as a Source of Finance; Place of Foreign Capital in the Overall Framework of Indian Financial System. The Regulatory Framework and NRI Investments.

SYLLABUS OF B.COM. (HONS.) IIIRD YEAR, UNIVERSITY OF DELHI

Optional Group EB: Finance II

Financial Institutions, Services and Insurance

Financial Markets, Institutions and Financial Services

Objectives: To provide the students an overview of financial markets and institutions in India and to familiarize them with important fee and fund-based financial services in India.

Course Contents

Unit-I:

1. **An Introduction to Financial System, its Components** — Financial Markets and Institutions. Financial Intermediation. Flow of Funds Matrix. Financial System and Economic Development. An Overview of Indian Financial System.

Unit-II:

2. **Financial Markets: Money Market** — Functions, Organization and Instruments. Role of Central Bank in Money Market. Indian Money Market — An Overview.

Capital Markets — Functions, Organization and Instruments. Indian Debt Market. Indian Equity Market — Primary and Secondary Markets. Role of Stock Exchanges in India. SEBI and Investor Protection.

Unit-III:

3. **Financial Institutions:** Commercial Banking — Introduction. Its Role in Project Finance and Working Capital Finance. Development Financial Institutions (DFIs) — Overview and Role in Indian Economy. Life and Non-life Insurance Organizations in India. Mutual Funds — Introduction, and Their Role in Capital Market Development. Non-banking Financial Companies (NBFCs).

Unit-IV:

4. **Overview of Financial Services Industry.** Merchant Banking — Pre- and Post-issue Management, Underwriting. Regulatory Framework relating to Merchant Banking in India.

Unit-V:

5. **Leasing and Hire-purchase** — Consumer and Housing Finance, Venture Capital Finance, Factoring Services, Bank Guarantees and Letter of Credit, Credit Rating, Financial Counselling.

Spreadsheet is the recommended software for doing basic calculations in finance and hence can be used for giving students subject-related assignments for their internal assessment purposes.

The weightage of the topics and the software to be used for practical work in this paper will be prescribed in the guidelines by the Committee of Courses and Studies in Commerce (Hons., P.G. and Research) every three years.

CONTENTS

1 Financial Markets

1.0 MEANING

A market as defined by economists is an institution or arrangement that facilitates the purchase and sale of goods and services and other things. A *Financial Market* is an institution or arrangement that facilitates the exchange of financial instruments including deposits and loans, corporate stocks and bonds, government bonds and **more exotic instruments such as options and future contracts.** A market wherein financial instruments such as financial claims/assets and securities are traded is known as a *Financial Market.*

A financial market transactions may take place either at a specific place or location, e.g., *stock exchange* or through other mechanisms such as telephone/fax/e-mail/mobile and other electronic media. In financial markets, the price for the use of investible funds is the interest paid on the funds transacted: wherever, a financial transaction takes place, it is deemed to have taken place in the financial market. Hence, financial markets are pervasive in nature since financial transactions are themselves very pervasive throughout the economic system.

1.1 CLASSIFICATION OR ORGANISATION OF FINANCIAL MARKETS (on the next page)

(A) Unorganised Markets

In these markets there are a number of moneylenders, indigenous bankers, traders, etc., who lend money to the general public. Indigenous bankers also collect deposits from the public. There are also private finance companies, chit funds, etc. whose activities are not controlled by the RBI. We can name such private companies as, *viz.,* Citifinancial/Manappuram Gold Loan/ Muthuswami, etc. Since 1998 the RBI has taken some steps to bring the unorganised sector under the organised fold. They charge exorbitant rates of interest on their advances.

1.1 CLASSIFICATION OR ORGANISATION OF FINANCIAL MARKETS

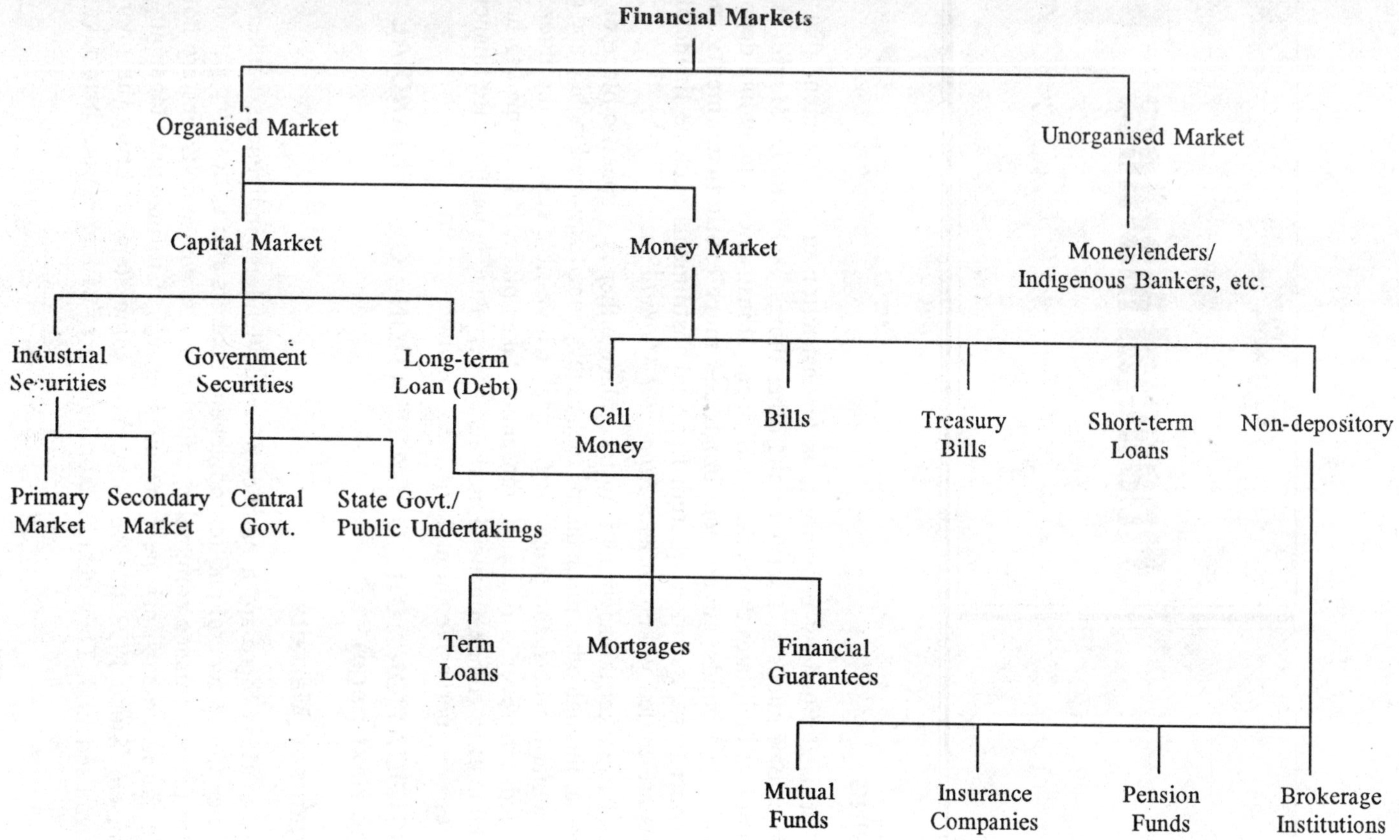

(B) Organised Markets

In the organised markets, there are standardised rules and regulations governing their financial dealings. There is also a high degree of institutionalisation and instrumentalisation. These markets are subject to strict supervision and control by the RBI and/or other regulatory bodies like Companies Act, 1956/SEBI Act, 1992, etc.

These organised markets can be further classified into two categories. They are —

Capital Market, and Money Market

Capital Market: It is the market for financial assets which have a long or indefinite maturity. Where long-term funds are borrowed and lent, mostly for the period of one year and above.

Features of this market are —

(*i*) **Demand for funds:** is made by individuals/institutions/governments and private sectors.

(*ii*) **Instruments:** Funds are raised through issue of shares/debentures/bonds.

(*iii*) **Supply of funds:** Supply of funds is made by households/institutions/banks and financial institutions.

(*iv*) **Price Mechanism:** The price mechanism prevalent in the active capital market ensures optimum allocation of scarce financial resources to the most productive sectors of the economy. Companies that operate efficiently can sell securities at premium (incentives). Conversely, companies with poor performance face problems in selling their securities and may have to issue securities at a discount to raise additional funds (penalties) or offer at higher rate of interest.

Capital market may be further divided into three sub-categories —

- Industrial securities
- Government securities
- Long-term loans.

(I) Industrial Securities Market: It is a market for equity shares/preference shares/debentures and bonds. It is a market where industrial corporates raise their capital or debt by issuing appropriate instruments. This market can further be subdivided into primary market and secondary market.

Primary Market deals with the issue of new issues to the public for the first time. Thus, primary market facilitates capital formation. The corporates can raise capital in the primary market by —

❖ Public Issue/Rights Issue/Private Placement

Sale of shares/securities to the public by new companies is called *Public Issue.* It is also called Initial Public Offering (IPO) and subsequent issue to public is called **Follow-up Public Offering** (FPO). When an existing company wants to raise additional capital/securities are *first offered* to the *existing* shareholders on a pre-emptive basis, it is called *Rights Issue.* Private placement of securities to a small or few group of investors is called private placement and are not sold or traded in the market.

Secondary Market: Secondary market is a market for secondary sale of securities. Market deals with existing claims. It provides ready market for trading in securities. The volume and the magnitude of the transactions taking place in the secondary market influences the activities in the primary market. For instance, if there is an active trading for the scrips of a particular company, it is possible for that company to raise additional capital with ease and convenience because of the goodwill already generated for the scrips. Such securities are traded in all 21 stock exchanges in India out of which Bombay Stock Exchange (BSE) and National Stock Exchange (NSE) are screen-based trading exchanges. Existing financial assets of a company are bought and sold in the secondary market. The existence of a secondary market for a financial asset enhances its *liquidity*. For example, suppose a person purchases a share of TCS in the primary market he/she can easily sell it for cash, after allotment of shares, the shares are actively traded in the secondary market. All that is required to inform a broker or sub-broker about the decision to sell the scrips. The presence of a secondary market helps lower the transaction costs, as finding buyers and sellers becomes an easy job.

In the absence of a secondary market for a stock, one has to personally locate someone willing to purchase the stock. This would not only take *considerable time*, but it may not to be possible to locate the buyer who is willing to pay the highest possible price for the stock. A secondary market is, therefore, that which allows dealing between buyers and sellers of existing shares which ultimately serves to enhance the liquidity of corporate stock.

(II) Government Securities Market: It is also called *Gilt-edged* securities market. It is the market where Government securities are traded. Only long-term securities are traded in this market ranging from seven years to 20 years. Securities issued by the Union Government/State Governments/semi-government undertakings like municipal corporations/port trusts, etc., city improvement trusts/state electricity boards, nationalised and public sector banks and financial institutions are dealt in this market. Government securities are issued in denominations of ₹ 100 and ₹ 1,000. Interest is payable half-yearly August and February every year. At present all of such securities are tax payable. Government securities are in many forms. These are generally:

(*i*) Stock certificates.

(*ii*) Promissory notes.

(*iii*) Bonds (bearer).

Government securities are sold through the Public Debt Office (PDO), Gilt-edged securities are also known as *Dated Government Securities* as the date of maturity is specified in the securities.

(III) Long-term Loans Market: In India, many industrial financing institutions have been created by the government both at the national and regional levels to supply long-term/medium-term loans to corporates, directly as well as indirectly. These development banks dominate the industrial finances. Such institutions are IFCI/EXIM Bank/NSIC/NIDC and 18 State Financial Corporations.

❖ Mortgage Market

The mortgages market refers to those centres which supply mortgage loan mainly to individual customers. A mortgage loan is a loan against the security of immovable property/real estate. The transfer of interest in a specific immovable property to secure a loan is called mortgage. This mortgage may be equitable/simple/registered or legal one. Again it may be first charged or secondly charged. Mortgage is a debt instrument used to finance the purchase of a home or other form of real estate, where the underlying real estate serves as a collateral for the loan, is known as a *mortgage*. There are two types of mortgage instruments, *viz.*, fixed rate and floating rate. Each type of mortgage specifies a term (the length of the mortgage) and a down payment (usually expressed as the fraction of the house value that must be paid upfront as prepaid interest). The fixed rate is not fixed during the term of the loan it changes every three years. The floating rate mortgage also stipulates a margin that reflects the premium.

Financial Guarantees Market: It is a centre where finance is provided against the guarantee of a reputed person in the financial circle. Guarantee acts as a security from the creditor's point of view. In case the borrower fails to repay the loan the liability falls on the shoulders of the guarantor. Hence, the guarantor must be known to both the borrower and the lender and he must have the means to discharge his liability. In India, the market for financial guarantees is well organised. The financial guarantees in India relate to —

- Deferred guarantees for imports and exports.
- Medium- and long-term loans raised abroad.
- Loans advanced by banks and other financial institutions.

❖ Money Market

Money market is a market where short-term instruments that mature in a year or earlier are traded. It facilitates short-term financing (and working capital requirements of industry/trade commerce), liquidity adjustment between individuals/institutions and governments, low capital risk with developed sub-markets like commercial banks/cooperative banks/discount houses and bill markets, etc. This market is divided into four sub-divisions —

- Call money market
- Commercial bills
- Treasury bills
- Short-term loan
- Non-depository markets/institutions

Call Money Market: It is a market for extremely short period loans from one day (overnight) to fourteen days. So, it is highly liquid. The loans are repayable on demand at the option of either the lender or the borrower. In India, call money markets are associated with the presence of stock exchanges and hence they are located in major industrial towns like Mumbai/Chennai/Kolkata/New Delhi/Ahmedabad/Bengaluru/Hyderabad/Jaipur/Ludhiana/Pune/Vadodara, etc. The special features of this market is that the interest rate varies from day-to-day and even from hour-to-hour and centre-to-centre. It is very sensitive to changes in demand and supply of call loans. Let us see the variations in call money rates on two different dates —

(on 3-3-2008)

	Volumes (₹ in Crore)	*Average rate*	*Range*
Call Money Market	10,275.61	7.25	5.60-7.50%
Notice Money Market	1.27	5.72	5.60-5.75%
Term Money Market	380.0	—	10-10.30%
		(on 24-4-2008)	
Call Money Market	12,715.42	5.99	4.75-6.15%
Notice Money Market	4.0	5.90	5.90-5.90%
Term Money Market	175.00	—	8.25-9.05%

(***Source:*** *DNA Newspapers* of 5-3-2008 and 26-4-2008) while inter-bank call rate on 24-4-08 was 5.99%.

Commercial Bills Market: It is a market for Bills of Exchange (BE) arising out of genuine trade transactions. In the case of credit sale, the seller may draw a bill of exchange on the buyer. The buyer accepts such a bill promising to pay at a later date the amount specified in the bill. The seller need not wait until the due date of the bill. Instead he can get the payment by discounting the bill. The Discount and Finance House of India Ltd., was set up in March 1988 to promote secondary market in bills, in terms of recommendations of Vaghul Committee (1987). The DFHIL quotes regular bid and offer rates (two way prices for purchase and sale) for Treasury Bills/ commercial bills for rediscounting. It also provides bid prices in respect of Certificates of Deposits and Commercial Papers. DFHIL takes part in auctions of Government dated securities from April, 1992.

The DFHIL undertakes REPO transactions in Treasury Bills and all dated Government securities.

Treasury Bill Market: It is a market the purchase and sale of Treasury Bills, which have short-term maturity (14 days/28 days/91 days and 364 days). TBs are in the nature of finance bills because they do not arise to any genuine commercial transactions in goods.

There are two types of TBs. They are ordinary Treasury Bills and *Ad hoc* TBs. The ordinary TBs are issued by the Government of India to the public/banks and other institutions for raising resources to meet the short-term financial needs.

Ad hoc TBs on the other hand, are issued in favour of the RBI only. They are used by the RBI as reserves against which the issue department issues currency notes. Besides *Ad hoc* TBs provide an investment avenue to state governments/semi-government departments and foreign central banks for parking their temporary surplus and for earning income. Ad hoc TBs are not marketable, the holders of these TBs can always sell them back to the RBI.

Period of Maturity of TBs

I. At the close of First World War	— 3/6/9 and 12 months
II. From 1935 started TBs of (Tap Bills)	— 91 days till Nov. 1986
III. From 1985	— 182 days till April 1992
IV. From April 1992	— 364 days
V. From May 1997	— 14 days
VI. From Oct. 1997	— 28 days
VII. From 26th May, 1999 (reintroduced)	— 182 days

Short-term Loan Market: It is a market where short-term loans are given corporate customers for meeting their *working capital* requirements. Commercial banks play a significant role in this market. It acts as the nerve centre of all the operations of the central bank of a country. It reflects the changes in short-term parameters such as interest rates/monetary policy/availability of short-term credit, etc. The flow of money and credit in the money market is regulated and controlled by the RBI (in India) through a plethora of qualitative and quantitative measures. This market offers a *low risk capital loss* (money risk) as instruments traded are short-terms in nature, besides offering a low risk of default (credit risk). This is because money market instruments are mostly in the form of the liabilities of the government/central bank and commercial banks.

❖ Non-depository Markets/Institutions

Non-depository comprises of institutions that *do not accept deposits* (cheques collection) to be with drawable by cheques. They carry out various functions in financial markets, ranging from financial intermediation to selling insurance. Such constituents are —

Mutual Funds: Trusts that sell units to investors and invest the proceeds in a variety of financial assets are called *Mutual Funds*. Owners of these units receive pro rata share of the earnings from these assets, minus management and other fees assessed by the fund. A mutual fund is nothing but a form of collective investment. It has emerged as a popular vehicle of creation of wealth due to high return/lower cost and diversified risk. The mutual funds can be broadly classified into many types as per table given below:

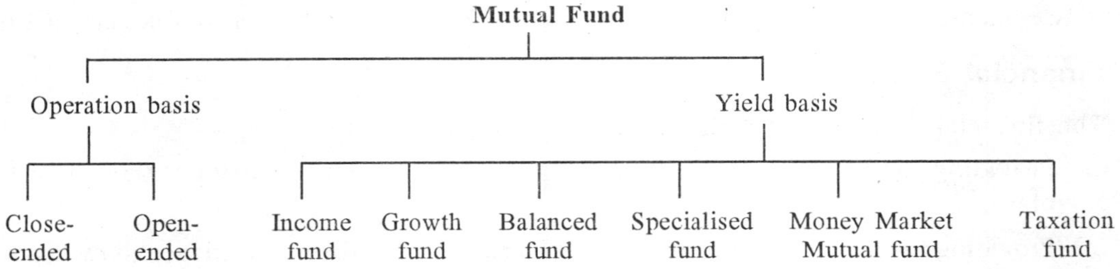

Insurance Companies: Companies that protect individuals against risk are called Life Insurance Companies. They accept regular payments, (monthly/quarterly/half-yearly/yearly or one time only) from individuals in exchange for contractual payments in the event of death of the issued before a maturity of the policy or even on maturity. These companies hold long-term assets like bonds/gilt-edged securities and traded shares. While general insurance companies, which deal in fire/theft/health/medical expenses/total loss of assets, due to accidents, etc.

Pension Funds: Funds that are operated by the private and government employers which provide retirement income to former employees are called pension funds. Money is collected by regular contribution from employees/employers.

These funds hold portfolios consisting mostly of shares and bonds. The return on these assets are paid-out to participating individuals when they reach the retirement age.

Brokerage Companies: Share brokers bring buyers and sellers of shares together for the purchase and sale of financial assets. They function as intermediaries, earning a fee for each transaction. Their main function is to serve as brokers in the secondary debt and equity markets.

1.2 FUNCTIONS

The functions of a financial market can be divided into two categories as below:

Intermediary functions: Intermediary function of financial market include —

(*i*) **Transfer of resources:** The market facilitates the transfer of real economic resources from lenders to ultimate borrowers.

(*ii*) **Enhancing income:** It makes lenders to earn interest/dividends/share in profits on their surplus investment funds, thus contributing to the enhancement of the individual and the natural income.

(*iii*) **Productive use of funds:** It allows for the productive use of the funds borrowed than enhancing the income and the gross national production.

(*iv*) **Capital formation:** Financial markets provide a channel through which new savings flow to aid capital formation of a country.

(*v*) **Price determination:** It allows for the determination of the price of the traded financial asset through the interaction of buyers and sellers. They provide a signal for the allocation of funds in the economy, based on the demand and supply, through the mechanism called *price discovery process.*

(*vi*) **Mechanism for selling:** It provides a mechanism for selling of a financial asset by an investor so as to offer the benefits of market ability and liquidity of such assets.

(*vii*) **Dissemination of information:** The activities of the participants in the financial market result in the generation and the consequent dissemination of information to the various segments of the market, so as to reduce the cost of transaction of financial assets.

❖ Financial Functions

The financial functions of a financial market include the following —

(*a*) Providing the borrowers with funds so as to enable them to carry out their investment plans.

(*b*) Providing the lenders with earning assets so as to enable them to earn wealth by deploying the assets in productive ventures.

(*c*) Providing liquidity in the market so as to facilitate trading of funds.

1.3 FINANCIAL INSTRUMENTS

The instruments that help in borrowing and lending of money are called financial instruments. Such instruments are as below:

- Treasury Bills
- Money at Call Notice
- Commercial Bills/Promissory Notes
- Commercial Papers
- Certificates of Deposits
- Inter-bank participation certificates
- Repo/Reverse repo instruments.
- Collateralised Borrowing and Lending Obligation (CBLO)

Treasury Bills: It is a market instrument for short-term maturity ranging from 14/28/91/182 and 364 days. These are promissory notes or finance bills issued by the government. It is highly liquid because its repayment is guaranteed by the government. These instruments do not make regular interest payments, instead they are sold at *discount*. The advantages of ready market and *zero default* risk makes this instrument very attractive.

Money at Call and Short Notice: The call money market is a market for extremely short period say one day to 14 days. So, it is highly liquid. The loans are repayable on demand at the option of either the lender or the borrower. The special feature of this market is that the interest rate varies from day-to-day. As against this if money is payable on notice then the interest rate is bit higher to call rate.

❖ Commercial Bills, Promissory Notes

These transactions arise out of genuine trade transaction. In the case of credit sale, the seller draws a bill of exchange (or Hundi) on the buyer. The buyer accepts such a bill promising to pay at a date stated in the bill of exchange 30/45/60/90 days or even other agreed days. The seller need not wait for money till due date and gets it discounted with their banker and gets immediate money less discount charges.

Commercial Papers: A form of direct short-term finance issued by large, creditworthy companies is called commercial paper. It contains a promise to pay back a higher specified amount at a designated time. Such papers are issued as bearer and issued at discount on the face value. These papers are unsecured. In India, such CPs can be issued by:

- Any creditworthy company having net asset of ₹ 5 crore or above.
- Minimum size of CP can be ₹ 25 lakh and is in minimum multiples of ₹ 5 lakh.
- Minimum maturity is seven days and less than twelve months.
- Debt-equity ratio be 1.5:1 and current asset ratio of 1.33:1 and shares are tradable in stock exchanges.
- CRISIL credit rating should not be below P-2.
- Minimum investment by investors should not be below ₹ one crore.

❖ Certificates of Deposits (CDs)

This is a short-term certificate of deposit which is issued by banks and financial institutions. These certificates are unsecured negotiable instruments/transferable by endorsement and delivery/ issued at discount on face value of amount/repayable, on maturity date without any days of grace. Its features are:

- Issued in the minimum amount of ₹ 10 lakh and in multiples of ₹ 5 lakh.
- Minimum maturity period is seven days with maximum period of one year.
- Minimum locking period is fifteen days.
- All commercial banks (except RRBs) can issue such certificates.
- This is very attractive to attract additional deposits from public/institutions for investment for short periods. The total ceiling for issue of such CDs by eligible banks (51 banks) is ₹ 20,552 crore.

❖ Inter-bank Participation Certificates

These certificates provide an additional instrument for even out short term liquidity within the perimeter of the banking system, particularly at time when there are imbalances affecting the maturity mix of assets in banking books.

Its features are:

(*i*) Minimum period for certificate is 91 days and maximum period of 180 days.

(*ii*) These certificates are *with risk* and *without risk*. With risks certificates can be issued for 90 days only.

(*iii*) With risk certificates can be issued only for advances under standard assets and the aggregate amount of such participation in any account should not exceed 40% of the outstandings in the account at the time of issue.

(*iv*) Rate of interest on these participants cannot be issued at more than 0.5% on the rate charged by bank to the borrowers.

(*v*) On the assent of both lenders and borrowers the participation can be enhanced by 30 days more.

(*vi*) The distinction between *with* and *without risk* for the borrower-bank is that under *with risk* participation the issuing bank will *reduce* the amount of participation from the *advances* outstanding while the participating bank will show the participation as *part* of its advances, whereas under the *without risk* sharing arrangement. The issuing bank will show the participation as a *borrowing* while the participating bank will show it as advances to banks. In the latter case the participation is treated as part of the *net demand* and *time liabilities* (NDTL) and net bank balances for purposes of SLR.

❖ Repo Instruments

Repo stands for repurchase. Under repo transactions the borrower parts with securities to the lender with an arrangement to repurchase them at the end of the fixed period at a specified price. At the end of the period, the borrower will repurchase the securities at the predetermined price. The interest charged on the original price is the cost of borrowings. This costs of borrowing is called *repo rate* which is little cheaper than pure borrowings. In India, RBI decides the repo rate which is 7.0% w.e.f. 26-7-2011. A transaction is called a *repo* when viewed from the perspective of the seller of the securities. Repo transactions are inducted in the money market to manipulate short term interest rate and manage liquidity levels. Repos are normally conducted for a period of three days. The eligible securities are government promissory notes/Treasury Bills and PSBs bonds. Repo transactions ensure stability is short-term interest rates in the money market. When the RBI wants to inject fresh funds in the market, it conducts *reverse repo* transactions with primary dealers against Government securities. The present reverse repo rate fixed by RBI is 7.0% from 26-07-2011, in Feb. 2008. RBI injected ₹ 33,075 crore through repo. In reverse repo operations averaged at ₹ 18,702 crore in Feb. 18, 2008.

Under a *repo* transactions, a holder of securities, sells them to an investor, with an agreement to *repurchase back* the same securities for a same amount at a predetermined date. Repo rate is the annualised interest rate for the funds lent by the buyer of the securities (lender) to the seller of the securities (borrower). Generally, the repo rate is lower than that offered on unsecured (or clean) inter-bank loan, for the reason that it is a collateralised transaction.

A reverse repo is the *mirror* image of repo. Repo is sometimes called a *ready forward* transaction as it is a means of funding by selling a security held on a spot (ready) basis and repurchasing the same on a forward basis. Banks can borrow funds from RBI by doing a *repo*. This is a reverse repo for RBI and it is known as LAF (Liquidity Adjustment Facility). RBI varies the repo rate frequently. The present repo rate is 8.0% since 26-07-2011.

When the repo rate is *greater* than the coupon, then the repurchase price is adjusted *upward* (with reference to the sale-price) to the extent of the difference between the two. And if the repo rate is *lower* than the coupon, then the repurchase price is adjusted *downward* (with reference to sale price). It should be particularly remembered that, whereas the price at the time of *first leg* is taken from the market, the second leg price is prefixed and may not be market related. As repo is also called a ready forward transaction, i.e., a transaction having a ready leg and a forward leg. Hence, the ready forward transaction is in two legs –

Example: The following example will clarify the repo transaction computation.

Allahabad Bank agrees to borrow approximately ₹ 10 crore from Bank of Baroda for a period of three days at an interest rate of 5%. Other details are as below —

Borrower	—	Allahabad Bank
Lender	—	Bank of Baroda
Tenor	—	Three days
Repo rate	—	5%
Security	—	6.85% GoI 2012
Ready Leg Date	—	15-11-2008
Forward Leg Date	—	18-11-2008
	Ready Leg Computation	
Ready Leg Price of Security	—	₹ 100
Face Value of Security	—	₹ 10 crore
Principal value of Security	—	₹ 10 crore (A)
Last interest date	—	5-10-2008
Accrued interest on Security	—	₹ 7,61,111.11 (B)
Ready Leg Proceeds (A+B)	—	₹ 10,07,61,111.11 (C)
	Forward Leg Computation	
Repo Interest Amount	—	(₹ 10,07,61,111.11) × 0.05 × 3/365
		= ₹ 41,408.68 (D)
Forward Leg Proceeds (C + D)	—	₹ 10,08,02,519.79 (E)
Accrued Interest on Security	—	₹ 8,18,194.44 (F)
Principal Value of Security (E–F)	=	₹ 9,99,84,325.35 (G)
Forward Leg Price of Security		G/10,00,00,000 × 100
	=	₹ 99.9843

❖ Types of Repo

Broadly, there are four types of repos available in the international market. When classified with regard to *maturity* of underlying securities/pricing/term of repo, etc. They comprise buy-sell back/classic/bond borrowing and lending/tripartite repos/hold in custody. Under a buyback (or normal) repo transaction the lender actually takes possession of the collateral. Here a security is sold out right and bought back simultaneously for settlement on a later date. In a buy-sell repo the ownership is passed on to the buyer and hence he retains any *coupon interest* due on the bonds. *Classic repo* is an initial sale of securities with a simultaneously agreement to repurchase them at a later date. In the case of this type of repo the start and end prices of the securities are the same and a separate payment of *interest* is made. Here the *coupon* income accrues to the seller of the security.

Under a *Hold in custody* repo the counterparties enter into an agreement, whereby the securities sold are held in custody by the seller for the buyer until maturity of the repo this eliminating the settlement requirements.

In a bond lending/borrowing transaction, the customer lends bonds for an open-ended or fixed period in return for a fee. The fee charged would depend on the type of underlying instrument/ size and term of the loan and the credit rating of the counterparty.

Under a *tripartite repo* a common custodian/clearing agency arranges for custody/clearing and settlement of repo transactions. The system starts with signing of agreements by all parties and the agreements include Global Master Repurchase and Tripartite Repo Service Agreements. This type of arrangement minimise credit risk and can be utilised when dealing with clients with low credit rating.

❖ Collateralised Borrowings and Lending Obligations (CBLOs)

Other than short-term transactions which are unsecured, this instrument is an artificial loan instrument which is secured by Accepted Bond of Government and public sector undertakings. These CBLOs are issued by Clearing Corporation of India Ltd., which is operational from 15-2-2002 (established in April 2001) to help to localise risks by preventing the contagion from spreading from a failed counterparty to others. CCIL is an ideal platform to the players in the debts/money and forex markets. The sellers of CBLOs are called debtors and their purchasers are called creditors. These instruments are issued in the parts of ₹ 50 lakh for short period of up to 90 days which are guaranteed by CCIL. CBLOs prepares a reference rate for inter-bank transactions.

CBLO rates were 4.51% in Jan. 2008 (in the earlier weeks it was 6.0%). CBLO is a product developed by CCIL for the benefit of the entities who have either been *phased out from inter-bank call money markets* or have been given restricted *participation* in terms of ceiling on call borrowing and lending transactions and who do not have access to the call money market. CBLO is a discounted instrument available in electronic book entry form for the maturity period ranging from *one day* to *ninety days* (can be made available up to one year as per RBI guidelines). CCIL provides the Dealing System through Indian Financial Network (*infinet*) a closed user group to the members of the Negotiated Dealing System (NDS) who maintain current account with RBI and through internet for other entities who do not maintain current account with RBI. Membership of CBLO segment is extended to banks/financial institutions/insurance companies/mutual funds/ primary dealers/NBFCs/non-government Provident Funds/corporates, etc. The members are required to open constituent SGL (CSGL) account with CCIL for depositing securities which are offered as collateral/margin for borrowing and lending of funds.

1.4 ROLE OF CENTRAL BANK IN MONEY MARKETS

The RBI assigns top priority in the introduction of effective money management and the coordination of the money market with a view to bringing indigenous bankers within the fold of its central banking policy. RBI is the central bank of the country. In order to exercise effective monetary management, the RBI has to introduce monetary discipline in the money markets. In this connection, its first and foremost task has been to consolidate commercial banking and extent banking facilities in the country. The apex bank stands committed today in this task. The nationalisation of banks in July 1969, and April 1980, setting up of various committees such as — Sukhmay Chakraborty Committee (1982), Vaghul Committee (1986) setting of Discount and Finance House of India Ltd., (1988) Securities Trading Corporation of India (1994) and the commencement of liberalisation and globalisation process in 1991 gave a further fillip for the integrated and efficient development of Indian money market. The branch expansion programme should be planned so as to meet the needs of various regions.

SELECTIVE DATA ON COMMERCIAL BANKS

Number of branches Population served by a branch Deposits (in ₹ crore) Advances (in ₹ crore) NPA of PSBs (in ₹ crore) 2.7% ratio to (advances)	73,836 *March 2007* (more than 85,000 in June 2011) 16,000 31,92,141 (March 08) 22,72,603 (March 08) 38,602 (March 07)

S.B. of India had opened its 10,000th branch in March 2008 and in June 2011 their number is above 11,000. The total ATMs of SBI were 8,500 (in March 2008) were more 25,000 in 2011. S.B. of India is now fully owned by government with 59% share with them since 2007. As per planning of S.B. of India, merged two of its subsidiaries in S.B. India, and the rest would be absorbed by March 2013. (***Source:*** *DNA News*). The total advances and deposits of S.B. India and its seven subsidiaries as on 31.3.2007 were as:

(₹ in crore)

	Deposits	***Advances***	***Income Total***
S.B. of India	4,35,521	3,37,336	46,990
Associate Banks	1,97,955	1,45,090	19,585
	6,33,476	4,82,426	66,585

(***Source:*** *DNA News*, Mumbai, dt. 26-12-2007).

Foreign branches were opened by S.B. India first in 1982 at California (U.S.) then in 1990 at Mauritius. Nepal State Bank formed as a Joint Venture in 1993. Acquired majority share in Indian Ocean Bank International Bank in Mauritius in 2005.

The organised money market includes various institutions — *viz.*, RBI/SBI and its five subsidiaries/20 PSBs/private sector banks/foreign banks/RRBs 83/non-scheduled commercial banks and other NBFCs comprising LIC/GIC/UTI, etc.

❖ Defects and Shortcomings of Indian Money Market

(1) Lesser control over unorganised money market: The presence of indigenous bankers (moneylenders/chit funds, etc.), in villages and semi-urban areas make the Indian money market highly unorganised. They follow their own rules and practices of finance and banking and are *not subject* to regulations and control of the RBI. But now in 2008, state governments and RBI are thinking to make their registration compulsory with RBI else they would not be allowed to recover their dues from borrowers and/or attach the lands/buildings given as securities.

(2) Absence of integration: This is the serious lacuna afflicting the Indian money market. Several sectors are very loosely connected with each other. Often there used to be hostility among the different sections of the money market. There is hardly any cohesive working relationship between the organised banking system and the unorganised indigenous bankers. Organised and unorganised markets are not properly integrated. This disabilitates the ability of the RBI in exercising effective control and supervision over the operations of the money market.

(3) Inadequate national market: Entry of DFHI and STCI, etc., in the money market, to a great extent, restarted the early growth of the money market. The so-called advancements in computerisation and telecommunications are also very limited and confined mostly to urban and semi-urban areas. It is imperative that a well coordinated and operationally uniform money market has to emerge in the country.

(4) Interest rate disparity: A major defect of the Indian money market has been that the *interest* rate varies from place-to-place, from time-to-time and from segment-to-segment. Wide disparity in money rate exists. This condition makes it difficult for any worthwhile regulatory mechanism to be put in place.

(5) Deficient bill market: Lack of popularity of bill-culture among the traders both at national and international arena, has given rise to a sick and deficient bill market. This has greatly affected the development of the money market. The transactions relating to bill-discounting and purchasing are limited. Besides, they also constitute only a small part of total money market operations in the country. It is a sad-commentary that the different sub-markets in the Indian bill market have not shown much development too. The investment in government securities is largely confined to institutional investors, comprising mainly the RBI/commercial banks/LIC in certain cases, Provident Fund Schemes and other trusts funds. This prevents the RBI from using these instruments effectively for influencing the level of liquidity in the money markets, through *open market operations*. Despite a series of measures initiated by the RBI over a period of time, the plight of Indian bill market largely remain secluded/constrained and underdeveloped.

(6) Seasonal variations: An essential characteristic of Indian money market is the existence of seasonality of the demand for money and short-term funds. This seasonal variation follows the pattern of the seasonal variations in agricultural activities. Accordingly, during the busy season from *October to April,* the demand for money is more, as more funds are needed for financing the post-harvest movement for the marketing of agricultural products, for the financing of seasonal industries such as sugar, etc.

(7) Constricted secondary market: The true development of a financial market depends on the extent of secondary market facilities that are available in the country. As far as the Indian money market is concerned, the secondary market for the money market instruments is mainly restricted to rediscounting of commercial bills and treasury bills. There is reluctance on the part of some of the big borrowers to avail finances against discounting of commercial bills.

❖ Measures for Development

Keeping in mind for a developed money market for a fast growing economy like India and based on a series of recommendations putforth by the committees such as Chakravarty Committee and Vaghul Working Group on money market, the following measures were initiated by the RBI towards developing Indian money market —

(1) Developing infrastructure: RBI took several measures for setting up institutions to help hasten the growth and development in the Indian money market. Accordingly, Discount and Finance House of India Ltd., was established to broaden the money market operations. It acts as a market-maker. Similarly, SEBI was set up to function as an apex regulatory body relating to security market activities. Credit rating agencies like CRISIL/ICRA/FITCH/DELPH were promoted for making possible easy raising of funds from the money market. Treasury Bills were introduced by RBI for various maturities such as 14 days/28 days/91 days and 364 days, to suit the requirements of varied people.

(2) Developing bill culture: The RBI, to develop the bill culture by promoting and encouraging credit transactions, made all our efforts by introducing rediscounting of bills, besides giving Stamp duty Exemption for rediscounting of derivative usance promissory notes arising out of genuine trade bill transactions. For encouraging bill culture banks were advised to ensure that their client traders make a credit purchase for a minimum of 25% and this should be through bills drawn on them.

(3) Innovative sub-markets: Innovative sub-markets like CDs/Call Money Market/Collateral Loan Markets/CPs/Money Market Mutual Funds, etc., were introduced to strengthen the money market.

(4) Credit control measures: Such measures are Cash Reserve Ratio (CRR) 6% from 24-04-2010 and Statutory Liquidity Ratio (SLR) 24% from 18-12-2010 which are efficiently manipulated to tone up and buoy the money market operations especially in the commercial banking sector.

(5) Repo and reverse operations: The reintroduction of repos (ready forward) was aimed at mopping up excess liquidity thus reducing volatility in Call Money Markets/Foreign Exchange Markets/corporate debt and PSU bonds. Reverse repo facility available to primary dealers (banks) in Government securities market at 7.0% from 26-07-2011.

(6) Money market mutual funds (MMMFs): MMMFs are required to invest in Call/Notice Money/CDs/CPs/Commercial Bills/Treasury Bills and dated Government securities having an unexpired maturity up to one year.

(7) Derivative products: Instruments such as options/futures/swaps/forwards/forward rate agreements, etc., are now available for trading by investors. Derivatives have the biggest advantage in them, in that they facilitate hedging and thereby help minimise the credit risks.

1.5 OVERVIEW OF INDIAN MONEY MARKET

The structure of Indian Money Market is as shown below:

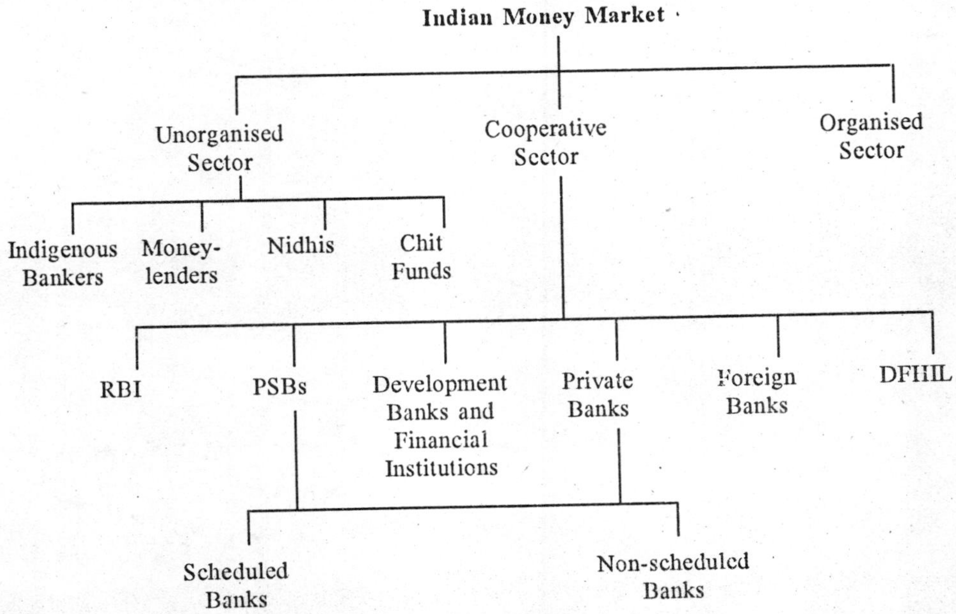

As per the above chart, the Indian money market is highly disintegrated and less developed. There are organised and unorganised sectors and in between these, exists the *cooperative sector*

In the organised sector the RBI/PSBs/private banks/development banks/other financial institutions play a dominant role. RBI is the leader of the Indian money market. Unorganised sector remains outside the purview of RBI even after 64 years of independence which dominates the 60% lending operations to agriculturists and other small borrowers. Such lending is generally without any productive purposes such as — marriage in the family/death or birth in the family/medical expenses meet out/some religious function/financial gap in needs of loans and their delivery by banks/unexpected expenses for agriculture production, etc. They charge interest in advance ranging from 50% to 200%. Though it is an unorganised market but deeply influences the life of the borrowers and they as such become landless labourers (from landlords of lands) Bandhua Mazdoors and/or unemployed and commit suicide due to shock and vicious circle of borrowings. This has largely happened in Andhra Pradesh and Maharashtra States in the last seven years.

◆ ◆ ◆

2 Capital Markets

2.0 WHAT IS CAPITAL MARKET?

It is an organised market mechanism for effective and efficient transfer of money capital or financial resources from the investing class (individuals or institutional savers) to the entrepreneur class (individuals or institutions engaged in industry, business or service) in the private and public sectors of the economy. Capital market is generally understood as the market for long-term funds. The capital market provides long-term debt and equity finance for the government and the corporate sector. By making long-term investments liquid, the capital market mediates between the conflicting maturity preferences of lenders and borrowers. The capital market also facilitates the dispersion of business ownership and the reallocation of financial resources among corporations and industries. Capital market is the market for financial assets that have long or indefinite maturity. It offers an ideal source of external finance.

2.1 FUNCTIONS

The capital market is directly responsible for the following functions:

- *Mobilisation* or concentration of national *savings* for economic development.
- *Mobilisation* and *import of foreign capital* and foreign investment capital plus skill to fill up the deficit in the required financial resources to maintain the expected rate of economic growth.
- *Productive utilisation* of resources, and
- Directing the *flow to funds of high yields* and also strive for balanced and diversified industrialisation.
- Capital market provides a means whereby buyers and sellers can exchange securities at mutually satisfactory prices. This allows a better *liquidity* for the securities that are traded.

- **Indicative function:** A capital market acts as a barometer showing not only the progress of a company, but also of the economy as a whole through share price movements.
- **Conversion of investments:** Capital market provides a means of quickly converting long-term investment into liquid funds, thereby generating confidence among investors and speeding up the process of savings and investment.
- **Transfer function:** Capital market facilitates the transfer of existing assets — tangible and intangible among individual economic units or groups.
- **Merger Function:** It encourages voluntary or coercive takeover mechanism to put the management of inefficient companies into more competent hands.

2.2 ORGANISATIONS

Indian Capital Market consist of the followings:

1. Industrial securities market
2. Gilt-edged market
3. Long-term loans market

(1) *Industrial Securities Market* — As the very name implies, it is a market for industrial securities namely —

- Equity shares
- Preference shares
- Debentures or bonds

and can be divided into two segments.

1. Primary Market.
2. Secondary Market.

Primary Market: It is also known as New Issues Market (NIM) is a market for raising fresh capital in the form of shares and debentures. Corporate enterprises, which are desirous of raising capital funds through the issue of securities, approach the primary market. Issuers exchange financial securities for long-term funds. The primary market allows for the formation of capital in the country and the accelerated industrial and economic development.

The following are the popular ways by which capital funds are raised in the primary market—

- **Public Issue:** Where securities are issued to the members of general public. It takes the form of public issue.
- **Rights Issue:** Where the issue of equity shares of a body corporate is made to the existing shareholders as a pre-emptive right, it takes the form of *Rights Issue*. Under this method, additional securities are offered for subscription to the existing shareholders at a rate which is lesser than the present market rate.
- **Private Placement:** Where the shares of a body corporate are sold to a group of small investors, it takes the form of private placement.

Secondary Market: A market which deals in securities that have been already issued by companies, is known as the secondary market. It is also called the stock exchange or the share market. The importance of the secondary market springs from the fact that it is the base upon which rests the edifice of the primary market. In other words, for the efficient growth of the primary market, a sound secondary market is an essential requirement. This is because the secondary market offers an important facility of transfer of securities. The settlement cycle, under rolling settlements is shortened to 1+2 days. This brings the securities settlement system in India at par with international standards.

(2) Gilt-edged Market: This market is also known as Government securities market, is the market for Government and Semi-government securities where securities are traded. The Government securities are in many forms. These are generally,

(*i*) Stock certificates

(*ii*) Promissory notes

(*iii*) Bearer bonds

Government securities are sold through public debt office. An important feature of the securities traded is that they are stable in value and are much sought after banks for their SLR requirements. Other special features are —

- Guaranteed return
- No speculation in securities
- Banks are investors in large amount.
- Heavy volume of transactions necessitating negotiation of each transaction.

Government securities (Central/State/Semi-government) City Corporations + Port Trusts + Improvement Trusts + State Electricity Boards) public sector enterprises, etc.), offer a good source of raising unexpensive finance for the government treasury and the payment of half-yearly interest, on these securities influences the prices and *yields* in this market. Hence, this market also plays a vital role in monetary management.

(3) Long-term Loans Market: The constituents of the capital market comprise of development banks/mutual funds/lease companies/financial service companies/commercial banks and other specialised institutions, *viz.*, SEBI/SHCIL/CRISIL/ICRA/AMC/OTCEI/NSE/factoring institutions/ venture funds/NSDL, etc., and they play a significant role in this market by supplying long-term loans to corporate customers. Term loans are provided by institutions like SIDBI/IFCI/TDICL/ LIC/UTI, etc., and other State Financial Corporations.

Mortgages market is where the long-term loans are provided on the mortgage of property by institutions like HUDCO/National Housing Bank/Land Development Banks/Public Sector Banks/ Private and Foreign Banks, etc.

Financial Guarantees Market: In India, financial guarantees relate to (in exports) —

- Export of goods on deferred payment terms
- Advance payment guarantee
- Performance guarantee.
- Guarantee for release of retention money.
- Guarantee for raising borrowings overseas.

Such guarantees are provided by institutions like EXIM Bank/ECGC/Commercial Banks, etc.

2.3 CAPITAL MARKET INSTRUMENTS

Financial instruments that are used for raising capital resources in the capital market are known as *capital market instruments*. The various capital market instruments used by corporate entities for raising resources are as follows:

1. Preference shares
2. Equity shares with voting rights
3. Equity shares with differential rights
4. Company fixed deposits
5. Warrants
6. Debentures and bonds

(1) Preference shares: Shares that carry preferential rights in comparison with equity shares are called *preference shares*. The preferential rights are the rights regarding payment of dividends and the distribution of assets of the company in the event of winding up in preference to equity shares.

❖ Kinds of Preference Shares

- **Cumulative preference shares:** They carry the right to cumulative dividends if the company fails to pay the dividend in a particular year. The accumulated arrears of dividends shall be paid, if dividend is declared in subsequent years before any dividend is paid to equity shareholders.
- **Non-cumulative preference shares:** Such shares do not carry the right to receive the arrears of dividend in a particular year, if the company fails to declare dividend in previous year or years. If no dividend is paid in any particular year, it *lapses*.
- **Participating:** These receive their fixed dividends in the normal way, but which then participate further in the distributed profits along with the equity shares after a *certain* fixed percentage has been paid to equity shareholders as well. The holders of such shares may also be entitled to get a share in the surplus assets of the company on its winding up.
- **Non-participating:** These shares are entitled to only a fixed rate of dividend.
- **Convertible:** Holders are given the right of conversion of their shares into *equity shares* at a later date.
- **Non-convertible:** Preference shareholders are not given the right of conversion of shares into equity shares. When the Articles of Association are silent, all preference shares are deemed to be non-convertible unless otherwise provided in the terms of issue.
- **Redeemable:** Section 80 of the Companies Act, 1956, authorises a company limited by shares to issue redeemable preference shares. The paying back of capital is called the redemption. But such redemption should be made for period less than 12 years.
- **Irredeemable:** preference shares has been banned as per Companies Amendment Act 1988 under Section 80A.
- **Cumulative Convertible Preference Shares (CCP):** Introduced in 1985 for the objects for setting up new projects/expansion or diversification of existing projects/capital expenditure

for modernisation and working capital requirements. The entire issue would be convertible into equity shares between the end of three and five years. The rate of dividend payable on CCP would be 10%. The face value of these shares would ordinarily be ₹ 100 each and the holders are entitled to receive arrears of dividend, if any, even after *conversion.*

(2) Equity shares with voting rights

The important features of equity shares are as follows:

(*i*) Equity shares carry voting rights at the general meeting of the company and have the right to control the management of the company.

(*ii*) Equity shares carry the right to share in the profits of the company in the form of distribution of dividend and bonus shares.

(*iii*) In the event of winding up of the company equity share capital is repayable only after repayment of the claims of the creditors and preference share capital.

(*iv*) Other rights available are:

❖ Right of Pre-emption Sec. 81

Right to apply to the court to have any variation of their rights set aside Sec. 107.

(3) Equity shares with differential rights (Sec. 86)

Shares issued with differential rights as to dividend/voting or otherwise in accordance with companies (issue of share capital with differential voting rights) Rules, 2001.

(4) Company's fixed deposits

The term deposit means any deposit of money with and includes any amount borrowed by a company but shall not include such categories of amount as may be prescribed as per Rule 2B of companies (acceptance of Deposits) Rules, 1975. Deposits from employees and ex-employees are also to be regarded as those falling in the category of *public* and the deposits accepted from them would as much attract the provisions of Section 50A.

❖ Features of public deposits are —

(*i*) No company shall accept or renew any deposit which is *repayable* on *demand* or on notice or after a period of less than 12 months or more than 60 months from the date of acceptance or renewal of such deposit.

(*ii*) No company shall invite or accept or renew any deposits in any form on a rate of interest exceeding 12½% p.a. at rests which shall not be shorter than monthly rests.

(*iii*) No company shall accept public deposits more than 25% of its paid-up capital and free reserves. Free reserves does not include balance in share premium account. However, in case of government company the ceiling of such public deposit is fixed at 35% of its paid-up capital and free reserves excluding share premium amount.

(*iv*) Where public deposits have been accepted from public amount not exceeding ₹ 25,000 in a financial year, from each depositor, those are considered as small depositors (Sec. 8AA). If there is any default committed by company in repayment of depositors' interest then company has to intimate to NCLT within 60 days of such default.

(*v*) Every company shall before the 30th day of April of each year *deposit* or *invest* a sum which shall not be less than 15% of the amount of deposits maturing during the financial year next.

- In a current or other deposit account with any scheduled bank, free from any charge or lien.
- In an encumbered securities of the Central Government/State Government.
- In an unencumbered securities of Section 20 of the Indian Trusts Act.
- In unencumbered bonds issued by the Housing Development Finance Corporation Ltd. Mumbai.
- Non-refund of deposits to be cognizable (Section 58AAA — Companies (Amendment) Act, 2000.
- No invitation of public deposits without advertisement in newspaper. But in the case of invitation of any deposit in contravention of the said rules, the minimum amount of fine is at least ₹ 50,000 and the maximum limit is ₹ 10 lakh. Besides every officer of the company who is in default shall be punishable with *imprisonment* for a term extending up to five years and also with fine.

(5) Warrants

It is a document which a public company issues in conformity with the statutory requirements. It is issued under the common seal of the company and states that the holder of the *warrant* is entitled to certain number of shares specified therein. *Its other features are*:

- It is a bearer document and title to the shares can be transferred by mere delivery of share warrant.
- The issue of such warrant can be made only if the company is so authorised by its Articles of Association and permission of the Central Government has been obtained (Section 114).
- Share warrants can be issued only in respect of fully paid shares.
- Dividend coupons are attached to the share warrants providing for the payments of future dividends on the specified shares.
- Share warrants have a life span of three to five years in India, whereas in USA it is five to ten years.
- Warrants are issued/sold to facilitate future financing.
- The exercise price of warrant, i.e., the price at which it can be exchanged for share is usually above the market price of the share so as to encourage existing shareholders to purchase it.
- Share warrants in India are called *sweetners* and are in existence since 1993.
- Share warrants have no floatation costs and when they are exercised, the company receives additional funds at a price *lower* than the current market price, yet higher than those prevailing at the time of issue.

(6) Debentures and bonds

As per Section 29(12) of Companies Act, 1956, debenture includes debenture stock/bonds and other securities of the company whether constituting a charge on the assets of the company or not. Debentures are bonds issued in acknowledgement of any indebtedness. It is an instrument which is drawn under company's seal. Debentures are the instruments that are generally used for raising long-term debt capital.

❖ Features of Debentures:

There are six kinds of debentures:

- **Naked or unsecured,** do not carry any charge on the assets.
- **Secured:** Secured by mortgage of the assets.
- **Redeemable:** Redeemable at the expiry of period.
- **Perpetual:** Issued (or indefinite period or happening of some specified events, i.e., winding up.
- **Bearer:** Payable to bearer and are transferable by delivery.
- **Regd.:** Payable to registered holders whose names are registered in company's books (Section 152).

- No charge is required to be registered when debentures are issued of maturity of *less than* 18 months, but such debentures are to be treated as deposits under Section 58A.
- secured debentures create a charge on the assets of the company. Such a charge may either be fixed or floating.
- Where debentures are given option of conversion into equity shares, after the expiry of certain period of time, such debentures are called *convertible debentures*.
- Earnings on debentures are regular and reasonable for the holders. There is legal obligation for the company to make payment of interest on debentures whether or not any profits are earned by it.
- Preferential claim at the time of winding up of company. Their claims rank prior to the claims of preference and equity shareholders.

❖ Types of Debentures:

There are various *types* of debentures, these are issued by the public linked companies in India, as below —

(*i*) **Participating debentureholders** are entitled to participate in its profits and are unsecured debt securities.

(*ii*) **Convertible debentures:** These debentures are various sub-types, *viz.,*

- **Convertible debentures** with *options* to both parties.
- **Third party convertible debentures** which allow the investor to subscribe to the equity of a third company at a preferential price *vis-a-vis* market price.
- **Convertible redeemable at a premium:** Issued at face value and with a put option entitling investors to sell the bond to the issuer at a premium.

(*iii*) **Debt equity swaps:** Offered from an issuer of debt to swap it for equity. The instrument is quite risky for the investor because the anticipated capital appreciation may not materialise.

(*iv*) **Zero-coupon convertible note:** These are converted into shares and on its conversion the investor *forgoes all accrued and unpaid interest.*

(*v*) **Secured premium notes with detachable warrants:** These are redeemable debentures that are issued along with with a detachable warrant. The warrant entitles the holder to apply and get equity shares allotted, provided the SPN is fully paid. The SPN holder has an option to sell back the SPN to the company at *par value*, after the lock-in period (no interest is payable during the lock-in period).

(*vi*) **NCDs with detachable equity warrants:** These entitle the holder to buy a specific number of shares from the company at a predetermined price within a definite time-frame.

(*vii*) **Zero interest FCDs:** These are zero interest fully convertible debentures on which no interest will be paid by the issuer during the lock-in period. However, there is a notified period after which fully paid FCDs will be automatically and compulsorily converted into shares.

(*viii*) **Secured zero interest PCDs:** These are issued in two parts. Part A is a convertible portion that allows equity shares to be exchanged for debentures at a fixed amount on the date of allotment. Part B is a non-convertible portion to be redeemed at part at the end of a specific period from the date of allotment. This part also carries a detachable and separately tradable warrant.

(*ix*) **Fully convertible debentures with interest:** There are debentures that will not *yield any interest* for an initial short period after which the holder is given an option to apply for equities at a premium. No additional amount needs to be paid for this.

(*x*) **Floating rate bonds (FRBs):** These are the bonds where the yield is linked to a benchmark interest rate as in the case of S.B. India's floating rate bond. Issue was linked to the maximum interest on term deposits that was 10% at that time. Interest rate linked to the *benchmark* ensure that neither the borrower nor the lender suffer from the changes in interest rates.

2.4 INDIAN DEBT MARKET

Importance of debt market: Public sector debt includes debt incurred by all levels of Central Government/State Governments/local bodies and public sector enterprises and public limited companies. The debt market enabled banks and financial institutions to shore up their Tier-II capital (under capital adequacy) by issuing bonds without diluting the equity base.

Public debt is raised by governments to meet the gap between budgeted receipts and payments. Public debt far-reaching consequences upon production and distribution of a country. Public debt is thus the debt of the union or states.

DEBT POSITION INTERNAL DEBTS OF THE GOVERNMENT (AS ON)

(Amt. ₹ in crore)

Debt	*2002-03*	*2003-04*	*2004-05*	*2005-06*	*2006-07*
Internal	1020689	1141706	1275971	1355943	1522031
Market	619105	707965	758995	867368	984645
Others	401584	433741	516976	488575	537386
GDP (as % of)	41.7%	41.4%	40.7%	39.9%	38.9%

Source: Ministry of Finance and RBI.

A market where fixed income securities of various types and features are issued and traded is known as a *debt market.*

In India, conventionally, debentures are debt instruments issued by corporates in private sector, while bonds are issued by institutions in public sector, which distinction really has no meaning in international market. Bonds, though issued by public sector companies, *do not* imply guarantee by the government, unless it is so mentioned specifically in the terms of issue, as also the face value of the bond. In *domestic market*, there are material differences in debentures and bonds. Debentures are governed by relevant provisions of Companies Act, 1956 and are transferable by registration (except when debentures are bearer one). Bonds on the other hand are *negotiable* instruments governed by Contract Act, 1872 and are generally transferable by endorsement.

❖ Advantages to Investors

Steady and constant income: The important advantage of the fixed income securities is that they ensure steady and constant return by way of interest and repayment of principal at the maturity of the instrument. Let us see list of such debts as on 28th April, 2008 —

GOVERNMENT SECURITIES (GS)

8.24% GS 2018
6.65% GS 2009
8.33% GS 2036
5.48% GS 2009
7.38% GS 2015
7.99% GS 2017
8.20% GS 2022
9.39% GS 2011
11.30% GS 2010
11.50% GS 2015

STATE GOVT. SECURITIES

8.45% Andhra GS 2018
8.43% MPGS 2017
8.68% Uttaranchal GS 2018
8.48% J&K GS 2018
8.40% W. Bengal SS. 2017
8.47% Tamil Nadu GS 2017
8.58% J&K GS 2017

SPECIAL SECURITIES

8.30% Fert. Co.GoI 2023
8.40% Oil Mktg. SB 2026
8.01% Oil Mktg. SB 2023
8.03% GoI FCI 2024
7.95% Oil Mktg. SB 2025

- **Safety of funds:** Such securities are issued by eligible entities of standing against the moneys borrowed by them from the investors. This guarantees safety of funds invested in these securities. Moreover, such debt is usually secured against the assets of the company.
- **Risk-free:** Some of the fixed income securities such as Government securities offer a risk-free return on the investor's moneys. The default on such securities in zero or near zero. Besides, there is government guarantee on those instruments.

❖ Advantages to Financial System

The following are the benefits accruing to the Indian financial system on account of the debt market —

1. Reduction in the borrowing costs thus facilitating mobilisation of resources at reasonable costs.
2. Providing greater funding avenues to public and private sector projects thereby reducing pressures on institutional financing.
3. Enhanced resource mobilisation by unlocking illiquid retail investments like gold.
4. Development of heterogeneity of market participants.
5. Assisting the development of a reliable yield centre.

2.4.1 Debt-instruments

(A) **Government Securities** include —

- Zero coupon bonds
- Coupon bearing bonds
- Treasury Bills
- Strips

(B) **Public Sector Bonds** include —

- Government guarantee bonds
- PSU bonds
- Commercial paper

(C) **Private Sector Bonds** include —

- Debentures
- Commercial paper
- Floating rate bonds
- Zero coupon bonds.
- Inter-corporate deposits
- Certificates of deposits

2.4.2 Role of Bond Market

Bond market plays an important role in the economic development of a counting in the following manner —

- Efficient mobilisation and allocation of financial and other resources in the economy.
- Financing the development activities of the government.
- Transmitting signals for the implementation of various monetary and other policies of the central bank of the country.
- Facilitating the efficient management in tune with the overall short-term and long-term objectives of the economic planning.

❖ Various fixed income securities and their uses

There are various fixed income securities based on the kinds of issuer and its purposes fixed income securities are SLR (Statutory and Liquidity Ratio as per RBI Act) and Non-SLR securities are classified for the purposes of banks. Such securities are:

Central Government Securities
State development loans
Other approved securities

While Non-SLR securities are —

Public Sector Undertaking Bonds
Corporate Debentures

2.4.3 Government of India Securities and their Issue System

These securities are issued by RBI as per powers vested with them of offering issues to institutions/public on an ongoing basis as per the notification issued by the Union (Central) Government in that connection. At the beginning of every half of the financial year, *viz.,* April-September and October-March, the government announces an issue calendar for dates. This calendar usually is for all or a major part of the budgeted borrowing programme. The calendar consists of approximate dates of issue, the amount and tenor (given in the range of years, e.g., 5-9 years/10-14 years/20 + years, etc.), of each issue. The security being issued could be security already in *existence* or it could be a new security. In the former case, it is a price based auction in which the investors *bid the price* at which they are *willing to buy* the security. In the latter case investors *bid for the coupon rate* for which they are willing to buy the security. The auction conducted by the RBI is usually a variable price auction (or *French Auction*) wherein applicants submit bids at their desired price. The cut-off price is usually the price at which the entire issue amount is fully bid. At times, as part of signalling RBI may indicate a cut-off (a higher price or a lower coupon) wherein the bids may not result in the issue being fully subscribed. In such cases the issue will partially or fully devolve on RBI. These securities could be later sold by RBI to market based on market movement of *rates*. All successful bidders, i.e., those bidders who have bid at or above the *cut-off prices* have to buy the securities at the prices at which they had bid. Thus, each bidder gets the security at a price which could be different from another bidder. Sometimes, the RBI conducts a *uniform price auction* (or Dutch Auction) In this case the successful bidders are allotted the security at the cut-off price or yield. This implies that every bidder gets the security at a uniform price or yield. In both the above auction methods, the bidders who have bid at a price higher than the cut-off price will get the full quantum of securities bid by them, while those who had bid at the *cut-off price* could get partial allotment of the quantity bid as the allotment is restricted to the notified amount.

The GoI issues are also underwritten, either fully or partially, by the primary dealers. Prior to the auction date each PD quotes amount and underwriting commission for the issue. The RBI determines the amount underwritten and the share of each PD in the underwritten amount. In case the issue is *undersubscribed* the undersubscribed portion devolves on the PDs in the ratio of their share in underwriting the issue. Any short fall over and above this is taken up by the RBI on its own risks. RBI could decide to reject all bids and take the entire amount of issue on its own books or even cancel an announced auction.

The RBI could also came out with an *on-tap* issue. Under this scheme of arrangements after the initial primary placement of a security, the issue remains open to yet further subscriptions. The period for which the issue remains open may be time specific or volume specific. The Central Government dated securities are accounted for in the Subsidiary General Ledger (SGL). This accounting is in the book form and not in the scrip form. The RBI, however, issues scrips to the investor *on request* where the investor is not having or is not permitted to have SGL account with the RBI or on the basis of specific request of the SGL accountholder. For all SGL accountholders all purchases and sales are dealt with in electronic form with delivery against payment (DVP). In August 2007, the average daily trading volumes were ₹ 11,792 crore.

2.4.4 State Development Loans

The quantum of the loans depends upon the estimated requirements to various state governments and notified by the Union Government to the RBI. The RBI while announcing the state loans issue notifies the quantum/the corporate/date of issue/date of redemption/calendar of interest payments, etc. On the issue date through auction mechanism, the successful holders are required to deposit money at the counters of RBI. On the basis of amount received the RBI decides to retain the notified amount and refund the excess received or to retain the entire subscription and allots the accounting of the state loans is in the SGL form.

❖ Other Approved Securities

The Central or State Government undertakings, while offering the issue for subscription would mention in the offer document that the particular security is eligible for SLR purposes and permission on that respect has been obtained from the Central Government. The second feature of this security is that the repayment of interest and principal on these securities are backed by the Central or State Government's guarantee. Generally, these securities *carry higher coupon* than offered for the Central/State Government loans for similar maturity. These securities are issued in demat forms. Examples of these institutions are NABARD/SIDBI/HUDCO, etc. Other issuers of such securities have been State Financial Corporations and State Electricity Boards. In recent times issue of such institutions are restricted to few institutions only.

❖ Non-SLR Securities

These are the securities which are *not eligible* for SLR. A bulk of these securities are issued by PSUs and private sector companies. These securities are medium- or long-term debt instruments issued by PSUs. Most of the PSU bonds are sold on private placement basis to the targeted investors at market determined interest rates. PSUs raise money for their projects or for their expansion programmes through issuance of bonds in an open market. The term or period of bonds is generally between five to ten years with or without options for early redemption. Sometimes the issue may be guaranteed by the Central and State Government to provide further financial strength. Such guarantees are called as *structured obligations.* Financial institutions are also allowed to issue bonds through public issues and private placements to large institutional investors. FIs offer bonds with different features to meet the different needs of investors, e.g., monthly return bonds/quarterly coupon bearing bonds/cumulative interest bonds/step up bonds, etc. Some of these FIs are allowed to issue bonds in the form of *book entry.* Hence, the institutions like EXIM Bank/National Housing Bank issue bonds in physical and in electronic form.

❖ Corporate Debentures

A debenture is a debt security issued by a company which offers to pay interest on the money borrowed for a certain period. In essence, it represents a loan taken by the issuer who pays an agreed rate of interest during the lifetime of the instrument and repays the principal normally, unless otherwise agreed on *maturity*. These are long-term debt instruments issued by private sector companies. These are issued in denominations as low as ₹ 1,000 and have maturities ranging between one and ten years. Long maturity debentures are rarely issued, as investors are not comfortable with such maturities. Debentures enable investors to reap the dual benefits of adequate security and good returns. Unlike other fixed income instruments such as fixed deposits/ debentures can be transferred from one party to another by using transfer form. However, it should be noted that debentures *are not negotiable*. Debentures are normally issued in physical form and also in demat form.

2.5 INDIAN EQUITY MARKET

A Public Litmited Company is managed by the Board of Directors appointed by the equity shareholders. A share is the interest of a shareholder in the company measured by a sum of money. Shares are transferable and therefore described as a movable property. Each share in the company shall be distinguished by its appropriate number. A share certificate is a document stating the person named therein as the registered holder of the shares and amount mentioned thereon. At present, the shares are being issued and traded in paperless or *dematerialised* form. There are two central depositories, *viz.*, National Security Depository Ltd., (NSDL) Central Depository Services (India) Ltd. Voting rights are granted under the Companies Act, 1956 (Sections 87 to 89) wherein each shareholder is eligible for votes proportionate to the number of shares held or the amount of stock owned. The share capital of the company is divided into equity shares. The share capital which authorises the company the maximum limit of issue of shares is called authorised capital/registered or nominal capital of the company.

Issued capital is the nominal value of shares offered for public subscription. In case shares offered for public subscription are not taken up, the portion of capital subscribed is called subscribed capital. This is less than the issued capital. Paid-up capital is the share capital paid-up by share owners which is credited as paid-up on the shares.

2.5.1 Issue of Equity Shares — SEBI Guidelines

The guidelines that have been issued by the SEBI as regards the offer of equity shares may be classified into those relating to regular issue and those relating to rights issue.

❖ Guidelines for regular issue

The issue of shares made by companies are classified into the following A to H categories.

Category 'A' : These are also called Initial Public Offering (IPO). Companies set up by individual promoters/entrepreneurs and that which have not completed 12 month of commercial operations, whose promoters do not have a track record in the sense of presence of profit are designated as new companies.

Category 'B' : These are the first public issues made by *existing companies* with a track record of five years of consistent profitability of seven years with profits during the last two years prior to the issue. Any fresh issue made by such companies constitutes *new issues.*

Category 'C' : These are the first public issues made by the existing private/closely held or other unlisted companies with a three-year track record of consistent profitability (two in case of public sector banks) out of five years with profits during the last two years prior to the issue.

Category 'D' : These are the first public issues made by the existing private/closely held or other listed companies without a three-year track record of consistent profitability.

Category 'E' : These are the first public issues made by existing private/closely held and other interested companies without a three-year track record of consistent profitability, but are promoted by existing companies with a five-year track record of consistent profitability.

Category 'F' : These are the public issues made by an existing listed company.

Category 'G' : These are the issues of shares made by existing private/closely held and other unlisted companies with the three-year track record that seek to offer fresh issue shares as a part of the disinvestments plan.

Category 'H' : These are the issues of shares made by existing private/closely held and other unlisted companies with the three-year record that seek to sell shares as a part of the disinvestments plan without issuing fresh capital.

❖ Pricing of issues

The pattern of selling the issue price is largely dependent on the kind of category to which a company belongs. The following is the position in this regard —

Category 'A' : The first issue can be made at *par.*

Category 'B' : The first issue can be made at premium, the reason to be disclosed in the prospectus.

Category 'C' : The first issue can be made at premium, with the disclosure of justification and NAV in the prospectus.

Category 'D' : The first issue can be made at *par.*

Category 'E' : The first issue can be made at *premium*, with the disclosure of justification and NAV in the prospectus. The companies can submit the draft prospectus to SEBI for vetting by mentioning as price band of 20% of the price fixed by them. The actual price shall be fixed within the band set by them and at the time of filing the prospectus with the RoC.

Category 'F' : Fresh capital can be raised by freely pricing their further issues in consultation with the lead managers to the issue, the NAV and justification for premium being disclosed in the prospectus. The gap between the closure dates of the public and *rights issues* should not exceed 30 days.

Category 'G' : The issue price can be set at a premium in consultation with their lead managers disclosing the justification for the same in the prospectus.

Category 'H' : Issues can only be made at *par.*

2.5.2 Promoters' Contribution

Following guidelines are relevant as regard the promoters' contribution.

❖ **Overall minimum contribution — for categories other than B and G**

The overall minimum contribution by promotors will be 25% and 20% of the total issued equity capital up to ₹ 100 crore and above ₹ 100 crore respectively. In the case of issues of fully convertible debentures (FCDs) or partly convertible debentures (PCDs) the respective (through equity subscription). Contribution by the promoters will be of the order of minimum of 1/3rd of the issue amount over and above the proposed issue of FCDs. Alternatively, the promoters' contribution in the case of FCD/PCD issues may be by way of equity or by way of subscription to *FCDs/PCDs* in such a manner that their minimum contribution is 25% or 20% of the equity, as the case may be, after conversion of FCDs/PCDs.

Group 'B': In respect of Category 'B' companies where shares are issued at a premium, the promoters' contribution subject to a minimum aggregate contribution of 21% of the expanded capital (size of issue including premium) will be determined by a slab rate as follows:

- First ₹ 100 crore = 50%
- Next ₹ 200 crore = 40%
- Next ₹ 300 crore = 30%
- Balance amount = 5%

The slab amount is to be adjusted such that the average does not exceed 21%.

Category 'G': The promoters' contribution must be minimum of 25% of the total issued capital w.e.f. May 1, 2002, the above promoters' quota cannot be applied to the shares in the general/unreserved category. Similarly, beginning from Oct. 1995, the mandatory requirement of minimum promotors' contribution is not applicable to issue of securities by a company, which is a listed company for at least three years and has a three-year track record of dividend payment out of the preceding five years.

The reservation of offer of issue made by a public company is known as *firm allotment.* This is also called preferential allotment. This represents the quantum of shares that are reserved for allotment to various categories of investors. Such reservations and firm allotments together with the promoters' contributions will be permitted to a maximum of 75% of the total issue amount. The maximum limit of firm allotment to various categories of investors —

- Indian and Multilateral Development finance institutions (QIBS) 15%
- Indian mutual funds 20%
- FII including NRIs and OCBs 15%
- Permanent regular employees (including working directors) of the issuing company 10%
- Lead merchant bankers 5%
- Other institutional investors 2.5%
- Small individual investors 12.5%
- Promoters' contribution 20%

2.6 INDIAN CAPITAL MARKET — MAJOR ISSUES

Indian capital market has over a period of time undergone rapid structural transformation during the last 60 years. With the vast and varied market reforms unleashed since 1992, primary market has emerged as a major source of funding for the corporate entities both in the public and private sectors and the secondary market has modernised itself through advanced technology and transparent trading practices. There are problems relating to investor protection/consolidation/ integration with other market segments/product innovation and technology, etc., which often came in the way of its efficient functioning. The major issues confronting the Indian capital market are as below:

Investors' protection: Investors constitute the pillars of the capital market. It is imperative that adequate protection is provided to them. This is of paramount importance. However, investors have been facing serious problems in view of the continuing market disturbances arising out of unscrupulous practices followed by many companies and market intermediaries. Some of the popular problems that are being faced by investors are as follows:

(1) Vanishing companies: No. of companies raised funds after taking advantage of market buoyancy under the impact of bulls like Harshad Mehta during 1991-92 who flourished with large funds, the origin and magnitude not being known at that time. Such companies left out of the market and vanished. Such vanishing companies still haunts investors and has affected their psyche very much.

(2) Lack of commitment: The incredibly lack of commitment shown by financial institutions and underwriters regarding the avoidance of project appraisal during the past issue period in relation to mega issues.

(3) Malaises: Like share price rigging and insider trading continue to afflict the Indian capital market, affecting the investors adversely.

(4) Lack of necessary professional expertise and integrity on the part of merchant bankers and other market intermediaries. In many cases merchant bankers act hand-in-gloves with companies to attract the gullible investors.

(5) Multiplicity of investor complaints—

The following is the position of investor grievances:

Year	*Cumulative Grievances Received*	*Redressed*	*Cumulative redressed rate %*
1999-00	2532969	2416218	95.39
2000-01	2629882	2501801	95.13
2001-02	2711482	2572129	94.86
2005-06	2880580	2723060	94.53

This shows that there is an increase in investors' complaints, which need more attention and strict penalty on corporates.

❖ Derivative Instruments

A derivative is a financial contract whose value depends on the values of one or more underlying assets or *indices* of asset value. Derivative instruments are forwards/futures/swaps and options, whose primary purpose is not to borrow and lend funds, but rather to transfer risks associated with fluctuations in asset/liability values. Derivatives have four broad uses — hedging/ speculation/investing and arbitrage. Derivative instruments help in deepening the capital markets by providing for risk hedging and guarded speculation.

In India, it is quite imperative that there is a need to provide sound capital foundation for the derivative market. However, the derivative trading is not a panacea for all that ails the Indian stock market if the experience of 2007 of some of the corporates and banks abroad (Citibank and ICICI Bank in India having major funds from abroad) suffered in foreign exchange hedging in millions and trillions US dollars.

❖ Integration of Capital Market

In order that the capital thrives well, it is important that it gets itself integrated with other segments of the financial system. Such an integration would lead to reduction of speculative movements of funds that may occur due to arbitrage that market segment offers. This in turn ensures efficient intermediation and optimal resource allocation. The borderlines between different market segments are fast getting obliterated in view of the rapid and varied development taking place in the realm of capital market. With banks being allowed greater flexibility so far as their *investment* activities are concerned, the traditional wall between banks and securities market is getting eliminated. Moreover, as banks are increasingly providing *long term loans* they enter capital market to raise resources through equity capital and subordinated debts. Banks have also been permitted to diversify into capital market activities by setting up of mutual funds.

❖ Rebound in Indian Capital Market

Although Indian capital market suffered bruises in the last part of the nineties owing to the manipulative trade practices of unscrupulous brokers and other participants, it has been witnessing fine times in the current past (2006/2007) thanks to many favourable conditions contributing to it. Some of the factors that are responsible for this phenomenon areas follows:

- Strong macroeconomic aggregates.
- Active participation of retail investors with reviewed vigour.
- Active FII buying especially futures market
- Active Indian institutional investors and mutual funds.
- Favourable sovereign rating by leading credit rating agencies like S&P Moody.
- Strong foreign exchange reserve position (US $ 314 billion as on 23-5-2008).
- Strong fundamentals of basic and other industrial segments such as steel/cement and FMCGs, etc.
- Favourable monsoons fuelling adequate demand for goods and services in the economy.
- Favourable and stable political and economic conditions.
- Forecasts of better prospects in future GDP growth estimates of 8% in the 12th Five-Year Plan.

2.7 PRIMARY AND SECONDARY MARKETS

SEBI has issued number of guidelines for primary market, those can be considered as under. Primary market also known as New Issues Market (NIM) is a market for *raising fresh capital* in the form of shares and debentures. Corporate enterprises which are desirous of raising capital funds through the issue of securities, approach the primary market issuers exchange financial securities for long-term funds. The primary market allows for the formation of capital in the country and the accelerated industrial and economic development. The main function of NIM is to facilitate the transfer of resources from savers to entrepreneurs to establish new enterprises through a complex of financial institutions. New issues are classified in various ways —

- Issues by new companies (IPO)
- Issues by old companies (FPO)
- Rights Issue
- Placement of shares

Since the major activity of the primary market is the mobilisation of funds from savings and heir channelisation into investment. The principal instruments are equity shares/preference shares/debentures and bonds.

The investors in the primary issue would be only buying in the primary market but *cannot sell* there. In the primary market, the brokers act as underwriters/managers/registrars and even merchant bankers to the issues. The securities issued by the companies and government are listed on the stock markets after they are flouted and issued to the public.

❖ Problems of Primary Markets

(1) Primary market does not mobilise adequate savings from the public as less than 10% financial savings of the household sector are mobilised for investment in shares/debentures. A large portion of the capital requirements of companies is placed on the market privately or with banks/financial institutions.

(2) Duping by Companies: There is ample scope for attracting investors by giving *misleading* informations. The issuing companies are often tempted to present a rosy picture about the prospective projects. They make exaggerated claims about prospects as well as over-subscription. The merchant banks responsibility is not played by them with the result that small investors are duped by the companies.

(3) Cost of Floatation: Cost of floatation has also been found to be abnormally high particularly for new and small sized companies.

(4) Lack of Post-issue Seriousness: There is absence of seriousness among majority of investors to check the performance of the company after the issue. Once the issue is subscribed their duty is over.

(5) Delay in Allotment Process: There is inordinate delay in receiving allotment letters (in demat accounts). All allotments have to be made within 30 days of the closure of the public issue which is time-consuming. (Now in 2008 SEBI desired to reduce it to seven days). If shares are not allotted, the investor suffers loss of interest (as happened in the case Reliance Power in 2007 when investors had to lose interest on about ₹ 1,00,000 crore. All these factors tend to affect the small investors who hesitate to approach a primary market for investing their funds (SEBI is now considering to *mark* the lien the amount of application money in bank accounts rather than issue of cheque/drafts at present). These hardships are more in rural/semi-urban areas and do great injustice to them *vis-a-vis* in metro-centres.

(6) Hefty Premium on Shares: Many new issues have become flops in raising subscriptions if their premiums are unreasonably high. It is now obvious that the experience of free-pricing will survive the criticism of the public. The problems of timing and bunching of new issues will also lead to investor problems in the form of scramble for limited resources and inadequate appraisal of the projects.

❖ Revival of Primary Market: Suggestions

(1) Revival of investor confidence: The first and foremost task before the authorities concerned is to allow for the restoration of confidence of investors, which remained largely, sagged. Most corporates enjoy little creditability with investors. This is one of the reasons for poor demand for scrips trading. The low creditability could be attributed to unhealthy companies entering the market without much difficulty. It calls for making the listing requirements stringent in phases so that the number of listed companies on the exchanges is pruned and only companies meeting the requirements are allowed to stay. Such a measure would send the right signals to investors. Moreover, the stock exchanges should be made accountable to defaults and violations committed by issuers.

(2) Investor protection: An efficient institutional arrangement shall be put in place for protection of small investors who are often at the mercy of brokers and who have no means of recovering the monetary losses suffered on account of default by market intermediaries. Such an arrangement would boast the investor-confidence and would substantially reduce the time loss in arbitration.

(3) Corporate governance: Corporates should be induced to move towards better corporate governance accounting to the code of conduct put in place by Confideration of Indian Industries (CII). Seps such as stricter enforcement of continuing disclosures by corporates/standardization of accounting norms in line with GAAP, consolidation of accounts are some measures which are bound to have profound effect on ensuring better compliance on transparency of information.

(4) Safety net: A mechanism of safety net/exit option can be offered on new issues to retail investors whereby the merchant banker or the issuer would buy the stock at the issue price if the price of a share falls below a certain level within a certain specified time. This would go a long way infusing the much needed confidence in the investors. Besides, the practice would also induce the market to move to a more realistic pricing.

(5) Greater participation: Greater participation by banks and insurance companies could activate the market. Although banks are permitted to invest up to 5% of their incremental deposits in the stock markets, there has not been much enthusiasm shown by banks and financial institutions. An overhauling of their internal rules/procedures is also called for so as to enable these institutions to enter the market. A part of their allowable limits could be earmarked for the primary market.

(6) Premium issues for domestic investor: GDR issues made by highly rated blue-chip companies are supposed to be prestigious in nature. Issuers could be persuaded to offer a part of this equity issue in the domestic market. This could be tried with the public sector equity that is being offered for divestment.

(7) Norms for issues: Norms for primary market issues could be made stricter. The criterion of dividend payment could be done away with. Instead a certain minimum net worth could be prescribed, as a *precondition* for corporates to make IPO. It is important that the size of the issue should be calculated on the GAAP format or a format to be designed in consultation with the Institute of Chartered Accountants of India. If a corporate does not satisfy the above criteria, it can be allowed to access the market on the existing condition of getting the project appraised and funded by commercial banks or financial institutions. The quality of information furnished by the corporates would be substantially better if the Auditors/Chartered Accountants are made accountable to the information certified by them.

(8) Action by SEBI: Intermediaries responsible for due diligence/disclosures/allotment, etc., must be made strictly *accountable* for *default* by client issuers. SEBI should be adequately empowered to take corrective/punitive action against defaulters. At present the monetary penalties for various violations are very *meagre* and these could be increased. The possibility of empowering SEBI under the Act to blacklist individuals could be examined. Simultaneously efforts should be made to institutionalise self-regulation among different class of market intermediaries.

(9) Infrastructure Investment: Investment in infrastructure issues may be made a part of *priority sector lending* (40% of total advances for banks and financial institutions) requirement for agencies like LIC/GIC, Commercial Banks and also for foreign banks, which are required to do priority sector lending.

(10) High Costs in Public Issues: The high cost of equity issue prevalent in India as compared to other developed markets must be reduced. It is this high cost of issue that derives the corporates to *resort to private placements* as well as turn to GDR market. The following steps need to be taken to *reduce the costs*:

- Popularising the book building practice (a method of marketing the shares of a company whereby the quantum and the price of the securities to be issued is decided on the basis of *bids* received from the prospective shareholders by the lead-merchant bankers.
- No mandating of installation of collection centres.
- Making it compulsory for the issuers to make the offer through the depository.
- Placing advertisement for the application form in the newspapers which would dispense with several crore of forms being printed.

(11) Innovative Instruments: Efforts must be made to encourage the Indian corporate enterprises to come out with the issue of innovative financial instruments. Some of these instruments can be —

- **Puttable Equity:** Where the investor has the option of selling the shares back to the company at a pre-specified price.
- **Equity Commitment Notes:** Where these notes are converted into equity shares at the then prevailing price which gives the advantage to the investor if the share *prices fall* at the time of conversion.

(12) Regulatory Need for Private Placement of Shares: Although private placements constitute one of the means of raising resources quickly and inexpensively, there is an imperative need for ensuring that public issues are not made under the name of private placements. This is also because private placements are *not subject* to any regulatory compulsions. Steps shall be taken to mandate the private placements to be traded in OTCEI and shall be brought under the larger supervisory-net of SEBI.

2.7.1 Secondary Markets

Investors in the primary issues or new issues would be only, *buying* in the primary market but cannot *sell* there. Investors or institutions and buyers and sellers would deal in the *secondary market* through the intermediaries or *brokers*. In the secondary market, investors can both buy and sell existing securities/invest and disinvest or rechannel funds from one company into another or one type of security into another. The secondary market is thus an important adjunct of the primary market. The market where existing securities are *traded* is referred to as the *secondary market* or *stock market*. The stock (secondary) market occupies a pivotal position in the financial system. It performs several economic functions and renders invaluable services to the investors/ companies and to the economy as a whole —

(1) Liquidity and marketability of securities: Stock market (or stock exchanges) provide liquidity to securities since securities can be converted into cash at any time according to the direction of the investor by selling them at the listed prices by providing continuous marketability to the investors in respect of securities they hold or intend to hold. Thus, they create a *ready outlet* for dealing in securities.

(2) Safety of funds: Stock markets ensure safety of funds invested because they have to function under rules/regulations and bye-laws overtrading/illegitimate speculations, etc., are prevented through carefully designed set of rules.

(3) Supply of Long-term funds: The securities traded in the secondary market are negotiable and easy transferable (due to demat facility) with minimum of charges (share transaction tax plus brokerage, etc.), and no short-term gaining transferred after one year. So, though there is substitution of investor but the company is assured of long-term availability of funds.

(4) Flow of capital to profitable ventures: The profitability and popularity of companies are reflected in stock prices. Normally, the prices quoted indicate the relative profitability and performance of companies.

(5) Motivation for improved performance: The performance of a company is reflected on the prices quoted in the stock market. These prices are more visible in the eyes of the public. This public exposure makes a company conscious of its status in the market and it acts as a motivation to improve its performance further.

(6) Reflections of business cycle: The changing business conditions in the economy are immediately reflected on the stock exchanges. Boom/depressions/inflation can be identified through the dealings on the stock exchanges (such as on 23-05-2008) the revised inflation rate March 2008, ending increased from 6.68 to 8.02% and it reflected in the present 10th May, 2008 which was 7.82% to 9% actually as against RBI permitted level of 5%). The result was that market fell by 238 points on 23-5-2008.

(7) Marketing of new issues: When the new issues are listed, there are readily accepted (normally) to the public, since listing presupposes their evaluation by concerned stock exchange regulatories.

(8) Diversification of securities: Stock market enables the investors to diversify their risks by a wider portfolio of investment. It should be noted that diversification should be restricted to less than 10 shares/securities so that observation becomes easy for the investors.

(9) Collection of daily margin from brokers: Stock exchanges to collect 100% daily margins on the notional loss of a broker for every scrip to restrict gross traded value to 33.33 times the brokers base. Minimum capital and to impose quarterly margins on the basis of concentration ratios in view of the falling percentage of deliveries.

(10) Share lending scheme: For short selling the sellers can borrow securities through an intermediary before making such sales. The approved intermediary should have minimum net worth of ₹ 50 crore.

2.7.2 Developments in Secondary Market

(a) Regulations for brokers: Brokers are expected to maintain minimum capital of ₹ 5 lakh, and

(b) Change in the management structure: As per SEBI requirements the 50% of directors of the stock exchange are required to be *non-brokers*, so there is professional change.

(c) Prohibition of insider trading: There is ban on insider trading and hence an insider is prevented from dealing in securities of any listed company on the basis of any unpublished price sensitive information available to them because of their position in the company. Thee is penalty for insider trading but imprisonment is also being considered recently (in May 2008) by SEBI. The present penalty up to ₹ 5 lakh can be imposed on an insider who indulges in dealing/ communicating or counselling on matters.

(d) Transparency is accounting practices: All attempts are taken to achieve *transparency* is trading and accounting procedures. Brokers are desired to show their prices/brokerage/security transaction tax and service charges separately in the contract notes and their accounts.

(e) Strict supervision of stock market: Strict rules have been framed with regard to recognition/ derecognition of stock exchanges membership/management/maintenance of accounts, etc. For example, Mangalore stock exchange was suspended in April 2007 due to non-operation. While Saurashtra stock exchange recognition was cancelled in July 2007.

(f) Prevention of price rigging: Greater powers have been given to SEBI to curb price rigging. In fact, the SEBI exercised its powers 'its' power by issuing show cause notices to the various promoters/brokers and clients involved in price rigging. It is an ongoing process and every year number of notices are issued even their tradings are suspended to protect the interest of genuine investors.

(g) Encouragement of market-making: Market-makers offer two-way quotations, i.e., buy as well as sell quotes for particular scrip, is known as market-making. Each quote mention the value or the quantity of scrip for which the quote is valid. The three types of market-making in OTCEI are —

Compulsory market-making: This is to be undertaken by the sponsor of scrip for a period of 18 months from the date of commencement of public trading in the specific scrip.

Additional market-making: It is undertaken by a dealer/member appointed by the sponsor for a period of at least three months from the date of commencement of public trading or commencement of market-making, whichever is applicable. Additional market-maker and compulsory market-maker hold between themselves up to 5% of the public offer.

Voluntary market-making: Any counter other than compulsory and additional market-makers in scrip can do voluntary market-making. Voluntary market-makers offer two-way quotes for the same scrip, but if they do not have adequate saleable stock of at least one market lot or any other quantity specified by OTCEI, then they may abstain from offering sale quote for the time-being.

Graded system of market-making: The Dave Committee recommended the graded system of market-making. According to the system, the market-making inventory between the compulsory market-maker and additional market-maker has row been graded. The inventory is 5% for companies with market capitalisation of less than ₹ 5 crore, 2% for capitalisation between ₹ 5 crore and ₹ 10 crore and 1% for market capitalisation of above ₹ 10 crore.

(h) Discouragement of price manipulation: SEBI takes all steps to present price manipulations in all stock exchanges. It has instructed all stock exchanges to keep special margins in addition to the normal ones on the scrips which are subject to wide price fluctuations. The SEBI itself insists upon a special margin of 25% or more (in addition to regular margin) on purchases of scrips which are subject to *sharp rise in prices.* This margin money is returned by the stock exchange concerned for a period of one to three months.

(i) Protection of investors' interest: SEBI has issued specific guidelines to deal with bad deliveries. For instance, in the case of bad deliveries, on account of *fake or stolen* shares, the responsibility is on the introducing broker and the exchange should file a case and take action against that broker immediately. Similarly, selling brokers are bound to rectify or replace defective share transfer deeds if they are returned under objection after book closure.

(j) Free pricing of securities: SEBI permits companies to issue shares below the face value of ₹ 10 to tap the market at a low price. Now the minimum value of shares can be not less than rupee one. SEBI is now started thinking of having uniform share price of rupee one instead of present various prices of shares (*DNA* Mumbai, April 2008) starting from rupees 1/2/3/5/7/ 10/100.

(k) Buyback of shares: Section 77A of the Companies Act provides for a company to purchase its own shares or other specified securities. As per Section 77B, a company may purchase its own shares or other specified securities out of —

- its free reserves, or
- the securities premium account, or
- he proceeds of any shares or other specified securities.
- buyback one or less than 25% of total paid-up capital and free reserves of the company.
- the ratio of the debt owed by the company is not more than twice the capital and its free reserves after such buyback.
- all the shares or other specified securities for buyback are fully paid-up.
- restricting the further issue of the same securities within six months (from amendment 2001) after the buyback.

(l) Trading in derivatives: Derivatives are financial investments that derive their value from the underlying financial assets. Index futures and options are traded. The scope of derivatives has widened and includes derivatives transactions covering a broad range of underlying assets such as interest rates/exchange rates/commodities/equities and other indices. There are different categories of derivatives, *viz.*:

- Forward contracts.
- Swaps
- Futures contracts.
- Forward rate agreements (FRAs).

(m) International listing of shares in USA: The first Indian software company, Infosys of Bangalore was listed on the NASDAQ exchange. Infosys issued American Depository Receipts (ADRs) at $ 34 each to *rake* in $70.38 million. One ADR is equivalent to half a share. It means that two ADRs represent the face value of an underlying share. There are Global Depository

Receipts (GDRs) which are issued in the global market to which India is a participant. The following figures tells us as to how many ADRs/GDRs were issued by Indian companies abroad yearly since 1992-93 to 2004-05.

Years	*Amt. in $ million*
1992-93	240
1993-94	1520
1994-95	2082
1995-96	683
1996-97	1366
1997-98	645
1998-99	270
1999-00	768
2000-01	831
2001-02	477
2002-03	600
2003-04	459
2004-05	613

Source: Treasury Management ICFAI University, September 2006, Issue.

2.8 ROLE OF STOCK EXCHANGES IN INDIA

Stock exchanges contribute in a huge measure to the growth and expansion of national business and to the ultimate benefit and well-being of the national economy and its people. They provide an ideal conduct through which enormous amounts of capital flows through the interconnected network of financing organisations to all the corporate enterprises in the country. Thus, stock exchanges ensure liquidity and transferability of financial assets that are dealt with. The efficient functioning of the *stock exchange* is responsible for creating a conducive climate for an active and growing primary market for new issues. Moreover, an active and a healthy secondary market in existing securities leads to a better psychology of expectations, considerably broadening the investment enquiries and thereby, rendering the task of raising resources by entrepreneurs easier.

❖ Barometers of Economy

Stock exchanges have come to occupy an important place in the economy of any country. Stock exchanges are very sensitive to the political and economic changes. They are appropriately called the *barometers* of the *state of economy* or the *mart of the world or business of business* and so on. The growth in the number and size of companies has increased the significance and the role of stock exchanges. Stock exchanges play an important role in the capital formation of an economy paving the way for the industrial and *economic development* of the country. It induces the public to save and invest in the *corporate sector* that is profitable to them. Companies depend upon stock exchanges for *raising finance*. Stock exchanges render many important services to the investors and the corporations alike.

Following are some of the functions/services/features and role by a stock exchange.

(1) Ideal meeting place for sellers and buyers: Stock exchange provides an ideal and convenient meeting place and a common platform for sellers and buyers or securities. It is the nerve centre when open *offers* and *bids* are made under free competition.

(2) Mobilisation of savings: It mobilises public savings and promote investment through capital formation and also channelise for productive purposes. Stock market provides an ample opportunity to all the investors (both individuals and institutions) to invest their surplus funds into various financial instruments and thus directs its flow towards *deficit units*. In case of prosperous and growing industries, the stock prices show a rising rend and more flow of funds, will take place and *vice versa*.

(3) Safety to investors: One of the fundamental functions of a stock exchange is to provide adequate safety to the genuine investors from fraud and manipulations caused due to activities of speculators/members/brokers, etc. For this purpose adequate and strict rules/regulations/bye-laws have been provided under the Securities Contract (Regulation) Act, 1956. The Securities and Exchange Board of India (SEBI) also regulates the working of stock exchanges with a view to provide safety to investors by periodically issuing guidelines on matters connected with securities trading.

(4) Marketing of new issues: As and when the new issues are listed they are readily accepted by the investor public, since listing pre-supposes their evaluation by concerned stock exchange. It also helps in the distribution of new issues.

(5) Ready market: Stock exchange provides a continuous/ready/open and broad based market for securities. This way maximum liquidity/marketability and price uniformity for securities is ensured. It is possible for the investors to sell their securities at the best quoted price and thus, convert their investments into cash, almost immediately and without much effort. The advantage of ready market encourages investment of funds in industrial enterprises besides enhancing the value of the investment as a *collateral* security for obtaining loans.

(6) Liquidity: Stock exchange provide liquidity to securities since securities can be converted into cash to anytime according to the discretion of the investors by selling them at the market price of the day. In fact, liquidity is related with depth/breadth and resiliency of the market. *Depth relates* to buy and sell orders around the price at which a share is transacted. *Breadth* refers to the adequate volume of orders and response of orders to price changes in a scrip is called *resiliency*.

(7) Speculative trading: An efficient functioning of stock market motivates investors to serve more and financial performance speculation also plays a dominant role in mobilisation of savings in an economy. For instance, healthy speculation on the stock exchanges based on scientific analysis and expert opinion, not only estimates fair price of the stock but also provides *adequate liquidity*. In fact, speculation adds life and agility to the working of a stock exchange by activating price movements, by expecting either rise or fall in prices.

(8) Sound price setting: The prices usually reflect (expect where there is more volatility in prices) the real worth of securities. Many factors such as limitless and free competition in open market, enlightened scientific trading based on accurate knowledge of present as well as future prospects of demand and supply, free flow of information, etc., contribute for the better price which benefits the investors ultimately.

(9) Dissemination of market data: Stock exchanges serve as information hub of trade and industry of an economy. They disseminate information about share prices, volume of trade — industry-wise, scrip-wise, etc. In addition, information is also provided on the financial aspects of the companies whose shares are traded widely in the stock market. The signals of impending financial or business booms or *distress* are first indicated in *advance* by stock exchanges very promptly.

(10) Perfect market conditions: Perfect market conditions prevail in the stock exchanges. On account of these reasons, the transaction and the carrying cost are the least. The activities are much standardised. They are well regulated by institutions of government. They facilitate a free and limitless competition among the dealers and the brokers of securities.

(11) Seasoning of securities: Stock market players such as, underwriters/dealers/brokers and speculators temporarily hold securities issues by new companies. This is called *seasoning of securities*. The securities are released then gradually at a time when the market is prepared to absorb the new issue.

(12) Flow of capital to profitable areas: The stock exchange mechanism enables judicious use of national savings by allowing the flow of savings into the profitable and desirable areas of investment. Funds tend to be attracted towards securities of profitable companies and this facilitates the flow of capital into profitable channels.

(13) Platform for public debt: By serving as an organised market for Government securities, stock exchanges allow for raising huge resources of finance required by the government for financing its development activities. Stock exchanges act as a platform for mopping up public debt to execute the schemes of planned projects. It works as over the counter market, consisting of dealers and brokers in Government securities Banks/LIC/Provident Fund/Pension Funds/Institutions are the chief buyers of Government securities.

(14) Clearing house of business informations: The business information supplied by corporate enterprises is allowed to be exchanged between investors and the issuers by the stock exchange. The informations provided by corporates by way of financial statements/annual reports and other reports, etc., helps ensure maximum publicity of corporate operations and working.

(15) True and fair value mechanism: The stock exchange provides liquidity and price continuity only to *listed* securities. Securities that the listed and allowed to be traded on a particular stock exchange are called *listed* securities. It is possible that a securities may be listed at more than one stock exchange for the purpose of trading. A stock exchange assists in determining the stock prices near to their *true* and *fair* market worth and prevent from violent and erratic fluctuations in such prices.

(16) Investor education: An important function of a stock exchange is to widen the share ownership base especially in developing countries. Stock exchanges play a significant role in educating the mass through various communication media by providing information relating to principles and advantages of investing in shares/debentures/bonds and other avenues. They also educate the people in selecting the securities and designing their own portfolio. Educating the public at large about the investment management has been popular in developed countries too. For example, the stock exchange like New York Stock Exchange/London Stock Exchange/Melbourne Stock Exchange/Sydney Stock Exchange/Toronto Stock Exchange, etc., have initiated various methods like *own your share* and other similar, to educate the masses and for widening the share ownership base.

(17) Company management regulations: The requirements of listing on a stock exchange (and more particularly with NSE or BSE) makes it possible for the stock exchange to run in on the corporate enterprises. Listing thus allows for the quoting and trading of securities of corporate enterprises on the floor of a stock exchange. Stock exchanges, thus exercise wholesome influence on the management and working of companies in public interest.

2.9 SEBI AND INVESTOR PROTECTION

(1) Restriction on takeover bids: Purchases or acquisition of shares beyond 5% to be notified to the stock exchange. Acquisition beyond 10% puts an obligation on the transferor and the transferee and intermediary to notify the stock exchange and the public and offer to the other shareholders of the company to buy at their price or the highest market price during the preceding six months.

(2) Restriction on insider trading: The investors have to guard themselves regarding the price and their investment.

(3) Complaint to SEBI: Complain to the grievance cell of the concerned stock exchange and to SEBI.

(4) Selecting the broker: Investors should deal with only SEBI registered broker after due diligence. Details of list of brokers can be procured from the members' list published by the exchange and also from the website of the exchange.

(5) Formal agreement: An investor is expected to enter into a formal agreement with the broker before transacting business. For this purpose, the investors advised to scrupulously adhere to the following procedure:

(*a*) *Registration:* Fill in a client registration form with broker/sub-broker.

(*b*) *Agreement:* Enter into broker/sub-broker client agreement. This agreement is mandatory for all investors for registering as a client of a BSE trading member. The agreement is to be executed on a valid stamp paper of the requisite value.

(6) Transacting business: The investor should keep in mind before transacting business.

(*a*) *Specifying exchange:* Specify to the broker/sub-broker, exchange through which investor's trade is to be executed and maintain separate account per exchange.

(*b*) *Contract note:* Obtain a valid contract note/confirmation memo within 24 hours of the execution of trade. Contract note is a confirmation of trade done on a particular day, for and on behalf of a client in a format prescribed by the exchange. Contract notes are made in duplicate and the member and the client keep one copy each. The client is expected to sign on the duplicate copy of the contract note for having received the original.

Contract Note: Form A — Issued where member is acting as *brokers* and *agents.*

Contract Note: Form B — Issued by members dealing with constituents as *principals.*

Confirmation Memo: Form C — Issued by registered sub-brokers acting for clients/constituents as sub-brokers.

The contract note/confirmation memo should contain details like:

SEBI Reg. No. of member/sub-broker

Order number

Trade number
Trade time
Quantity
Price
Brokerage
Settlement number
and details of other levies/taxes.

(7) Brokerage: As stipulated by SEBI the maximum brokerage that can be charged is 2.5% of the trade value. This maximum brokerage is inclusive of brokerage charged by sub-broker. (1.5% maximum) of trade value). Any additional charges that the member can charge are service tax @ 5% of the brokerage and any penalties arising on behalf of the investor.

(8) Ensuring settlement: For smooth settlement it is required.

(*a*) Delivery of securities/payment of money to the broker is to be ensured immediately upon getting the contract note for sale/purchase, before the prescribed pay in day. The member should pay the money or deliver the securities to the investor with 48 hours of the payout.

(*b*) Open demat account.

(*c*) Depository participant to be given delivery *out* instructions to transfer the shares from the beneficiary account to the pool account of broker through whom shares and securities have been *sold*. For receiving shares in the demat account, give the *DP delivery in* instructions to accept shares in beneficiary account from the pool account of broker through whom the shares have been purchased.

(9) Investors' grievances solving: BSE (Bombay Stock Exchange) has established a full-fledged investors' services cell (ISC) to redress investors' grievances against listed companies/members.

Grievances against listed companies: ISC forwards the complaints to the respective company and directs them to solve the matter within 15 days. In spite of the above efforts, if the company fails to resolve the complaints and the total number of pending complaints against the company exceeds 25 and are pending for more than 45 days, after issue of show cause notice for seven days, the scrip of the company is suspended from trading till grievances are resolved. ISC also transfers such scrip to 'Z' category for non-resolution of investors complaints.

❖ Grievances Against Members:

The nature of complaints received by the exchange can be broadly classified into the following categories —

(*a*) Non-receipt of delivery of shares/non-removal of objection/non-receipt of sales proceeds of shares/non-receipt of dividend/non-receipt of rights/bonus shares.

(*b*) Dispute regarding rate difference.

(*c*) Disputes relating to non-settlement of accounts.

(*d*) Miscellaneous complaints.

(10) Investors' protection fund: BSE is the first exchange to have set up the *stock exchange customers's protection fund* in the interest of the customers of the definite members of the exchange. This fund is registered with the Charity Commissioner, Government of Maharashtra as a Charitable Fund. BSE is the only exchange in India, which offers the highest compensation of ₹ 10 lakh in respect of the approved claims of any investor against the defaulter members of the exchange. The members at present contribute ₹ 1.50 per ₹ 10 lakh of turnover. The BSE contribute 2.5% of the listing fees collected by it. Also the entire earned by the exchange on 1% security deposit kept with it by the companies making public/rights issues is credited to the fund.

(11) Trade guarantee fund: In order to introduce a system of guarantee settlement of trades and ensuring that market equilibrium is maintained in case of payment default by the members, the trade guarantee fund is constituted and it has come into force from 12th May, 1997 with the following objectives –

(*a*) *Guarantee settlement:* To guarantee settlement of bonafide transactions of members of the BSE which form part of the stock exchange settlement system, so as to ensure timely completion of settlements of contracts and thereby protect the interest of investors and the members of exchange.

(*b*) *Create confidence in secondary market:* To inculcate confidence in the minds of secondary market participants generally and global investors, particularly to attract larger number of domestic and international players in the capital market.

(*c*) *To protect investors:* To protect the interest of investors and to promote the development of and regulation of the secondary market.

(12) Ombudsman regulations, 2003: The purpose is to redress the grievance of the investors in securities and for matters connected therewith or incidental thereto — the various Acts of the stipendiary Ombudsman are —

(*a*) Stipendiary ombudsman means any person appointed for a specific matter and for which he/she may be paid such expenses/honorarium or sitting fees as may be determined by the bond from time-to-time.

(*b*) The ombudsman has the powers of —

- Receiving complaints specified in regulation 13 against any intermediary or a listed company or both.
- To consider such complaints and facilitate resolution thereof by amicable settlement.
- To approve a friendly or amicable settlement of the dispute between the parties.
- to adjudicate such complaints in the event of failure of settlement thereof by friendly or amicable settlement.

Procedure: Any investor who has a grievance against a listed company or an intermediary, may himself or through his/her authorised representative or any investors association recognised by the board, shall make a complaint against a listed company or an intermediary to the ombudsman within whose jurisdiction the registered or corporate office of such listed company or intermediary is located. This complaint should be made within six months from the date of receipt of communication of rejection of his complaint by the company.

◆ ◆ ◆

3 Life and Non-life Insurance, Mutual Funds and NBFCs

3.1 DEFINITION

The term financial system is a set of interrelated activities/services working together to achieve some predetermined purpose or goal. It includes different markets/institutions/instruments/ services and mechanisms which influence the generation of savings/investment/capital formation and growth. According to Robinson, the primary function of the system is "To provide a link between savings and investment for the creation of new wealth and to permit portfolio adjustment in the composition of the existing wealth." Hence the primary function of the financial system is the mobilisation of savings. Their distribution for individual investment and stimulating capital formation to accelerate the process of economic growth. It can be shown asunder —

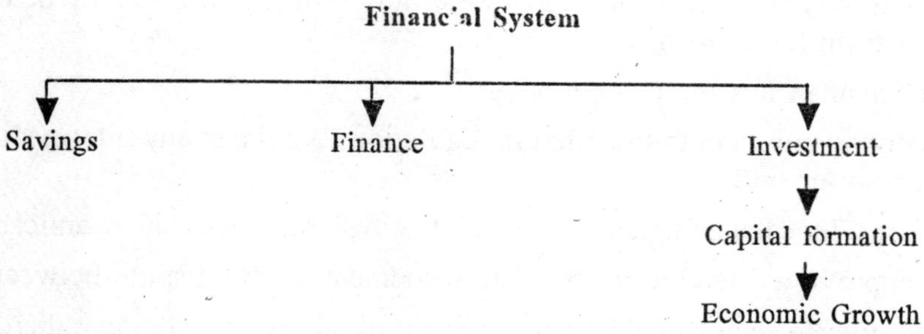

The process of savings/finance and investment involves financial institutions/markets/instruments/ intermediaries and services. Thus, financial management is an integral part of the financial system.

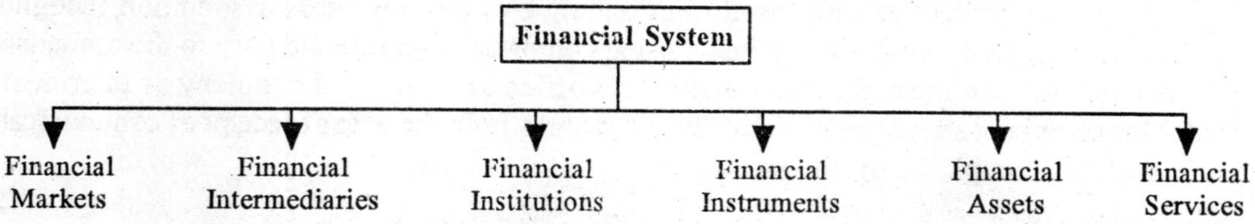

The financial system consists of many institutions/instruments and markets. Financial instruments range from moneylenders to banks pension funds/insurance companies/brokerage houses/investment trusts and stock exchanges. Financial instruments range from the common currency/cheques/ mortgages/debentures/bonds and share to the *more exotic* — futures and swaps of high finance.

The understanding of the financial system requires an understanding of the following important concepts:

(1) Financial assets: The basic product of any financial system is the financial asset. A financial asset is one which is used for *production* or consumption or for further *creation of* assets. For example, Aditya buys equity shares of TCS Ltd., and these shares are financial assets since they *earn income* in future. The distinction between financial assets and physical assets should be understood here. Unlike financial assets, physical assets are not useful for further production of goods or for *earning income.* For example, Rajesh purchases lands and building or gold and jewellery. These are physical assets since they cannot be used for further production. Many physical assets are useful for consumption only. It is interesting to note that the objective of investment decides the nature of the asset. For instance, if a building is bought for residential purposes, it becomes a physical asset. If the same is bought for hiring, it becomes a financial asset.

Financial assets can be classified differently under different circumstances. Such asset classification is marketable and Non-marketable.

Marketable assets — Marketable assets are those which can be easily transferred from one person to another without much hindrance such as equity shares of listed companies/government bonds/debentures of public companies.

Non-marketable assets: But when the assets cannot be transferred easily, they come under this category such as bank deposits/provident funds/pension funds/NSCs/Kisan Vikas Patra/Life Insurance policies/public deposits of companies, etc.

The other kind of classification is —

Debt asset: Debt asset is issued by a variety of organisations for the purpose of raising their debt capital. Debt capital entails a fixed repayment schedule with regard to interest and principal. There are different ways of raising debt capital such as debentures/term loans and working capital finance, etc.

Share asset: Shares are issued by business corporates for the purpose of raising their fixed or permanent capital. There are three types of shares *viz.:* equity with voting rights/equity with differential rights/preference shares.

Equity shareholders are the real owners of the business and they enjoy the fruits of ownership and at the same time they bear the risks as well. While preference shareholders get a fixed rate of dividend and at the same time they retain some characteristics of equity shares. Preference shares can no longer be issued for more than 20 years period (Section 80 Companies Act).

(2) Financial intermediaries: The term financial intermediary includes all kinds of organisations which intermediate and facilitate financial transactions of both individuals and corporate customers. Thus, it refers to all kinds of financial institutions and *investing institutions* which facilitate financial transactions in financial markets. Such intermediaries may be in the organised sector and also in unorganised sector as shown in the following chart:

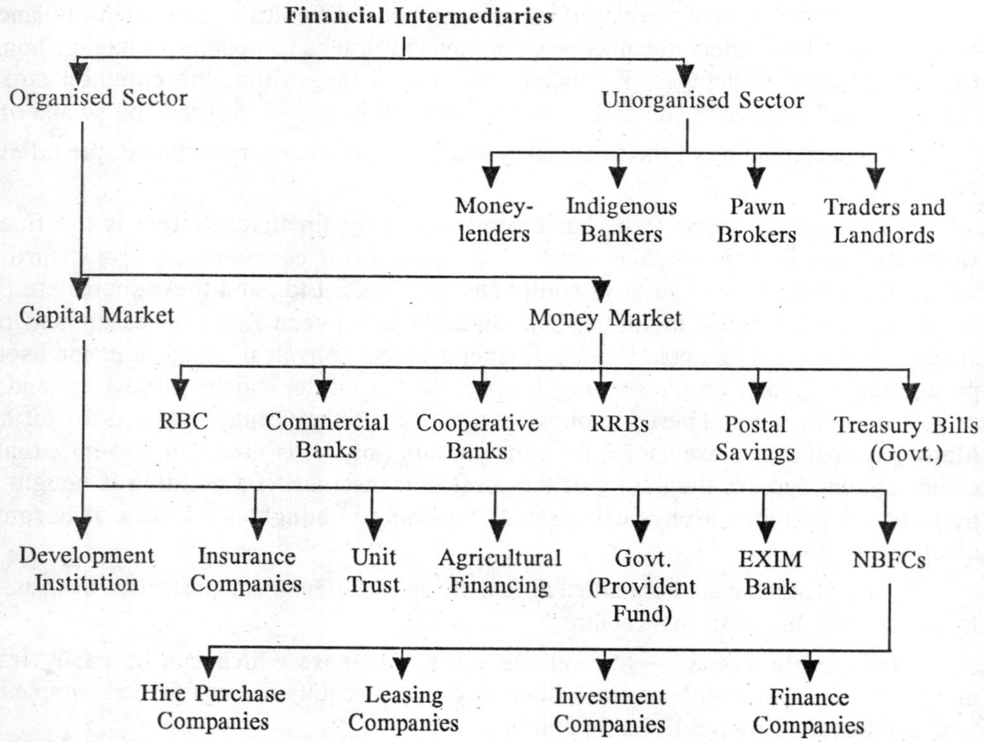

❖ Organised Sector

In the organised sector, there are standardised rules and regulations governing their financial dealings. There is also a high degree of institutionalisation and instrumentalisation. These markets are subject to strict supervision and control by the RBI or other regulatory bodies. This sector is sub-divided into capital market and money market. The capital market and money markets have their own different intermediaries such as

❖ Capital Market Intermediaries

These intermediaries mainly provide long-term funds to individuals and corporate customers. They consist of term lending institutions like financial corporations and investing institutions like LIC/GIC/Unit Trust of India/EXIM Bank/NBFCs.

❖ Money Market Intermediaries

Money market intermediaries supply only short-term funds (less than a year) to individuals and corporate customers. They consist of commercial banks/cooperative banks/RRBs/Treasury Bills, etc.

(3) Financial Markets

Generally speaking, there is no specific place or location to indicate a financial market. Wherever a financial transaction takes place, it is deemed to have taken place in the financial market. Hence, financial markets are pervasive in nature since financial transactions are themselves very pervasive throughout the economic system. For instance issue of equity shares/granting of loan by term lending institutions/bank deposits/sale of debentures/shares and so on. However, financial markets can be referred to as those centres and arrangements which facilitate buying and selling of financial assets/claims and service. Sometimes, we do find the existence of a specific place or location for a financial market as in the case of stock exchange.

(4) Financial Rates of Return

As per the need of time, most households prefer to invest on assets like land/buildings (flats)/gold/silver, etc., where transactions/investments are done for longer period and for which daily trading is not required. But when stock-market is rising, investment in financial assets like equity shares in capital market, fetches *higher return* than *investments on gold*. The return on Government securities an bonds are comparatively less than one corporate securities due to lower risk involved therein. The government and RBI determined the interest rates on Government securities. Thus, the interest rates on Government bonds/securities are administered and controlled. The peculiar feature of the interest rate structure is that the interest rates do not reflect the *free market forces*. Most of these rates are fixed on an *ad hoc* basis depending upon the credit and monetary policy of the government. Generally, the interest rate policy of the government is designed to achieve the following:

- To enable the government to borrow comparatively *cheaply*.
- To ensure stability in the macroeconomic system.
- To support certain sectors through preferential lending rates.
- To mobilise substantial savings in the economy.

The interest rate structure for bank deposits and bank credits is (freely decided by banks) but to some extent influenced by the RBI. Normally, interest is a reward for risk undertaken through investment and at the same time it is a return for abstaining from consumption. The interest rate structure should allocate scarce capital between alternative uses. Unfortunately, in India, the administered interest rate policy of the government fails to perform the role of allocating scarce resources between alternative uses. Now with the passage of time interest rate on company deposits/364 days Treasury Bills/coupon rates on government loans revised upward, etc., have attempted to adopt a realistic interest rate policy so as to give positive return in real terms adjusted for inflation (on 10th May, 2011 the inflation was 9.11% subject to more than 1% revised inflation, i.e., about 10%) the proper functioning of any financial system requires a good interest rate structure.

(5) Financial Instruments

Financial instruments refer to those documents which represent financial claims on assets and can also be called financial securities. Such securities are of two categories —

(a) Money Market Instruments

These are most liquid, short-term debt obligations that are traded in the money market. Such instruments are —

Commercial Paper: A typical debt instrument sold by one company to another company for the period less than a year.

Certificates of Deposits: These are debt instruments sold by banks and other depository institutions up to 91 days.

Treasury Bills: These are short-term debt instruments for 14/28/91/182/364 days used by government to obtain funds.

Repos/Reverse Repos: An agreement in which borrower sells and agrees to buyback a financial instrument, a government bond/note or Treasury Bills, is called Repo agreement and is used by banks (RBI).

(b) Capital Market Instruments

Equity shares are issued to mobilise capital required for taking up new investment projects or for modernisation and expansion of projects.

Corporate Bonds: It is a debt instrument issued by a corporate entity that contains a promise that the firm will make specified interest payment, and a principal amount or the face value on the maturity of the instrument.

3.2 FINANCIAL SYSTEM AND ECONOMIC DEVELOPMENT

❖ Introduction

Some developing countries have taken advantage of the favourable world environment. Most countries in Asia did well; in several the gross national product (GNP) grew at an estimated annual rate of 10 per cent. Some countries, however, continued to suffer from misdirected domestic policies, excessive indebtedness, and the economic shock of the 1990s. The growth rate of many African nations remained near zero. The heavily indebted economies also continued to stagnate. The governments of creditor countries agreed at the Toronto Summit in 1991 to grant debt relief to the poorest and most heavily indebted countries, such as the countries of Sub-Saharan Africa, and early in 1989, took the first official steps to sanction debt relief for the middle-income countries. But despite a rise in the disbursement of funds to the highly indebted countries in 1997, net transfers to these countries continued to be negative.

Future growth in the developing countries will depend in part on the policies of high-income countries. By ensuring the success of the Uruguay Round of trade negotiations, the high-income countries if positive, are in a position to create a favourable environment for the exports of developing countries. Tighter fiscal but easier monetary policy in high-income countries would bring international interest rates down, which would ease the burden of debt. This would benefit developing and high-income countries alike. But far more important will be the policies pursued by the developing countries themselves. They can improve their economic growth prospects by continuing to seek fiscal balance and trade reforms. The decline in foreign capital flows has placed a premium on policies that encourage domestic saving and investment and direct the flow of resources to profitable activities — in other words, on policies that will improve the performance of domestic financial systems.

In developing countries like India, the financial system has another and more important function of promoting growth in the economy. Investment in an economy takes the form of either inventories or fixed capital assets. The growth of fixed capital formation is necessary for the development of the economy. The types of financial assets provided by the financial system would influence the types of capital formation in the economy and *vice versa.* Thus, the economic development of a country depends *inter alia* on the growth of the financial system. The larger the proportion of financial assets to real assets, the greater is the scope for development because, as referred to earlier, growth in the economy requires, adequate investment which only the financial system can facilitate. Finance is an important input in the productive process and as such developed financial system is an important prerequisite for economic growth.

The financial system should have proper width and resilience so that the rate of growth of the financial assets and their structure are in tune with the optimal characteristics of the real capital stock needed for growth. The optimal composition of wealth in an economy is achieved by the promotion of such financial assets as provide incentives to savers and the public to hold a growing part of their wealth in financial form. The rate of saving and the rate of growth in the economy are highly correlated with the proportion of savings held in the form of financial assets relative to non-financial assets.

3.2.1 Role of the Financial System

The financial sector plays a crucial role in the functioning of the economy because it allows a more efficient transfer of resources from savers to investors as well as facilitates the use of funds by households, businesses, traders and governments. In fact, an efficient financial sector spurs economic growth.

Conditions that support the development of a more robust and balanced financial structure will improve the ability of domestic financial systems to contribute to their growth. By restoring macroeconomic stability, building better legal, accounting, and regulatory systems, specifying rules for fuller disclosure of information, and levying taxes that do not fall excessively on finance, governments can lay the foundations for smoothly functioning financial systems. This study reviews the lessons of experience of the key financial sectors and tries to identify the measures that will enable domestic financial systems to provide the services needed in the next decade.

The forces of change unleashed in the Indian economy over the last decade have transformed the operational environment across the entire spectrum of businesses. This coincided with rapid developments in technology that created both an opportunity and a challenge for businesses worldwide — the opportunity to innovate in product offerings to customers and improve operating efficiency, and the challenge of keeping pace with change and gaining first-mover advantage. These two developments catalysed significant shifts in the structure of the Indian economy, perhaps the most visible and far-reaching or which was the increased share of the services sector in the economy.

The liberalisation of the financial sector, which formed a key part of the overall liberalisation process, blurred the distinction between various financial intermediaries and promoted greater efficiency and competitiveness in the financial markets. The structure of the financial markets itself began to change — with the growth of the debt capital markets and the entry of new market participants like mutual funds, disintermediation gradually set in. This started the process of evolution of the financial intermediary into a provider of services in addition to an originator of credit.

Development involves not merely economic change but also social and institutional changes. In many developing and underdeveloped countries, it calls for new sets of values and new concepts of society and government. As a continuous process, it calls for structural adjustments, innovations as well as new institutions to fulfil the aspirations of the people as well as national objectives.

For more than four decades, there has been growing awareness of the development process associated with certain aspects of economic growth. Challenges of persistent poverty, degradation of natural resources are leading to radically new ways of assessing economic development. The direction of global thinking is towards sustainable development.

The Brundtland Commission defined sustainable development as:

"... a process of change in which the exploitation of resources, the direction of investments, the orientation of technological development and institutional change are all in harmony and enhance both current and future potential to meet human needs and aspirations."

The concept of economic development is itself complex, including not only simply growth in total monetary production but also additional concerns for equity, the quality of life and less tangible human aspirations for education, security and aesthetic values.

3.2.2 Financing Development

The economic development depends upon a multiplicity of factors. Amongst these varied factors, the *rate of capital formation* is one of the most important determinants of the rate of growth of an economy. It is one of the key inputs of development.

The economic development of a country depends *inter alia*, on its financial structure. In the long-run, the larger the proportion of the financial assets to real assets, the greater will be the scope for economic growth. Investment is a precondition of economic growth. To sustain growth, continued investment in the growth process is necessary. Since finance is an important input in the growth process, it plays a crucial role in the economy. A more efficient composition of real wealth is obtained by the promotion of financial assets which provide incentives to savers to hold a large part of their wealth in the financial form. An increasing rate of savings correlates with the increase in the proportion of savings held in the form of financial assets — relative to tangible assets.

A major function of financial institutions, whether short-term or long-term, is to provide the maximum financial convenience to the public. This can be done in the three ways:

(*i*) Promotion of the overall savings in the economy by an authentic widening of the financial structure;

(*ii*) Purveying the existing savings in a more efficient manner so that those in greater need, from the social and economic points of view, get priority in allotment; and

(*iii*) Monetary financial institutions assist by creating credit and deposit money and facilitating transactions in trade, production and distribution in the economy.

The financial sector plays a major role in the mobilisation and allocation of financial savings in the economy and in facilitating funds flow among the various sub-sectors. Financial institutions, instruments and the financial markets together act to transfer financial resources from net savers to net borrowers. The resultant gains to the real sector of the economy depend on the efficiency of the financial sector to perform the function of financial intermediation.

The process of socio-economic change is an intrinsic part of human civilization. Man has been striving endlessly to discover the secrets of nature and thereby benefit immensely in creating a peaceful, rich life for himself and his fellow-beings. Man has benefited by agricultural, industrial and information activities. According to J.K. Galbraith, there are three types of economic development that are currently in vogue. These are symbolic modernisation, maximised economic growth and selective growth. Economic growth is the *sine qua non* of change and better living standards. Over the years, middle-of-the-road social democratic thinking is becoming consolidated.

3.2.3 Primary Objective of Development

The primary objective of developing countries like India is to achieve rapid, balanced and sustained rate of economic growth. Hence, efforts are directed towards the creation of conditions in which a fast development of productive resources can take place. This inevitably necessitates the transformation of social and economic structures which will not restrain the potential productivity forces and inhibit the development of resources. The state has therefore, to devise efficient and effective strategies, at once political economic, social, technological and cultural, so as to ensure a desirable coordination of all sectors of the economy and assure deliberate and requisite interest and involvement of the people. This is largely secured by adopting politically, the technique of planning and economically, the tool of management. Countries on an individual basis in the underdeveloped world are progressively and intensively resorting to centralised state management of the economy and to restructured and neo-cultured society.

Economic development, if conceived without appropriate social changes, soon becomes stultified and stagnated. Social change cannot be achieved, if political, technological and cultural aspects are not combined and woven strategically into the fabric of economic planning. Comprehensive national planning is increasingly becoming an instrument of socio-economic transformation in developing countries. Planning delineates strategies.

3.2.4 Trends in Economic Development

There are seven major trends affecting the direction of economic development:

- Technology as a resource
- Competition in domestic and international markets
- The role of invention
- Government as stimulator
- Entrepreneurial and intrapreneurial development
- Innovative capital formation
- Collaborative relationships

Technology is more than a thing, a gadget, or even a process. It is a *self-generating resource that is not consumed in the process* of use. Consequently, it is an important form of economic wealth.

Competition is forcing a reassessment of our individual and collective responses to the marketplace. Fierce domestic and international competition for scientific, technological, and economic preeminence is forcing communities and regions to leverage all their resources — human, technological and financial — to compete effectively for vibrant and diversified economies.

The countries are experiencing an unprecedented burst of invention. Myriad technological advances are occurring with incredible speed and frequency. The ability to commercialize these inventions will have direct and immediate economic consequences.

The governments are trying to find positive non-interventional approaches to encouraging entrepreneurship and technological diversification. They seek to create jobs, provide benefits to the small business sector, and push technology for maximum benefits. The creation of an environment that promotes entrepreneurial activity has become a more important focal point in the government's policy on development.

People with raw energy and a proclivity for risk-taking built and sustained the countries. They are continuing to build it today — in new ways and, with new approaches. These entrepreneurs and intrapreneurs are breaking tradition and providing a dynamic source of creative and innovative enterprises. In simple words, they are giving a boost to their local economies.

Innovative capital formation is providing the catalyst for the entrepreneurial process. Mechanisms for providing seed capital and venture capital as well as an expanding venture capital industry are helping to chalk out new ventures. If the entrepreneurial process is to succeed, it is essential to continue to support and expand the formation of capital and its strategic utilization in new business development.

Finally, creative collaborative relationships are being formed between business, government, and the academicia on a large-scale. These ties are forging new opportunities for commercialization, thus accelerating the technology transfer process.

❖ Economic Growth and Financial System

The economic development of a country depends, *inter alia*, on the growth of the financial system. The larger the proportion of the financial assets (money and monetary assets) to real assets (physical goods and services), the greater the scope for economic growth in the long-run. For growth to take place, investment is necessary which flows from the financial system. Besides, as a scarce factor of production in the less developed countries (LDCs), finance has a crucial role to play in these economies.

The growth objective of the financial system is to achieve the structure and rate of growth of various financial assets and liabilities in consonance with the optimal characteristics of real capital stock. The more efficient composition of real wealth is obtained through the promotion of such financial assets which provide incentives to savers and the public to hold a growing part of their wealth in financial form. Increasing rate of savings correlates well with the increase in the proportion of saving held in the form of financial assets relative to tangible assets. There is a direct correlation between growth of the economy and the growth of the financial assets. Investment in the real sector depends on the functioning of the financial sector, as the latter collects and channels savings into investment which is necessary for growth. It would be pertinent to note here that economic growth is a function of the level of investment, capital-output ratio in each activity of productive process, the level of investment determines the increase in output of goods and services and incomes in the economy.

There is another aspect of the financial system which is relevant to growth, namely, the absorption of liquidity and its use for productive purposes. A well developed financial system with adequate institutions would not only promote savings but encourage these savings to flow into financial assets as against physical assets. The flow of liquidity into physical assets such as gold, silver, real estate and commodities — particularly the sensitive commodities of a speculative nature — would feed inflation while the same flowing into financial assets is not only non-inflationary but would aid growth in the economy and reduce inflationary pressures. In LDCs with inadequate and underdeveloped financial systems, increasing government deficits and growing liquidity could not be absorbed in the financial system and this leads to the well-known phenomenon of money chasing goods and to investment in unproductive physical goods and assets feeding further inflation.

3.2.5 Financial System and Economic Development

The Indian financial system comprises of an impressive network of banks, other financial and investment institutions, offering wide range of products and services, which together function in fairly developed capital and money markets. As such, financial system has come to occupy an important role in the process of economic development.

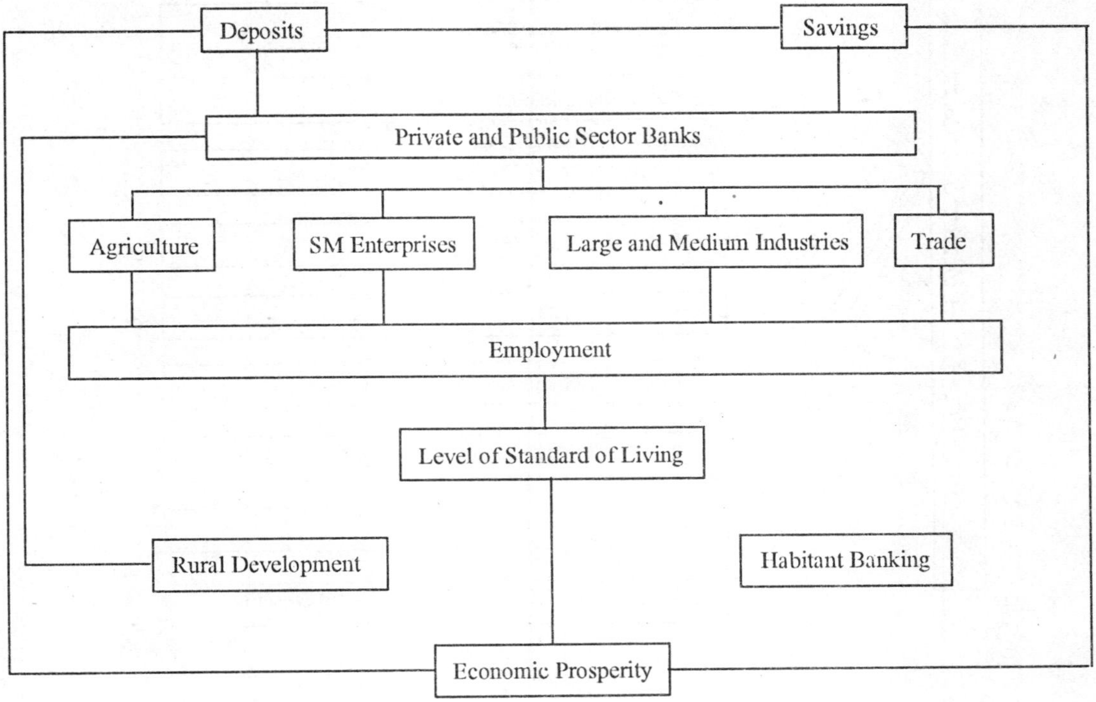

The economic development of a country depends *inter alia,* on its financial structure. In the long-run, the larger the proportion of financial assets to real assets, the greater the scope for economic growth. Investment is a precondition of economic growth. This apart, to sustain growth, continued investment in the growth process is essential. Since finance is an important input in the growth process it has a crucial role to play in the economy. The more efficient composition of real wealth is obtained by the promotion of financial assets which provide incentives to savers to hold a large part of their wealth in financial form. The increasing rate of savings is correlated with the increase in the proportion of savings held in the form of financial assets relative to tangible assets.

The major function of financial institutions, whether short-term or long-term, is to provide the maximum financial convenience to the public. This maybe done in three ways:

(*i*) Promoting the overall savings of the economy by deepening and widening the financial structure;

(*ii*) Distributing the existing savings in a more efficient manner so that those in greater need, from the social and economic point of view, get priority in allotment;

(*iii*) Creating credit and deposit money and facilitating the transactions of trade, production and distribution in furtherance of the economy.

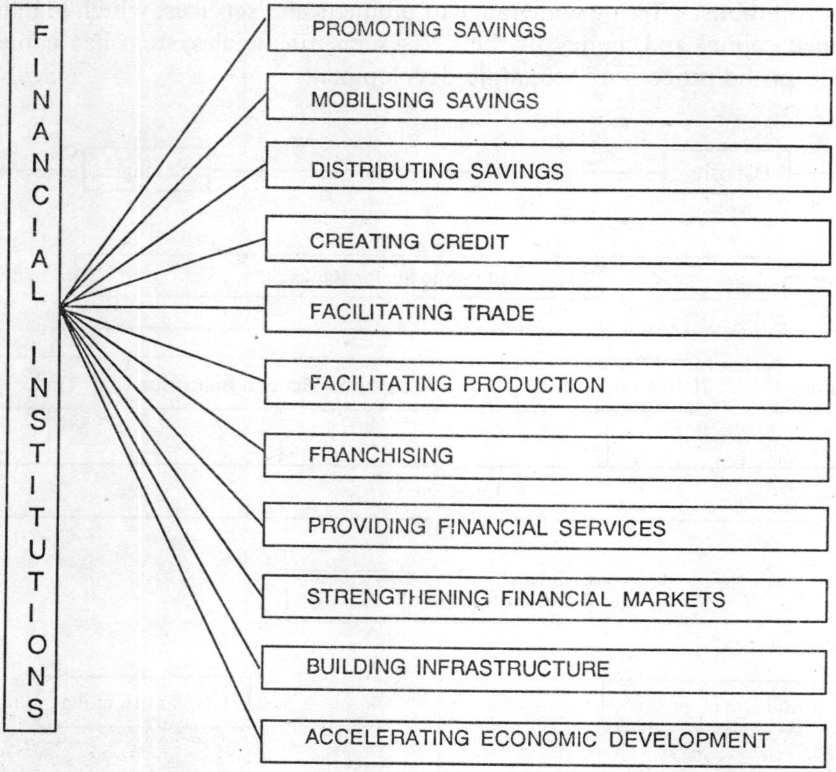

Specialised financial investment and banking institutions are established on an ongoing process in India, as integral parts of the capital market on account of the following reasons:

1. Need for promotion services;
2. Need for higher capital formation;
3. Need for replacement finance;
4. Need for organised capital market;
5. Need for long-term finance;
6. Planned economic development;
7. Finance for small business, and
8. Finance for priority sectors.

A sound and efficient financial system can contribute to economic growth and development in a number of ways:

(i) By providing a spectrum of financial assets to meet diverse preferences of household and, thus, enabling them to choose their asset portfolios to achieve a preferred mix of return, liquidity and risk.

(ii) By raising productivity of capital through efficient allocation.

In the post-independence period, the Indian financial system has augmented well significantly and has demonstrated considerable ability to mobilise savings and meeting the needs of agriculture, industry and trade. In short, it is a catalytic agent of development and change.

The process of economic development will make continued demands on the banking system. The banking system has to be integrated with the process of economic development both in terms of mobilising savings and utilising them to the best advantage. Together with other specialised financial institutions and the active participation of the financial markets, the process of economic development is likely to be accelerated during the next millennium.

❖ Lessons and Agenda

- **Imagination** and out-of-the-box thinking is essential for coping with resource constraints.
- **Strategy** is about discovery and innovation, breaking away from conventional wisdom.
- **Business** and organizational models that work best are those that are indigenously developed.
- **Transactions** must be based strictly on commercial considerations to be successful.
- **Deployment** of high technology must be as innovative as the technology itself.
- **World-class** standards are what Indian operations can — and must strive to — attain
- **Access to credit** must become a birthright. It is critical to bring the poor into a monetised economy.
- **Distribution efficiencies** must be dramatically altered. The capital that can be released is staggering.
- **Relieving choke points** by understanding productivity-levels along the value chain is critical.
- **Development efforts** must be entrusted to private enterprise, both indigenous and transnational.
- **Scaling up is important** in the choice of technology, the business model, and the managerial skills.
- **State-of-the-art** solutions using new and unique technology, not dated methods, must be provided.

3.2.6 Financial System *vis-a-vis* Corporate Sector

Industrialisation is *sine qua non* for economic progress. In the post-independence era, the base of the industrial structure has been broadened. *In this, the corporate sector has been in the lead.* More importantly, "*Finance is the life blood of industry.*"

The corporate sector depends on the financial system for:

(i) Risk Capital

Risk capital is an important source of raising the promoters' contribution. Financial institutions provide venture/seed capital to entrepreneurs.

INDIAN BANKING IN ECONOMIC DEVELOPMENT

Indian banking is the life line of the nation. Its network over 74,000 offices is spread across the length and breadth of the country, servicing nearly 100 crore depositors. Financing diverse needs of more than 20 crore entrepreneur customers. Providing a nationwide framework for payments, clearing and settlements. Developing vital sectors of the economy. Bolstering agriculture, industry, trade and commerce.

- **Savings:** Mobilised savings of ₹ 31,92,141 crore deposits as on 31-03-2008 from 100 crore depositors.
- **Credit:** ₹ 23,48,493 (March 2008) crore credit to 11 crore loan customers.
- **Investments:** ₹ 7,22,115 crore investment in government and approved securities towards planned development.
- **Agriculture:** Loans amount over ₹ 1,01,808 crore to about 1,000 lakh farmers.
- **Industry:** ₹ 2,72,626 crore of financial assistance to medium and large industries. Around ₹ 67,177 crore loan assistance to 37 lakh small-scale industrial units.
- **Exports:** Around ₹ 59,222 crore provided to the export sector, the engine of the nation's growth.
- **Trade:** ₹ 32,447 crore assistance to 310 lakh wholesale traders, ₹ 18,800 crore to 303 lakh retail traders.
- **NPA** — Non-performing Assets of PSBs (till 31-3-2007) ₹ 38,602 crore.

In addition, banks have extended financial assistance to artisans, professionals, small entrepreneurs, education, housing, small business self-help groups, transport, infrastructure, software personnel and consumption.

(ii) Equity

A good equity base ensures the financial health of a unit. It provides flexibility, favourable financial leverage and increases its debt raising capacity. Financial institutions' share in the equity holding varies from 44.5 per cent in ACC to 75.5 per cent in Alfa Laval.

(iii) Debt — Long- and Short-term Capital

Financial institutions are generally the major lenders of borrowed funds of the corporate sector.

(iv) Working Capital

The commercial banks are a major source of working capital for the industry. In a way, adequate and timely working capital ensures smooth functioning of production.

Financial institutions provide related financial services as well as promotional services to the corporate sector. They are more than equal partners in the success of corporate projects. Today, the corporate sector's dependence on the financial system has expanded its area of performance.

Broadly, financial institutions are grouped into types of finance provided for development:

1. *Seed Capital:* IDBI, IFCI, ICICI Bank, SIDBI, SFCs, State Government, venture capital companies.
2. *Refinance:* SIDBI, NABARD, EXIM Bank.
3. *Term Loans:* IDBI, IFCI, SIDBI, SFCs, SIDCs Banks, NABARD, EXIM Bank.
4. *Machinery Loan:* IFCI, NSIC, SSIDC, SIDBI.
5. *Working Capital:* Commercial Banks, Coop. Banks, RRBs, SSIDCs, SFCs.
6. *Subsidy and AID:* Central and State Governments, KVIC.

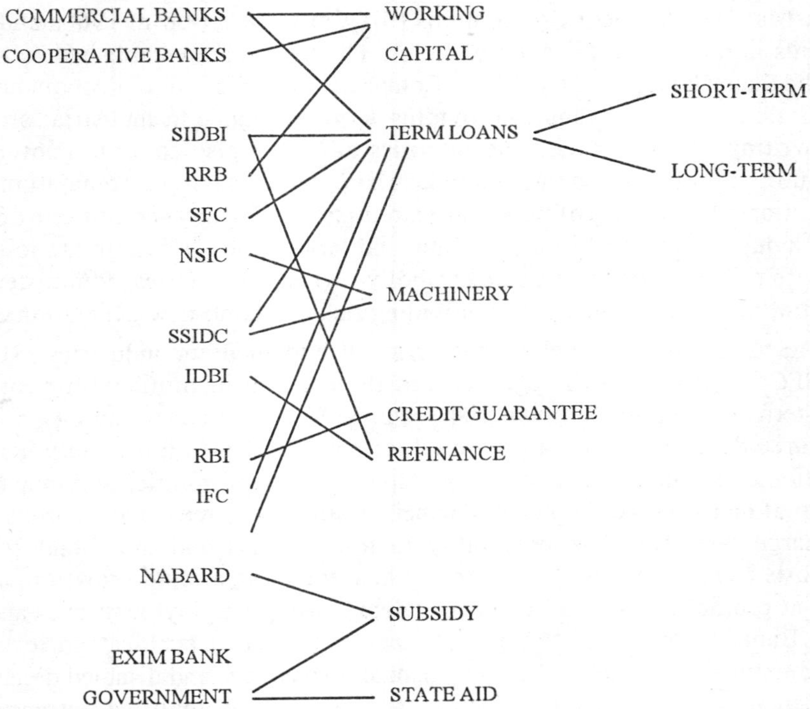

Although such development corporations like the (IDBI), (IFCI), Small Industrial Development Bank (SIDBI), State Industrial Development Corporations (SIDCs) and State Financial Corporations are basically constituted to provide industrial finance, particularly to medium and large units, their role in assistance is by no means less important. These institutions, together with the Life Insurance Corporation of India (LIC), General Insurance Corporation of India (GIC) and the Unit Trust of India (UTI) play a significant role in the rapid growth of the small-scale industry. The emergence of small-scale units on a sizeable scale in the last decade has given a real impetus to the industrialisation of underdeveloped areas.

Among the term-lending institutions, financial assistance to small-scale industries is mainly provided by SFCs, SSIDCs, SIDCs/SIICs and by the IDBI under its refinance of industrial loans and bills rediscounting schemes. Assistance sanctioned and disbursed by these institutions to projects and ventured entrepreneurs are discussed in the following pages.

The network of commercial banks, cooperative banks and Regional Rural Banks, State Financial Corporations (SFCs), State Industries Development Corporations and National Small Industries Corporation (NSIC) provide the framework for financial assistance to small-scale and medium-scale industries. The Industrial Development Bank of India (IDBI) provides funds to the commercial banks and SFCs through its scheme of refinance of industrial loans and rediscounting of machinery bills. The commercial banks are the main source of short-term loans/advances while SFCs provide long-term loan advances to entrepreneurs. The National Bank for Agriculture and Rural Development (NABARD) has been set up for the supply of credit to entrepreneurs in agriculture and for the small village and cottage industry sector in rural areas.

State Industrial Development Corporations (SIDCs) were set-up in 1960s and 1970s to act as catalytic agents in the industrialisation of states. The SIDCs are established as wholly-owned undertaking of the State Governments under the Companies Act, 1956 or as autonomous corporations under specific State Acts. In addition to providing term assistance to industrial projects by way of loans, underwriting and guarantees, the activities of SIDCs also cover promotional functions such as formulation of project ideas through industrial potential surveys, preparation of feasibility reports and selection and training of potential entrepreneurs. Further, activities of SIDCs extend to setting up of industrial projects in the medium and large sectors either in the joint sector, i.e., in partnership with private entrepreneurs or as wholly-owned subsidiaries, administering incentive schemes of Central/State Governments and providing risk capital to new generation entrepreneurs.

Designed to assist in the development of small and medium industries, State Financial Corporations (SFCs) constitute an integral part of the national institutional network engaged in extending long-term finance to the industrial sector. SFCs have been playing an effective role for more than three decades in the rapid growth of small and medium-scale units and through them have contributed significantly in creating employment opportunities and in achieving wider regional dispersal of industrial development. Financial institutions have made vigorous and sustained efforts to discharge their social responsibility to the business and the social sector at large community. Efforts have constantly been directed at stimulating a rapid growth in all the sectors of the industry, at promoting new entrepreneur talent, raising employment level and developing backward areas. Banks have formulated special schemes to finance such categories of the weaker sections of the community as cobblers, hawkers, handloom weavers, and disabled defence personnel, and formulate schemes for financing craftsmen and technically qualified entrepreneurs. They, however, believe in tailoring credit to suit the specific requirements of each case because requirements vary from unit-to-unit. Also, new situations arise from time-to-time; to meet them new credit instruments have to be devised. Thus, for schemes for craftsmen and technically qualified entrepreneurs, all that the banks require today is a worthwhile project which is technically feasible and economically viable, backed by technical competence and the ability to manage an enterprise. Credit from a banker is no problem today, even when the entrepreneur is not in a position to bring in the normal owner's equity.

The second phase of financial sector reform has to be set against broader macroeconomic changes. One important aspect of this is that we are now on a higher growth trajectory. This would call for a continuing and indeed expanding role of the financial system in mobilising savings and allocating these savings in an efficient and effective manner. Meanwhile, a major policy development affecting the financial sector has been the increasing importance being given to indirect monetary instruments of control in place of direct discretionary action and, in this process, acting on the cost of money to impact on its availabilty. Financial liberalisation calls for a measure of market determination of interest rates.

Another institutional and policy development has been the considerable measure of relaxation in foreign exchange transactions with our acceptance of the full obligations of current account convertibility and our movement to a not inconsiderable extent towards capital account convertibility as well. There is, as a result of these developments, greater integration between the money, securities and foreign exchange markets. What these developments have meant for the financial system is the greater exposure to market risks either in the form of security price variations or of foreign exchange risks and, which in turn, calls for greater measure of risk management and the deployment of newer forms of risk management techniques.

One of the aspects of the macropolicy environment that has constrained the operations of the financial system in India is the continued high level of fiscal deficit which tend to restrict the boundaries for the operation of the system by crowding out non-governmental claimants to the national pool of financial savings. The continuance of the high fiscal deficit is a major element in the measure of macroeconomic imbalance, the correction of which along with a strong and healthy financial system should be regarded as a *sine qua non* for moving towards capital account convertibility.

3.2.7 Promotional Role of the Financial System

These mutual interactions between the financial and real system may take promotional or development forms. It is in this context that the development role of the financial system is to be emphasised.

This role assumes two forms: innovation and promotion, which are inter-related. The innovatory role relates to the creative activity of these institutions. Thus, dynamisms as well as creative imagination can be in both the assets and liabilities side of the activities of financial institutions. This takes the form of improving the quality of assets as well as showing new and more profitable activities or keeping pace with the developmental priorities of the government.

This creative element in the case of commercial banks can be seen in the Lead Bank Scheme, financing of neglected sectors, opening of branches in the rural areas, etc. The creative role in the case of development banker takes the form of a critical examination of the appraisal and follow-up actions including the application of social cost and benefit analysis. The development banker follows sound appraisal techniques including the economic and financial tools both from the point of the view of the company as well as the economy. The industrialist finds a contractive partner in the banker who will help him in improving his project plan and prospects of investment.

The financial institutions by virtue of long experience, expertise and information, which they acquire during the course of their project appraisal are in a better position to play the promotional role in the economy. Firstly, they can share their expertise with their clients and improve the project preparation, plug up the loopholes in their schemes and advise them on improving project prospects as well as on the new areas they can explore. Secondly, these institutions have established their own training institutions or schools as in the case of IFC (Management Development Institute) and ICICI (Institute of Financial Management), etc. Thirdly, they are instrumental in setting up consultancy companies, accounting firms, leasing companies and industrial estates, etc. The IDBI with the help of other institutions have set up at state levels various consultancy services centres. Iran and Greece have also set up similar institutions. Fourthly, development bankers can share their experience with the government in the formulation of their financial policy as their experience with projects and project implementation would help the government. Their day-to-day market knowledge about the demand pattern, export market, etc., would also enable the development bankers to advise the government.

Financial institutions can also undertake what William Diamond calls "directed efforts" in the sense that the efforts are directed toward achieving the specific objectives of the government which of course change from time-to-time. Thus, when the government's intention was to encourage small and cottage industries, development bankers geared themselves to this task. When development bankers are directed to give priority to development of backward areas, concessional finance as well as special efforts are made to encourage entrepreneurship in the backward areas.

The creation of enterprise is, no doubt, costly and expansive and the return will be delayed and meagre. But these are the risks which are to be undertaken along with the financial and moral implications of it.

3.2.8 Critical Appraisal

The role of the Indian financial system has clearly established that they constitute the backbone of industrial development. There are, however, certain aspects which merit critical appraisal.

The mushrooming of financial institutions with overlapping activities has given rise to speculation, scans and distortion.

Inter alia, it has eroded the financial discipline among the borrowers on the one hand, and more effective public control of private enterprise on the other hand.

Financial control and management of the financial institution has touched its bottom.

The Indian financial system has failed to meet the financial needs of small enterprises and businesses.

Again, while most of the financial institutions are in the public sector, various areas of operation are linked with the growth of the private sector.

In the process, the system has helped various industrial groups rather than the millions of first generation entrepreneurs.

The Indian financial system also failed in its effort to create a healthy and aggressive capital market.

In spite of these lacunae, the financial system is a catalytic agent of economic development.

The experiences of the 1980s have led India to reconsider their approach to economic development. All along with the introduction of the liberalisation policy in the 1990s, the financial sector needs to be restructured, supervision improved so that the financial institution plays a catalytic role in accelerating the process of development. The financial sector is attuned to the needs of the economic development. They are made more efficient by improving their management systems and increasing the competition they face.

Efforts are being made to create appropriate financial institutions, financial instruments and services, develop better systems of prudential regulations and supervision, improve the flow of financial information, develop human skills for managing complete financial operations, which would result in substantial economic process.

3.3 REFORMS IN FINANCIAL SECTOR IN INDIA

The financial sector plays a major role in the mobilisation and allocation of financial savings in the economy and in facilitating funds flow among the various sub-sectors. Financial institutions, instruments and the financial markets together act to transfer financial resources from net savers to net borrowers. The resultant gains to the real sector of the economy depend on the efficiency of the financial sector to perform the function of financial intermediation.

A feature of the Indian financial system is the dominance of public sector institutions be it in banking, term lending or insurance. The financial system has thus been subjected to a high degree of regulatory control. This regulatory mechanism, originally devised keeping in view certain socio-economic considerations, defined the various activities in the financial sector. Thus, both entry and expansion of the financial institutions remained for a long time subjected to control. Credit deployment policies were determined at the apex, with mandatory allocations for specific sectors such as government, small-scale industries, agriculture, etc. An element of cross subsidisation was introduced, providing concessionality in interest rates, within the overall framework of the administered interest rate structure. The regulatory policy and the direct controls placed in the planning process were necessary during the initial underdeveloped state of the financial sector to ensure flow of necessary funds to the socially desirable sub-sectors of the real economy.

The progress made thereafter by the financial sector in terms of growth as well as in meeting the financial needs of the economy has certainly been commendable. Banking statistics (number of offices, population per bank office, overall business growth, financial assistance to weaker sections of society, etc.), performance of term lending and investment institutions and the growing equity cult reflected in capital market activities, indicate the tremendous strides the financial sector has taken in facilitating economic growth.

In the process of this growth, the financial system, however, developed certain rigidities and deficiencies, hampering operational efficiency. In particular, the banking industry witnessed

STRUCTURAL POLICIES IN THE FINANCIAL SECTOR

Objectives	*Measures*	*Countries*
To improve the monetary control system	Improvements in financial programming framework	Algeria, China, and Egypt
	Adequacy of monetary policy instruments; switch from direct to indirect controls	Botswana, China, Costa Rica, Hungary, Indonesia, Mauritius, the Philippines, and Sri Lanka
To improve the mobilization and allocation of domestic savings	Development of money and government securities markets	Indonesia, Malaysia, Oman, Sri Lanka, Yemen Arab Republic, and Zaire
	Reduction of selective credit policies; integration of unregulated financial institutions; promotion of term finance and capital market development	Costa Rica, Dominican Republic, Indonesia, Malaysia and Papua New Guinea
	Improvement in supervision of financial institutions and creation of deposit insurance schemes	Chile, Dominican Republic, Panama, and Trinidad and Tobago
	New financial institutions and instruments, and adequacy of bank regulation and legislation	Aruba, Bolivia, Hungary, Kenya, and Republic of Nepal (from 28-5-2008)
To improve the level and structure of interest rates	Reduction of interest rate subsidies and of bad debts	Bangladesh, Chile, Malaysia, Mauritania, Senegal, and Uruguay
	Liberalization of interest rates; introduction of prime rate or base lending rate system	Bolivia, Burundi, The Gambia, Haiti, Indonesia, Malaysia, the Philippines, and Sierra Leone

Source: International Monetary Fund

The list under each category comprises countries which have received advice in the indicated areas, either in the context of the use of Fund resources and consultation missions, or direct Fund technical assistance. Countries receiving technical assistance through the placement of experts are not covered in the list.

perceptible decline in productivity and profitability and a substantial increase in its non-performing assets (NPAs). This led to inadequate provisioning for bad and doubtful assets making the financial position of some of the banks delicate. Incidence of sickness in the industrial sector and tardy recovery of agricultural and other rural advances largely contributed to the problem, resulting in large accumulation of bank losses. The term lending and investment institutions performed better in comparison, probably due to the limited nature of their operating activities. Capital markets (both primary and secondary) also showed differing performance. The heartening response from the investing public in the capital market was not matched by removal of inadequacies in the market operations. As such, investor protection, settlement system, and inculcation of uniform trading practices left much to be desired. In the absence of a proper regulatory system and a single regulatory authority, in the aftermath of sizeable expansion in the volume of business, the market witnessed events which could not be adequately controlled. The development of the short-term money market has, besides, picked up only over the last 20 years.

❖ Challenges of Financial Sector

The Indian financial system has shown considerable widening and deepening since the initiation of the present phase of financial sector reforms in 1992-93. In the years to come, the financial sector would grow not only in size but also in complexity as the forces of reform gather momentum. Over the last few years, the macropolicy framework conducive to growth and development of the financial system has been put in place. Now a range of issues relating to micromanagement need to be addressed. In this regard, improving organizational effectiveness of banks and financial institutions assumes importance.

Risk management is an important area where improvements are needed. All major component of risk, *viz.,* credit risk, interest rate risk and foreign exchange risk will become much more critical than in the past. Credit risk will call for tackling the risk of non-performance and non-repayment by improving management efficiency. For managing interest rate risk, necessity expertise will have to be developed for asset-liability management. Exchange rate risk will call for developing appropriate risk-hedging techniques. Banks and financial institutions, therefore, need to develop relevant expertise in risk management backed by appropriate management information system and sound treasury management framework.

From the policy perspective, maintaining integrity and credibility of financial entities is a crucial prerequisite for smooth functioning of the financial system. In a competitive environment wherein profits are subject to pressures from assets as well as liability sides, financial entities often tend to venture into new areas of activities which are disproportionately risky relative to capital deployed, which may, if unimpeded, affect the financial system. For avoiding such occurrence, strict adherence to prudential norms and effective system of supervision are necessary.

Over the last few years, Indian financial system has been going through a process of transformation. To match with the changing environment, the financial entities have to readjust their system of functioning. It calls for shifting emphasis from traditional areas of financing and venturing into new areas, improving efficiency level by inclusion of trained manpower and restructuring their organizations.

The reform process so far can be considered as first phase of reform. The thrust of the second phase of reforms is on improvement in the organizational effectiveness of banks and other financial entities. More specifically, future trends of banking development will be: (*i*) greater specialization by banks in different niches of the market such as retail, agriculture, export, small-scale and corporate sector, (*ii*) greater reliance on non-fund business such as advisory and consultancy services, guarantee and custody services, (*iii*) greater overlap in product coverage between commercial banks and non-bank financial intermediaries, (*iv*) greater financial disintermediation with large companies accessing securities debt domestically and in the financial market abroad. The areas needing special attention are: asset-liability management, risk management, ability to work under deregulated interest rate environment, customer service and housekeeping. In other words, the banks are to revamp their structure and system of functioning to meet the challenges of reform.

❖ Financial Reforms vs. Economic Reforms

The financial sector reforms in India is an integral part of the overall programme of economic reforms aimed at improving productivity and efficiency. A major lesson to be learnt from the experiences of other countries which have gone through a programme of financial sector reform is that reforms are successful only if accompanied by fiscal consolidation, moderate inflation and no sharp appreciation in the real effective interest rate. The problem into which the financial sector reforms ran into in the Southern Cone countries were because of uncontrolled inflation and sharp appreciation in real exchange rates. In those circumstances, interest rate deregulation faced even more difficulties. Also, in those countries, no effective prudential guidelines had been put in place either prior to or simultaneous with the introduction of the reforms.

On the contrary, the Indian financial sector reform has gone hand-in-hand with fiscal reforms, trade reforms and exchange rate reforms. The three major building blocks of the financial sector reform in our country have been: (*i*) removing or relaxing the external constraints; (*ii*) introduction of prudential norms; and (*iii*) institutional strengthening. The chief merit of our reform process has been the cautious sequencing of reforms and the consistent and the mutually reinforcing character of the various measures taken. Even as the new prudential norms are reportedly being introduced, the capital base of the banks has been strengthened and organisational improvements are said to be in place.

Improving the profitability and viability of banks is only one aspect of enhancing their performance. The other is how adequately and satisfactorily banks are able to meet the demand of customers. The ultimate test of success of the financial sector reforms is truly customer satisfaction; customer — as a borrower and a depositor. Through the various reform measures, we are laying the foundation for an efficient and a well-functioning banking system. A renewed and a reinvigorated banking system can play an important role in accelerating economic growth. Significant changes have already taken place. It has however miles to go. But the steps that are being taken are in the right direction. The first phase of the banking sector reform concentrated on such factors as pre-emptions, interest rate structure, prudential norms and supervisory oversight. The second phase of banking reform must lay stress on the improvement of the organisational effectiveness of banks, for which the initiative has to come largely from banks themselves.

The financial system should have to redouble efforts to adapt to the advances in technology which are changing the contours of financial intermediation worldwide. Unless they catch up, the technology lag could widen with adverse implications for efficiency and costs, the system also need to imbue our financial institutions with flexibility to absorb and adapt to institutional change. Banks must shed their inward-looking focus and develop an outward orientation. And, most important of all, we have to invest more resources into human resource development with a focus on the quality, timeliness and delivery of financial services. The human resource model of the future will require professionals to be both driving and anticipating change, understanding the complexities of the new business environment and forces shaping it.

In financial systems worldwide, today's buzzwords are competition, consolidation and stability. Proactive strengthening of prudential regulations, enhanced transparency and accountability, initiatives in setting best practices of corporate governance, and comprehensive, sound and effective regulation and supervision have together played a key role in creating a secure and conducive environment for the functioning of the financial system. There is currently a strong emphasis on upgrading the technological infrastructure for our financial institutions and markets. This is expected to provide significant gains in terms of the efficiency and cost of intermediation. The full benefits of technological transformation, especially in terms of dealing with the vulnerabilities that persist in our system, will hinge upon enabling changes in the legal architecture.

Financial sector reforms have supported the transition of the Indian economy to a higher growth path while significantly improving the stability of the financial system. In comparison of the pre-reform period, the Indian financial system today is more stable and efficient. However, the gains of the past decade have to be consolidated, so that these could be translated to drive the institutions, markets and practices into a mature financial system that can meet the challenges of sustaining India on a higher growth trajectory. The financial system would, therefore, not only need to be stable but would also need to support still higher levels of planned investments by channeling financial resources more efficiently from deficit to surplus sectors. The banks would need to reassess their core banking business to view how best they could undertake maturity transformation to step up the lendable resources in support of real economic activity. Competitive pressures as well as prudential regulatory requirments have made banks risk-averse and their investment in relatively risk-free gilt instruments have far exceeded the stipulated requirements. The behaviour and strategies of bank business would need to change from the present so that they can factor in their own risk assessment even while performing their core activities. There is a need to ensure long-term finance to support development and growth in the economy, even as restructuring takes place through mergers and universal banking. Also, the functioning of the capital markets requires to be toned up so that the levels of primary resource mobilisation seen in the early years of reform period are reached and perhaps surpassed. The key to attaining higher levels of investments by way of direct finance routed through capital markets lie in bringing about institutional improveinent. Improved corporate governance practices can go a long way in bringing the retail investors back to capital markets. Institutional reforms supporting risk capital is important in broad-basing the entrepreneurship culture in the economy. While financial sector reforms till date have been helpful, more needs to be done so that greater gains from the financial sector reforms could be realised for the real economy.

3.3.1 Financial Sector Reforms

The Principle objective of financial sector reform is to improve the allocative efficiency of resources and accelerate the growth process of the real sector by removing structural deficiencies affecting the performance of financial institutions and financial markets, At the same time, create competition in the finance sector and give customers a wide choice of products. And to increase interlinkages across financial institutions and markets and bring in stability in the financial system.

The main thrust of reforms in the financial sector is on the creation of efficient and stable financial institutions and markets. Reforms in respect of the banking as well as non-banking financial institutions focused on creating a deregulated environment and enabling free play of market forces while at the same time strengthening the prudential norms and the supervisory system. In the banking sector, the particular focus is on imparting operational flexibility and functional autonomy with a view to enhancing efficiency, productivity and profitability, imparting strength to the system and ensuring financial soundness. The restrictions on activities undertaken by the existing institutions are gradually relaxed and barriers to entry in the banking sector were removed. In the case of non-banking financial intermediaries, reforms focused on removing sector-specific deficiencies. Thus, while reforms in respect of DFIs focused on imparting market orientation to their operations by withdrawing assured sources of funds, in the case of NBFCs, the reform measures brought their asset side also under the regulation of the Reserve Bank. In the case of the insurance sector and mutual funds, reforms attempted to create a competitive environment by allowing private sector participation.

Reforms in financial markets focused on removal of structural bottlenecks, introduction of new players/instruments, free pricing of financial assets, relaxation of quantitative restrictions, improvement in trading, clearing and settlement practices, more transparency, *etc.* Reforms encompassed regulatory and legal changes, building of institutional infrastructure, refinement of market microstructure and technological upgradation. In the various financial market segments, reforms aimed at creating liquidity and depth and an efficient price discovery process.

In response to reforms, the Indian financial sector has undergone radical transformation over the 1990s. Reforms have altered the organisational structure, ownership pattern and domain of operations of institutions and infused competition in the financial sector. The competition has forced the institutions to reposition themselves in order to survive and grow. The extensive progress in technology has enabled markets to graduate from outdated systems to modern market the speed of execution of trades and the transaction costs. However, despite substantial improvements in the financial sector, some issues have to be addressed overtime as the reform process is entrenched further. Whether the public sector character of the banking sector is affecting its performance adversely? Whether dilution of the government stake would have a positive impact on the efficiency of the banking sector? As a result of various reform measures aimed at enhancing stability of financial institutions, there is a possibility that such measures might have affected the efficiency of financial institutions. Whether DFIs have lost their relevance? The relevant issue, however, is how to fill the vacuum that would be created when DFIs withdraw from the scene. The role of mutual funds in promoting savings continues to be insignificant. There is also an issue of availability of adequate risk capital with the resource mobilisation from the primary capital market showing a sharp decline in the second half of 1990s and the early 2000s. It has also been argued by some that various markets are still segmented. With blurring of boundaries among providers of various financial services, the issue as to what should be the appropriate supervisory framework for regulating them has also arisen.

As wide-ranging reforms have been initiated in the financial sector with a view to making it more efficient and stable, the main focus of this chapter is to assess the impact of reforms on efficiency and stability of financial institutions and financial markets. Besides, this chapter attempts to seek answers to the following three questions: (*i*) whether ownership pattern (public or private) impinges on the efficiency of the banking sector; (*ii*) whether various stability enhancing measures introduced in the Indian banking system have had any adverse impact on its efficiency; and (*iii*) whether the various market segments have become integrated.

❖ Policy Instruments

Effective monetary control through reserve money management requires the development of adequate instruments and their proper use and coordination. For instance, reserve requirements for banks and other financial institutions may be ineffectual because penalties for reserve shortfalls are set too low. In any case, the lack of coordination of reserve requirements with the management of the discount window allows banks to borrow easily and cheaply from the central bank to meet reserve needs. (Credit is channeled by the central bank through its discount window by rediscounting particular types of eligible bills and securities.) If required reserves earn little or no interest, an increase in reserve requirements may cause banks to raise effective loan rates, for example, through higher service charges and/or lower deposit rates, with adverse effects on savings mobilization and allocation. Structural measures to tighten penalties for reserve shortfalls, to improve coordination with the discount window, and to pay appropriate interest rates on required reserves will make reserve requirements an effective instrument of monetary control and promote the efficiency of financial intermediation.

A reform of the discount window operations of central banks can also enhance the efficiency of short-term bank liability management, and encourage the use of money markets.

The key objective of reforms in the financial sector in India has been to enhance the stability and efficiency of financial institutions. To achieve this objective, various reform measures were initiated that could be categorised broadly into three main groups: enabling measures, strengthening measures and institutional measures. The enabling measure were designed to create an environment where financial intermediaries could respond optimally to market signals on the basis of commercial considerations. Salient among these included reduction in statutory pre-emptions so as to release greater funds for commercial lending, interest rate deregulation to enable price discovery, granting of operational autonomy to banks and liberalisation of the entry norms for financial intermediaries. The strengthening measures aimed at reducing the vulnerability of financial institutions in the face of fluctuations in the economic environment. These included, *inter alia,* capital adequacy, income recognition, asset classification and provisioning norms, exposure norms, improved levels of transparency, and disclosure standards. Institutional measures were aimed at creating an appropriate institutional framework conducive to development of markets and functioning of financial institutions.

3.3.2 Recent Reforms

In reforming the financial sector, three broad issues need to be addressed:

- The adequacy of instruments to improve the implementation of monetary policy and to facilitate increased reliance on indirect, rather than direct, controls.
- Institutional and regulatory reforms to improve the efficiency and soundness of the financial system.
- The adequacy of the level and structure of interest rates. The rest of this article analyses these issues and, in the light of Fund experience, identifies structural policies in the financial sector that could help achieve macroeconomic objectives and the needed growth-oriented adjustment.

To analyse problems which the financial sector faced and to suggest remedial measures, various study groups and committees were set up in the recent past which went into the problems and suggested steps to vitalise the underdeveloped sub-sectors of the system to function in a deregulated environment. A major committee to go into the functioning of the system was appointed in 1985 with late Prof. S. Chakravarty as its chairman. It studied various aspects of the Indian monetary system and proposed measures to improve its functioning. The other major committee, which had a wider canvass was set up in 1991 under the chairmanship of Mr. M. Narasimham. It went into the different aspects of the entire financial system and offered suggestions to revamp it, to improve its functioning. There were also the various study groups which suggested setting up new institutions, introduction of new products, regulation of capital market institutions and so on. Many of the recommendations of these committees and groups have been implemented; a few are at different stages of implementation.

❖ Second Phase

The first phase of India's financial reforms highlighted above may be termed as "Curative" inasmuch as they were addressed to the issue of cleansing the balance sheet of banks and putting them on recovery path. The second generation reforms will be "Preventive", aimed at building a strong and robust banking system which can withstand the pressures of globalisation.

The broad tenor of the recommendations of the second Narasimham Committee (1998) is to move towards universal banking. This view has also been echoed by the RBI. The opening of the Indian insurance sector will usher in bancassurance. The Development Finance Institutions (DFIs) like IDBI, ICICI have moved for converting themselves into universal banks. They have already set up commercial bank ventures. Commercial banks, especially in the private sector, have entered the insurance business with joint ventures. Some of the public sector banks have also taken up distribution of insurance products, so as to realise cross-sell opportunities by leveraging on their large branch network. In a way, it also indicates that the Indian banking system is not immune from the trends holding sway in the global financial scenario.

It has been suggested that the twin forces of consolidation and convergence need to be reckoned in the Indian context. Possibilities of convergence have been envisaged through universal banking to lead to one-stop financial supermarkets providing a range of services such as commercial, merchant and investment banking and even insurance. Risk diversification is also expected to be achieved through convergence resulting in strengthening of the system. In essence, the suggestions are aimed at establishing financial conglomerates through a process of mergers and diversification.

The first and foremost condition for attainment of capital account convertibility after year 2011 will be strengthening the banking system, which in turn would call for higher size of balance sheet so that Indian banks can withstand the pressures of international competition. But it is felt that attainment of bigger size should not be seen as a major driver of consolidation, especially from the point of view of systemic soundness.

At the same time, supervisory structure will have to allow financial diversification and innovation while attempting to contain risks within individual financial affiliates and preferably prevent any spillage of financial difficulties originating in a non-bank affiliate overflowing into the parent bank. It may be mentioned that Reserve Bank of India, following the BIS model has started moving towards the *Three-Pillar Approach* to regulation by strengthening internal governance, official oversight and market discipline.

With interest rates more or less deregulated, competition gaining is apace in different market segments. So far the public sector banks have been beneficiaries of state protection and rule-based regulation and direction from the monetary authority. With the reforms and the gradual freedom that they have now been bestowed with, adjustment to the market-led conditions will have to be completed. The logical outcome of the strategy of deregulation and competition will be financial innovations and introduction of risk hedging mechanisms.

The process of financial innovations has also commenced recently with the introduction of interest rate swaps. But this needs to be followed up by other derivative instruments. However, development of full-fledged OTC market will take longer time. Near absence of technology and skills have impaired the development of such markets and these impediments cannot be just wished away. There is a need to systematically address the structural issues so that the financial markets can attain full integration. With suitable supervisory structure including proper legal systems and investor protection measures, Indian financial market can graduate from an "emerging" market to an "efficient" market. It may be noted that the bi-annual Monetary and Credit Policy announced by the RBI in the recent period has shown a pronounced shift towards addressing the structural issues.

As part of rationalisation of manpower in public sector banks, the Narasimham Committee has suggested scheme for voluntary separation. Following the government's encouragement, public sector banks have implemented, the Voluntary Retirement Scheme (VRS). This has been a major step as this was one of the most contentious issues facing the banking industry. Nearly one lakh employees of banks, constituting about 11% of the total staff strength have accepted VRS, the severance package had been estimated to cost over ₹ 10,000 crore. Although, banks had been allowed to amortise the VRS outgo over a period of three years, the financial burden had been significant. This had reflected in the profit performance of most of the banks during 2000-01. No doubt, the reduction in staff is likely to reduce establishment expenses over the medium term. With this, the 'golden handshake' has been accepted as a downsizing (rightsizing) tool in the public sector. The real managerial challenge lies in the aftermath of the VRS. Firstly, rationalisation of manpower will have to be achieved at the earliest so that the vacuum arising out of the exit of employees is filled up. This could also require relocation of staff in large numbers. Secondly, this could lead to 'de-layering' aimed at cutting down organisation tiers and closure of unviable branches and merger of branches. With interest rates moving southwards, banks will have to learn to work with leaner staff and thinner margins. Banks should also ensure that due to shortage of manpower, the quality of customer service does not suffer. In balance, it appears that VRS could at best provide a partial solution to the issue of reduction in intermediation costs as banks which are burdened with a backlog of NPAs will not be in a position to cut interest rates to the desired extent.

But by far, the most challenging task before banks in the post-VRS situation will be changing the mindset of employees to face the competitive pressures. This will call for thorough reorientation of the HR initiatives in the banks. The HR strategy, *inter alia*, will have to deal with career path, provision of incentives for better performance, training in areas like risk management, technology, marketing, relationship management, etc. In other words, employees should be able to adopt a commercial orientation to business so that they can service existing clients well and recruit new customers.

The reduction in manpower could also give a push to the use of technology. Public sector banks have been relatively late entrants in respect of technology, with the result, their level of technology absorption has been low. However, recognising the need for using IT, the banks have gone for large-scale computerisation of branches in a rapid pace. Almost all the public sector banks have been able to capture 70% of their business through computerisation in compliance with the guidelines of the Central Vigilance Commission. They are offering various electronic banking products like Electronic Fund Transfer (EFT), Electronic Clearing Services, Electronic Data Interchange, etc. Besides, as part of alternative channels of delivery, they have established ATMs and in a limited scale offer telebanking and remote access facility to customers. Some of the banks have also established connectivity between select branches and provide "Anytime Anywhere" banking. However, considering the vast customer base they serve, such strategies are inadequate. Further lack of standardisation and non-availability of a reliable and safe inter-bank and intra-bank communication backbone have hampered any significant development of technology. With the establishment of INFINET (Indian Financial Network) by RBI, using V-SAT technology has begun. The INFINET will provide inter-bank connectivity and would eventually help introduction of various electronic banking products addressed to different market segments. It is also envisaged, the implementation of the Real Time Gross Settlement (RTGS) system will be completed soon bringing the payment systems in the country on par with other developed countries. It may be mentioned that the Information Technology Bill,'99 *inter alia* provides for legal recognition of electronic records, digital signatures and books of account maintained in electronic form by a bank.

While the efforts of banks to evolve alternative channels of service delivery like ATMs, Internet banking, etc., is laudable, adding another channel of delivery without pruning the existing channels like branch will only add to overheads. Since electronic service channels will drastically cut costs of transactions, banks will be required to optimise their branch network.

Closely linked to the use of technology is innovations. In fact, in the developed economies, technology has been a key-driver of financial innovations. It was the advancement in computing and communications technology that spurred the growth of derivative instruments and cross-border transactions. In fact, technology is credited with 'ending geography', as funds today flow in a seamless world. In fact, unbundling of risks has become possible by use of technology based solutions, a task which derivatives perform. As the process of deregulation is pursued and structural barriers are lowered, new opportunities will emerge. But in every opportunity, there is an inherent risk as well. Banks cannot perform in a competitive environment unless there are means of mitigating the inherent risks. Derivative instruments like swaps, options, futures, etc., enable such risk mitigation. As the Indian financial market moves towards more sophistication, some of these instruments have emerged as in the case of interest rate swaps, futures, etc. Securitisation is in its infancy. But there is a need for more such instruments considering globalisation of the corporate sector and as the Indian economy integrates with the world economy. Acquiring the skills to offer such products will pose a major challenge to the public sector banks. But as mentioned earlier, development of full-fledged OTC markets will take sometime till the structural rigidities in the financial markets are addressed.

At the retail level, public sector banks will have to make further inroads into electronic banking. It could be through card-based mechanisms like stored-value products (Smart Cards), internet based banking, telebanking, remote banking, etc. This will lead to innovative technology-based products and services.

As the Indian banks move gradually towards universal banking and as they position themselves as financial service providers, banking business is getting redefined. Technology is unsettling the earlier business processes and customer behaviour is undergoing change. To survive under these conditions, the public sector banks will have to undertake business process re-engineering, re-define their strategy and align their organisational structure. They have to understand their core competencies and dovetail their strategies to exploit such strengths. Besides, banks will have to develop IT and HR strategies which are aligned to the overall business strategy. Banks which are successful in restructuring their operations will be better placed to face the onslaught of competition.

3.3.3 Banking Institutions

The measures adopted aim at introducing an element of competitive efficiency in the Indian banking system. It would improve their operational efficiency and strengthen the financial position of banks, which is a pre-requisite of their exposure to the globalised banking environment. Banking, nine-tenth of which is in the public sector, has been subjected to administrative controls in respect of interest rates, directed lending, personnel policies, expansion of offices, etc., over the years. These controls are now sought to be eased in a gradual manner.

Both the deposit rates structure and the lending rates structure were determined by the regulatory authority in the past. In addition, banks used to be subjected to various guidelines on priority sector lending, investment in Government securities, etc., which were a part of the policy to ensure that a certain percentage of credit went to specified sub-sectors. Till recently, banks were required to keep investment in Government and other approved securities at 24% of their net demand and time liabilities by way of Statutory Liquidity Ratio (SLR), which investments in effect were banks' funds lent to the government at concessional rates. In the 'private' sector category also, banks were required to dispense 40% of credit to 'predefined' priority sectors, again most of it at concessional rates. The concessionality in interest charged and a high level of pre-empted funds, affected bank profitability adversely, despite a measure of cross-subsidisation. As to the interest structure, fixed rates have been done away with. Banks enjoy the freedom to offer deposit rates subject to a maximum and charge lending rate subject to a minimum on their non-priority advances. Significantly, the banks can now charge interest at commercial rates on priority advances, if the amount advanced exceeds ₹ 2,00,000 except education loans for higher studies. These steps should help banks shore up profitability to a large extent. In respect of larger industrial advances, the erstwhile Credit Authorisation Scheme has been replaced by a relaxed Credit Monitoring Arrangement which permits individual banks to avail of the opportunity to tone up their credit appraisal skills.

To rationalise banking presence on efficient lines, banks have been given permission to open, close or relocate branches in non-rural areas without prior approval of the Reserve Bank of India subject to their fulfilling certain norms, thus virtually doing away with the branch licensing policy. A proposal is also under active consideration to segregate the regional rural bank subsidiaries of the commercial banks and reorganise them into separate units with different norms to judge their viability.

To restore financial health of banks, prudential norms have been set, adherence to which will reflect, in the first phase, the true picture of their financial condition. Guidelines have been issued on the transparency of their financial statements, on income recognition, asset classification as well as on provisioning for bad and doubtful assets. Simultaneously, capital adequacy norms have been prescribed for various banks.

The guidelines are to be implemented over a period of time. One other important aspect of banks' health which will need to be dealt with is the present accumulation of their Non-performing Assets (NPAs) and their present comparatively weak capital base. It is essential that the accumulated NPAs be removed from the banks' balance sheets by means of a mechanism like the Asset

Reconstruction Fund, recommended by the Narasimham Committee. This undoubtedly would involve substantial separate funding. But, without it, touching capital adequacy norms will pose a very difficult problem for banks.

A *major structural change* in our financial system is the *infusion of competition*. The enabling conditions for a more competitive environment initially took the form of shifts in the policy regime. Statutory pre-emptions were progressively lowered, interest rates were deregulated and restrictions on entry and exit were eased. Financial markets were developed to enable financial intermediaries to deal in assets and liabilities of varying maturities and risk profiles. Activity restrictions were eased and banks can now undertake various types of activities reserved earlier for development financial institutions. Likewise, the term-lending financial institutions have been allowed to undertake working capital financing. Elements of this growing convergence have determined the pace and sequencing of the approach to universal banking in the recent years.

Within the banking system, there is heightened competition with the introduction of new generation private sector banks. Foreign banks have also been a source of competition, at least potentially, given their use of sophisticated technology, risk monitoring analysis and exposure management. In recent years, the policy thrust has been to level the playing field for domestic and foreign banks. For example, foreign banks that were earlier allowed to operate only branches but not subsidiaries, are now free to choose to set up either branches or subsidiaries under common banking regulations including lending norms. Appropriate legislative changes are also under consideration of the government. Foreign direct investment up to 49% has been allowed in private sector banks and up to 20% in nationalised banks. Guidelines have been issued for the entry of banks into insurance business for providing infrastructure and services support without any contingent liability.

3.3.4 Issues in Supervision and Regulation

Recent international financial developments have underscored the critical role of the regulatory and supervisory function in ensuring the health and stability of the financial system. There is now a worldwide debate on how to strengthen financial regulation even further, including proactively, to contend with the dangers posed by creative accounting practices, even as the depressed state of economic activity exerts conflicting pulls on the extent of supervisory rigour. At the same time, the impact of technological advancement, financial liberalisation and the degree of integration between domestic and international financial markets has rendered the conduct of oversight of the financial system a highly complex task.

Regulatory and supervisory authorities need to be regarded as providing a range of services to the community. This includes the establishment of specific rules of behaviour for participants in the financial system, monitoring the observance of the rules, and general supervision of the behaviour of financial entities. The primary need for regulation arises from the fact that consumers of financial services are not in a position to evaluate the soundness and safety of financial entities since even the most stringent laws regarding enforceability of contracts cannot protect for post-contract-signing behaviour. Therefore, the rationale for financial regulation lies in the economic costs imposed on society by the external effects of financial market failure which can threaten systemic stability. There is also a potential for gridlocks in the financial system due to adverse selection and moral hazard problems. At the same time, substantial benefits can accrue from correction of market imperfections, reduced transaction costs, and in general, providing people with a financial system they can trust.

In India, progressive strengthening of the regulatory and supervisory framework has been a key element of financial sector reforms since their inception. There has been progress in achieving international best practices in banking supervision and this has been noted even convergence with the best practices, fine-tuning is undertaken keeping in view the country-specific circumstances. An example of this is the approach being evolved towards consolidated supervision and the compliance of banks with accounting standards.

In the past 10 years, there has been a shift in emphasis from microregulation to macro-management, supported by a tightening of prudential norms and improvements in the functioning of financial markets. A clearer definition of the regulatory role of the Reserve Bank is also being considered within the broader debate on the conflict of interest between ownership and regulation. The supervisory strategy of the Board for Financial Supervision, which is entrusted with the supervision of banks, all-India financial institutions, non-bank financial companies and systemically important institutions, consists of combining a restructured system of on-site inspection with off-site surveillance, enhancing the role of external auditors and strengthening corporate governance, internal controls and audit information on exposure to sensitive sectors, market risks and macroprudential early warning indicators. Banks need to prepare for switching to risk-based supervision by identifying information gaps in the compilation of risk profiles and training to personnel. The supervisory follow-up process will then involve a monitorable action plan including remedial actions and timely corrective steps.

Banks are being encouraged to improve the reliability and robustness of their risk management, management information and supervisory reporting systems. A scheme of prompt corrective action based on early warning triggers is being developed as a supervisory tool. Trigger points would be set for three parameters — capital, non-performing assets, return on assets — and for each trigger a set of mandatory and discretionary prompt corrective actions would be laid down. Financial soundness indicators have been proposed for monitoring the health and soundness of financial institutions and markets. The legal reforms to enable the regulatory and supervisory regime to keep pace with advancements in information and communication technology. The envisaged reforms relate to electronic cheques, cheque truncation, securitisation and reconstruction of financial assets, the payment system and money laundering. With regard to the cooperative banking sector, the Reserve Bank has proposed that there is need for an apex supervisory body to deal with the existing regulatory overlap among multiple agencies. In respect of the financial institutions, the Reserve Bank has been in favour of divesting all or part of its holdings to mitigate the conflict of interest that could potentially arise in regulating the entities. However, it is necessary to recognise that there are distinct limits to what regulation and supervision can achieve. In particular, it does not provide a foolproof of assured contract of safety and does not absolve either management or consumers of their responsibilities.

❖ Capital Market

Activities on the capital market are increasing, consistent with government's liberalisation policy in other spheres, liberalised operations were permitted on the capital market and the market was opened to potential global investment. Over the past 20 years, major liberalisation measures were taken in this regard.

(*a*) The office of the *controller of capital issues* was disbanded. Corporates are now allowed to enter the market directly, without prior approval. For the purpose of control and regulation in the process, SEBI has laid down certain guidelines for disclosures, etc.

(*b*) A new company set up by an existing company with a five-year track record of consistent profitability is now free to price its issue (in the past, such issues used to be at par). Similarly, private or closely held companies, with a 3-year track record of consistent profitability, can now *price their issues* freely.

(*c*) *Stringent disclosure norms* have been prescribed for compliance by corporates by SEBI.

(*d*) For debentures, companies are now allowed to determine interest rates, the premium amount on fully convertible debentures, etc. *Credit rating* has been made mandatory for issue of debentures or any debt instrument by a company.

(*e*) The *capital market* has now been *opened to foreign institutional investors*. An earlier issue of this publication carried a feature on the scheme.

(*f*) New institutions, *viz.,* Stock Holding Corporation of India Ltd., Over-the-counter Exchange of India (OTCEI) have been set up to cater to investor requirements and improve the working of stock exchanges.

With growing equity cult and investment awareness among savers, the capital market is poised to play a much enlarged role in the financial sector.

In the short-term money market, many new instruments have been introduced such as certificates of deposit, commercial paper, up to 364 days treasury bills, etc. To regulate activities in the money market, which is not as developed as the capital market, Discount and Finance House of India was set up. Commercial banks and financial institutions have been permitted to set up Money Market Mutual Funds. Steps have also been taken to regulate the activities of Mutual Funds set up by banks and financial institutions. They have been brought under the purview of SEBI.

3.3.5 Private Sector Non-banking Financial Companies (NBFCs)

A committee recently went into the functioning of NBFCs and its recommendations are under consideration. Major recommendations are: enactment of suitable new legislation, compulsory registration with SEBI for NBFCs of certain minimum size, stipulations regarding profit appropriation, risk exposure, portfolio management, etc. A policy announcement is expected shortly.

The financial sector plays an important role as fulcrum for the activities in the real sector of the economy. It has to perform its functions most efficiently. Alive to this need, many structural and operational reforms have been and are being implemented and the financial system is being liberalised to let market forces determine their operational efficiency. The sector has an ambitious agenda ahead whose objective is a vibrant, internationally competitive financial system which is adequately responsive to the needs of India's economic and social development.

The financial sector has a vital role in promoting efficiency and growth. It intermediates in the flow of funds from those who want to save a part of their income to those who want to invest in productive assets. The efficiency of intermediating depends on the width, depth and diversity of the financial system. Till about two decades ago, a large part of household savings was either invested directly in physical assets or put in bank deposits and small saving schemes of the government. Since late eighties, however, equity market started playing an important role.

Other markets such as the medium to long-term debt markets and short-term money market remained relatively segmented and underdeveloped. In the past decades, the government and its subsidiary institutions and agencies had an overwhelming and all encompassing role, which has played a part in slowing the evolution and development of these markets. The extensive system of controls, rules, regulations and procedures, directly or indirectly affected the development of these markets.

Major problems in the financial system were lack of flexibility in intermediary behaviour and segmentation of various markets and sets of financial intermediaries. Well developed markets are inter-connected; demand-supply imbalances in one market overflow into related markets, thereby dampening shocks and disturbances. The interconnection also ensures that interest rates and returns in any market, reflect the broad demand supply conditions in the overall market of savings. A rise in the demands for funds for investment, above the existing flow of funds from savings, leads to rise in the interest rate or rate of return in all markets. The time lag may differ from market-to-market depending on economic factors. Conversely, a decline in demand for funds for investment below savings leads to a fall in interest rates across the board. This does not happen in segmented markets. Adjustment in interest rates is also delayed by the slow speed of response of intermediaries and their lack of flexibility.

❖ Deregulation of Interest Rates

Rationalisation of the interest rate structure has been carried out gradually with the ultimate objective of total deregulation of interest rates. The most important reform in interest rate structure was the deregulation of lending rates on advances above ₹ 2 lakh. With predominant portion of loans falling in this category, banks have been given freedom to fix the interest rates, depending upon the risk-perception of the loan. For this, banks have to evolved Base Rate (B.R.) which is the rate offered to the first-class clients of the banks and peg the interest rates to be charged for other borrowers to this rate. Banks have been required to declare the maximum spread they earn over the B.R. loans in the ₹ 25,000 – ₹ 2 lakh category are to be charged at Base Rate or even below base rate.

In order to switch to signal-based tools of monetary control, the RBI has more recently activated the Bank Rate which is the rate at which the central bank discounts eligible bills. Interest rates are getting gradually linked to the Bank Rate and with inflation at high levels in the recent three years period, the Bank Rate has been reduced to 6%. Keeping with such a increasing interest rate regime, many banks have also increased their Base Rate to the highest at 11%. Loans up to ₹ 2 lakh will be charged below base rate. More recently, keeping with international practice, RBI has provided freedom to banks to provide loans at below base rates to exporters. Thus, lending rates have been deregulated for all loans and advances excepting those under Differential Rate of Interest (DRI) scheme, export credit and advances up to ₹ 2 lakh. Banks have also been permitted to announce their base rate for term loans over ₹ 2 lakh.

In respect of deposit rates also, interest rates have been mostly deregulated with banks given freedom to determine interest rates on term deposits of all tenors. Interest rates on saving deposits, however, continue to be regulated and this is also expected to be deregulated eventually.

Thus, the process of deregulation of interest rates has been more or less achieved, save for certain categories of loans and saving deposits. The deregulation process during the last decade has provided valuable lessons to banks, particularly in regard to the cost-consciousness in resource mobilisation.

❖ Directed Credit and Rural Finance

Considering the contribution of agriculture and the rural sector to the national economy, a multi-agency approach to rural credit and development has been adopted. The rural credit system in the Indian context has been a product of both *evolution* and active *intervention* by the government. Bank credit to the rural sectors are denominated under "Priority Sector" credit under which various target groups of beneficiaries are included. These *inter alia* include credit to agriculture and allied activities, small-scale industries, credit to weaker sections, professionals and self-employed. At the end of March 2001, lending to priority sector credit extended by public sector banks amounted to ₹ 1,47,478 crore and formed 43.2% of net bank credit as against the national goal of 40%. Advances to agriculture stood at ₹ 54,100 crore, while SSI credit was to the tune of ₹ 48,000 crore.

Important changes have been brought in the definition of priority sector by broadening the coverage and combining sub-goal relating to direct/indirect agriculture credit. Concessionality element in interest rates on these loans have also been largely done away thereby reducing the burden of cross-subsidisation. To provide a level playing field, foreign banks are also now required to dispense PS credit as will be the new private sector banks. Balancing social orientation with achievement of adequate profits is a challenge before the banks.

❖ Financial Supervision

With deregulation, the supervisory role of the Reserve Bank of India has been enhanced. Following the recommendations of the Narasimham Committee, a separate Board for Supervision (BFS) has been established. Besides, a Department of Supervision (DoS) headed by a Deputy Governor has been established. The DoS has been entrusted with the task of supervising the banks and other non-banking financial companies. A process of rating banks on the *CAMELS (Capital adequacy, Management, Earnings, Liquidity and Systems)* format has been put in place.

Keeping with the shift towards prudential regulation, emphasis is being laid on off-site supervision which will supplement on-site supervision. The off-site supervision system comprises 12 returns focussing on the supervisory concerns like Capital adequacy, asset quality, credit concentration, connected lending, risk exposure, etc. The role of reporting accountants has been enhanced so as to improve the authenticity of the data reported, while measures have also been initiated to strengthen internal governance in banks. Particular mention may be made of the system of Concurrent Audit of large branches of banks and the constitution of the Audit Committee of the Board (ACB). Banks have already the system of Executive Committee (EC) and Management Committee (MC) to make important operational decisions.

Following the adoption of international financial standards and codes, the RBI has put in place a system of Prompt Corrective Action (PCA) which will help in addressing financial distress in banks in a pro-active manner. Under the PCA framework, which is modelled on the lines existing in USA, three main parameters have been proposed, *viz.,* Capital to Risk Asset Ratio (CRAR), Net NPAs and Return on Assets (RoA). Trigger points have been set up under these three parameters and for every trigger point, a set of mandatory and discretionary preventive corrective actions have been prescribed. The PCA will pre-empt further deterioration in the soundness of the banks and bring about improvement in their functioning. RBI has also proposed to move over to risk-based supervision which aims at allocation of supervisory resources according to the risk perception of the supervised institution. This will also facilitate adoption of one of the pillars of the New Capital, Accord, *viz.,* Supervisory Review. Also, the RBI has proposed to adopt Consolidated Supervision which will allow bank supervisors to get a consolidated view of the operations of banking groups, apart from that of the parent bank.

❖ Financial Market Interlinkages

Indian financial market till recently was characterized by market segmentation among its various constituents on account of variety of regulations including barriers to entry. This impaired free flow of resources. Since the introduction of reform measures in early 1990s, broad segments of the market, *viz.*, money market, Government securities market, and foreign exchange market have responded favourably with growing interlinkages among them, thus facilitating faster liquidity pass through. This is borne out by the fact that improvements in liquidity in 1996-97 were translated in significant softening of various money market rates, interest rates on Government papers, particularly those on shorter end, and forward premia in the foreign exchange market. The increasing complementarity between credit market and capital market on the one hand, and credit market and external sources of financing on the other, has become evident in the availability of a wider choice among alternate sources of funds to the corporates. The integration between yield rates of Government papers and those of other debt market instrument is, however, currently at a formative stage on account of, *inter alia*, narrow investor base and lack of depth in secondary markets. While these changes are symptomatic of a greater interplay of market forces, the thrust of the present policy is on elimination of the factors constraining free flow of resources among these segments and to facilitate opportunities for larger arbitrage, so that pricing and allocation of resources become more efficient. These interlinkages, however, have also added another dimension to the conduct of monetray policy in view of the necessity to assess, on a continuous basis, the liquidity in the system and to adopt appropriate measures minimizing volatility in financial markets.

❖ Continuing Process

There can be no finite end to the process of financial sector reform and liberalisation. Financial sector reform is a process rather than an event. Strengthening the financial system has to be a continuing effort. If India has been spared the ravages of the type of financial crisis that has overtaken some countries as far apart as East Asia, Russia and some Latin American countries, it is because of an element of prudence that has marked our policies. Our banks have not been exposed to lending to the bubble sectors such as real estate and the stock market nor have they been involved in the dangerous type of assets-liability mismatches that characterised the financial systems in some East Asian countries.

The Indian financial services sector is witnessing unprecedented changes, fuelled by economic deregulation and technological and financial innovation. The emergence of the internet as an alternative service delivery platform has profound implications for the way that business is conducted. The availability of online real-time information implies considerably lower switching costs for customers and places a premium on customer retention. Also, traditional entry barriers are rendered redundant to a large extent. As a result, traditional entities increasingly have to focus on technology adoption as a means of retaining competitive advantage.

The internet has changed the competitive dynamics of the financial services business in the United States with nearly all traditional-service providers setting up parallel online delivery channels. Competition has been heightened by the emergence of certain internet-only banks and online brokerage service providers. However, the internet has not yet had the same kind of impact in India, owing to the absence of an enabling regulatory framework and a lack of adequate infrastructure, resulting in low levels of internet penetration particularly in rural areas.

Following a decade of reform, the Indian financial sector is gradually moving towards attainment of global standards, through the proactive role played by the RBI and other regulatory bodies. The RBI has adopted the Core Principles for Effective Banking Supervision suggested by the Basle Committee and is working out further improvements to prudential norms, particularly in the areas relating to asset classification and provisioning standards. It has also brought disclosure standards almost at par with global best practices by requiring data on important performance indicators including provisions and non-performing loans to be added as notes to accounts. In a free-interest-rate regime, asset-liability management (ALM) is of paramount importance, and the RBI has instituted an ALM reporting system beginning this financial year. Further, the RBI has also moved towards more stringent capital adequacy norms and adopted the CAMELS (capital adequacy, asset quality, management, earnings, liquidity and systems and control) system for evaluating the soundness of banks. All these measures are aimed at ensuring the stability and health of the Indian financial system, which is imperative in a global financial environment marked by increasing capital mobility.

3.4 FINANCIAL GLOBALISATION

During the past two decades, financial markets around the world have become increasingly interconnected. Financial globalisation has brought considerable benefits to national economies and to investors and savers, but it has also changed the structure of markets, creating new risks and challenges for market participants and policymakers.

Globalisation — the process through which an increasingly free flow of ideas, people, goods, services, and capital leads to the integration of economies and societies — has brought rising prosperity to the countries that have participated. It has boosted incomes and helped raise living standards in many parts of the world, partly by making sophisticated technologies available to less advanced countries.

The *globalisation of national economies* has advanced significantly as real economic activity — production, consumption, and physical investment — has been dispersed over different countries or regions. Today, the components of a television set may be manufactured in one country and assembled in another, and the final product sold to consumers around the world. New multinational companies have been created, each producing and distributing its goods and services through networks that span the globe, while established multinationals have expanded internationally by merging with or acquiring foreign companies. Many countries have lowered barriers to international trade, and cross-border flows in goods and services have increased significantly.

The liberalisation of national financial and capital markets, coupled with the rapid improvements in information technology and the globalisation of national economics, has catalyzed financial innovation and spurred the growth of cross-border capital movements. The globalisation of financial intermediation is partly a response to the demand for mechanisms to intermediate cross-border flows and partly a response to declining barriers to trade in financial services and liberalised rules governing the entry of foreign financial institutions into domestic capital markets.

Competition among the providers of intermediary services has increased because of technological advances and financial liberalisation. The regulatory authorities in many countries have altered rules governing financial intermediation to allow a broader range of institutions to provide financial services and new classes of nonbank financial institutions, including institutional investors, have emerged. Investment banks, securities firms, asset managers, mutual funds, insurance companies, speciality and trade finance companies, hedge funds, and even telecommunications, software and food companies are starting to provide services similar to those traditionally provided by banks.

❖ Benefits versus Risks

All in all, the radical change in the nature of capital markets has offered unprecedented benefits. But it has also changed market dynamics in ways that are not yet fully understood. One of the main benefits of the growing diversity of funding sources is that it reduces the risk of a "credit crunch". When banks in their own country are under strain, borrowers can now raise funds by issuing stocks or bonds in domestic securities markets or by seeking other financing sources in international capital markets. Securitisation makes the pricing and allocation of capital more efficient because changes in financial risks are reflected much more quickly in asset prices and flows than on bank balance sheets. The downside is that markets have become more volatile, and this volatility could pose a threat to financial stability. For example, the OTC derivatives markets, which accounted for nearly $100 trillion in notional principal and $3 trillion in of Balance sheet credit exposures in June 2001, has grown up to $ 370 trillion market in 2006. Accordingly, those in charge of preserving financial stability need to better understand how the globalisation of finance has changed the balance of risks in international capital markets and ensure that private risk-management practices guard against these risks.

Another benefit of financial globalisation is that, with more choices open to them, borrowers and investors can obtain better terms on their financing. Corporations can finance physical investments more cheaply, and investors can more easily diversify internationally and tailor portfolio risk to their preferences. This encourages investment and saving, which facilitate real economic activity and growth and improve economic welfare. However, asset prices may over-shoot fundamentals during booms and busts, causing excessive volatility and distorting the allocation of capital. For example, real estate prices in Asia soared and then dropped precipitously before the crises of 1997-98, leaving many banks with nonperforming loans backed by collateral that had lost much of its value. Also, as financial risk becomes actively traded among institutions, investors, and countries, it becomes harder to identify potential weaknesses and to gauge the magnitude of risk. Enhanced transparency about economic and financial market fundamentals, along with a better understanding of why asset market booms and busts occur, can help markets better manage these risks.

Finally, creditworthy banks and firms in emerging market countries can reduce their borrowing costs now that they are able to tap a broader pool of capital from a more diverse and competitive array of providers.

❖ Technology

The widespread application of computer and telecommunications technology to financial markets has permitted markets to process a significantly larger volume of transactions, to communicate developments more rapidly and more widely, to react more quickly to new information, to devise innovative instruments and trading procedures, and to link markets in different time zones.

Communications technology has also increased the global integration of financial markets by making possible round-the-clock trading. In addition, improved computer technology has allowed the use of new methods for hedging against risks, including financial options and futures, and has opened up arbitrage opportunities based on computer-generated and computer-executed transactions — computer trading.

❖ Liberalization

Financial liberalization has also diminished the segmentation of domestic financial markets and increased the integration of international financial centres. Liberalization has been prompted by official policies to promote greater efficiency in domestic financial markets and to increase the access of domestic institutions to international sources of finance. Moreover, the expanding Euro markets have led to competitive pressures on domestic financial markets and have made it easier to circumvent regulations.

Liberalization has proceeded along two basic lines: relaxation of price and quantity restrictions and the easing of limitations on certain types of financial activities.

❖ New instruments

Innovative instruments are the third major force transforming financial markets. These instruments fall into two broad categories, *credit- or liquidity-creating,* and *risk-transferring.* Under the first category, the greater use of tradable assets issued directly by the borrower — securitization — has been the most important element. In particular, syndicated loans have been displaced to a large degree by issues of international bonds, by the use of note issuance facilities, and by issues of Eurocommercial paper, not underwritten by financial institutions.

Risk-transferring innovations have occurred in the area of hedging instruments such as *financial options, financial futures, and interest rate and currency swaps.* These new instruments permit various risks to be unbundled, separately priced, and sold to new portfolios willing to assume the risk. Swaps have furthered the integration of international capital markets by allowing access to markets in maturity ranges that previously were uneconomic. For example, currency swaps have effectively extended the maturity range for which forward cover is available to about ten years. Thus, intermediation opportunities that were previously unattractive, because of the inability to hedge currency risk, have become possible.

Reforms in financial sector in India is a continuous process. With the global integration, technological advancement, the reforms are focused on new instruments and policy measures.

The changed financial environment has also had important implications for the conduct and effectiveness of national monetary policy. The analysis of financial market conditions, the meaning of monetary aggregates, the linkage of monetary policy to the real economy, and inflation can all be influenced to varying degrees by structural changes in financial markets. The transparency of conditions in financial markets has been lessened considerably in recent years because markets have developed in areas where statistical coverage is as yet weak. In particular, the relative importance of bond markets and off-balance sheet activities of financial institutions (such as interest and currency swaps) has increased substantially. New instruments for credit or liquidity creation, as well as increased access to international markets, have made it more difficult to evaluate conditions in financial markets and judge the proper course for policy.

The revolutionary nature of the changes in financial markets wrought by financial liberalization measures and the recent wave of financial innovations. These changes have enhanced market efficiency, hedging opportunities, and blurred the traditional distinctions in financial markets, both domestically and internationally.

The design of growth-oriented adjustment programmes can benefit from a systematic review of financial sector issues. Three broad areas for such review are: an analysis of how well the instruments work in order to improve the effectiveness of monetary policy and facilitate a switch away from direct controls; the formulation of institutional and regulatory reforms to improve the efficiency and soundness of the financial sector; and an examination of the adequacy of the level and structure of interest rates. Significant measures to reform the financial sector in these areas have been introduced in one form or another in a number of countries, resulting in major shifts in the balance sheet positions of savers and investors. The monetary policy component of a growth-oriented adjustment programme with financial sector reform has two elements:

- In choosing monetary and credit targets, the effects of the reforms themselves on the demand for money and domestic savings are taken into account.
- Appropriate benchmarks are devised to monitor the progress of financial sector reform and developments in the efficiency of financial intermediation.

3.5 FINANCIAL INSTITUTIONS

3.5.1 Commercial Banking — Its Introduction

The importance of commercial banks in the process of economic development has been stressed from time-to-time by the economists and progressive bankers in India. Commercial banks play a very important role in India. In fact it is difficult to imagine how our economic system could function efficiently without many of their services. They are the heart and brain of our financial structure, since they have the ability in cooperation with the RBI, to add to the money supply of the nation and thus create additional purchasing power. Banks' lending/investing and other related services facilitate the economic processes of production/distribution/and a consumption.

❖ What is a Commercial Bank?

In earlier times, it was easy to identify a bank. It was an institution which took deposits from the public and lent money to needy individuals and institutions. Of course, there have always been institutions of rather different character which fell within the definition — UK discount houses. There have also been banks which have developed extensively into other areas of financial activity such as the *Universal* Banks. And it is universally acknowledged that because of the special nature of banking, the institutions involved needed special supervisory treatment for the protection, both of the public and of the financial system as a whole.

There is the *securitisation* of banking, effectively by passing the accepted banking practice in a way which leads to marketable instruments superseding *traditional borrowing* and lending.

Banking is different from moneylending but the two terms usually carry the same significance to the general public. The moneylender advances money out of his own private wealth, hardly accepts deposits from general public and usually charges high rate of interest. More often, the rates of interest relate to the needs of the borrower and at times the rates may be exorbitant. On the other hand banking has two important functions to perform one of accepting deposits and other of lending money and/or investment of funds and the rates 'of interest allowed on deposits and charged on advances generally remain known and reasonable. Accepting of deposits for lending and investments have been the original functions of banking but gradually these functions were extended, and others were added from time-to-time and presently banks perform a number of economic activities which may affect all walks of economic life.

Banks play a very important role in a nation's economy. Banks play a pivotal role in the economic development of a country and directing the affairs of the economy in various ways. The operations of the banking system in a country record the economic pulse of the country. The dependence of commerce upon banking has become so great that in modern economy and the period of globalization, the cessation, even for a day or two, of the banker's activities, would completely paralyse the economic life of a nation.

With globalization of economic activities taking place and enormous growth in international trade and cross-border economic activities the activities of banking have grown manifold and banks are now entering into new fields of economic activities.

❖ Different types of Banks

Banks can be classified in various types of categories depending upon their ownership pattern, nature of operations, structure of operations, etc.

For example, in India the banking sector may be classified into two categories, *viz.*, commercial banks and cooperative banks. While commercial banks cater to the needs of industry and trade to a great extent, the cooperative banks play a major role in financing agriculture and allied activities in rural areas, and trade and services in urban areas.

The commercial banks may be further classified into two categories such as — banks incorporated in India and banks incorporated outside India. Banks incorporated in India may be further classified as per their ownership pattern such as Public Sector Banks, Private Sector Banks, Regional Rural Banks, etc. The commercial banks may also be classified on the basis of their inclusion in the second schedule to the Reserve Bank of India Act, 1934 in two categories such as Scheduled Commercial Bank or Non-scheduled Commercial Banks. Public Sector Banks may be classified in two categories such as State Bank Group Banks (SBI and Associate Banks) or Nationalized Banks. Banks incorporated outside India and having branches in various countries are also termed as Multi-national Banks.

❖ Structure of a Commercial Bank

The banks may have a single unit operation or multi-unit operations. The operations may either be restricted to a single country or may spread to a number of countries. If the operations are generally restricted/confined to a single office .or in very rare cases restricted to branches within a strictly limited area the banks are described as Unit Bank. The practices of Unit Banks are prevalent mainly in USA.

In the case of chain banking a single bank operates in the country through a countrywide network or branches and the areas in which they operate vary depending on the size or the bank. This is the system followed in UK.

In the Indian banking scenario also the system of branch/chain banking is followed and banks have a network of branches spread far across the country or in restricted compact geographic areas. Regional Rural Banks operate in the specified regions of the country. Under the system the controls over branches are exercised by the Head Office through Circle or Regional Offices, etc. The branches extend all kinds of banking services and the Head Office/Regional Offices exercises administrative control over operations.

❖ Foreign Banks/Multinational Banks

Another important segment of the commercial banking system is that of Foreign Banks, also known as Multinational Banks. These banks registered and headquartered in overseas centres, open branches in other countries and thus acquire the status of Multinational Banks. The Central Bank of the host country frames rules for governance of such banks and the banks have to follow the rules applicable to them.

❖ Universal Banks

The term "Universal Banks has different meanings, but in a very broad sense it refers to those banks that offer a wide range of financial services such as — commercial banking (collecting deposits and making loans) and investment banking, i.e., issuing, underwriting and trading in securities and other activities, especially insurance. In universal banking, linkages can be downstream (a case when a bank undertakes non-banking activities, such as investment banking or insurance) or upstream (a case when a non-banking financial intermediary, such as, an investment banker or an insurance company undertakes the banking business). Universal banking usually takes one of the three forms, i.e., in-house, through separately capitalized subsidiaries or through a holding company structure. Three well-known countries in which these structures prevail are Sweden and Germany, the UK and the US. Universal banking in its fullest and purest form would allow a banking corporate to engage in-house in any activity associated with banking, insurance, securities, etc.

❖ Universal Banking in the Indian Context

In India, the financial system has traditionally been compartmentalized with three main types of financial intermediaries operating being commercial banks, DFIs and investment institutions. All these institutions were required to confine their operations strictly to their own areas, barring commercial banks which were allowed to undertake some investment/merchant banking activities and project finance within the prescribed limits. However, in the 1980s and the 1990s many significant changes took place which increasingly blurred the distinctions between the commercial banks and the DFIs. In 1983, the Banking Regulation Act was amended and banks were allowed to undertake leasing activity through separate subsidiaries. In the late 1980s commercial banks were allowed to set up subsidiaries for undertaking other non-traditional activities. Accordingly, many commercial banks set up subsidiaries in the field of investment banking, mutual funds, factoring, hire-purchase, etc., either wholly-owned or jointly in collaboration with other banks/DFIs. In the mid-1990s, all restrictions on project finance activity by commercial banks were removed. Banks were allowed to undertake hire-purchase and leasing activities in-house. Major DFIs, such as IDBI, ICICI and IFCI also set up subsidiaries in various fields, including commercial banking, including commercial banking. They were also allowed to accept deposits, within limits and subject to some conditions. DFIs, which traditionally extended only long-term project finance have started extending short-term loans including working capital. Banks and DFIs have also been allowed to undertake insurance business. Thus, the practice of universal banking is already prevalent in India and presently DFIs are being allowed to convert themselves into Universal Banks.

❖ Regional Rural Banks (RRBs)

In order to meet the needs of the weaker sections of the rural population, namely, small and marginal farmers, agricultural labourers, artisans and small entrepreneurs such banks were set up in 1975. Such banks mainly orient their operations in accordance with the declared objectives of their setting up, but may also allow financing to other categories of borrowers in exceptional circumstances which are incidental to their normal functioning. With a view to facilitating their operations in the context of their catering exclusively to the weaker sections various concessions are granted by the Central Bank of the country, i.e., the Reserve Bank of India. For instance, RRBs are included in the Second Schedule to the Reserve Dank of India Act immediately on their establishment and they are required to maintain a lower level of Statutory Liquidity Ratio (SLR) and Cash Reserve Ratio (CRR).

RRBs were required to be sponsored by a Scheduled Commercial Bank and that bank was statutorily required to provide managerial and financial assistance to the RRBs. The capital in RRBs is contributed by Central Government, State Government and the sponsoring bank in the ratio of 50:15:35 and the sponsoring bank is required to provide staff training support to RRBs. There are 82 RRBs in the country at the end of June 2010.

3.5.2 Role of Commercial Banks

Banks play a positive role in economic development of a country as repositories of community's savings and as purveyors of credit. Indian banking has aided the economic development during the last 62 years (1949 to 2011) in an effective way. The banking sector has shown remarkable responsiveness to the needs of planned economy. It has brought about a considerable progress in its efforts at deposit mobilisation and has taken a number of measures in the recent past for accelerating the rate of growth of deposits. As a recourse to this the commercial banks opened a number of branches in urban/semi-urban and rural areas and have introduced a number of attractive schemes to foster economic development. The scheduled commercial banks in the country comprise the SB India and its associate banks/nationalised banks* private sector banks and RRBs and foreign banks.

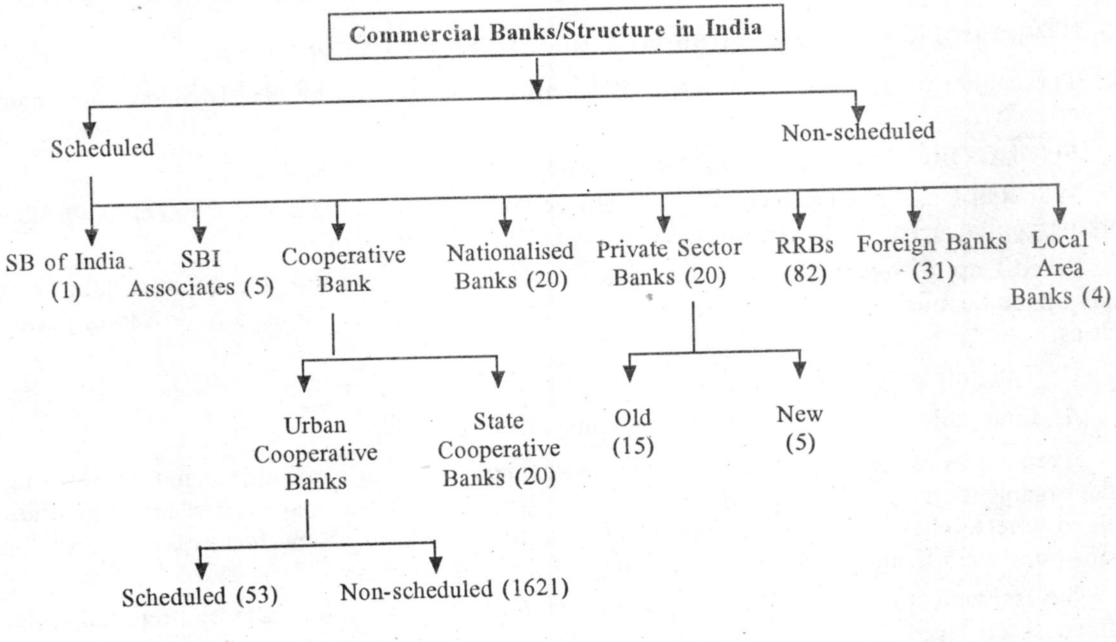

* Including IDBI Bank from 2003 year.

Commercial banks provide short-term and medium-term financial assistance. The short-term credit facilities are granted for *working capital* requirements (up to one year only) while the medium-term loans are for construction of premises/purchases of machineries and equipments (ranging from five to seven years). They also establish letters of credit on behalf of their clients favouring suppliers of raw-materials/machinery (both Indian and foreign) which extend the bankers' assurance for payment and thus help their delivery. Guarantees in lieu of security/earnest deposit/release of advance money/full payment of bills, etc., are also issued on behalf of customers. The various services provided by commercial banks are charted below:

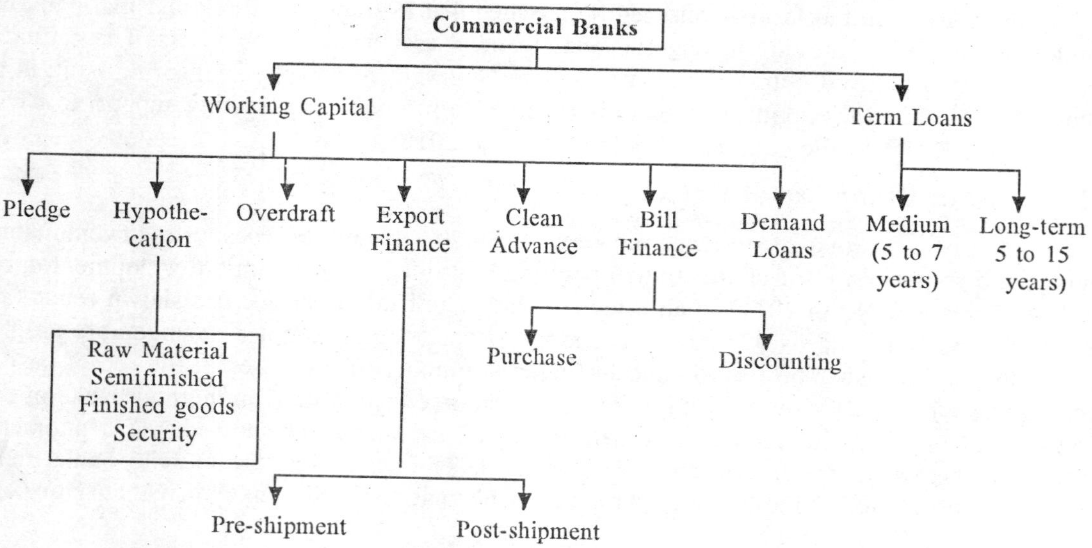

3.5.3 Types of Capital Requirements of a Business Enterprise

The capital requirements of a business enterprise can broadly be classified into two main categories, *viz.,*

Fixed Capital Requirements, i.e., for acquisition or fixed assets; and

Working Capital Requirements, i.e., for acquisition of current assets to meet day-to-day working capital needs of the business enterprise.

Fixed Capital means the capital, which is meant for meeting the permanent or long-term needs of the business, i.e., for acquiring those assets, which are to be used over a long period such as:

(*i*) Tangible assets like land, buildings, plant and machinery, furniture and fixtures, etc.

(*ii*) Intangible assets like goodwill, patents, copyrights, etc.

Fixed assets cannot be withdrawn from the business without disturbing the normal working of the organization and, therefore, it is necessary that sufficient funds are raised for acquisition or fixed assets. These funds ale required not only for setting up a new business, but also for expansion, diversification, etc., of the existing business activities.

The assessment or fixed capital requirement for a business can be made by preparing a list of fixed assets needed by the business and making assessment of the value for each of the components of the fixed capital required by the business organization. While making assessment of requirements of fixed capital various factors which have a direct impact on the requirements of a business organization, e.g., nature of business, size of the business, types of products, diversity of product-lines, method or production, method of acquisition of fixed assets, etc., should be carefully examined.

❖ Basic Principles for Management of Fixed Capital

While managing fixed capital in a business enterprise, some of the important points which should be observed are as under:

(*i*) Generally, only such assets should be purchased which are likely to increase productive and earning capacity of the business.

(*ii*) Investment in fixed assets should have a proper relationship with sales and profits.

(*iii*) Obsolete or outdated fixed assets should not be purchased even if the same are available at lower prices.

(*iv*) There should not be any idle capacity. In other words new fixed assets should be acquired if the existing capacity is fully utilized.

(*v*) The requirements of fixed assets should be met out of long-term sources of funds such as capital, term-loans, etc.

(*vi*) Proper depreciation should be provided out of profits to enable timely replacement of the fixed assets.

(*vii*) Fixed assets should be maintained properly with a view to increase the working life of the assets.

Working Capital means the capital required for day-to-day operations of a business organization. Working capital constitutes of current assets such as inventory, receivables, cash in hand and balances with banks, advance payments, etc. It is necessary for any organization to run successfully its affairs, to provide for adequate working capital. In fact management of working, capital require more attention than management or fixed capital. Mismanagement of current assets can be costly as on the one hand large investment in current assets may block the costly capital, whereas on the other non-availability/insufficiency of current assets at the time when the same are required may hamper productive activities. Proper estimation or the working capital requirements is a must for running the business efficiently and profitably. While making assessment of requirements of working capital various factors which have a direct impact on the requirements of a business organization, e.g., production policies, nature of business, time involved in manufacturing process, policy for extension or credit, rapidity of turnover, seasonal fluctuations, fluctuation of supply, credit available on purchases, etc., are to be kept in view.

❖ Basic Principles for Management of Working Capital

While managing working capital in a business enterprise, some of the important points, which should be observed, are as under:

(*i*) The projections on the basis of which requirements arc assessed should be realistic.

(*ii*) The projections should be based on proper assessment of available capacity, expected capacity utilization, and demand/supply position, general conditions of the economy and industry, other players in the market, etc.

(*iii*) Trade practices followed by supplier of inputs and buyers of the product should be carefully analyzed to assess the position of credit available on purchases, credit extended on sales and cost benefit analysis of the same.

(*iv*) For making assessment of holding level assessment of supply of various materials, economic quantity, transportation cost, lead period for receipt of material, etc., should be carefully analyzed.

The *working capital* should neither be *short of requirements nor in excess of requirement.* While shortage of working capital may hamper the production capacity, excess of working capital imposes avoidable costs and therefore a realistic assessment is very necessary.

❖ Types of Finance (Sources of Funds)

Finance is the lifeblood of a business. The business cannot run efficiently if it does not have adequate finance to meet its requirements. The financial requirements of business can be classified in two categories:

(*i*) Short-term financial requirements.

(*ii*) Long-term financial requirements.

Short-term funds are required to meet working capital needs. They are usually required for a period up to one year and are raised from sources, which can provide funds only for a short period quickly and at reasonable cost. The requirement of these funds is usually met by taking short-term loans or getting bills discounted from commercial banks.

The long-term funds are required to a great extent for meeting the fixed capital requirement or the business. They are required for a period exceeding one year and are further classified as medium- or long-term asunder:

- Medium-term for funds required for a period exceeding one year but up to five years.
- Long-term for funds required for a period exceeding five years.

These funds are raised by business organizations from sources, which provide the use of funds for a long period, *viz.*, shares, debentures, term loans from Specialized Financial Institutions, etc. Presently, commercial banks have also started to provide such finance for medium- and long-term to trade and industry either independently or sometimes in collaboration with one or more specialized financial institutions.

The types of finance available can be classified into various categories as under:

According to period —

- Long-term — such as shares, debentures, term loans, etc.
- Short-term — such as advances from commercial banks, advances from customers, trade creditors, public deposits, etc.

According to ownership —

- Owned Funds — such as share capital, retained earnings and surpluses, etc.
- Borrowed Funds — such as loans, debentures, public deposits, trade creditors, etc.

According to source of generation —

- Internal Sources — such as retained earnings, depreciation funds, etc.
- External Sources — such as shares, debentures, loans, etc.

These sources or finance can also be classified into following three categories:

(*a*) Security financing which includes financing through issue of shares (equity/preference shares), debentures, etc.

(*b*) Internal financing which includes financing through retained earnings and financing through depreciation funds.

(*c*) Loan financing which includes financing through short-term and long-term loans raised from banks/FIs, obtaining public deposits, trade creditors, etc.

3.5.4 Project Financing — Cost of Project and Sources of Finance

Let us now discuss the main components of project financing, i.e., project cost and sources of finance.

1. Project Cost

This include the cost of land, site development, building, civil works, plant and machinery, equipment for power, technical know-how, utilities, miscellaneous assets, preoperative and preliminary expenditure, provisions and contingencies and margin money for working capital.

Estimation of the project cost provides the basic information to decide its pattern of financing and viability of the project. If project cost is not estimated correctly, the entire financial planning for the project will go wrong and will be a futile exercise and may also create difficulties in tie-up of funds for financing the project cost. The following table gives an idea for estimation of project cost:

Sl. No.	*Nature of Asset*	*Item to be included*
1.	Land and Site Development	Cost of land, legal charges for registration, cost of levelling, cost of laying roads, cost of fencing, cost of gates, etc.
2.	Buildings	Main factory building, ancillary building, administrative building, godowns, canteen, guesthouse, quarters for essential staff, drainage, architect's fees, etc.
3.	Plant and Machinery	Cost of imported/indigenous plant and machinery, machinery stores and spares, related import duty/sales tax, transportation charges, installation charges, etc.
4.	Technical Know-how	Expenses of foreign technicians, expenses of training, technical know-how fee, consultancy fees for preparing project report, etc.
5.	Misc. Fixed Assets	Furniture, office equipment, vehicles, laboratory equipment, workshop equipment, fire-fighting equipment, effluent disposal equipment, etc.
6.	Preliminary and pre-operative expenses	Brokerages, commission, commitment charges, interest on term loan during construction period, Misc. expenses during construction period, etc.
7.	Provisions and Contingencies	Probable increase in cost due to new additions; due to rise in prices, etc.
8.	Margin Money for working capital	Margin money for financing of indigenous/imported raw material, consumable stores, stock of goods in process, finished goods, receivables, etc. Only margin money for working capital is included in the cost of project, which represent the organization's/contribution in the working capital as the rest amount is expected to be financed by financing agencies.

The aforesaid items are not exhaustive and depending upon the nature of project different items may be included in various categories of assets mentioned above which may form part of fixed capital requirement of an organization. Each project is different from the other project and cost of one project should not be blindly followed for other similar projects. The cost of project provides a basis for making financial arrangements to finance the project.

II. Sources of Finance

A project can be financed by anyone or more than one of the following sources:

(i) Issue of equity/preference shares: A share is the share in the capital of the company (and may be defined as one of the units into which the share capital of the company) is divided. A company can issue two types or shares, *viz.,* equity (ordinary) shares or preference shares. Equity capital does not involve any preferential right or fixed charge for payment of dividend. Preferential capital, however, carry preferential rights in respect of payment of a fixed dividend and also for repayment of capital in the case of winding up of the company in priority to equity shares.

(ii) Issue of secured debentures: A debenture is a document issued by a company as an evidence of a debt due from the company with or without a charge on the assets of the company. If the debenture carry a charge on the assets of the company the same are known as secured debentures. The debentures carry fixed rate of interest which is payable prior to payment of any dividend by the company.

While equity shares are part of the capital of the company, debentures constitute loan to the company. Shareholders are owners of the company but debentureholders are creditors of the company. Shareholders enjoy rights or membership of the company such as right to vote, etc., similar rights are not available to debentureholders. Debentures do not carry any voting rights.

(iii) Issue of convertible debentures and bonus: Issue of convertible debentures/bonds is another method of raising loan funds which combine certain benefits of equity capital and loan capital. The holder has the option to convert the debentures into equity shares at a later stage as per the terms of issue or the bond. Till conversion the bondholder remains entitled for payment of interest.

(iv) Term loans from financial institutions/banks: Banks/FIs grant term loans to finance technically feasible and financially viable and bankable projects. The term loans constitute borrowings by an organization and is repayable as per the terms of sanction stipulated by the concerned bank/FI along with interest thereon.

(v) External commercial borrowings/foreign direct investment: These have been discussed separately in details in the chapter on the subject of cross-border banking.

(vi) Deferred payment guarantee: Many times, the machinery suppliers provide the facility of deferred credit. In such cases banks may extend DPG facility in favour of the supplier and the business organization is able to procure assets there against.

(vii) Leasing finance: Under the leasing finance the business organization (lessee) enter into a contract with the leasing company (lessor) to acquire an asset for a fixed period during which the lessee pays periodical lease rent to the lessor for the use of the asset.

(viii) Unsecured loans/deposits: For financing of a project a business enterprise may resort to obtain unsecured loans/deposits from various sources. However, for raising deposits from public the organization has to comply with various statutory requirements prescribed by regulatory agencies.

(ix) Internal accrual: These are the sources generated by internal operations of the company, which are retained in the business to meet the business requirements of the company.

❖ Role of Banks in Business Finance

As has been discussed above business finance is that business activity which is concerned with the acquisition and conservation of capital funds in meeting financial needs and overall objectives of a business enterprise and covers planning, raising, controlling and administering of the funds used in the business, The business finance functions include financial planning, funds requirement decision, financing decision, investment decisions, etc.

Commercial banks play a very important role in these functions through variety of services provided by them. Various functions performed by commercial banks which describe their useful role in business finance/financial management or business enterprises have been discussed in other chapters. As has been mentioned earlier **"Banking means the accepting, for the purpose of lending or investment, of deposits of money from the public, repayable on demand or otherwise, and withdrawable by cheque, draft, order or otherwise" and 'Banking Company' means any company, which transacts the business of banking.** Banks accept deposits of different types — current, fixed, savings, etc., for the purpose of lending or investment. Making advances and investments of funds are equally important functions for banks. These basic functions of banking, *viz.*, acceptance of deposits for the purpose of lending or investment are helpful in financial management by business organizations as they can manage their business affairs efficiently through the channels of banking.

Banks perform, various fund-based and fee-based functions which help a lot in financial management. Fund-based functions of a bank are those in which banks make deployment of their funds either by granting advances or by making investments for meeting gaps in funds requirements or their customers/borrowers. Find-based functions or a bank may be classified in to two parts:

- Granting of loans and advances
- Making investments in shares/debentures/bonds.

Lending of funds to the constituents, mainly traders, business and industrial enterprises constitute the main business of any bank. Banks may allow loans and advances to its customers in any of the following manners:

— By sanctioning cash credit limit

— By allowing overdrafts (clean/secured)

— By purchasing/discounting bills

— By way or demand loan

The fund-based functions of banks include making of investments in various capital, debt market or money market instruments. The investments may be made in Equity Shares, Convertible Debentures, Govt. Securities, Non-convertible Debentures, etc. Lending and investment constitute a very important source of finance and helps in financial management for business organisations.

Fee-based functions of a bank are those in which banks extend various services to their customers or add their commitments to certain transactions undertaken by their clients and charge their fees/commissions for the services rendered by them/their commitments added to the transactions undertaken by the clients. These services provided by banks play a very important role in financial management functions of their customers. The total advances granted by all commercial banks were ₹ 23,48,493 crore ending 31-3-2008, while NPA at the end of (March 2007) were ₹ 38,602 core. The total advances were managed by their 73,836 branches (as on 31-3-2007). Out of this, SB India and its seven subsidiaries share was ₹ 4,82,426 crore (as on 31-3-2007).

3.5.5 Development Financial Institutions

Specialised and hybrid financial institutions that are engaged in the provision of financial and other assistance for the purpose of undertaking long-term developmental activities in certain identified sectors of the economy such as small-scale industrial sector/export promotion/industrial development/agricultural development, etc., are known as Development Financial Institutions or Development Banks.

Many factors are responsible for the emergence and the growth of development banks and the world over and in India in particular. They are —

Fostering industrial growth: An important factor that was responsible for the growth of development banks was the requirement of institutional machinery for fostering industrial growth in the country, especially after the World War II. This caused the need for supplying the basic ingredients of development/capital/knowledge and entrepreneurship for the rapid industrial growth of the country.

Long-term assistance: Another factor that caused the growth of development banks in India and the world over was the need for long-term assistance to business undertakings in the form of loans/underwriting and investment.

Balanced development: The need for promoting balanced and viable development by assuming the promotional role of discovering project, ideas/undertaking feasibility studies/providing technical/ financial and managerial assistance for the implementation of projects, etc., also enhanced the growth of development banks.

Promotional services: The need for the provision of financial assistance and rendering of promotional services such as the development of infrastructure and social utilities, etc., also prompted the development in the realm of development banking.

Infrastructure building: A strong reason for the phenomenal growth of the development banks was the need for building up the infrastructure required for the accelerated industrial development and economic growth.

Economic policies: The growth of development banks was also driven by the need for assisting in the process of implementation of economic policies formulated by the government.

Other factors: In addition to the above factors the following factors also contributed to the growth of development banks.

- Need for providing assistance for reconstruction/modernisation/development of war-shattered industries.
- Scientific and technological innovations leading to the need for venture capital funds.

❖ Functions of Development Financial Institutions

1. **Catalysts:** DFIs act as catalysts for quickening the pace of industrial development of the country in order to help alleviate endemic problems of poverty and unemployment.

2. **Entrepreneurial cult:** DFIs help promote the development of entrepreneurial cult by facilitating such activities as identification of growth projects/preparation of feasibility reports and provision of technical/managerial and other assistance to interested entrepreneurs right from the stage of project formulation to the commissioning and operation of the project.
3. **Socio-economic objectives:** DFIs assist in the realization of the socio-economic objectives of the country so as to ensure equitable distribution of income and wealth contributing to the promotion of social justice/self-reliance/prevention of concentration of economic power and regional balanced growth.
4. **Balanced development:** DFIs assist in the promotion of balanced regional and economic development. This is accomplished by assisting the development of priority areas such as SSI sector/export promotion/import substitution, etc.
5. **Optimal utilisation:** Development banks allow for the optional use of available resources of the country. They also cause development in the infrastructure such as transport/ telecommunications/banking, etc.
6. **Financial functions:** DFIs carry-out financial functions such as granting loans to industrial enterprises/subscribing to the shares and debentures of companies/guaranteeing the loans raised by them from other sources/guaranteeing deferred payments for the import of plant and equipment and underwriting the issue of industrial stocks/shares/bonds and debentures. They also provide technical/managerial and other services to entrepreneurs with a view to widening the entrepreneurial base.

3.5.6 Overview and Role in Indian Economy — Various DFIs in India

(a) Industrial Finance Corporation of India (IFCI): The IFCI was first financial institution, set up in 1948, for financing development projects in India. It was set up to provide medium and long-term finance to industrial concerns in the economy.

The following are the functions that are performed by the IFCI.

1. Granting loans and advances to industrial concerns.
2. Subscribing directly to the shares of industrial concerns.
3. Subscribing to the issues of debentures, repayable within a period of 20 years.
4. Guaranteeing loans raised from scheduled banks or state cooperative banks repayable within 25 years.
5. Underwriting of shares/debentures/bonds or stocks and disposable within seven years.
6. Acting as an agent for Central Government and the World Bank in respect of loans granted by them to industrial concerns in India.

❖ RIL-StanChart set to bid for IFCI to control and Sterlite consortium may go head-to-head

Reliance Industries (RIL) and Standard Chartered Bank may be the surprise co-bidders for a strategic stake in IFCI Ltd.

The New Delhi-based financial institution revived its plan to get on board a strategic investor, after its earlier plan in December 2007 fell apart.

Sources familiar with the situation said StanChart had expressed interest in the first round of IFCI bid in February, 2007.

This time, StanChart and RIL will be making a joint bid, revealed an investment banking source, who preferred not to be quoted.

Competing with the powerful duo would most probably be a consortium led by the Sterlite group.

The foreign bank withdrew from the bidding process after the IFCI share price went through the roof buoyed by expectations arising out of the bids made by several suitors.

Roughly during that time the ICI share hit a 52-week high to ₹ 121.70 per share.

In Feb. in a cryptic message to the premier stock exchanges, IFCI informed of a meeting of its board of directors, "to consider the issues relating to the induction of strategic investor and optionally convertible debentures held by Government of India".

StanChart's earlier bid to acquire a strategic stake in IFCI was structured by the 'strategic initiatives group' within the bank.

If is not known whether the same group is involved now.

❖ RIL in Joint IFCI bid

Some portfolios within the bank saw a change with PR Somasundaram, who led the strategic initiatives group being moved in an internal reshuffle. He now leads (in 2008) StanChart's brokerage business.

It is not clear whether RIL will be directly involved in the bids or the bid will be routed through associates of the group.

In recent times, many conglomerates including the Tatas and the Aditya Birla group have infused more men and funds into reviving their financial services business. RIL has been eyeing the retail finance business, in a strategy that is in sync with their retail business.

On 29th May, 2008, IFCI shares were among the biggest gainers in the stock exchanges. The shares finally ended at ₹ 62.30, a gain of 6.5%, when the main stock market index was down 209 points.

Analysts were not sure of RIL's gameplan as they were never keen on the financial business, which is said to be the preserve of Mukesh Ambani's younger brother Anil's flagship company Reliance Capital.

In December last year, the other bidders that expressed interest apart from the Anil Agarwal's Sterlite consortium were GE Capital, Natixis, Blackstone, Cargill Financial Services, Japan's Shinsei Bank, Punjab National Bank, Goldman Sachs and Standard Chartered bank.

Some weeks before the rejection of Sterlite bid, the IFCI board had approved issuing 123.7 million shares at ₹ 107 each on conversion of zero-coupon optionally convertible debentures held by banks and institutions.

(6) IDBI (now IDBI Bank)

The IDBI was set up with the goal of reorganising and integrating the structure of the existing financial institutions in the country so as to gear them up to cater to the demands of rapid industrialisation for medium- and long-term finance.

The financial functions of the Bank include —

(*i*) providing financial assistance to industrial concerns directly in the firm of loans.

(*ii*) providing indirect financial assistance by way of discounting and rediscounting of commercial papers.

(*iii*) Underwriting or purchase of shares and debentures.

(*iv*) Guaranteeing deferred payments and loans raised from other financial institutions by extending refinancing facilities and subscribing to the securities of such institutions.

IDBI was first established in July 1964. In September 1994, IDBI Bank was born. IDBI was registered as a bank on July 2, 2004. In March 2005, IDBI merged with IDBI Bank. The 51% shareholding is with government as such this bank is considered as nationalised bank. This is the total assistance sanctioned by IDBI in 2004-05 (April-Sept.) was ₹ 6,314.4 crore while total sanctions assistance in previous year was ₹ 5,630.8 crore (2003-04).

(c) State Financial Corporations: SFCs came to be set up in each state with the enactment of State Financial Corporations Act, 1951. At present, there are 18 SFCs for 28 states. SFCs were established to provide financial assistance to medium and SSIs which are outside the scope of IFCI. The scope of the SFCs activities includes public limited companies and also private limited companies/partnership firms and proprietary concerns.

The main functions of SFCs are —

(*i*) The financial assistance of SFCs takes the form of granting of loans or advances or subscribing to the debentures of industrial concerns repayable within 20 years.

(*ii*) Underwriting of issue of shares/bonds and debentures of industrial concerns repayable within seven years.

(*iii*) Guarantees loans raised by industrial concerns repayable within 20 years.

(*iv*) Acts as agents of the Central and State Governments.

Financial resources of SFCs comprise the followings —

- Capital structure of SFC being determined by the state government concerned, the minimum and maximum capital are ₹ 50 lakh and ₹ 500 lakh respectively.
- Contribution of capital funds by respective state governments/scheduled commercial banks/state cooperative banks/insurance companies/investment trusts and public.
- Issuing bonds and debentures and resorting to borrowings from the RBI to augment its financial resources.
- Accepting public deposits for periods *not less than one year* and such deposits could be accepted up to paid-up capital of SFC.

(d) EXIM Bank: The important functions of the EXIM Banks are as follows:

(*i*) Providing finance to export-oriented industries by way of preshipment finance and guarantees as well as rediscounting facilities.

(*ii*) Conducting export feasibility studies.

(*iii*) Providing international merchant banking services.

(*iv*) Assisting overseas Indian joint ventures and turnkey construction projects.

(*v*) Assisting exporters of capital goods/software and consultancy services.

(*vi*) Providing financial assistance to joint ventures in foreign countries and for the importation of machinery.

(*vii*) Conducting forfeiting operations in order to enable Indian exporters to have the advantage of access to quick financial assistance.

The EXIM Bank operates 14 lending schemes at present to help Indian exporters. Non-funded assistance is provided mainly for construction of projects which accounted for about 88% of sanctions and 72% issues. EXIM Banks is fully owned by the Central Government and is managed by nominees from government/financial institutions/banks and business community. EXIM Bank issues following guarantees directly or in participation with other banks, for project export contracts. Bid-bonds/advance payment guarantee/performance guarantee/guarantee for raising borrowings overseas, etc. EXIM Bank normally does not take up cases of exports involving credit requirement below ₹ 50 lakh and provides exports requirements up to ₹ 20 crore.

(e) National Small Industries Corporation (NSIC): Started in 1955 as financing and developmental agency. The functions of NSIC are also as follows:

(*i*) Securing government orders for the products manufactured by the SSIs.

(*ii*) Providing financial/technical and other assistance to enable the SSIs to execute such orders.

(*iii*) Constructing and managing industrial estates for SSIs.

(*iv*) Assisting SSI in the marketing and exporting of their products.

(*v*) Working for the linkage of SSI with large units so as to enable the former to serve as ancillaries to the later.

(*vi*) Underwriting and coordinating loans from banks and financial institutions to SSIs.

NSIC has six divisions each looking after a particular function. Such divisions are:

Store Purchase Division
Marketing Division
Projects Division
Hire Purchase Division
Industrial Estate Division
General Administration/Loans/Guarantees, etc.

(f) National Industrial Development Corporation (NIDC): NIDC was set up essentially for securing a balanced and integrated development of industries in the private as well as public sector. The NIDC also aimed at promoting and developing heavy industries that are essential for filling up gaps in the industrial structure of the country.

The NIDC renders the following functions for securing and filling up gaps in the industrial structure of the company:

(*i*) Providing financial assistance in the form of loans and advances/guarantees/discounting of bills and notes/underwriting of securities and direct subscriptions.

(*ii*) Providing consultancy services through the formulation of projects for setting up new industries and for developing new lines of production.

(*iii*) Undertaking the study and investigations of industrial schemes in order to ensure the best possible utilisation of natural resources.

(*iv*) Promoting/establishing and executing industries which lead to the growth of ancillary industrial development.

(*v*) Granting special loans to industries as an agency of the government.

(*vi*) Securing foreign assistance to carry-out studies for the purpose of preparation of reports for projects of national importance.

(*vii*) Providing various types of assistance to public and private sector concerns that are engaged in the manufacture of capital goods like machinery and equipment.

(*viii*) Providing both financial and entrepreneurial assistances for the rehabilitation and modernisation.

(g) State Industrial Development Corporations (SIDCs): These are established under the Indian Companies Act, 1956 as wholly-owned State Government undertakings for development of medium and large-scale industries. They undertake a range of promotional activities such as preparation of feasibility reports/conducting industrial potential surveys and entrepreneurship development programmes and developing industrial areas/estates. SIDCs are acting as agent for providing, tax benefits under the state government's package scheme incentives and acting as Agents of SIDBI for their Seed Capital Scheme. There are 28 SIDCs in the country out of these 11 SIDCs also function as SFCs to provide assistance to SSIs while seven SIDCs are involved in infrastructure development and provide extension services for the SSI sector. Council of Society of State Industrial Development Corporation, State Financial Corporations is the apex level organisations for SIDCs and SFCs both.

(h) Small Industries Development Bank of India (SIDBI): It was established in April 1990. The business domain of SIDBI consists of SSI units which contribute significantly the national economy in terms of production/employment and exports. SSIs are the industrial units in which the investment in plant and machinery does not exceed ₹ one crore. This limit is ₹ 5 crore in case of pharmaceutical/construction companies from July 2003.

The total number of working SSI units as on 31.3.05 were 1,18,60,997 (***Source:*** *Navbharat Times* dt. 5-11-05). Out of the total production 36% account for exports. SIDBI assistance flows to the transport, health care and tourism sectors alongwith professional and self-employed persons setting up SSI units. SIDBI delinked from IDBI in the year 2005. The total assistance sanctioned at the end of April-Sept. (2004-05) by SIDBI was ₹ 2,991.8 crore and ₹ 8,223.7 crore in 2003-04. SIDBI had decided to open its ten retail branches (*News,* Dec. 2005) and had targeted assistance of ₹ 13,500 crore for 2005-06. Refinance to SFCs is available from SIDBI at band of 7.5% to 8%. SIDBI directly assists SSIs under project finance scheme/equipment finance scheme/marketing scheme/vendor development schemes/infrastructural development scheme/ISO-9000 Technology Development of Modernisation Fund/Venture capital scheme assistance for leasing to NBFCs/SFCs/SIDCs.

Indirect assistance schemes under its indirect finance schemes SIDBI extends refinance of loans of SSI by primary lending institutions, *viz.,* SFCs/SIDCs and commercial banks with a view to up-scaling credit flows to the sector and raising resources for the SME fund.

3.6 LIFE AND NON-LIFE INSURANCE ORGANISATIONS IN INDIA

It is estimated that between the year 2005-2010 the business growth of life and non-life insurance was as below —

	(2005 Jan.)	(2010 Dec.)
Life Insurance	₹ 60,000 crore	₹ 1,40,000 crore
Non-life Insurance	₹ 20,000 crore	₹ 40,000 crore
Pension Business	₹ 4,000 crore	₹ 14,000 crore

The various (total 23 till June 2011) Life Insurance Companies in India were —

(*i*) Life Insurance Corporation
(*ii*) Tata-AIG Life Insurance
(*iii*) Bajaj Allianz Life Insurance
(*iv*) Birla Sun Life Insurance
(*v*) HDFC Standard Life Insurance
(*vi*) ICICI Prudential Life Insurance
(*vii*) SBI Life Insurance
(*viii*) ING Vysya Life Insurance
(*ix*) MET Life Insurance
(*x*) Reliance Life Insurance
(*xi*) Aviva Life Insurance
(*xii*) Kotak Mahindra Life Insurance
(*xiii*) Max New York Life Insurance
(*xiv*) Aegon Relegare Life Insurance
(*xv*) Star Union Daichi Life Insurance
(*xvi*) IDBI Federal Life Insurance Co. Ltd.,
(*xvii*) Sahara India Life Insurance
(*xviii*) Canara HSBC Life Insurance Company
(*xix*) Bharati Axa Life Ins.
(*xx*) Future Generali India Life
(*xxi*) Shriram Life Insurance Co. Ltd.,
(*xxii*) India First Life Insurance
(*xxiii*) DLF Pramerica Life Insurance

The share of LIC in the total life insurance business was 79% in 2009-10 and the rest was occupied by other private insurance companies.

Life Insurance business: In life insurance business, a long-term policy is issued for several years (ranging from 15 years to 30 years) or even for whole of life. A life policy covers risk of death due to natural causes as also due to accidents. In life insurance a level premium is payable generally throughout the policy period, even though the risk of death will be increasing with the advancing age of the life assured. During the policy period, the amount being determined by hi'/her age, at the time of effecting the policy and of course, the type of policy taken. The premiums may be paid by a single payment or annually/half-yearly/quarterly or even monthly. The life insurance authority carries out an actual valuations of its liabilities on is books, annually. The assets of the organisation are also *valued* as per Insurance Act, 1938, the excess of value of assets thus arrived at, cover the amount of the total policy liabilities is called *valuation surplus*. As per LIC Act, 5% of the valuation surplus is paid to the Government of India, whilst the remaining 95% is credited *with profits* policyholders as bonus. LIC made a profit in its business to the extent of ₹ 26,628 crore (year 1999-2000) @ 20.9% being the excess over expenditure. Total investments in the same year have grown from ₹ 56,182 crore in 1994-95 to ₹ 1,39,032 crore (in 1999-2000).

❖ Investment Norms

The investment policy of LIC is broadly guided by Section 27-A of LIC Act. Following criterias are followed as per the guidelines —

1. 50% of the total funds to be invested in Central and State Government securities.
2. 25% of total funds to be invested in socially-oriented projects like housing/sewage/water supply/slum clearance/electricity distribution, etc., of the Central and State Governments.
3. 25% in other investments at the discretion of LIC.
4. Subscription up to 30% of the equity capital of any company which limit may be exceeded with the prior approval of the Central Government.
5. 24% of its funds to be invested in socially-oriented sectors approved securities and 1% in Unapproved Securities (approved securities consist of equity shares/preference shares and mortgage debentures of companies, shares or debentures of cooperative societies and fixed deposits with scheduled banks or cooperative societies) immovable properties and loans on policies of LIC policies own with their surrender value.

❖ General Insurance (or Non-life Insurance)

The general insurance is conducted by 23 companies, out of which four companies are Public Sector companies. Names of such companies are:

1. Bajaj Allianz General Insurance
2. Cholamandalam General Insurance
3. ICICI-Lombard General Insurance
4. IFFCO-TOKIO General Insurance
5. Royal Sundaram Alliance General Insurance
6. Reliance General Insurance
7. Tata-AIG General Insurance
8. HDFC General Insurance

9. Future Generali General Insurance
10. Universal Sompo General Insurance
11. Shriram Generali Insurance
12. Bharati Axa General Insurance
13. Apollo DKV General Insurance
14. Star Health and Allied Insurance
15. Raheja QBE General Insurance
16. L&T General Insurance
17. United India General Insurance Ltd.,
18. Oriental Insurance Co. Ltd.,
19. New India Assurance Co. Ltd.,
20. National Insurance Co. Ltd.,
21. Max General Insurance
22. Canara HSBC General
23. SBI General Insurance

The existing general insurance products can be grouped as follows:

- Fire Insurance
- Marine Insurance
- Motor Insurance
- Health Insurance
- Engineering Insurance
- Rural Insurance
- Professional Indemnity Cover
- Videsh Yatra (Overseas Mediclaim Policy)
- Package Insurance cover for domestic travellers
- Office Umbrella Policy (comprehensive risk coverage)
- Personal Accident Insurance
- Other miscellaneous policies (Goods in transit/money lost/fidelity insurance/interruption insurance/live stock, etc.). Out of the above categories first 3 categories together constitute around 75% of total general insurance premium each year.

The share of insurance sector in household financial savings moved up from 10.1% during the 1990s and further to about 12% during 2000-01, however, the insurance penetration (share of premium as percentage of GDP) in India remained low at 2.3% at the end of 1999-2000 in comparison with the world average of 7.8% and the emerging market average of 3.2%.

INSURANCE BUSINESS

(₹ *in crore)*

	2000-01	2001-02
Life Insurance		
Premium	36,070	50,094
of which: Private Insurers	7	273
Total investments	1,94,010	2,46,869
of which Government and other approved securities	1,00,037	1,32,177
Other than Approved Investments	18,584	16,521
General Insurance		
Gross – Direct Premium Income	10,087	12,383*
of which: Private insurers	7	466
Total investments	24,462	26,373
of which: Government and other guaranteed securities	7,703	15,910
Other than approved investments	3,761	2,972
* excluding GICs four companies		

Source: IRDA.

The general insurance business has increased substantially in the period ending *March 2008,* by 14% as compared to previous year. This increase was due to increase in premium collection by Bajaj Allianz and Reliance General and other eleven private insurance companies. The total premium collection in April 2008 was ₹ 3,593 crore which it was ₹ 3,141 crore in April 2007. In the same period four public sector insurance companies total premium collection was ₹ 2,015 crore as against previous April-2007 collection of ₹ 1,864 crore. Percentage-wise private insurance companies business growth was recorded 23% as against government owned GIC business of 8%. In terms of higher collection amount, New India Assurance Co. Ltd. collected premium of ₹ 694 crore in April 2008 and remained number one, while on the second place was private company, ICICI-Lombard with premium collection of ₹ 543 crore while Bajaj Allianz could collect only ₹ 276 crore in the same period.

(***Source:*** *Navbharat Times,* Mumbai 6-6-2008)

3.7 MUTUAL FUNDS

❖ Introduction and Their Role

Of late, mutual funds have become a hot favourite of millions of people all over the world. The driving force of mutual funds is the 'safety of the principal' guaranteed, plus the added advantage of capital appreciation together with the income earned in the form of interest or dividend. People prefer mutual funds to bank deposits, life insurance and even bonds because with a little money, they can get into the investment game. One can own a string of blue chips like ITC, TISCO, Reliance, etc., through mutual funds. Thus, mutual funds act as a gateway to enter into big companies hitherto inaccessible to an ordinary investor with his small investment.

❖ What is a Mutual Fund?

To state in simple words, a mutual fund collects the savings from small investors, invest them in government and other corporate securities and earn income through interest and dividends, besides capital gains. It works on the principle of 'small drops of water make a big ocean'. For instance, if one has ₹ 5,000 to invest, it may not fetch very much on its own. But, when it is pooled with ₹ 5,000 each from a lot of other people, then, one could create a 'big fund' large enough to invest in a wide varieties of shares and debentures on a commanding scale and thus, to enjoy the economies of large-scale operations. Hence, a mutual fund is nothing but a form of collective investment. It is formed by the coming together of a number of investors who transfer their surplus funds to a professionally qualified organisation to manage it. To get the surplus funds from investors, the fund adopts a simple technique. Each fund is divided into a small fraction called "units" of equal value. Each investor is allocated units in proportion to the size of his investment. Thus, every investor, whether big or small, will have a stake in the fund and can enjoy the wide portfolio of the investment held by the fund. Hence, mutual funds enable millions of small and large investors to participate in and derive the benefit of the capital market growth. It has emerged as a popular vehicle of creation of wealth due to high return, lower cost and diversified risk.

The Securities and Exchange Board of India (Mutual Funds) Regulations, 1993 defines a mutual fund as "a fund established in the form of a trust by a sponsor, to raise monies by the trustees through the sale of units to the public, under one or more schemes, for investing in securities in accordance with these regulations."

These mutual funds are referred to as Unit Trusts in the UK and as open end Investment companies in the USA. Therefore, Kamm, J.O. defines an open-end investment company as "an organisation formed for the investment of funds obtained from individuals and institutional investors who in exchange for the funds receive shares which can be redeemed at any time at their underlying asset values".

According to Weston J. Fred and Brigham, Eugene, F., Unit Trusts are "Corporations which accept dollars from savers and then use these dollars to buy stocks, long-term bonds, short-term debt instruments issued by business or government units; these corporations pool funds and thus reduce risk by diversification".

Thus, mutual funds are corporations which pool funds by selling their own shares and reduce risk by diversification.

Fund Unit Vs. Share

Just like shares, the price of units of a fund is also quoted in the market. This price is governed basically by the value of the underlying investments held by that fund. At this juncture, one should not confuse a mutual fund investment on units with that of an investment on equity shares. Investment on equity share represents investment in a particular company alone. On the other hand, investment on an unit of a fund represents investment in the parts of shares of a large number of companies. This itself gives an idea how safe the units are. If a particular company fails, the shareholders of that company are affected very much, whereas the unitholders of that company are able to withstand that risk by means of their profitable holdings in other companies shares.

Again, investment on equity shares can be used as a tool by speculators and inveterate stock market enthusiasts with a view to gaining abnormal profits. These people play an investment game in the stock market on the basis of daily movement of prices. But, mutual funds cannot be invested for such purposes and the mutual fund is not at all concerned with the daily ebbs and flows of the market. In short, mutual fund is not the right investment vehicle for speculators. Mutual funds are, therefore, suitable only to genuine investors, whereas shares are suitable to both the genuine investors and the speculators.

❖ Origin of the Fund

The origin of the concept of mutual fund dates back to the very dawn of commercial history. It is said that Egyptians and Phoenicians sold their shares in vessels and caravans with a view to spreading the risk attached with these risky ventures. However, the real credit of introducing the modern concept of mutual fund goes to the Foreign and Colonial Government Trust of London established in 1868. Thereafter, a large number of close-ended mutual funds were formed in the USA in 1930s followed by many countries in Europe, the Far East and Latin America. In most of the countries, both open- and close-ended types were popular. In India, it gained momentum only in 1980, though it began in the year 1964 with the Unit Trust of India launching its first fund, the Unit Scheme 1964.

3.7.1 Types of Funds/Classification of Funds

In the investment market, one can find a variety of investors with different needs, objectives and risk taking capacities. For instance, a young businessman would like to get more capital appreciation for his funds and he would be prepared to take greater risks than a person who is just on the verge of his retiring age. So, it is very difficult to offer one fund to satisfy all the requirements of investors. Just as one shoe is not suitable for all legs, one fund is not suitable to meet the vast requirements of all investors. Therefore, many types of funds are available to the investor. It is completely left to the discretion of the investor to choose anyone of them depending upon his requirement and his risk taking capacity.

Mutual fund schemes can broadly be classified into many types as given below:

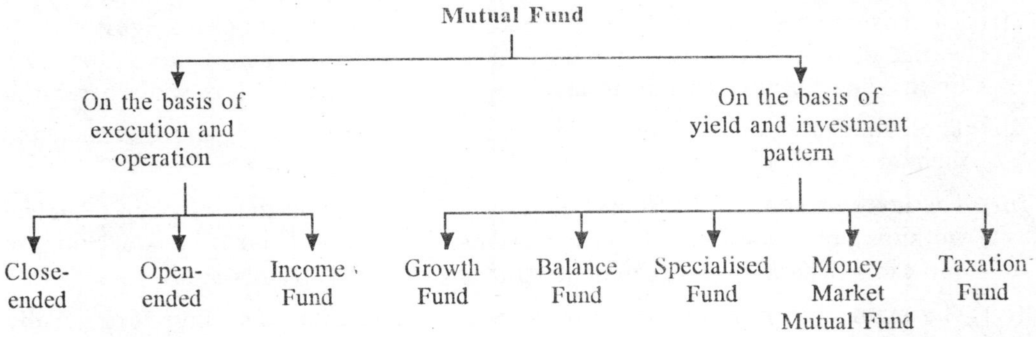

(I) Close-ended Funds

Under this scheme, the corpus of the fund and its duration are prefixed. In other words, the corpus of the fund and the number of units are determined in advance. Once the subscription reaches the predetermined level, the entry of investors is closed. After the expiry of the fixed period, the entire corpus is disinvested and the proceeds are distributed to the various unit-holders in proportion to their holding. Thus, the fund ceases to be a fund, after the final distribution.

Features: The main features of the close-ended funds are:

(*i*) The period and/or the target amount of the fund is definite and fixed beforehand.

(*ii*) Once the period is over and/or the target is reached, the door is closed for the investors. They cannot purchase any more units.

(*iii*) These units are publicly traded through stock exchange and generally, there is no repurchase facility by the fund.

(*iv*) The main objective of this fund is capital appreciation.

(*v*) The whole fund is available for the entire duration of the scheme and there will not be any redemption demands before its maturity. Hence, the fund manager can manage the investments efficiently and profitably without the necessity of maintaining and liquidity.

(*vi*) At the time of redemption, the entire investment pertaining to a closed-end scheme is liquidated and the proceeds are distributed among the unitholders.

(*vii*) From the investor's point of view, it may attract more tax since the entire capital appreciation is realised in to at one stage itself.

(*viii*) If the market condition is not favourable, it may also affect the investor since he may not get the full benefit of capital appreciation in the value of the investment.

(*ix*) Generally, the prices of close-ended scheme units are quoted at a discount of up to 40 per cent below their Net Asset Value (NAV).

(II) Open-ended Funds

It is just the opposite of close-ended funds. Under this scheme, the size of the fund and/ or the period of the fund is not predetermined. The investors are free to buy and sell any number of units at any point of time. For instance, the unit scheme (1964) of the Unit Trust of India is an open-ended one, both in terms of period and target amount. Anybody can buy this unit at any time and sell it also at any time at his discretion.

The Main Features of the Open-Ended Funds are:

(*i*) There is complete flexibility with regard to one's investment or disinvestment. In other words, there is free entry and exit of investors in an open-ended fund. There is no time limit. The investor can join in and come out from the Fund as and when he desires.

(*ii*) These units are not publicly traded but, the Fund is ready to repurchase them and resell them at any time.

(*iii*) The investor is offered instant liquidity in the sense that the units can be sold on any working day to the Fund. In fact, the Fund operates just like a bank account, wherein one can get cash across-the-counter for any number of units sold.

(*iv*) The main objective of this Fund is income generation. The investors get dividend, rights or bonuses as rewards for their investment.

(*v*) Since the units are not listed on the stock market, their prices are linked to the Net Asset Value (NAV) of the units. The NAV is determined by the Fund and it varies from time-to-time.

(*vi*) Generally, the listed prices are very close to their Net Asset Value. The Fund fixes a different price for their purchases and sales.

(*vii*) The fund manager has to be very careful in managing the investments because he has to meet the redemption demands at any time made during the life of the scheme.

To put it in a nutshell, the open-ended funds have a perpetual existence and their corpus is ever-changing depending upon the entry and exit of members.

❖ On the Basis of Income

(A) Income Funds: As the very name suggests, this Fund aims at generating and distributing regular income to the members on a periodical basis. It concentrates more on the distribution of regular income and it also sees that the average return is higher than that of the income from bank deposits.

The main features of the Income Funds are:

(*i*) The investor is assured of regular income at periodic intervals, say half-yearly or yearly and so on.

(*ii*) The main objective of this type of Fund is to declare regular dividends and not capital appreciation.

(*iii*) The pattern of investment is oriented towards high and fixed income yielding securities like debentures, bonds, etc.

(*iv*) This is best suited to the old and retired people who may not have any regular income.

(*v*) It concerns itself with short run gains only.

(B) Pure Growth Funds (Growth-oriented Funds): Unlike the Income Funds, Growth Funds concentrate mainly on long-run gains, i.e., capital appreciation. They do not offer regular income and they aim at capital appreciation in the long-run. Hence, they have been described as "Nest Eggs" investments.

The Main features of the Growth Funds are:

(*i*) The growth-oriented Fund aims at meeting the investors' need for capital appreciation.

(*ii*) The investment strategy therefore, conforms to the Fund objective by investing the funds predominantly on equities with high growth potential.

(*iii*) The Fund tries to get capital appreciation by taking much risks and investing on risk bearing equities and high growth equity shares.

(*iv*) The fund may declare dividend, but its principal objective is only capital appreciation.

(*v*) This is best suited to salaried and business people who have high risk bearing capacity and ability to defer liquidity. They can accumulate wealth for future needs.

(C) Balanced Funds: This is otherwise called "income-cum-growth" fund. It is nothing but a combination of both income and growth funds. It aims at distributing regular income as well as capital appreciation. This is achieved by balancing the investments between the high growth equity shares and also the fixed income earning securities.

(D) Specialised Funds: Besides the above, a large number of specialised funds are in existence abroad. They offer special schemes so as to meet the specific needs of specific categories of people like pensioners, widows etc. There are also funds for investments in securities of specified areas. For instance, Japan Fund, South Korea Fund, etc. In fact, these funds open the door for foreign investors to invest on the domestic securities of these countries.

Again, certain funds may be confined to one particular sector or industry like fertilizer, automobiles, petroleum, etc. These funds carry heavy risks since the entire investment is in one industry. But, there are high risk taking investors who prefer this type of fund. Of course, in such cases, the rewards may be commensurate with the risk taken. At times, it may be erratic. The best example of this type is the Petroleum Industry Funds in the USA.

(E) Money Market Mutual Funds (MMMFs): These funds are basically open-ended mutual funds and as such they have all the features of the open-ended fund. But, they invest in highly liquid and safe securities like commercial paper, banker's acceptances, certificates of deposits, Treasury bills, etc. These instruments are called money market instruments. They take the place of shares, debentures and bonds in a capital market. They pay money market rates of interest. These funds are called 'money funds' in the USA and they have been functioning since 1972. Investors generally use it as a "parking place" or "stop gap arrangement" for their cash resources till they finally decide about the proper avenue for their investment, i.e., long-term financial assets like bonds and stocks.

Since MMMFs are a new concept in India, the RBI has laid down certain stringent regulations. For instance, the entry to MMMFs is restricted only to scheduled commercial banks and their subsidiaries. MMMFs can invest only in specified short-term money market instruments like Certificate of Deposits, Commercial Papers and 182 days Treasury bills. They can also lend to call market. These funds go for safe and liquid investment. Frequent realisation of interest and redemption of fund at short notice are the special features of this fund. The funds will not be subject to reserve requirements. The repurchase could be subject to a minimum lock-in period of three months.

Since the RBI has fixed the minimum amount of investment as ₹ one lakh, it is out of the reach of many small investors. In the USA the minimum amount is only $100. Recently, the private sector funds have been permitted to deal in money market mutual funds. Generally, it is best suited only to institutional investors like banks and other financial institutions.

(F) Taxation Funds: A taxation fund is basically a growth-oriented fund. But, it offers tax rebates to the investors either in the domestic or foreign capital market. It is suitable to salaried people who want to enjoy tax rebates particularly during the month of February and March. In India, at present the law relating to tax rebates is covered under Section 80C of the Income Tax Act, 1961. An investor is entitled to get rebate in income tax for investments made under this fund subject to a maximum investment of ₹ 30,000 per annum. The Tax Saving Magnum of SBI Capital Market Limited is the best example for the domestic type. UTI's US $60 million India Fund, based in the USA, is an example for the foreign type.

❖ Other Classification

(G) Leveraged Funds: These funds are also called borrowed funds since they are used primarily to increase the size of the value of portfolio of a mutual fund. When the value increases, the earning capacity of the fund also increases. The gains are distributed to the unitholders. This is resorted to only when the gains from the borrowed funds are more than the cost of borrowed funds.

(H) Dual Funds: This is a special kind of close-ended fund. It provides a single investment opportunity for two different types of investors. For this purpose, it sells two types of investment stocks, *viz.,* income shares and capital shares. Those investors who seek current investment income can purchase income shares. They receive all the interest and dividends earned from the entire investment portfolio. However, they are guaranteed a minimum annual dividend payment. The holders of capital shares receive all the capital gains earned on those shares and they are not entitled to receive any dividend of any type. In this respect, the dual fund is different from a balanced fund.

(I) Index Funds: Index funds refer to those funds where the portfolios are designed in such a way that they reflect the composition of some broad based market index. This is done by holding securities in the same proportion as the index itself. The value of these index linked funds will automatically go up whenever the market index goes up and *vice versa.*

Since the construction of portfolio is entirely based upon maintaining proper proportions of the index being followed, it involves less administrative expenses, lower transaction costs, less number of portfolio managers, etc. It is so because only fewer purchases and sales of securities would take place.

(J) Bond Funds: These funds have portfolios consisting mainly of fixed income securities like bonds. The main thrust of these funds is mostly on income rather than capital gains. They differ from income funds in the sense income funds offer an average returns higher than that from bank deposits and also capital gains lesser than that in equity shares.

(K) Aggressive Growth Funds: These funds are just the opposite of bond funds. These funds are capital gains oriented and thus the thrust area of these funds is 'capital gains'. Hence, these funds are generally invested in speculative stocks. They may also use specialised investment techniques like short-term trading, option writing, etc. Naturally, these funds tend to be volatile in nature.

(L) Offshore Mutual Funds: Offshore mutual funds are those funds which are meant for non-residential investors. In other words, the sources of investments for these funds are from abroad. So, they are regulated by the provisions of the foreign countries where those funds are registered. These funds facilitate flow of funds across different countries, with free and efficient movement of capital for investment and repatriation. Offshore funds are preferred to direct foreign investment, since, it does not allow foreign domination over host country's corporate sector. However, these funds involve much currency and country risk and hence they generally yield higher return.

In India, these funds are subject to the approval of the Department of Economic Affairs, Ministry of Finance and the RBI monitors such funds by issuing directions then and there. In India, a number of offshore funds exist. 'India Fund' and 'India Growth Fund' were floated by the UTI in UK and USA respectively. The State Bank of India floated the India Magnum Fund in Netherlands. 'The Indo-Suez Himalayan Fund NV' was launched by Canbank Mutual Fund in collaboration with Indo-Suez Asia Investment Services Ltd. It also floated 'Commonwealth Equity Fund'.

3.7.2 Importance and Role of Mutual Funds in Capital Market

The mutual fund industry has grown at a phenomenal rate in the recent past. One can witness a revolution in the mutual fund industry in view of its importance to the investors in general and the country's economy at large. The following are some of the important advantages of mutual funds:

(i) Channelising Savings for Investment

Mutual funds act as a vehicle in galvanising the savings of the people by offering various schemes suitable to the various classes of customers for the development of the economy as a whole. A number of schemes are being offered by MFs so as to meet the varied requirements of the masses, and thus, savings are directed towards capital investments directly. In the absence of MFs, these savings would have remained idle. Thus, the whole economy benefits due to the cost efficient and optimum use and allocation of scarce financial and real resources in the economy for its speedy development.

(ii) Offering Wide Portfolio Investment

Small and medium investors used to burn their fingers in stock exchange operations with a relatively modest outlay. If they invest in a select few shares, some may even sink without a trace never to rise again. Now, these investors can enjoy the wide portfolio of the investment held by the mutual fund. The fund diversifies its risks by investing on a large varieties of shares and bonds which cannot be done by small and medium investors. This is in accordance with the maxim 'Not to lay all eggs in one basket'. These funds have large amounts at their disposal, and so, they carry a clout in respect of stock exchange transactions. They are in a position to have a balanced portfolio which is free from risks. Thus, MFs provide instantaneous portfolio diversification. The risk diversification which a pool of savings through mutual funds can achieve cannot be attained by a single investor's savings.

(iii) Providing Better Yields

The pooling of funds from a large number of customers enables the fund to have large funds at its disposal. Due to these large funds, mutual funds are able to buy cheaper and sell dearer than the small and medium investors. Thus, they are able to command better market rates and lower rates of brokerage. So, they provide better yields to their customers. They also enjoy the economies of large-scale and can reduce the cost of capital market participation. The transaction costs of large investments are definitely lower than that of small investments. In fact, all the profits of a mutual fund are passed on to the investors by way of dividends and capital appreciation. The expenses pertaining to a particular scheme alone are charged to the respective scheme. Most of the mutual funds so far floated have given a dividend at the rate ranging between 12% p.a. and 17% p.a. It is fairly a good yield. It is an ideal vehicle for those who look for long-term capital appreciation.

(iv) Rendering Expertised Investment Service at Low Cost

The management of the Fund is generally assigned to professionals who are well trained and have adequate experience in the field of investment. The investment decisions of these professionals are always backed by informed judgement and experience. Thus, investors are assured of quality services in their best interest. Due to the complex nature of the securities market, a single investor cannot do all these works by himself or he cannot go to a professional manager who manages individual portfolios. In such a case, he may charge hefty management fee. The intermediation fee is the lowest being one per cent in the case of a mutual fund.

(v) Providing Research Service

A mutual fund is able to command vast resources and hence it is possible for it to have an in-depth study and carry-out research on corporate securities. Each fund maintains a large research team which constantly analyses the companies and the industries and recommends the fund to buy or sell a particular share. Thus, investments are made purely on the basis of a thorough research. Since research involves a lot of time, efforts and expenditure, an individual investor cannot take up this work. By investing in a mutual fund, the investor gets the benefit of the research done by the fund.

(vi) Offering Tax Benefits

Certain funds offer tax benefits to its customers. Thus, apart from dividends, interest and capital appreciation, investors also stand to get the benefit of tax concession.

The mutual funds themselves are totally exempt from tax on all income on their investments. But, all other companies have to pay taxes and they can declare dividends only from the profits after tax. But, mutual funds do not deduct tax at source from dividends. This is really a boon to investors.

(vii) Introducing Flexible Investment Schedule

Some mutual funds have permitted the investors to exchange their units from one scheme to another and this flexibility is a great boon to investors. Income units can be exchanged for growth units depending upon the performance of the funds. One cannot derive such a flexibility in any other investments.

(viii) Providing Greater Affordability and Liquidity

Even a very small investor can afford to invest in mutual funds. They provide an attractive and cost-effective alternative to direct purchase of shares. In the absence of MFs, small investors cannot think of participating in a number of investments with such a meagre sum. Again, there is greater liquidity. Units can be sold to the fund at any time at the Net Asset Value and thus quick access to liquid cash is assured. Besides, branches of the sponsoring bank is always ready to provide loan facility against the unit certificates.

(ix) Simplified Record Keeping

An investor with just an investment in 500 shares or so in three or four companies has to keep proper records of dividend payments, bonus issues, price movements, purchase or sale instruction, brokerage and other related items. It is very tedious and consumes a lot of time. One may even forget to record the rights issue and may have to forfeit the same. Thus, record keeping is the biggest problem for small and medium investors. Now, a mutual fund offers a single investment source facility, i.e., a single buy order of 100 units from a mutual fund is equivalent to investment in more than 100 companies. The investor has to keep a record of only one deal with the mutual fund. Even if he does not keep a record, the MF sends statements very often to the investor. Thus, by investing in MFs, the record keeping work is also passed on to the fund.

(x) Supporting Capital Market

Mutual funds play a vital role in supporting the development of capital markets. The mutual funds make the capital market active by means of providing a sustainable domestic source of demand for capital market instruments. In other words, the savings of the people are directed towards investments in capital markets through these mutual funds. Thus, funds serve as a conduit for disintermediating bank deposits into stocks, shares and bonds. Mutual funds also provide a valuable liquidity to the capital market, and thus, the market is made very active and stable. When foreign investors and speculators exit and re-enter the markets en masse, mutual funds keep the market stable and liquid. In the absence of mutual funds, the prices of shares would be subject to wide price fluctuation due to the exit and re-entry of speculators into the capital market en masse. Thus, it is rendering an excellent support to the capital market and helping in the process of institutionalisation of the market.

(xi) Promoting Industrial Development

The economic development of any nation depends upon its industrial advancement and agricultural development. All industrial units have to raise their funds by resorting to the capital market by the issue of shares and debentures. The mutual funds not only create a demand for these capital market instruments but also supply a large source of funds to the market, and thus, the industries are assured of their capital requirements. In fact the entry of mutual funds has enhanced the demand for India's stocks and bonds. Thus, mutual funds provide financial resources to the industries at market rates.

(xii) Acting as Substitute for Initial Public Offerings (IPOs)

In most cases investors are not able to get allotment in IPOs of companies because they are often oversubscribed many time. Moreover, they have to apply for a minimum of 500 shares which is very difficult particularly for small investors. But, in mutual funds, allotment is more or less guaranteed. Mutual funds are also guaranteed a certain percentage of IPOs by companies. Thus, by participating in MFs, investors are able to get the satisfaction of participating in hundreds of varieties of companies.

(xiii) Reducing the Marketing Cost of New Issues

Moreover, the mutual funds help to reduce the marketing cost of the new issues. The promoters used to allot a major share of the Initial public offering to the mutual funds and thus they are saved from the marketing cost of such issues.

(xiv) Keeping the Money Market Active

An individual investor cannot have any access to money market instruments since the minimum amount of investment is out of his reach. On the other hand, mutual funds keep the money market active by investing money on the money market instruments. In fact, the availability of more money market instruments itself is a good sign for a developed money market which is very essential for the successful functioning of the central bank in a country.

Thus, mutual funds provide stability to share prices, safety to investors and resources to prospective entrepreneurs.

3.8 NON-BANKING FINANCIAL COMPANIES (NBFCs)

NBFCs are largely operating in India. It is estimated that there are as many as more than 45,000 NBFCs operating at present.

The reason for such fast growth, as compared to banking sector, are many as stated below:

(*i*) Banking system has been subject to comprehensive and strict regulations while NBFCs regulations are *not so rigid*.

(*ii*) NBFCs have got simple procedure and lesser response time, to meet the needs of the customers.

(*iii*) Higher rates of interest are offered @12.5% to depositors in the present low-rate on bank deposits which is between 10% to 11%.

Non-deposit taking NBFCs and repay the deposits held by them to depositors within five years 21-05-2007 (i.e., up to 20-5-2012).

Source: *DNA Money Newspaper,* 22-5-07)

On 17-6-2008, the RBI has set a deadline of March 2009 for NBFCs to increase their net worths at least ₹ 200 crore and freeze fresh deposit mobilisation till the net worth target is achieved.

(*ii*) This specification of higher Net Owned Fund (i.e., ₹ 200 crore) was not applicable to such company, whose application for certificate of registration under Section 45-IA was submitted to RBI on or before 20-4-1999.

3.8.1 NBFCs Exempted from Registration/NOF Requirements

The following institutions are not required to comply with registration/NOF requirements:

(*i*) Insurance companies/stock exchanges/stock broking companies/mutual benefit financial companies (Nidhis) notified under Section 620-A of the Companies Act/Chit Fund Companies/ Housing Finance Companies/merchant banker registered in SEBI and into accepting public deposits and registration with RBI. Net owned funds means the aggregate of equity capital/free reserves minus losses/preference/deferred revenue expenses/intangible assets.

(*ii*) Existing NBFCs have also to apply for registration. Their business can, however, be carried on unless registration is refused.

(*iii*) NBFCs have to maintain *liquid assets* in specified securities on a daily basis. Liquid assets would have to be maintained as per the current norms of 15% of their deposits, outstanding at the end of *last working day* of second previous quarter depending on the category and regulating status of NBFCs w.e.f. 1st April, 1998.

(*iv*) NBFCs have to create *reserve fund* and transfer not less than 20% of their net profit to the reserve fund every year.

(*v*) For violation of any provision of the RBI Act, the RBI not only can prohibit NBFC from accepting deposits, but also ask *not to sell, transfer,* etc., their properties and assets without RBI prior permission for a period of six months.

(*vi*) Failure to pay debts and disqualified from carrying on business, winding up petition can be filed by RBI.

(*vii*) Nomination facilities to NBFCs depositors.

(*viii*) Unincorporated bodies cannot issue advertisement for soliciting deposits.

(*x*) NBFCs below *credit rating* of A — Minus, BBB/BBB - minus are allowed to accept public deposits.

(*xi*) Failure to comply any norms, the NBFC can be ordered to make immediate repayment of deposits.

(*xii*) Interest rate on deposits capped at 12.5% and brokerage at 2% of maximum.

(*xiii*) Capital adequacy stipulated at 12% and SLR stipulated at 15% w.e.f. Jan. 2000.

3.8.2 Bigger 'CAR' to NBFCs by April 1, 2012

Higher capital adequacy ratio (CAR) mooted by RBI in its guidelines for non-banking financial companies (NBFCs), including microfinance institutions (MFIs), will put the organisations under pressure to boost their capital requirements by half to 15% by March 2012. MFIs in the country are highly leveraged since they are dependent on borrowings. They may find it difficult to bring in additional capital to meet the norms. The guidelines have increased CAR of systemically important non-deposit-taking NBFCs from 10% to 12% by April 2009, and to 15% by 31st March, 2012. This would limit the way the NBFCs leverage their capital. Some experts say that with a 15% CAR, MFIs can leverage only up to five times.

"Many MFIs that are struggling to achieve economies of scale will find it difficult to meet capital adequacy norms. MFIs classified as NBFCs do not have access to deposits and, therefore, their capital is highly leveraged." The regulator's concern was triggered because NBFCs raised short-term resources to fund their asset books. "Strong MFIs with large capital bases will be able to meet the requirements. Equity infusion is not a problem for the MFIs because, if they were not strong enough, debt financing for the MFIs would have dried up." So far, only deposit-taking NBFCs were subject to prudential regulations on income recognition, asset classification and provisioning capital adequacy, among others, while non-deposit-taking NBFCs were subject to minimal regulation. Most of the systemically-important NBFCs are those promoted by banks. There were 311 systemically-important deposit-taking NBFCs at the end of March 2010.

According to RBI, "In view of international developments, the risk associated with highly-leveraged borrowings and the reliance on short-term funds by some NBFCs, there have been concerns regarding the enhanced systemic risk associated with the activities of the entities".

Non-deposit-taking NBFCs total number of 267 at the end of March 2010 with an asset size of over ₹ 100 crore are considered NBFC-ND-SL and a new regulatory framework involving prescription of capital adequacy and exposure norms for such NBFC-ND-SI was put in place from April 1, 2007. The companies were advised to maintain a minimum capital-to-risk weighted assets (CRAR) ratio of 15% and were maintaining the same till March 2011. The number of total NBFCs at the end of June 2010 was 12,630 which were registered with RBI.

(*xiv*) Exposure by an NBFC, in credit, to each entity and group restricted to 25% and 40% respectively.

(*xv*) Loans against the security of NBFCs own shares, banned.

(*xvi*) Filling of half-yearly returns compulsory if accepting public deposits.

(*xvii*) Resultant excess deposits in case of downgrading of rating, has to be repaid or regulated within a period of 12 months.

(*xviii*) RBI is empowered to impose *penalty* on NBFCs for carrying on business without certificate of registration, fine up to ₹ 5 lakh or twice the amount involved, in such contravention. Continuing default involves a further penalty of ₹ 25,000 for every day, after the first day of such default and also imprisonment *not less than one year* which may extend to five years.

(*xix*) Residuary NBFCs (also known as *parabank*) have been disallowed to lend from April 2006. They were required to invest all their deposits in government and other approved securities at least 90% up to April 2005 and 100% by April 2006. These companies were prohibited to accept retail deposit from October 2004 as per RBI directions.

3.8.3 RBI Bans Sahara from Raising Deposits

One of the country's largest finance companies, Sahara India Financial Corporation (SIFCL) — known for the political connections and proximity to Bollywood stars of its somewhat enigmatic supremo Subrata Roy — has been banned from raising money through public deposits with immediate effect.

Banking regulator Reserve Bank of India, which issued the order late and has asked Sahara — which has an outstanding deposit liability of over ₹ 18,000 crore — to lodge all securities held in its custody with the designated bank. The decision, according to the central bank, was in "public interest", aimed at protecting the "interests of depositors". According to market circles, a possible distress sale of securities by the Lucknow-headquartered SIFCL, in the coming days could hurt the broader financial market. SIFCI directly and indirectly employs 30,000 people.

Asking its depositors not to panic, SIFCL, in a strongly-worded statement said that the RBI order is "legally unsound" and is "wanting in prudence and application of mind." The company said it will initiate legal proceedings very soon, adding it was "sanguine" about its changes of success. It also said depositors would be paid as and when the deposits mature, and other activities like insurance and mutual funds would not be affected by the order.

The central bank, which had long been building a case against the residuary non-banking company (RNBC), said Sahara "had continuously violated directions/guidelines" related to directed investments, payment of minimum interest rates to depositors, anti-money laundering norms and intimating depositors in time of maturity of their deposits.

RBI has always found it difficult to regulate RNBCs, which have had no limit on the amount of deposits they could mobilise. In the early 1990s, RBI had come down heavily on another RNBC, Peerless General Finance & Investment, sacking its chairman PC Sen who had become a cult figure by bailing out cash-starved state governments. Peerless, which is currently changing its business model, will stop accepting deposits from 2011.

Unlike non-banking finance companies whose deposit mobilisation is linked to their net-owned funds. RNBCs have no cap on the quantum of deposits they can raise but are required to follow a strict investment regime. Under this, RNBCs are allowed to use their discretion to invest only 20% of the money.

However, in April 2007, RBI had scrapped this discretionary investment headroom for Sahara. As a result, Sahara was forced to invest entirely in Government securities and other lower-yielding bonds, which squeezed its margins. RNBCs have to offer minimum interest rates to depositors, which could be 3.5% for daily deposits and 5% for fixed deposits. Sahara, which has a presence across India, operates through an army of agents. According to the RBI circular, SIFCL shall forthwith notify all its agents and employees that it has been prohibited from accepting deposits, and shall paste a copy of the order in a conspicuous place at each of its branches and offices.

(*xx*) A general guidelines for lending to NBFC by bank which is applicable to all NBFCs, except NBFCs complying with the requirements of registration/credit rating and prudential norms (for which there is no overall ceiling) requires that the total outside borrowings including public debentures/bonds and borrowings from banks and financial institutions should not exceed 10 *times* of their *net owned funds* (NOF).

3.8.4 Position of NBFCs

In June 2007, of the 12,968 NBFCs registered with RBI. 401 were deposit-taking ones. Of these, 218 NBFCs have a deposit base of less than ₹ 0.5 crore while 89 NBFCs have deposit base between ₹ 0.5 crore and ₹ 2 crore. RBI has further said that from March 2009, asset finance companies (AFC) with a minimum investment credit rating and capital adequacy ratio of 12% will be allowed a deposit level of 1.5 times the NOF down from four times NOF allowed earlier. An AFC's principal business is that of financing the physical assets supporting productive or economic activity such as automobiles, tractors, generator sets, earth-moving and material handling equipment moving on own power and general-purpose industrial machines.

BASE EFFECT	
13000 Total number of NBFCs	**2cr** Prescribed net worth of NBFCs
401 Deposit-taking NBFCs listed with RBI	**89** NBFCs with Deposit base of ₹ 0.5-2 crore

Other AFCs with CAR of 15% but without credit rating and NOF of above ₹ 25 lakh but less than ₹ 2 crore will be allowed to have a deposit base equivalent to their NOF. Other NBFCs-primarily giving loans and making investments — with a CAR of 15% with minimum investment-grade rating and NOF of more than ₹ 25 lakh but less than ₹ 2 crore will be allowed to raise deposits equivalent to their NOF.

3.8.5 Specific Legal Sections for Regulations

Sec. 45-1B — Maintenance of Percentage of assets

NBFCs are required to invest in *Approved Unencumbered Securities,* a sum not less than 5% and not more than 25% of the deposits. The bank may specify *Different Percentage* of investment for different NBFC. In case of shortfall of investment, a penal interest @ 3% p.a. above the bank rate (at present 6%) on the amount of shortfall. If the shortfall continues to persist in subsequent quarters, the rate of penalty would be raised to 5% above Bank Rate (i.e., 11% as on today in 2008). The penal interest is payable within 14 days from the date of receipt of notice from the bank. In case of failure to pay the penal interest, the RBI can approach the city civil court of the place for a certificate which would be equal to a *Decree of the Court.*

Approved securities connotes, securities of State/Central Government while *unencumbered approved securities* indicates these securities against which, no loans or advance has been availed.

Sec. 45-1C-Reserve Fund.

Every NBFC shall transfer a sum not less than 20% of its disclosed *net profit,* before declaration of dividend. Appropriation of amount from Reserve Fund shall be for specified purposes only and shall be reported to RBI within 21 days from the date of such withdrawal. In case the amount of Reserve Fund along with Share Premium Account is *not* less than the paid-up capital of NBFC, the RBI may declare that the Reserve Fund provisions may not be applicable, for such period as specified in the order.

Sec. 45-J — Prohibition to Soliciting Deposits by Advertisement

It prohibits the issue by any NBFC of any prospectus or *advertisement,* soliciting deposits of money from the public. The RBI may specify the conditions, subject to which, any such prospectus or advertisement, *if not prohibited,* may be issued.

Sec. 45-JA — Power to Determine Policy and Issue Directions

The RBI can issue directions regarding income recognitions/accounting standards/provision for bad and doubtful debts/capital adequacy/credit conversion factors for off-balance sheet items, as also deployment of funds by an NBFC or a class of NBFC or NBFCs generally in the following circumstances, *viz.*,

In the public interest/NBFC's affairs conducted detrimental to the interest of its depositors or its company/the purposes for which advances may not be made/ceiling on advances/investments in a company or a group of companies — as per position of the NBFC.

Sec. 45-K — To Collect Information from NBFC as to the Deposits

The information may relate to amount of deposit/purpose of deposit/period of deposit/and rate of interest payable on the deposits. The RBI may prohibit, acceptance of deposit by the NBFC, in case of their failure to comply with any direction given to the bank.

Sec. 45-L — Call for Information from Financial Institutions and Give Direction

The information may relate to paid-up capital/reserves and other liabilities/investments in Government securities or otherwise the persons, to whom and the purposes and periods for which finance is provided and the terms and conditions on which it is provided.

Sec. 45-MC — Power of Bank to File Winding Up Petition

RBI had started closure of 84 NBFCs due to frauds committed by companies with the investors.

(*Times of India,* 5-12-06). As per details submitted in the Rajya Sabha in New Delhi that RBI has so far submitted applications for liquidation/closure of 84 NBFCs and criminal complaints have been lodged against 70 such NBFCS while 27 such criminal complaints have been lodged under Section 420 of IPC.

Such actions have been taken against those companies who have failed to comply RBI directions and whose financial position to be very weak.

(As per RBI Act, Section 45 MC).

Sec. 45-N — Inspection of a Non-banking Institutions

Sec. 45-NA — Deposits not to be solicited by unauthorised persons.

Sec. 45-NB — Disclosure of information with the permission of RBI, if it is necessary in the public interest and may be in accordance with the practice and usage customary among such companies.

Section 45-NC — Power of the Bank to exempt any or all the provisions from being applied to an NBFC, for such periods and in such conditions/limitations as it may impose.

Sec. 45-Q — Chapter 3b to override other laws.

Sec. 45-QA — Power of the National Companies Law Tribunal to order repayment of deposits.

Sec. 45-QB — Nomination by depositors, to receive the deposits in case of death of the depositor or the death of all the depositors. This is similar to Sec. ZA.

General Provisions regarding repayment of *Public Deposits*.

(*a*) No NBFC shall repay any public deposit within a period of three months, from the date of acceptance.

(*b*) For premature withdrawal after first three months the rate of interest would be —

In between three to but less than six months	@ Nil
In between six but less than 12 months	@ Not exceeding 10% p.a.
In between 12 months but less than the date of maturity	@ 1% less than the rate of stipulated in the deposit

On and from Jan 13, 2000, *no NBFC shall open its branch or appoint agents* to collect deposits except as provided may open its branch, within the state, where it is registered office is situated, if NOF is up to ₹ 50 crore. If NOF is more than ₹ 50 crore and credit rating is AA or above, can open branches anywhere in India.

The above directions are not applicable to certain types of NBFCs.

(*a*) An insurance company registered under Insurance Act, 1938.

(*b*) A loan company/investment company/a hire purchase finance company/or an equipment leasing company, not accepting/holding any *public deposits.*

(*c*) Nothing shall apply to an NBFC being a Government Company.

3.8.6 Master Guidelines for Lending to NBFCs by Banks

(*i*) In respect of NBFCs which do not require to be registered with RBI, namely:

- Insurance Companies registered under Section 3 of the Insurance Act, 1938.
- Nidhi Companies notified under Section 620A of the Companies Act, 1956.
- Chit Fund Companies carrying on chit funds business as their principal business.
- Stock Broking Companies/Merchant Banking Companies registered under Section 12 of the SBI Act.
- Housing Finance Companies being regulated by the National Housing Bank.

(*ii*) Residuary NBFCs are also required to be mandatory registered with RBI. The bank finance would be restricted to the restructed to the extent of their NOF.

(*iii*) **Assessment of Working Capital:** Banks may assess and provide need-based finance to NBFCs referred to above, within the prudential guidelines and exposure norms prescribed by the RBI, subject to the condition that the activities indicated in subsequent paragraphs are *not financed by banks.*

(*iv*) **Activities not Eligible for Bank Credit:** Bills discounted/rediscounted by NBFCs except for rediscounting of bills discounted by NBFCs arising from sale of —

(*a*) Commercial vehicles (including light commercial vehicles), and

(*b*) Two-wheeler and 3-wheeler vehicles, subject to the following conditions —

- The bills should have been drawn by the manufacturer on *dealers only.*
- The bills should represent genuine sale transactions as may be ascertained from the chassis/engine number, and

- Before rediscounting the bills, banks should satisfy themselves about the bonafides and track record of NBFCs which have discounted the bills.
- Investments made by NBFCs in shares/debentures, etc., of a current nature, i.e., stock-in-trade. However, stock broking companies may be provided need-based credit against shares and debentures held by them as *stock-in-trade*.
- Investments of NBFCs in and advances to subsidiaries group companies or other entities.
- Investments of NBFCs in other companies and inter-corporate loans/deposits to/in other companies.
- Finance to NBFCs for further lending to individuals for subscribing to Initial Public Offerings (IPOs).
- Banks should not enter into lease agreements departmentally with equipment leasing companies as well as other NBFCs, engaged in equipment leasing.
- Lease rentals receivables arising out of sub-lease of an asset by an NBFC (undertaking nominal leasing activity) or by an NBFC should be excluded for the purpose of computation of bank finance for such company.
- Banks should not grant *bridge-loans* of any nature or interim finance against capital/ debenture issues and/or in the form of loans of a bridging nature pending raising of long-term funds from the market by way of capital/deposits, etc., to all categories of NBFCs.
- Banks should strictly follow these instructions and ensure that these are not circumvented in any manner whatsoever by purport and/or intent by sanction of credit under a different nomenclature like unsecured negotiable notes/floating rate interest bonds/ short-term loans, the repayment of which is proposal/expected to be made out of funds to be or *likely to be mobilised* from external/other sources and not out of the surplus generated by the use of the assets.

3.8.7 Miscellaneous NBFCs (Reserve Bank) Directions 1977 (MNBC)

In terms of powers conferred by Sections 45J/45K and 45L of RBI Act, 1934, the directions are issued by RBI which have become effective from 01-07.1977.

(*i*) **Applicability of Directions:** To every financial institution carrying on business in the state of Jammu & Kashmir and to every financial institution, which is a company and which carries on, in any place in India, any types of business as specified in sub-paragraphs below:

(*a*) Collecting as a promoter/foremen/agent or in any other capacity, monies in one lump sum or instalments, by way of contributions or subscriptions or by sale of units/certificates or other instruments and the purposes for utilizing the monies as—

- giving or awarding periodically, prizes or gifts in cash or kind.
- refunding to subscribers or such of them as have not won any prize or gift, the whole or part of the subscriptions or contributions with or without any bonus, premium or interest.

(*b*) Managing/conducting or supervising as a promoter, foreman or agent of any transaction.

(*c*) Conducting any other form of Chit or Kuri or executing any other business similar to the business.

(*ii*) **Acceptance of Deposits by MNBC** — No MNBC shall receive any deposit repayable on demand on or notice after a period of less than six months and more than 36 months, from the date of receipt of such deposit or renew any deposit.

(*iii*) **Rules for Furnishing Receipts** duly signed by an officer authorised and keeping of register for deposits are the same as for other NBFC.

(*iv*) **Ceiling on the Rate of Interest and Brokerage:** On and from 01-11-2001, no MNBC shall invite or accept or renew deposit on a rate of interest exceeding 12½% p.a. Interest may be paid or compounded at rests which shall not be shorter than monthly rests. And also shall not pay to any broker for deposits collected by or through him, brokerage in excess of ratio specified as —

- Deposits less than one year — 1%
- Deposits exceeding one year — 1.5%
- Deposits exceeding two years — 1.5%.

(*v*) In submission of balance sheets/directors' reports/returns to RBI like other NBFCs.

CHIT FUNDS OR NIDHI COMPANIES FORM PART OF NBFCs

The features of Chit Fund Companies are —

- Chit means a transaction whether called chit/chit fund/chitty/kuri or by any other name, under which a person enters into an agreement with a specified number of persons that everyone of them shall subscribe a certain sum of money by way of periodical instalments over a definite period.
- Period not to exceed five years.
- Effective in 16 States and six Union Territories except the State of Maharashtra.
- Minimum capital requirement is ₹ one lakh.
- Legal provisions are governed by Chit Fund Act, 1982.
- No foreman can conduct chits, the amount of which exceeds ₹ one lakh. But for association of individuals or firms (Not less than four associations of individuals, such amount can be ₹ 6 lakh.

◆ ◆ ◆

4

Overview of Financial Services

4.1 POSITION OF ECONOMIC SCENE

The economic scene in the post-independence period has seen a sea change; the end result being that the economy has made enormous progress in diverse fields. There has been a quantitative expansion as well as diversification of economic activities. The experiences of the 1980s have led to the conclusion that to obtain all the benefits of greater reliance on voluntary, market-based decision-making, India needs efficient financial systems.

The financial system is possibly the most important institutional and functional vehicle for economic transformation. Finance is a bridge between the present and the future and whether it be the mobilisation of savings or their efficient, effective and equitable allocation for investment, it is the success with which the financial system performs its functions that sets the pace for the achievement of broader national objectives.

This chapter makes an in-depth analysis of the structure of the Indian financial system.

The word 'system' stands for a set of bodily organs like composition or concurring in function, a scheme of classification and a method of organisation.

The term financial system is a set of inter-related activities/services working together to achieve some predetermined purpose or goal. It includes different markets, the institutions, instruments, services and mechanisms which influence the generation of savings, investment capital formation and growth.

Van Horne defined the financial system as the purpose of financial markets to allocate savings efficiently in an economy to ultimate users either for investment in real assets or for consumption. *Christy* has opined that the objective of the financial system is to *"supply funds to various sectors and activities of the economy in ways that promote the fullest possible utilisation of resources without the destabilising consequence of price level changes or unnecessary* interference with individual desires".

According to Robinson, the primary function of the system is "to provide a link between savings and investment for the creation of new wealth and to permit portfolio adjustment in the composition of the existing wealth".

From the above definitions, it may be said that the primary function of the financial system is the mobilisation of savings, their distribution for industrial investment and stimulating capital formation to accelerate the process of economic growth.

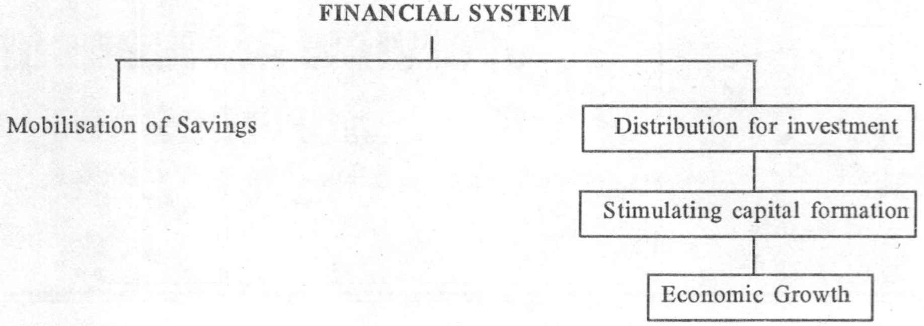

The Concept of the Financial System

The process of savings, finance and investment involves financial institutions, markets, instruments and services. Above all, supervision control and regulation are equally significant. Thus, financial management is an integral part of the financial system. On the basis of the empirical evidence, *Goldsmith* said that "... a case for the hypothesis that the separation of the functions of savings and investment which is made possible by the introduction of financial instruments as well as enlargement of the range of financial assets which follows from the creation of financial institutions increase the efficiency of investments and raise the ratio of capital formation to national production and financial activities and through these two channels increase the rate of growth...."

Thus, the inter-relationship between varied segments of the economy are illustrated below:

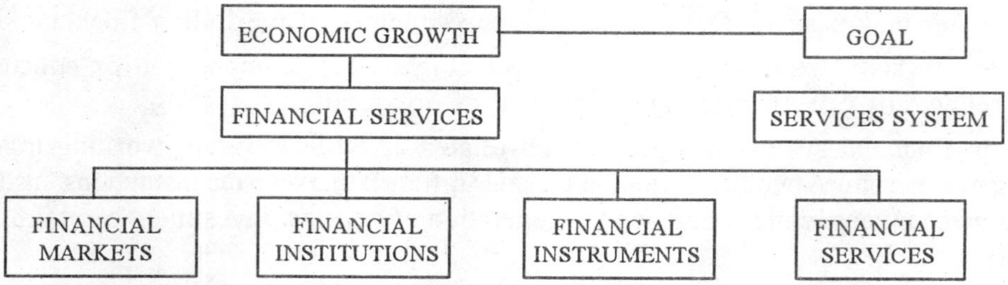

❖ Inter-relationship in the Financial System

A financial system provides services that are essential in a modern economy. The use of a stable, widely accepted medium of exchange reduces the costs of transactions. It facilitates trade and, therefore, specialization in production. Financial assets with attractive yield, liquidity and risk characteristics encourage saving in financial form. By evaluating alternative investments and monitoring the activities of borrowers, financial intermediaries increase the efficiency of resource use. Access to a variety of financial instruments enables an economic agent to pool, price and exchange risks in the markets. Trade, the efficient use of resources, saving and risk taking are the cornerstones of a growing economy. In fact, the country could make this feasible with the active support of the financial system. The financial system has been identified as the most catalysing agent for growth of the economy, making it one of the key inputs of development.

The Indian financial system has established a strong link between savings and investments by creating a unique mechanism through which varied economic activities are created, sustained and developed. In this background, the Indian financial system becomes the rock foundation of our economy. The financial system and the economy are complementary and have made enormous progress. It is against this backdrop that the scenario for the Indian financial system unfolds itself. The study, therefore, assumes special prominence in this context.

4.2 STRUCTURE OF FINANCIAL SYSTEM

The financial system consists of many institutions, instruments, and markets. Financial institutions range from pawnshops and moneylenders to banks, pension funds, insurance companies, brokerage houses, investment trusts, and stock exchanges. Financial instruments range from the common — coins, currency notes, and cheques; mortgages, corporate bills, bonds, and stocks — to the more exotic — futures and swaps of high finance. Markets for these instruments may be organized formally (as in stock or bond exchanges with centralized trading floors) or informally (as in over-the-counter or curb markets). For analytical purposes, the system can be divided into users of financial services and providers.

❖ Users of Financial Services

Financial institutions sell their services to households, businesses and government.

The household sector includes small mainly unregulated firms and individuals. Their main financial needs are for payment of services, saving and small credit. They seek convenience, liquidity and security.

Businesses have more complicated financial needs. It needs short-term credit to finance inventories and long-term funds to finance capital expansion.

All governments use payment services. In most developing countries, governments, like businesses, are net borrowers, and they use the financial system as a source of funding for current and capital spending. In industrial countries, government deficits are financed mainly by selling securities to the public. In developing countries they are usually financed by borrowing from banks. Governments have also used the financial system to serve development or other goals.

❖ Providers of Financial Services

Different financial institutions provide services that are both complementary to and competitive with each other. Deposit institutions offer payment and liquid deposit facilities, and contractual savings institutions provide illiquid savings opportunities that cater to the longer-term needs of customers. Collective investment institutions offer small investors the benefits of professional management and low-cost risk diversification, encouraging them to diversify their savings into marketable securities. On the lending side, commercial banks have traditionally provided working capital and trade finance, but longer-term lending is gaining with the spread of universal banking. Factoring companies provide long-term investment finance.

Money and capital markets provide investment instruments appropriate for contractual savings and collective investment institutions, whose services to the saving public are thereby improved. The efficient functioning of financial markets also depends on institutions that lend and borrow little on their own account: investment banks, securities brokers, and credit rating agencies. Commercial banks also improve the working of financial markets by providing credit and payment facilities to market-markers and other market participants.

Different financial institutions and markets compete for a limited pool of savings by offering different instruments. Money and capital markets increase competition between suppliers. Money markets give merchant banks, or commercial banks with limited branch networks, greater access to funds. Because such banks specialize in lending to larger corporations, the corporate loan market may be highly competitive, even though few large domestic banks may continue to dominate the retail deposit market.

Money markets also provide large corporations and non-blank financial institutions with efficient short-term instruments for investing their liquid funds and thus compete directly with commercial banks' traditional deposit facilities. They also enable large corporation to issue short-term securities in the form of commercial paper and thus further reduce the market power that large banks may have in the domestic banking sector. Finally, capital markets enable contractual savings and collective investment institutions to play a more active role in the financial system.

The complementary and competitive interaction of financial institutions has policy implications. To promote an efficient financial system there must be competition, but the system must also offer an array of services. Rather than restrict the growth and diversification of the main banking groups, governments in the greater competition by encouraging money and capital markets, specialized credit institutions (such as leasing and factoring companies), and contractual savings and collective investment institutions. Economies too small to support such specialized institutions can spur competition by allowing economic agents to buy.

❖ Structure of the Financial System in India

The Indian financial system is broadly classified into two broad groups:

(*i*) organised sector, and (*ii*) unorganised sector.

The financial system is also divided into users of financial services and providers.

Financial institutions sell their services to households, businesses and government. They are the users of the financial services. The boundaries between these sectors are not always clear-cut.

In the case of providers of financial services, although financial systems differ from country-to-country, there are many similarities.

(*i*) Central bank (*ii*) Banks (*iii*) Financial institutions (*iv*) Money and capital markets, and (*v*) Informal financial enterprises.

❖ Organised Indian Financial System

The organised financial system comprises of an impressive network of banks, other financial and investment institutions and a range of financial instruments, which together function in fairly developed capital and money markets. Short-term funds are mainly provided by the commercial and cooperative banking structure. Nine-tenth of such banking business is managed by twenty-eight leading banks which are in the public sector. In addition to commercial banks, there is the network of cooperative banks and land development banks at state, district and block levels. With around two-thirds share in the total assets in the financial system, banks play an important role. Of late, Indian banks have also diversified into areas such as merchant banking, mutual funds, leasing and factoring, treasury management/lease financing.

The Indian financial services industry has undergone a metamorphosis since 1990. During the late seventies and eighties, the Indian financial services industry was dominated by commercial banks and other financial institutions which cater to the requirements of the Indian industry. In fact the capital market played a secondary role only. The economic liberalisation has brought in a complete transformation in the Indian financial services industry.

Prior to the economic liberalisation, the Indian financial service sector was characterised by so many factors which retarded the growth of this sector. Some of the significant factors were:

(*i*) Excessive controls in the form of regulations of interest rates, money rates, etc.

(*ii*) Too many control over the prices of securities under the erstwhile controller of capital issues.

(*iii*) Non-availability of financial instruments on a large-scale as well as on different varieties.

(*iv*) Absence of independent credit rating and credit research agencies.

(*v*) Strict regulation of the foreign exchange market with too many restrictions on foreign investment and foreign equity holding in Indian companies.

(*vi*) Lack of information about international developments in the financial sector.

(*vii*) Absence of a developed Government securities market and the existence of stagnant capital market without any reformation.

(*viii*) Non-availability of debt instruments on a large-scale.

However, after the economic liberalisation, the entire financial sector has undergone a sea-saw change and now we are witnessing the emergence of new financial products and services almost everyday. Thus, the present scenario is characterised by financial innovation and financial creativity and before going deep into it, it is imperative that one should understand the meaning and scope of financial services.

4.3 MEANING OF FINANCIAL SERVICES

In general, all types of activities which are of a financial nature could be brought under the term 'financial services'. The term "Financial Services" in a broad sense means "mobilising and allocating savings". Thus, it includes all activities involved in the transformation of saving into investment.

The 'financial service' can also be called 'financial intermediation' Financial intermediation is a process by which funds are mobilised from a large number of savers and make them available to all those who are in need of it and particularly to corporate customers. Thus, financial services sector is a key area and it is very vital for industrial developments. A well developed financial services industry is absolutely necessary to mobilise the savings and to allocate them to various investable channels and thereby to promote industrial development in a country.

4.4 CLASSIFICATION OF FINANCIAL SERVICES

The financial intermediaries in India can be traditionally classified into two:

(*i*) Capital market intermediaries, and

(*ii*) Money market intermediaries.

The capital market intermediaries consist of term lending institutions and investing institutions which mainly provide long-term funds. On the other hand, money market consists of commercial banks, cooperative banks and other agencies which supply only short-term funds. Hence, the term 'financial services industry' includes all kinds of organisations which intermediate and facilitate financial transactions of both individuals and corporate customers.

❖ Scope of Financial Services

Financial services cover a wide range of activities. They can be broadly classified into two namely:

(*i*) Traditional activities, and

(*ii*) Modern activities

❖ Traditional Activities

Traditionally, the financial intermediaries have been rendering a wide range of services encompassing both capital and money market activities. They can be grouped under two heads *viz.*;

(*i*) Fund-based activities, and

(*ii*) Non-fund-based activities.

❖ Fund-based Activities

The traditional services which come under fund-based activities are the following:

(*i*) Underwriting of or investment in shares, debentures, bonds, etc., of new issues (primary market activities)

(*ii*) Dealing in secondary market activities.

(*iii*) Participating in money market instruments like commercial papers, certificate of deposits, treasury bills, discounting of bills, etc.

(*iv*) Involving in equipment leasing, hire purchase, venture capital, seed capital, etc.

(*v*) Dealing in foreign exchange market activities.

❖ Non-fund-based Activities

Financial intermediaries provide services on the basis of non-fund activities also. This can also be called "fee-based" activity. Today, customers whether individual or corporate are not satisfied with mere provision of finance. They expect more from financial service companies. Hence, a wide variety of services, are being provided under this head. They include the following:

(*i*) Managing the capital issues, i.e., management of pre-issue and post-issue activities relating to the capital issue in accordance with the SEBI guidelines and thus enabling the promoters to market their issues.

(*ii*) Making arrangements for the placement of capital and debt instruments with investment institutions.

(*iii*) Arrangement of funds from financial institutions for the clients' project cost or his working capital requirements.

(*iv*) Assisting in the process of getting all government and other clearances.

4.5 MODERN ACTIVITIES

Besides the above traditional services, the financial intermediaries render innumerable services in recent times. Most of them are in the nature of non-fund-based activity. In view of the importance, these activities have been discussed in brief under the head 'New financial products and services'. However, some of the modern services provided by them are given in brief hereunder:

(*i*) Rendering project advisory services right from the preparation of the project report till the raising of funds for starting the project with necessary government approval.

(*ii*) Planning for mergers and acquisitions and assisting for their smooth carry-out.

(*iii*) Guiding corporate customers in capital restructuring.

(*iv*) Acting as Trustees to the debentureholders.

(*v*) Recommending suitable changes in the management structure and management style with a view to achieving better results.

(*vi*) Structuring the financial collaboration/joint ventures by identifying suitable joint venture partner and preparing joint venture agreement.

(*vii*) Rehabilitating and reconstructing sick companies through appropriate scheme of reconstruction and facilitating the implementation of the scheme.

(*viii*) Hedging of risks due to exchange rate risk, interest rate risk, economic risk and political risk by using swaps and other derivative products.

(*ix*) Managing the portfolio of large Public Sector Corporations.

(*x*) Undertaking risk management services like insurance services, buyback options, etc.

(*xi*) Advising the clients on the question of selecting the best source of funds taking into consideration the quantum of funds required, their cost, lending period, etc.

(*xii*) Guiding the clients in the minimisation of the cost of debt and in the determination of the optimum debt-equity mix.

(*xiii*) Undertaking services relating to the capital market such as:

(a) Clearing services,

(b) Registration and transfers,

(c) Safe-custody of securities,

(d) Collection of income on securities.

(*xiv*) Promoting credit rating agencies for the purpose of rating companies which want to go public by the issue of debt instruments.

❖ Sources of Revenue

Accordingly, there are two categories of sources of income for a financial service company namely: (*i*) fund-based, and (*ii*) fee-based.

Fund-based income comes mainly from interest spread (difference between the interest paid and earned), lease rentals, income from investments in capital market and real estate. On the other hand, fee-based income has its sources in merchant banking, advisory services, custodial services, loan syndication, etc. In fact, a major part of the income is earned through fund-based activities. At the same time, it involves a large share of expenditure also in the form of interest and brokerage. In recent times, a number of private financial companies have started accepting deposits by offering a very high rate of interest. When the cost of deposit resources goes up, the lending rate should also go up. It means that such companies should have to compromise the quality of its investments.

Fee-based income, on the other hand, does not involve much risk. But, it requires a lot of expertise on the part of a financial company to offer such fee-based services.

4.6 CAUSES FOR FINANCIAL INNOVATION

Financial intermediaries have to perform the task of financial innovation to meet the dynamically changing needs of the economy and to help the investors cope with an increasingly volatile and uncertain marketplace. There is a dire necessity for the financial intermediaries to go for innovation due to the following reasons:

(i) Low profitability: The profitability of the major financial intermediary, namely the banks has been very much affected in recent times. There is a decline in the profitability of traditional banking products. So, they have been compelled to seek out new products which may fetch high returns.

(ii) Keen competition: The entry of many financial intermediaries in the financial sector market has led to severe competition among themselves. This keen competition has paved the way for the entry of varied nature of innovative financial products so as to meet the varied requirements of the investors.

(iii) Economic liberalisation: Reform of the financial sector constitutes the most important component of India's programme towards economic liberalisation. The recent economic liberalisation measures have opened the door to foreign competitors to enter into our domestic market. Deregulation in the form of elimination of exchange controls and interest rate ceilings have made the market more competitive. Innovation has become a must for survival

(iv) Improved communication technology: The communication technology has become so advanced that even the world's issuers can be linked with the investors in the global financial market without any difficulty by means of offering so many options and opportunities. Hence, innovative products are brought into the domestic market in no time.

(v) Customer service: Nowadays, the customer's expectations are very great. They want newer products at lower cost or at lower credit risk to replace the existing ones. To meet this increased customer sophistication, the financial intermediaries are constantly undertaking research in order to invent a new product which may suit to the requirement of the investing public. Innovations thus help them in soliciting new business.

(vi) Global impact: Many of the providers and users of capital have changed their roles all over the world. Financial intermediaries have come out of their traditional approach and they are ready to assume more credit risks. As a consequence, many innovations have taken place in the global financial sector which have its own impact on the domestic sector also.

(vii) Investor awareness: With a growing awareness amongst the investing public, there has been a distinct shift from investing the savings in physical assets like gold, silver, land, etc., to financial assets like shares, debentures, mutual funds, etc. Again, within the financial assets, they go from 'risk free' bank deposits to risky investments in shares. To meet the growing awareness of the public, innovation has become the need of the hour.

❖ Financial Engineering

Thus, the growing need for innovation has assumed immense importance in recent times. This process is being referred to as financial engineering. Financial engineering is the lifeblood of any financial ability. "Financial engineering is the design, the development and the implementation of innovative financial instruments and processes and the formulation of creative solutions to problems in finance."

4.7 NEW FINANCIAL PRODUCTS AND SERVICES

Today, the importance of financial services is gaining momentum all over the world. In these days of complex finance, people expect a Financial Service Company to play a very dynamic role not only as a provider of finance but also as a departmental store of finance. With the injection of the economic liberation policy into our economy and the opening of the economy to multinationals, the free market concept has assumed much significance. As a result, the clients both corporates and individuals are exposed to the phenomena of volatility and uncertainty and hence they expect the financial service company to innovate new products and services so as to meet their varied requirements.

As a result of innovations, new instruments and new products are emerging in the capital market. The capital market and the money market are getting widened and deepened. Moreover, there has been a structural change in the international capital market with the emergence of new products and innovative techniques of operation in the capital market. Many financial intermediaries including banks have already started expanding their activities in the financial services sector by offering a variety of new products. As a result, sophistication and innovations have appeared in the arena of financial intermediations. Some of them are briefly discussed below:

(i) Merchant Banking: A merchant banker is a financial intermediary who helps to transfer capital from those who possess it to those who need it. Merchant banking includes a wide range of activities such as management of customers securities, portfolio management, project counselling and appraisal, underwriting of shares and debentures, loan syndication, acting as banker for the refund orders, handling interest and dividend warrants, etc. Thus, a merchant banker renders a host of services to corporates and thus promotes industrial development in the country.

(ii) Loan Syndication: This is more or less similar to 'consortium financing'. But, this work is taken up by the merchant banker as a lead-manager. It refers to a loan arranged by a bank called lead manager for a borrower who is usually a large corporate customer or a Government Department. The other banks who are willing to lend can participate in the loan by contributing an amount suitable to their own lending policies. Since a single bank cannot provide such a huge sum as loan, a number of banks join together and form a syndicate. It also enables the members of the syndicate to share the credit risk associated with a particular loan among themselves.

❖ Steps for Syndicated Loans

Over the years, the drill for the finalisation of syndicated loans has become well settled. Some of the more important steps in the process are summarised hereunder —

1. The borrower decides upon the size and currency of the loan he decides to borrow and invites bids from banks for arranging finance on the basis of the business plan, purpose of the loan, etc.
2. Several banks or groups of banks come forward with offers indicating the brand terms on which they are willing to arrange the loan. The bank or banks are referred to as the lead managers. In their offers the lead managers indicate the front end fees, commitment and other charges and spreads and LIBOR (or Prime Lending Rate in India) on which (or lesser than PLR in India) they are willing to arrange the loan.
3. After comparing the bids received from the various banks or group of banks, the borrower will choose the one that seems best for him in terms of the total cost of the package, the other terms and conditions and the relationship factor. Once the borrower has chosen the bid, he would mandate the lead managers to arrange the loans.
4. The next step is the finalisation of an information memorandum. This is the basis on which the lead managers would solicit participation in the loan from other banks and financial institutions.
5. The invitation to participate would also specify the basis on which the front end fees would be split between the lead managers and the other participants. The greater the amount a participant is willing to take up, the higher will be his share.
6. Once the response to the participation invitation is known, the lead managers are required to take up the balance themselves. If the response is too poor and the offer to arrange the financing was initially made on a best efforts rather than commitment basis the lead managers could back out, but in practice this rarely happens.
7. Once all the participants have been finalised the lead managers and the borrower and the guarantor, finalise the loan agreement. There is generally one loan agreement document running with 50/60 pages or longer, which the borrower, guarantor and all the participants banks sign. Syndicated loans are generally used for balance of payments purpose, to finance domestic budget deficit or to refinance existing external debt.

The loan agreement specifies the commitment fees, front end (or management) fees and interest payable by the borrower. As for interest, the borrower has got the option of choosing interest period say 1/3/6 or 12 months where the borrower chooses the 12-month interest persons, actual payment is made at 6 monthly intervals.

❖ Arranger of Syndicated Loans

The functions of the arranging banks are:

1. The arranges agrees to finalise the terms of the loan or facility with the borrowers.
2. It also underwrites the loan, so that if no other banks agree to join the syndicate, the arranger, as underwriter would be required to provide all the funds.
3. In case of large loan or facility, arranger will find other banks willing to share the underwriting of the loan or faci'ity. These may be called underwriting banks, or lead

managers or co-arrangers. The lead managers between them will provide the loan funds if they cannot find other banks. The sub-underwriting banks may be called managers in the syndicate.

4. The lead managers may sub-underwrite a part of the loan that they have underwritten to other banks. The sub-underwriting banks may be called managers in the syndicate.
5. The managers may find other banks willing to join the syndicate (participants). A hierarchy committing itself to lending some finds however, and delegating some, but not all, of its commitment to other banks. A large syndicate is built-up not solely by the arranger, but by the arranger together with other banks in the sub-underwriting hierarchy. The names given to banks in the syndicate hierarchy vary, and terminology is not standard. There may, for example, be an arranger, three or four senior lead managers, six or seven lead managers, a dozen managers and a number of participating banks. Every bank in the hierarchy usually will agree to lead some funds to the borrower. The borrower usually will require the arranger to provide a large proportion of the loan funds partly because it is important that the arranger should have a direct interest in the lending, and partly because the arranger invariably is a bank with which the borrower has a good relationship. The borrower is likely to be disappointed if the arranger did not lend some of the more. Being a member of a syndicate is often regarded as a matter of some status and prestige. The borrower will be a well established organisation, and the reason for the syndicated loan might be a prominent news item. The arranger often will have little difficulty in assembling a syndicate for the loan.

❖ Arrangement for Syndicated Loan

There is always an agreement on how a company should borrow funds within a standby credit facility or revolving credit facility. Broadly, there are two types of arrangement. In an old-fashioned facility, a company might borrow funds from a small syndicate of banks, and draw down the facility from each bank *pro rata* to its total commitment. For example, suppose that a company has a $ 80 million facility from a syndicate of five banks whose individual commitments are —

Bank A	$ 12 million
Bank B	$ 24 million
Bank C	$ 22 million
Bank D	$ 14 million
Bank E	$ 08 million
Total	**$ 80 million**

If the company draws down $40 million of the facility (50% of the total) it would borrow from each bank (50% of sanctioned limit) in the syndicate as follows:

Bank A	$ 06 million
Bank B	$ 12 million
Bank C	$ 11 million
Bank D	$ 07 million
Bank E	$ 04 million

Another arrangement is for each bank in the syndicate to agree to lend up to a specified maximum but for the borrower to decide within these limits which banks to borrow from, and how much from each, when it wants to draw down funds. The borrower has the opportunity under this arrangement, to get the banks to compete amongst themselves for the lending business. In this way, the borrower might be able to obtain better interest rates. In the previous example, a company drawing down $ 40 million of an $ 80 million facility might borrow as follows:

Underwritten	*($ million)*	*Lent*
Bank A	12	—
Bank B	24	24
Bank C	22	02
Bank D	14	14
Bank E	08	—
	80	40

❖ Multiple-option Facility (MOF)

Syndicated bank facilities can have different structures. One such structure is a Multiple-option Facility (MOF). This is a facility for large corporate borrowers typically for a term of five to ten years. A MOF is a form of revolving credit facility, provided by a syndicate of banks. The term multiple option refers to the flexibility within the facility for the borrower to choose in what form to borrow the funds.

- There may be choice in the currencies in which to borrow. The permitted currencies will be specified in the facility agreement.
- More importantly, there will be choice of debt instruments that can be used within the facility. The borrower will be allowed to borrow for short periods like a few weeks or a few months or for longer periods from one year to 5 years. Also, there may be the option of a Bankers' Acceptance facility whereby the borrower can draw bills on a bank in the syndicate. Alternatively, there might be a commercial paper issue whereby the borrower can issue commercial paper and sell it to banks in the syndicate. An MCF is structured in a similar way to a syndicate for a straightforward syndicated loan. There will be an arranger who initially will underwrite the entire facility. It will appoint other underwriting banks to sub-underwrite a part of the facility; they may be called lead managers or managers for the facility. The underwriting banks will undertake to provide plain-vanilla loans to the borrower in the event that other participating banks cannot be found for the facility. Plain-vanilla loans are straightforward term loans. These loans would be made available, if required in the form of a revolving credit facility, and the funds may be referred to as the backstop facility, committed facility or standby facility.

The arranger and underwriter banks will find banks that are prepared to join a syndicate or Tender Panels of Banks when the company wants to borrow funds, it decides, possibly in consultation with the arranger, in what form the funds should be raised, for example as a 3 months/6 months/two-year loan. The banks on the tender panel are invited to tender for the business, and the company can select the bank or banks offering the best rates. Banks on the tender panel do not have to offer to lend money, but if they do, they can quote rates of their own choice, *i.e.*, rates at which they would be prepared to lend commercially to the company.

The advantage of an MOF to a company are —

- **Its size:** It is a facility that might be too large to arrange bilaterally with a single lending bank.
- **Its flexibility:** The company borrows only the funds that it needs and for as long as it needs them. It also has flexibility in the choice of method for raising funds, e.g., loans, bankers' acceptances, etc.
- **The MOF is a committed facility:** The underwriting banks undertake to provide loans up to the limit of the facility, in the event that the tender panel banks are unwilling to do so.
- Because tender panel banks are invited to compete to lend funds to the company, the company should be able to borrow at very competitive rates.
- The company can borrow short-term/long-term within facility and so should be able to choice the most favourable method of raising funds at the time. For example, it may be able to benefit from low short-term interest rates by borrowing short-term and then borrowing short-term again when the old loan reaches maturity.

❖ Syndicated Facilities and Covenants

A major drawback to a multibank syndicated facility is the potential consequence of a determination in the company's financial health to a state where an event of default occurs or is likely to occur in the near future, and the Company's funding has to be renegotiated. A syndicated facility borrower agrees to the same covenants for all the banks in the tender period. This can give rise to difficulties in the event of default and the borrower needs either refinancing or a rescheduling of loan payments. Banks in the syndicate, that are not owed money by the customer could refuse any lending on the grounds of the breach of covenant. Banks in the syndicate that have loans outstanding are in much the same position as any lending bank when the customer defaults. However, the banks might disagree about whether the customer should be offered a refinancing package and if so, which of the syndicate banks should provide the extra money. For example, when a customer breaches a loan covenant, a small bank that has lent a large amount relative to its size could be very keen on refinancing for the customer in order to protect its loan. On the other hand, a larger bank that is owed very little, might disagree and argue that no further financial report should be given. Obtaining an agreement from all the banks on the tender panel can be very difficult, and could take a long time. If the company's problem is a short-term liquidity shortage rather than a long-term issue of profitability and solvency, and delay by the banks in agreeing to a refinancing package could have disastrous consequences. Any one bank, out of total that could be as high as 100 or more, can hold out for terms that one neither acceptable in which case the company could go into liquidation, nor by accepted, would apply automatically to all other syndicate members. From the bank's point of view a requirement for unanimity gives each bank a reassurance that decision will not be taken that adversely affect its interests. A bank should not agree to be bound by a majority decision of the banks in the syndicate unless it feels able to depend on than to reach decisions that are in the best interest of all the banks. If a company is funded by a member of Bilateral facilities discrete negotiations with each bank can be conducted in refinancing crises without any single bank having the power to veto.

❖ M&A deals drive up Syndicated Loans

Volume of such offerings rose by 13.2% in 2007

India Inc's mergers and acquisitions (M&A) play has given a further push to the raising of syndicated loans in the country. The total volume of syndicated loans by Indian entities has advanced by 13.2% in the first five months of year to $8.5 billion from $7.5 billion in the corresponding period a year ago, according to a report by Thomson Financial. M&A deals in the country rose by 48% in the period.

The list of the top ten bookrunners of syndicated loans features three Indian players — ICICI Bank, UTI and IDBI. The other lead issuers are Citigroup, Calyon, Standard Chartered, ABN-Amro, HSBC Holdings, DBS Group Holdings and ING, Jerome Ongtiapco and Ulysses Roque of Thomson Financial said in the report.

However, the total number of loans issued has fallen by 45.45% to 33 issues in the period. This indicates that the loans of a higher amount are being sought by companies.

But, analysts say that, considering the prevailing interest rate levels, a further drop in the number of loans issued is expected. "With multiple rate hikes, we are seeing a drop in credit growth. While we expect the total loan issuances to drop this year, demand will continue to rise", said Rajesh Mokashi, executive director of CARE Ratings.

The growth in manufacturing sector would continue to be robust, adds Allen Pereira, executive director of Oriental Bank of Commerce. Banks will now start deploying funds for steel, cement and textile sector, he points out.

ICICI Bank and IDBI, which have been focussed on retail lending, have witnessed a slow down in loan issuances owing to multiple rate hikes and also the central bank asking banks to re-balance their credit portfolio to focus on priority sector lending.

"Banks have started re-scheduling their credit portfolio. Though we expect a slowdown in loan issues during the year, it might not be drastic", said Sejal Doshi, CEO of Finquest Securities.

TOP ARRANGERS

Syndicated loans in India

Jan 1, 2007 to June 1, 2007

Bookrunner	*Proceeds ($ million)*	*Rank*	*Market share*
ICICI Bank	861.1	1	10.1
Citigroup	713.9	2	8.4
Calyon	665.1	3	7.8
StanChart Plc	640.4	4	7.5
UTI	580.8	5	6.8
IDBI	549.6	6	6.4
ABN-Amro	473.9	7	5.6
HSBC Holdings Plc	387.1	8	4.5
DBS Group Holdings	352.9	9	4.1
ING	292.9	10	3.4
Industry total	**8,538.5**		**100.0**

Market share in %.

$8.5 billion of syndicated loans were raised by Indian entities in the first five months of year.

The top ten bookrunners of syndicated loans features three Indian players — ICICI Bank, UTI and IDBI Bank.

The total number of loans issued has, however, fallen by 45.45% to 33 issues in the period.

Other Asia-Pacific countries have shown a mixed performance on the loan front. Australian loan volumes increased by 18%, while that in China grew by 32%. On the other hand, Japan witnessed a decline of 24.2% in the loan volume.

❖ Transfers, Assignments and Subparticipation

A lender might not want to wait until the end of the loan period to recover the money lent. The borrower does not have to repay the debt until the redemption date. A lender can recover the money lent, perhaps with some profit or loss on the transaction by transferring it or selling it to someone else. A loan is a contractual agreement between the lender and the borrower and when a lender transfers a debt to someone else, he/she is transferring to receive interest from the borrower. These rights have a money value, and the bank making the transfer can sell the loan. The market for selling loans is known as the secondary loan market. It might seem strange that a bank, having agreed to grant a loan to a borrower, might want to transfer the loan to someone else, but there are several reasons why this might occur. It might seem strange that a bank, having agreed to grant a loan to a borrower, might want to transfer the loan to someone else, but there are several reasons why this might occur:

1. The bank might want to change the portfolio of loans in its loan book. For example, a bank might decide that an excessive proportion of its loans have been made to companies in the telecom sector. It might want to reduce its loans to telecom companies and lend more to retailing companies. To do this, it can sell or transfer, some of its loans to telecom companies and use the money from the sale to lend to retailing companies.
2. A bank might be required to reduce the size of its loan book, *i.e.,* reduce the total amount it makes, for regulatory reasons. As per Basel II, a bank must have a minimum of capital to support, a given volume and quality of assets. If the capital is nearing the minimum acceptable level, it will have to increase its capital or reduce its activities, probably by reducing the volume of its loans. It can do this by transferring or selling loans on to another bank or investor.
3. A bank might decide that some individual loans are too difficult to manage. A corporate borrower might get into financial difficulties and struggle to meet its loan payment commitments. A bank might decide to sell the debt to another bank that specialises in handling distressed debt.

When a bank transfers its loan rights to a third party, it might not want the barrier to know about the transfer. If the bank has a long established commercial relationship with the borrower, or is trying to develop a better commercial relationship it might prefer to keep quiet about the fact that it is offloading the customer's debt on to someone else for the sake of good customer relations.

❖ Transfer

There are three ways for a lender to transfer a loan novation/arrangement and sub-participation. Novation means cancelling the original contract between the old lender and the borrower and creating a new contract between the new lender and the borrower on the same terms and conditions as the old contract. As a result of novation, effectively the contract remains as it was before, except that the new lender has become a party to the loan agreement in place of the old lender. Novation can be arranged only with the consent of all three parties, the old lender, the new lender and the borrower.

Assignment: A party to a loan can assign the loan rights to another person. Assignment is the sale of those rights to the other person. A party to a contract can only assign rights not obligations. A lender can assign his/her rights to be paid by a borrower, but he/she cannot assign any remaining obligations under the loan agreement for example to provide further runs under a committed loan facility arrangement. Under it, the borrower must be notified in writing, but the borrower's consent is not required.

Sub-participation: It is another arrangement for transferring all or part of a loan that leaves the original loan agreement unchanged in all respects. The lending bank takes a deposit from another bank, the sub-participant, equal to all or part of the original loan. The terms of the deposit match the terms of the original loan or part of it. For example, a bank has lent $ 10 million to a company that is repayable in four years' time. Interest is payable six months at LIBOR plus 1$ on set dates up to the redemption date. The bank might decide to transfer the loan by sub-participation. The sub-participation bank will pay a deposit to the lending bank. The deposit will be for the whole amount of the loan ($ 10 million) or just part of it. The term of the deposit will match the remaining term of the loan. Interest payments on the deposit also will reflect the interest payments on the loan, *i.e.,* at LIBOR plus 1% on set dates. It is an example of a non-recourse finance agreement.

(iii) Leasing: A lease is an agreement under which a company or a firm, acquires a right to make use of a capital asset like machinery, on payment of a prescribed fee called "rental charges". The lessee cannot acquire any ownership to the asset, but he can use it and have full control over it. He is expected to pay for all maintenance charges and repairing and operating costs. In countries like the USA, UK and Japan equipment leasing is very popular and nearly 25% of plant and equipment is being financed by leasing companies. In India also, many financial companies have started equipment leasing business. Commercial banks have also been permitted to carry on this business by forming subsidiary companies.

(iv) Mutual Funds: A mutual fund refers to a fund raised by a financial service company by pooling the savings of the public. It is invested in a diversified portfolio with a view to spreading and minimising risk. The fund provides investment avenue for small investors who cannot participate in the equities of big companies. It ensures low risks, steady returns, high liquidity and better capital appreciation in the long-run.

(v) Factoring: Factoring refers to the process of managing the sales ledger of a client by a financial service company. In other words, it is an arrangement under which a financial intermediary assumes the credit risk in the collection of book debts for its clients. The entire responsibility of collecting the book debts passes on to the factor. His services can be compared to a *del credere* agent who undertakes to collect debts. But, a factor provides credit information, collects debts, monitors the sales ledger and provides finance against debts. Thus, he provides a number of services apart from financing.

❖ Cash-flow financing route back in vogue for SMEs as firms chase capital

Many small- and mid-sized firms are once again taking the *factoring route to raise short-term funds. Factoring, or cash-flow financing,* is an arrangement in which receivables created out of sale of goods or services are sold to an agency, known as a factor. Here, goods are sold on credit to a solvent buyer and the seller gets the invoices accepted for payment from the buyer, usually within 90-120 days. The factor then discounts the invoices to pay the seller of the goods. On due date, the factor to collects the entire payment (due to seller) from the buyer of goods.

The factoring business, which had shrunk by half in 2009, is growing again due to increased production and better cash flows.

"Cash-flow financing frees the much-needed working capital. It provides credit protection for the receivables and helps the business to meet increasing sales demand and expand production.

According to officials with factoring firms, capital raised through factoring has gone up from 9,690 crore in 2003 to 11,940 crore in 2005 and 30,330 crore and 31,200 crore in 2007 and 2008 respectively. Capital raised through factoring fell in 2009 to ₹ 15,900 crore but recovered in 2010 following an up-tick in production. If one goes by estimates, companies will raise about 15% more funds through factoring this year.

MONEY RAISED THROUGH FACTORING

	China (Mne)	*Japan (Mne)*	*Thailand (Mne)*	*India (₹ cr)*
2003	2,640	60,550	1,425	9,690
2004	4,315	72,535	1,500	9,750
2005	5,830	71,220	1,640	11,940
2006	14,300	74,530	1,925	21,360
2007	32,976	71,721	2,240	30,330
2008	55,000	1,06,500	2,367	31,200
2009	67,300	83,700	2,107	15,900

Fund-raising through factoring converted to ₹ cr.

Factoring helps companies save time as it is the factor that works to collect money from the counterparty. It is an option that can substitute debt financing significantly, he added. As per Prime Database, there has been over 690 debt issuances aggregating to 1,84,000 crore since January this year. India's share in the Asian factoring market is only 2.2%. The lower volumes, among other things, can be attributed to the large share of agriculture and services in the economy. Globally, factoring business grew at a CAGR of 15% in 2005-09 *vis-a-vis* 7.4% in India during the same period.

"Large companies also benefit from cash-flow financing as it is less cumbersome and the processes are faster compared to bank finance. It (factoring) is a good option to turn around big and fundamentally good businesses, that finds difficult to work within the constraints of their bank covenants."

(vi) Forfaiting: Forfaiting is a technique by which a forfaitor (financing agency) discounts an export bill and pay ready cash to the exporter who can concentrate on the export front without bothering about collection of export bills. The forfaitor does so without any recourse to the exporter and the exporter is protected against the risk of non-payment of debts by the importers.

Forfeiting is a form of trade financing undertaken to facilitate export transactions The process of forfeiting thus has a lot of significance as it undertakes to solve the cash flow problem of the exporter taking the benefit of factoring. In a forfeiting transaction the exporter surrenders his right for claiming the payment for services rendered or goods supplied to the importer in favour of the forfeiter. A deed is prepared stating the same and the exporter receives cash payment from the facilitator. All the transaction of forfeiting are performed with the support of a bank which assumes the default risk possessed by the importer. The exporter before extending finance for a forfeiting transaction looks into several critical aspects of the underlying goods or commodity. For example, the bank would pay special attention towards the durability/ perishability nature of the goods, authentication of the product (date of manufacturing, product code, etc.), packaging arrangements and other precautions adopted during the stage of shipment, etc. After these checks and verifications the banker provides the exporter with the funds. In other words, the forfeiting transaction helps an exporter with instant cash and eliminates his cash-flow problems. Forfeiting is a relatively new concept. It is a specialized forms of factoring, which is undertaken on export transactions on a *Non-recourse Basis*.

The process of forfeiting gets underway the moment an exporter asks for quotations from the overseas buyer on the issue of price, delivery, interest structure, currency involved, etc. Once the exporter is satisfied with the data received/quotation, he approaches the EXIM Bank, furnishes the name of the overseas party, name of the country, description of goods, order details, base price, payback period, and the details of the export Agency who will facilitate the transaction for the exporter. To make a complete transaction of forfeiting, the forfeiter asks for the details of the banker of the overseas importer. The overseas banker accepts and validates the documents of the transaction. This is known as the banker's Coacceptance. The Coacceptance serves as a yardstick for the forfeiter as to the credit quality and the marketability of the instrument accepted. EXIM Bank then collects from the overseas forfeiting agencies the representative quotes on rates of discount, documentation charges, commitment charges and informs the same to the exporter. If the terms are acceptable for the exporter, he requests the EXIM Bank to obtain a firm quote from the forfeitor.

Fees and charges of forfeiting are classified into three broad categories, *viz.*:

- **Commitment charges:** Range 0.5 to 1.5% p.a. calculated on the unutilized amount of the forfeiting transactions.
- **Discount fees:** It is payable for the total period of credit under consideration and based on L1BOR Rate.
- **Documentation fees:** Charged for elaborate legal formalities and complexities, if any (or when essentially required).

Forfeiting transaction is considered where the consignment is for a minimum value of $2,50,000 or its equivalent. The normal duration of the receivables in a forfeiting contract ranges from one to five years.

(vii) Venture Capital: A venture capital is another method of financing in the form of equity participation. A venture capitalist finances a project based on the potentialities of a new innovative project. It is in contrast to the conventional "security based financing". Much thrust is given to new ideas or technological innovations. Finance is being provided not only for 'start-up capital' but also for 'development capital' by the financial intermediary.

(viii) Custodial Services: It is yet another line of activity which has gained importance, of late. Under this, a financial intermediary mainly provides services to clients, particularly to foreign investors, for a prescribed fee. Custodial services provide agency services like safe keeping of shares and debentures, collection of interest and dividend and reporting of matters on corporate developments and corporate securities to foreign investors.

(ix) Corporate Advisory Services: Financial intermediaries particularly banks have set up corporate advisory service branches to render services exclusively to their corporate customers. For instance, some banks have extended computer terminals to their corporate customers so that they can transact some of their important banking transactions by sitting in their own office. As new avenues of finance like Euro loans, GDRs, etc., are available to corporate customers, this service is of immense help to the customers.

(x) Securitisation: Securitisation is a technique whereby a financial company converts its ill-liquid, non-negotiable and high value financial assets into securities of small value which are made tradable and transferable. A financial institution might have a lot of its assets blocked up in assets like real estate, machinery, etc., which are long-term in nature and which are non-negotiable. In such cases, securitisation would help the financial institution to raise cash against such assets by means of issuing securities of small values to the public. Like any other security, they can be traded in the market. It is best suited to housing finance companies whose loans are always long-term in nature and their money is locked up for a considerable long period in real estates. Securitisation is the only answer to convert these ill-liquid assets into liquid assets.

(xi) Derivative Security: A derivative security is a security whose value depends upon the values of other basic variables backing the security. In most cases, these variables are nothing but the prices of traded securities. A derivative security is basically used as a risk management tool and it is resorted to cover the risks due to price fluctuations by the investments manager. Just like a forward contract which is a derivative of a spot contract, a derivative security is derived from other trading securities backing it. Naturally, the value of a derivative security depends upon the values of the backing securities. Derivative helps to break the risks into various components such as credit risk, interest rates risk, exchange rates risk and so on. It enables the various risk components to be identified precisely and priced them and even traded them if necessary. Financial intermediaries can go for derivatives since they will have greater importance in the near future. In India, some forms of derivatives are in operation. Example: Forwards in forex market.

(xii) New Products in Forex Market: New products have also emerged in the forex markets of developed countries. Some of these products are yet to make full entry in Indian markets. Among them, the following are the important ones:

(a) Forward Contracts: A forward transaction is one where the delivery of a foreign currency takes place at a specified future date for a specified price. It may have a fixed maturity for, e.g., 31st May or a flexible maturity for, e.g., 1st to 31st May. There is an obligation to honour this contract at any cost, failing which, there will be some penalty. Forward contracts are permitted only for genuine business transactions. It can be extended to other transactions like interest payments.

(b) Options: As the very name implies, it is a contract wherein the buyer of the option has a right to buy or sell a fixed amount of currency against another currency at a fixed rate on a future date according to his option. There is no obligation to buy or sell, but it is completely left to his option. Options may be of two types namely call options and put options. Under call options, the customer has an option to buy and it is the option to sell under put options. Options trading would lead to speculation and hence there are much restrictions in India.

(c) Futures: It is a contract wherein there is an agreement to buy or sell a stated quantity of foreign currency at a future date at a price agreed to between the parties on the stated exchange. Unlike options, there is an obligation to buy or sell foreign exchange on a future date at a specified rate. It can be dealt only in a stock exchange.

(d) Swaps: A swap refers to a transaction, wherein a financial intermediary buys and sells a specified foreign currency simultaneously for different maturity dates — say, for instance, purchase of spot and sale of forward or *vice versa* with different maturities. Thus, swaps would result in simultaneous buying and selling of the same foreign currency of the same value for different maturities to eliminate exposure risk. It can also be used as a tool to enter arbitrage operations, if any, between two countries. It can also be used in the interest rate market also. It is explained in detail under the chapter derivatives.

(xiii) Letter of Credit (LoC): It is an innovative funding mechanism for the import of goods and services on deferred payment terms. LoC is an arrangement of a financing institution/ bank of one country with another institution/bank/agent to support the export of goods and services so as to enable the importers to import no deferred payment terms. This may be backed by a guarantee furnished by the institution/bank in the importing country. The LoC helps the exporters to get payment immediately as soon as the goods are shipped, since, the funds would be paid out of the pool account with the financing agency and it would be debited to the account of the borrower agency/importer whose contract for availing the facility is already approved by the financing agency on the recommendation of the overseas institution. It acts as conduct of financing which is for a certain period and on certain terms for the required goods to be imported. The greatest advantage is that it saves a lot of time and money on mutual verification of bonafides, source of finance, etc. It serves as a source of forex.

4.8 MERCHANT BANKING

❖ Meaning

The term merchant banking is used differently in different countries and so there is no precise definition for it. In London, merchant banker refers to those who are members of British Merchant Banking and Securities House Association who carry on consultation, leasing, portfolio services, assets management, euro credit, loan syndication, etc. In America, merchant banking is concerned with mobilising savings of people and directing the funds to business enterprise.

There is no universal definition for merchant banking. It assumes diverse functions in different countries. So, merchant banking may be defined as, 'an institution which covers a wide range of activities such as management of customer services, portfolio management, credit syndication, acceptance credit, counselling, insurance' etc.

The Notification of the Ministry of Finance defines a merchant banker as, "any person who is engaged in the business of issue management either by making arrangements regarding selling, buying or subscribing to the securities as manager, consultant, adviser or rendering corporate advisory service in relation to such issue management".

Merchant banking originated through the entering of London merchants in financing foreign trade through acceptance of bill. Later, the merchants assisted the government of under developed countries in raising long-term funds through flotation of bonds in London money market. Over a period, they extended their activities to domestic business of syndication of long-term and short-term finance, underwriting of new issues, acting as registrars and share transfer agents, debenture trustees, portfolio managers, negotiating agents for mergers, take over, etc. The post-war period witnessed the rapid growth of merchant banking through the innovative instrument like Euro dollar and the growth of various financial centres like Singapore, Hong Kong, Bahrain, Kuwait, Dubai, etc.

❖ Merchant Banking in India

In India prior to the enactment of Indian Companies Act, 1956, managing agents acted as issue houses for securities, evaluated project reports, planned capital structure and to some extent provided venture capital for new firms. Few share broking firms also functioned as merchant bankers.

The need for specialised merchant banking service was felt in India with the rapid growth in the number and size of the issues made in the primary market. The merchant banking services were started by foreign banks, namely the National Grindlays Bank in 1967 and the City Bank in 1970. The Banking Commission in its report in 1972 recommended the setting up of merchant banking institutions by commercial banks and financial institutions. This marked the beginning of specialised merchant banking in India.

To begin with, merchant banking services were offered first by a foreign bank in 1967 by National Grindlays Bank along with other traditional banking services. In the mid-eighties, the Banking Regulations Act was amended permitting commercial banks to offer a wide range of financial services through the subsidiary rule. The State Bank of India was the first Indian Bank to set up Merchant Banking Division in 1972. Later ICICI set up its Merchant Banking Division followed by Bank of India, Bank of Baroda, Canara Bank, Punjab National Bank and UCO Bank.

❖ Merchant Banks and Commercial Banks

There are differences in approach, attitude and areas of operations between commercial banks and merchant banks. The differences between merchant banks and commercial banks are summarised below:

1. Commercial banks basically deal in debt and debt-related finance and their activities are appropriately arrayed around credit proposals, credit appraisal and loan sanctions. On the other hand, the area of activity of merchant bankers is 'equity and equity-related finance'. They deal with mainly funds raised through money market and capital market.
2. Commercial banks are asset-oriented and their lending decisions are based on detailed credit analysis of loan proposals and the value of security offered against loans. They generally avoid risks. The merchant bankers are management-oriented. They are willing to accept risks of business.

3. Commercial bankers are merely financiers. The activities of merchant bankers include project counselling, corporate counselling in areas of capital restructuring, amalgamations, mergers, takeover, etc., discounting and rediscounting of short-term paper in money markets, managing, underwriting and supporting public issues in new issue market and acting as brokers and advisers on portfolio management in stock exchange. Merchant banking activities have impact on growth, stability and liquidity of money markets.

4.8.1 Services of Merchant Banks

The financial institutions in India could not meet the demand for long-term funds required by the ever expanding industry and trade. The corporate sector enterprises, therefore, meet their requirements through issue of shares and debentures in the capital market. To raise money from capital market, promoters bank upon merchant bankers who manage the whole show by rendering multifarious services. The merchant bankers also advise the investors of the incentives available in the form of tax reliefs and other statutory obligations.

The services of merchant bankers are described in detail in the following section.

(i) Corporate Counselling

Corporate counselling covers the entire field of merchant banking activities, *viz.*, project counselling, capital restructuring, project management, public issue management, loan syndication, working capital, fixed deposit, lease financing, acceptance credit, etc. The scope of corporate counselling is limited to giving suggestions and opinions to the client and help taking actions to solve their problems. It is provided to a corporate unit with a view to ensure better performance, maintain steady growth and create better image among investors.

(ii) Project Counselling

Project counselling includes preparation of project reports, deciding upon the financing pattern to finance the cost of the project and appraising project report with the financial institutions or banks. Project reports are prepared to obtain government approval, get financial assistance from institutions and plan for the public issue. The financing mix is to be decided keeping in view the rules, regulations and norms prescribed by the government or followed by financial institutions. The projects are appraised, as to the location, technical, commercial and financial viability of the project. Project counselling also includes filling up of application forms with relevant information for obtaining funds from financial institutions.

(iii) Loan Syndication

Loan syndication refers to assistance rendered by merchant banks to get mainly term loans for projects. Such loans may be obtained from a single development finance institution or a syndicate or consortium. Merchant bankers help corporate clients to raise syndicated loans from commercial banks.

Merchant banks help clients approach financial institutions for term loans. The decision as to which financial institution should be approached depends on industry, location of the unit and size of project cost. The merchant bankers, first, make an appraisal of the project to satisfy that it is viable. The next step is designing capital structure, determining the promoter's contribution and arriving at a figure of approximate amount of term loan to be raised. The merchant banker has to ensure that the project adheres to the guidelines for financing industrial projects. After verifications that the project would be eligible for term loan, a preliminary meeting is fixed with financial institution. If the financial institution agrees to consider the proposal, the application is filled in and submitted along with other documents. The merchant bankers involvement enables the company to state that it has exercised due diligence in the exercise of obligations under various regulations.

(iv) Issue Management

Management of issue involves marketing of corporate securities, *viz.,* equity shares, preference shares and debentures or bonds by offering them to public. Merchant banks act as intermediary whose main job is to transfer capital from those who own it to those who need it.

The issue function may be broadly divided into pre-issue management and post-issue management. In both the stages, legal requirements have to be complied with and several activities connected with the issue have to be coordinated:

The pre-issue management is divided into:

(*i*) Issue through prospectus, offer for sale and private placement.

(*ii*) Marketing and underwriting.

(*iii*) Pricing of Issues.

(i) Public Issue through Prospectus

(*a*) The most common method of public issue is through prospectus.

(*b*) Offers for sale are offers through the intermediary of issue house or firm of stock broker. The company sells the entire issue of shares or debentures to the issue house at an agreed price which is generally below the par value.

(*c*) The direct sale of securities by a company to investors is called private placement. The investors include LIC, UTI, GIC, SFC, etc.

To bring out a public issue, merchant bankers have to coordinate the activities relating to issue with different government and public bodies, professionals and private agencies. They have to ensure that the information required by the Companies Act and SEBI are furnished in the prospectus and get it vetted by reputed solicitor.

The copies of consent of experts, legal adviser, attorney, solicitor, bankers, bankers to the issue, brokers and underwriters are to be obtained from the company making the issue, to be filed along with prospectus to the Registrar of Companies. After the prospectus is ready, it has to be sent to SEBI for vetting. It Is only after clearance by SEBI, the prospectus can be filed with the Registrar of Companies.

Brokers to the issue canvass subscription by mailing the literature to the clients and undertaking wide publicity. Members of stock exchange are appointed as brokers to issue.

Principal brokers, in addition to the functions of brokers assist merchant bankers to devise strategy for success of the public issue, keep liaison between merchant banker and stock exchanges and canvass support for the issue among stock brokers. Sometimes, they undertake centralised mailing of prospectus, application forms and other publicity material at the instant of the merchant banker.

Bankers to the issue accept applications along with subscriptions tendered at their designated branches and forward them to the Registrar.

The brokers to the issue, principal agent and bankers to issue are appointed by merchant bankers.

(ii) Marketing

After despatch of prospectus to SEBI, the merchant bankers arrange a meeting with company representatives and advertising agents to finalise arrangements relating to date of opening and closing of issue, registration of prospectus, launching publicity campaign and fixing date of board meeting to approve and sign prospectus and pass the necessary resolutions.

Publicity campaign covers the preparation of all publicity material and brochures, prospectus, announcement, advertisement in the press, radio, TV, investors conference, etc. The merchant bankers help choosing the media, determining the size and publications in which the advertisement should appear.

The merchant bankers role is limited to deciding the number of copies to be printed, checking accuracy of statements made and ensure that the size of the application form and prospectus conform to the standard prescribed by the stock exchange. The merchant banker has to ensure that the material is delivered to the stock exchange at least 21 days before the issue opens and to brokers to the issue, branches of brokers to the issue and underwriters on time.

Security issues are underwritten to ensure that in case of under subscription the issues are taken up by the underwriters. SEBI has made underwriting mandatory for issues to the public. The underwriting arrangement should be filed with the stock exchange. Particulars of underwriting arrangement should be mentioned in the prospectus.

The various activities connected with pre-issue management are a time-bound programme which has to be promptly attended to. The execution of the activities with clock work efficiency would lead to a successful issue.

(iii) Pricing of Issues

The SEBI guidelines, 1992 for capital issues have opened the capital market to free pricing of issues. Pricing of issues is done by companies themselves in consultation with the merchant bankers. Pricing of issue is part of pre-issue management.

An existing listed company and a new company set up by an existing company with five-year track record and existing private closely held company and existing unlisted company going in for public issues for the first time with two-and-a-half years track record of constant profitability can freely price the issue. The premium has to be decided after taking into account net asset value, profit earning capacity and market price. Justification of price has to be stated and included in the prospectus.

(iv) Post-issue Management

The post-issue management consists of collection of application forms and statement of amount received from bankers, screening applications, deciding allotment procedure, mailing of allotment letters, share certificates and refund orders.

Registrars to the issue play a major role in post-issue management. They receive the applications, verify them and submit the basis of allotment to the stock exchange. After the basis of allotment is approved by the stock exchange and allotted by the Board, the auditor/company secretary has to certify that the allotment has been made by the company as per the basis of allotment approved by the exchange. Registrars have to ensure that the applications are processed and allotment/refund orders are sent within 70 days of the close of the issue. The time limit of 70 days has proved difficult to adhere and applicants have to wait for anytime between 90 to 180 days. Merchant bankers assist the company by coordinating the above activities.

(v) Underwriting of Public Issue

Underwriting is a guarantee given by the underwriter that in the event of under subscription the amount underwritten, would be subscribed by him. It is an insurance to the company which proposes to make public offer against risk of undersubscription. The issues backed by well known underwriters generally receive a high premium from the public. This enables the issuing company to sell securities quickly.

All public issues have to be fully underwritten Only Category I, II and III merchant bankers are permitted to underwrite an issue subject to the limit that the outstanding commitments of any such individual merchant banker at any point of time do not exceed five times of his net worth (paid-up capital and free reserves excluding revaluation reserves). This criteria is applicable to brokers also. Lead managers have to underwrite mandatorily 5% of the issue Banks/Merchant banking subsidiaries cannot underwrite more than 15% of any issue.

By ensuring a direct stake in the underwriting, the merchant bankers make raising of external resources easy.

(vi) Managers, Consultants or Advisers to the Issue

The managers to the issue assist in the drafting of prospectus, application forms and completion of formalities under the Companies Act, appointment of Registrar for dealing with share applications and transfer and listing of shares of the company on the stock exchange. Companies are free to appoint one or more agencies as managers to the issue. SEBI guidelines insist that all issues should be managed by at least one authorised merchant banker. Ordinarily, not more than two merchant bankers should be associated as lead managers, advisers and consultants to a public issue. In issues of over ₹ 100 crore, up to a maximum of four merchant bankers could be associated as managers.

(vii) Portfolio Management

Portfolio refers to investment in different kinds of securities such as shares, debentures or bonds issued by different companies and securities issued by the government. It is not merely a collection of unrelated assets but a carefully blended asset combination within a unified framework. Portfolio management refers to maintaining proper combination of securities in a manner that they give maximum return with minimum risk.

Merchant bankers provide portfolio management service to their clients. Today the investor is very prudent. Every investor is interested in safety, liquidity and profitability of his investment. But investors cannot study and choose the appropriate securities. They need expert guidance. Merchant bankers have a role to play in this regard. They have to conduct regular market and economic surveys to know.

(*i*) monetary and fiscal policies of the government.

(*ii*) financial statements of various corporate sectors in which the investments have to be made by the investors.

(*iii*) secondary market position, i.e., how the share market is moving.

(*iv*) changing pattern of the industry.

(*v*) the competition faced by the industry with similar type of industries.

The merchant bankers have to analyse the surveys and help the prospective investors in choosing the shares. The portfolio managers generally will have to classify the investors based on capacity and risk. They can take and arrange appropriate investment. Thus, portfolio management plans successful investment strategies for investors.

The portfolio management service is very important need of the day since 1/8th of our investment at present comes from rural areas. Eventhough on July 2007, there are 21 stock exchanges in our country, 23 nationalised banks with network of about 74,000 branches, only 1/8th of the savings is mobilized from the rural areas. By establishing portfolio management centres at various areas more investments can be augmented from villages. Instead of concentrating on large investors, there is immediate need to develop small investors which could be done through portfolio management.

The role which can be played by non-resident Indians in the economic development of a country is not small. With their technical skill and foreign exchange and also with their knowledge of foreign market they can contribute much for the country. In order to utilise this opportunity government is offering number of facilities and incentives. But the NRI investment is not showing any signs of substantial improvement for corporate sector. This is due to the NRI accounts being scattered with various branches of banks throughout the country and no institution is taking action to pool these resources. The non-resident themselves for investment will have to follow many rules and regulations which are complicated. In this regard merchant bankers should help the NRI in selecting right type of securities and offering expertise guidance in fulfilling government regulations. By this service to NRI accountholders, merchant bankers can mobilise more resources for the corporate sector.

(viii) Advisory Service Relating to Mergers and Takeovers

A merger is a combination of two or more companies into a single company where one survives and others lose their corporate existence. A takeover is the purchase by one company acquiring controlling interest in the share capital of another existing company. Merchant bankers are the middlemen in setting negotiation between the offeree and offeror. Being a professional expert they are apt to safeguard the interest of the shareholders in both the companies. Once the merger partner is proposed, the merchant banker appraises merger/takeover proposal with respect to financial viability and technical feasibility. He negotiates purchase consideration and mode of payment. He gets approval from the government/RBI, drafts scheme of amalgamation and obtains approval from financial institutions.

(ix) Offshore Banking

The merchant bankers help their clients in the following areas involving foreign currency.

(*i*) long-term foreign currency loans

(*ii*) joint venture abroad

(*iii*) financing exports and imports, and

(*iv*) foreign collaboration arrangements.

The bankers render other financial services such as appraisal, negotiations and compliance with procedural and legal aspects.

(x) Non-resident Investment

The services of merchant bankers include investment advisory services to NRI in terms of identification of investment opportunities, selection of securities, investment management, etc. They also take care of the operational details like purchase and sale of securities, securing necessary clearance from RBI for repatriation of interest and dividend.

4.8.2 Merchant Bankers as Lead Managers

As per SEBI guidelines it is mandatory that all public issues should be managed by merchant bankers in the capacity of lead managers. Only in the case of right issues not exceeding ₹ 50 lakh such an obligation is not necessary. The number of lead managers to be appointed by a company depends upon the size of the issue as shown below:

S. No.	*Size of the Issue*	*Maximum Number of Lead Managers*
1.	Less than ₹ 50 crore	2
2.	₹ 50 crores to ₹ 100 crore	3
3.	₹ 100 crores to ₹ 200 crore	4
4.	₹ 200 crores to ₹ 400 crore	4
5.	Above ₹ 400 crore	5 or more as prescribed by SEBI

4.8.3 Duties and Responsibilities of Lead Managers

The most important aspect of merchant banking business is to function as lead managers to the issue management. As lead managers, they have to exercise reasonable care and diligence in issue management by paying attention to the following:

(*i*) It is the duty of every lead manager to enter into an agreement with the issuing companies stating the details regarding their responsibilities, liabilities, mutual rights, functions, disclosures, refund, allotment, etc. A copy of this agreement should be submitted to the SEBI at least one month before the opening of the issue for subscription.

(*ii*) One merchant banker cannot have association with another merchant banker who does not hold a certificate of registration with the SEBI.

(*iii*) Similarly, a lead manager cannot undertake the work of issue management if the issuing company is its associate.

(*iv*) In case there are more than one lead managers to an issue, the responsibilites of each of item should be clearly defined in the agreement.

(*v*) A lead manager is under an obligation to accept a minimum underwriting obligation of 5 per cent of the total underwriting or ₹ 25 lakh whichever is less. If he is not able to comply with the above provision it is his duty to make managements with another merchant banker associated with that issue to underwrite the said amount. Of course, it must be duly intimated to the SEBI.

(*vi*) A lead manager has to exercise due care and diligence in the verification of prospectus or letter of offer.

(*vii*) He has to submit due diligence certificate rating that the prospectus or letter of offer is in conformity with the documents relevant to the issue, the disclosures are true, fair and adequate and all legal requirements connected with the issue have been duly complied with.

(*viii*) Every lead manager has to submit all the particulars of an issue, draft prospectus or letter of offer, etc., to the SEBI at least two weeks before the date of filing with the Registrar of Companies or regional stock exchanges or both.

(*ix*) In case of any suggestions or modifications given by the SEBI, he has to ensure that they are properly incorporated in the appropriate areas.

(*x*) In the case of development, the lead manager has to ensure the collection of the specified amount from the underwriters.

(*xi*) Every lead manager is responsible for ensuring timely refund of excess application money received from the applicants.

(*xii*) It is his duty to mail the share/debenture certificate immediately on allotment or inform it to the depository participant.

REQUIRED QUALITIES OF MERCHANT BANKERS

Merchant bankers play a significant role as a catalyst to transform the project ideas into industrial ventures. They help promotion of the enterprise by undertaking various activities such as market surveys, choice of suitable location and its size, preparation of documents and obtaining consent from various authorities. They help in taking important decisions such as financing mix, management of public issues, credit syndication, etc. The success of the merchant bankers depends on the quality of service and soundness of advice to clients. To perform these services, effectively the merchant bankers are expected to possess certain qualities which are described below:

1. Ability to analyse various aspects such as technical, financial and economic aspects concerning the formation of an industrial project.
2. Knowledge about the various aspects of capital markets, trends in stock exchange, psychology of investing public, change in the economic and technological environment in the country.
3. Ability to build-up the bank-client relationship and live up to the clients expectations with total involvement in the project assigned to them.
4. Innovative approach in developing capital market instruments to satisfy the ever-changing needs of investing public.
5. Integrity and maintenance of high professional standards are the essential requisites for the success of merchant bankers present scenario.

4.8.4 Guidelines for Merchant Bankers

Merchant banking has been statutorily brought within the framework of the Securities and Exchange Board of India under SEBI (Merchant Bankers) Regulations, 1992.

(1) In terms of the guidelines issued during April 1990, all merchant bankers will require authorisation by SEBI to carry-out business.

The criteria for authorisation include:

(*i*) professional qualification in finance, law or business management;

(*ii*) infrastructure like adequate office space, equipment and manpower;

(*iii*) employment of two persons who have the experience to conduct business of merchant bankers;

(*iv*) capital adequacy;

(*v*) past track of record, experience, general reputation and fairness in all transactions.

(2) SEBI issued further guidelines classifying the merchant bankers into four categories based on the nature and range of activities and their responsibilities to SEBI investors and issuers of securities. SEBI has issued revised guidelines on December 22, 1992 classifying the activities of merchant bankers as follows:

The first category consists of merchant bankers who carry on any activity of issue management which will *inter alia* consists of preparation of prospectus and other information relating to the issue, determining financial structure, tie-up of financiers and final allotment and refund of subscription and to act in the capacity of managers, advisor or consultant to an issue, portfolio manager and underwriter.

The second category consists of those authorised to act in the capacity of co-manager/advisor, consultant, underwriter to an issue or portfolio manager.

The third category consists of those authorised to act as underwriter, advisor or consultant to an issue.

The fourth category consists of merchant bankers who act as advisor or consultant to an issue.

Minimum net worth for first category is ₹ 5 crore, second category ₹ 50 lakh, third category ₹ 20 lakh and fourth category is nil.

(3) An initial authorisation fee, an annual fee and renewal fee may be collected by SEBI.

(4) All issues must be managed at least by one authorised banker, functioning as the sole manager or the lead manager. Ordinarily not more than two merchant bankers should be associated as lead managers. But, for issues over ₹ 100 crore and above, the number of lead managers may go up to a maximum of 5. The specific responsibilities of each lead manager must be submitted to EBI prior to the issue.

(5) The lead merchant banker holding a certificate under category I shall accept a minimum underwriting obligation of 5% of the total underwriting commitment or ₹ 25 lakh whichever is less.

(6) Each merchant banker is required to furnish to the SEBI half-yearly unaudited financial results when required by it with a view to monitor the capital adequacy of the merchant banker.

(7) SEBI has prescribed a code of conduct to the merchant bankers. The banker must perform his duties with highest standards of integrity and fairness in all his dealings. He will render at all times high standards of service, exercise due diligence, ensure proper care and exercise independent professional judgement. The merchant banker and his personnel will act in an ethical manner in all his dealings with the investors, clients and fellow bankers. All merchant bankers must adhere to the code of conduct.

(8) The above guidelines will be administered by SEBI and it will supervise the activities of merchant bankers.

(9) SEBI has been vested with power to suspend or cancel the authorisation in case of violation of the guidelines.

(10) To ensure transparency and accountability in the operation of merchant bankers and to protect the investors, a number of obligations and responsibilities have been imposed on them. It has been decided to ask merchant bankers to enter into agreement with corporate body setting out their mutual rights, liabilities and obligations relating to an issue particularly on disclosure, allotment and refund, maintenance of books of accounts and submission of half-yearly reports to SEBI.

(11) Inspections will be conducted by SEBI to ensure that provisions of the regulations are properly complied with and to investigate the complaints from customers. It is obligatory on the part of merchant bankers to furnish all the details sought by the investigating team. The regulations, however, indicate that the Board would give reasonable notice to merchant bankers before undertaking inspection. On the basis of inspection report, the Board will communicate the contents of the report to the concerned merchant banker to give him/her an opportunity to put forth his/her submissions. On receipt of the explanations, if any, of the merchant bankers, the SEBI would advise merchant bankers to take any measures that it may deem fit, and to comply with the provisions of the regulations.

The notification procedure relating to action to be initiated against merchant banks in case of default has been detailed out. The regulations empower SEBI to take action against defaulting banker such as suspension/cancellation of registration. In case of deliberate manipulation, or price rigging or cornering activities or deterioration in the financial position, the Board is empowered to cancel the registration of the merçhant banker. Under the regulation, the SEBI is empowered to suspend a registration of a member banker in case the merchant banker furnishes wrong or false information, fails to resolve the complaints of the investors, etc. The penalty or suspensation or cancellation of registration can be imposed by SEBI only after holding an enquiry and giving sufficient opportunity to the merchant banker of being heard. Any merchant banker aggrieved by an order of SEBI, can, however, appeal to the Union Government.

In September, 1997, SEBI brought about some major changes in SEBI (Merchant Bankers) Rules and Regulations, 1992. Accordingly, only Corporate bodies will be allowed to function as merchant bankers. Moreover, the multiple categories of merchant bankers shall be abolished and there will be just one entity, *viz.*, merchant banker. The merchant bankers presently functioning as Merchant Bankers Category II, III and IV shall have an option to either upgrade themselves as merchant bankers (presently Merchant Banker Category I) or seek separate registration as underwriters or portfolio managers under the respective regulations. The merchant bankers will be prohibited from carrying out fund based activity other than those related exclusively to the capital markets. In effect, the activities undertaken by NBFCs such as accepting deposits, leasing and bill discounting would not be allowed to be undertaken by a merchant banker.

4.8.5 Merchant Bankers Commission

As determined by the Finance Ministry, Government of India, merchant bankers are eligible to charge commission/fee from their clients as detailed below:

(*i*) A merchant banker can charge 0.5% as the maximum as commission for whole of the issue.

(*ii*) They can charge project appraisal fees.

(*iii*) A lead manager can claim a commission of 0.5% up to ₹ 25 crore and 0.2% in excess of ₹ 25 crore.

(*iv*) Underwriting Commission.

Type of Security	*On Amount Subscribed by Public*
1. Equity shares	55
2. Preference shares/debentures	2½%

(*v*) Brokerage commission 1.5%.

(*vi*) Other expenses like advertising, printing, Registrar's expenses, stamp duty, etc., in connection with the issue can be reimbursed from its clients.

❖ Merchant Bankers in the Market Making Process

The Securities and Exchange Board of India (SEBI) has stated that merchant bankers must be involved more closely in the market making process as share brokers do not have the requisite expertise to evaluate the fundamentals of the scrips before taking over the role of market-makers. Further, share brokers generally being partnership firms, do not have the financial clout which is necessary for market making activity. Resultantly, the SEBI has suggested that any member of the stock exchange, along with one merchant banker registered with SEBI could act as a market-maker.

The SEBI has felt that to ensure liquidity of scrips, it was necessary to facilitate greater movement, which could only be achieved through the institution of market-makers. Market-makers would also create a market for the scrips by offering two-way quotes to the investors. A minimum of ten scrips have been proposed by SEBI for the market-makers.

4.8.6 Progress of Merchant Banking in India

Up to 1970, there were only two foreign banks which performed merchant banking operations in the country. SBI was the first Indian commercial bank and ICICI the first financial institution to take up the activities in 1972 and 1973 respectively. As a result of buoyancy in the capital market in 1980s some commercial banks set up their subsidiaries to operate exclusively in merchant banking industry. In addition, a number of large stock broking firms and financial consultants also entered into business. Thus, by the end of the 1980s there were 33 merchant bankers belonging to three major segments, *viz.*, commercial banks, all India financial institutions, and private firms. Merchant banking functions of these institutions was related only to management of new capital issues.

Merchant banking industry which remained almost stagnant and stereotyped for over two decades, witnessed an astonishing growth after the process of economic reforms and deregulation of Indian economy in 1991. The number of merchant banks increased to 123 by the end of March 2000, 128 by the end of 2004-05. All merchant bankers registered with SEBI under four different categories include 50 commercial banks, six all India financial institutions — ICICI, IFCI, IDBI, IRBI, Tourism Finance Corporation of India, Infrastructure Leasing and Financial Services, Ltd., and private merchant bankers.

In addition to Indian merchant bankers, a large number of reputed international merchant bankers like Merrill Lynch, Morgan Stanley, Goldman Sachs, Jardie Fleming, Kleinwort Benson, etc., are operating in India under authorisation of SEBI. As a result of proliferation, Indian merchant bankers are faced with severe competition not only among themselves but also with the well developed global players.

The chart presents the merchant bankers registered with SEBI classified according to the category till March 2010.

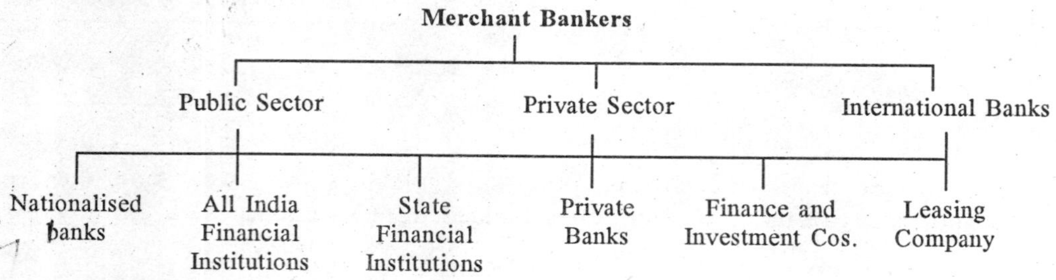

❖ Problems of Merchant Bankers

1. SEBI guidelines have authorised merchant bankers to undertake issue related activities only with an exception of portfolio management. These guidelines have made the merchant bankers either to restrict their activities or think of separating these activities from the present one and float new subsidiary and enlarge the scope of its activities.

2. SEBI guidelines stipulate a minimum net worth of ₹ 5 crore for authorisation of merchant bankers. Small but professional and specialised merchant bankers who do not have a net worth of ₹ 1 crore may have to close down their business. The entry is denied to young, specialised professionals into merchant banking business.

3. Non-cooperation of the issuing companies in timely allotment of securities and refund of application money is another problem of merchant bankers. The guidelines have put the responsibility on the merchant bankers. They have to seek the cooperation of the issuing company to shoulder the responsibility.

4.8.7 Scope for Merchant Banking in India

In the present day capital market scenario, the merchant banks play the role of an encouraging and supporting force to the entrepreneurs, corporate sectors and the investors. There is vast scope for merchant bankers to enlarge their operations both in domestic and international market.

(i) Growth of New Issues Market

The growth of new issue market is unprecedented since 1995-96. The amount of annual average of capital issues by non-government public companies was only about ₹ 90 crore in the 70s, the same rose to over ₹ 1,000 crore in the 80s, and further to ₹ 12,700 crore in the first four years of 1990s.

Issues	*1996-97*	*1997-98*	*1998-99*	*1999-2000*	*2000-01*	*2001-02*	*2002-03*	*2003-04*	*2004-05*
Domestic Issue	33,872	37,738	59,044	68,963	74,198	72,061	71,814	71,752	1,05,944
Non Govt. Public Co.	10,410	3,138	5,013	5,153	4,890	5,692	1,877	3,675	13,482
Public Co. Bonds	3,394	2,982	—	—	—	—	—	—	—
Govt. Com.	650	430	—	—	—	350	—	100	2,684
Banks/Financial Institutions	4,352	1,476	4,350	2,551	1,472	1,070	2,989	4,076	5,726
Private Placements	15,066	30,099	49,679	61,259	67,836	64,950	66,948	63,901	84,052
Euro Issues	5,594	4,009	1,148	3,487	4,197	2,342	3,442	3,098	3,353

Source: Annual Report, RBI.

(ii) Entry of Foreign Institutional Investors (FIIs)

An outstanding development in the history of Indian capital market was its opening up in 1992 by allowing foreign institutional investors to invest in primary and secondary market and also permitting Indian companies to directly tap foreign capital through euro issues. Within two years to March 1994, the total inflow of foreign capital through these routes reached to about $5 billion. Foreign direct investment as also investment by NRIs have risen considerably due to number of incentives offered to them. They need the services of merchant bankers to advise them for their investment in India. The increasing number of joint ventures abroad by Indian companies also require expert services of merchant bankers.

FIIs Investments are increasing year-after-year. In primary and secondary securities market FIIs investments are increasing. Although their limit in individual industries, have been fixed although it is increasing day-by-day. This is clear from the table below:

Areas	*Maximum Investment*	*Investment Way/Conditions*
Ceiling		
Coal mines	50%	Export Investment Promotion Council
Coal Processing	100%	Up to 50% automatic and thereafter export promotion council
Electricity	100%	Up to 50% automatic and thereafter export promotion council
Non-electricity	74%	- do -
Green leaves (excluding tea)	100%	Export promotion council
Television uplinking	49%	- do - (except News Channel where it is maximum 26%)
Cable Network	49%	- do -
Direct to Store	20%	- do -
Telecom (Mobile)	74%	After 49% at export promotion council
ISP (with Gateway)	74%	
ISP (Without gateway)	100%	
E-mail/Voice mail	100%	
Radio Paging	74%	
Band width	74%	
Dark Fibre	100%	
Aerodromes	100%	above 74% on clearance from export promotion council
Domestic Air Service	49%	Automatic
Petroleum Products Marketing	100%	Automatic out of which 26% is given to Indian investors in 5 years.

Source: DNA Money Newspaper, Mumbai dt. 8-5-2007.

Foreign Direct Investment was $ 19 million in 2006-07 (out of which 15 billion (equal to ₹ 61,000 crore) in new issues and $ 4 billion in retained dividends. While in earlier years, it was standstill at $5 billion which is apparent from the following figures —

Year	*Amount*	*Amt. in ₹ Crores*
2002-03	$ 3.13 billion	
2003-04	$ 2.63 billion	
2004-05	$ 3.75 billion	₹ 1,44,596
2005-06	$ 5.50 billion	₹ 1,93,396
2006-07 (till Feb. 2007)		₹ 2,24,200

Even their the above investments were 1/4th share of total direct investment of China. Total investment in China in the year 2006 were $ 63 billion.

While the FIIs total registered number was 685 in March 2005 and their investments in Euro Issue was ₹ 3,353 crore and cumulative amount (ADRs + GDRs) amount were $ 36.93 billion.

(iii) Changing Policy of Foreign Direct Investments

With the changing emphasis in the lending policies of financial institutions from security orientation to project orientation, corporate enterprises would require the expert services of merchant bankers for project appraisal, financial management etc. The policy of decentralisation and encouragement of small and medium industries will further increase the demand for technical and financial services which can be provided by merchant bankers.

(iv) Development of Debt Market

The concept of debt market has set to work through National Stock Exchange and the Over the Counter Exchange of India.

Debt Market Development — Total amount collected from Public Issue and debts, the details are as below:

Areas	*2003-04*		*2004-05*	
	Number	*Amount in Cr.*	*Number*	*Amt. in Cr.*
IPOs	21	3434	23	13749
Listed companies Issue	36	19838	37	14507
Total	57	**23272**	60	**28256**

4.8.8 Arranging International Finance including Loan Syndication

External Commercial Borrowings (ECBs) envisages a cap to ensure that debt is kept at a sustainable level. Priority is accorded to INFRASTRUCTURE and core sectors/Export-oriented and import substitution units and also medium sized/SSI units. ECBs are to be used for only meeting the foreign exchange cost of capital investment. ECBs have minimum final maturity of 5 years. ECB can be defined to include suppliers credits and credits from officially sponsored agencies but excludes all borrowings with a maturity of less than one year. In August 2007, India capped the foreign debt an Indian company could bring home at $ 20 million a year and made RBI approval mandatory. However, a company could still raise a loan up to $500 million abroad under the automatic route, without taking specific RBI permission. This is the time to make it easier to borrow from outside, as high input costs and high domestic interest rates are heavily weighing on industrial output. Despite the credit sequence in international markets, the arbitrage is still favourable to overseas restrictions in a gradual manner. On 29-5-2008 the government has tried to give leg up to economic growth by relaxing ECB Norms.

ECB window widened to prop rupee flows with the external commercial borrowing (ECB) norms.

In doing so, it also counters two other pressing problems: tapering foreign inflows and an extremely weak rupee. While that could be good for corporates, it may not be so for domestic banks because their prime lending rates are 200·300 basis points more than the cost of borrowing abroad. Domestic credit growth, thus, could be impacted negatively; said analysts.

The Centre allowed infrastructure companies to borrow five times more — $100 million instead of an earlier limit of $20 million, for their rupee expenditure.

Other companies have got for narrower window: two-and-a half times more at $50 million instead of $20 million earlier. However, the limit per company for borrowings through the automatic route (or without government approval) from abroad remains the same at $500 million, it was announced on Friday. The new rules will take effect when the Reserve Bank of India notifies them. What could be the motive behind the measures?

"The corporate sector has been facing problems of credit availability and the rupee is getting weaker. This is an attempt to address the issues."

For this an "immediate appreciation" of the local currency to about 42.5 per dollar, would benefit the beleaguered oil companies who pay for their oil purchase in dollars.

❖ Steps Required:

FII investment limit in bond markets raised.

Infrastructure companies to borrow five times more — $ 100 million instead of an earlier limit of $20 million for their rupee expenditure.

Other companies have got a narrower window; two-and-a-half times more; $50 million instead of $20 million earlier.

Ceiling on the cost of borrowings for overseas loans raised by 50-100 bps.

NEW ECB CEILINGS

Average Maturity Period	*All-in-cost ceilings over six months Libor*	
	Existing	*Proposed*
Three years and up to five years	150 bps	200 bps
More than five years	250 bps	350 bps.

The local currency had dropped by a per cent to 42.785 dollar on 29-5-2008 and has enhanced in January 2011 to ₹ 46.375 per dollar.

The government also raised the limit on holdings of government bonds by overseas investors to $5 billion from $3.2 billion in an attempt to deepen the debt market.

The limit on the ownership of corporate bonds was doubled to $3 billion.

But not everyone agrees, the limit 'insignificant' to have an impact.

The government also raised the ceiling on the cost of borrowings for overseas loans to six-month Libor plus 200 basis points from six-month Libor plus 150 basis points for a loan of average maturity period of three years and up to five years. A basis point is 0.01 percentage point. For overseas borrowings with an average maturity period of more than five years, the government raised the limit on the cost of borrowing to six-month. Libor plus 350 basis points from six-month. Libor plus 250 basis points.

This has helped Indian corporates get better access to credit abroad.

Libor is a benchmark rate that's an average derived from 16 quotations provided by banks determined by the British Bankers Association.

The four highest and lowest are eliminated an average of the remaining eight is calculated to arrive at the fix.

The Hong Kong and Shanghai Bank Corp. said, "It is clearly a step in the right direction... but it is not enough. We need to wait and see what the government does in the coming weeks."

RBI RAISES LOAN LIMIT FOR OIL MARKETERS

The Reserve Bank on Thursday liberalised the policy governing borrowings by oil companies, a move aimed at helping them muster funds to meet their crude import requirements.

In a notification, the central bank said: "It has been decided to revise with immediate effect... exposure limit to 25% of the capital funds (from the existing 15%)."

It also allowed banks, in exceptional circumstance, to consider enhancement of exposure to oil companies up to a further five per cent of capital funds. This enhancement in borrowing limit is applicable only to those oil companies who have been issued oil bonds by the govemment and do not have SLR (statutory liquidity ratio) status.

The move comes amid state-run oil companies reporting that they would run out of cash in 2-3 months to import crude, whose price has doubled since the last retail fuel price hike in February. The petroleum ministry has been pushing for an immediate hike in retail prices of petrol, diesel and LPG cylinders to pull out oil companies from a financial sinkhole.

4.8.9 Loan Syndication

The syndication technique in the Eurodollar market (consists of international banks/finance companies/foreign exchange banks and special institutions) arose because of the large size of the loans and wide variety of banks providing the funds. The procedure also helps the banks to diversify some of the unique sovereign-risks that arose in international lending. The funds availability in Eurodollar market is on an average is about $ 500 billion. The Eurodollar market is not constrained by funds availability like national markets where credit rationing is adopted during periods of tight credit or credit squeeze. Further, firms raising funds in the Eurodollar market can deploy anywhere as long as the lender is satisfied that the intended purpose will not jeopardise the prospects for servicing the loan. Lead banks assemble a management group of other banks to underwrite the loan and to market shares in it to other participating banks. In a syndicate there are three levels of banks, *Lead Banks/Money Banks,* and *Participating Banks.* The mandate to organise the loan is awarded by the borrower to one or two major banks after a competitive procedure. The lead bank assembles a management group to underwrite the loan. The share of the loan underwritten by the lead bank is at least as large as any other lender. Once the lead bank receives the mandate from the borrower, a placement memorandum is prepared by the lead bank and the loan is marketed to other banks who may be interested in taking up shares. The placement memorandum helps the banks to understand the transaction and provides information about the borrower. On the basis of the data in the placement memorandum banks make a reasonable appraisal of the credit before deciding about participation in the loan.

Lead bank keeps normally 50-70% initial underwriting share. In the case of smaller loans to frequent borrowers, *Club loans* are often arranged. The club loan is funded by lead bank and managers. In such cases, no placement memorandum is prepared. Club loans are common in periods of market uncertainty when large multinational banks are reluctant to do business. The size of the loan could vary from a small sum of $ 5,00,000 to several billions. The normal duration for syndication is about 6 weeks. But it could take less time say 15 days in the case of small loans and in the case of a familiar borrower where the terms can be settled quickly and placement memorandum prepared. Common type of *Syndicated loan* is *term loan* with a grace period before repayment of principal commences. Grace period is one of the factors that determines the cost of the loan. Syndicated loans are normally denomination in US dollars, but loans in Euros/Japanese Yens and other currencies are also granted.

4.9 PRICING OF EURODOLLAR LOAN

The pricing practices in the Eurodollar market reflect the nature of the market in which funds are bought and sold. The banks which lend to do not have a deposit base. The lenders are wholesale banks that rely on a sole funding source, large time and call deposits from banks and other depositors. The lending bank's cost of funds varies directly with the level of short-term rates. There is thus mismatch between source of funds and term loans. While banks are obtained more or less from the money markets, syndicated loans are for periods of 5/7 or eight years. The resulting interest rate risk from the mismatch is covered by the technique of rollover credit pricing. Interest on syndicated loans is altered every three or six months bearing fixed relationship to the *Libor*. The rollover Eurodollars bear a rate tied directly to money market and inter-bank cost of funds and the rate is changed at fixed intervals. Beyond the *Libor* is the 'spread' which is negotiated with the borrower before the loan is granted. The spread remains constant over the life of the loan or changed after a set number of years. The spread could be as fine as 1/8% and can group to 1.5%. There are also Praecipium commitment fees/front end fees and sometimes an annual agent's fee. Praecipium is the lead manager's fee for assuming responsibility for setting up and co-ordinating the syndication of the loan. It is 1/8% of the loan commitment fees of 0.5% is payable only on the undrawn amount of loan. Front-end and management fees of 0.5 to 1% of the value of the loan are one time charges negotiated in advance and imposed when the loan agreement is signed front end charges are an important component of the banks total return on credit. The front end fees include participation and management fees. Participation fees are devided among the banks in proportion to share of the loan. Management fees are divided between underwriting banks and lead banks. Agent's fee, where applicable is an yearly charge and on a large credit may amount to $ 10,000 p.a. The *annual charges* on syndicated loans are charged as below:

Libor + Spread × Loan amount + praecipium × Loan amount + Commitment fee × Undrawn loan amount + annual agent's fees. While *Front end charges* are calculated

Participation fee × Loan amount

Management fee × Loan amount + Initial agent's fee

For example:

Loan of $ 100 million

Term seven years, no grace period

Interest 100 basis points over Libor of 10%.

Annual payment of interest and principal = $ 21 million

1% fee on $ 100 million loan = $ 1 million

Paid to the banks in the syndicate at the outset. This raises effective rate to 11.31%. If lending banks pay 9.75% for their funds, the front end fees increase their margin on loan from 125 to 155 basis points as 25% increment to their return on credit.

❖ Agreement Provisions

As compared to loans from domestic financial institutions Eurodollar loan agreement are *simple* and contain *fewer restrictive covenants*. In the case of loans to multinational companies, affiliates are regarded as obligation of the parent company. There is a cross-default-clause which stipulates that the loan is in default if and when the parent is in default on its loans. The other aspect in the loan document reflects the international character of the loan. The borrower may be in one country, the booking of loan is another country and the funding is yet another country. First relates to jurisdiction. New York is often chosen because of the extensive case law on banking matters even in cases involving lenders and borrowers not residents of the USA. Judgement currency clauses are necessary because courts in several countries render judgement in domestic currency only.

Payment of interest and principal on loan is normally affected by means of transfer of funds from one bank account to another in the country of the currency in which the loan is denominated. Borrowers normally receive funds in the place of their choice.

Bank Guarantee: The syndicated loans have no collateral. A bank guarantee is required and the bank should satisfy capital adequacy norms as per Basel-II requirements.

The lending banks in the Eurodollar markets are free of any reserve regulations imposed when subject to a central bank jurisdiction. The *reserve requirement clause* stipulates that the borrower has to absorb any additional cost the lender incurs when interest free reserve requirements are imposed.

Free of Income Tax: Lending banks insist on payments of principal and interest should be free of taxes.

Eurobonds are also sold in more than one market simultaneously usually through international syndicates. The Eurobond market and Eurodollar market overlap. Eurobonds are usually for a duration of 10 to 15 years period. Eurobonds are defined as bonds issued by a borrower who is of a nationality different from the country of the capital market in which the securities are *issued*.

Companies and governments prefer to raise a bank loan or a syndicated loan rather than tap the international bond market. *Loans* are *cheaper* and larger amounts can be raised even beyond $ 100 million. The interest rates in Eurobond markets are based mainly on fixed interest rates and Eurodollar markets, where medium and long-term credits are priced on a *short-term rollover basis.*

◆ ◆ ◆

5 Lease Financing

5.1 INTRODUCTION OF LEASE FINANCING

Traditionally firms acquire productive assets and use them as owners. The sources of finance to a firm for procuring assets may be internal or external. Over the years there has been a declining trend in the internally generated resources of Indian companies due to low profitability. The financial institutions experience paucity of funds at their disposal to meet the increasing needs of borrowers. Further, modern business environment is becoming more and more complex. To succeed in the situation, the firms aim at growth with stability. To accomplish this objective, firms are required to go for massive expansion, diversification and modernisation. Essentially such projects involve a huge amount of investment. High rate of inflation, severe cost escalation, heavy taxation and meagre internal resources forced many companies to look for alternative means of financing the projects. Leasing has emerged as a new source of financing capital assets.

❖ Concept of Leasing

Leasing, as a financing concept, is an arrangement between two parties, the leasing company or lessor and the user or lessee, whereby the former arranges to buy capital equipment for the use of the latter for an agreed period of time in return for the payment of rent. The rentals are predetermined and payable at fixed intervals of time, according to the mutual convenience of both the parties. However, the lessor remains the owner of the equipment over the primary period.

By resorting to leasing, the lessee company is able to exploit the economic value of the equipment by using it as if he owned it without having to pay for its capital cost. Lease rentals can be conveniently paid over the lease period out of profits earned from the use of the equipment and the rent is cent per cent tax deductible.

A Lease is defined as follows:

— **Dictionary of Business and Management** —

'Lease is a form of contract transferring the use or occupancy of land, space, structure or equipment, in consideration of a payment, usually in the form of a rent.'

— **James C. Van Horne** —

'Lease is a contract whereby the owner of an asset (lessor) grants to another party (lessee) the exclusive right to use the asset usually for an agreed period of time in return for the payment of rent.'

— **Equipment Leasing Association of UK** —

'A contract between lessor and lessee for the hire of a specific asset selected from a manufacturer or vendor of such assets by the lessee. The lessor retains the ownership of the asset. The lessee has possession and use of the asset on payment of specified retain over the period.'

Thus, in a contract of lease there are two parties involved: (*i*) lessor and the lessee. The lessor can be a company, a cooperative society, a partnership firm or an individual in manufacturing or allied activities. The lessee can be even a doctor or any other specialists who use costly equipment for the practice of his profession.

❖ Leasing as a Source of Finance

Leasing is an important source of finance for the lessee. Leasing companies finance for:

1. Modernisation of business.
2. Balancing equipment.
3. Cars, scooters and other vehicles and durables.
4. Items entitled to 100% or 50% depreciation.
5. Assets which are not being financed by banks/institutions.

❖ Steps Involved in Leasing Transaction

The steps involved in a leasing transaction are summarised as follows:

1. First, the lessee has to decide the asset required and select the supplier. He has to decide about the design specifications, the price, warranties, terms of delivery, servicing, etc.
2. The lessee, then enters into a lease agreement with the lessor. The lease agreement contains the terms and conditions of the lease such as,
   (*a*) The basic lease period during which the lease is irrecoverable.
   (*b*) The timing and amount of periodical rental payments during the lease period.
   (*c*) Details of any option to renew the lease or to purchase the asset at the end of the period.
   (*d*) Details regarding payment of cost of maintenance and repairs, taxes, insurance and other expenses.
3. After the lease agreement is signed the lessor contacts the manufacturer and requests him to supply the asset to the lessee. The lessor makes payment to the manufacturer after the asset has been delivered and accepted by the lessee.

5.2 TYPES OF LEASE

The lease agreement can be classified broadly into four categories:

1. Financial Lease

A financial lease is also known as Capital lease, Long-term lease, Net lease and Close lease. In a financial lease, the lessee selects the equipments, settles the price and terms of sale and arranges with a leasing company to buy it. He enters into a irrevocable and non-cancellable contractual agreement with the leasing company. The lessee uses the equipment exclusively, maintains it, insures and avails of the after-sales service and warranty backing it. He also bears the risk of obsolescence as it stands committed to pay the rental for the entire lease period.

The financial lease could also be with purchase option, where at the end of the predetermined period, the lessee has the option to buy the equipment at a predetermined value or at a nominal value or at fair market price. The financial lease may also contain a noncancellable clause which means that the lessor transfers the title to the lessee at the end of the lease period.

Under a financial lease, the rate of lease would be fixed based on the kind of lease, the period of lease, periodicity of rent payment, and the rate of depreciation and other tax benefits available. The leasing company also charges nominal service charges to cover legal and other costs. The leasing company may also insist on collaterals or bank's guarantee in individual cases. In a large number of cases, the financial leases are used as financing cum tax planning tool.

The financial lease is very popular in India as in other countries like USA, UK and Japan. On an all India basis, at present, approximately a lease worth ₹ 75 to ₹ 100 crore is transacted as a tax planning device. The high cost of equipments such as office equipment, diesel generators, machine tools, textile machinery, containers, locomotives, etc., are leased under financial lease.

The following table shows the direct cash flow consequences of signing the least contract:

- Lessee does not have to pay for the asset. This is equivalent to a cash inflow of ₹ 10 lakh.
- Lessee no longer owns the asset, and so it cannot depreciate it. Therefore, it gives up a valuable depreciation tax shield.
- Lessee pays ₹ 1,69,000 per year for eight years to the lessor. The first payment dues immediately.

(Amt. in thousand ₹)

Year	*0*	*1*	*2*	*3*	*4*	*5*	*6*	*7*
Cost of asset	1,000							
Lost depreciation shield tax		–70	–112	–67.2	–40.3	–40.3	–20.2	0
Lease payment	–169	–169	–169	–169	–169	–169	–169	–169
Tax shield of lease payment	+59.2	+59.2	+59.2	+59.2	+59.2	+59.2	+59.2	+59.2
	+ 890.2	–179.9	–221.9	–177.1	–150.2	–150.2	–130	–109.80

❖ Operating Lease

An operating lease is also known as Service lease, Short-term lease or True lease. In this lease, the contractual period between lessor and lessee is less than the full expected economic life of equipment. This means that the lease is for a limited period, may be a month, six months, a year or few years. The lease is terminable by giving stipulated notice as per the agreement. Normally, the lease rentals will be higher as compared to other leases on account of short period of primary lease. The risk of obsolescence is enforced on the lessor who will also bear the cost of maintenance and other relevant expenditure. The lessor also does the services like handling warranty claims, paying taxes, scheduling and performing maintenance and keeping complete records lease is suitable for,

(*i*) Computers, copy machines and other office equipments, vehicles, material handling equipments or plants installation, etc., which are sensitive to obsolescence; and

(*ii*) Where the lessee is interested in tiding over temporary problem.

DISTINCTION BETWEEN A FINANCIAL LEASE AND OPERATING LEASE

Financial Lease	*Operating Lease*
1. A financial lease is like an instalment loan. It is a legal commitment to pay for the entire cost of the equipment plus interest over a specified period of time. The lessee commits to a series of payment which in total exceed the cost of the equipment.	1. An operating lease is a rental agreement. The lessee is not committed to paying more than the original cost of equipment during contractual period.
2. It excludes provisions for maintenance or taxes which are paid separately by the lessee.	2. Operating lease provides for maintenance expenses and taxes of the lessor.
3. The risk of obsolescence is assumed by the lessee.	3. Leasing company assumes risk of obsolescence.
4. Contract period ranges from medium to long-term.	4. Contract period ranges from intermediate to short-term.
5. Contracts are usually noncancellable.	5. Contracts are usually cancellable either by the lessor or by the lessee.
6. Aircrafts, land and building, heavy machinery are leased.	6. Computers, office equipments, automobiles, truck, etc., are leased.
7. The lease involves a financial commitment similar to a loan by a leasing company. It places the lessee in a position of a borrower	7. The financial commitment is restricted to regular rental payment. The rentals find a place in the P & L A/c of the lessee.
8. The lessor fulfils financial function.	8. The lessor fulfils service function.

❖ Leverage Lease

A leverage lease is used for financing those assets which require huge capital outlay. The outlay for purchase cost of the asset generally varies from ₹ 50 lakh to ₹ 2 crore and has economic life of ten years or more. The leverage lease agreement involves three parties, the lessee, the lessor and the lender. The lessor acquires the assets as per the terms of the lease agreement but finances only a part of the total investment, say 20% to 50%. The balance is provided by a person or a group of persons in the form of loan to the lessor. The loan is generally secured by mortgage of the asset besides assignment of the leased rental payments. The position of the lessee under a leveraged leasing agreement is the same as in the case of any other type of lease. In leveraged lease, a wide range of equipments such as rail road, rolling stock, coal mining, electricity generating plants, pipelines, ships, etc., are acquired.

Under a leverage lease, there are some attractive investment features in the form of after-tax consequences for the owner of the equipment. By investing 20% or 25% of the cost of an asset, the lessor is entitled to 100% allowance for depreciation plus the investment allowance. In addition, interest expenses related to his borrowings are also tax deductible. From the point of view of lessee/lease rentals are deductible in full as an operating expense.

❖ Sale and Lease Back

Under this type of lease, a firm which has an asset sells it to the leasing company and gets it back on lease. The asset is generally sold at its market value. The firm receives the sale price in cash and gets the right to use the asset during the lease period. The firm makes periodical rental payment to the lessor. The title to the asset vests with the lessor. Most of the lease back agreements are on a net — net basis which means that the lessee pays all maintenance expenses, property taxes and insurance. In some cases, the lease agreement allows the lease to repurchase the property at the termination of lease.

The sale and lease back agreement is beneficial to both lessor and lessee. The lessor gets immediate cash which becomes available for working capital or for further expansion and lessor gets tax benefits. Retail stores, office buildings, multipurpose industrial building and shopping centres are financed under this method.

❖ Cross-border Lease

Cross-border lease is international leasing and is known as transnational leasing. It relates to a lease transaction between a lessor and lessee domiciled in different countries and includes exports leasing. In other words the lessor may be of one country and the lessee may be of another country. To illustrate, if a leasing company in USA makes available an Air bus-387 on lease to Air India, there would be a cross border lease.

Indian leasing industry is unlikely to deal in export border leases for big ticket items such as aircraft but it is well placed to contribute to India's export earnings by offering the lease option. First Leasing Company had initiated discussions with Bulgar Leasing of Bulgaria to export bull dozers and shovels in significant number of an export lease to that country. RBI has made certain regulations under RBI Act, 1974 Section 45-J and Sec. 45-K. These regulations are called Residuary Non-banking Companies (Reserve Bank) 1987. Lease financing comes under it.

❖ Instalment Buying, Hire Purchase and Leasing

In instalment buying, the property passes on to the buyer immediately as soon as the first instalment is made. The balance amount is payable in instalments. Under the contract of instalment the buyer has no right to return the goods. In case of default, the seller has the right to file a suit in the court of law to recover his dues.

Hire purchase is an agreement under which the owner delivers the goods to the buyer who agrees to make periodical payment as hire charges. The possession of goods vests with the hirer but the ownership remains with the seller. On full payment of hire charges, the buyer gets the option of purchasing the goods. On default, the seller can reclaim the goods, subject to certain provisions of Hire Purchase Act.

Hire purchase resembles leasing in certain ways. In both the cases the right to use the equipment is transferred to the hirer/lessee.

In leasing, the entire lease rentals represents a hire charge and it is treated as expense and hence tax deductible. Under hire purchase, a part of instalment represents capital payment and hence it is not an expense. A part of the instalment is interest on the loan which is considered as revenue expenditure and hence it is tax deductible.

In leasing, rental charges are debited to profit and loss account and the leased asset is not shown in the balance sheet of the lessee. As against this, the hire purchaser capitalises the asset brought under hire purchaser contract. The liability for future hire purchase instalments not yet due is shown separately in the balance sheet.

5.3 ADVANTAGES AND DISADVANTAGES OF LEASE

The following are the advantages of leasing:

1. Permit Alternative Use of Funds: A leasing arrangement provides a firm with the use and control over asset without incurring huge capital expenditure. The firm is required only to make periodical rental payments. It saves considerable funds for alternative uses which would otherwise be tied up in fixed capital.

2. Faster and Cheaper Credit: Depending on tax structure of the lessee it costs less than other methods of acquiring assets. It permits firms to acquire new equipment without going thorough formal scrutiny procedure. Hence, acquisition of assets under leasing agreement is cheaper and faster than any other source of finance.

3. Flexibility: Leasing arrangements may be tailored to the lessee's needs more easily that ordinary financing. Lease rentals can be structured to match the lessee's cash flaws. It can be skipped during the months when the cash flows are expected to below.

4. Facilitates Additional Borrowings: Leasing may increase long-term ability to acquire funds. The lessee can utilise more funds for working capital needs. Moreover, acquisition of assets under the lease agreement does not alter debt equity ratio. Hence, the lessee can go for additional borrowings in case need arises.

5. Protection Against Obsolescence: A firm can avoid risk of obsolescence by entering into operating lease agreement. This is highly useful in respect of assets which became absolute at a faster rate.

6. No Restrictive Covenants: The restrictive cavenants such as debt equity ratio, declaration of dividend, etc., which are usually imposed under debenture or loan agreement are absolutely absent in a lease agreement.

7. Hundred Per Cent Financing Lease Financing enables a firm to acquire the use of an asset without having to make a down payment. So, hundred per cent financing is assured to the lessee.

8. Boon to Small Firm: The firms which are either small or have uncertain records of earning are able to obtain the use of asset through lease financing. It is a boon to small firms and technocrats who are able to make promoter's contribution as required by financial institutions.

9. Leases may be Off-balance Sheet Financing: In some countries, such as Germany financial leases are Off-balance Sheet financing, that is, a corporate can acquire an asset, finance it through a financial lease, and show neither the asset nor the lease contract on its Balance Sheet.

While in the USA, the Financial Accounting Standards Board (FASB) requires that all capital, (i.e., financial) leases be capitalised. This means that the present value of the lease payments must be calculated and shown alongside debt on the Right Hand Side of the Balance Sheet as (Asset) to be amortized over the life of the lease.

Leasing can make the corporate's Balance Sheet and income statement *Look Better* by increasing book income or decreasing book asset value or both.

A lease which qualifies as *Off-balance Sheet* financing affects book income in one way. The lease payments are an expense. If the corporate buys the asset instead and borrows to finance it, both depreciation and interest expenses are deducted. Leaves are set up so that payments in the early years are *less* than *depreciation* plus interest under the buy and borrow alternative. Consequently, leasing increases book income in the early years of an asset life. The book rate of return can increase even more dramatically, because the book value of assets (the denominator) in the book rate of returns calculation is understated if the leased asset never appears on the Corporate's Balance Sheet.

❖ Disadvantages of Leasing

1. Lease is not suitable mode of project finance. This is because rentals are repayable soon after entering into lease agreement while in new projects cash generations may start only after a long gestation period.
2. Certain tax benefits/incentives such as subsidy may not be available on leased equipment.
3. The value of real assets such as land ·and building may increase during lease period. In such a case the lessee loses the advantage of a potential capital gain.
4. The cost of financing is generally higher than that of debt financing.
5. A manufacturer who wants to discontinue a particular line of business will not in a position to terminate the contract except by paying heavy penalties. If it is a owned asset the manufacturer can sell the equipment at his will.
6. If the lessee is not able to pay rentals regularly, the lessor would suffer a loss particularly when the asset is a sophisticated one and less liquid.
7. In case of lease agreement, it is lessor who has purchased the asset from the supplier and not the lessee. Hence, the lessee by himself is not entitled to any protection in case the supplier commits breach of warranties in respect of the leased assets.
8. In the absence of exclusive laws dealing with the lease transaction, several problems crop up between lessor and lessee resulting in unnecessary complications and avoidable tension.

5.4 HISTORY AND DEVELOPMENT OF LEASING

The history of leasing dates back to for the first time in 1877 when the Bell Telephone Company began renting telephones in the USA. In 1832, Cottrell and Leonard leased academic caps, gowns and hoods. Subsequently, during 1930s the Railway Industry used leasing service for its rolling stock needs. In the post-war period, the American Air Lines leased their jet engines for most of the new aircrafts. This development ignited immediate popularity for the lease and generated growth of leasing industry.

Since World War II the use of leasing has been greatly expanded and is constantly used for new products and new industries. In May 1952, Henry Scholfeld set up a separate Corporation in the USA to handle lease transaction. He founded the US Leasing Corporation with a capital of $20,000. Since 1963, commercial banks have been allowed to engage themselves in direct leasing. In the early 1960s leasing entered the United Kingdom following its successful and rapid development in the USA.

The concept of financial leasing was pioneered in India during 1973. The First Leasing Company was set up by the Chidambaram group in 1973 in Madras. The company undertook leasing of industrial equipment as its main activity. The Twentieth Century Leasing Company Limited was established in 1979. By 1981, four finance companies joined the fray. The performance of First Leasing Company Limited and the Twentieth Century Leasing Company Limited motivated others to enter the leasing industry. In 1980s financial institutions made entry into leasing business. Industrial Credit and Investment Corporation was the first all India financial institution to offer leasing in 1983. Entry of commercial banks into leasing was facilitated by an amendment of Banking Regulation Act, 1949. State Bank of India was the first commercial bank to set up a leasing subsidiary, SBI capital market, in October 1986. Can Bank Financial Services Ltd., BoB Financial Service Ltd., and PNB Financial Services Limited followed suit. Industrial Finance Corporation's Merchant Banking division started financing leasing companies as well as equipment leasing and financial services. In 2000, G.E. Capital Aviation Services leased out 970 commercial aircrafts.

In the subsequent years, the adverse trends in capital market and other factors led to a situation where apart from the institutional lessors, there were hardly 20 to 25 private leasing companies who were active in the field. The total volume of leasing business transacted by both private and public sector leasing companies was ₹ 50,000 crore in 2007 and it is expected to cross ₹ 1,00,000 crore by March 2015.

❖ Legal Aspects of Leasing

As there is no separate statute for equipment leasing in India, the provisions relating to bailment in the Indian Contract Act govern equipment leasing agreements as well Section 148 of the Indian Contract Act defines bailment as:

"The delivery of goods by one person to another, for some purpose, upon a contract that they shall, when the purpose is accomplished, be returned or otherwise disposed of according to the directions of the person delivering them. The person delivering the goods is called the 'bailor' and the person to whom they are delivered is called the 'bailee'."

Since an equipment lease transaction is regarded as a contract of bailment, the obligations of the lessor and the lessee are similar to those of the bailor and the bailee (other than those expressly specified in the lease contract) as defined by the provisions of Sections 151 and 157 of the Indian Contract Act. Essentially these provisions have the following implications for the lessor and the lessee.

1. The lessor has the duty to deliver the asset to the lessee, to legally authorise the lessee to use the asset, and to 'leave the asset in peaceful possession of the lessee during the currency of the agreement.
2. The lessee has the obligation to pay the lease rentals as specified in the lease agreement, to protect the lessor's title, to take reasonable care of the asset, and to return the leased asset on the expiry of the lease period.

5.5 CONTENTS OF A LEASE AGREEMENT

The lease agreement specifies the legal rights and obligations of the lessor and the lessee. It typically contains terms relating to the following:

1. Description of the lessor, the lessee, and the equipment.
2. Amount, time, and place of lease rental payments.
3. Time and place of equipment delivery.
4. Lessee's responsibility for taking delivery and possession of the leased equipment.
5. Lessee's responsibility for maintenance, repairs, registration, etc., and the lessor's right in case of default by the lessee.
6. Lessee's right to enjoy the benefits of the warranties provided by the equipment manufacturer/ supplier.
7. Insurance to be taken by the lessee on behalf of the lessor.
8. Variation in lease rentals if there is a change in certain external factors like bank interest rates, depreciation rates, and fiscal incentives.
9. Option of lease renewal for the lessee.
10. Return of equipment on expiry of the lease period.
11. Arbitration procedure in the event of dispute.

❖ Income Tax Provisions Relating to Leasing

The principal income-tax provisions relating to leasing are as follows:

1. The lessee can claim lease rentals as tax-deductible expenses.
2. The lease rentals received by the lessor are taxable under the head of 'Profits and Gains of Business or Profession'.
3. The lessor can claim investment allowance (this may be doubtful) and depreciation on the investment made in leased assets.

❖ Sales Tax Provisions Pertaining to Leasing

The major sales tax provisions relevant for leasing are as follows:

1. The lessor is not entitled for the concessional rate of central sales tax because the asset purchased for leasing is meant neither for resale nor for use in manufacture. (It may be noted that if a firm buys an asset for resale or for use in manufacture it is entitled for the confessional rate of sales tax).
2. The 46th Amendment Act has brought lease transitions under the purview of 'sale' and his empowered the Central and State Government to levy sales tax on lease transactions. While the Central Sales Tax Act has yet to be amended in this respect, several State Governments have amended their sales tax laws to impose sales tax on lease transactions.

5.6 ACCOUNTING TREATMENT OF LEASE

Presently, the accounting treatment of lease transactions in India is as follows:

1. The leased asset is shown on the Balance Sheet of the lessor.

2. Depreciation and other tax shields associated with the leased asset are claimed by the lessor.
3. The entire lease rental is treated as income in the books of the lessor and as expense in the books of the lessee.

In a nut shell, from the point of view of the lessee, a lease transaction represents an Off-balance Sheet transaction and this appears to be an important advantage associated with leasing. It may be noted that in countries like the United States and the United Kingdom, where leasing is very popular, leases which meet certain criteria are capitalised in the books of the lessee. This essentially implies that:

(*a*) the leased asset and the corresponding liability (reckoned at the present value of the stream of rental payments) are shown on the Balance Sheet of the lessee,

(*b*) depreciation charges are claimed by the lessee, and

(*c*) the lease rental is split into two parts, the interest component (which is charged to the profit and loss statement) and the principal repayment component.

5.7 STRUCTURE OF LEASING INDUSTRY

The present structure of leasing industry in India consists of (*i*) Private Sector Leasing, and (*ii*) Public Sector Leasing.

The *private sector* leasing consists of:

(*i*) Pure Leasing Companies,

(*ii*) Hire Purchase and Finance Companies, and

(*iii*) Subsidiaries of Manufacturing Group Companies.

The *public sector* leasing organisations are divided into:

(*i*) Leasing divisions of financial institutions,

(*ii*) Subsidiaries of public sector banks, and

(*iii*) Other public sector leasing organisations.

(*i*) Pure Leasing Companies

These companies operate independently without any link or association with any other organisation or group of organisation. The First Leasing Company of India Limited. The Twentieth Century Finance Corporation Limited, and the Grover Leasing Limited, fall under this category.

(*ii*) Hire Purchase and Finance Companies

The companies started prior to 1980 to do hire purchase and finance business especially for vehicles added leasing to their activities during 1980. Some of them do leasing as major activity and some others do leasing on a small-scale as a tax planning device. Sundaram Finance Limited and Motor and General Finance Limited belong to this group.

(iii) Subsidiaries of Manufacturing Group Companies

These companies consist of two categories,

(a) Vendor leasing, and

(b) In house leasing

(a) Vendor Leasing: This type of companies are formed to boost and promote the sale of its parent companies' products through offering leasing facilities.

(b) In House Leasing: In house leasing or capture leasing companies are set up to meet the fund requirements or to avoid the income tax liabilities of the group companies.

❖ Public Sector Leasing

(i) Financial Institutions: The financial institutions such as IFCI, ICICI, IRBI and NSIC have set up their leasing divisions or subsidiaries to do leasing business. The Shipping Credit and Investment Company of India offers leasing facilities in foreign currencies for ships, deep seas fishing vehicles and related equipments to its clients.

(ii) Subsidiaries of Banks: The commercial banks in India can, under Section 19(1) of the Banking Regulation Act, 1949, set up subsidiaries for undertaking leasing activities. The SBI was the first bank to start a subsidiary for leasing business in 1986.

Leasing in SBI is transacted through, Strategic Business Unit (SBU) of the bank. Each SBU is manned by specially trained staff and is equipped with the latest technological aids to meet the needs of top corporate clients. For the bank as a whole, leasing is considered as a high growth area. Now the bank is concentrating only on 'Big Ticket Leasing' which is generally of ₹ 5 crore and above.

(iii) Other Public Sector Organisations: A few public sector manufacturing companies such as Bharat Electronics Limited, Hindustan Packaging Company Limited, Electronic Corporation of India Limited have started to sell their equipment through leasing.

5.8 PROBLEMS OF LEASING

Leasing has great potential in India. However, leasing in India faces serious handicaps which may mar its growth in future. The following are some of the problems.

(i) Unhealthy Competition: The market for leasing has not grown with the same pace as the number of lessors. As a result, there is over supply of lessors leading to competition. With the leasing business becoming more competitive, the margin of profit for lessors has dropped from four to five per cent to the present 2.5 to 3 per cent. Bank subsidiaries and financial institutions have the competitive edge over the private sector concerns because of cheap source of finance.

(ii) Lack of Qualified Personnel: Leasing requires qualified and experienced people at the helm of its affairs. Leasing is a specialised business and persons constituting its top management should have expertise in accounting, finance, legal and decision areas. In India, the concept of leasing business is of recent one and hence it is difficult to get right man to deal with leasing business. On account of this, operations of leasing business are bound to suffer.

(iii) Tax Considerations: Most people believe that lessees prefer leasing because of the tax benefits if offers. In reality, it only transfers, the benefit, i.e., the lessee's tax shelter is lessor's burden. The lease becomes economically viable only when the transfer's effective tax rate is low. In addition, taxes like sales tax, wealth tax, additional tax, surcharge, etc., add to the cost of leasing. Thus, leasing becomes more expensive form of financing than conventional mode of finance such as hire purchase.

(iv) Stamp Duty: The states treat a leasing transaction as a sale for the purpose of making them eligible to sales tax. On the contrary, for stamp duty, the transaction is treated as a pure lease transaction. Accordingly a heavy stamp duty is lived on lease documents. This adds to the burden of leasing industry.

(v) Delayed Payment and Bad Debts: The problem of delayed payment of rents and bad debts add to the costs of lease. The lessor does not take into consideration this aspect while fixing the rentals.

◆ ◆ ◆

6

Other Financial Services

Hire Purchase/Factoring/Forfaitiing/ Securitisation of Debts/Mutual Funds/ Venture Capital/Credit Rating Agencies/ Indemnity and Guarantee/ Letters of Credit

6.1 HIRE PURCHASE

Hire purchase is a method of selling goods. In a hire purchase transaction the goods are let out on hire by a finance company (creditor) to the hire purchase customer (hirer). The buyer is required to pay an agreed amount in periodical instalments during a given period. The ownership of the property remains with creditor and passes on to hirer on the payment of last instalment.

❖ Features of Hire Purchase Agreement

1. Under hire purchase system, the buyer takes possession of goods immediately and agrees to pay the total hire purchase price in instalments.
2. Each instalment is treated as hire charges.
3. The ownership of the goods passes from buyer to seller on the payment of the instalment.
4. In case the buyer makes any default in the payment of any instalment the seller has right to repossess the goods from the buyer and forfeit the amount already received treating it as hire charge.
5. The hirer has the right to terminate the agreement any time before the property passes. This is, he has the option to return the goods in which case he need not pay instalments falling due thereafter. However, he cannot recover the sums already paid as such sums legally represent hire charge on the goods in question.

❖ Legal Position

The Hire Purchase Act, 1972 defines a hire purchase agreement is, an agreement under which goods are let on hire and under which the hirer has an option to purchase them in accordance with the terms of agreement under which:

1. Payment is to be made in instalments over a specified period.
2. The possession is delivered to the purchaser at the time of entering into a contract.
3. The property in the goods passes to the purchaser on payment of the last instalment.
4. Each instalment is treated as hire charge so that if default is made in payment of any one instalment, the seller is entitled to take away the goods.
5. The hirer/purchaser is free to return the goods without being required to pay any further instalments falling due after the return.

6.2 HIRE PURCHASE AGREEMENT

There is no prescribed form for a hire purchase agreement, but it has to be in writing and signed by both parties to the agreement.

A hire purchase agreement must contain the following particulars:

(*i*) The description of goods in a manner sufficient to identify them.

(*ii*) The hire purchase price of the goods.

(*iii*) The date of commencement of the agreement.

(*iv*) The number of instalments in which hire purchase price is to be paid, the amount, and due date.

❖ Hire Purchase and Credit Sale

Higher purchase transaction is different from credit sale.

In case of actual sale, the title in the property, i.e., ownership and possession is transferred to the purchase simultaneously, in hire purchase, the ownership remains with the seller until last instalment is paid.

❖ Hire Purchase and Instalment Sale

Hire purchase transaction is different from instalment system. In case of instalment system it is not only the possession but also the ownership of goods which is transferred to the buyer immediately at the time of agreement. Further, when the buyer stops payment of dues, the seller has no right to repossess the goods. He has the only right to sue the buyer for the non-payment by returning the goods but has the right of disposing of the goods in any manner as he likes. Any loss of goods should be borne only by the buyer as risk lies with the ownership.

❖ Hire Purchase and Leasing

Hire purchase is also different from leasing.

(*i*) **Ownership:** In a contract of lease, the ownership rests with the lessor throughout and the lessee (hirer) has no option to purchase the goods.

(*ii*) **Method of Financing:** Leasing is a method of financing business assets, whereas hire purchase is a method of financing both business assets and consumer articles.

(*iii*) **Depreciation:** In leasing, depreciation and investment allowance cannot be claimed by the lessee. In hire purchase, depreciation and investment allowance can be claimed by the hirer.

***(iv)* Tax Benefits:** The entire lease rental is tax deductible expense. Only the interest component of the hire purchase instalment is tax deductible.

***(v)* Salvage Value:** The lessee, not being the owner of the asset, does not enjoy the salvage value of the asset. The hirer, in purchase, being the owner of the asset, enjoys salvage value of the asset.

***(vi)* Deposit:** Lessee is not required to make any deposit, whereas 20% deposit is required in hire purchase.

***(vii)* Rent-purchase:** With lease, we rent and with hire purchase we buy the goods.

***(viii)* Extent of Finance:** Lease financing is invariably 100 per cent financing. It requires no immediate down payment or margin money by the lessee. In hire purchase, a margin equal to 20-25 per cent of the cost of the asset is to be paid by the hirer.

***(ix)* Maintenance:** The cost of maintenance of the hired asset is to be borne by the hirer himself. In case of finance lease only, the maintenance of leased asset is the responsibility of the lessee.

***(x)* Reporting:** The asset on hire purchase is shown in the balance sheet of the hirer. The leased assets are shown by way of footnote only.

6.2.1 Origin and Development

The growth and development of hire purchase system can be traced back to the advent of industrial development in UK, Henry Moore, a Bishogate piano-maker introduced the system of hire purchase in 1846 in UK. Cowperwait & Sons, a furniture dealer introduced the hire purchase system in USA in 1807. The Singer Manufacturing Company started selling sewing machine under hire purchase agreement. The idea was developed by Wagon Companies which were formed to finance the purchase of wagons by collieries. The Wagon Companies bought the wagons and then let them out collieries under hire purchase agreement.

All early hire purchase transactions were financed by manufacturers or dealers themselves. Subsequently, independent finance house came into existence to offer hire purchase of wide variety of consumer articles, automobiles and industrial machinery on hire purchase.

In India, hire purchase finance started only after I World War. However, it was only after II World War that its growth assumed visible dimension. The concept of hire purchase was not quite popular in the pre-independence period though a few were endeavouring to increase the volume of their business with the provision of extending credit to intending buyers. With the increase in economic activity, many non-banking Financing Companies entered the scene in the fifties and sixties.

The pioneer in the field were Commercial Credit Corporation Limited, Motor and General Finance Limited and Investments Supply Limited. These companies were set up predominantly to finance road transport sector. The volume of hire purchase business was around ₹ 635 crore in 1987-88, out of which automobiles accounted for 55 per cent. Today about 80 per cent of sale of commercial vehicles is accounted by hire purchase. It is estimated by the Federation Hire Purchase Association that the stock-on-hire of hire purchase companies comprising corporate and non-corporate entities would be approximately ₹ 1,00,000 crore now.

In addition to commercial vehicles, purchase of consumer articles like household appliance, air-conditioners, refrigerators, office furniture and equipment are financed through hire purchase. In recent years, the consumer durable goods market is experiencing an unprecedented boom,

The growing Indian middle class – 301 to 451 crore, growing at a rate of 20 per cent per annum and their willingness to mortgage the future for todays enjoyment have led to spectacular growth in hire purchase business.

The institutions engaged in the hire purchase business in organised sector include commercial banks, cooperatives banks, State Finance Corporations, National Small Industries Corporations and in the unorganised sector they comprise a large number of partnership firms and individuals.

The National Small Industries Corporation supplies machineries to small-scale industries under hire purchase. The Industrial Development Bank of India indirectly participates in financing hire purchase business by way of rediscounting usance bills/promotes arising out of sale of indigenous machinery on hire purchase basis. The ICICI has a discounting scheme of usance bills under hire purchase scheme.

6.2.2 Bank Credit for Hire Purchase Business

The subsidiary of commercial banks lend to the dealer or to finance intermediary who has already financed articles sold by the dealer to the hirer under a hire purchase contract. While considering proposals from dealers or hire purchase financing companies, the bank subsidiary has to take extra precautions, looking to the particular nature of transaction under hire purchase contract.

When offered this type of business, the bank subsidiary would make an assessment of the standing and financial position of the dealer or of the hire purchase company, and take into consideration the principles of good lending and carry-out the procedure below:

1. Customer

When approached for hire purchase facility the subsidiary should take care to make the assessment of the standing and financial position of the business customer.

2. Purpose

The type of goods being used to finance in the hire purchase transaction is of great importance. In the event of default the bank may reconsider repossessing the goods and selling them to clear the advance. Thus, if the goods can be readily sold elsewhere (e.g., a relatively new car), then these agreements are better security than those for (say) cameras which will have a lower resale value.

3. Amount

Bank subsidiaries taking up hire purchase business would do well to discourage small individual loans. In order to ensure proper servicing and monitoring, it is also essential to a have floor limit in the amount of individual hire purchase transactions. While it may be about ₹ 8 lakh automobile sector, it may be about ₹ 50,000 for consumer durables.

4. Period

The facility will normally be extended over to three to five years.

5. Repayment

Repayment are spread evenly, or agreed, over the loan period. The repayment should be adaptable to the hirer's needs. The repayment can usually be tailor-made to suit the income generated from the use of asset so that it is self-financing. Sometimes, repayment holidays can be allowed and repayment is delayed until the asset is operational or producing profit. To ensure timely recovery in the case of car, two-wheeler, and consumer durable financing, it would be preferable to have institutional tie-ups with employers/employees' cooperative societies for which eligibility criteria can be laid down.

6. Security

Technically hire purchase advance is against hypothecation of equipment/vehicles and pledge of hundis/pronotes and lodgements of hire purchase agreements. The bank subsidiary will ask the borrower to complete the bank's form of security to charge the security under an equitable/ hypothecation charge. If the borrower is a limited company which is not of sufficient strength to allow equitable/hypothecation facility and if suitable security is not of sufficient strength to allow equitable/hypothecation facility and if suitable security is not available it is normal to obtain a debenture over the assets of the company under which a floating charge is obtained.

If necessary the bank subsidiary will ask the hirer to furnish a guarantor of means and the bank would in such a case insist that the guarantor should also accept the hundies. It is a practice with some banks to insist for insurance policy to indemnify the bank against the default of the hirer. The premiums will be charged to the hirer.

In view of the cost and difficulty of the repossession of a fast depreciating asset, the customer's ability to repay is vital and no reliance is placed on security.

7. Monitoring and Control

The bank needs to exercise control over the on-going situation. A periodical certificate should be obtained from the finance company at the monthly intervals, stating the total amount of outstanding but excluding those hire purchase agreements which have become in arrears and are, therefore, suspects. One or two months in arrears may be acceptable but more than suggest that the particular hirer is in permanent default and encourages tendency towards NPA. The bank will keep a running total of these amounts, returning agreements which have become lapsed to their customers.

6.3 FACTORING — CONCEPTUAL FRAMEWORK

In absence of any uniform codified law, the term "factoring" has been defined in various countries in different ways. Many efforts have been made to arrive at a consensus regarding uniform meaning and define a well laid scope for such a type of service contract. The study group appointed by International Institute for the Unification of Private Law (UNIDROIT), Rome during 1988 recommended, in general terms, the definition of factoring asunder:

"Factoring means an arrangement between a factor and his client which includes at least two of the following services to be provided by the factor:

— Finance

— Maintenance of accounts

— Collection of debts

— Protection against credit risks".

However, the above definition applies only to factoring in relation to supply of goods and services:

(*i*) Across national boundaries,

(*ii*) To trade or professional debtors,

(*iii*) When notice of assignment has been given to the debtors.

1. Report of International Institute for the Unification of Private Law (UNIDROIT)

This means that domestic factoring is not yet a well defined concept and it has been left to the discretion of legal framework as well as trade usage and convention of the individual country.

Nevertheless, following the development of factoring concept in various developed countries of the world, some broad agreement has been arrived at towards defining the term. Factoring can broadly be defined as an arrangement in which receivables arising out of sale of goods/ services are sold to the "factor" as a result of which the title to the goods/services represented by the said receivables passes on to the factor. Henceforth, the factor becomes responsible for all credit control, sales accounting and debt collection from the buyer(s). In a full service factoring concept (without recourse facility), if any of the debtors fails to pay the dues as a result of his financial inability/inolvency/bankruptcy, the factor has to absorb the losses.

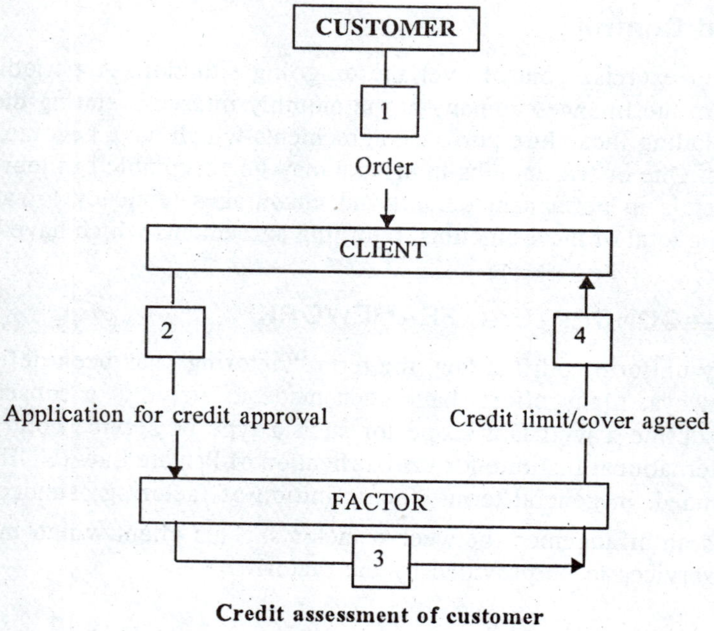

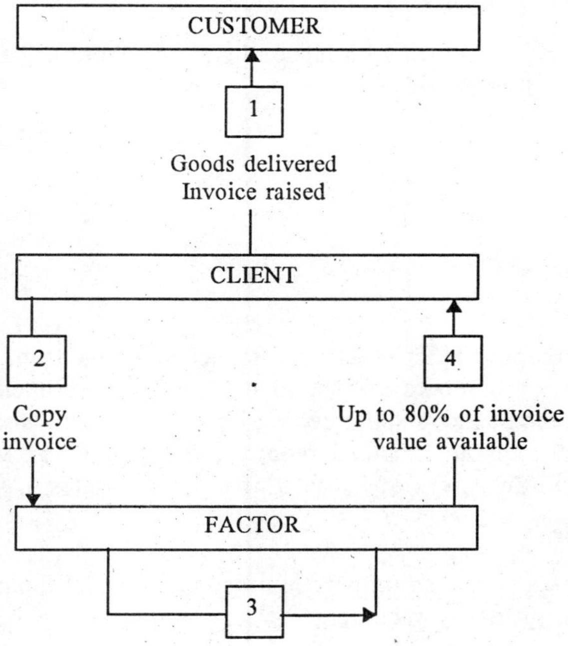

Sales ledger updated

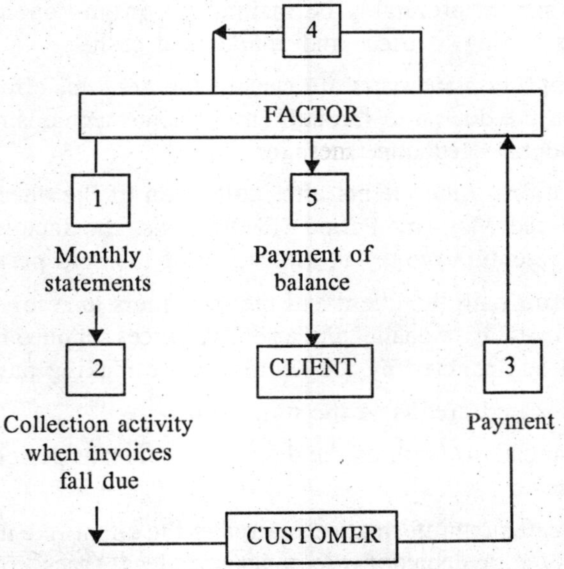

Payment Collection

6.3.1 Functions of a Factor

Thus, in a full service factoring parlance, the main functions of a factor can be grouped in the following four broad categories:

1. Finance
2. Administration
3. Credit Risk
4. Consultancy

(1) Finance

As business develops, higher stocks are to be maintained and greater quantum of credit provided to an increasing numbers of customers. These developments result in higher demand for working capital as the business starts getting into cash crunch. One of the important functions of the factor is to cater to the financial requirements of such growth-oriented enterprises by providing finance up to an extent of 80-85% of the credit sales.

(2) Administration

— The entire sales ledger administration responsibility of the client gets transferred to the factor. These primarily include:

— To ensure that invoices raised represent genuine trade transactions in respect of goods sold or services provided.

— To maintain sales ledger of the client in a scientific manner up dated with latest invoices raised and cash received.

This sales ledger should preferably be maintained on an **"open item system"** which shows all the outstanding invoices and unallocated cash.

— To ensure that monthly statements are sent to the debtors, efforts are being made to collect the dues on the due dates through an efficient mechanism of personal contacts, issuance of reminders, telephone messages, etc.

— To remit the retention to the clients after collection of the dues. Where the factoring is operating on Fixed Maturity Period (FMP) basis, the factor is to ensure that the client is paid the retention money at the expiry of the said period.

— To have close liaison with the client and the customers to resolve the various disputes raised in respect of quantity or quality of the goods/services supplied besides the unauthorised discounts claimed or deducted by the debtors while making payment.

— To keep the unallocated credits to the minimum.

— To review the financial strength of the debtors at constant periodic intervals to ensure collectibility of debts.

— To submit the management information returns to the client like up to date aged balance reports, details of overdue unpaid invoices, disputes, legal cases, etc., at periodic intervals.

(3) Credit Risk

Assuming credit risk responsibility is one of the important functions of a factor where transaction is on "without-recourse" basis. Normally, in such cases, "credit limits" on individual debtor are approved by the factor based on the financial strength and past track record of the customers. Thus, in case of finance provided up to such limit, the factor has to absorb the shock of losses in case of financial inability or insolvency of any of the customers. Thus, in addition to the other administrative responsibility, the factor assumes debt insurance risk. However, where a factor purchases accounts receivable but does not offer credit cover, he will operate "recourse" which gives him the right to have payment guaranteed or the receivables repurchased by the client. This will happen if the debtor does not make payment in full by agreed period.

(4) Consultancy

Besides the aforementioned services, the factor in today's world also often provides advisory services guiding the client in areas relating to marketing, finance and production. Is there recession in the market? Is there any need for diversification? Should the products be continued to be sold to the particular debtors with whom the client is dealing at present? How the profitability should be improved? These are some of the areas in which the factor can assume the responsibility as a counsellor.

❖ Distinction between Bills Finance and Factoring

Both the facilities — bills finance and factoring are, in fact, aimed at augmenting the cash flow position of the seller as regards availability of working capital at post-sales stage. However, the approach and the operational mechanism are totally different between the two concepts.

The main points of difference are:

1. Bills finance comprises of providing only finance to the entrepreneur while factoring is a much broader concept encompassing the total service approach — rendering sales ledger administration, collection of and protection against bad debts besides providing financial facilities. Thus, factoring is an ideal tool for growth and development of expanding small and medium enterprises.
2. In conventional bills financing, advance is given against bills of exchange raised, whereas in factoring, there is an outright purchase of trade debts after providing for returns, allowances and settlement discounts.
3. As a corollary to the above, legally speaking, bills financing involves advance against security, whereas factoring implies outright purchase of a debt for a consideration value.
4. In case of bills finance provided to a corporate client, charge of the lender can be got registered with company house (Registrar of Companies). But, since the factor is the owner of trade debt, the question of registering the charge does not arise.
5. In respect of bills finance, the drawee or the acceptor of the bills is in full knowledge of the bank's charge on the receivables arising from sale of goods/services, whereas some variations of factoring services like 'Undisclosed Factoring' are confidential in nature, i.e., the debtors are not aware of the arrangement. Thus, the large industrial houses availing of such facility can successfully claim of running business of their own without any outside financial support.

6. Financing against bills is individual transaction-oriented, i.e., each bill of exchange is singly assessed on its merit and got purchased/discounted. On the contrary, factoring follows the principle of *"whole turnover"* meaning thereby that bulk finance is provided against several unpaid, trade generated invoices in batches.
7. Bills finance is always *"In-balance sheet"* financing, i.e., both the amounts of receivables and bank credit are reflected in the balance sheet of the client as current assets and current liabilities respectively. This is because of the *"With recourse"* nature of the facility, i.e., the bank reserving the right to fall back upon the client (the drawer of the bill) in case of dishonour of the same by the acceptor or the drawee. However, full factoring service facility is "off-balance sheet" arrangement, as the client company completes his double entry accounting by crediting the factor for consideration value.

6.3.2 Advantages of Factoring

(1) Benefits from Sales Management Service

The distinct advantage of factoring arrangement is that the client need not undertake any more the responsibility of collecting the dues from the buyers of the goods/services. Similarly, the functions of sales ledger administration including accounting and asset management are also performed by the factor. Thus, the industrial/service units, especially in the small/medium-scale sector, need not have any administrative set up for credit management including collection resulting in substantial savings by way of salaries and wages to the concerned personnel besides economy in infrastructural expenditure like postage, telephone, telegram, telex, etc. The firm also no longer remains bogged down with disturbing feature of control and collection aspects of bad debts. It can, as it ought to, concentrate on production, finance and marketing. Thus, the axiom is — **"Factoring best suits the clients who produce goods which can be sold and forgotten".**

Thus, the main benefits under the above category include:

- Savings in the cost of maintaining own sales ledger.
- Saving of management time towards supervising sales accounts or chasing slow paying customers.
- Quicker payment by customers as a result of endeavour of professional, (i.e., the factor) resulting in cash flow improvement.
- Cost of realisation being brought down as a result of the automated and bulk efforts by the factor.
- Relationship with customers not damaged by sales and management requesting payment.
- More time for business development and quality production.
- Improvement in quality of lending as apart from *"Supplier-risk"*, the appraisal involves judgement of *"Debtor-risk"* also.

(2) Benefits from Financing Facility and Credit Protection Service

Under factoring arrangements, flexible financial facility by way of prepayment is provided to the client, which grows with a company's sales. Usually, after execution of the factoring agreement, an amount equivalent to previously agreed per cent (say 80-85%) of the eligible trade debts is released to the client on an ongoing basis based on the invoices submitted. The remaining portion, known as retention, is made available on realisation of debts or if the arrangements is on Fix Maturity Period (FMP) basis, at the end of the said period. Further, in the case of full factoring (without recourse) service, the factor provides 100% credit protection on all approved sales, thus guaranteeing payment in the event of a bad debt. Thus, the primary benefits to the client under the above system include:

— Obtaining off-balance sheet finance on more flexible terms for maintaining higher level of sales. Gearing of the client is also not disturbed.

— Payment to suppliers more promptly giving enhanced credit reputation.

— Getting cash and quality discount on supplier thus improving profit margin.

— Coping with seasonal and other peak demands for cash.

— Improving return on capital without giving up equity or control.

— Elimination of problem of bad debts.

(3) Benefits from Consultancy Service

One of the key aspects of factoring service is providing expert credit and other advice to the clients. The factor by virtue of his dealings with several clients operating with a number of debtors, is in a unique position to advise the former about the creditworthiness of the latter.

Expert advice can also be offered in a number of other matters like production, marketing, etc., which are not directly connected with the main service. Thus, the main benefits under this category include:

— No time and expenses spent investigating customer credit standing.

— Poor quality risky customers avoided.

— Ability to develop sales to sound and better quality customers.

— Ready availability of information regarding product design/mix, prices, market conditions and economic prospects.

❖ Limitations

The above discussions do not mean that the factoring operations are totally free from any limitation — the attendant risk itself is of very high degree. Some of the main inherent limitations of such transactions are enumerated hereunder:

1. It may result in over-complacency in the behaviour of the client resulting in overtrading or mismanagement.

2. The risk-element in factoring gets accentuated due to possible fraudulent acts by the client in furnishing the main instrument "invoice" to the factor. Invoicing against non-existent goods, pre-invoicing, (i.e., invoicing before physical despatch of goods), duplicate-invoicing, (i.e., making more than one invoice in respect of single transaction) are some commonly found frauds in such operations, which had brought many factors in early 60s allover the world into difficulty.

3. In a developing economy like ours, the factoring in its nascent stage may have teething problems arising from lack of professionalism and competence, under developed expertise, resistance to change, etc.

4. One of the major limitations in factoring is regarding right of the factor resulting from purchase of trade-debts. In the words of Fredrick Salinger, one of the leading legal experts on factoring in UK, "Whereas, the holder in due course of bill of exchange has the right to recover payment in full, free from any countervailing rights of the acceptor or any third party claims, the assignee of a debt on open credit owns a pure intangible claim with no such special rights". Thus, the rights of the assignee in a factoring arrangement are uncertain not as strong as that in Bills of Exchange and are subject to settlement of discounts, returns and allowances.
5. All companies, may not be suitable for entering into factoring contracts. Some of the limiting factors may be as follows:
   (*a*) Small companies with less turnover, say up to ₹ 50 lakh per annum, as in such cases, the cost of factoring may be disproportionately high and uneconomic.
   (*b*) Companies having high concentration on a few debtors.
   (*c*) Companies selling a large number of small products of various types to general public or companies having large number of debtors for small amounts.
   (*d*) Units manufacturing and selling highly specialised items because the factor may not have sufficient expertise to assess the credit risk.
   (*e*) Companies with speculative business.
   (*f*) Companies which have inefficient or weak management or which have high bad debt/dispute experience.

❖ Overall Compromise

From the above deliberations, it can be observed that there are both advantages and disadvantages in factoring transactions, the former being more applicable to clients and the latter primarily denoting the risk to the factor. Nevertheless, there is no denying that factoring suits best the clients with a developing business in an expanding economy. Scope for choice for clients for choosing a factoring company in India, at least, for a few years to come will be very limited meaning thereby that the market will predominantly be a seller's one as far as the factor is concerned. Therefore, the factor will have ample opportunity to appraise the risk-factors associated with a client company with a view to accepting only the desired proposals. For instance, some of the pertinent questions could be:

— Which industries are providing most growth?

— Which industries provide most secure clients?

— Which industries have an inherent need for debtor based finance, etc.?

Another limitation could be the clients having acute cash flow crunch on the verge of becoming sick approaching the factor for immediate relief, being shed-of by the bank(s) to the factoring counterparts. Factors have to be on guard against such clients. As such, it is felt that at the initial stage of development, there has to be some compromise but definitely not at the cost of the very viability of the factor.

6.3.3 Pricing of Factoring Services

The pricing of factoring services primarily comprises of following two components:

(1) Administrative Charges/Factoring Fees

This is charged towards providing various services to the clients namely:

(*a*) Sales ledger administration, (*b*) Credit control including processing, operational overheads and collection of debts, and (*c*) Providing protection against bad debts.

This charge is normally computed with reference to the projected sales turnover of the client during next twelve months, being a per cent of the same. Normally all over the world, this charge varies between 1-25% of the projected turnover. The quantum levied depends on several factors such as,

(*a*) Type of industry

(*b*) Strength of the client as well as of the debtors

(*c*) Volume of sales

(*d*) Average invoice value

(*e*) Terms of trade

(*f*) Type(s) of service(s) offered

(*g*) Extent of competition

(*h*) Required profit margin to the factor

(*i*) Security to the factor, etc.

There can be many variations to the above suggested approach. One can be a minimum handling charge per proposal plus certain per cent of the projected turnover. The latter, since it is based on many assumptions, may not fructify and cause less return than anticipated to the factor. As such, for a new client, if the factor's appraisal indicates any doubt regarding the ability of the client to achieve the projected turnover, a minimum administrative charge, in absolute terms can also be stipulated. Similarly, if any segment of service is not provided, for example, bad debt protection, the fees are correspondingly reduced by a certain per cent (say .5 to 1%) for credit protection element (CPE).

(2) Discount Charges

This is levied towards providing instant credit to the client by way of prepayment. This is normally linked with the base rate of the parent company or the bank from which the factoring institution is borrowing money, say, 1 to 2.5% above the said rate.

6.3.4 Costing and Pricing Techniques

These two are interlinked issues as the resources are always mobilised at a cost and the pricing of the services should provide a reasonable spread for the continued viable operations by the factor. Classical concepts of pricing strategies have been defined by G. Michael Moebs as under: "Four pricing strategies for pricing anything whether a good or a service."

(*a*) Cost-plus pricing has an internal focus, and adds a profit margin or mark-up to the production cost of the good or service in order to set the price.

(*b*) Competition pricing focuses entirely on other firms, examines their prices, and sets prices in order to place one's own firm relative to the competition.

(c) Relationship pricing aggregates all the services used by a household or a company and singularly prices the entire amount of services purchased. This pricing strategy allows some products to be priced at a loss, since the relationship as a whole is profitable.

(d) Value pricing is an external strategy which prices products and services based on the perceived due as determined by market research."

Though competition pricing and value pricing have their role to play, normally the pricing strategy adopted in factoring is on the basis of the cost-plus, i.e.:

Selling price = cost + profit

Total costs are again bifurcated in two components:

(i) Fixed cost which remains fixed irrespective of volume of business till the time major reorganisation is required, and

(ii) Variable cost which varies directly with the volume of business transacted.

The pricing strategy to be followed depends on the costing technique adopted, i.e., either absorption costing or marginal costing.

Absorption costing is based on the principle that the client would pay for the entire fixed cost as well as the variable cost. The principle followed in respect of marginal costing is that the pricing would recover the variable cost in full and part of fixed cost only.

Costing Computation: This is normally done as under:

(a) Direct Cost		
Per invoice amount	....	
Per active account	....	
Per debtor amount	....	
Per client	....	% of turnover
Bad debt provision	....	% of turnover
Total direct cost	....	
(b) Administrative cost	....	% of turnover
(c) Total factoring cost	= (a) + (b)	
(d) Profit	....	% of turnover

(e) Required service charge $= \dfrac{(c) + (d)}{\text{Total Turnover}} \times 100$

= % of turnover

Illustration:

The computation of costing and the resultant pricing for an individual client are shown in the following illustrative example.

Say turnover during last 12 months = ₹ 10 lakh.

(₹)

Description	*No. of Instruments*	*Cost per Instrument*	*Total Cost*
Invoices	875	1.50	1,312.00
Active accounts	40	50.00	2,000.00
No. of customers	50	3.50	175.00
Per client		.1% (of turnover)	1,000.00
Transmission cost		.01% (of turnover)	100.00
Total Direct Cost (A)			4,587.00
Administrative Cost (B)		.15% (of turnover)	1,500.00
Total Operative Cost (C) = (A + B)			6,087.00
Profit required		1% (of turnover)	10,000.00
Therefore, total required income			16,087.00

As such, required service charge would be 1.61% of turnover,

$$\left(\frac{16,087}{10,00,000}\times 100\right)=1.61$$

❖ Accounting System

Primarily, a factoring company maintains four heads for its factoring transactions:

— Sales Ledger Control A/c – Main asset account of various debtors on behalf of clients.

— Debt Purchased A/c — Mirror account of sales ledger control account. In operations under pay-as-paid basis, sales ledger control account and debt purchased account would depict the same balance.

— Client Current A/c — Statement of account of the client depicting all debits and credits.

— Bank account (Nominal account).

The various journal entries to be passed at different stages are:

1. Assignment or invoices

Sales Ledger Control Account, Dr.

To Debt Purchased Account

2. Payment to client

Client current account, Dr.

To Bank Account

3. Payment by customer Dr.

(*a*) Bank Account Dr.

To Client Current Account

(*b*) Debt Purchased Account Dr.

To Sales Ledger Control Account

4. **Assignment or credit notes**

Debt purchased Account Dr.

To Sales Ledger Control Account

Notes:

(*i*) Sales Ledger Control Account to be maintained separately for each customer and also Master Control Account,

(*ii*) Periodic balancing involves :
Total of each of customer's balance = Sales Ledger
Master Control Account = Debt Purchased Account,

(*iii*) At each month end, copy of debt purchased account and client current account to be sent to the client.

6.3.5 Organisational Set Up

There is no classical way of laying down an ideal organisational structure for a factoring company. Allover the world, the factoring companies have developed either as a wing of banking/ financial institutions or as separate subsidiary of theirs with a small set up expanding gradually with growth of business. New ventures have naturally resulted in setting up new divisions resulting in horizontal or vertical dispersion. However, the different functional aspects in a full service factoring arrangement can be summarised as under:

Marketing and Business Development:

1. Developing new products and/or modifying existing ones to meet the changing needs of clients.
2. Conducting market research on an ongoing basis.
3. Identification of new prospects, (i.e., prospective clients).
4. Promotion of new business.
5. Advertising and publicity.
6. Public relations with branch managers of the bank and outside professionals for tapping new business.

Thus, in brief, there are three major components of the above service, namely: (*a*) Marketing, (*b*) Sales, and (*c*) Product development.

Credit Management:

1. Appraisal of client's proposal.
2. Conducting survey.
3. Credit underwriting, i.e., assessment of debtor's risk and approval of limits.
4. Take on survey.
5. Putting up notes to sanctioning authority/credit committee for approval of limit
6. Offer of quotation to the client.
7. Documentation formalities.

Client Relations (Operations):

1. Liaison with client on day-to-day basis.
2. Processing invoices/credit notes.
3. Computation of availability and disbursal of funds.
4. Transmission of information — returns to client.
5. Review, monitoring and follow-up.
6. Annual review.
7. Reconciliation.

Credit Control:

1. Maintenance of sales ledger.
2. Follow-up with customers.
3. Collection of debts and allocation of cash.
4. Raising and solving disputes.

Legal:

1. Handling cases relating to insolvency/bankruptcy of the client/customers.
2. Initiating legal proceedings against customers.

Finance and Accounts:

1. Raising resources and treasury functions.
2. Financial accounting including supplier accounting and preparation of annual accounts after due provision as well as normal routine matters like payroll, purchase ledger, nominal ledger, etc.
3. Preparation of management accounts for the top management on periodic basis.
4. Preparation and monitoring of supplier costing, new business pricings, etc., on an ongoing basis.

Besides the above, a factoring company may also have separate wings for the undermentioned job specifications:

(*a*) Personnel and general administration

(*b*) Computers

Thus, normally, the organisational flow chart of a medium sized factoring establishment will look like as on the next page.

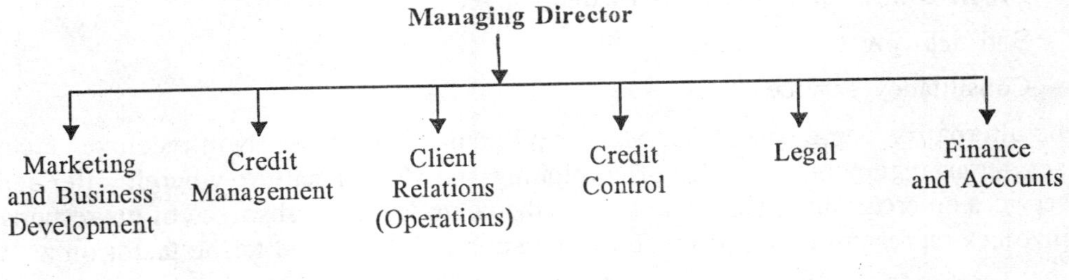

However, the above is only an illustrative design and many variations are possible. At the initial stage, the divisions relating to credit management and credit control could probably be clubbed together. Similarly, the functions relating to general administration and computers may be brought under either "marketing and business development" or "finance and accounts". There is yet another approach to the organisational design which is being practised by some of leading factoring institutions of the world known as "Group-concept". Under this approach, a group of clients based on either activity or geographical distribution are allotted to a particular group of personnel, wherein all the activities relating to these clients namely, (*i*) assessment and appraisal of debtors, (*ii*) daily operations including calculation of prepayment and disbursal, and (*iii*) credit control, collection of debts, monitoring and follow-up, are undertaken. This is the extended concept of single window approach.

Similarly, many factoring companies have two separate divisions for dealing with clients having: (*a*) With recourse, and (*b*) Without recourse facilities. Many of the large factoring houses have a separate department to deal in International Factoring both export and import, which has also a specialised cell to undertake the exchange risk management functions.

6.3.6 Types of Factoring Services

There is no universal model of factoring which can satisfy all segments of clientele. Over the years, various services have been experimented to meet the expectations and needs of different categories of clients. Security of a factor is another consideration that has given rise to different variations. Some of the issues that primarily determine the type of service required are:

— Nature of client's business

— Volume of client's business

— Transactions, whether domestic or international or combination of the both

— Cost of service that is acceptable to both the parties, and

— Factor's security.

Nevertheless, based on global experience for more than last there decades, several classical packages have been in vogue, which to a major extent have satisfied the needs of various groups of clients. These services are:

(1) Full Service Factoring

This is the most standard and comprehensive of all the packages, wherein all the ingredients of factoring service are present, namely:

— Providing finance

— Sales ledger administration

— Credit control and collection of debts

— Bad debt protection, and

— Consultancy service

The alternative name of this service is 'Without-recourse' or 'Non-recourse' factoring. It is, in fact, an arrangement, normally of continuing and regular nature, wherein after selling the goods/services on credit on open account basis, the client is totally absolved of his responsibilities as the invoices representing the receivables/trade debts are assigned to the factor on a 'Without-recourse' basis. Being the owner of the trade debt, the entire responsibility relating to credit management, credit control and debt collection is with the factor. Since the ownership has been passed on unequivocally and without recourse basis, the factor has to absorb the shock of potential losses, if any, arising from financial inability on part of any of the debtors.

However, this does not mean that the recourse element is totally absent. This has to be viewed from two dimensions —

(*a*) Without-recourse facility is available only towards financial inability of the debtors. Any dispute in respect of quality, quantity, pricing terms, non-availability of goods, etc., are outside its purview and they have to be settled between the principal contracting parties, namely, the seller and the buyer. If the dispute is not resolved amicably within a reasonable period, say 60 days, the non-recourse facility is automatically converted into a recourse one and the corresponding invoice is assigned back to the client.

(*b*) Without-recourse facility is available only for agreed sales to approved debtor(s) up to the specified amount. At the initial stage itself, an approved limit is set up for each of the debtors and the debt protection facility is available only for sale up to the agreed quantum. Any prepayment over and above the said limit or any transaction to an unapproved debtor is at client's risk meaning thereby that the facility automatically becomes recourse one.

(2) With-recourse Factoring

The name itself indicates that the arrangement operates on pedestal of having recourse against the client. This means that debt protection facility is not available under such agreement notwithstanding the causes of the non-payment by any of the debtors and any invoice remaining outstanding beyond a predetermined period, normally, 60-90 days from the due date is automatically assigned back to the client. Now the debt collection responsibility for the outstanding invoice is with the seller and he has to independently pursue the same with the defaulting debtor(s). Thus, under such an arrangement, the services offered by a factor comprise of:

— Providing finance.

— Sales ledger administration, asset management and collection of debts, and

— Consultancy services.

However, in such a type of facility also debtor wise limits are approved by the factor primarily with a view to restricting the quantum of prepayment.

Another important concept in recourse factoring parlance is "Refactoring Charges", which is akin to the original factoring fees levied on all trade-debts remaining outstanding beyond 60-90 days after due date. This is normally levied when the client requests the factor to continue the collection efforts without reassignment or asks the latter to initiate legal proceedings, however, at his own cost, for recovery of the outstanding dues.

Since the entire edifice of transaction is on recourse model, the recourse factoring normally operates on Pay-as-paid method rather than on FMP.

(3) Maturity Factoring

The alternative name given to this arrangement is "Collection Factoring". In such an agreement, no prepayment is accorded to the client at the initial stage at the time of assignment of invoice.

The entire amount less the factoring fees is paid to the client as and when the dues are collected from the debtors (in pay-as-paid model) or after the expiry of the predetermined maturity period (FMP model). The responsibilities relating to sales ledger administration, asset management, credit control including collection of debts and debt protection, however, remain vested with the factor. Thus, under such a type of arrangement, there is no "client risk" to the factor as no financing is involved. The success of such venture depends on the evaluation of the credit-risk of the debtors.

(4) Invoice Discounting

This involves simple financing against invoices without assumption of any other risk or responsibility on part of the factor. All other responsibilities, namely, sales ledger administration, accounting and collection of debts remain with the client himself. The client sells the goods/ services and invoices are directly sent to the customer(s). Bulk invoices are sent to the factor with a covering schedules normally reading as under:

"We have already executed invoice discounting agreement with you in terms of which the following debts are absolutely assigned in your favour. We will forward the payment to you as and when they are received".

On strength of the corresponding invoices, after maintaining the required retention, the prepayment is accorded to the client, who after collecting the debts passes on the same to the factor. Another interesting feature is that such arrangement is totally confidential in nature meaning thereby that the customers are not aware of the financing arrangement. Therefore, the popular alternative name of this facility is "Confidential Invoice Discounting" or "Undisclosed Factoring". As can be seen from the mechanics of operation, the facility is high risk in nature and normally, therefore, no credit protection facility is available. However, for selected highly rated clients with a very sound and professional sales ledger administration with no bad debt experience in the past, credit cover is sometimes provided, though to a lesser extent, say 70-80%. Such a type of arrangement is known as "Protected Invoice Discounting". The lesser coverage is obviously to induce the clients to make their collection endeavour in a more systematic and aggressive manner.

(5) Bulk Factoring

This word has been coined from *"Eigen Service Factoring"* (Own Service Factoring) — a German terminology. As can be seen from the discussion above, invoice discounting is a high risk venture primarily on account of its confidentiality, i.e., non-notification of the assignment to the debtors. A minor variation of the above results in the concept of bulk factoring. When the factor is not fully satisfied with the financial eligibility criteria of the client required for invoice discounting, he, under this arrangement agrees to provide the prepayment but with notification to debtors. However, the responsibilities relating to sales ledger administration, asset management and even the credit control including collection of debts remain with the client himself. Since notification of debts has been given to the debtors, the amount automatically is collected by the factor on behalf of the client and is passed on to the latter at periodic intervals. As such, this system makes an effort towards strengthening the security of the factor. This arrangement mainly runs on with-recourse basis, i.e., protection against bad debt is not available.

(6) Agency Factoring

This is yet another variation in the factoring world. The word "agency" is a misnomer and has separate meanings in the factoring parlance in different countries. However, mainly under this system, the risks and responsibilities of the client and the factor are bifurcated as follows:

Client: (*a*) Sales ledger administration, and

(*b*) Collection of debts.

Factor: (*a*) Prepayment facility, and

(*b*) Protection against bad debts.

As such, agency factoring is no different from the bulk factoring except that the former operates on a without recourse basis compared to the recourse nature of the latter.

❖ Comparative Evaluation

As already stated in the discussions at the beginning of the chapter, there is a combination of issues which determine the nature of services to be offered and availed. The list of six services discussed above is not an exhaustive one but only illustrative. Any number of variations can be introduced to satisfy specific needs of a client *vis-a-vis* the security of the factor. Nevertheless, for smaller growing companies in a competitive environment, full service factoring can offer the best and comprehensive package. However, if a prospective client is used to sell to solvent customers and has no bad debt experience in the past, probably he may not require protection against bad debt facility, which will push down the pricing structure at least by 1 to 1.5%. He may have the problem of growing debt turn and getting finance in which case he would prefer to avail of recourse factoring only. A very sound company with computerised and well managed sales ledger administration selling to a number of good customers may like to avail of only invoice discounting facility. This may serve two purposes namely, uninterrupted and predicted cash flow and an "ego" satisfaction of demonstration of running business with his own funds to outside world as notification of debts is not there. Bulk factoring is a unique package to those clients who do not satisfy the strict financial criterion stipulated to become eligible for invoice discounting but still have sufficient resources at command to carry-out their business.

Pricing is yet another important consideration for choosing which service to go in for. Obviously, due to absence of credit protection element, the administrative fees are reduced by 1-1.5% in respect of with recourse facility compared to the full service package, discounting charge, nevertheless, remaining the same in both the cases. This is indeed a substantial saving which, however, has to be compared with the actual write-off and provision for bad and doubtful debts in the past. Invoice discounting primarily involves discounting charges and small per cent of administrative fees (say ½ - ¾% of turnover) due to the processing work involved. The charges for bulk factoring are substantially higher compared to that of invoice discounting owing to increased administrative cost to the factor as the proceeds of debts are to be collected, processed, apportioned and remitted back to the client at periodic intervals. Agency factoring is still costlier in view of the presence of debt protection element. Full service package is obviously the costliest but most attractive at the same time, as all ingredients are bundled together and offered whereby the client can produce and sell the goods and can then afford to forget about the same.

The types of services to be offered, to certain extent depends on the prevailing socio-economic environment of the country, industrial usage and practices as well. For instance, in

India, cases of bankruptcy/insolvency of medium/large industrial houses are relatively unknown phenomenon. The problem here is non-adherence to the promise to make payment on due date enjoying interest free credit from the suppliers. Since, the market is primarily a buyer's one, wherein a large number of small-scale industries are supplying the same goods to a select few big houses, payment can deliberately be delayed or disputes "Created". Therefore, need in India is not debt protection facility but a professionally-managed factoring house which can perform the credit management functions in a better manner thereby reducing the debt-turn, besides providing finance. Historically also, it would be unwise to go ahead in a big way with full service package having high risk potential.

All over the world, different factoring companies are adopting various approaches to meet the expectations of the clientele without, however, jeopardising their own security position. Again, some of the factoring institutions do have a tendency to specialise in a particular field. For instance, Alex Lawrie Factors Ltd., subsidiary of Lloyds Bank in UK only undertakes recourse business, whereas their counterpart, International Factors Ltd., subsidiary of the same bank is primarily engaged in without-recourse factoring.

The various facilities along with the services available to the clients are given.

Both the factoring company and the prospective clients are required to have full information regarding various packages of services that are available with the former along with suitability of a particular type of service to the latter.

	Administration	*Credit Control*	*Finance*	*Risk Assumption*
Package 1 (Full Service factoring)	✓	✓	✓	✓
Package 2 (Recourse factoring)	✓	✓	✓	
Package 3 (Maturity factoring)	✓	✓		
Package 4 (Invoice discounting)			✓	
Package 5 (Bulk factoring)			✓ (with notification)	
Package 6 (Agency factoring)			✓	✓
Package 7 (Protected Invoice discounting)			✓	✓ (To a lesser extent)

✓ denotes availability of facility.

6.3.7 Evaluation of Factoring Proposals

Evaluation of factoring proposals, emanating from the prospective clients, is definitely a more complicated exercise compared to that of normal bank lending especially for post-sales bills finance. This is primarily on account of the rationale that in conventional bills financing, banks are more concerned about the financial strength of the sellers. Since the facility by its very nature is with recourse, normally, weightage for evaluation of the debtor-risk is minimal.

Further, banks can adopt a comprehensive and integrated approach for the entire working capital needs of the client, of which bills financing is only a part.

But, the edifice of sound factoring decision comprises of primarily, assessment of three dimensional aspects:

- Financial, operational and managerial competence of the client along with his capability of assigning valid debts.
- Collectibility of debts, i.e., the strength of the debtors.
- Continued profit earning capacity of the client-business.

There is also additional risk arising from the facility of protection against bad debts.

As such, normally, the evaluation of factoring proposals comprises of two broad facets:

1. Client Risk Assessment, and
2. Debtor Risk Assessment

1. Client Risk Assessment

The primary objective of the assessment is to evaluate the strength and weakness of the client in respect of all parameters with a view to come to rational judgement regarding his creditworthiness. The important aspects which are looked into are:

(a) Nature of Business

This is of primary concern to the factor. The economic environment within which the industry, in general, and the client business, in particular, is operating throws much light on the future prospects. Product should be easily marketable, competition should not be too severe and the product should have a long-term perspective. Government policies, rules and regulations, incentives, taxation aspects, etc., should also be conducive for the industry's growth. The present stage of the industry in the overall project life cycle is another important consideration; if it is in "matured stage" or "decaying stage", it is better not to accept the proposal or induce the prospect for diversification or an alternate product mix. Some of the industries which may not be suitable for factoring are as under:

- Companies having a high concentration on a few debtors.
- Consumer product-oriented units producing a variety of household goods and selling directly to public at large.
- Companies with speculative business.
- Units manufacturing and selling highly specialised items.
- Units manufacturing volatile items susceptible to changes like high-fashion garments, etc.
- Companies engaged in construction or similar activities where part/progress payment system is in vogue.

(b) Past Performance of the Business

Past happenings though not fully conclusive, may be an important indicator for future likely events to come. This past performance scanning is being carried out in a number of ways, the most important amidst them being as follows:

(i) *Financial Statement Analysis*

Normally, trend analysis for last three years is being done based on audited P and L a/c and balance sheet submitted by the client. The important and critical areas which are looked into are:

Debt turn: This is the average of normal period of credit allowed to the debtors. This is computed by the following formula:

$$\text{Debt turn in days} = \frac{\text{Sundry Debtors}}{\text{Average Credit Sales during the year}}$$

$$= \frac{\text{Sundry Debtors}}{\text{Average Credit Sales}} \times 360$$

Note: (*i*) No. of days in a year have been taken as 360 for simplicity of calculation.

(*ii*) Instead of taking sundry debtors as on the balance sheet date, it is preferable to have the average thereof as at the end of every month throughout the year.

However, there can be several limitations of the above ratio which may creep in as a result of, (*i*) Non-writing-off of bad debts, (*ii*) Long outstanding debts which are in dispute, and (*iii*) Growth of deliberate credit to some debtors, etc.

Say, for example, the historical debt turn of a client as computed above, for last three years is as under:

Year I	Year II	Year III (No. of days)
50	60	75

The figures by themselves do not reveal anything. May be the credit control mechanism of the client is ineffective only because of which factor has been approached. Or the client is entering into new segments of market and endeavouring to induce higher sales by giving liberal credit.

Similarly, gradual reduction in historical debt turn over the years may also not always be happy indicator as it may signify overtrading and constraint of cash flow resulting in the client's efforts to realise the debts by price-slash.

Nevertheless, the debt turn provides some vital information to the factor in respect of (*i*) its comparative position within the industry, (*ii*) steadiness of debtor realisation, (*iii*) effectiveness of credit control mechanism, etc.

Liquidity: This is of vital importance to the factor in as much as information is available regarding the liquid surplus (Working Capital) available within the unit. Some of the important ratios calculated in this regard are:

$$\text{Current Ratio} = \frac{\text{Current Assets}}{\text{Current Liabilities}} \text{ (Ideal Ratio 2:1)}$$

$$\text{Liquid Ratio} = \frac{\text{Current Assets} - \text{Stocks}}{\text{Current Liabilities}} \text{ (Ideal Ratio minimum 1:1)}$$

$$\text{Creditor Turnover Ratio} = \frac{\text{Sundry Creditors for Goods}}{\text{Annual Credit Purchases}} \times 360$$

(should be comparable to that of the industry)

(ii) Profitability: The client's business should have sustained profitability — both in terms of gross and net margin. This classification is essential to identify whether poor profit track record is due to incorrect pricing strategy or because of poor control of overheads. The profit index can be computed by either or more of the following methods:

(*i*) Return on Capital Employed (ROCE)

(*ii*) Profit on Sales (both gross and net)

(*iii*) Value added per employee

and compared with the industry average to come to a positive conclusion.

Adequacy of Financial Structure: Financial structure of the client unit should be well balanced and gearing ratio should be optimum. The basic ratios analysed during the process are:

(*i*) Debt equity ratio $= \dfrac{\text{Long-term Debt}}{\text{Tangible Net Worth}}$

(*ii*) Borrowing ratio $= \dfrac{\text{Total Borrowings}}{\text{Tangible Net Worth}}$

(*iii*) Interest coverage ratio $= \dfrac{\text{Profit after Taxes}}{\text{Interest on Total Borrowings}}$

(*iv*) Security coverage ratio $= \dfrac{\text{Net Fixed Assets}}{\text{Long-term Debt (incl. Debentures)}}$

There are no ideal parameters as far as the above ratios are concerned. They may differ from case-to-case. However, some basic norms can be prescribed as under:

(*i*) Debt equity ratio should not be more than 3:1 for SSI units and 2:1 for medium/large scale industries.

(*ii*) Borrowing ratio should not be more than 6:1.

(*iii*) Interest coverage ratio should be minimum 2:1.

(*iv*) Security coverage ratio should be minimum 1.5:1.

(iii) Ledger Analysis: Financial statement analysis is only one aspect of appraisal which must be supplemented by a more detailed inspection of a company's business to ensure the viability of the proposal. This is what is technically known as "Survey" in the factoring parlance. This simply means that on receipt of a factoring proposal, a team of experts belonging to the factoring company should study the various aspects of working of the unit, which *inter alia*, may include the following:

— Financial compatibility

— Managerial competence

— Credit control mechanism

— General functional aspects.

The various aspects which are normally looked into by the factor during such an operation are:

(iv) Sales Ledger Scrutiny

— Names and addresses of major debtors (At least top ten).

— Spread of debtors. This is very important because any substantial concentration on a few debtors may result into problem at a later date arising from insolvency or disputes raised by anyone of such major customers. Normally, the concentration on a single debtor should not be more than 20-25%. This itself implies that the proposals emanating from small-scale industrial ancillary units have to be given a cautious consideration.

— Past payment record of various debtors. This should be scrutinised with reference to standard terms on which sales were effected. Non-payment, delayed payment, part payments, continued correspondence for effecting payments, etc., are to be looked in detail. Similarly, history of disputed debts in the past and the reasons thereof have to be analysed. Write-off of bad debts and provision for bad and doubtful debts in the past, say for last 2-3 years have to be looked into. Potential bad debts, if any, still outstanding in sales ledger should also be scanned.

— Existence of onerous condition like *"Ban on Assignment"*. This concept will be discussed in detail in later chapters. However, it is suffice to appreciate that many buyers, especially the larger ones may stipulate a condition in the purchase agreements prohibiting any assignment to third party including a factor. Under such circumstances, the title to the factored debt continues to remain with the client and the debtor is not obliged to make payment, in the legal sense, to the factor resulting in distortion in the very edifice of sound factoring.

Normal Terms of Trade and Condition of Sale: This should have some correlation with prevalent trade practices within the industry. The client should not be offering excessive discounts to induce more sales. At the same time period of credit normally allowed should also be reasonable as longer the period, higher is the risk. Normally, the due date should not be more than 30-45 days from the invoice-date; relaxations, however, can be made to certain specific customers to whom special terms are applicable. However, there are no rigid guidelines and the terms are always industry specific; for instance, in textile trade, the usual period normally varies from 90-120 days. But, certain types of sales are definitely outside the purview of factoring, the most important among them being as under:

(*a*) Sales to sister/allied/associate/group companies

(*b*) Sales on approval basis

(*c*) Sales or Return (SoR)

(*d*) Sales on consignment basis

(*e*) Long-term contracts

(*f*) Contra-accounts (where suppliers and debtors are the same) (*g*) Cash sales

(*h*) Sales to individuals, etc.

(v) Purchase Ledger Scrutiny: This is very important from the factor's view point as uninterrupted supply of raw materials can only ensure smooth production and sustained profitability. Some of the vital areas which are looked into in this regard are as follows:

(*a*) Whether there is excess dependence on one or two suppliers?

(*b*) Whether payments are made to the suppliers in time?

(*c*) Existence of onerous condition like *"Reservation of Title"*. This concept will be discussed, in detail, in the ensuing chapters. Here, it is suffice to understand that under certain occasions, the unpaid suppliers reserve the right to be reimbursed from out of the proceeds of the goods supplied thereby jeopardising the interest of the factor. Thus, the factor should scan through one or two purchase contracts to ensure whether this covenant exists in the same or not and how it affects his rights.

(*d*) Position regarding existence of any pressing sundry creditors including any suit/claim/ petition filed by anyone of them.

(*e*) Payment of up to date statutory liabilities including income tax, wealth tax, PF, ESI, etc.

(*f*) Existence of contra-accounts.

(c) *Existing Credit Management Practices*

This relates to analysis of existing credit control mechanism. The various aspects that are normally looked into in this regard are:

Present system of maintaining books of accounts and placing the orders. Are the books maintained properly? Are they reconciled? How purchase orders are received — orally, by letters or any other means? How goods are despatched? Is there any proof of delivery (PoI)? What is the system of drawing the invoices, etc.?

The existing criteria for giving credit (in terms of both quantum and time-limit) to the customers should be analysed in detail and cross-checked with the trade practices and sound accounting principles.

The collection procedure of the client requires enough scrutiny in terms of:

(*i*) Strengths and Weaknesses of the exiting system.

(*ii*) Whether constant touch is maintained with the debtors through personal contact/written follow-up or efforts are on *ad hoc* basis?

(*iii*) Whether regular statements are sent to the debtors?

(*iv*) Whether any "hard measures" are also undertaken sometimes to recover dues, like taking the help of legal notice or withholding further deliveries, etc.?

(*v*) Whether there are any specific debtors who are excluded from normal collection procedure and the reason why?

(*vi*) Are the disputes resolved promptly?

(d) Efficiency of Management

The capability of the management to run the business profitably, handle the funds efficiently and being able to work with factoring agreement have to be analysed in detail. Some of the points for judging the quality of the management can be summarised as under:

— Experience, background and the qualification of the entrepreneur.

— Existence of balanced, professional, broad based and independent Board of Directors.

— Depth of management in terms of sound organisational set up, well defined objectives and policies, extent of delegation and communication channels and proper management information system (MIS).

— Strong Finance Dept. to be headed by an able Finance Director.

— Presence of sound accounting policies, *viz.*, (*a*) Management accounting reports, (*b*) Budgetary and control system, (*c*) Internal cost system for product and departments, and (*d*) proper cash flow control mechanism.

— The efficiency level of the employees, in terms of their productivity, morale of the staff in general, employee turnover, problems regarding absenteeism, industrial unrest, etc.

2. Debtor Risk Assessment

As already stated, the edifice of sound factoring is collectibility of debts. Therefore, the assessment of debtor risk assumes substantial importance in the overall parlance of factoring.

The various information that are obtained in respect of the debtors are:

(*i*) Name and constitution.

(*ii*) Business and line of activity. As with supplier's product, the same observations apply to debtor's product. Some of the pertinent questions could be:

(*a*) Is it cyclical or vulnerable to recession?

(*b*) Is it susceptible to change in fashion, technology, social attitudes, overseas competition, exchange rate fluctuations?

(*c*) Does it belong to a declining or volatile industry?

(*d*) What has been the profitability track record?

(*e*) Is it a new or well established unit?

(*iii*) Standing in the market with a view to assessing its strength and creditworthiness.

(*iv*) *Financial stability:* The various ratio-analysis approach applicable for client(s) are also applied in such cases.

(*v*) *Terms of sale:* Length of credit extended must be considered in assessing the debtor(s). The most important aspect that is to be seen is whether the terms are longer than the industry average.

If so, there can be two issues:

(*a*) Strong debtor exercising financial muscle, or

(*b*) Weak debtor with financial problems.

Either of the two is a potential danger for the factor.

(*vi*) *Location of the debtor:* This is of vital importance if the debtor is situated at a very far flung place at a difficult approachable location which may make the collection a problem at a later date.

The various sources of information to be relied on for the different facets of debtor risk analysis are:

(*a*) Bank reports

(*b*) Trade/market references

(*c*) Reports of the rating agencies

(*d*) Past payment performance

(*e*) Past history of disputes and non-payment

(*f*) Published financial statements.

A detailed check list for evaluation of factoring proposals is given at Annexure II.

Thus, creditworthiness of both the clients and customers has to be analysed, processed and established before factoring decisions are taken.

6.3.8 Factoring in India

In India, the idea of providing factoring services was first thought of by the Vaghul Working Group. It had recommended that banks and private non-banking financial companies should be encouraged to provide factoring services with a view to helping the industrialists and traders to tide over their financial crunch arising out of delays in the realisation of their book debts. The RBI subsequently constituted a study group in January 1988 under the chairmanship of Mr. C.S. Kalyanasundaram, former Managing Director of the SBI, to examine the feasibility of starting factoring services. On the recommendation of the committee, the Banking Regulations Act was amended in July 1990 with a view to enabling commercial banks to take up factoring services by forming separate subsidiaries.

In the public interest and in the interest of banking policy, the RBI is of the view that:

(*i*) The banks should not directly undertake the business of factoring.

(*ii*) The banks may set up separate subsidiaries or invest in factoring companies jointly with other banks.

(*iii*) A factoring subsidiary or a joint venture factoring company may undertake the factoring business. But, they should not finance other factoring companies.

(*iv*) The banks can invest in the shares of factoring companies not exceeding 10% of the paid-up capital and reserve of the bank concerned.

But, recently in February 1994, the RBI has permitted all banks to enter into factoring business departmentally. Perhaps, this step would have been taken with a view to giving further impetus to the factoring system. Since factoring requires special skills and infrastructure, the RBI has further stipulated that:

(*i*) Factoring activities should be treated on par with loans and advances and should accordingly be given risk weight of 100 per cent for calculation of capital to risk asset ratio.

(*ii*) A bank's exposure shall not exceed 25% of the bank's capital funds to an individual borrower and 50% to a group of borrowers. Factoring would also be covered within the above exposure ceiling along with equipment leasing and hire purchase finance.

(*iii*) Factoring services should be provided only in respect of those invoices which represent genuine trade transactions.

In India, the factoring service was first started by the State Bank of India in association with the Small Industries Development Bank of India, Union Bank of India, State Bank of Sourashtra and State Bank of Indore. The pioneering factoring company founded by the SBI is called "SBI-Factors and Commercial Services Pvt. Ltd., (SBI FACS)". It was started in July 1991 with a subscribed capital of ₹ 25 crore. It has been allotted the Western Zone composing of Maharashtra, Gujarat, Goa, Madhya Pradesh, The Union Territories of Dadra, Nagar Haveli, Daman and Diu. Similarly, the RBI has allotted the Southern Region to the Canara Bank, the Northern Region to the Punjab National Bank and the Eastern Region to the Allahabad Bank for providing necessary factoring services to the clients of those regions. This zonal restriction has been removed by the RBI in 1993. In South, Canara Bank has already established Can Factors Ltd. Now, these two factoring companies can operate in the centres outside their given zones. Besides the above, some non-banking companies also have made a bid for entering into factoring services. Thus, factoring service has got a very bright future in India due to its superiority over other forms of financing.

6.3.9 International Factoring

Generally, factoring services are very popular for domestic business. They are gradually entering into export business also.

Just as domestic suppliers, the exporters also find that there is a considerable delay in receiving payments from the importers. As a result, they are hard pressed for money to ensure their profitability as well as to maintain and expand their export business. In this situation, international factoring comes really handy to them to find the required resources.

The International Institute for the Unification of Private Law in 1988 has defined international factoring as follows:

"Factoring means an arrangement between a factor and his client which includes at least two of the following services to be provided by the factor: (*i*) Fiance, (*ii*) Maintenance of Accounts, (*iii*) Collection of debts, and (*v*) Protection against Credit Risks".

As the definition points out, the services of a factor in a domestic business are simply extended to international trade. However, the functioning of this scheme is different depending upon the type of export factoring and the arrangement made by the exporter and the factor.

❖ Types of Export Factoring

Generally, in the absence of factoring, all export finance transactions are backed by Letters of Credit. But, factoring relates purely to 'Open Account Transactions' with no promissory notes and collaterals. Factoring is done entirely on the basis of the invoice prepared by the exporter and so it is purely an "invoice-based export finance" technique.

In an international factoring transaction, there are four parties namely:

(*i*) The exporter who is taking the place of a client in a domestic transaction.

(*ii*) The importer who is taking the role of a customer in a domestic transaction.

(*iii*) Export Factor (EF), and

(*iv*) Import Factor (IF)

The exporter (client) and the factor enter into an agreement for export factoring which may take anyone of the following types:

(*i*) Two factor system.

(*ii*) Single factor system.

(*iii*) Direct Export factor system.

(*iv*) Direct Import factor system.

❖ Two Factor System

There are two factors under this system — one in the exporter's country and the other in the importer's country. When the exporter wants to do business with some importer or importers, he approaches the factor in his country and informs him of his business proposal, the likely size of the business, the number of invoices likely to be raised, the value of the consignment and the currency involved.

This export factor in turn informs the same to his counterpart, i.e., import factor in the importing country. The import factor makes enquiries regarding the financial position of the importer and his dealings and, if satisfied, he conveys the message to the export factor. He also indicates the limit for factoring and his commission for undertaking this work. Then, the export factor contacts the exporter and conveys the positive findings and his readiness to cover the credit risk through factoring. If the rates are acceptable to the exporter, he signs an agreement with the export factor.

Once this factoring relationship is established, the exporter sends the goods to the importer along with the invoice with a condition that the payments should be made to the import factor. Two copies of the invoices are sent to the export factor along with a notification that the debts have been assigned to the import factor. At this stage, the export factor makes payment immediately to the extent of 80% of the invoice amount to the exporter.

Thereafter, the export factor informs the import factor about the financial deal by sending a copy of the invoice. Now, it becomes the responsibility of the import factor to monitor and maintain the account and take all possible efforts to collect the amount at the due date. When the amount is collected, it is sent to the export factor. In case of any default, the import factor has to pay the amount to the export factor from his own sources.

When the amount is realised from the import factor, the export factor pays the balance of 20% of the invoice amount to the exporter. The cost of factoring is debited to the exporter's account and the commission due to the import factor is also sent. Thus, the financial dealing has to be carried out with the help of two factors and hence it is called 'Two factor system'.

❖ Single Factor System

Under this system also, two factoring companies, as stated earlier, are involved. However, the responsibility of making the payment, maintenance of books of accounts, its administration, etc., initially rest with the export factor. But, just to cover the credit risk, the export factor enters into an agreement with the import factor to collect the debt from the importer, in case the export factor is not able to realize the amount. If such a contingency arises, the export factor has to assign the debt in favour of the import factor. Thus, the import factor is called upon to assist the export factor only during the times of difficulties in realising the debt. Otherwise, the export factor himself will do all the work. So, it is called 'Single factor system'.

❖ Direct Export Factor System

Under the system, there is a factoring agreement directly between the exporter and this export factor and no other party is involved. The entire export credit risk, the administration of the account, the advance payments, etc., have to be done only by the export factor. Hence, it is called 'direct export factor system'.

❖ Direct Import Factor System

It is just the opposite of direct export factor system. The agreement is between the exporter and the import factor in the importer's country. The import factor assumes all responsibilities for the collection of the debt from the importer.

6.3.10 Factoring in Other Countries

In European countries, factoring organizations have an option to finance both domestic and export business. The tough business conditions and continued recession across Europe have affected the factoring business of late. Hence, some factoring organisations had to wind up their business in UK as well as in the USA. Again, there has been merger of factoring companies. Now, more than 700 factoring companies are operating in some forty countries. Nine out of ten of the world's strongest banks now have their own foothold in the factoring industry.

In the USA, the Fuji Bank's Chicago based Heller financial has taken over the CIT Group factoring. It has become the biggest US factor. Similarly, BNY Financial acquired BT Factors in 1990. Again, Citizen's and Southern Commercial acquired the Security Pacific in 1989 and it is now called 'National Bank Commercial'. In all, there were 17 big factors and the total US factoring business volume was more than $51 billion in 1991. In the USA the factoring organisations specialise in financing the apparel business which accounts for nearly 75% of the total volume of factoring business.

6.4 FORFAITING

Forfaiting is another source of financing against receivables like factoring. This technique is mostly employed to help an exporter for financing goods exported on a medium term deferred basis.

The term 'a forfait' is a French word denoting 'to give something' or 'give up one's rights' or 'relinquish rights to something'. In fact, under forfaiting scheme, the exporter gives up his right to receive payments in future under an export bill for immediate cash payments by the forfaitor. This right to receive payment on the due date passes on to the forfaitor, since, the exporter has already surrendered his right to the forfaitor. Thus, the exporter is able to get 100% of the amount of the bill minus discount charges immediately and get the benefits of cash sale. Thus, it is a unique medium which can convert a credit sale into a cash sale for an exporter. The entire responsibility of recovering the amount from the importer rests with the forfaitor. Forfaiting is done without any recourse to the exporter, i.e., in case the importer makes a default, the forfaitor cannot go back to the exporter for the recovery of the money.

Forfaiting has been defined as "the non-recourse purchase by a bank or any other financial institution, of receivables arising from an export of goods and services."

❖ Factoring Vs. Forfaiting

Both factoring and forfaiting are used as tools of financing. But there are some differences:

(*i*) Factoring is always used as a tool for short-term financing, whereas forfaiting is for medium-term financing at a fixed rate of interest.

(*ii*) Factoring is generally employed to finance both the domestic and export business. But, forfaiting is invariably employed in export business only.

(*iii*) The central theme of factoring is the purchase of the invoice of the client, whereas it is only the purchase of the export bill under forfaiting.

(*iv*) Factoring is much broader in the sense it includes the administration of the sales ledger, assumption of credit risk, recovery of debts and rendering of consultancy services. On the other hand, forfaiting mainly concentrates on financing aspects only and that too in respect of a particular export bill.

(*v*) Under factoring, the client is able to get only 80% of the total invoice as 'credit facility', whereas the 100% of the value of the export bill (of course deducting service charges) is given as credit under forfaiting.

(*vi*) Forfaiting is done without recourse to the client, whereas it may or may not be so under factoring.

(*vii*) The bills under forfaiting may be held by the forfaitor till the due date or they can be sold in the secondary market or to any investor for cash. Such a possibility does not exist under factoring.

(*viii*) Forfaiting is a specific one in the sense that it is based on a single export bill arising out of an individual transaction only. But, factoring is based on the "whole turnover", i.e., a bulk finance is provided against a number of unpaid invoices.

❖ Working of Forfaiting

In a forfaiting transaction, the exporter is 'the client' and the financial institution is called 'the forfaitor' and the importer is 'the debtor'. When an exporter intends to export goods and services, he approaches a forfaitor and gives him the full details of his likely export dealing such as the name of the importer, the country to which he belongs, the currency in which the export of goods would be invoiced, the price of the goods and services, etc. He discusses with him the terms and conditions of finance. If it is acceptable, a sale contract is signed between the exporter and the importer on condition that the payment should be made by the importer to the forfaitor.

As usual, bills or promissory notes are signed by the importer. Such notes are guaranteed by the importer's bank and forwarded to the exporter's bank. Generally, such notes would be released to the exporter only against shipping documents. When goods are exported, the shipping documents are handed over to the exporter's bank. The exporter's bank, then forwards the shipping documents to the importer's bank after releasing the notes/bills to the exporter. These documents finally reach the hands of the importer through his bank.

Thereafter, the exporter takes these notes to the forfaitor, who purchases them and gives ready cash after deducting discount charges.

❖ Cost of Forfaiting

The cost of forfaiting finance is always at a fixed rate of interest which is usually included in the face value of the bills or notes. Of course, it varies depending upon the arrangements duration, creditworthiness of the party, the country where the importer is staying, the denomination of the currency in which the export deal is to be done and the overall political, economic and monetary conditions prevailing in the importer's country. Since the forfaitor has to assume currency fluctuation risk, interest rate fluctuation risk and the country's risk, he charges a fee and obviously it varies according to the risk factor involved in the deal.

6.4.1 Benefits of Forfaiting

(i) Profitable and Liquid: From the forfaiter's point of view, it is very advantageous because he not only gets immediate income in the form of discount charges, but also, can sell them in the secondary market or to any investor for cash.

(ii) Simple and Flexible: It is also beneficial to the exporter. All the benefits that are available to a client under factoring are automatically available under forfaiting also. However, the greatest advantage is its simplicity and flexibility. It can be adopted to any export transaction and the exact structure of finance can also be determined according to the needs of the exporter, importer and the forfaitor.

(iii) Avoids Export Credit Risks: The exporter is completely free from many export credit risks that may arise due to the possibility of interest rate fluctuations or exchange rates fluctuations or any political upheaval that may affect the collection of bills. Forfaiting acts as an insurance against all these risks.

(iv) Avoids Export Credit Insurance: In the absence of forfaiting, the exporter has to go for export credit insurance. It is very costly and at the same time it involves very cumbersome procedures. Hence, if an exporter goes for forfaiting, he need not purchase any export credit insurance.

(v) Confidential and Speedy: International trade transactions can be carried out very quickly through a forfaitor. It does not involve much documentary procedures. Above all, it is very confidential. The speed and confidentiality with which deals are made are very beneficial for both the parties namely the exporter and the importer. No banking relationship with the forfaitor is necessary, since, it is a one time transaction only.

(vi) Suitable to all Kinds of Export Deal: It is suitable to any kind of goods — whether capital goods exports or commodity exports. Any export deal can be subject to forfaiting.

(vii) Cent per cent Finance: The exporter is able to convert his deferred transaction into cash transaction through a forfaitor. He is able to get 100 per cent finance against export receivables.

(viii) Fixed Rate Finance: Forfaiting provides finance always at a fixed rate only. So, there is no need to enter into any hedging transactions to protect against interest rate and exchange rate risks.

❖ Benefits to the Banker under Forfaiting

The advantages are:

(*a*) The banker gets the financing charges, the commitment charges and EXIM Bank charges. The first two charges would be shared between the international forfaitor and Indian Agency while the last type of charge will be earnings of EXIM Bank.

(*b*) Secondary market for forfaited receivables.

6.4.2 Drawbacks

(i) Non-availability for Short and Long Periods: Forfaiting is highly suitable to only medium-term deferred payments. Forfaitors do not come forward to undertake forfait financing for long periods, since, it involves much credit risks. Similarly, it cannot be used for availing short-term credit or contracts involving small amounts because they do not give rise to any bills or notes. Hence, exporters who require short-term and long term credit have to seek some other alternative source.

(ii) Non-availability for Financially Weak Countries: Similarly, forfaitors generally do not come forward to undertake any forfait financing deal involving an importer from a financially weak country. Generally, the forfaitor has a full grasp of the financial and political situation prevailing in different countries, and hence, he would not accept a deal if the importer stays in a risky country. In exceptional cases, it can be undertaken at a higher price.

(iii) Dominance of Western Currencies: In International forfaiting, transactions are dominated in leading Western currencies like US Dollar, Pound Sterling, Euro, Canadian Dollars. Hence, our trade contracts have to be in foreign currencies rather than in Indian rupees.

(iv) Difficulty in Procuring International Bank's Guarantee: Forfaitors do not normally finance an export deal unless it is supported by an unconditional and irrevocable guarantee from an international bank known to the forfaitor. Generally, it is the duty of the exporter to procure a guarantee of this kind and it is a stupendous task for an exporter to do so.

6.4.3 Forfaiting in India

Forfaiting, as a source of finance, has gained substantial momentum abroad. Though it had its origin in 'Zurich', it has been well established in all the financial centres of the world. Some of the important forfaiting centres are London, Zurich, Hong Kong, Singapore and Frankfurt. It has become a popular source of finance among Europeans.

In India, forfaiting is slowly emerging as a new product in the liberalised financial market. It was approved by the Union Government only in January, 1994. The existing scheme available for exporters like concessional finance by commercial banks, insurance cover against export credit risks by ECGC, etc., are available mainly to large and well established exporters. In this context, forfaiting may be a real boon to the small, as well as, new exporters.

In India, forfaiting is done by the EXIM Bank. The minimum value of a forfaiting transaction is ₹ 5,00,000. A special form of promote/Bill has to be used for forfaiting transactions. An Indian exporter who wants to avail of this service has to approach the EXIM Bank through his bank. The EXIM Bank would obtain the forfaiting quotation from the forfaiting agency abroad. Based on this, the exporter would workout his price to be quoted to the importer. If the importer accepts the price and the payment terms, the contract would be finalised and executed. The exporter would then get cash through forfaiting arrangements for which he has to enter into a separate contract with the forfaitor through the EXIM Bank.

However, in order to encourage forfaiting finance business, it is necessary to designate export contracts in leading international currencies. In the wake of economic liberalisation and opening of our economy to the global market, there are good prospects for forfaiting business in India. To promote forfaiting business, it is essential that we should denominate our trade contracts in foreign currencies rather than in Indian rupees. Now, since the rupee has gained strength, it is time for us to denominate our trade obligations in foreign currencies so that the pace of forfaiting business may be accelerated mainly to boost our export trade.

6.5 SECURITISATION OF DEBT

The financial system all over the world is in the process of rapid transformation. As a result, the capital market, money market and the debt market are getting widened and deepened. It is interesting to note that new instruments and new products are emerging in the debt market too. In fact the development of a debt market increases the efficiency of a capital market to a greater extent. Again, along with the equity market, there is bound to be a natural growth in the debt market also. Thus, it is obvious that a debt market should also have both primary and secondary markets. In this context, debt or asset securitisation assumes a significant role and it is one of the most innovative techniques introduced in the debt market to achieve the above objective. Moreover, it is the debt market which has provided more impetus for capital formation than the equity market in the economically advanced countries.

❖ What is Securitisation?

Securitisation of debt or asset refers to the process of liquidating the illiquid and long-term assets like loans and receivables of financial institutions like banks by issuing marketable securities against them by any reconstruction company. In other words, it is a technique by which a long-term, non-negotiable and high valued financial asset like hire purchase is converted into securities of small values which can be tradable in the market just like shares.

Thus, it is nothing but a process of removing long-term assets from the balance sheet of a lending financial institution and replacing them with liquid cash through the issue of securities against them by any reconstruction company. Under securitisation, a financial institution pools its illiquid, non-negotiable and long-term assets, creates securities against them, gets them rated and sells them to investors. It is an ongoing process in the sense that assets are converted into securities, securities into cash, cash into assets and assets into securities and so on.

Generally, extension of credit by banks and other financial institutions in the form of bills purchase or discounting or hire purchase financing appears as an asset on their balance sheets. Some of these assets are long-term in nature and it implies that funds are locked up unnecessarily for an undue long period. So, to carry on their lending operations without much interruptions, they have to rely upon various other sources of finance which are not only costly but also not available easily. Again, they have to bear the risk of the credit outstandings. Now, securitisation is a ready-made solution for them. Securitisation helps them to recycle funds at a reasonable cost and with less credit risk. In other words, securitisation helps to remove these assets from the balance sheets of financial institutions by providing liquidity through tradable financial instruments.

Again from another angle also, securitisation is a boon to financial institutions. From the risk management point of view, the lending financial institutions have to absorb the entire credit risk by holding the credit outstandings in their own portfolio. Securitisation offers a good scope for risk diversification.

It is worthwhile to note that the entire transaction relating to securitisation is carried out on the asset side of the Balance Sheet. That is one asset (ill-liquid) is converted into another asset (cash).

As stated earlier, securitisation helps to liquify assets mainly of medium- and long-term loans and receivables of financial institutions. The concept of securitisation can be defined as follows:

"A carefully structured process whereby loans and other receivables are packaged, underwritten and sold in the form of asset backed securities."

Yet another simple definition is as follows:

"Securitisation is nothing but liquifying assets comprising loans and receivables of an institution through systematic issuance of financial instruments."

According to Hendersen, J. and Scott, J.P. "Securitisation is the process which takes when a lending institution's assets are removed in one way or another from the balance sheet of that lending institution and are funded instead, by investors who purchase a negotiable financial instrument evidencing this indebtedness without recourse, or in some cases with limited recourse, to the original lender". Thus, financial assets can be made liquid through securitisation, i.e., through packaging loans and selling them in the market. It is very clear from the above definitions that securitisation is nothing but the packaging of a pool of financial assets into marketable securities. In brief, ill-liquid assets are converted into tradable securities.

❖ Structured Securities Vs. Conventional Securities

Securitisation is basically a structured financial transaction. It envisages the issue of securities against ill-liquid assets and such securities are really structured securities. It is so because, they are backed by the value of the underlying financial asset and the credit support of a third party also. At this stage, one should not confuse such structured securities with conventional securities like bonds, debentures, etc. They differ from each other in the following respects.

(1) Source of Repayment: In the case of conventional securities, the primary source of repayment is the earning power and cash flow of the issuing company. But, under securitisation, the issuing company is completely free from this botheration since the burden of repayment is shifted to a pool of assets or to a third party.

(2) Structure: Under securitisation, the securities may be structured in such a way so as to achieve a desired level of risk and a desired level of rating depending upon the type and amount of assets pooled. Such a choice is not available in the case of conventional securities.

(3) Nature: In fact, these structured securities are basically derivatives of the traditional debt instruments. Of course, the credit standing of these securities is well supported by a pool of assets or by a guarantee or by both.

❖ Securitisation Vs. Factoring

At this stage, one should not confuse the term 'securitisation' with that of 'factoring'. Since both deal with the assets, *viz.*, book debts and receivables. it is very essential that the differences between them must be clearly understood. The main differences are:

(*i*) Factoring is mainly associated with the assets (book debts and receivables) of manufacturing and trading companies, whereas securitisation is mainly associated with the assets of financial companies.

(*ii*) Factoring mainly deals with trade debts and trade receivables of clients. On the other hand, securitisation deals with loans and receivables arising out of loans like Hire purchase finance receivables, receivables from Government departments, etc.

(*iii*) In the case of factoring, the trade debts and receivables in questions are short-term in nature, whereas they are medium-term or long-term in nature in the case of securitisation.

(*iv*) The question of issuing securities against book debts does not arise at all in the case of factoring, whereas it forms the very basis of securitisation.

(*v*) The factor himself takes up the 'collection work', whereas it can be done either by the originator or by a separate servicing agency under securitisation.

(*vi*) Under factoring, the entire credit risk is passed on to the factor. But under securitisation, a part of the credit risk can be absorbed by the originator by transferring the assets at a discount.

6.5.1 Modus Operandi of Securitisation

For the operational mechanics of securitisation, the following parties are required:

(*i*) The originator

(*ii*) A Special Purpose Vehicle (SPV) or a trust

(*iii*) A merchant or investment banker

(*iv*) A credit rating agency

(*v*) A servicing agent — Receiving and Paying Agent (RPA)

(*vi*) The original borrowers or obligors

(*vii*) The prospective investors, i.e., the buyers of securities.

The various stages involved in the working of securitisation are as follows:

1. Identification stage/process
2. Transfer stage/process
3. Issue stage/process
4. Redemption stage/process
5. Credit rating stage/process

❖ Identification Process

The lending financial institution either a bank or any other institution for that matter which decides to go in for securitisation of its assets is called the 'originator'. The originator might have got assets comprising of a variety of receivables like commercial mortgages, lease receivables, hire purchase receivables, etc. The originator has to pick-up a pool of assets of homogeneous nature, considering the maturities, interest rates involved, frequency of repayments and marketability. This process of selecting a pool of loans and receivables from the asset portfolios for securitisation is called 'identification process'.

❖ Transfer Process

After the identification process is over, the selected pool of assets are then "passed through" to another institution which is ready to help the originator to convert those pools of assets into securities. This institution is called the special purpose vehicle (SPV) or the trust. The pass through transaction between the originator and the SPV is either by way of outright sale, i.e., full transfer of assets in question for valuable consideration or by passing them for a collateralised loan. Generally, it is done on an outright sale basis. This process of passing through the selected pool of assets by the originator to a SPV is called transfer process and once this transfer process is over, the assets are removed from the balance sheet of the originator.

❖ Issue Process

After this transfer process is over, the SPV takes up the onerous task of converting these assets of various types of different maturities. It is on this basis, the SPV issues securities to investors. The SPV actually splits the package into individual securities of smaller values and they are sold to the investing public. The SPV gets itself reimbursed out of the sale proceeds. The securities issued by the SPV is called by different names like 'Pay through Certificates', 'Pass through Certificates'. Interest only Certificates, Principal only Certificates, etc. The securities are structured in such a way that the maturity of these securities may synchronise with the maturities of the securitised loans or receivables.

❖ Redemption Process

The redemption and payments of interest on these securities are facilitated by the collections received by the SPV from the securitised assets. The task of collection of dues is generally entrusted to the originator or a special servicing agent can be appointed for this purpose. This agency is paid a certain percentage of commission for the collection services rendered. The servicing agent is responsible for collecting the principal and interest payments on assets pooled when due and he must pay a special attention to delinquent accounts. Usually, the originator is appointed as the servicer. Thus, under securitisation, the role of the originator gets reduced to that of a collection agent on behalf of the SPV, in case he is appointed as a collection agent. A pass through certificate may be either 'with recourse' to the originator or 'without recourse'. The usual practice is to make it 'without recourse'. Hence, the holder of a pass through certificate has to look to the SPV for payment of the principal and interest on the certificates held by him. Thus, the main task of the SPV is to structure the deal, raise proceeds by issuing pass through certificates and arrange for payment of interest and principal to the investors.

❖ Credit Rating Process

Since the pass through certificates have to be publicly issued, they require credit rating by a good credit rating agency so that they become more attractive and easily acceptable. Hence, these certificates are rated at least by one credit rating agency on the eve of the securitisation. The issues could also be guaranteed by external guarantor institutions like merchant bankers which would enhance the creditworthiness of the certificates and would be readily acceptable to investors. Of course, this rating guarantee provides a sense of confidence to the investor with regard to the timely payment of principal and interest by the SPV.

Pass through certificates, like debentures, directly reflect the ownership rights in the assets securitised, their repayment schedule, interest rate, etc. These certificates, before maturity, are tradable in a secondary market to ensure liquidity for the investors. They are negotiable securities and hence they can be easily tradable in the market.

❖ Role of Merchant Bankers

Merchant or investment bankers can playa big role in asset securitisation. They generally act as Special Purpose Vehicle. There are many issues involved in securitisation namely the timing of the issue of pass through certificates, pricing of these certificates for marketing and above all underwriting of these issues. In private placement, they act as agents for the issuer connecting the sellers and buyers. They can also involve in structuring the issue to see that the issue meets all legal, regulatory, accounting, tax and other requirements. In all these aspects, merchant bankers have a definite role to play. The mere fact that an issue has been underwritten by a popular merchant banker will add credit to that issue and it would become more attractive from the investor's point of view. Thus, securitisation enlarges the activities of the merchant bankers too.

❖ Role of Other Parties

The other parties in the game of securitisation are the original borrowers and the prospective investors. The original borrowers refer to those who have availed of the loan facilities from the lending institution, i.e., the originator. They are also called obligors. In fact the success of the securitisation process depends upon these original borrowers. If they fail to meet their commitments on the due dates, the securitisation process will be at danger. In fact the receipts of cash flows from the original borrowers are passed through to the investors. The prospective investors are nothing but the public at large who are willing to purchase the pass through certificates.

6.5.2 Structure for Securitisation/Types of Securitisation

Securitisation is a structured transaction, whereby the originator transfers or sells some of its assets to a SPY which breaks these assets into tradable securities of smaller values which could be sold to the investing public. The appropriate structure for securitisation depends on a variety of factors like quality of assets securitised, default experience of original borrowers, amount of amortisation at maturity, financial reputation and soundness of the originator, etc. The general principle is that the securities must be structured in such a way that the maturity of these securities may coincide with the maturity of the securitised loans. However, there are three important types of securities as listed below:

(*i*) Pass through and pay through certificates,

(*ii*) Preferred stock certificates, and

(*iii*) Asset based commercial papers.

(i) Pass through and Pay through Certificates

In the case of pass through certificates, payments to investors depend upon the cash flow from the assets backing such certificates. In other words, as and when cash (principal and interest) is received from the original borrower by the SPV, it is passed on to the holders of certificates at regular intervals and the entire principal is returned with the retirement of the assets packed in the pool. Thus, pass through certificates have a single maturity structure and the tenure of these certificates is matched with the life of the securitised assets.

On the other hand, pay through certificates have a multiple maturity structure depending upon the maturity pattern of underlying assets. Thus, two or three types of securities with different maturity patterns like short-term, medium-term and long-term may be issued. The greatest advantage is that they can be issued depending upon the investor's demand for varying maturity patterns. This type is more attractive from the investor's point of view because the yield is often inbuilt in the price of the securities themselves, i.e., they are offered at a discount to face value as in the case of deep-discount bonds.

(ii) Preferred Stock Certificates

Preferred stocks are instruments issued by a subsidiary company against the trade debts and consumer receivables of its parent company. In other words, subsidiary companies buy the trade debts and receivables of parent companies, convert them into short-term securities, and help the parent companies to enjoy liquidity. Thus, trade debts can also be securitised through the issue of preferred stocks. Generally, these stocks are backed by guarantees given by highly rated merchant banks and hence they are also attractive from the investor's point of view. These instruments are mostly short-term in nature.

(iii) Asset-based Commercial Papers

This type of structure is mostly prevalent in mortgage backed securities. Under this type, the SPY purchases portfolio of mortgages from different sources (various lending institutions) and they are combined into a single group on the basis of interest rates, maturity dates and underlying collaterals. They are, then, transferred to a Trust which, in turn, issues mortgage backed certificates to the investors. These certificates are issued against the combined principal value of the mortgages and they are also short-term instruments. Each certificate holder is entitled to participate in the cash flow from underlying mortgages to the extent of his investments in the certificates.

❖ Other Types

Apart from the above, there are also other types of certificates namely:

(*i*) Interest only certificates, and

(*ii*) Principal only certificates.

In the case of Interest only Certificates, payments are made to investors only from the interest incomes earned from the assets securitised. As the very name suggests, payments are made to investors only from the repayment of principal by the original borrowers, in the case of principal only certificates. These certificates enable speculative dealings since the speculators know well that the interest rate movements would affect the bond values immediately. For instance, the principal only certificates would increase in value when interest rates go down. It is so because, it becomes advantageous to repay the existing debts and resort to fresh borrowings at lower cost. This early redemption of securities would benefit the investors to a greater extent. Similarly, when the interest rates go up, interest only certificate holders stand to gain since more interest would be available from the underlying assets. One cannot exactly predict the future movements of interest, and hence, these certificates give much scope for speculators to play their game.

Thus, securitisation offers much scope for the introduction of newer and newer instruments so as to meet the varying requirements of investors. Debt securitisation offers a variety of investment instruments to the investing public at large as well as to the financial intermediaries like mutual funds, insurance companies, etc.

❖ Securitisable Assets

As stated earlier, all assets are not suitable for securitisation. For instance, trade debts and receivables are not generally suitable for securitisation, whereas they are readily acceptable to a factor. Only in rare cases, they are securitised. Example: Preferred Stock Certificates.

The following assets are generally securitised by financial institutions:

(*i*) Term loans to financially reputed companies

(*ii*) Receivables from Government Departments and Companies

(*iii*) Credit card receivables

(*iv*) Hire purchase loans like vehicle loans

(*v*) Lease Finance

(*vi*) Mortgage Loans, etc.

6.5.3 Benefits of Securitisation

Debt securitisation provides many benefits to all the parties, such as, the originator, investors and the regulatory authorities. Some of the important benefits are the following:

(i) Additional Source of Fund: The originator (i.e., the lending institution) is much benefitted because securitisation provides an additional source of funds by converting an otherwise illiquid asset into ready liquidity. As a result, there is an immediate improvement in the cash flow of the originator. Thus, it acts as a source of liquidity.

(ii) Greater Profitability: Securitisation helps financial institutions to get liquid cash from medium-term and long-term assets immediately rather than over a longer period. It leads to greater recycling of funds which, in turn, leads to higher business turnover and profitability. Again, the cash flow could be recycled for investment in higher yielding assets. This means greater profitability. Moreover, economies of scale can be achieved since securitisation offers scope for the fuller utilisation of the existing capabilities by providing liquid cash immediately. It results in additional business turnover.

Again, the originator can also act as the Receiving and Paying agent. If so, it gets additional income in the form of servicing fee.

(iii) Enhancement of Capital Adequacy Ratio: Securitisation enables financial institutions to enhance their capital adequacy ratio by reducing their assets volume. The process of securitisation necessitates the selection of a pool of assets by the financial institutions to be sold or transferred to another institution called SPV. Once the assets are transferred, they are removed from the balance sheet of the originator. It results in the reduction of assets volume, thereby increasing the capital adequacy ratio. Capital adequacy ratio can also be improved by replacing the loan assets with the lesser risk weighted assets. Thus, the removal of assets from the balance sheet under a true sale improves the capital adequacy norms.

(iv) Spreading of Credit Risk: Securitisation facilitates the spreading of credit risk to different parties involved in the process of securitisation. In the absence of securitisation, the entire credit risk associated with a particular financial transaction has to be borne by the originator himself. Now, the originator is able to diversify the risk factors among the various parties involved in securitisation. Thus, securitisation helps to achieve diversification of credit risks which are greater in the case of medium-term and long-term loans. Thus, it is used as tool for risk management.

(v) Lower Cost of Funding: In view of enhancement of cash flows and diversification of risk factors, securitisation enables the originator to have an easy access to the securities market at debt ratings higher than its overall corporate rating. It means that companies with low credit rating can issue asset backed securities at lower interest cost due to high credit rating on such securities. This helps it to secure funds at lower cost. Moreover, the criteria for choosing the pool of assets ensures an efficient cost of funds. In the present context of scarcity of funds and higher interest rates, securitisation provides a good scope for cheap funding.

(vi) Provision of Multiple Instruments: From the investor's point of view, securitisation provides multiple new investment instruments so as to meet the varying requirements of the investing public. It also offers varieties of instruments for other financial intermediaries like mutual funds, insurance companies, pension funds, etc., giving them many choices.

(vii) Higher Rate of Return: When compared to traditional debt securities like bonds and debentures, securitised securities offer better rate of return along with better liquidity. These instruments are rated by good credit rating agencies and hence more attractive. Being structured assets based securities, they offer more protection and yield a good return. The bankruptcy/winding up of the originator does not affect the investors since the payment is guaranteed by the SPV.

(viii) Prevention of Idle Capital: In the absence of securitisation, capital would remain idle in the form of ill-liquid assets like mortgages, term loans, etc., in many of the lending institutions. Now, securitisation helps recycling of funds by converting these assets into liquidity, liquidity into assets, assets into liquidity and so on by means of issuing tradable and transferable securities against these assets. Thus, it provides impetus for capital formation.

(ix) Better than Traditional Instruments: Certificates are issued to investors against the backing of assets securitised. The underlying assets are used not only as a collateral to the certificates but also to generate the income to pay the principal and interest to the investors. It does not entail any servicing needs and hence does not require much costs. It is better than even mutual fund units because it is issued against the backing of collateral securities, whereas there is no such backing for mutual fund certificates. Thus, these instruments, being structured asset backed securities, afford a greater protection to investors.

Again, there is much transparency from the investor's point of view. They can very well see the collateral pool that a particular issue represents and this transparency reduces uncertainty as to the risk element.

(x) Other Benefits: Securitisation, if carried out in true spirit, leads to greater economy in the use of capital with efficiency and cost-effectiveness in both funding and lending. This is a great boon to the regulating authorities as well since their primary objective is to prevent the accumulation of capital where it is not needed.

In the long-run, it is beneficial to the borrowers also. They will be able to get funds at cheaper rates since the originators are likely to pass on the benefit to the ultimate borrowers. There is no doubt that securitisation is a low cost and innovative funding source ensuring economy in the use of capital.

6.5.4 Securitisation and Banks

There is a vast scope for commercial banks to go in for securitisation due to the following factors:

(i) Innovative and Low Cost Source of Fund: Traditionally deposit has been the only dependable source of funds for banks over the years. But, in recent times, banks have to face severe competition from other non-banking institutions in deposit mobilisation. Now, securitisation offers an excellent source of funds at cheaper rates. Unlike deposits, it will not entail any servicing needs and the consequent increase in costs.

(ii) Better Capital Adequacy Norms: Securitisation has the effect of improving the capital adequacy norms of banks. Generally, commercial firms utilise the cash flow from securitisation for repayment of their borrowings, and thus, they can achieve a good debt-equity ratio. But, in the case of banks, borrowings are limited. So, they can better utilise the cash flow to create lower risk weighted assets. Hence, high risk weighted assets can be easily converted into lower risk weighted assets. Thus, it helps banks to achieve better capital adequacy norms.

(iii) Creation of More Credit: In India, banks are subject to high statutory pre-emptions for which more liquid cash is essential now and then. This has necessarily impaired the capacity of banks to create credit. In fact, securitisation is not at all affected by these factors. The cash flow from securitisation could be very well used for further expansion of credit without any statutory restrictions.

(iv) Increased Profitability: The profitability of banks has been very much affected to a greater extent in these days due to many factors. In this context, securitisation has a salutary impact on the profitability of banks. It provides for more liquidity, quicker recycling of funds and greater economy in the use of capital. This has the effect of improving the profitability of banks. Besides, they can also earn income in the form of service fee by acting as Receiving and Paying agent.

(v) Tool for Asset-liability Management and Risk Management: Securitisation can be better used as a tool to avoid mismatch in the asset-liability management. It would reduce the overdependence of banks on the market for money at call and short notice as well as the refinancing agencies for recycling of funds. Again, it can be used as a risk management tool also. It completely eliminates the interest risks and thus it provides a hedge to banks against interest risks which are inherent in the free interest rate market.

❖ Conditions for Successful Securitisation

If securitisation of debt has to be successful, the following conditions must have been fulfilled.

(*i*) Ultimately, the success of securitisation depends upon the ability of the original borrower to repay his loan. Therefore, selection of assets to be securitised requires utmost care. The assets should be ranked and selected on the basis of least losses and to provide for maximum protection to the investor.

(*ii*) The credit rating is an integral part of securitisation. Hence, credit rating must be done by credit rating agencies on a scientific basis and the ratings should be unquestionable. Then only, the prospective investor's confidence can be built. The credit rating agencies should take into account the various types of risks such as credit risk, interest risk, liquidity risk, etc., along with other usual factors.

(*iii*) The SPV should be a separate organisation from that of the originator. It should be completely insulated from the parent corporate entity so that SPV could be protected from the danger of bankruptcy.

(*iv*) The pass through certificates or any other similar instruments arising out of securitisation must be listed in stock exchanges so that they may be readily acceptable to investors. It would provide instant liquidity and moreover, its price could also be easily ascertained.

(*v*) Alternatively, it is also advisable to provide two-way quotations for facilitating the buying and selling of the pass through certificates in the market as in the case of mutual fund units.

(*vi*) There must be standardised loan documentation for similar loans so that there may be uniformity between different financial institutions. It must carry a right to assign debts to third parties, so that, it could be sold or transferred to the SPV.

(*vii*) There should be a proper accounting treatment for the various transactions involved in asset securitisation. Suitable accounting norms for the recognisation of the trust created for securitised debt should be evolved. The accounting system should provide for the removal of the securitised assets from the balance sheet of the originator. Only then, the real benefit will go to the originator.

(*viii*) Above all, there should be proper and adequate guidelines given by the regulatory authorities dealing with the various aspects of the process of securitisation.

6.5.5 Securitisation Abroad

The credit of introducing the concept of securitisation goes to America where the first structured asset securitised financing came into being in 1970. In 1970, the newly created Government National Mortgage Association (Ginnie Mae) began its operations by publicly trading in securities, backed by a pool of mortgage loans. It was followed by Federal National Mortgage Association and similar organisations. These organisations bought residential mortgage loans, made pools out of them and issued mortgage-backed securities against them. The payment of principal and interest of these instruments was also guaranteed. The securities issued by it were called "Mortgage pass through securities". A pool of mortgages was created by putting together assets that had similar characteristics in terms of duration, interest rate and quality. The pool was then placed with a trust which actually sold the certificates drawn against such mortgages to the investors either directly or through private placement. Thus, the concept of securitisation was confined to mortgages only.

However, in March 1985, non-mortgage collaterals started getting securitised in the USA. For instance, the first offering of 192 million of lease backed certificates for Sperry Lease Finance Corporation was underwritten by The First Boston. Now it has become a popular mode of financing in America. It is slowly becoming a global phenomenon covering transactions relating to various modes of finance.

Securitisation is gaining popularity in UK also in recent years only. Like America, this concept started with mortgage securitisation. The Bank America Finance Ltd., UK issued mortgage securities in January, 1985 against the residential property mortgages as underlying assets. The first mortgage securitisation issue for the international market arranged was MINI in London in 1985. Now, clearing banks and building societies have entered into this market under the supervision of the Bank of England. Securitisation of debt and the consequent debt instruments are now popular in countries like Italy, Australia, Canada, France, Spain, and Japan. In many of these countries, the process of securitisation has been encouraged by passing suitable legislations.

6.5.6 Securitisation In India

The concept of asset securitisation is slowly entering into the Indian soil. Financial institutions have not yet come forward to make use of this avenue for financing on a large-scale. However, there is a tardy movement of the financial institutions in resorting to this mode of financing. The securitisation of the ICICI's receivables by the Citibank in February 1991 is the first attempt in this direction. A sum of ₹ 15 crore was raised by means of securitisation of assets. Following this, the Hire purchase portfolio of TELCO was securitised by the Citibank. Again, the Retail Residential Receivables of DLF International were also securitised by the Citibank in June 1992. The Citibank's own portfolio of "Citimobile Scheme" was subject to securitisation. In fact the Citibank has pioneered this trend in India. Now, the HDFC has taken up this route along with the Citibank. The HDFC securitised its housing loan portfolio around ₹ 50 crore. Infrastructure Leasing and Financial services is also expected to enter into this field by setting up a SPV. If securitisation has to become popular in India, the commercial banks should enter into this field in a big way. In fact, the commercial banks can remove the non-performing assets from their balance sheet by resorting to this technique. At the same time, they can recycle the funds for greater profitability. If financial institutions have to meet their ever-increasing capital requirements, securitisation would go a long way in mobilising adequate resources. Earlier in 1994-95, SBI Cap structured an innovative deal where a pool of future cash flaws of high value customers of Rajasthan State Industrial and Development Corporation was securitised. An oil monetisation deal was structured where the future flows of oil receivables accruing to a company was securitised. Real estate developers have securitised receivables arising out of instalment sales. The recent securitisation deal of Larsen & Toubro opened a new vista for financing power projects. The deal was a securitisation of lease receivables even before the plant was completed. Thus, this securitisation deal financed even the asset creation.

The ICICI had securitised assets to the tune of ₹ 2,750 crore in its books at the end of 31-3-1999. Assets to the tune of ₹ 1,200 crore is in the process of being bought over CRISIL is reported to have rated about ₹ 200 crore of securitised transactions up to 1998 (***Source:*** RBI monthly Bulletin, May 1999).

Towards the end of August 2002, IDBI had floated a securitised product to raise resources by transferring loan assets of L&T and Natural Hydroelectric Power Corporation to a special purpose vehicle (SPV), SBI Capital Markets was appointed as an advisor for the ₹ 265 crore Issue. Since IDBI was finding tough to raise resources through the bond market due to its poor rating and lack of appetite for IDBI paper among investors, it thought it proper to sell the loan assets to SBI Capital Markets which enjoyed credit rating of AA+ from CRISIL as against the AA rating of IDBI. In October 2002, Reliance Industries approached the LIC for mopping up about ₹ 1,500 crore through a securitisation deal. The India's largest private sector company would raise the fund against energy receivables or cash flows from the *Panna Mukta* and Tapi oil and Gas Fields.

Securitisation is the process of acquisition of large Non-performing Assets (NPAs) loan or portfolio of loans such as housing by Securitisation or Reconstruction Company from a bank or financial institution on mutually agreed terms and conditions, i.e., the sale or transfer price, *with or without recourses* transfer/sale, etc. The SCRC transfers the acquired loans to a SPV set up by it that manages the assets for the purpose of realisation or holds them as investments till maturity. The SPV issues the consideration of transfer price to the originator bank in the form of cash or debentures/bonds as mutually agreed. To provide banks and financial institutions a summary procedure for recovery of their secured dues which have been classified as NPA on their books, and also for setting up of Securitisation Company Reconstruction Company (SCRC) for taking over the defaulted loans of banks and financial institutions and recovery thereof. Parliament passed the Securitisation and Reconstruction of Financial Assets and Enforcement of Security Interest Act SRFAESI and enacted the Act with effect from 21-06-2002.

The Act deals with 3 aspects.

1. Enforcement of security interest by secured creditor (Banks/financial institutions)
2. Transfer of NPA to Securitisation Company or Reconstruction Company (SCRC) which will then dispose of those assets and realise the proceeds.
3. To provide a legal framework for securitisation of asset.

SCRC can either *Finance* the acquisition from their own resources or raise resources from Qualified Institutional Buyers (QIB) by securitising the financial assets and issuing them security receipts as per mutually agreed terms and on assessment of risks involved. The guidelines for acquisitions have been prescribed by RBI.

❖ Exclusions

The provisions of the Act shall not apply to the following:

(*i*) A lien on any goods/money or security given by or under the Indian Contract Act, 1872 or the Sale of Goods Act or any other law for the time-being in India.

(*ii*) A pledge of movables within the meaning of Section 172 of Indian Contract Act.

(*iii*) Creation of any security in any aircraft as defined u/s 2(1) of Aircraft Act.

(*iv*) Creation of any security interest in any vessel as defined in Section 3(5) of Merchant Shipping Act.

(*v*) Any conditional sale/hire purchase/or lease or any other contract *in which No security interest has been created.*

(*vi*) Any right of Unpaid Seller u/s 47 of Sale of Goods Act.

(*vii*) Any properties *Not liable to Attachment* or Sale under first provision to Section 60(1) of Code of Civil Procedure.

(*viii*) Any *security interest creating in Agricultural land.*

(*ix*) Any case in which the amount due to *less than* 20% of the principal amount and interest thereon, i.e., where borrower has *repaid more than 80% of principal amount and interest.*

❖ Measures of Asset Reconstruction

A SCRC may, for the purpose of asset reconstruction, with regards to the guidelines formed by RBI, provide for any one or more of the following measures.

- Proper management of the business of borrower by *change in, or takeover* of the business of the borrower.
- The *sale* or *lease* of a part or whole of the *Business* of the *Borrower.*

- Rescheduling of payment of debts payable by the borrower.
- Enforcement of security interest in accordance with the provisions of this Act.
- *Settlement of Dues* payable by the borrower.
- *Taking possession of secured assets* in accordance with the provisions of this Act.

6.5.7 Norms for Sale of Financial Assets by Banks/Financial Institutions

RBI has laid down guidelines, to be followed by Banks or FIs, for sale of financial assets. These guidelines are as follows:

1. Setting up of a system for *Sale/Valuation* and *Pricing*.
2. Setting up valuation/capital adequacy/exposure and disclosure requirements.
3. Any NPA, including a Non-performing Bond/Debenture, can be sold.
4. Bonds or debentures offered by SCRC should ensure as follows:
    - Securities must not have a term in excess of six years.
    - Interest on securities should not be less than 1.5% above the bank rate (present bank rate is 6% since 2003). Hence interest should be 7.5%.
    - It should be secured by an appropriate charge on the assets transferred.
    - Full or part payment to be given in the event the SCRC sells the assets before maturity.
    - Commitment to redeem securities must be unconditional.
    - Notice of transfer of security should be issued to the SCRC.

6.5.8 Incentives and Benefits for Asset Securitisation

The main benefit from asset securitisation is that it enables banks to pass the risks of lending on to other parties, this freeing capital resources to back new lending which would other wise beyond their capacity. The funding and liquidity benefits of the securitisation process derive from the conversion of illiquid assets into liquid funds available for additional lending. Because of the credit enhancements, the rating of asset backed securities is often higher than that of the originator who is therefore able to tap funding sources not normally accessible to him. Asset securitisation also helps banks in their asset and liability management. Passing it on to the investors can reduce interest rate risk, a bank wishing to extend its lending but not having funds of adequate maturity can *Avoid a Maturity Mismatch* by securitising the new loans. Securitisation offers a bank, which is heavily exposed to a particular region or economic sector an ability to transfer part of its loan portfolio and also to purchase with the proceeds other types of ABS (asset bank securities) thus achieving a more diversified loan portfolio. Banks engaging in one or more of the securitisation roles, such as lender/service provider/trustee or enhancer/can increase and diversify their sources of fee and interest income. By transferring assets banks can contribute their existing types of lending or invest the proceeds in other lines of business and avoid concentration in a single type of credit risk. Asset securitisation can also have important benefits for borrowers. Since such securitisation generally helps to improve the liquidity of credit markets. It can increase the availability of credit to borrowers and can allows borrowers to obtain funds at a lower cost.

❖ Offences and Penalties

According to Section 27, if a default is made —

(*i*) in filing under Section 23, the particulars of every transaction of any securitisation or asset reconstruction or security interest created by a securitisation company or reconstruction company or secured creditor, or

(*ii*) in sending under Section 24, the particulars of the modification referred to in that section, or

(*iii*) in giving intimation under Section 25. Every company and every officer of the company or the secured creditor.

6.5.9 The Economic Logic of Securitisation

Why are so many organisations going through so much trouble (and cost) to securitise their portfolios? Simply because the benefits accruing from it merit the efforts. Chief among these are —

❖ Capital Relief

Financial institutions have to maintain mandatory capital adequacy ratio. As asset portfolios grow, the CAR requirements force FIs to increase capital via either additional equity infusion (which may dilute share price, limit future investments, etc.), or additional debt (worsens leverage, increases cost, etc.), both of which may often be undesirable. Securitisation often offers the ideal alternative by removing the assets from the FIs balance sheet, and reducing capital requirement.

❖ Cheap, Off-balance Sheet Financing

Upon securitisation, organisations unlock the value of the transferred portfolio in the form of the further in asset creating activities. Further, the rating of PTCs can often be superior to that of the originator (rating is for a selected asset portfolio and not the entire business and also. Key risks like prepayment or concentration risks get reallocated) which permits it to raise funds from investors, via. securitisation at lower rates than from corporate debt.

❖ Balance Sheet Management

Depending upon corporate capital structure strategy, securitisation leads to improved financial ratios (like debt-equity) and also smaller, leaner and better managed balance sheets.

❖ NPA Management

Securitisation deals can also be used by banks to transfer their NPA to specialized Asset Reconstruction Companies (ARCs — 13 ARCs in India at the end of year 2010 and ARCIL is the first company and largest shares in business) who either manage these portfolios using specialised expertise or aggregate and restructure these loans to sell them to other buyers as PTCs, freeing up the balance sheets of banks and allowing them to focus on core banking activities.

Within Asia, India, Japan and South Korea are the major players of securitisation, with South Korea and India being the first movers among the rest of Asia. In 2004, India was one of the leading securitisation issuance nations in the Asian Region. The financial year 2005, has also witnessed the securitisation of new assets, namely used vehicle loan (cars or motor cycles) and two-wheeler loan portfolios, in addition to increased activity on the traditional asset classes.

In India, two sectors are the principal beneficiaries of securitisation — banking and the infrastructure sector.

1. *Bank credit* grows faster than deposits.
2. Banks are capital starved and are expected to require ₹ 600 billion over the next few years.
3. Basel II compliance by 2007 and with it more stringent norms on capital adequacy would apply. Banks must sell off their portfolio of bad-loans to ARC to free up their balance sheets and focus on their core banking activities. Recent development like the Government of India's decision to permit 49% FDI in ARCs would widen the market and appetite for such loans.
4. *For infrastructure* sector the stumbling blocks are:
   (*a*) *Small investor Base:* The market for securitisation is rather shallow and shackled by small investors. The only ARC in India at present is *Arcil.*
   (*b*) *Double taxation* — which escalate the cost of the structure and may lend a shade of uncertainty to the process and every officer of the secured creditor who is in default shall be punishable with fine which may extend to ₹ 5,000 for every day, during which the default continues. The provisions of SRFAESI Act, 2002 do not apply when the amount of secured loan does not exceed ₹ One lakh and unsecured dues ₹ 10 lakh.

❖ Asia's 75% Securitised Floats in India

India has emerged as the largest issuer of securitised products in the year 2007 with a market share of 75% in Asia and accounting for one-third of the global emerging markets issuances. This was indicated in a report issued by international rating agency Moody's Investor Service on securitisation in emerging markets.

Moody's had pointed out that despite the US sub-prime crisis, the global volume of securitisation in new markets increased by 23% to $46.6 billion in 2007 from $38 billion in 2006. The new markets include Russia, Turkey, Middle East, central and eastern Europe, Brazil, Mexico and Argentina.

However, growth was not equally distributed across regions. For instance, the new securitisation markets within the Europe, Middle East and Africa (EMEA) region recorded a 23% year-on-year decline.

The emerging markets in Asia saw 68% rise to $19.8 bn. with growth driven mainly from India which accounted for 75% of volumes in Asia or transactions valuing $14.8 bn. Moody's had taken India, China (excluding Hong Kong), Malaysia, Thailand and Indonesia as emerging markets. India saw about 400 transactions, with average issue size of $36 million.

Malaysian issuance ranked second (11% of the region's total), with one-third of this issuance being Sukuk transactions. However, activity decreased in China and Thailand while Indonesia recorded no new transactions. Sukuk (or Islamic bonds) are the fastest-growing segment of the market and have seen phenomenal growth in the past six years. By 2007, Sukuk global volumes had reached $97.3 billion, with the majority coming from Malaysia and the Arabian Gulf.

In terms of asset classes, collaterlised debt obligation, single-loan collaterlised loan obligation and asset backed securities dominated the market, accounting for a combined 86%.

Moody's feel that in 2008, issuance volumes may be constrained by the fragile state of global capital markets and with cross-border issuance in particular likely to decrease significantly. At the same time it is likely many more countries may get active in securitisation and the further diversification of asset classes into CDOs, auto loans, leases and commercial mortgage backed loans may take place.

Several other factors may mitigate the negative impact of credit crisis such as large pipeline of deals that were postponed during second half of 2007. Also, legal improvements regarding securitisation in countries like Turkey, Russia, Ukraine, Poland and India. Further securitisation can also get a boost if the portfolio from emerging market performance well and if they offer attractive high yields on emerging market bonds.

RACING AHEAD
75% INDIA'S SHARE IN ASIA ISSUES
14.8 TOTAL VALUE IN BILLION DOLLARS
400 TOTAL NUMBER OF TRANSACTIONS
36 AVERAGE DEAL SIZE IN MILLION DOLLARS

6.6 VENTURE CAPITAL

Venture capital is a growing business of recent origin in the area of industrial financing in India. The various financial institutions set-up in India to promote industries have done commendable work. However, these institutions do not come up to the benefit of risky ventures when they are undertaken by new or relatively unknown entrepreneurs. They contend to give debt finance, mostly in the form of term loans to the promoters and their functioning has been more akin to that of commercial banks. The financial institutions have devised schemes such as seed capital scheme, Risk capital Fund, etc., to help new entrepreneurs. However, to evaluate the projects and extend financial assistance they follow the criteria such as safety, security, liquidity and profitability and not potentiality. The capital market with its conventional financial instruments/ schemes does not come much to the benefit or risky venture. New institutions such as mutual funds, leasing and hire purchase company's have been established as another source of finance to industries. These institutions also do not mitigate the problems of new entrepreneurs who undertake risky and innovative ventures.

India is poised for a technological revolution with the emergence of new breed of entrepreneurs with required professional temperament and technical know-how. To make the innovative technology of the entrepreneurs a successful business venture, support in all respects and more particularly in the form of financial assistance is all the more essential. This has necessitated the setting up of venture capital financing Division/companies during the latter part of eighties.

6.6.1 Concept of Venture Capital

The term 'Venture Capital' is understood in many ways. In a narrow sense, it refers to, investment in new and tried enterprises that are lacking a stable record of growth.

In a broader sense, venture capital refers to the commitment of capital as shareholding, for the formulation and setting up of small firms specialising in new ideas or new technologies. It is not merely an injection of funds into a new firm, it is a simultaneous input of skill needed to set up the firm, design its marketing strategy and organise and manage it. It is an association with successive stages of firm's development with distinctive types of financing appropriate to each stage of development.

❖ Venture Capital Overview

Venture Capital is a financial innovation of 20th century. It is generally synonymous with high risk capital. It is often considered as financing start-up ventures of new and young enterprises seeking to grow rapidly. There is also a popular misconception that high technology is the principal driving force behind the investment decisions of the venture capitalists. There is no doubt that high-tech companies who are not in a position to offer suitable collateral for securing capital from conventional sources would approach venture capitalist for funding.

❖ Key Factors Determining Venture Capital

- It is an investment in the form of equity, quasi-equity and sometimes debt.
- It is an investment made in new untried technology or high risk venture promoted by a technically or professionally qualified entrepreneur.
- The enterprise expects to have a very high growth rate.
- The venture capitalist provides management and business skills to enterprise.
- The venture capitalist does not expect any collateral to cover the capital provided.

❖ Small Business Dilemma

Small business especially trying out a new idea requires support in the early stages. Venture capital is risk money. Banks make loans where the risk of loss is negligible. In the absence of venture capital, the entrepreneur is left with no alternative but to approach individual or family members for capital. This source of funding may prove dangerous for the entrepreneur as the individual investor's approach may be unprofessional. Further investor's objective may be to own the business which may be detrimental to the interest of the investee firm.

❖ Venture Capital Mantra

The venture capitalist operates on the principle "I'll back you if you have a good idea that will make money for both of us". The venture capitalist must be convinced that the firm and its management team can make the idea happen and make money doing it. The investee therefore has to perform the most difficult task of explaining why the firm and its team are the ones who can make it all happen.

6.6.2 Stages in Venture Financing

1. **Early Stage Financing:**
   - Seed financing for supporting a concept or idea.
   - R&D financing for product development.
   - Start-up capital for initiating the operations and developing prototype.
   - First Stage financing for full-scale production and marketing.
2. **Expansion Financing:**
   - Second stage financing for working capital and initial expansion while the company may be operating at a loss.
   - Development financing for major expansion and the company may have started operating at a profit.
   - Bridge or Mezzanine financing for facilitating public issue.
3. **Acquisition/Buyout Financing:**
   - Acquisition financing for acquiring another firm for further growth.
   - Management buyout financing for enabling operating group to acquire firm or part of its business.
   - Turnaround financing for turning around a sick unit.

❖ Major Task before Venture Funds

- Building the investor group
- Reviewing and helping to formulate business strategy
- Filling in the management team

Venture capitalists generally keep in constant touch with the assisted companies. They monitor their performance and activities on a regular basis. They become more involved in enterprises which are not able to perform satisfactorily. They form part of the management team and provide valuable support to the investee companies.

❖ Financing Technology Oriented Firms

Most developing countries, India being no exception, have followed the strategy of importing foreign technology in a regulated manner for promoting technological development. Technology transfer is considered essential for the economic development of a country. The office of Technology Assessment (OTA) of the USA has identified twelve emerging technologies broadly classified as materials, electronics and information systems, manufacturing systems, and life science application technology. They have potential global markets worth billions of dollars. Of the emerging technologies, India has taken initiatives in biotechnology which have potential to influence the economy of the country. But lot needs to be done. Biotechnology is expected to result in increased agricultural production, improved comparative advantage in production of some commodities, new opportunities for the use of marginal lands and a reduced need for agrochemicals. Venture capital companies will be able to provide fillip to the development of biotechnology in the country in view of the high risk of failure associated with the research.

India can also take lead in production of electronics under advanced material research as India has a growing electronic industry which requires a variety of electronics materials which are imported. The venture capitalist can help to develop indigenous advanced material in electronics required for the industry.

Similarly, India is witnessing high growth in computers, telecommunications and informatics, etc. This field can also be tapped by the venture capitalist by their proactive financing approach.

The Government of India has identified nine business sectors for considering tax incentives to venture capital undertakings. The nine areas are biotechnology, information technology relating to software and hardware development, R&D of new chemical entities in the pharma sector, dairy industry, poultry industry, production of bio-fuels and hotel-cum-convention centres with a capacity of at least 3,000 persons.

Presently venture funds are not permitted to invest in financial services and gold financing.

❖ Financing of Small and Medium Enterprises

Small and medium-size enterprises (SMEs) deserve special treatment since it is quite difficult for them to raise funds from the capital markets. SMEs are unable to raise funds because they are considered as high risk ventures as they do not possess adequate tangible assets to offer as security. Venture capitalist can offer finance to SME segments as they play a major role in export performance of the country and also in the domestic sector.

6.6.3 Categories of Venture Capital

Venture capitalist can be categorized into four main groups as prevailing in US.

1. Private venture capital firm (PVCFs)
2. Small business investment companies (SBICs)
3. Subsidiaries of finance corporations, and
4. Subsidiaries of non-finance corporations

PVCFs include family firm and private partnership firms. They account for about 60 per cent of venture capital in US. In US expansion stage financing is much higher than the seed stage or the later stage of acquisition or buyout financing. This shows the preference of the venture capitalist in financing business which has successfully tested its products.

One of the first steps toward a professionally-managed venture capital industry was the passage of the Small Business Investment Act of 1958. The 1958 Act authorized the US Small Business Administration (SBA) to license private "Small Business Investment Companies" (SBICs) to provide financing and management assistance to small entrepreneurial businesses in the United States.

❖ Features of Venture Capital

Some of the features of venture capital financing are as under:

1. Venture capital is usually in the form of an equity participation. It may also take the form of convertible debt or long-term loan.
2. Investment is made only in high risk but high growth potential projects.

3. Venture capital is available only for commercialisation of new ideas or new technologies and not for enterprises which are engaged in trading, booking, financial services, agency, liaison work or research and development.
4. Venture capitalist joins the entrepreneur as a co-promoter in projects and share the risks and rewards of the enterprise.
5. There is continuous involvement in business after making an investment by the investor.
6. Once the venture has reached the full potential the venture capitalist disinvests his holdings either to the promoters or in the market. The basic objective of investment is not profit but capital appreciation at the time of disinvestment.
7. Venture capital is not just injection of money but also an input needed to set up the firm, design its marketing strategy and organise and manage it.
8. Investment is usually made in small and medium-scale enterprises.

❖ Disinvest Mechanism

The objective of venture capitalists to sell of the investment made by him at substantial capital gains. The disinvestment options available in developed countries are:

(*i*) Promoter's buyback

(*ii*) Public issue

(*iii*) Sale to other venture capital funds

(*iv*) Sale in OTC market, and

(*v*) Management buyouts.

In India, the most popular investment route is promoter's buyback. This permits the ownership and control of the promoter in tact.

The Risk Capital and Technology Finance Corporation, CAN-VCF, etc., in India allow promoters to buyback equity of their enterprise.

The public issue would be difficult and expensive since first generation entrepreneurs are not known in the capital market. The option involves high transaction cost and also less feasible for small ventures on account of high listing requirements of the stock exchange.

The OTC Exchange in India has been set up in 1992. It is hoped that OTCEI would provide disinvestment opportunities to venture capital firms.

The other investment options such as management buyout or sale to other venture capital fund are not considered appropriate in India.

6.6.4 Scope of Venture Capital

Venture capital may take various forms at different stages of the project. There are four successive stages of development of a project, *viz.*, development of a project idea, implementation of the idea, commercial production and marketing and finally large-scale investment to exploit the economies of scale and achieve stability. Financial institutions and banks usually start financing the project only at the second or third stage but rarely from the first stage. But venture capitalists provide finance even from the first stage of idea formulation. The various stages in the financing of venture capital are described below:

(1) Development of an Idea: Seed Finance: In the initial stage venture capitalists provide seed capital for translating an idea into business proposition. At this stage investigation is made in-depth which normally takes a year or more.

(2) Implementation Stage: Start up Finance: When the firm is set up to manufacture a product or provide a service, start up finance is provided by the venture capitalists. The first and second stage capital is used for full scale manufacturing and further business growth.

(3) Fledging Stage: Additional Finance: In the third stage, the firm has made some headway and entered the stage of manufacturing a product but faces teething problems. It may not be able to generate adequate funds and so additional round of financing is provided to develop the marketing infrastructure.

(4) Establishment Stage: Establishment Finance: At this stage the firm is established in the market and expected to expand at a rapid pace. It needs further financing for expansion and diversification so that it can reap economies of scale and attain stability. At the end of the establishment stage, the firm is listed on the stock exchange and at this point the venture capitalist disinvests their shareholdings through available exit routes.

Before investing in small, new or young hi-tech enterprises, the venture capitalists look for percentage of key success factors of a venture capital project. They prefer projects that address these problems. An idea developed for these success factors has been presented in Table 1.

After assessing the viability of the projects, the investors decide for what stage they should provide venture capital so that it leads to greater capital appreciation.

All the above stages of finance involve varying degrees of risks and venture capital industry, only after analysing such risks, invest in one or more. Hence, they specialize in one or more but rarely all. .

6.6.5 Importance of Venture Capital

Venture capital is of great practical value to every corporate enterprise in modern times.

I. ***Advantages to Investing Public***

1. The investing public will be able to reduce risk significantly against unscrupulous management, if the public invest in venture fund who in turn will invest in equity of new business. With their expertise in the field and continuous involvement in the business they would be able to stop malpractices by management.
2. Investors have no means to vouch for the reasonableness of the claims made by the promoters about profitability of the business. The venture funds equipped with necessary skills will be able to analyse the prospects of the business.
3. The investors do not have any means to ensure that the affairs of the business are conducted prudently. The venture fund having representatives on the Board of Directors of the company would overcome it.

KEY SUCCESS FACTORS OF VENTURE CAPITAL PROJECTS

Sl. No.	*Key Factors*	*Developed Country*				*Developing Country*			
		VI	*I*	*LI*	*NI*	*VI*	*I*	*LI*	*NI*
1.	Management skill of entrepreneurs	100	—	—	—	100	—	—	—
2.	Management skills of venture capitalists	14	72	14	—	40	40	20	—
3.	Affinity of interests between both parties	57	20	14	—	40	40	20	—
4.	Financial commitment of entrepreneurs	57	29	—	14	60	40	—	—
5.	Projects potential for rapid growth	57	14	29	—	80	—	20	—
6.	Project's potential to generate above average capital appreciation	72	28	—	—	60	40	—	—
7.	Project's potential to generate current income	14	43	29	14	40	60	—	—
8.	Availability of tech. expertise	14	72	14	—	60	20	20	—
9.	Possibility of exit offered by project	14	72	14	—	40	60	—	—
10.	Value of underlaying assets	—	43	29	28	—	80	20	—
11.	Strength of credit backing	14	43	14	29	40	60	—	—
12.	Involvement of a multilateral institution (e.g., IFC)	—	—	—	—	—	60	20	20

Keys:

VI. Absence of this constitutes an insurmountable obstacle for an institution to develop venture capital activities in the country.

I. The presence of this factor constitutes a clear to an incentive to an institution for developing venture capital activities in the country.

LI. The presence of this factor may influence favourable the decision of an institution for, but doe not constitute a decisive factor.

NI. Not Important.

II. Advantages to Promoters

1. The entrepreneur for the success of public issue is required to convince tens of underwriters, brokers and thousands of investors but to obtain venture capital assistance, he will be required to sell his idea to justify the officials of the venture fund.
2. Public issue of equity shares has to be preceded by a lot of efforts, *viz.*, necessary statutory sanctions, underwriting and brokers arrangement, publicity of issue, etc. The new entrepreneurs find it very difficult to make underwriting arrangements require a great deal of effort. Venture fund assistance would eliminate those efforts by leaving entrepreneur to concentrate upon bread-and-butter activities of business.
3. Costs of public issues of equity share often range between 10 per cent to 15 per cent of nominal value of issue of moderate size, which are often even higher for small issues. The company is required, in addition to above, to incur recurring costs for maintenance of share registry cell, stock exchange listing fee, expenditure on printing and posting of annual reports, etc. These items of expenditure can be ill afforded by the business when it is new. Assistance from venture fund does not require such expenditure.

III. General Advantages

1. A developed venture capital institutional set up reduces the time lag between a technological innovation and its commercial exploitation.
2. It helps in developing new processes/products in conducive atmosphere, free from the dead weight of corporate bureaucracy, which helps in exploiting full potential.
3. Venture capital acts as a cushion to support business borrowings, as bankers and investors will not lend money with inadequate margin of equity capital.
4. Once venture capital funds start earning profits, it will be very easy for them to raise resources from primary capital market in the form of equity and debts. Therefore, the investors would be able to invest in new business through venture funds and, at the same time, they can directly invest in existing business when venture fund disposes its own holding. This mechanism will help to channelise investment in new high-tech business or the existing sick business. These business will take-off with the help of finance from venture funds and this would help in increasing productivity, better capacity utilisation, etc.
5. The economy with well developed venture capital network induces the entry of large number of technocrats in industry, helps in stablising industries and in creating a new set of trained technocrats to build and manage medium and large industries, resulting in faster industrial development.
6. A venture capital firm serves as an intermediary between investors looking for high returns for their money and entrepreneurs in search of needed capital for their start ups.
7. It also paves the way for private sector to share the responsibility with public sector.

6.6.6 Origin of Venture Capital

Venture capital as a new phenomenon originated in USA and developed spectacularly world-wide since the second half of the seventies. American Research and Development Corporation, founded by Gen. Doriot soon after the Second World War, is believed to have heralded the institutionalisation of venture capital in the USA. Since then the industry has developed in many other countries in Europe, North America and Asia. The real development of VC took place in 1958. When the Business Administration Act was passed by the US congress. In USA alone there are 800 venture capital firms managing around $40b. of capital with annual accretions of between $1b and 5b. It is reported that some of the present day giants like Apple, Microsoft, Xerox, etc., are the beneficiaries of venture capital.

UK occupies a sécond place after US in terms of investment in VC. The concept became popular in late sixties in UK. The Government's Business Expansion Scheme which permitted individuals to claim tax reliefs for investment in companies not listed in stock exchange led to the success of VC in UK. The CHARTER House Development Limited is the oldest venture capital company established in 1934 in UK. The Bank of England established its venture capital company in late 40s. The UK witnessed a massive growth of industry during 70s and 80s. During 1988 there were over 1,000 venture capital companies in UK which provided ₹ 3,700 crore to over 1,500 firms.

The success of venture capital in these countries prompted other countries to design and implement measures to promote venture capital and their total commitment have been rising.

❖ Initiative in India

Indian tradition of VC for industry goes back more than 150 years when many of the managing agency houses acted as venture capitalists providing both finance and management skill to risky projects. It was the managing agency system through which Tata Iron and Steels and Empress Mills were able to raise equity capital from the investing public. The Tatas also initiated a managing agency house, named Investment Corporation of India in 1937 which by acting as venture capitalist, successfully promoted hi-tech enterprises such as CEAT Tyres, Associated Bearings, National Rayon, etc. The early form of venture capital enabled the entrepreneurs to raise large amount of funds and yet retain management control. After the abolition of managing agency system, the public sector term lending institutions met a part of venture capital requirements through seed capital and risk capital for hi-tech industries which were not able to meet promoters contribution. However, all these institutions supported only proven and sound technology while technology development remained largely confined to government labs and academic institutions. Many hi-tech industries, thus, found it impossible to obtain financial assistance from banks and other financial institutions due to unproven technology, conservative attitude, risk awareness and rigid security parameters.

Venture capital's growth in India passed through various stages. In 1973, R.S. Bhatt Committee recommended formation of ₹ 100 crore venture capital fund. The Seventh Five Year Plan emphasised the need for developing a system of funding venture capital. The Research and Development Cess Act was enacted in May 1986 which introduced a cess of 5% on all payments made for purchase of technology from abroad. The levy provides the source for the venture capital fund.

United Nations Development Programme in 1987 on behalf of government examined the possibility of developing venture capital in private sector. Technology Policy Implementation Committee in the same year also recommended the same provisions. Formalised venture capital took roots when venture capital guidelines were issued by Comptroller of Capital Issues in November 1988.

❖ Guidelines

The following are the guidelines issued by the Government of India.

1. The public sector financial institutions, State Bank of India, scheduled banks, foreign banks and their subsidiaries are eligible for setting the venture capital funds with a minimum size of ₹ 10 crore and a debt equity ratio of 1:1.5. If they desire to raise funds from the public, promoters will be required to contribute a minimum of 10 per cent of capital. Foreign equity up to 25 per cent subject to certain conditions would be permitted.

   The guidelines provide for Non-resident Indians investment up to 74 per cent on a repatriable basis and 25 per cent to 40 per cent on a non-repatriable basis. It should invest 60 per cent of its funds in venture capital activity. The balance amount can be invested in new issue of any existing or new company in equity, cumulative convertible preference shares, debenture bonds or any other security approved by SEBI.

2. The venture capital companies and venture capital funds can be set up as joint venture between stipulated agencies and non-institutional promoters but the equity holding of such promoters should not exceed 20 per cent and should not be largest single holder.
3. Venture capital assistance should go to enterprises with a total investment of not more than ₹ 10 crore.
4. The venture capital company (VCC/Venture Capital Fund (VCF) should be managed by professionals and should be independent of the parent organisation.
5. The VCC/VCF will not be allowed to undertake activities such as trading, brooking, money market operations, bills discounting, inter-corporate lending. They will be allowed to invest in leasing to the extent of 15 per cent of the total funds developed. The investment on revival of risk units will be treated as a part of venture capital activity.
6. Listing of VCCs/VCF can be according to the prescribed norms and underwriting of issues at the promoter's discretion.
7. A person holding a position or full-time chairman/president, chief executive, managing director or executive director/whole-time director in a company will not be allowed to hold the same position simultaneously in the VCC/VCF.
8. The Venture Capital assistance should be extended to:
   (*i*) The enterprise having investment up to ₹ 10 crore in the project.
   (*ii*) The technology involved should be new and untried or it should incorporate significant improvement over the existing technologies in India.
   (*iii*) The promoters should be new, professionally or technically qualified with inadequate resources.
   (*iv*) The enterprise should be established in the company form employing professionally qualified persons for maintenance of accounts.

9. Share pricing at the time of disinvestment by a public issue or general sale offer by the company or fund may be done subject to this being calculated an objective criteria and the basis disclosed adequately to the public.

POSITION OF VARIOUS VENTURE CAPITAL FUNDS

Sl. No.	*Funds Name*	*Established in*	*Promoter's Contribution*	*Assistance Areas*
1.	IDBI Venture Capital Fund finances by Central Government	1986	10% up to ₹ 50 lakh 15% above this	Chemicals products/ computer electronic equipments, clinical (Medical) equipments
2.	Risk capital and Technology Finance Corporation Ltd., capital by IFCI and Risk Capital Fund by IDBI	1988	Risk share with promoters	Short-term loans/interest free conditional/loans

3.	Technological Development Development and Information Co. of India Ltd., Capital by — ICICI Bank and Unit Trust	1998	Professionally technical persons for small and medium units. Maximum finance ₹ 2 crore period 5 to 8 years.	Computers/machines/ tissue culture/chemicals and feed and fodder techniques/environment engineering
4.	Credit Capital Venture Fund Ltd., Capital by Credit Capital Corporation Ltd., Bank of India/Asian Development Bank and general investors.	April 1989		Primary sector and subsidiary industries
5.	Gujarat Venture Finance Ltd., - Capital by - Gujarat Industrial Investment Corporation and IDBI	1990	Minimum ₹ 21 lakh and maximum ₹ 2 crore	Risk Technique/Medical equipment/electric savings/food processing industries.
6.	Andhra Pradesh Industrial Development Venture Capital Ltd., Capital by above Corporation + IDBI + World Bank + Andhra Bank	June 1990	Minimum ₹ 25 lakh Maximum ₹ 100 lakh and share with a project not exceeding 49%	Finance recorded in share capital save times in loan form.
7.	20th Century Capital Corporation Fund Ltd., Capital by ICICI Bank + 20th Century Finance	1990	For small business men.	
8.	Indus Venture Capital Fund Ltd., Finance by Mafatlal Group + IFCI	1992	Share not to exceed more than 10% in the project. Share capital not to exceed 50%	Health care products/ electrical equipments/ computer techniques
9.	Canbank Venture Capital Fund (Trust) Finance by Canara Bank + Canbank financial + Loan from World Bank	1991		For industrial technique projects/computer software/biotechnique chemicals
10.	SBI Capital Markets Ltd.		Share capital for 3 years and not to exceed 49%.	Import substitution/High export probabilities/High technique options.

❖ Methods of Venture Financing

Venture capital is available in four forms in India:

1. Equity Participation
2. Conventional Loan
3. Conditional Loan
4. Income Notes.

6.6.7 Venture Capital in India

With the opening of economy the Indian industries have come under great pressure to continuously upgrade knowledge and technology so as to operate effectively in the highly competitive domestic and international environment. Indian industries need generous funding to acquire state-of-the-art technology, research and development and better interconnection between public research institutions and corporate R&D.

Entrepreneurs need capital at different stages of their company's growth. But, it is not always possible for them to raise funds from capital markets. They are unable to raise funds through the capital market because some of them are high risk ventures and they may not possess adequate tangible assets to offer as security though their requirement of funds may generally be small. Besides, they are also reluctant to raise outside equity because of high transaction costs, increased discloser requirement and more importantly the fear of loss of control. Lack of access to capital markets and high transaction costs make it almost impossible for enterprises to obtain outside equity.

Venture capital is the most appropriate mechanism for funding such innovative enterprises. Venture capitalists provide funds for innovative ideas which have potential for high growth and return, but also inherent risks. It is an equity or quasi equity investment in highly potential business promoted by innovative entrepreneurs. The VC financing is however different from traditional financing. The difference lies in the norms and methods of financing, in the type of security and in the magnitude of risks involved. The VCs not only provide financial support to enterprises, they play a much greater and active role in providing technology, managerial and marketing support to enterprises. Venture Capital has helped in creating several highly successful companies in the USA. Apple, which was started by 21 years old Steven Jobs and 26 years old Stephen Wozniak, and assisted by A. C. Markkula, marketing expert, is one of them. Similarly, a number of multinational corporations such as Digital Equipment Corporation, Dysan, INTEL, Compaq, Sun Micro Systems, etc., were initiated with the assistance of VC funds. In India also, a number of high technology companies of today such as Wipro, Mastek Software System, Microland, Sun Pharmaceuticals and some others were financed by VC Funds.

❖ Historical Perspective

The development of venture capital is a recent phenomenon in India. It is still at its nascent stage and requires promotional efforts and policy initiatives for faster growth. Until very recently in the absence of an organized venture capital industry, individual investors and development financial institutions played the role of venture capitalists. Entrepreneurs have largely depended upon private placements, public offerings and lending by financial institutions.

The venture capital industry made a beginning in India in late 70s at the initiatives of the Government, when a Committee under the Chairmanship of Shri R.S. Bhatt was set up to examine the strategies for funding small and medium sized enterprises. The Committee drew attention to the problems faced by new entrepreneurs and technologists in setting up industries. The VC Financing was first introduced in 1975 with the setting up of IFCI sponsored Risk Capital Foundation (now known as IFCI Venture Capital Funds Ltd.) In 1975, Seed Capital Scheme was introduced by the IOBI. Till 1984, the Venture Capital took the form of Risk and Seed Capital. A VC Fund was set up by the GoI in 1985 for providing equity capital for projects attempting commercial application of the indigenous technology.

In 1988, the Indian government issued its first guidelines to legalize venture capital operations (Ministry of Finance, 1988). These regulations were aimed at allowing public sector banks to establish venture capital subsidiaries though it was possible for other investors to create a venture capital firm.

The most important feature of the 1988 Government guidelines was that venture capital funds received the benefit of a relatively low capital gains tax rate which was lower than the corporate tax rate. They were also allowed to exit investments at prices without obtaining permission from the Controller of Capital Issues, Ministry of Finance, GoI (which otherwise did not permit exit at a premium over book value). Funds' promoters had to be banks, large financial institutions, or private investors. Private investors could own no more than 20 per cent of the fund management companies (although a public listing could be used to raise the needed funds). The funds were restricted to investing in small amounts per firm (less than 100 million rupees); the recipient firms had to be involved in technology that was "new, relatively untried, very closely held or being taken from pilot to commercial stage, or which incorporated some significant improvement over the existing ones in India". The government also specified that the recipient firm's founders should be "relatively new, professionally or technically qualified, and with inadequate resources or backing to finance the project". There were also other features including a list of approved investment areas. At least one of the two government-sponsored development banks, ICICI and IDBI, were required to vet every portfolio firm's application to a venture capital firm to ensure that it met the requirements. Also, the Controller of Capital Issues of the Ministry of Finance had to approve every line of business in which a venture capital firm wished to invest.

The World Bank supported the venture capital project, noting that "the guidelines reflect a cautious approach designed to maximize the likelihood of venture capital financing for technology-innovation ventures during the initial period of experimentation and thereby demonstrate the viability of venture capital in India. For this reason, during the initial phase, the Guidelines focused on promoting venture capital under the leadership of well-established financial institutions (World Bank Report: 1989)."

Four state-owned financial institutions accordingly established venture capital subsidiaries under government guidelines and received a total of $45 million from the World Bank. The World Bank however sought to ensure a level of professionalism in the four new venture capital funds, two of which were established by two well-managed state-level financial organizations (Andhra Pradesh and Gujarat), one by a large nationalized bank (Canara Bank) and one by a development finance organization (ICICI). The World Bank loaned the money to the Indian government that would then on-lend it at commercial rates to these institutions for 16 years, including a 7-year moratorium on interest and principal repayments. The venture capital funds were expected to invest principally in equity or quasi-equity. Some monies were allocated for training personnel through internships in overseas venture capital funds.

In 1988, Technology Development & Information Company of India Ltd., (TDICI), was established in Bangalore as a subsidiary of ICICI, towards venture capital operation. Many of today's renowned Software/ IT companies were funded by TDICI.

❖ Regulatory Framework

In the late 1990s, the Indian government became aware of the potential benefits of a healthy venture capital sector. In 1999 a number of new regulations were promulgated. Some of the most significant of these related to liberalizing the regulations regarding the ability of various financial institutions to invest in venture capital. The most important of these was allowing banks to invest up to 5 per cent of their new funds annually in venture capital, with effect from April 1999. But no venture capital investment was made by these institutions as of 2001 probably they considered that extending such venture capital loans would be unwise.

There were several statutes governing the venture capital in India which included the SEBI's 1996 Venture Capital Regulations, the 1995 Guidelines for Overseas Venture Capital Investments issued by the Department of Economic Affairs of the Ministry of Finance, and the Central Board of Direct Taxes (CBDT) 1995 Guidelines for Venture Capital Companies (later modified in 1999). In early 2000, domestic venture capitalists were regulated by three government bodies: the Securities and Exchange Board of India (SEBI), the Ministry of Finance, and the CBDT. For foreign venture capital firms the Foreign Investment Promotion Board (FIPB) was required to approve every investment, and the Reserve Bank of India (RBI) had to approve every exit.

The aim of the Indian regulatory regime was to be neutral with regard to the risk profile of investment recipients. However, in sharp contrast to the US, where a venture capital fund could invest in any industry it wished, in India only six industries were opened to investment, *viz.*, software, information technology, pharmaceuticals, biotechnology, agriculture and allied industries.

In June 2000, the Ministry of Finance issued further guidelines that only SEBI should regulate and register venture capital firms. The only criterion would be the technical qualifications of their promoters, whether domestic or offshore.

With moderate liberalization effected in 2000, there are indications that investments had increased. This indicates that further liberalization could elicit even greater venture capital activity. Unofficial figures gathered by SEBI showed that over $1 billion was invested in 2000, although the flow substantially declined thereafter in next 2 months of 2001 due to global tightening of venture capital investments.

6.6.8 Current Scenario

According to Indian Venture Capital Association (IVCA) yearbook, in the year 2001, India ranked as the third most active venture capital market in Asia-Pacific region).

- Venture Capital Fund invested was US$ 907.58 million (i.e., ₹ 4,500 crore) in Indian companies in 2001, down 21.8 per cent from US$ 1,160.2 million (i.e., about ₹ 5,750 crore) in 2000. However, it may be noted that, the world over, the venture capital industry registered a decline of about 50 per cent during this period.
- The number of Indian companies receiving investment declined 62.6 per cent to 101 in 2001 from 270 in 2000.
- 65.4 per cent of companies that raised venture capital in 2001 were in information technology and communications.
- Overall India saw a shift to later stage investing with expansion stage funds, accounting for 60 per cent of disbursements in 2001, compared to 44.3 per cent in 2000.

As per data available with SEBI, 43 domestic venture capital funds registered with SEBI had about 400 investors, who were largely corporates, qualified institutional buyers (QIBs) and high net worth individuals. According to provisional data available, SEBI registered VFCs and FVCIs had made a total investment of about ₹ 2,000 crore, i.e., US$430 million approximately, in Indian companies as on March 2003. Thus, the investment made by SEBI registered VCFs was much less compared to data compiled by IVCA, which shows that major part of VCF industry is not registered with SEBI. (Report of Advisory Committee on Venture Capital, October 2003, SEBI). In India, the venture capitalist have invested US $4.4 billion between Jan. 2003 and Dec. 2005. In Jan. 2006 industry estimates suggest that about $7.4 billion stands invested in Indian companies by private equity and venture capital firms. As 90% of India's funds come from overseas, notably the US. Private Equity in India has made in roads into infrastructure/financial services/manufacturing/engineering and utilities.

Evalueserve research shows that an interesting phenomenon is beginning to emerge. Over 44 US-based VC firms are now seeking to invest heavily in start-ups and early-stage companies in India. These firms have raised, or are in the process of raising, an average of US $100 million each. If these 40-plus firms are successful in raising money, they would garner approximately $4.4 billion to be invested during the next 4 to 5 years.

Evalueserve's research further indicates that several US-based VC funds have also been investing in the Indian market for the last six years. So far, these funds have been investing in early and mid-stage technology companies dealing primarily with consumer Internet, mobile devices, wireless and wire-line, IT services, BPO services, software and hardware products, electronics and semiconductors. The details of US based VC Funds investing in India is given in Table below.

US BASED VC FUNDS INVESTING IN INDIA

	Venture Capital Firm	*Key Principals*	*US-India Cross Border India-based Companies in their Portfolios*
1.	Westbridge (now a part of Sequioa Capital India)	Sumir Chadha K. P. Balaraj Surendra K. Jain Sandeep Singhal	AppLabs, Astra, Brainvisa, Celetron, ICICI OneSource Indecomm, Induslogic, MarketRX, ReaMatrix Tarang, Zavata, Dr. Lal Pathlabs Royal Orchid Hotels, Bharti TeleSoft Mauj, Nazara, Shaadi, Times Internet Travelguru, Emagia, July Systems, Strand Life Sciences, Zenasis
2.	Oak Investment Partners	Ranjan Chak	Talisma, Sutherland
3.	Matrix Partners	Shirish Sathaye Avnish Bajaj Rishi Navani	Not available
4.	Sherpalo Ventures (now, a part of Kleiner Perkins, Caufield and Byers, KPCB)	Ram Sriram Sandeep Murthy	Cleartrip, Paymate, Naukri.com, 247 Customers

5.	The View Group	Mintoo Bhandari Gopal Jain Mehool Parekh Manish Sabharwal	Integreon, Ingenero, TWS, Tracmail, Peerless India
6.	Bessemer Venture Partners	Rob Chandra	Shriram EPC, Sarovar Hotels & Resorts, Rice Auto Industries, Motilal Oswal Financial Services Ltd.
7.	Trident Capital	Venetia Kontogouris	Cognizant, Microland, Outsourced Partners International
8.	Walden International	In process of hiring more Principals after Dinesh Vaswani left	Headstron, e4e, Info Tech, Mindtree Venture Info Tek
9.	New Enterprise Associates (NEA)	Vinod Dham Vani Kola	Indus Logic, Sasken
10.	Canaan Partners	Alok Mittal	e4e
11.	Softbank Asia International	Ravi Adusumalli	SIFY, Slashsupport, Intelligroup
12.	International Finance	Paul Asel	Indecomm Global Services
13.	Artiman Ventures	Amit Shah Yatin Mundkur M. J. Aravind Saurabh Srivastava	Biolmagine, Net Devices, Opsource
14.	Columbia Capital	Hemant Kanakia Arun Gupta	Net Devices, Approva
15.	Gabriel Venture Partners	Navin Chaddha	Allsec,IL&FS Investment, MakeMy Trip, Persistent Systems, Tejas
16.	Norwest Venture Partners	Pramod Haque Vab Goel	Persistnet Systems, Yatra
17.	Austin Ventures	Venu Shmapant Krishna Srinivasan	Siperia
18.	Sigma Partners	Mark Pine	Emagia Solutions, Kirusa, Senasis Technologies, Virtusa
19.	Charles River Ventures	Izhar Armony	July Systems, Virtusa Net Customer
20.	Financial Technology Ventures	Eric Byunn	Exlservice
21.	Telesoft Partners	Arjun Gupta Santhil Durairaj	Bombay Cellular
22.	Draper, Fisher, Jurvetson	Raj Atluru	Personiva (f.k.a. Pictureal) Seventymm

Source: Evalueserve.

6.6.9 Issues

❖ Structure of Indian Venture Capital Industry

The venture capital firms in India can be categorized into the following four groups:

1. All India Development Financial Institutions (DFIs) sponsored Venture Capital Funds (VCFs) such as Technology Development and Information Company of India Limited (TDICI) by ICICI, Risk Capital and Technology Finance Corporation Limited (RCTFC) by IFCI and Risk Capital Fund by IDBI.
2. State Finance Corporation (SFC) — sponsored VCFs promoted by the State level developmental financial Institutions such as Gujarat Venture Capital Limited (GVCL) by Gujarat Industrial Investment Corporation (GIIC) and Andhra Pradesh Venture Capital Limited (APVCL) by Andhra Pradesh State Finance Corporation APSFC.
3. Banks-sponsored VCFs promoted by the public sector banks such as Canfina and SBI Caps
4. Private VCFs promoted by the foreign banks/private sector companies and financial institutions such as Indus Venture Capital Fund, Credit Capital Venture Fund and Grindlays India Development Fund.

❖ Understanding Venture Capitalists Preference

Most venture capital would prefer to invest their funds in high technology products. That usually means that they prefer industrial products rather than retail products such as new toasters or new cameras. A new robot designed to be used in steel industry is an example of high technology industrial product.

Further venture capitalist prefers products rather than services. There are four types of product categories to choose from. Revolutionary, innovative, evolutionary and substitute products. Revolutionary products are extremely difficult to finance. These products absorb enormous amounts of capital. They have a very long development time before one can realize a substantial profit.

Venture capitalist prefers innovative products such as next generation products. They also prefer evolutionary products which are ahead of the competition. Still other group of venture capitalist prefers substitution products.

❖ Venture Capitalist Involvement

When it comes to venture capitalist's involvement in the investee's business, there are two types of venture capitalists: passive advisers and active directors. Most venture capital companies are passive advisers. They limit their advice to areas in which they have a strong expertise. Their involvement is particularly more when the business they have financed faces operating trouble.

On the other hand the active directors provide part of the management team to the investee companies. They do not involve on a day-to-day basis but they review the business situation once or twice a week.

Some venture capital companies take a more active part than just direction. They seek to control the investee company directly or through the board of directors.

❖ Myths about Venture Capital

(*i*) Venture capital firms want to own control of your company and tell you how to run the business. No venture capital intentionally sets out to own control of a small business.

(*ii*) You must have an introduction to the venture capitalist from one of his friends in order to obtain financing. The business proposal that is well prepared is a best introduction as venture capitalists are interested in good investment opportunities

(*iii*) Venture capital firms are interested only in new technological discoveries The venture capitalists are more interested in an add-on technology rather than revolutionary areas which are indeed difficult to finance.

(*iv*) Venture capitalists are satisfied with a reasonable return on investments. In fact the truth is, the venture capitalists expect very high, exorbitant, unreasonable returns.

(*v*) Venture capitalists are quick to invest. On the contrary it takes long time to raise venture capital. On an average it will take 6 to 8 weeks from the initial interface.

(*vi*) Venture capitalists are interested in backing new ideas or high technology inventions. Management is secondary consideration. Venture capital only back good management. They believe that a good idea is important but a good management team is even more important.

(*vii*) Venture capitalists only need basic summary information before they make an investment — A detailed and well-organized business proposal is the only way to gain a venture capital investor's attention and obtain funding.

❖ Appraisal by the Venture Capitalist

The venture capitalist will gather information on four basic areas namely management, uniqueness, projections and an exit. As regards management the most important characteristics that the venture capitalists will be looking for is honesty. He will also look at the business experience of the management team, their motivations and achievements record.

As regards uniqueness the venture capitalists will look at the growth possibilities of the investee company. He will look for the answer to the question what makes the business different? "Why will it succeed?". "Does business has high growth potential?". In the case of projections the venture capital will try to determine how realistic are the projections and how reasonable are the assumptions? The projections should not be only optimistic but must be aggressive enough to attract the venture capitalists.

Finally the venture capitalist will have to decide on the question of exit. The business proposal must tell the venture capitalists how he will exit from the financial investment.

❖ Business Proposal Seeking Venture Capital

Under the business proposal the venture capitalist will seek the following information.

1. Business and its future

— General information about the company

— Nature of the Business

— Business history

— Business of the future – milestones to be achieved in future

— Uniqueness – out of the ordinary which will make the business succeed.

— Product or service – the products which are sold and needs that it satisfies.

— Customers or purchasers of the product

— Industry or Market

— Competition

— Marketing – description of the marketing strategy

— Production

— Production characteristics – critical factors in the production processes

— Labour force and employees

— Suppliers

— Subcontractors

— Equipment

— Property and Facilities

— Patents and Trademarks

— Research and Development

— Litigation – any legal actions that are in existence or that are being contemplated.

— Government Regulations

— Conflicts of interest or potential conflict between company and board of directors, management, key employees, large stockholders and so on.

— Backlog – nature of orders backlog

— Insurance

— Taxes

— Corporate Structure — form of organization.

Publications and Associations — primary publications that cover the industry.

2. Management

— Directors and Officers

— Key Employees

— Management Fidelity – information regarding management honesty and credit check.

— Remuneration – compensation of key management teams.

— Stock Options

— Stock Option Plan

— Principal Shareholders

— Employment Agreements

— Conflicts of interest between employee and company.

— Consultants, Accountants, Lawyers, Bankers, and Others

3. Description of the Financing
   — Proposed Financing
   — Capital Structure
   — Collateral for the Financing
   — Guarantees
   — Conditions – to be fulfilled for loan disbursements
   — Reporting – periodicity and nature of reporting
   — Use of Proceeds – end-use of funds lent
   — Ownership – pattern existing and proposed.
   — Dilution
   — Fees Paid
   — Investor Involvement – terms of management participation.
4. Risk Factors
   — Limited Operating History – no previous experience.
   — Limited Resources – problem of not enough money for initial investment and expansion.
   — Limited Management Experience
   — Market Uncertainties
   — Production Uncertainties
   — Liquidation – process as also issues relating to liquidation.
   — Dependence on Key Management
   — What Could Go Wrong?
   — Other Items
5. Return on Investment and Exit
   (*a*) Public Offering
   (*b*) Sale
   (*c*) Buyback
   (*d*) Return on Investment
6. Analysis of Operations and Projections
   (*a*) General
   (*b*) Ratio Analysis
   (*c*) Results of Operations
   (*d*) Financial Conditions
   (*e*) Contingent Liabilities
7. Financial Statements
8. Financial Projections

9. Product Literature, Brochures, Articles, and Pictures
10. Other Information the Venture Capitalist Will Need
    — References on the Business
    — References on Key Employees
    — Bankers, Lawyers, Accountants, and Consultants
    — Largest Suppliers
    — Largest Purchases
    — Backlog
    — Aging of Accounts Receivable
    — Aging of Accounts Payable
    — Debts and Terms Summarized
    — Lease
    — Taxes
    — Tax Returns
    — Other Government Data
    — Union Contract
    — Personal Financial Statements
    — Long Resume of key employees
11. Summary of the proposal

Having broadly seen what a Venture Capital Fund is, their promotional role and their mindset when vetting a proposal, the investee company or an entrepreneur can confidently approach the venture fund for assistance. The investee company can prepare business plan incorporating the various information answering the basic questions in the minds of venture capitalist.

These questions are:

1. How much money is required by the venture?
2. How the money will be utilized?
3. How much money will be made from the venture?
4. How much will be returned to venture capitalist at the end?

It is important to note that at the heart of every investment decision is the question of trust. As the old saying goes, investor invests in people, not in business plans. In the partnership with the venture capitalist, many entrepreneur-engineers have built successful business. In doing so, they have made the transition from analytical style of thinking to a synthetic style. The contrasting style of analytical thinking involves breaking down the problem into its constituent parts and focusing on details, while the synthetic style of communication involves explaining the goals and objectives to investors effectively and succinctly without great technical detail that is painting the big picture. The investee companies must master both the style of communication to be successful entrepreneur.

6.6.10 Challenges

There are several challenges before the Venture Capital Funds. Some inherent issues relating to VC and entrepreneurs development could be as under:

1. Profitability

Focus on early profitability might be counter productive for a product company: As most of companies are in the service sector, the mindset of entrepreneurs in India is on making their companies profitable as quickly as possible, unlike most start up companies in US, which are usually product-based and expect 2-3 stages of investments. There are several reasons which could be attributed to such a mindset for Indian entrepreneurs, as given here:

(*a*) Indians by tradition have founded service and trading companies,

(*b*) the scarcity of available venture capital in India,

(*c*) reluctance in offloading too much equity, and

(*d*) the requirement of venture capital funds significantly smaller as most of start-up companies are in the service sector.

The disadvantages of any obsessive focus on profitability could lead to:

(*a*) a possibility that an Indian start-up company may not grow very quickly or realize its full potential in terms of turnover and profit, and

(*b*) the possibility of an Indian start-up being upstaged by some other firm somewhere else in the world.

The VCs can play a much greater role here in educating Indian entrepreneurs to think differently in the context of product-based companies compared to how they have traditionally run their companies.

2. Funding

As the Indian start-ups companies still continue to be created in the service business and even those who are in product based start-ups, wish to achieve profitability quickly, the VCs should look beyond distinct stages of funding to Indian companies, (i.e., seed funding, Stage A funding, Stage B funding, mezzanine funding, etc). They should provide "continuous" funding based on continued attainment of predefined metrics such as revenues, profits, development expenses, etc. This would mean a much greater involvement of VCs operationally with the Indian start-up, and act as a "bank" that provides money in exchange for equity, as and when needed.

3. Marketing

Indian entrepreneurs are quite adept technically and are at par with similar entrepreneurs in developed countries. However, what entrepreneurs in India generally lack are: expertise in marketing, sales and business development area. Indian start-ups need help in finding the appropriate marketing, sales and business development people. This problem has further gained importance as most start-ups have to compete for talent not only with other companies who are exporting similar or dissimilar products and services but also with many Indian domestic companies. In fact, finding and retaining the 'right talent' has become an issue not only in marketing, sales and business development but also in research, technical and advanced development areas.

4. Management Control

Indian entrepreneurs are usually hesitant about giving up control. In fact, most of the entrepreneurs in India currently receive their initial funding from family and friends, and even if they do not do so, the Indian social system is such that relatives and friends still end up being a major influence. Many Indian entrepreneurs would rather list their companies on BSE than give up a substantial share to the VCs. Thus, the VCs will have to provide a very clear value proposition to the start-ups.

5. Disclosure and Transparency

There is ostensible lack of financial transparency in Indian entrepreneurs. One reason for this may be that the Indian economy was a "socialistic and closed" economy, and for the other, it may be because Indian entrepreneurs are not as proficient at business development as their counterparts in the US. Indian start-ups lack financial transparency and often have limited experience in implementing effective financial processes. This usually makes the task of the VC much more difficult at the due diligence phase, and also in helping the start-up grow rapidly. Hence, in such circumstances, the VCs may have to get actively involved in "process-sizing" the company.

The venture capital industry in India is at an early stage. However, with the opening of the economy and clear policy guidelines, VC financing activity has boosted up recently. The VC financing activities, which started with financing the Technology Companies in India, are now exploring other non-IT areas, such as transport, hospitality, BPO, bio-technology, real estate, infrastructure, etc. India is therefore rightly poised for a big leap. What is needed is a vibrant venture capital sector, which can leverage innovation, promote technology and harness the ongoing knowledge explosion. India certainly needs a large pool of risk capital from home and abroad. But to attract VC funds and to build-up a strong venture capital industry we need to have the right regulatory, legal, tax and institutional environment; the risk taking capacities among the budding entrepreneurs; start-up access to R&D flowing out of national and state level laboratories; support from Universities, so also infrastructural support such as telecom, technology parks, etc.

US CONSORTIUM LAUNCHES $ 5 BILLION INDIA INFRA FUND

Citigroup, Infrastructure Development Finance Company (IDFC), India Infrastructure Finance Company (IIFC) and Blackstone Group Holdings launched recently, a dedicated Infrastructure fund for financing projects in India. The companies are coming together in an effort to pump in around $ 5 billion for infrastructure projects in India.

As per the plan, $2 billion will be deployed as equity capital and the remaining $3 billion will be mopped up through long-term debt financing with maturities exceeding 10 years. The equity financing programme will be managed by IDFC which will invest in green-field, brown-field and operating projects in roads, power, airports and industrial and commercial infrastructure.

Source: *Economic Times.*

6.7 MUTUAL FUNDS

The economic progress of a country is, to a certain extent, linked with the growth of the capital market. Capital market growth depends on the savings of the nation. In India, notwithstanding a high rate of savings by the community, the capital market is not in a position to grow fast because the common man has not acquired the necessary know-how himself to select appropriate avenues of investment which will serve his needs. Therefore, the savings are mainly directed towards bank deposits/real estate/gold, etc. If he is assured that there are organisations of repute which have necessary expertise to select appropriate avenues of investment where the yield is attractive enough, with utmost security of the capital invested, it would create a proper climate for diversion of a part of the savings which at present goes into sectors where there is either only capital appreciation but with little or no scope for regular periodical return on investment or no capital appreciation at all, but with a periodical small return on the investment.

On the other hand, insurance — life and general, have been an important segments of the Indian financial system. Insurance segment and mutual funds together have a corpus of over ₹ 5,60,000 crore of savings. They play a crucial role in the capital market, while providing security to people. This chapter discusses the role and other related issues indepth.

In these circumstances, there is enough scope for Mutual Funds to operate, which would not only assure a reasonable capital appreciation on his investment but also provide a regular dividend at periodical intervals with also a facility for easy encashment of the principal.

Mutual fund is a scheme where the investor, invests in the schemes issued by mutual funds on regular monthly basis a fixed instalment. This is equal to saving schemes of banks like recurring deposit, saving bank deposits. The only difference is both these schemes is that one can invest in purchase of units of the accepted mutual fund schemes and such investment can be as small as ₹ 500.

The total amount managed by all mutual funds in India ending June 2006 was ₹ 2,65,534 crore.

❖ Name of Funds

As per SEBI guidelines the mutual funds cannot use the word *"Relief Bond"* with their scheme names. Sometimes name of the scheme is entirely different than its objects, e.g., Prudential ICICI has one scheme. Spice Fund, which has nothing to do spices but it is an index fund.

Sometimes names of schemes are similar of two different mutual fund companies, *viz.,* Birla Income Plus is purely an income fund which incorporates in its portfolio, various range of debt-securities. The similar type of name of scheme is *Kotak Income Plus* which is a kind of conservative balanced fund. Similarly, MIP - *Monthly Income Plans* of mutual funds do not provide monthly income to investors. MIP is a kind of balanced fund, wherein major portion is invested in debt securities.

Another example of deceptive name of the scheme is K-30 (by Kotak Mahindra Mutual Fund). The investor should not think that it contains 30 stocks of BSE in the scheme. In fact K-30 is a kind of diversified equity fund.

❖ Evolution of Mutual Funds

Historically, mutual fund investment traces its origins to the early pioneering investments of Scottish and English investors in the American West in the 1800s, and later of the early global portfolio investors in Japan in the 1960s.

6.7.1 Origins of Mutual Funds

Sure, the stock market is the best place for your money to make more money. But only if you start out with a lot of money in the first place, and if you understand financial manoeuvring. In 1822, royalty (in the form of King William I of the Netherlands) came up with an option for the rest of us. The closed-end fund. It was a stratlingly simple idea. A group of investors, individuals and institutions with common investment goals, pooled their investment and placed them with fund managers. These professional money managers then invested these funds in securities, and distributed the profits among the fund members. Rubert Fleming's first investment trust set up in the 1870s promised to manage the finances of the moneyed classes of Scotland. Fleming's Trust called Foreign and Colonial Investment Trust was formed as a limited company, to invest in a selection of 18 overseas Government Stocks, at an average yield of 8 per cent. The moneyed people latched on to the trust idea in a period of falling interest rates. The 'investment trust' concept spread rapidly through Europe, and the first American fund was created in 1893. The idea spread quickly around the world, but it came to India only in the 1960s. Today, there are over 100 distinct schemes in the market, and more being introduced every year.

6.7.2 What is a Mutual Fund?

Mutual Funds are financial intermediaries in the investment business. They collect funds from public and invest on behalf of the investors as "pass through entities" with losses and gains accruing to the investors only. Mutual fund sell their shares to the investors, invest the proceeds in a wide choice of securities in the financial market. Owners of shares receive pro rata shares of the earnings from these assets, minus management and other fees assessed by the fund.

Mutual funds are defined by the different authors in different words meaning one and same thing, i.e., it is a non-banking or non-depository financial intermediary which acts as an important vehicle for bringing wealthholders and deficit units together indirectly. Mutual funds are pooling funds together and then investing that fund to different securities thus reduce risk by diversification.

Mutual Fund units are investment vehicles that provide a means of participation in the stock market for people who have neither the time, nor the money, nor perhaps the expertise to undertake direct investment in equities successfully. On another level, they also provide a route into specialist markets where direct investment often demands both more time and more knowledge than an investor or his financial adviser may possess.

The basic idea is simple: A large number of investors pool their money in order to obtain a spread of professionally managed Stock Exchange investments that they cannot obtain individually. The advantage is that the investor in a mutual fund is taking much less of a risk than a direct equity investor, because increase in the number of stocks held obviously reduces the effect that any one stock can have on the overall performance of the equity portfolio. Professional management has two main benefits: it provides specialist investment expertise which should ensure greater success than the inexperienced investor can achieve on his own and it reduces the administrative burden of investment.

A mutual fund is divided into equal portfolios called units. The price of units is calculated regularly by the managers, rather than being determined by supply and demand in the market. The prices are quoted for units — the higher (offer) price being the price the investor pays to buy units, and the lower (bid) price being the price he will receive for units sold back to the managers.

Mutual fund managers are the only people allowed to make a market in mutual fund units, and they must be prepared to buy units from and sell units to the public at any time.

The price of the units in any mutual fund is governed by the value of the underlying securities. The price will therefore fluctuate with the movements of the market sector in which a fund is invested. The value of an investor's holding in a unit can therefore, like an investment in shares, go down as well as up. In India, excepting UTI, all other mutual funds are organised and set up under Indian Trust Act, 1882. And UTI is set up under special Act, the UTI Act, amended by the Parliament in 1963.

6.7.3 Types of Mutual Funds

No single gun is suitable for all types of hunting. Nor is one fishing rod suitable for all types of fishing. Similarly, no one mutual fund is suitable to the vast variety of investors' needs and objectives. The needs and the risk-taking capacity of an old widow may differ significantly from those of a young businessman. In the funds market, many types of funds are offered to the investor. His choice of a fund will depend on what he wants his money to earn for him and how much risk he is willing to take. Most of the funds will fall in one of the following four categories:

(*i*) *Open and Close-ended Funds:* If the period and/or target amount of the fund is definite, the fund is called close-ended. If indefinite, it is called open-ended. For instance, the Unit Scheme (1964) of the Unit Trust of India (UTI) is an open-ended fund, both in terms of period as well as target amount.

(*ii*) *Income and Growth-oriented Fund:* The income-oriented fund aims at distribution of income periodically amongst investors. Consequently, its investment strategy conforms to the fund objective by deployment of investors' monies into fixed income yielding securities. On the other hand, the growth-oriented fund meets the investors' need for appreciation, high risk-bearing capacity and ability to defer liquidity. As such, the investment by growth-oriented funds are predominantly made in equities. The fund which partially meets the needs for income and growth are called 'balanced' or 'income-cum-growth' fund.

(*iii*) *Area, Industry, Customer Group Funds:* The funds may have, at the international level, investments in securities of specified areas, e.g., Japan Fund, Thailand Fund or South Korea Fund, etc. These funds provide access to foreign investors into domestic securities of these countries. Similarly, certain funds may invest their resources in specified industry or industries like Rail Road or Petroleum Industry funds in the US. Certain mutual funds may be confined to a high-tech and high-growth industry, which may attract risk taken in such cases. The fund may also aim at a specific customer target group to meet their major needs, like funds for pensioners, widows, etc.

(*iv*) *Taxation Funds:* Certain funds are designed to avail certain tax-exemptions, whether in the domestic or foreign capital markets. Tax Saving Magnum of SBI Capital Markets Limited is an example of the domestic type. UTI's US $60 million India Fund, based in the US, is an example of the latter type offshore mutual fund to avail the tax exempt status in tax havens.

(*v*) *Balanced Funds:* They divide their investments between equity shares and bonds in order to meet the objectives of safety, capital appreciation and regularity of income.

(*vi*) *Index Funds:* These funds invest only in those shares which are included in the market indices and in exactly the same proportion, so that the value of such index funds varies with the market index.

(*vii*) *Hedge Funds:* Mutual funds which employ their funds by speculative trading, i.e., by buying shares whose prices are likely to rise and selling shares whose prices are likely to fall, are called hedge funds.

(*viii*) *Money Market Mutual Funds:* Specialise in investing in short-term money market instruments like certificate of deposits. The emphasis is on liquidity with low rate of return.

(*ix*) *Special Funds:* These funds invest only in specialised channels like a specific country (India Fund, Japan Fund, Korea Fund, etc.), a specific category of companies, Real Estate.

(*ixA*) *Gold Exchange Traded Fund (GETF):* The idea originated in Jan. 2006 and UTI Mutual Funds and Benchmark Mutual Fund had applied to SEBI for such schemes. This is valued on London Metal Exchange price, import duties and exchange rates. This was originated by passing the SEBI (Mutual Funds) Amendment Regulations 2006.

(*ixB*) *Real Estate Fund:* To attract investment in property market, this fund scheme has been originated. The BSE index for realty which was 8077.67 on 19-7-2007 have variations for substantial amount.

(A) Valuation: Since physical gold and other permitted instruments linked to gold are denominated in gold tonnage, it will be value-based on the market price of gold in the domestic market, and will be marked to market on a daily basis. The market price of gold in the domestic market on any business day would be arrived at as under:

Domestic price of gold = (London Bullion Market Association AM fixing in US$/ounce × conversion factor for converting ounce into kg. for 0.995 fineness × rate for US $ into INR + custom duty for import of gold + sales tax/octroi and other levels applicable.

(B) Determination of NAV:

NAV of units under the scheme shall be calculated as —

$$\text{NAV}(₹) = \frac{\text{Market or Fair Value of scheme's investments + current assets Minus Current Liabilities and provisions}}{\text{No. of units outstanding under the scheme on the valuation date}}$$

The NAV shall be calculated up to four decimals.

(C) Recurring expenses:

For a GETF, the limits applicable to equity schemes shall be applicable.

(D) Benchmark for GFTF:

The necessary amendments to SEBI (Mutual Funds) Regulations, 1996 in regard to indices catering to the gold sector/securities linked to gold, shall be made.

❖ Guidelines for Real Estate Mutual Funds (REMFs)

The SEBI has approved the guidelines for REMFs. REMF scheme means a scheme of a mutual fund which has investment objective to invest directly or indirectly in real estate property and shall be governed by the provisions and guidelines under SEBI (Mutual Funds) regulations. The structure of REMFs is to be *close-ended.* The units of REMFs shall be compulsorily listed on the stock exchanges and NAV should be declared *daily.* These scheme can:

1. invest directly in real estate properties within India.
2. mortgage (housing loans) backed securities.
3. invest in equity shares/bonds/debentures of listed/unlisted companies which was in properties and undertake property development, and
4. invest in other securities.

6.7.4 Geographical Classification of Mutual Funds

1. *Domestic Funds:* Domestic funds are the saving schemes, which are opened for mobilising savings of the investors in household sectors in the country. They can invest only in the securities in the financial markets within the country.

2. *Offshore Funds:* Such mutual funds can invest in securities of foreign companies and such investments require RBI permission.

The Advantages of Investing in Mutual Funds are:

1. *Professional Management:* You avail of the services of experienced and skilled professionals who are backed by a dedicated investment research team which analyses the performance and prospects of companies and selects suitable investments to achieve the objectives of the scheme.

2. *Diversification:* Mutual Funds invest in a number of companies across a broad cross-section of industries and sectors. This diversification reduces the risk because seldom do all stocks decline at the same time and in the same proportion. You achieve this diversification through a Mutual Fund with far less money than you can do on your own.

3. *Convenient Administration:* Investing in a Mutual Funds reduces paperwork and helps you avoid many problems such as bad deliveries, delayed payments and unnecessary follow-up with brokers and companies. Mutual funds save your time and make investing easy and convenient.

4. *Return Potential:* Over a medium to long-term, Mutual Funds have the potential to provide a higher return as they invest in a diversified basket of selected securities.

5. *Low Costs:* Mutual Funds are a relatively less expensive way to invest compared to directly investing in the capital markets because benefits of scale in brokerage, custodial and other fees translate into lower costs for investors.

6. *Liquidity:* In open-ended schemes, you can get your money back promptly at net asset value related prices from the Mutual Fund itself. With close-ended schemes, you can sell your units on a stock exchange at the prevailing market price or avail of the facility of direct repurchase at NAV related prices which some close-ended and interval schemes offer you periodically.

7. *Transparency:* You get regular information on the value of your investment in addition to disclosure on the specific investments made by your scheme, the proportion invested in each class of assets and the fund manager's investment strategy and outlook.

8. *Flexibility:* Through features such as regular investment plans, regular withdrawal plans and dividend reinvestment plans, you can systematically invest or withdraw funds according to your needs and convenience.

9. *Choice of Schemes:* Mutual Funds offer a family of schemes to suit your varying needs over a lifetime.

10. *Well Regulated:* All Mutual Funds are registered with SEBI and they function within the provisions of strict regulations designed to protect the interests of investors. The operations of Mutual Funds are regularly monitored by SEBI.

6.7.5 Net Resource mobilisation by Mutual Funds

(₹ in crore)

Category	2005-06	April '05	April '06	Mar. '06
UTI	3,424	2.0	–210	4,030
Other public sector	6,378	917	2,236	1,684
Private Sector	**42,977**	**10,357**	**18,802**	**30,113**
Total	**52,779**	**11,275**	**20,828**	**35,827**
Cumulative Assets under Management	2,31,863	1,58,422	2,57,499	2,76,343

June 06 July 06
– 4603 / 20302

Source: SEBI Bulletin – May/June 2006.

The net investment by the foreign institutional investors FII in mutual funds have been as below:

(Amt. in ₹ crore)

Year	Equity	Debt	Total	Asset under Management
2004-05	448	16,981	17,429	1,49,600
2005-06	14,308	36,486	50,794	2,31,863
April '06	3,121	4,503	7,624	2,57,499

6.7.6 Precautions before Investments

In every advertisement, there remains a warning that "mutual fund investments are subject to market risk, please read the offer document carefully before investing". So, we should know the risks, what for such warning is statutorily given in the advertisement, but to a small investor, it is very difficult to read such offer document which runs into 80 to 100 pages. Most of the investors also do not understand the clauses given in the offer document. Hence, in view of such difficulties it is proper to know and give attention to the precautions needed before any investments in mutual funds. Though, the SEBI has incorporated in the offer document, abridged form which give full details about memorandum to the would be investors. The ten precautions to be taken care of are:

Offer document: It contains the objects of the fund group and its strategy is defined in detail. By this document one comes to know the previous performance, details about fund manager record and financial informations. Persons can know such details directly through e-mail and website.

1. Date of issue of fund.
2. Minimum subscription amount and its multiples, e.g., the minimum subscription can be for individuals can be ₹ 5,000 while for institutional premium liquid plans it can to ₹ 2 crore.
3. Read fund's objective carefully as to their plans — whether plans are for short-term or long-terms, the ratio of equity and debt.
4. Investment policy be seen. Fund manager provide details of investment, their strategies — whether investments in Government Bonds or in equities of blue chips or ordinary

companies, credit rating of bonds and the names of the companies where investments are to be made.

5. Quantum of risk be also studied. Risk section contains credit risk/market risk/interest rate risk, which are discussed in detail. It should be noted the higher the proportion in equity higher risk. Suppose the fund has invested 20% in equity and the sensex in BSE/NSE is on high jump then fund will get profit and it would be your advantage.
6. What has been previous performance of the fund, should also be seen. For comparison of performance the offer document contains data per share and its net asset value (NAV) as per SEBI directives which should be compared for your decision.

   Further the performance should also be seen in short-term and long-term categories.
7. The amount of Exit Load and Entry Load should be known and what are other fees and other charges. And if you want to switch another fund, what could be the charges, be also seen.
8. What has been the experience of fund manager and CEO and how is their management team? See also the style of the fund manager in investment.
9. One gets advantage of Section 23D and 115, of Income Tax Act, for the investments in mutual funds but should be seen in the equity fund.
10. On the last page of the document, the various services offered to investors could be available its systems, are told. Specific answer is required in case of reinvestment of dividend, or systematic investment or advantage of Exit plan. Annual reports can be had from the fund company and get comments from any financial planner, all mutual funds' investors w.e.f 2nd July, 2007, are required to tender their PAN number and residence proof, if they invest ₹ 50,000 or more as per SEBI guidelines. The mutual fund companies would issue Mutual Identification Number to investors which would be quoted in all schemes where investment would be made by investors.

6.7.7 Whether to Invest in Mutual Funds or Direct in Shares?

Generally, the small investors are guided to invest in mutual funds rather than directly in share market. Even the Finance Minister of India had on various occasions in the year 2006, advised the small investors for investing only in mutual funds for better security and minimising risks. But this does not appear to the correct since the purpose of mutual funds is to grab the money from strangers or unknown investors.

Now, we would see the working of mutual funds. Most of the funds invest their funds in *short-terms* funds and has become a centre for wholesale investors. Fund Managers work only for big companies. For retail investors, the promises and details are only lip-service to them. Actually, mutual funds have gone against the retail investors due to 4 reasons:

(*a*) Another exploitation of investor is the charging of *"management fee"* in lieu of expenses of Asset Management Company. The purpose of this fee is to earn margin in order to make happy to the shareholders of the AMC. The wholesale investors is not charged entry load but only management fee while retail investors are charged both; so double expenses.

When the fund incurs any losses, which happens many times, the exit of retail investors would cost again, even less than principle amount. While the AMC is not affected at all whether there was any loss or profit to the fund.

(*b*) Company's contribution remains more in the mutual funds hence the fate of these are decided with the attitude of companies and actual sufferer is the retail investor. Suppose, if there is demand by company for withdrawal of money, they sell the units; and for payment of amount to sellers, the fund managers sell the assets at any cost resulting reduction in NAV and loss falls on the retail investors.

(*c*) Presently, there are over 800 mutual funds and due to their options, about 1,200 NAVs are published daily. If you derive to invest in mutual funds then you have to study all the 1,200 schemes which cannot be done by a small investor, at all due to their limitations.

In view of above there is need to curtail the undesirable activities of mutual funds if the Finance Minister actually wants to see growth of retail investors.

6.7.8 Past Performance of Certain Mutual Funds

Due to increase in sensex (18,407 Mark on 3-2-2011) mutual funds performance has been excellent till 2009, resulting high returns to the retail investors as below:

(*i*) Equity Oriented Mutual Fund schemes totalling 45 have paid dividend 100% to their investors.

(*ii*) While 29 schemes have given return in between 90 to 100%.

Such schemes include diversified equity schemes and equity linked saving schemes and even sector fund schemes.

If we look at the sensex, we observe that there has been increase in it, in a year, by about 93% in BSE while 83% in NSE index during 2007 and 2008.

The mutual funds scheme of Prudential ICICI FMCC Space, in one year has given return of about 108% while Reliance diversified power sector infrastructure has given return of 107%. In the same way, the HDFC-Tax saver, Ing-Vysya Tax Saving, ICICI Tax plan and Sundaram Tax Saver have also given return in between 100 to 105%.

6.7.9 Misconcepts about Mutual Funds

There are about 10 concepts (or misconcepts) about mutual funds which needs to be explained to the retail investors, as follows:

(1) All mutual funds schemes are the same.

Mainly mutual fund schemes are of 3 types, *viz.*,

(*a*) equity scheme, total investment in equity shares.

(*b*) debt schemes, investments in bonds, commercial papers, debentures and call money, etc.

(*c*) balanced scheme (partly in debts and partly in equities.

(2) Balanced fund consists of 50% equity and 50% debt.

Presently, there are about 23 balanced funds in which there has never been allotment of 50-50%. Normally, investment in such funds has been in between 60 to 70% in equity and the balance in debt form.

(3) Fund Agent better cares investor's profitability

Agents advise or praises those fund-schemes, wherein they get higher rate of commission hence do not depend upon your fund's agent for advice.

(4) Investment in mutual funds is costly

Investment in mutual funds needs professional advice and the fund manager keeps eye over investment. There does not arise any need for opening Demat account and brokerage account.

(5) Investment in mutual funds IPO is cheaper — Mutual funds units face value is ₹ 10. Due to higher quantum of amount, mutual funds charge high NAV for old schemes. Due to this investors move towards new schemes where those are considered cheap. This is their concept. Actually objects of old/new schemes are equal. If the old scheme performance is good their investment in it is better.

(6) Investment in mutual funds increases lower than the investment in stocks.

There always remain risk in investment in private stocks which require up to date information. It is correct that shares giving better results/dividends do also give better/higher return than the mutual funds.

But the position becomes reverse in case of downmarket in shares while mutual funds have no such risks.

(7) Investment in mutual funds require only seeing *the past performance.*

Investment in mutual funds need only to look at the objectives of the fund schemes, cost of investment, ratio of risk-return and previous performance.

(8) No need to look at the performance subsequently of mutual funds after investment.

Constant vigil on the performance of mutual funds is essential at least once a quarter.

(9) Investment of entire money in better managed mutual funds only.

Diversification in mutual funds is essential your capital reaches to fund-houses and fund managers. When portfolio of mutual fund is considered see that the share in equity and loan portions is as you require.

(10) Valuation of mutual funds is easy and does not need any adviser.

Today, when there are over 1,200 mutual fund schemes, it is very difficult to examine schemes carefully and then to invest. But when investment in any particular mutual fund is desired then continuous availability of information is essential along with professional advice.

6.7.10 Care to be Taken

Before one turns to invest in mutual funds, it is essential to get all informations and do not get attracted from the returns (dividends) declared/paid by mutual funds. As per research made by Value Research in Aug. 2006, out of 137 diversified equity funds, only 18 funds could do well performance in BSE Sensex, as this is clear from the following table.

Fund Name	*Return in one year %*	*Rank in one year*	*Net Assets (Amt. in ₹ crore)*
1. Reliance NRI equity	50.95	2/137	101.06
2. DWS Alpha equity	48.70	4	87.22
3. Franklin India Opportunity	46.13	8	424.45
4. Sundaram BNP select focus	44.80	9	109.97
5. DSPML T.I.GER	44.78	10	1032.65
6. Prudential ICICI power inst.	44.29	11	1400.00

7. DSPML Top 100 equity	43.12	14	248.50
8. Franklin India Flexi Cap	42.91	15	2974.53
9. Reliance equity opportunity	42.78	16	1937.80

These funds did better because special theme or special sector during this period. One year period is very important because during this there were many corrections and recoveries. Many of the investors were depressed because of low return by mutual funds. The reasons for such low return was given that these funds invested more in stocks and kept them hold for longer period. Since focus fund invested in few stocks, they performed better and higher, hence reached in top 18 funds. As per report submitted by Indian Mutual Fund Association the total assets of mutual funds in Oct. 2006 were of ₹ 3.09 lakh crore while it were of ₹ 2.90 lakh crore in Sept. 2006. Unit Trust of India is at the top level with AUM of ₹ 37,789 crore. The position of other mutual funds have been as under whose total assets have increased in Oct. 2006.

1. UTI MF	37789 (AUM)
2. ICICI Prudential MF	32664
3. Rel. Mutual Fund	31577
4. HDFC MF	27552

While there are other nine funds which have reduced their total assets in the same period, *viz.*,

BOB Mutual Fund
DBS Chola MF
DWS MF
ING Vaishya MF
Kotak Mahindra MF
Principal MF
Sahara MF
Tata MF
Torus MF

While position/rank of 18 equity funds in March 2007 in terms of returns was as below:

		Yearly Return
1.	Reliance Media Star - D	104.09
2.	Reliance Media Bonus	103.70
3.	Reliance Media & Entertainment Fund - G	103.70
4.	JM Basic Fund	101.56
5.	Reliance Banking Fund - G	100.41
6.	Reliance MF Banking - Bonus	100.41
7.	Reliance MF Banking - D	100.37
8.	Reliance Diversified Power Fund - G	99.34
9.	DSP MC Technology.Com Fund - G	97.05
10.	UTI Thermatic Banking Sector Fund - G	95.80

11.	Standard Chartered Premier Equity Fund - G	89.45
12.	ICICI Emerging Star - D	89.75
13.	ICICI Prudential Ser. Ind. - D	89.45
14.	ICICI Prudential Service Ind. Fund - G	89.45
15.	Principal Personal Tax Saver	87.30
16.	DBS Chola Opportunities Fund - G	83.43
17.	DBS Chola Opp. QD	83.38
18.	SBI Mag. Mid Cap - G	75.74

Source: *DNA Money Newspaper*, dt. 23-07-07.

The investors those desire to get higher return they should keep in mind three things, *viz.*,

(*i*) What has been the record of performance of their fund managers?

(*ii*) What is their risk taking capacity?

(*iii*) If the fund is diversified equity fund then how many stocks have been chosen by the fund manager?

6.7.11 Other Essentials

The popularity of mutual funds is enhancing and in view of this it is essential to look into 5 essentials before investment —

(a) It is an investment and not a product: When one invests in mutual funds, it is utilised either in equities or in debt. When it is invested in equities, then it goes to share market. Hence, it is an investment and not a product. Means you are not investing in Mutual Fund but investing through mutual funds.

(b) Legal disclaimer: Before you invest in mutual funds get all details about rules/conditions. There is one clause of legal disclaimer in the offer document, which contains details about sector of utilisation of money and the availability of returns.

(c) Separate scheme, separate risk: Every mutual fund has got different category of risk. What is the quantum of risk depends on the performance of fund manager. In fact, fund manager decides as to which companies the money would be invested and what amount would be invested. He also decides about the time of sale and purchase of shares. Hence, knowledge of track record of fund manager is essential.

(d) Track record of fund manager: To know this, find out the previous performance of the scheme, in how many companies shares the money s invested, if the number of such companies is large, then there is risk to your investment, in how many sectors, the money is invested. When investment is more sectors then more risk. What is the percentage of investment in one company? If major share is invested in one or few companies then the risk is higher since depending on the profitability of companies. If investment is in debt-fund then what is the average investment period. For example, if the investment is from 6 months to 36 months in 10 debt securities, then average period would be in between 6 to 36 months. Debt fund is having higher risk if invested other than gilt-funds.

(e) Investment not for full money: Whatever the amount you invest is not fully and entirely invested in. Out of this, certain percentage is deducted for administration, marketing, sales, fund management, etc. Some amount is also kept as security and the balance is invested. You should know as to what is the actual investment.

(f) Services are not free: When you are investing through mutual funds then you have been certain expenses which is paid in the form of *Load*. Such loads are of two kinds: (*i*) entry load, and (*ii*) exit load. Such loads at present are in the range of 0.5 to 2.25% (for entry load) and in between 0.5 to 4.0% (for exit load) are charged by mutual funds.

6.7.12 Position of Monthly Income Mutual Funds

Take a look at some monthly income Mutual Fund schemes that aim to generate regular returns through investment primarily in debt and money market instruments.

Scheme Name	*Returns (%)*			
	1 Month	*3 Months*	*6 Months*	*1 Year*
ABN-AMRO Monthly Income Plan-Growth	1.66	7.01	12.49	14.5
DSP Merrill Lynch Savings Plus Moderate Plan-Growth	1.26	3.17	7.67	11.14
HDFC Monthly Income Short-term Plan-Gth	1.23	2.12	6.11	6.39
Alliance Monthly Income Plan-Growth	0.95	2.31	9.12	12.47
Kotak Mahindra Income Plus-Growth	0.91	2.75	6.06	8.19
Templeton Monthly Income Plan-Growth	0.87	1.79	7.35	9.73
HSBC MIP Savings-Gth	0.83	2.93	9.17	12.06
Prudential ICICI Monthly Inc Plan-Gth	0.76	2.7	8.01	11.49
LIC Monthly Income Plan-Growth	0.75	3.2	7.69	10.75
Principal Monthly Income Plus-Growth	0.75	2.14	7.37	7.36
Chola Monthly Inc-Gth	0.71	2.57	6.65	8.05
Magnum Monthly Income Plan-Growth	0.69	1.49	4.85	8.04
Birla Monthly Income Plan-Growth	0.62	1.6	7.29	9.79
ING Vysya Monthly Income Plan B-Growth	6.59	2.31	7.83	7.8
UTI Monthly Income Scheme-Growth	0.52	1.95	6.17	8.94
Sundaram Monthly Income Plan-Growth	0.41	1.83	5.36	7.1
BoB MIP Fund-Growth	0.37	1.7	3.06	6.76

6.7.13 PAN (Permanent Account Number)

❖ Mandatory Requirement

PAN has been made mandatory for transacting in the futures and options market as well as for operating a Beneficiary Owner (BO) account in the depository system.

In continuation of the above and to further strengthen the *Know Your Client* (KYC) norms in the cash market with a view to facilitate sound audit trail, it is decided that PAN is mandatory for all the entitles/persons who are desirous of transacting in the cash market with effect from *1st Oct., 2006*.

❖ Clarifications for PAN

1. All entities registered under SEBL Act, 1992 (Sec. 12) and having some difficulty in producing PAN CARD for verification at the time of opening the BO account may be permitted to open a DD account without producing the PAN CARD. However, such

entities would be required to submit the Pan Card to the DPs within a period of 30 days from the date of opening of the BO account for verification, *failing which* the DP shall freeze such accounts with remark *suspended for debit.*

2. As regards proof of address of FIIs, a copy of the Power of Attorney given by the FIIs to the custodians that gives the registered address of the FIIs can be accepted as proof of address.
3. NRIs/PIOs are required to comply with the mandatory requirement of producing PAN card at the time of opening a BO account.
4. United Nations entitles/multilateral agencies which are *exempt* from paying taxes/filing tax returns in India are *exempted* from the *mandatory requirement of PAN.*
5. In case of HUF, association of persons, partnership firm, unregistered trust, etc., through the BO account would be in the name of natural persons, PAN of respective units shall be obtained.
6. As regards registered trust, corporate bodies and minors, PAN of the respective entities shall be obtained when accounts are opened is their respective names.
7. In case where there is differences in the maiden name and current name of the investor (particularly in the case of married women) DPs can collect the PAN card proof as submitted by the accountholder, subject to the DPs verifying the veracity of the claim of such investors by collecting sufficient, documentary evidence in support of the identity of the investors.
8. The mandatory requirement of PAN is exempted in the Sikkim State as per High Court of Sikkim dt. 31-3-2006. But the DPs in Sikkim's investors are subject to the sufficient documentary evidence in support of their address.

❖ Considerations before Investments

A typical dilemma faced by investors today is to choose between safety of capital and the opportunity to earn higher returns. Sticking to traditional fixed income investments might be *safe* option but also means relatively lower inflation-adjusted returns. On the other hand, while equities have the potential to deliver higher returns, one may be concerned about market volatility Funds facts should be noted which consist the following.

Scheme	— Capital protection or guaranteed returns
Offer price	— at ₹ 10.
Minimum investment amounts	— ₹ 5,000/10,000/50,000
Plan period	— 3 years/5 years
Liquidity	— Whether mutual fund will repurchase the units before maturity
Load Structure	— No entry load only charging of ₹ 100 fee for ₹ 10,000 — from Aug. 2011) (in open-ended schemes) exit load rate.
Rating of scheme	— highest CRISIL Rating be there for repayment of face value on maturity.
Name of fund manager for	— equity and/or debt portion.
Share in debt/equity	— to know stability of return on investment

Due to change in fund offer in mutual funds are given 5 days for allotment during the year 2010 July resulting reduction in subscription. The following figures speak themselves:

2010 — ₹ 3,000 crore in – 24 NFO

2009 — ₹ 7,284 crore in – 33 NFO

2008 — ₹ 12,722 crore in – 48 NFO

2007 – ₹ 39,327 crore in – 64 NFO.

From July 2010, as per instructions of SEBI subscription to mutual funds remains open for 15 days (as against earlier 30 days).

6.7.14 Beware of Mutual Fund Returns

The returns declared by Mutual Fund Managers are many times misleading. There is one process known Black-Scholes Merton Process which has a huge influence on the way that traders price and hedge options. This has also been pivotal to the growth and success of financial engineering in the last 3 decades. In mutual fund there are two essentials —

- Expected returns on share per year (m)
- Volatily of the share price per year (s)

Suppose the sequence of yearly returns by the mutual fund over the last 5 years are:

15%, 20%, 30% - 20%, 25%

The arithmetic mean of the returns, calculated by taking the sums of the returns and dividing by 5 is 14%. However, an investor would actually earn less than 14% p.a. by leaving the money invested in the fund for 5 years. The value of ₹ 100 at the end of the 5 years would be —

$$100 \times 1.15 \times 1.20 \times 1.30 \times 1.20 \times 1.25 = ₹\ 179.40$$

By contrast, a 14% p.a. return with annual compounding gives

$$100 \times 1.145 = ₹\ 192.5^4$$

Hence, the return that gives ₹ 179.40 at the end of 5 years is 12.4%. This is because

$100 \times (1.124)5 = ₹\ 179.40$

Hence, the statement made in advertisement by Mutual Funds are misleading. Hence, while calculating returns on investment the geometric mean should be considered which is (1.124) in the example rather than arithmetic mean which is (1.140) which is misleading —

6.7.15 How to Handle Mutual Funds Paperwork?

1. Through online transactions ask for common folio number to consolidate MF holdings (even across different schemes).
2. Use Electronic Clearing Service (ECS) or direct credit facility to do away with physical deposit of dividend cheques.
3. Demand annual statements from mutual funds for tax-filing purposes.
4. Use trigger facility.
5. SIP investors insist on common folio number on renewal.
6. Inform mutual fund houses about any changes to bank account or address.

7. Register online with mutual fund houses to print statements anytime or receive updates through e-mails.
8. Use the online equity broking account to buy mutual fund units too.
9. Know that in case of common folio holdings, FIFO (First in First Out) methodology is followed for tax proposes while redeeming partial units.
10. Verify that the fund house has a direct credit tie-up with banks where you have your account.
11. Reducing paperwork is one of the most important steps undertaken to make investment less cumbersome and acceptable. This would also enable mutual funds in cost reductions in terms of paperwork, which would lower expense ratios to unitholders.

❖ How to Read Offer Document of MF?

There are seven steps to be taken by any investor to read the offer document of any mutual fund as under:

(*a*) Check whether the fund in question is *equity balanced* or *debt-fund.*

(*b*) The offer document *mentions the objectives* with its broad equity ad debt allocation. For instance, it gives a band of equity allocations of 80-100% which means that the fund manager would invest in equities anywhere within that range.

(*c*) Analyse the *performance track-record* of the fund have in question. Often there is a mention of performance of its other schemes, which when compared to its peers would give an inkling of its relative performance.

(*d*) Check if the fund is trying to *take extra-risk.*

(*e*) *Open or close-ended:* Most funds are open-ended giving its investors, option to buy or sell units at any point in time. But some of the small cap funds launched are close-ended too.

(*f*) *Entry* and *exit load* for a fund reduces the overall units you would own.

(*g*) *Expense ratio:* Are the same around 2-2.5% p.a. for equity funds and other debt-based funds. The ratio vary which could affect returns. Investors should check for any deviations.

6.7.16 When to *quit out* of Mutual Funds Schemes?

1. When you feel that market is on its full rise.
2. When your mutual funds performance is not better continuously in rising prices of equities.
3. Investment return should be checked every quarterly and can use mutual fund tracker which is available on private financial websites.

❖ Whether to Invest in MFs or Directly in Share Markets?

The answer is to invest directly in shares, because:

1. Mutual funds becomes the source of investments of corporates, in short-term investments and as such is moulded as per wholesale investors needs. MFs work as per requirements of big companies and they do not have any thinking for small investors.

2. There is levy of *load factor* by MFs. All investors are charged *entry load,* those who invest less than prescribed limits. For example, those who invest less than ₹ 5 crore are charged with entry load of 2¼%. We can clarify the same again. Suppose you have invested ₹ 10,000 in units of ₹ 10 each. These units, due to entry load will not cost you ₹ 10 but ₹ 10.225 resultantly, you will get 977 units as against 1,000 applied.
3. MFs charge *management fees* in lieu of Asset Management Company. The purpose is to earn margins so that shareholders of asset management company are made happy due to higher dividends fee is charged on all assets which includes both wholesale and retail investors. While retail investors do not pay any entry load, the retail investors are charged two levies (fees) and as such bear double expenses. Bigger the size of the fund, bigger is the income to asset management company.
4. If the MF scheme starts incurring losses then the investor has to come out of the scheme and suffer losses due to lower NAV.
5. More influence of the big companies who have invested on wholesale. If they draw, out the investment, they drew out not only from one scheme but from various schemes. Total sums of which goes with hundreds and thousands of crore of rupees which compels the MF to sell their assets to refund the amount. This means heavy loss to MF in their liquidity and deduction of exit charge.
6. Study of 1,200-1,300 schemes daily, by retail investors is impossible task. There are at present about 800 fund schemes.
7. SEBI Regulator of MFs overlooks the doubtful activities of MFs and as such retail investors suffer, till such things come to limelight.

6.7.17 How to Build a Mutual Fund?

Picking the right mutual fund out of more than 3,000 options in the market is tricky enough. But it can be truly daunting to figure out-how to bring the right one together to make a portfolio that can outperform the index, while also being in sync with your personal risk tolerance, investment objectives and tax situation. There's just no one-size-fits-all strategy, nor one "correct" way, to build a mutual fund portfolio.

Putting together a group of mutual funds is a matter of your personal preferences and goals. But there are some universals you should think about when choosing and combining funds to create your portfolio. You can use the following steps as a guide to building and monitoring your mutual fund portfolio.

❖ Starting with Asset Allocation

One starts out by selecting an asset allocation plan designed to meet your goals and risk tolerance. The rest of the investment process includes picking funds — either for taxable or tax-advantaged accounts — putting them together in a portfolio, monitoring the portfolio overtime, and rebalancing it so it remains in line with your risk tolerance.

The foundation of your portfolio is asset allocation — your preferred combination of large-cap and small-cap Indian stocks, international stocks, bonds, and cash. It determines the broad risk level of your portfolio, which should match your risk profile, and is the first step towards constructing a diversified portfolio.

The basic premise of diversification — which is to reduce certain risks unique to an asset class, sector or security by combining different securities together — works because different asset classes, sectors and securities don't move in tandem. Even when well-known asset classes such as large-cap stocks are dropping, other asset classes may be rising.

❖ Outperforming the Benchmark

When you put together a portfolio of mutual funds, your goal should be to outperform the relevant benchmarks for each asset class in your portfolio (evaluated using index returns) without taking on excessive risk of underperformance. This guiding principle implies that we're not going to be so conservative in our investment decision-making that we completely eliminate any upside opportunity versus the benchmark, which would be the case if we selected all index mutual funds, for example. But we're not going to be so aggressive that we fail to adequately diversify the portfolio within asset classes. The key to achieving that goal is picking the right funds.

6.7.18 Picking Funds Wisely

When you select funds for portfolios, you should look for funds that will do well in the future and that will work well together. These need not necessarily be funds that have been at the very top of their categories in the past. You should consider the following factors when picking the right funds: past performance, including past risk-and style-adjusted performance (a measure of the fund manager's security selection skill), the fund's operating expense ratio assets under management, and cash flows. Use a blend of quantitative and qualitative analysis.

The first thing to remember in evaluating a mutual fund scheme's performance is to separate performance luck from skill. A fund's return is what it is for a variety of reasons, some having to do with luck and some with skill. You should see the fund's year-on-year performance to see if it has been doing consistently well, or if this is just a one-time good performance which has boosted returns. A fund heavily invested in technology stocks might have performed well in years past, but remaining heavily invested in tech now could have greatly hurt returns. So check whether the fund's strategy is flexible, and whether the fund manager shuffles the portfolio regularly.

The second thing to keep in mind is to look beyond past performance. Non-performance-related characteristics for instance, expenses, assets under management, and cash flows into the fund can influence future performance. For example, conventional wisdom says it's difficult for small-cap managers with many assets under management to do well, because it's hard to put large sums of money to work in management's best investment ideas without negatively affecting the price of those small-cap stocks. Generally, small-cap funds with low expense ratios and few assets under management eventually significantly outperform their peers with high expense ratios and many assets under management. But keep in mind that this theory is relevant for evaluating small-cap funds, and not, for example, large-cap funds.

Which brings us to point number three: don't use a one-size-fits-all approach. The amount of consideration, or weight, that should be given to each factor varies depending on the category. A fund's operating expense ratio, for example, is always an important consideration. But it's more important for categories such as intermediate-term bonds, where returns are low and the underlying investments are traded in very efficient markets, versus, say, international funds, where returns are higher and the underlying investments are traded in both efficient and less efficient markets. In other words, expenses take a bigger bite out of bond fund returns, and managers have less opportunity to make it up by security selection.

The fourth thing to remember when evaluating fund performance is to remember to look at the whole story: The numbers are important, but qualitative considerations matter too. Look at the fund manager's profile, the performance of his/her other funds, and his/her investment strategy. For instance, it could happen that the fund is categorised as a low risk investment, but the fund manager is actually taking an aggressive stance.

6.7.19 Making a Portfolio of Funds

The most critical task is, of course, creating the portfolio. It entails analysing your profile — your risk capacity, objectives for investment, time horizon, and the amount to be invested. Different factors determine the appropriate mix for you, how much exposure you should have to any asset class, and what the time horizon should be for your investment.

Equity markets are too volatile in the short-term, but can give good returns in the long-run. Debt funds, on the other hand, give steady but low returns. Therefore, depending on your goal and risk profile, the asset class will be determined.

If, say, your retirement is 15 years away, an equity-dominated portfolio would be a good option. But if you have taken a personal loan, which you have to pay up in just one year, debt funds will be more suitable. If you have a medium-term goal, like a trip abroad, balanced funds may be the right answer. And generally, liquid funds are a nice place to park very short-term funds.

Depending on the corpus, you could invest in an average of 4-7 funds for an equity portfolio, and maybe 3-4 funds for the debt and balanced category. If you invest in too few funds, it could make your portfolio concentrated and risky. If you invest in too many, the portfolio becomes unmanageable and doesn't really serve the purpose. So it's important to strike the right balance.

Also, while selecting funds, study each one's portfolio mix to ensure that the funds are not all similar. If most of them are similar, you will .not achieve the desired diversification even with 6-7 funds. In order to achieve diversification across asset classes, consider options such as real estate fund, gold fund, international fund, and so on. Once these factors are decided, a portfolio plan can be created that includes an appropriate mix of funds.

❖ Rebalancing and Monitoring

Discipline is a highly desirable trait, because it can lead to success in many aspects of our lives. Just as a disciplined diet and an exercise routine are critical to your physical health, a disciplined rebalancing strategy is critical to your financial well-being. Unfortunately, many of us don't rebalance our portfolio on a regular schedule, because we're either too busy or because we let our emotions get the better of us, choosing to hold on too long to investments that have performed well. Following a disciplined rebalancing strategy means you are more likely to sell higher-priced assets in favour of lower-priced ones — which makes plenty of sense. We recommend rebalancing back to your target allocation at least annually. You may want to rebalance sooner if there is an extreme change in value in some part of your portfolio.

Portfolio management doesn't stop with the creation of your portfolio. It's important to monitor funds on an ongoing basis. You should consider selling a fund if there is a change in management, organisation, or strategy, or if you foresee a significant deterioration in the fund's prospects. If you don't have the time, desire and expertise to construct, monitor and rebalance a diversified portfolio of mutual funds, a mutual fund advisor can help.

6.7.20 When do you Jump into a Mutual Fund?

Every time you exit a fund and re-enter a new one, someone is making a good buck.

Pune-based retirees Sushma and Ramesh Malani were recently approached by their "relationship manager" — no, this was not someone armed to give them man-woman relationship advice, but a self-appointed financial advisor from their bank branch. His advice: "I propose that you put your money in X equity mutual fund. It is a good performer", he told them, "Your money will grow well".

Nothing wrong with this story, except that seven months earlier, the same gentleman had come to the Malanis peddling another fund. Now, he was telling them to exit the earlier fund and get into the new one. His reason? The first fund had done well, but the second one he was recommending would do even better, he advocated. Also, it was a new fund and he told them they would get in at 'face value'.

Face value? Oh dear! The Malanis were nicely hooked. They had been raised in the IPD investment generation, and had made money investing in shares at face value, so they applied the same logic to mutual fund new issues as well, not realising that this is one of the most common cons faced by individuals who invest in mutual funds.

The subtext of this in-out drama is that the advisor stands to make enormous commissions every time you enter a fund. Plus, when you exit a scheme within a year of getting in it, another penalty comes into play: So what is a bonus for the advisor, could end up being a double hit for you!

So often, your relationship manager takes a look at the funds you already own, shakes his head, tut-tutting. When you ask him in alarm, what the matter is, he will point at your list and say how badly your funds are doing.

In some cases, such as in equity funds, the commission can be higher than 2%. And guess what? Banks earn even more because they are bulk sellers of funds. In new fund offers, they can earn up to 5%. For those who are not good at math, when you invest ₹ 1 lakh, your bank could be earning ₹ 5,000 — for merely getting you to sign the form!

The head of a retail channel at a major mutual fund house explains what is going on: "Banks earn their revenues from two areas — one is their core banking business, the other is from fees from referring their clients to third-party products like mutual funds or insurance products. Sometimes, the advice given to customers may be driven by the bank's revenue model rather than the customer's best interest."

The Malanis still have not caught on to the fact that they are being 'churned'. Their charming relationship manager has now become vice-president at the same bank.

When the same thing was happening to Prakash Mehta, a Mumbai-based entrepreneur, he decided to get a perspective from a relative who was in the financial planning field. That was when he learned that he was being taken for a nice ride. He was also being 'churned'.

His cousin sat him down and explained to him how to evaluate when to sell a fund by listing a few reasons. She suggested that if some of these reasons were applicable, then he could consider selling. One, is if it is genuinely a dog. She helped him check the performance of a fund, comparing it with other funds in the same category. An aggressive equity fund must only be compared with other aggressive equity funds. An infrastructure fund has to be seen against other similar funds. One easy place to get information is by going online into a site like www.valueresearchonline.com or www.moneycontrol. com. Such sites have objective and regularly-updated data on mutual funds and other schemes. Better still, ask your advisor to provide these inputs for you. If your fund is one of the worst performers, consider selling. However, you need to look at more than just· fund's rating.

She also recommended that Prakash should evaluate whether to sell the fund based on his original objective. For instance, Prakash had invested in an equity index fund over the last six years, to help fund his daughter's IB school, education. This year she has finished her 10th standard and is waiting her results. He needed to review whether to sell that fund or not based on his current financial situation.

Finally, she advised him that the most important thing to remember is that the person who repeatedly calls you from your bank, supposedly giving you advice, has probably been put through superficial training on the subject over a short period and then thrown out into the big bad world to achieve 'targets'. To be fair to these young 'turks', they often believe that selling a ULIP (Unit Linked Insurance Plan) or an NFO (New Fund Offer) is the best thing for you, their investor.The brain washing they get is hugely convincing. So is the pressure to achieve targets in order to retain their jobs. And that's the basis of their 'relationship'!

TIMING IT RIGHT

- **Does it still meet your objectives?** Sometimes a fund does not stick to its original investment objectives. In that case it's not meeting your objectives either. This can become problematic if this drifting fund spoils your efforts at diversification and doesn't meet your asset allocation goals. Each fund has to publish its holdings once a quarter so this data can be provided by your advisor and/or the fund house.
- **Vet the performance of comparable MFs:** Ask your advisor to provide you with performance data over a good length of time. If a similar fund's overall performance is down 10%, your fund is down 16% and your fund's performance consistently trails its peers, your fund may be a loser.
- **Keep track of changes in your fund's management:** If the fund hires a new fund manager, he/she may have a different investment outlook or strategy.
- **Check for overlapping stocks in your portfolio:** Ask your financial advisor to research whether, for example, the two diversified growth mutual funds that you own hold shares in the same set of companies. There will always be some like Reliance or L&T which are liquid stocks; other than these avoid having the same stocks to stay diversified, sell one of the MFs and replace it with another.
- **Can you deal with the volatility?** In a volatile market, you may discover that you're a more conservative investor than you imagined. If you can't sleep at night, sell your fund.
- **Monitor performance:** If the fund increases by three or four times its original size in a short period and its performance starts to decline, you may want to sell. As the fund grows, the professional money manager can't invest in the securities he/she knows best, so the fund may start to acquire poor-performing assets.
- **Consider your needs:** If you bought the fund for a specific purpose and your life circumstances change, sell the fund and buy one that meets your needs — even if the fund is doing well.
- **Is it becoming too expensive?** If your MF's expenses have been creeping up, you may want to sell. The higher the expenses, the less you earn. However, expenses are limited by SEBI rules.

6.8 CONSUMER FINANCE

India is experiencing the rise of service economy and the culture of *living off debt.* In the recent past, the conservative middle class debt-averse Indians are increasingly growing for spending on conspicuous consumption. The low rate of inflation, high interest rates (during 2010 and 2011) TV or media bombardment, internet access, greater availability of choice in buying consumer durables, due to globalization have contributed to this new culture. Commercial and cooperative banks, NBFCs have liberalized access to credit for the consumers. Consumers are now in a position to buy everything from TV, fridge, car, scooter, computers, furniture, home or flat, through instalment and hire purchase credit. The manufacturers, financiers, banks, NBFCs are coming together to make attractive credit offers to the potential buyers. They have come up with new schemes such as zero interest scheme, 100% finance schemes, instantaneous loan approval scheme. (Housing loan in 48 working hours), step-up and step-down repayment (monthly instalment increases or decreases each year) scheme, and front-ended and back-ended (higher repayment at the beginning and higher repayments towards the end) scheme, which have help to expanded Consumer Finance Market in India also. The consumers loan are SECURED and UNSECURED; the former include. Home loans/vehicle loans/TV, fridge, air-conditioners, furniture, computer loans, while the latter include credit card, personal loans and so on. The official estimates of the size of consumer finance are not available. Once estimate puts the consumer finance to be of the order of about ₹ 70,000 crore (in the year 2003) and its annual rate of growth to be about 30%. The receivables in the economy are growing at a higher rate. The expansion in consumer finance has been accompanied by the need for risk management or containing deliquencies and losses in repayments of loans. Banks have developed their techniques to manage risk, such as using past repayments of previous loan, turnover in the deposit operative account and credit card volume of transactions to gauge the financial creditability of the borrower. The consumer financier has to deal with operational risks like frauds also.

❖ Features of Consumer Finance

- It can be availed by individuals, are 18 years of age partnership firms and public or private limited companies and are either existing depositors of the bank or consumers with proven ability and willingness to repay.
- It is offered for worthwhile purchase or approved purposes to purchase article of either personal use.
- The loan amount can be minimum ₹ 10,000 and maximum ₹ 10 lakh.
- The purpose can be besides consumer durables good, to peruse higher education or for holiday-tour or meeting wedding expenses.
- The security for good articles is its hypothecation or personal integrity of the borrower.
- The repayment is in equated monthly instalments (EMI) which is to be repaid over a period of 12 months to 60 months and for having loan up to 10 years. This is arrived at after verifying the costumers income, having potential and the life of the asset/ goods so purchased.
- The repayment or loans is done either through standing instructions or receipt or post-dated cheques from the customer.
- Interest rates are charged in between 9% to 15%, as per purpose of the consumer loan.

- Such loans enable banks to channelise their loanable funds or adding more depositors giving more float funds and ensuring more profit for the bank.

The common credit (finance) encompasses all asset-based financing plans that are offered primarily to individuals for acquiring consumer durables. The typical form of a customer credit transaction is one where the individual pays a fraction of the cash purchased price on taking delivery of the asset and agrees to pay the balance with interest over a specified (1 year to 5 years) period of time.

❖ Determinations of Flat and Effective Rates of Interest

For example: The EMI (Equated monthly instalments) for a consumer loan of ₹ 20,000 under three repayment options are as under:

Repayments in Months	EMI (₹)
12	1,900
24	1,070
36	799

Calculate the Flat and Effective Rates of interest for each option.

Solution:

I. Repayment Period = 12 Months

Total Charge of Credit = (1900 × 12) – 20,000 = 2800

Flat Rate of Interest $= \dfrac{2,800}{20,000} \times 100 = 14\%$

While Effective Rate of Interest $= \dfrac{n}{n+1}.2F = \dfrac{12}{13}$

$= 25.85\%$

II. Repayment Period = 24 months

Total Charges for credit = (1070 × 24) – 20,000 = 5680

Annual Charges (for 12 Months) = 2840

Flat Rate of Interest $= \dfrac{2,840}{20,000} \times 100 = 14.2\%$

Effective Rate of Interest $= \dfrac{24}{25} \times 28.4 = 27.26\%$

III. Repayment Period = 36 months

Flat Rate = 14.61%

Effective Rate = 28.43%

6.8.1 Truth Behind a Personal Loan

The incident of a Mumbaikar committing suicide after being harassed by a bank's recovery agents has brought into focus the pitfalls of personal loans.

One newspaper decided to locate the strands that weave a Debt trap for loan-seekers. We found that even though financiers offered 'attractive interest rates' the only thing attractive was the way it was put across to the customer.

What would your reaction when a financer tells you, "Sir, you can get a loan for just two per cent interest". There's a good chance that you would readily accept the 'lucrative' offer. But, before jumping into such a deal, there are questions one must ask in order to unveil the devil that as they say, lies in the details.

The first thing to confirm is the duration of the period for which the bank is charging interest. Is the two per cent interest being charged monthly, half-yearly or annually? The financier, who told us that the interest was two per cent, admitted that it was two per cent monthly. A two per cent interest, which compounds monthly, works out to a annual rate of almost 27 per cent.

One must also question the method used to calculate the interest. A leading private sector bank that we visited told us that one can get a personal loan of ₹ 50,000 at an interest of 12 per cent per annum, to be repaid over a period of three years or 36 months. The equated monthly instalment (EMI) to repay the loan worked out to ₹ 1,890 per month, we were told.

How was this bank offering a personal loan at an interest of 12 per cent per annum, when the interest rate being charged on most personal loan was at around 20 per cent? This is the logic the bank gave us: An EMI of ₹ 1,890 per month means that for three years you have paid the bank, ₹ 68,040 (₹ 1,890 × 46). Of this the principle amount, i.e., the loan you have taken amounts to ₹ 50,000. What remains is the interest. So, over a period of three years, the interest paid amounts to ₹ 18,040 (₹ 68,040 – ₹ 50,000), So interest per year amounts to ₹ 6,013 (₹ 18,040/3).

An interest of ₹ 6,013 per annum on a loan amount of ₹ 50,000 means an interest rate of around 12 per cent (this figure is arrived at by dividing ₹ 6,013 by ₹ 50,000 and expressing this as a percentage). This method of expressing interest is known as the flat rate of interest. But this is not the right way to calculate interest. The actual interest the individual taking this loan would have paid is 21.25 per cent, which is almost nine per cent higher than what the bank makes it out to be. But, why distort the interest rate figure and not disclose the real rate? "Traditionally Indians have been averse to borrowing, but, when they hear that the rate is 12 per cent, he will. But, if he is told the rate is 21 per cent he would decline." says the head of a finance firm.

In order to repay the loan, every month an EMI is paid. Every time an EMI is paid, a certain part of the principle amount, i.e., the actual loan that you had taken gets repaid. Hence, the interest at any point of time has to be calculated on the principle or the loan outstanding. This is the correct way of calculating interest and is known as the reducing balance method. This is the method we used when we arrived actual interest rate of 21 per cent.

A part from the disguised interest rate, one should keep a watch on the processing fee, which banks usually deduct from the loan they grant. So, if you have been granted a loan of ₹ 50,000, you will be handed over ₹ 49,000 as two per cent of the loan might be deducted as processing fees.

Sujan Sinha, senior vice-president of retail assets at AXIS Bank, says one has a choice to either pay the processing fee from their OWD pocket or ask the bank to deduct it from the disbursed loan. "People usually resist paying the processing fee and ask us to deduct it from the loan itself", he said.

Banks also say that they offer a discounted rate to the employees of certain organisations, But a few customers, who fell for the bait claim that they were later denied the rebate in the interest rate, stating they did not belong to the class of employees eligible for the rebate.

Finance companies say that their loan targets in the class A cities are aware of what they are purchasing. In areas less urban, where Mahindra Finance operates, managing director Ramesh Iyer, says, "We ask the customer what amount would he be comfortable to pay each month". These questions also help the financier decide what interest rate should be offered to the customer.

"Rates are never common to all. The rate depends on the purpose of the loan, the ability of the person to repay the period and the size of the loan. The interest has a relation to risk. Personal loan is a security free loan, where the security is your ability to repay".

6.9 CREDIT RATING AGENCIES

The role of financial markets in a market economy is that of an efficient intermediator, mediating between savers and investors, mobilizing capital on one hand and efficiently allocating them between competing uses on the other. Such an allocative role hinges crucially on the availability of reliable information. The doctrine of "efficient market allocation" in fact has as its bedrock, what economists label "perfect information". An investor in search of investment avenues has recourse to various sources of information — offer documents of the issuer(s), research reports of market intermediaries, media reports, etc. In addition to these sources, Credit Rating Agencies have come to occupy a pivotal role as information providers, particularly for credit related opinions in respect of debt instruments; a role that has been strengthened by the perception that their opinions are independent, objective, well researched and credible.

The factors leading to the growing importance of the credit rating system in many parts of the world over the last two decades are:

1. the increasing role of capital and money markets consequent to disintermediation;
2. increased securitisation of borrowing and lending consequent to disintermediation;
3. globalisation of the credit market;
4. the continuing growth of information technology;
5. the growth of confidence in the efficiency of the market mechanism; and
6. the withdrawal of Government safety nets and the trend towards privatisation.

It was this growing demand on rating services that enable credit rating agencies to charge issuers for their services. This was much in variance with the mode of financing used hitherto — with no fees charged to the issuers, a credit rating agency used to provide rating information through the sale of their publication and other materials.

The concept of credit rating originated in America in the Southern Hemisphere in 1895.

Credit rating serves as a valuable input in the decision-making process of different participants in the capital market including the regulators. Although credit rating is relatively new in India, the level of awareness as well as its actual use are increasing steadily. With the liberalisation and consequent restructuring of the financial services sector, credit rating is becoming even more important. In this context, it is essential that the major players in the market, particularly the investors, understand the significance as well as the limitations of credit rating. This article attempts to answer some questions that are frequently asked about credit rating.

6.9.1 What is Credit Rating?

Credit rating is a symbolic indicator of the current opinion of a rating agency and of the relative capability and willingness of an issuer of a debt programme to service the debt obligations as per the terms of the contract. This groups together a large number of similar (but not necessarily identical) debt instruments under different categories according to their credit quality as judged by their inherent protective factors.

❖ Credit Rating: Concept

Ratings, usually expressed in alphabetical or alphanumeric symbols, are a simple and easily understood tool enabling the investor to differentiate between debt instruments on the basis of their underlying credit quality. The credit rating is thus *a symbolic indicator of the current opinion of the relative capability of the issuer to service its debt obligation in a timely fashion, with specific reference to the instrument being rated*. It is focused on communicating to the investors, the relative ranking of the default loss probability for a given fixed income investment, in comparison with other rated instruments.

A *rating is specific* to a debt instrument and is intended as a grade, an analysis of the credit risk associated with the particular instrument. It is based upon the relative capability and willingness of the issuer of the instrument to service the debt obligations (both principal and interest) as per the terms of the contract. Thus, a rating is neither a general purpose evaluation of the issuer, nor an overall assessment of the credit risk likely to be involved in all the debts contracted or to be contracted by such entity.

The primary objective of rating is to provide *guidance* to investors/creditors in determining a credit risk associated with a debt instrument/credit obligation. It does not amount to a recommendation to buy, hold or sell an instrument as it does not take into consideration factors such as market prices, personal risk preferences and other considerations which may influence an investment decision. The rating process is itself based on certain 'givens'. The agency, for instance, does not perform an audit. Instead, it is required to rely on information provided by the issuer and collected by analysts from different sources, including interactions in-person with various entities. Consequently, the agency does not guarantee the completeness or accuracy of the information on which the rating is based.

"In determining a rating, both quantitative and qualitative analysis are employed. The judgement is qualitative in nature and the role of the quantitative analysis is to help make the best possible overall qualitative judgement because, ultimately, a rating is an opinion." Standard & Poor's.

❖ Credit Rating as Elucidated by the Leading Rating Agencies of the World

"A rating is an opinion on the future ability and legal obligation of the issuer to make timely payments for principal and interest on a specific fixed income security. The rating measures the probability that the issuer will default on the security over its life, which depending on the instrument may be a matter of days to 30 years or more. In addition, long-term ratings incorporate an assessment of the expected monetary loss should a default occur." *Moody's*

"Credit ratings help investors by providing an easily recognizable, simple tool that couples a possibly unknown issuer with an informative and meaningful symbol of credit quality."

Standard & Poor's

❖ Meaning of Credit Rating

To understand the meaning of credit rating, let us look at some definitions offered by well-known rating agencies.

Moody's: *"Ratings are designed exclusively for the purpose of grading bonds according to their investment qualities".*

Australian Ratings: *"A Corporate Credit rating provides lenders with a simple system of gradation by which the relative capacities of companies to make timely repayment of interest and principal on a particular type of debt can be noted".*

According to CRISIL, *"Credit rating is an unbiased and independent opinion as to issuer's capacity to meet its financial obligations. It does not constitute a recommendation to buy/sell or hold a particular security".*

According to ICRA, *"Ratings are opinions on the relative capability of timely servicing of corporate debt and obligations. These are not recommendations to buy or sell .... neither the accuracy nor the completeness of the information is guaranteed".*

From the above definitions it is understood that:

(*i*) Credit rating is an assessment of the capacity of an issuer of debt security, by an independent agency, to pay interest and repay the principal as per the terms of issue of debt. A rating agency collects the qualitative as well as quantitative data from a company which has to be rated and assesses the relative strength and capacity of company to honour its obligations contained in the debt instrument throughout the duration of the instrument. The rating given is based on an objective judgement of a team of experts from the rating agency.

(*ii*) The ratings are expressed in code number which can be easily comprehended even by the lay investors. The ratings are the quickest way of understanding a company's financial standing without going into the complicated financial reports. Credit rating is only a guidance to the investors and not a recommendation to a particular debt instrument. The important element for investment decision-making in debt security are: (*i*) yield to maturity (*ii*) risk tolerance to investor, and (*iii*) credit risk of the security. Clearly the focus of credit rating is on anyone of these three elements, *viz.,* credit risk of the security and hence it cannot by itself be a basis for investment decision-making. It is only a current opinion on the relative capacity of firms to repay debt in time.

(*iii*) Credit rating, as it exists in India, is done for a specific debt security and not for a company as a whole. No rating agency tells that it is an indicator of the financial status of the company. All that a rating agency claims is that the rating symbols indicate the capacity of the company to honour the terms of contract of a debt instrument.

(*iv*) A debt rating is not a one time evaluation of credit risk, which can be regarded as valid for the entire life of the security. It is an ongoing appraisal. Changes in dynamic world of business may imply a change in the risk characteristics of the security. Hence debt rating agencies monitor the business and financial conditions of the issuer to determine whether modification in rating is warranted.

(*v*) A credit rating does not create a fiduciary relationship between the rating agency and the users of rating since there is no legal basis for such relationships.

6.9.2 Functions of Credit Ratings

The credit rating firms are supposed to do the following functions:

1. Superior Information

Rating by an independent and professional firm offers a superior and more reliable source of information on credit risk for three inter-related risks:

(*a*) it provides unbiased opinion.

(*b*) due to professional resources, a rating firm has greater ability to assess risks.

(*c*) it has access to lot of information which may not be publicly available.

2. Low Cost Information

A rating firm which gathers, analyses, interprets and summarises complex information in a simple and readily understood format for wide public consumption represents a cost-effective arrangement.

3. Basis for a Proper Risk-return Trade Off

If debt securities are rated professionally and if such ratings enjoy widespread investor acceptance and confidence, a more rational risk — return trade off would be established in the capital market.

4. Healthy Discipline on Corporate Borrowers

Public exposure has healthy influence over the management of issuer because of its desire to have a clear image.

5. Formulation of Public Policy Guidelines on Institutional Investment

The public policy on the kinds of securities that are eligible for inclusion in different kinds of institutional portfolios can be developed with great confidence if securities are rated professionally by independent agencies.

❖ Origin

The credit rating concept originated in the USA. In 1860, Henry Vannum poor started publishing financial statistics of railroad companies. In 1909, Moody's Investors Agencies started rating rail-road giving more thrust to the concept. Since then the importance has grown extensively in the global market. System of ratings got institutionalised following the Great Depression. In 1933, the US controller of currency enacted a rule that banks could purchase securities rated only BBB/BAA or above. In 1970, Penn Central, the then largest Railroad company in the world went bankrupt with just under $ 100 million in outstanding commercial paper. This forced the investors to ask for rating for commercial paper. Consequently, today, almost 100% of the commercial paper volume and 99% of the corporate bond volume are rated in the USA.

6.9.3 Credit Rating in India

The environment that prevailed in America when first ratings were assigned, prevails in many developing countries today. The Indian capital market has witnessed a tremendous growth in the past few years. Companies are relying on capital markets for financing existing operations as well as for new projects rather than on institutions. In this process, the average size of debenture issued by companies, the number of companies issuing debentures and the number of investors have grown substantially.

As the number of companies borrowings directly from capital market increases, investors find that the company's size or name is no longer a sufficient assurance of the timely payment of interest and principal. Default by large and well-known companies recently in payment of interest on fixed deposits or debentures has reinforced this belief among investors. They felt the need for an independent and credible agency which judges the quality of debt obligations of different companies' and assists individual and institutional investors in making investment decisions.

In this context, the Credit Rating Information Services of India Limited (CRISIL) was set up in 1987. Following this, Investment Information and Credit Rating Agency of India (ICRA) was promoted in 1991 and Credit Analysis and Research Limited (CARE) was floated in 1993. All the three credit rating agencies have been approved by the Reserve Bank of India.

6.9.4 Benefits of Credit Rating

(*i*) Low Cost Information

Credit rating is a source of low cost information to investors. The collection, processing and analysis of relevant information is done by a specialised agency which a group of investors can trust.

(*ii*) Quick Investment Decision

In the present day complex world ratings enable investors to take quickest possible decisions based on associated ratings.

(*iii*) Independent Investment Decision

For rated instruments, investors need not depend upon the advice of the financial intermediaries. As the rating symbol suggests the creditworthiness of the instrument and indicates the degree of risk involved in it, the investors can make direct investment decisions.

(*iv*) Investors Protection

Hiring of credit agency implies that the management of the company is ready to show its operations for independent scruting. So, the investors who are not provided with confidential information can have overall assessment based on ratings. The creditable and objective rating agency can provide increased disclosure, better accounting standard and improved investor protection.

❖ Benefits to Rated Companies

(*i*) Sources of Additional Certification

Credit rating agency provides additional information to the issuers of debt/ financial instruments. A highly rated firm can enter the market with great confidence. Indian experience shows that use of rating, benefit a great deal by getting larger amount of money from a wider audience at a lower cost.

(*ii*) Increase the Investors Population

A sound credit rating system gives an alternative method to name recognition as a determining factor in making investment and helps increase the population of those investing in debt obligations of the company.

(*iii*) Forewarns Risks

Credit rating acts as a guide to companies which get a lower rating. It forewarns the management of the perception of risk in the market and prompts to take steps on their operating and marketing risks and thereby changes the perception in the market.

(*iv*) Encourages Financial Discipline

Ratings also encourage discipline among corporate borrowers to improve their financial structure and performance to obtain better rating for their debt obligations.

(*v*) Merchant Bankers Job Made Easy

Merchant bankers and brokers will be relieved of the responsibility of guiding investors as to the risk of a particular investment. Merchant bankers and brokers, in the absence of objective information, go on the basis of name recognition in guiding their clients. With the advent of credit rating, what they would be required to do is to bring to the attention of their clients the ratings of debt obligations.

(*vi*) Foreign Collaborations Made Easy

The foreign collaborators always ask for credit rating while negotiating with an Indian company. Credit rating enables to identify instantly the relative credit standing of the company. The importance of credit rating is being increasingly recognised in the Euro-markets.

(*vii*) Benefits the Industry as a Whole

Relatively small and unknown companies use ratings to instill confidence in investors. Higher rate companies get larger amount of money at a lower cost. Thus the industry as a whole can benefit from ratings by direct mobilisation of savings from individuals rather than from intermediary lending institutions.

(*viii*) Low Cost of Borrowing

A company with highly rated instrument has the opportunity to reduce the cost of borrowing by quoting lesser interest rate on fixed deposits or debentures as the investors with low risk preference would invest in safe securities though yielding low rate of return.

(*ix*) Rating as a Marketing Tool

Companies with rated instruments, use rating as a marketing tool to create better image in dealing with their customers, lenders and creditors.

6.9.5 Credit Rating Agencies in India

Currently there are five credit rating agencies in India:

1. Credit Rating Information Service Ltd., (CRISIL).
2. Investment Information and Credit Rating Agency of India (ICRA).
3. Credit Analysis and Research (CARE).
4. Duff Phelps Credit Rating Agency of India Ltd., (DCR India).
5. Onida Individual Credit Rating Agency Ltd., (ONICRA)
6. SME Rating Agency (SMERA)

To assess the future prospects, CRISIL studies the industry or industries in which the company operates and the company's position within the industry. It also makes an evaluation of the management and cash flow projections of the company and identifies the key issues concerning the company.

The industry is studied by analysing demand and supply growth, nature and basis of competition, Government policy for the company and the effect of change in Government policy on the future of the company. The position of the company within the industry is studied to understand how the company would fare in the future.

(*i*) CRISIL, therefore, looks at the operating efficiency in terms of locational advantage, raw material, power and labour situation; its cost structure as compared to that of its nearest competitors and the company's market position in terms of its market share, product strength, selling and distribution arrangements, competitive advantage, customer delivery, etc.

CRISIL, evaluates the management of the company with reference to its track record, the recruitment and training system, planning and control system, depth of managerial talents and succession plans, goals for the company, the philosophy of doing business, attitudes towards taking business risks and the strategies for the company. The tenacity, determination and drive of the management to overcome problems as they arise in the company is yet another factor assessed by the CRISIL.

Then, CRISIL makes its own assessment of cash flows and decides the degree of comfort available from the cash flows to meet cash needs of the company for capital expenditure, working capital growth and debt servicing obligations. In addition, it assesses the company's ability to raise funds quickly in various ways in times of necessity to meet the requirements of servicing debt.

The rating process seeks to identify the key issues concerning the company. For instance, if a company is putting up a new project, the key issue in the rating is the likelihood of timely completion of the project. The rating is a composite assessment of all these factors with the key issue getting greater attention from the Rating agency.

In evaluating the ratings, CRISIL employs both qualitative and quantitative criteria. The judgement made by the CRISIL is necessarily subjective and the quantitative analysis is meant to assist in making best possible overall qualitative judgement.

CRISIL employs a multi-layered decision-making process in assigning ratings. When it receives a request for rating, it assigns two teams on the job. The first team meets the officials and makes an assessment of the industry, company and management. The second team is also required to make its own study of the industry. Then the first team interacts with the back-up team. The findings of the interactions are presented simultaneously in a detailed note to the Branch Internal Committee comprising at least three senior analysts of CRISIL and an Internal Committee of six senior executives and thereafter the note is presented with the recommended ratings to the Rating Committee comprising six directors of the company who are not connected with any shareholders of CRISIL. The Rating Committee members are chosen carefully so that they do not have any links with industries or investment agencies connected with the units being rated. This multi-layered process ensures that no individual decides on rating and that prejudices and biases are eliminated.

The evaluation of the company is made on a confidential basis. The rating process ensures complete confidentiality of information that may be provided by the company.

SEBI GUIDELINES 1999

1. No credit rating agencies shall rate a security issued by its promoters.
2. It has barred rating agencies from rating securities issued by any borrower, subsidiary or associate of the promoter if it has a chairman, director, employee of any such firm.
3. Dual rating is compulsory for public and rights issue of debt instruments of ₹ 100 crore or more.
4. SEBI has decided to incorporate a clause in the listing agreement of stock exchanges requiring companies to cooperate with agencies by providing correct information. Refusal to do so may lead to breach of contract between rating agencies and client.
5. The issues would be required to incorporate an undertaking in their offer documents promising necessary cooperation with the rating agency in providing factual information.
6. It is also suggested that a penal clause be introduced in the listing agreement of the information provided is proved to be incorrect at a later stage, to protect investors' interest.
7. The net worth of rating agencies has been fixed at ₹ 5 crore.
8. Rating agencies can choose their methodology of operation but self-regulatory mechanism will give a better maturity status for agencies.
9. No chairman, director or employee of the promoters shall be a chairman, director or employee of the CRA or its rating committee. Promoter of a CRA is a person who holds more than 107 of holdings of the CRA.
10. Period of validity of registration shall be 3 years.

❖ Practical Problems

1. The absence of widespread branch network of the rating agency may limit its skills in rating.
2. Inexperienced, unskilled or overloaded staff may not do justice to their job and the resulting ratings may not be perfect.
3. Since rating exercise involves a number of factors, a rigid mathematical formula can not be applied to finalise rating and some element of subjectivity creeps in, thereby giving scope for bias.

4. The time factor greatly affects rating and gives misleading conclusions. A company which experiences adverse conditions temporarily will be given a low rating judged on the basis of temporary phenomenon.
5. Since the rating agencies receive a sizable fee from the companies for awarding ratings, a tendency to inflate the ratings may develop.
6. The rating is not permanent but subject to changes and moreover the agencies cannot give any guarantee for the investors.
7. Investments which have the same rating may not have identical investment quality because the number of rating categories is limited and hence cannot reflect small but meaningful differences in the degree of risk.
8. Borrowing entities give misleading advertisements about the rating symbols of their instruments. For example, 'X' Co. Ltd., which has got AAX for its debenture may mobilise fixed deposits instead of revealing the low rating for fixed deposits. Such kind of window dressing should be curtailed.

6.9.6 Purpose of Credit Rating

Credit rating is neither a general purpose evaluation of a corporate entity nor an overall assessment of the credit risk likely to be involved in all the debts contracted or to be contracted by such an issuer. A rating is specific to a debt instrument and is intended to grade different and specific debt instruments in terms of credit risks associated with the particular instruments. A rating does not amount to any recommendation to buy, hold or sell an instrument as it does not take into consideration factors such as market prices, personal risk preferences of an investor and such other considerations, which may influence an investment decision.

The credit ratings assess the debt servicing capabilities and guide the investors as to the degree of certainty of timely payment of principal and interest on the debt instrument under consideration. These ratings are not recommendations but are carefully assessed opinions.

❖ Types of Credit Rating

Credit ratings are of different types, depending upon the requirements of the rater and the rated. The following are the common types of rating:

(i) *Bond Rating:* Rating the bonds or debt securities issued by a company, government or quasi-government body is called bond rating. This occupies the major business of credit rating agencies.

(ii) *Equity Rating:* The rating of equity of capital market is called equity rating.

(iii) *Commercial Paper Rating:* It is mandatory on the part of a corporate body to obtain the ratings of an approved credit rating agency to issue commercial paper. In USA, 100% of commercial paper volume is rated. In India, P1 rating is prescribed for issue of commercial paper by corporate bodies.

(iv) *Sovereign Rating:* This includes rating a country as to its creditworthiness, probability to risk, etc.

❖ Credit Rating Vs. Financial Analysis

Credit rating is, essentially, business analysis, which has a much broader connotation than financial analysis. One significant factor which adds value to the analysis of a rating agency is that the rating is normally done at the request of and with the active cooperation of the issuer. So, the rating agency had access to unpublished information and the discussions with the senior management of issuers give meaningful insights into corporate plans and strategies. The rating agencies also make necessary adjustments to published accounts for the purpose of their analysis and juxtapose the issuer against the backdrop of the industry in question and the general economic environment. And, at the culmination of this detailed process, the rating emerges as the well-considered view of a dozen or more highly qualified and experienced professionals. The rating agencies zealously safeguard their independence and scrupulously avoid any conflict of interest with the various players in the capital market. If any analyst or group of analysts are able to ensure all these, we probably have another rating agency in the making. And this has happened with credit rating agencies analysing, assessing and rating the participants in the capital market.

6.9.7 Factors Contributing to Success of Rating System

The driving force behind the rating industry is essentially the question of reputation for analytical credibility. Wilson (1994) sums it up succinctly. "Every time a rating is assigned, the agency's name, integrity and credibility are on line and subject to inspection by the whole community." This section focuses on the ingredients essential for the rating system to function effectively and serve the interests of all market participants and regulators.

(a) Credible and Independent Structure and Procedures

To quote from Standard & Poor's:

"Ratings are of value only as long as they are credible. Credibility arises primarily from the rater being independent of the issuer's business. The investor is willing to accept the rater's judgement only where such credibility exists. When enough investors are willing to accept the judgement of a particular rater, that rater gains recognition as a rating agency."

According to Moody's:

"The Rating Agency must do all it can to preserve its credibility and integrity in the market-place. As a primary ingredient of credibility, the agency must maintain independence from all interested market forces — including issuers, securities underwriters, or government."

A few other critical factors that serve to enhance the credibility of a rating agency are:

- objectivity and impartiality of opinions;
- analytical integrity and consistency;
- professionalism and relevant expertise across industry;
- strict rules of confidentiality relating to the sensitive and confidential information of the issuer;
- timeliness of rating review and announcement of changes;
- ability to reach a wide range of investors by means of press reports, print or electronic publications and more investor-friendly research services.

(b) Reliance on the Market Mechanism

Reliance on the capital market for resource allocation generates a strong demand for investment related information. Rating agencies provide this information. An investor would be willing to look at rating as an important input for his investment decision only when there is a perceived default risk.

(c) Corporate Disclosure and Credit Education

Rating agencies are not and should not assume the role of regulators. They are mostly carrying out an assignment on the mandate of an issuer and, in some countries, the issuer has the option of publishing or not publishing the rating assigned. This may result in investors not having all essential information required for his decision. The regulatory guidelines for mandatory disclosure of ratings could ensure that the information reaches the users. However, it is not sufficient for the information to reach the investor, he must be capable of arriving at meaningful conclusions by interpreting the assigned rating. He should also be aware of the limitations of credit rating and should not assume that the rating amounts to an insurance or guarantee against default risk.

(d) Creation of Active Debt Market

The continued growth and evolution of the credit rating business would depend on the size and growth of the debt market. An active primary and secondary debt market is crucial for rating agencies to continue to provide their services.

❖ Benefits of Credit Rating

The benefits to various parties concerned with credit rating are listed below:

Investors

(*i*) It enables the investors to get superior information at low cost.

(*ii*) It enables the investors to take calculated risk in their investment decisions.

(*iii*) It encourages the common man to invest his savings in corporate securities and get high returns.

❖ Corporate Borrowers

(*i*) It facilitates companies with good rating to enter the capital market confidently and raise funds at comparatively cheaper rates.

(*ii*) It can be used as a marketing tool.

(*iii*) It facilitates foreign collaborations.

(*iv*) It encourages discipline among the corporate borrowers.

❖ Credit Rating Companies

The existence and development of credit rating companies largely depends upon their performance. Honest and impartial credit rating agencies would definitely thrive, as long as they sustain their credibility.

❖ Government

(i) Fair and good ratings motivate the public to invest their savings in good shares, deposits and debentures. Thus, the idle savings of the public are channelised for productive uses.

(ii) It facilitates the formulation of public policy guidelines on institutional investments.

(iii) Credit rating system plays a vital role in investor protection without casting burden for that responsibility on the Government.

6.9.8 Rating Methodology

The rating exercise commences at the request of a company. A rating applies to a particular debt obligation of the company and is not a general purpose evaluation of the company. The focus of the evaluation is on the ability and the willingness of the company to meet the financial obligations on the debt instrument in a timely manner.

In evaluation and monitoring ratings, both qualitative and quantitative criteria are employed. The methodology involves an analysis of the past performance of the company and an assessment of its future prospects, which involves judgement of the company's competitive position and evaluation of its management and strategies. In order to eliminate subjectivity, a multi-layered decision-making process is applied in assigning a rating, which ensures that no single individual decides on a rating.

The key factors considered are:

❖ Business Analysis

- Industry Risk (nature and basis of competition; key success factors; demand-supply position; structure of industry; cyclical seasonal factors; government policies; etc.)
- Market position of the company within the industry (market share; competitive advantages; selling and distribution arrangements; product and customer diversity; etc.)
- Operating efficiency of the company (locational advantages; labour relationships; cost structure; technological advantages and manufacturing efficiency as compared to those of competitors; etc.)
- Legal position (terms of prospectus, trustees and their responsibilities; systems for timely payment and for protection against forgery/fraud; etc.)

THE RATING PROCESS

Review of the public information on the client

↓

Questionnaire

↓

Meeting with client

↓

Preparation of draft report

↓

Draft report sent to subject client for review as to factual accuracy

↓

Amended report (following client comments) sent to rating committee members

↓

Rating committee meeting/discussion and assignment of rating

↓

Client advised of rating

↓

Rating made public

❖ Financial Analysis

- Accounting quality (overstatement/understatement of profits; auditors' qualifications; method of income recognition, inventory valuation and depreciation policies; off-balance sheet liabilities; etc.)
- Earnings protection (sources of future earnings growth; profitability ratios; earnings in relation to fixed income charges; etc.)
- Adequacy of cash flows (in relation to debt and fixed and working capital needs; sustainability of cash flows; capital spending flexibility; working capital management; etc.)
- Financial flexibility (alternative financing plans in times of stress; ability to raise funds; asset redeployment potential; etc.)

❖ Management Evaluation

- Track record of the management; planning and control systems; depth of managerial talent; succession plans.
- Evaluation of capacity to overcome adverse situations.
- Goals, philosophy and strategies.

The above factors are considered for companies with manufacturing activities. The assessment of finance companies lays emphasis on the following factors in addition to the financial analysis and management evaluation as outlined above.

❖ Regulatory and Competitive Environment

- Structure and regulatory framework of the financial system.
- Trends in regulation/deregulation and their impact on the company.

❖ Fundamental Analysis

- Capital Adequacy (assessment of true net worth of the company, its adequacy in relation to the volume of business and the risk profile of the assets).
- Asset Quality (quality of the company's credit-risk management; systems for monitoring credit; sector risk; exposure to individual borrowers; management of problem credits; etc.)
- Liquidity Management (capital structure; term matching of assets and liabilities; policy on liquid assets in relation to financing commitments and maturing deposits).
- Profitability and Financial Position (historic profits; spreads on fund deployment; revenues on non-fund based services; accretion to reserves; etc.)
- Interest and Tax Sensitivity (exposure to interest rate changes; tax law changes and hedge against interest rate, etc.)

❖ Ratings

The ratings are symbolic presentation of the agency's opinion. The ratings can be classified according to the merit into four main categories: High Investment grade, Investment grade, Speculative grade and Poor grade. The symbols used by CRISIL, CARE and ICRA are different, but their thrust and interpretations are identical. These can be best summarised as follows:

Notes:

ICD = Inter Corporate Deposit, CD = Certificate of Deposit, CP = Commercial Paper, FD = Fixed Deposit, PCD/NCD/OCD = Parity Convertible/Non-convertible/Optionally Convertible Debentures, OFCD = Optionally Fully Convertible Debentures, FRD = Floating Rate Debentures, SO = Structured Obligation, FRN = Floating Rate Note, PTC = Pass Through Certificates, PCN = Partly Convertible Note, FRB = Floating Rate Bond, ARN = Auction Rated Note, RUF = Revolving Underwriting Facility, CCPS = Cumulative Convertible Preferential Share.

The suffix of a '+' (Plus) or '–' (Minus) sign reflects comparative standing within the category. 'F' is used as a prefix for Fixed Deposit Ratings. Prefixes "L" and "M" denote long and medium term instruments, respectively. "P" suffixed in parentheses after symbol indicates that instrument is being issued to raise resources for new company for financing a project and the rating assumes successful completion of project. ↑ Indicates upgrade and ↓ indicates a downgrade. CRISIL uses prefix of "pf" to its long-term rating symbols for preference shares.

CRISIL

AAA/FAAA	= Highest Safety	P1	=	Very Strong
AA/FAA	= High Safety	P2	=	Strong
A/FA	= Adequate Safety	P3	=	Adequate
BBB	= Moderate Safety			
BB/FB	= Inadequate Safety			

CARE

CP = Commercial Paper		NCD/ PCD/ OCD	FD = Fixed Deposits		
Symbol	*Explanation*	*Symbol*	*Symbol*	*Explanation*	
PR1	Superior	CARE AAA	CARE AAA (FD)	Best Quality	High Investment grade
PR2	Strong	CARE AA	CARE AA (FD)	High Quality	-do-
PR3	Adequate	CARE A	CARE A (FD)	Adequate Safety	Investment Grade
PR4	Risk Prone	CARE BBB	CARE BBB (FD)	Moderate Safety	-do-
PR5	Default	CARE BB	CARE BB (FD)	Inadequate	Speculative Safety Grade
		CARE B	CARE B (FD)	Risk Prone	-do-
		CARE C	CARE C (FD)	High Risk	Poor Grade
		CARE D	CARE D (FD)	Default	-do-

ICRA

CP = Commercial Paper	*FCD/PCD/NCD = Fully/Partly Non-convertible Debentures*	*CD/FD = Certificate of Deposit/Fixed Deposit*
A1 Highest Safety	LAAA Highest Safety	MAAA Highest Safety
A2 High Safety	LAA High Safety	MAA High Safety
A3 Adequate Safety	LA Adequate Safety	MA Adequate Safety
A4 Risk Prone	LBBB Moderate Safety	MB Inadequate Safety
	LBB Inadequate Safety	MC Risk Prone
	LB Risk Prone	
	LC Substantial Risk	
	LD Default	

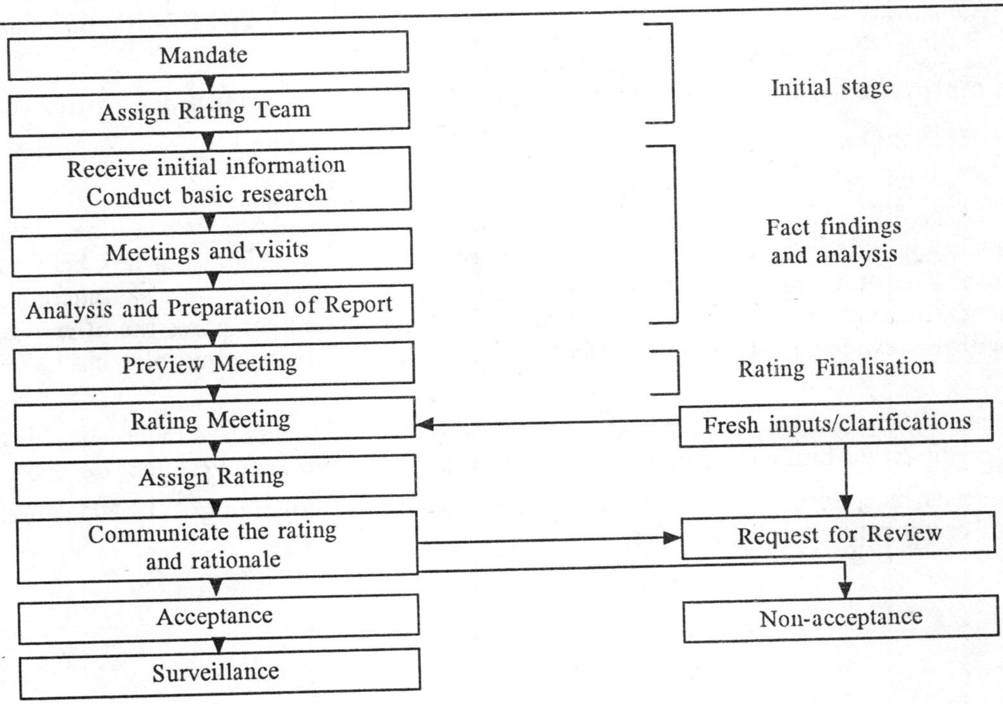

6.9.9 Working of Credit Rating Agencies

In India, the first rating agency CRISIL, Credit Rating Information Services of India Ltd., was promoted by ICICI in 1987 followed by ICRA (Investment Information and Credit Rating Agency) promoted by IFCI in 1991 and (CARE) Credit Analysis and Research promoted by IDBI. With economic liberalisation, industrial development and increasing trend of financial disintermediation, there is a genuine need for authentic investment information specifically designed to facilitate the decision-making process of investors and other participants of the financial services world.

❖ Credit Rating Information Services of India Limited (CRISIL)

The Credit Rating Information Services of India Limited (CRISIL), the first rating agency in India, was promoted in 1987 by the Industrial Credit and Investment Corporation of India Limited (ICICI) and Unit Trust of India (UTI). Other shareholders include Asian Development Bank, Life Insurance Corporation of India, State Bank of India, Housing Development Finance Corporation Limited, General Insurance Corporation of India and its subsidiaries, Standard Chartered Bank, Banque IndoSuez, Sakura Bank, Bank of Tokyo, Hong Kong and Shanghai Banking Corporation, Citibank, Grindlays Bank, Duetsche Bank, Societe Generale, Banque Nationale de Paris, Bank of India, Bank of Baroda, UCO Bank, Canara Bank, Central Bank of India, Allahabad Bank, Indian Overseas Bank, Vysya Bank Ltd., and Bank of Madhura Ltd.

CRISIL's principal objective is to rate debt obligations of Indian companies. Its ratings provide a guide to the investors as to the degree of certainty of timely payment of interest and principal on a particular debt instrument. CRISIL rates debentures, fixed deposit programmes, short-term instruments like commercial paper, structured obligations and preference shares.

Since its inception in March 31, 1994, CRISIL has rated in all 926 debt instruments issued by 668 companies. CRISIL has introduced CRISIL Card, CRISIL View, CRISIL Ban Card and CRISIL Rating Digest Service.

❖ Investment Information and Credit Rating Agency of India Limited (ICRA)

The IFCI and a number of other financial institutions set up ICRA in 1991 at Delhi. ICRA undertakes rating of debt instruments.

ICRA credit rating provides an investor with a simple indicator expressing the underlying credit quality in a debt issue programme. ICRA credit ratings also establish a link between risk and return. They thus provide a yardstick against which to measure the risk inherent in an instrument. An investor uses the rating to assess the risk-level and compares the offered rate of return with his expected rate of return (for the given level of risk) to optimise his risk-return trade off.

The relatively unknown issuer is also benefitted by having access to a much wider investor base as credit rating minimises the role of 'name recognition' in an investment decision.

Since its inception, ICRA has rated 273 debt instruments involving ₹ 12,295 crore. The details of credit rating by ICRA are as follows:

Instruments	*No.*	*Amount (₹ crore)*
1. Debentures	112	8,595.8
2. Fixed Deposit Programme	81	1,433.9
3. Commercial Paper Programme	80	2,265.0
Total	273	12,294.7

In addition, ICRA provides 'general assessment' report on different aspects of the company's operations and management.

❖ Credit Analysis and Research Limited (CARE)

The Industrial Development Bank of India (IDBI) jointly with Canara Bank, UTI, private sector banks and financial services companies promoted the Credit Analysis & Research institution to offer credit rating information and equity research services to the Indian industry and business institutions. CARE, incorporated on April 21, 1993, commenced its operations in October 1993.

CARE undertakes rating of all types of debt instruments like commercial paper, fixed deposits, bonds, debentures and structural obligations, involving an independent and professional assessment of debt servicing capabilities of companies.

❖ Duffs and Phelps Credit Rating Agency of India Ltd., (DCR-India)

The Duffs and Phelps is a leading international credit rating agency. The J.M. Financial and Alliance Group in joint venture with Duffs and Phelps has set up DCR in India in 1996. Its main objective is to give credit rating to debt instruments. On special request it may undertake rating of (NBFCs) companies and countries as well. The popular symbol employed by DCR is D-1, D-2, D-3, etc., depending upon the credit status. For example, the RBI has stipulated a minimum credit rating of D-2 OCR India for the purpose of issuing commercial papers by instructions. The minimum investment grade credit rating to be assigned by DCR-India and acceptable to RBI has been fixed at BBB.

❖ Onida Individual Credit Rating Agency Ltd., (ONICRA)

Almost all credit rating agencies established in India undertake credit analysis work of corporate bodies only. Unlike these agencies, the ONICRA Ltd., has taken up the individual borrowers. It has been sponsored by the Onida Finance Ltd. In all credit transactions relating to credit cards, Housing Finance, Rental/H.P. agreements, personal loan, etc., it becomes imperative that one should know the quantum of default risk associated with such transactions before entering into those transactions. It is where the ONICRA comes into the picture. It does not rate the individual as such but the risk associated with entering into those credit transactions with that individual at a certain period. Thus, it helps the users of this rating to know risks associated with credit transactions while dealing with individuals. It is gaining popularity among financial institutions.

❖ SMERA

It is the first new credit rating agency for SMEs. It is sponsored by Dun and Bradstreet Credit Information Bureau (India) Ltd., and public and private banks. Till 31st March, 2007 SMERA completed ratings of over 546 SME units.

❖ Credit Rating Mandatory in India

Credit Rating is mandatory in India for the issuance of certain debt instruments of the following nature:

- Public issue of debentures/bonds with conversion/redemption period exceeding 18 months.
- Commercial paper can be issued in India, *inter alia*, if the programme has a rating not below 'A2' from ICRA (or its equivalent from the other rating agencies), and
- Fixed deposit programmes of all non-banking finance companies with net owned funds above ₹ 200 lakh need to be compulsorily rated by March 31, 1995, as per the recent Reserve Bank of India guidelines. The non-banking finance companies with net owned funds between ₹ 50 lakh and ₹ 200 lakh should also get their fixed deposit programmes rated within March 31, 1996.

Having regard to the fact that fixed deposits are unsecured debts and are subscribed by the unorganised sector, i.e., the common people, who are most vulnerable, the Government is considering an amendment in the Companies Act, to provide for mandatory credit rating of fixed deposits.

❖ Use of Rating by Regulators in India

The RBI prescribes a number of regulatory uses of ratings. The RBI requires that a NBFC must have minimum investment grade credit rating if it intends to accept public deposits. Furthermore, unrated or underrated NBFCs in the category of equipment leasing and hire purchase finance companies are required to disclose the fact of their being unrated, to the public, if they intend raising deposits. Finally, as per money-market regulations of RBI, a corporate must get an issue of CP rated and can issue such paper subject to a minimum rating.

In the area of investments, SEBI stipulated that ratings are compulsory on all public issues of debentures with maturity exceeding 18 months. SEBI has also made ratings mandatory for acceptance of public deposits by Collective Investment Schemes. If the size of the issue is larger than ₹ 100 crore, two ratings are required.

Pension funds can only invest in debt-securities that have two ratings, as per the stipulations of Government of India.

6.9.10 Risks of Use of Ratings by Regulators

Of particular interest to policymakers and of course to market participants is implications of use of ratings by regulators.

First, reputed rating agencies feel that when regulators rely on ratings, there is a potential of laxity. It tends to create demand for easy and accommodating raters. In other words, it stimulates 'rating shopping', i.e. issuers will be inclined to seek the cheapest and least demanding credit rating agency.

Second, and following from the earlier point, it creates a continuous revenue source for rating agencies.

Third, the ratings induced by regulatory requirement could induce ritualism and even enhance risk. Thus, issuers will get rated because they are required to do so and investors will tend to use it as a proxy for internal analysis. It is argued that in such situations, ratings may actually end up increasing the risk.

Fourth, regulatory use of ratings tends to provide official sanction for rating agencies' assumptions and their ratings, thus increasing the risk of moral hazard. Sometimes, it is argued that while assessing creditworthiness of Government owned banks or public sector units, ratings may be higher than justified, though there is no evidence to support this argument.

Fifth, the more profuse use of ratings would increase the demand for ratings and, therefore, indirectly also increase the influence of CRA on financial markets. Thus, there is a potential challenge to the financial stability by CRA.

Sixth, it is held that when regulators tend to rely on ratings, often it seems to be under an assumption of uniform/standard ratings and rating criteria by different rating agencies, an assumption that is not necessarily valid at all times.

Seventh, there is an expectation, especially among some developing countries that ratings by themselves can be used as a stimulus to developing financial markets without realizing that the requirement of mandatory ratings on domestic debt instruments, etc., are no substitutes to a strong regulatory framework, transparency, accounting and disclosure standards. There is indeed the bigger issue of institutional factors relevant to debt and ratings at best is one aspect.

Finally, it is clear that there are many dilemmas for regulators in using the ratings. Prescription of eligibility criteria based on reputation of the rating agency, length of service, acceptability by market participants, and actual track record would only entrench the oligopolistic nature of the market. On the other hand, easy eligibility criteria would increase the laxity and moral hazard. There have been suggestions to develop official substitutes for regulatory induced rating, and this idea is not favoured by many since there is a fear of possible political influence on official bodies.

Another suggestion to increase accountability of CRAs whose ratings are used by regulators is prescription of codes of conduct for rating agencies to enhance market discipline. CRAs could be encouraged to disclose relevant aspects of their organization, including among others, their ownership, staff, etc. They could be asked to disclose a record of their assessments and results. They may also be asked to publicise more explicitly their methodologies. The entire process of ratings could be codified by developing modalities for consultation, sharing of preliminary ratings, detailed explanations, etc.

Use of ratings in regulation: As ratings have gained greater acceptance in the market-place, regulators of financial markets and institutions have increasingly used ratings to simplify the task of prudential oversight. Today we have regulations governing new issuance and purchase of securities by investors and financial institutions, and ratings for securities issuance or investment purposes.

Selectively applied, regulations may also help to foster the development of the rating system. It should be remembered, however, that regulations alone cannot force market participants to utilise the rating agency's service, particularly if they serve to limit the range of securities issued. Credibility cannot come from regulations. The rating agencies in such a scenario have to prove their credibility.

❖ Regulation of Credit Rating Agencies

The question of regulation of credit rating agencies evokes mixed response. While a section of people believe that ratings, being opinions, should not be regulated, others feel that given the critical role rating agencies are supposed to play in the market, there must be a regulator overseeing their functioning. But probably, the ideal solution would be to have guidelines for the formation of credit rating agencies ensuring that people who do the rating are independent and the method followed is transparent. For example, rating agencies may be required to be registered with the regulator, say SEBI.

Such 'registrations' as a nationally recognised organisation would lend additional credibility in the eyes of the investors and other users of the ratings, provided of course, the criterion for registration are transparent and based on sound logic.

6.9.11 Rating Challenge

Borrowers, be it an individual or a corporate entity, are rated for their creditworthiness. And why not? The banks themselves are now entering the capital market to raise funds. It has become all the more important in the context of the new code of greater transparency and prudential norms. While ratings act as a guide to the average investor, it also enhances the credibility of the rated organisation.

Presently, credit rating is mandatory in India for debt instruments with conversion/redemption exceeding 18 months for fixed deposit programmes of all non-banking finance companies. It is optional for PSU Bonds and privately placed non-convertible debentures. Rating of equity has been left out. However, with the deepening of the capital market and globalisation, equity must also be brought into the purview.

Are the Indian rating agencies able to meet evaluation standards and eliminate influence of vested interests? For this, it is imperative that they are independent. In the Indian case, the existing three rating agencies, *viz.*, CRISIL, ICRA and CARE are promoted by financial institutions. They may well serve as in-house rating agents to assess credit risk of their customers. But what would be the yardsticks and whether they would remain impartial when their promoters themselves would be the clients? We may think of other independent rating agencies in the field but there is every likelihood that industrial groups may start their own rating agencies, on the patterns of their own financial agencies. In such an eventuality, there is every danger of such agencies becoming an in-house sort of entity thereby compromising on objectivity in rating standards. Multiple agencies may increase competition in rating but it may also land up in indifferent rating standards and there is also the risk of succumbing to pressures for attracting business.

There have been three criticisms of Indian credit rating agencies. First, that they assign ratings which are not comparable against international standards; secondly, the rating symbols they assign are internally inconsistent, and thirdly, agencies are not kept at arm's length from their sponsors.

The first is accepted even by the rating industry itself, but it is hard for the Indian agencies to match international ratings. That is since both Moody's and Standard & Poor's had, for a long time, put India's sovereign rating in the speculative grade. Meanwhile, no corporate can get ratings exceeding the sovereign rating. That way, not even the best Indian corporates could get ratings higher than 'BB'.

Unless agencies have a longer term view and keep off short-term profitability considerations, the industry will not mature. If one of the agencies thinks that a corporate has walked off with a higher rating just because it could arm-twist the rating agency, could not the other agencies publish their own ratings and let the market decide which rating they would use? Internationally, it is accepted that corporates are rated by more than one agency and the lower of the ratings are usually used.

6.9.12 Future Scenario

As our economy opens up and is exposed to competitive climate of international finance and as investment decisions will involve more and more complex considerations, the rating system will gain strong foothold. Very soon, the ratings will become an accepted and inevitable norm in the market. In a deregulated system, such an objective and credible system has an important role to play. The ratings have gained good acceptability with various investors and this trend is expected to consolidate itself.

With the emergence of debt markets and the imminent introduction of security instruments for mortgaged debts, the work of rating agencies is bound to multiply. The credit rating agencies will have to develop their own support systems to evaluate debts. Additional skill will need to be developed for an access to overseas debt markets. Moody's has set up an establishment in India and Standard and Poor is said to have decided to do so in the near future.

Other areas of new developments include Equity Research and Credit Analysis Ratings of various companies. The rating agencies will provide opinions about prospects of a company, estimates about EPS and P/E ratio, future projections, etc. With the available expertise and data banks, the rating agencies are eminently suited to undertake such an exercise.

The primary benefit of credit rating has been to enable the investor to identify the risks associated with various debt obligations. The other benefits, include decreasing the potential conflict between the underwriters and the investors, providing greater liquidity in secondary markets, encouraging increased disclosure on the part of companies, better accounting standards and improved financial information for the promotion of individual and institutional investor protection.

Nevertheless, the analysis has highlighted the fact that, at present, ratings are not widely used by individual investors. With the eruption of new financial instruments and the realisation on the part of the investor of the invaluable service that credit rating agencies provide, credit rating is bound to find its niche in the investment decision-making process and act as a positive step in the direction of increasing investor protection. Thus, credit rating has firmly docked itself on the shores of the Indian capital market and is definitely here to stay.

6.10 CONTRACTS OF INDEMNITY AND GUARANTEE

- Contract of Indemnity.
- Rights of Indemnity-holder.
- Contract of Guarantee.
- Nature of surety's liability.
- Continuing Guarantee
- Discharge of surety
- Rights of surety
- Guarantee when invalid
- Contribution as between co-sureties
- Distinction between a contract of indemnity and a contract of guarantee.
- Summary
- Self-examination questions

❖ Learning Objectives

1. Be conversant with the two special type of contracts, i.e., indemnity contracts and guarantee contracts governed under Contract Act also the nature of obligations and rights of each of the parties to the contract.
2. Be clear about distinction between these contracts.

6.10.1 Contract of Indemnity

A contract of indemnity is a type of contingent contract. The nature of such contract is stated in Section 124 which is reproduced below:

A contract by which one party promises to save the other from loss caused to him by the conduct of the promisor himself, or the conduct of any person, is called a "contract of indemnity".

For example, A may contract to indemnity B against the consequences of any proceedings which C may take against B in respect of a sum of ₹ 5,000 advanced by C to B. In consequence, when B who is called upon to pay the sum of money to C fails to do so, C would be able to recover the amount from A as provided in Section 124.

❖ Rights of the Indemnity Holder When Sued (Section 125)

The promisee in a contract of indemnity, acting within the scope of his authority, is entitled to cover from the promisor:

1. all damages which he may be compelled to pay in any suit in respect of any matter to which the promise to indemnify applies;
2. all costs which he may be compelled to pay in any such suit, if in bringing or defending it, he did not contravence the orders of the promisor, and acted as it would have been prudent for him to act in the absence of any contract of indemnity, or if the promisor authorised him to bring or defend the suit.
3. all sums which he may have paid under the terms of any compromise of any such suit, if the compromise was not contrary to the orders of the promisor, and was one which it would have been prudent for the promisee to make in the absence of any contract of indemnity, or if the promisor authorised him to compromise the suit.

Section 125 is by no means exhaustive, which deals only with his rights in the event of his being sued. The indemnity holder has other rights besides those mentioned above. If he has incurred a liability and that liability is absolute he is entitled to call upon his indemnifier to save him from that liability and to pay it off.

6.10.2 Contract of Guarantee (Section 176)

A contract of guarantee is a contract to perform the promise made or discharge liability incurred by a third person in case of his default. Thus, if A applies for shares in a limited company and B agrees with the company that any amount which remains unpaid on the call shall be paid by him, it is a contract of guarantee.

Implied promise to indemnify surety: This principle is contained in Section 145 which is reproduced below:

"In every contract of guarantee there is an implied promise by the principal debtor to indemnify the surety; and the surety is entitled to recover from the principal debtor whatever sum he has rightfully paid under the guarantee, but no sums which he has paid wrongfully."

It would be observed that the right of the surety to recover the amount paid by him from the original debtor is limited to amounts 'rightfully' paid by him. The right however, is not affected by the fact that the creditor has refused to sue the principal debtor or that he has not demanded the sum due from him.

Consideration in case of a guarantee: What constitutes consideration in case of a guarantee is stated in Section 127 which is reproduced below:

"Anything done or any promise made, for the benefit of the *principal debtor may be a sufficient consideration to the surety for giving the guarantee."*

Illustration: A had advanced money to B on a bond hypothecating B's property stating that C is the surety for any balance that might remain due after realisation of B's property. C was not a party to the bond. He, however, signed a separate surety bond two days subsequent to the advance of the money. It was held that the subsequent surety bond as void for want of consideration: (*Nanak Ram vs. Mehinlal 1877, I Allahabad 487*).

❖ Nature of Surety's Liability

It is stated in Section 128 which is reproduced below:

"The liability of the surety is co-extensive with that of the principal debtor, unless it is otherwise provided by the contract".

The language of the Section suggests that the surety is liable to the same extent as the principal debtor. When the debtor cannot be held liable to any defect in the document executed by him, the surety also ceases to be liable on the contract entered into by him. However, a surety's liability to pay the debt is not discharged even if the creditor omits to sue the principal debtor since the surety is separately liable on the promise of guarantee. On that account though the principal debtor has not been sued, the action is maintainable against the surety.

❖ Continuing Guarantee

The law in this regard is contained in Sections 129 and 131 which are reproduced below:

A guarantee which extends to a series of transactions is called a "continuing guarantee" (Section 129). For example, A, in consideration that B will employ C in collecting rents of B's estate promises B to be responsible, to the amount of ₹ 5,000 for the due collection and payment by C of those rents. This is a continuing guarantee.

"The continuing guarantee may at any time be revoked by the surety as to future transactions, by notice to the creditor" (Section 130). But where a continuing relationship is established on the faith of a guarantee the guarantee cannot be annulled during the continuance of that relationship. Thus, when A becomes surety of C for B's conduct as manager in C's bank and B is appointed on the faiths of this guarantee, A is precluded from annulling the guarantee so long as B acts as manager in C's banks.

"The death of the surety operates, in the absence of any contract to the contrary, as a revocation of a continuing guarantee, so far as regards future transactions' (Section 131).

6.10.3 Discharge of Surety

The law on the subject is contained in Sections 133 to 139. The provisions of these Sections are as follows:

(*i*) Any *variance* made without the surety's consent in the terms of the contract, between the principal debtor and the creditor, discharges the surety as to the transactions taking place subsequent to the variance (Section 133). Thus, if A becomes a surety to C for payment of rent by B under a lease and aforesaid B and C contract, without A's consent, that B will pay rent a higher rate, A would be discharged from his liability as a surety for rent accruing subsequent to the variance.

(*ii*) The surety is discharged by any contract between the principal debtor and the creditor by which the *principal debtor* is released or by any act or *omission* of the creditor the legal consequence of which is the discharge of the principal debtor (Section 134). For example, A contracts to build a house for B, and C stands surety to B for due performance of the contract by A. Thereafter, if B, by a contract releases A from the performance of the contract, C's liability as surety also shall come to an end. For instance, A contracts with B to build a house for B on the condition that B will supply the necessary timber; C guarantees A's performance of the contract, B fails to supply the timber. It would discharge both A and C.

But mere *forbearance on the part of the creditor to sue the principal debtor* or to enforce any other remedy against him would not, in the absence of any provision in the guarantee to the contrary, *discharge the surety* (Section 137). Accordingly, the liability of the surety continues even when the claim against the principal debtor becomes barred by limitation. *In Krish to Kishore vs. Radha Romun* I.L.R. 12 Cal. 330, the plaintiff sued the principal debtor and the surety for arrears of rent, and the plaintiff on discovering during the trial that the principal debtor had died before the institution of the suit, impleaded the legal representative of the principal debtor after the right to recover the arrears from the principal debtor had become barred by limitation. Held, the surety was still liable. The same was the view of the *Privy Council in Mahant Singh vs. U Bai* A.I.R. 1939 P.C. 110,41 Bomb. L.R. 742 in which it was confirmed that omission of the creditor to sue within the period of limitation does not discharge the surety.

(*iii*) Where a creditor makes a composition, (i.e., settlement) with, or promises to give time to the principal debtor, or promises not to sue the principle debtor, by a contract between the creditor and the principal debtor the surety is absolved from the liability under the guarantee, unless the surety assents to such new contract (Section 135).

Where, however, a contract to give time to the principal debtor is entered into by the creditor with a third person and not with principal debtor, the surety will not be discharged (Section 136). For example, C, a holder of an overdue bill of exchange drawn by A as surety for B, and accepted by B, contracts with M who is not a party to the bill, to give time to B. In such a case, A would not be discharged.

It may further be noted that if there are co-sureties, a release by the creditor of one of them does not discharge the other co-surety or co-sureties; also that as between the other co-sureties *per se* it does not absolve the surety so released from his responsibility to another or others (Section 138).

(*iv*) The *surety is also discharged* when the creditor does any act which is inconsistent with the *rights of surety* or omits to do any act which, his duty to the surety requires him to do, an eventual remedy of the surety against the principal debtor is thereby impaired (Section 139).

For example, A puts M as an apprentice under B and gives a guarantee to B for M's fidelity. B promises on his part that he will, at least once a month, see M make-up the cash. B defaults in keeping up his promise to see that this is done and M embezzles cash in his custody. A would not be liable on his guarantee, because B, the creditor, had omitted to check-up the cash once a month, which he had undertaken to do.

6.10.4 Rights of Surety against Principal Debtor and/or Creditor

These are contained in Sections 140 and 141.

(1) *Against principal debtor:*

(*a*) Where a guaranteed debt has become due or default of the principal debtor to perform a guaranteed duty has taken place, the surety upon payment or performance of all that he is liable for is vested with all the rights which the creditor had against the principal debtor (Section 140). The right of the surety is known as the right of subrogation the right to stand in the shoes of the creditor.

(*b*) The surety is entitled to the benefit of every security which the creditor has against the principal debtor at the time when the contract of suretyship was entered into whether or not the surety was aware of the existence of such security.

(*c*) In every contract of guarantee, there is an implied promise by the principal debtor to indemnify the surety; and the surety is entitled to recover from the principal debtor whatever sums he has rightfully paid under the guarantee but not sums which he has paid wrongfully (Section 145). In *Reed vs. Norris* it was held that if the surety has, by 'accord and satisfaction' paid the creditor a smaller amount than that guaranteed, he is entitled to recover such a smaller amount only from the principal debtor and not the full amount as the surety's right is merely to claim indemnity from the principal debtor. If in performing his obligation the surety has suffered any special damage, he can claim indemnity from the debtor for that too. There is a conflict of decision as to whether when a surety pays a time-barred debt to the creditor he can be said to have made the payment rightfully. The better view appears to be to hold that it is a rightful payment.

The surety can claim the amount only when he has actually paid it so that if he executes a promissory note in favour of the credit, he cannot immediately claim an indemnity from the principal debtor. He can do so only upon actually paying the amount due on the note as it is only then that he can be said to have been indemnified [*Pautti Narayanamurthy vs. Narimuthu* (1902) 26 Mad, 322, 328].

In *Muthu Raman vs. Chinna Vellayan* (1916) 39 Mad. 965 it was held that if a person becomes a surety without the knowledge and consent of the principal debtor, the only rights which he acquires against him are those given by Sections 140 and 141 and not those given by Section 145, i.e., he does not, in such a case, have the right to claim an indemnity from the principal debtor.

(2) *Against creditor:*

(*a*) On payment of the amount guaranteed by the surety or performance of all that he is liable for, the surety is subrogated to all the rights that the creditor had against the debtor (Section 140). For example, if the creditor had the right to stop the goods in transit or had a seller's lien, the surety would be entitled to exercise the right after he had paid all he was liable for [*Imperial Bunk vs. London & St. Kathereine Docks* (1877) 5 Ch. D. 195]. But this right accrues to a surety only on discharge in full, and not in part, of the whole of his liability.

(*b*) A surety is entitled the benefit of every security which the principal debtor had provided to the creditor at the time the contract of suretyship was entered into whether or not the fact was within the knowledge of the surety. If the creditor by his negligence or default had lost any such security, the liability of the surety to the creditor would abate proportionately (Section 141). However, the surety is not entitled to the benefit of any security provided by the debtor to the creditor subsequent to the contract of guarantee if the creditor had parted with the security before the surety has performed all that he is liable for. If such a security, however, is in the possession of such a security. Thus, where a loan is secured by the mortgage of a property along with a surety, the persons standing surety on payment of the amount would be entitled to the benefit of the mortgage provided by the principal debtor. Likewise, where a mortgage of leasehold to the benefit of the mortgage provided by the principal debtor. Likewise, where a mortgage of leasehold premises and a policy of both the securities, on payment of the amount guaranteed and the fact that on the same security the creditor had subsequently advanced another sum of money would not defeat his rights [*Forbes vs. Jackson* (1882) 19 Ch. D. 615, 619]. If the creditor does not hand over security to which the surety is entitled, he can be compelled to do so.

(*c*) At the time before the guaranteed debt has become due and before the surety is called upon to pay the amount he has guaranteed, he has the right to require the creditor to sue for and recover the guaranteed debt. Such a right is described as a right to file a *"Quia timet action"* against the debtor. However, in such a case, the surety must undertake to indemnify the creditor for the risk, delay and expense which he may incur in doing so.

(*d*) It has been held in *Sanderson vs. Aston* that where a surety has guaranteed the fidelity of person and he finds that such a person is persistently dishonest, he can call upon the creditor to dismiss him from his service.

(*e*) When the creditor calls upon the surety to pay the guaranteed amount, the surety is entitled to plead any set-off which the principal debtor may have against the creditor; or he may compel the creditor who has a claim on two funds one of which is not available to the surety, to resort first to that fund. This principle follows from the surety's right to be indemnified by his principal, combined with the equitable maxim of avoiding circuity of action.

(*f*) The last right of the surety against the creditor is to claim that he is to liable on the guarantee if the principal debtor at the date of the guarantee was a person who was incapable of entering into a contract (say, because he was a minor). This is so because under Section 128 of the Act the liability of the surety is co-extensive with that of principal debtor.

(It may be pointed out that though this appears to be the better view, there is a conflict amongst the various High Courts on this point.)

6.10.5 Guarantee When Invalid

The conditions under which the guarantee is void are stated in Sections 142, 143 and 144.

Although the contract of guarantee is "one in which there is no universal obligation to make disclosure", i.e., it is not, like a contract of insurance, a contract *uberrimae fidei*, liable to be avoided by mere non-disclosure of any material fact nevertheless, the surety is entitled to know so much as would disclose to him the nature of the transaction for which he is rendering himself answerable.

The *circumstances* under which a guarantee is *invalid* are:

(*i*) When the guarantee has been obtained by *means of misrepresentation* made directly by the creditor or made with his knowledge and assent concerning a material part of the transaction. (Section 142).

(*ii*) When the creditor has obtained any guarantee by means of *keeping silence* as to material circumstances. (Section 143).

The expression "keeping silence" implies intentional concealment of a material fact, as distinct from a mere non-disclosure thereof. There must exist some element of fraud. [*Balakrishna vs. Bank of Bengal* (1891) 15 Bom. 585]. Thus, A engages B as clerk to collect money for him and B fails to account for some of his receipts. Thereupon, A calls upon B to furnish security for his duly accounting the receipts. C gives the required guarantee. A does not apprise C of the fact of a previous defalcation by B and thereafter B again makes a default. The guarantee would be invalid.

(*iii*) When a contract of guarantee is entered into on the condition that the creditor *shall not act upon it until another person has joined* in it as cosurety and that other party fails to join as such. (Section 144).

❖ Contribution as between Cosureties

The principle is laid down in Section 146 which is reproduced below:

"When two or more persons are co-sureties for the same debt, or duty, either jointly, or severally and whether under the same or different contracts and whether with or without the knowledge of each other, the co-sureties in the absence of any contract to the contrary, are liable, as between themselves, to pay each an equal share of the whole debt, or of that part of it which remains unpaid by the principal debtor."

A cosurety is entitled to recover from other sureties the amount that he has paid but the right answers only if the surety has paid an amount beyond his share of the debt to the creditor, for only then does it become certain that there is ultimately a case for contribution at all. A judgement against the surety at the suit of the creditor for the full amount of the guarantee will have the same effect as payment made for these parties and would entitle the surety or his representative to a declaration of the right to contribution on the very same principle by which the rights of cotrustees in respect of amount which they are made liable to pay are settled.

Liability of two sureties is not affected by mutual arrangements

The law in this regard is laid down in Section 132 which is reproduced below:

"Where two persons contract with a third person to undertake a certain liability, and also contract with each other that one of them shall be liable only on the default of the other, the third person not being a party to such contract, the liability of each of such two persons to the third person under the first contract is not affected by the existence of the second contract, although such third person may have been aware of its existence."

The foregoing is the position of law applicable when the liability is undertaken jointly by two parties in respect of the same debt. But it is not so when it is in respect of different debts. For example, a party who accepts a bill of Exchange for the accommodation of another would plead that he was the accommodating party. This is because the liability undertaken by the acceptor and drawer of a bill is in no sense a joint liability. Though they contract to pay the same sum of money, they contract severally in different ways and subject to different conditions. [*Pages vs. Bank of Bengal* (1877) 3 Cal. 174].

❖ Distinction between a Contract of Indemnity and a Contract of Guarantee

A contract of guarantee is a contract to perform the promise or discharge the liability of a third person in the case of this default. The distinction between a contract of indemnity and a contract of guarantee should be noted. In a contract of indemnity the promisor undertakes an independent liability; whereas a contract of guarantee is a contract to discharge the liability of a third person in case of a default made by him. A contract of guarantee requires the concurrence of three persons, *viz.*, the principal debtor, the creditor and the surety; whereas a contract of indemnity requires the concurrence of only two persons, *viz.*, the indemnifier and the indemnity-holder. The promise of the indemnifier is to save the person indemnified from a contingent risk; whereas the surety undertakes to discharge the liability of the principal debtor, which is not contingent, but is subsisting. In a contract of guarantee, the surety, after he has discharged the debt owing to the creditor, can proceed against the other case, the guarantor is totally unconnected with contract guaranteed except through the medium of his guarantee. In the case of indemnity, there is one contract, but in the case of guarantee there are at least three contracts. The contract of indemnity is for the reimbursement of the loss, whereas the contract of guarantee is for the security of the creditor.

6.10.6 Guarantee Facility

❖ Need for the Facility

It is customary for the Bank, in normal course of business, to is issue and execute guarantees in favour of third parties on behalf of customers. The Bank guarantees are governed by various provisions as contained in The Indian Contract Act, 1872. In commercial transactions Bank's customers are sometimes required to give a Bank Guarantee. This is mostly as an alternate to keep cash as a security deposit. The third party who seeks the guarantee, not being aware of the customer's financial standing prefers a bank guarantee. In turn the bank, which very well understands the financial standing of the customer, undertakes to guarantee the customer's financial commitments or the performance of contracts by him. The bank charges commission for this service, which depends on the security available and the financial stability of the customer. In this unit you will learn what is a bank guarantee, various types of bank guarantees, precautions to be taken while issuing bank guarantee and all making payment on a bank guarantee, the distinction between a bank guarantee and an ordinary guarantee, why in a bank guarantee the bankers duty to honour the guarantee is of prime importance and the limit to which this duty can be extended.

❖ Contract of Guarantee and Contract of Indemnity (Definition)

A "Contract of guarantee" is a contract to perform the promise, or discharge the liability (enforceable at law) of a third person in case of his default. In a contract of guarantee given by Bank there are three parties. One is surety, i.e., the Bank issuing the guarantee, second is the principal debtor, i.e., the Bank's customer, on whose behalf the guarantee is issued and third is the creditor, i.e., the beneficiary of the guarantee, i.e., to whom guarantee is issued. (Section 126 of the Indian Contract Act).

A contract by which one party promises, to save the other (beneficiary) from losses caused by himself: or by the conduct of any other person, is called a contract of indemnity (Section 124 of the Indian Contract Act). There are only two parties in the indemnity, *viz.*, the indemnifier and the indemnified or the beneficiary.

Sometimes, beneficiaries desire indemnities in the guise of guarantees. One must understand the distinction between a guarantee and an indemnity. Though for the bank issuing the guarantee or indemnity, there is no difference in the type of liability assumed, yet they are governed by different articles of The Indian Stamp Act, 1899 (Stamp Act). Whereas guarantee attracts Stamp duty under Article 37, an indemnity attracts Stamp duty under Article 34. Stamp duty on indemnity is higher.

6.10.7 Types of Bank Guarantees

The Bank guarantees may be classified broadly into three categories.

❖ Financial Guarantees

This type of guarantee is intended to secure purely monetary obligations. These are guarantees issued by banks on behalf of the customers in lieu of the customer being required to deposit cash security or earnest money. These kinds of guarantees are generally issued on behalf of customers dealing with Govt. departments. Specifically the following types of guarantee may be classified as financial guarantees:

(*a*) Bid bond/tender money guarantee.

(*b*) Security deposit guarantee.

(*c*) Advance payment guarantee.

(*d*) Guarantee given to court, custom, excise, and sales-tax authorities.

❖ Performance Guarantee

These are guarantees issued by banks on behalf of its customers, whereby the banks assures a third party that the customer will perform the contract entered into by the customer as per the condition stipulated in the contract, failing which the bank will compensate the third party up to the amount specified in the guarantee. In this type of guarantee due performance or fulfilment by the principal debtor is guaranteed and the bank undertakes to make good the financial loss caused to the beneficiary on account of non-performance or short performance of the guaranteed obligation.

Illustrations of performance guarantees are:

(*a*) Performance for installation of plant and machinery within a given timeframe and with agreed specifications.

(*b*) Performance of plant and machinery up to the agreed level.

(*c*) Performance relating to supply of agreed material within stipulated period.

Although these guarantees are for performance, the quantum of the pecuniary obligations is reduced to monetary terms and a guarantee is issued for the amount.

❖ Deferred Payment Guarantees

These guarantees normally arise in the cases of purchase of machinery or such other capital equipment by industries (from suppliers in India or abroad) on deferred payment basis. The manufacturer/supplier of the machinery supplies the machinery against a down payment of say 10% to 20% of the cost and gets usance bills, for the balance amount in instalments extending over the deferred payment period. Such usance bills are duly accepted by the purchaser's banker for payment on due date, or alternatively the purchaser's bank may guarantee to pay the agreed deferred payment instalments on the due dates, if not paid by the purchaser. Such guarantees or acceptance or usance bills for the amount of instalments by the bankers are popularly known as Deferred Payment Guarantees.

❖ Statutory Guarantee

These are guarantees issued by banks favouring courts and other statutory authorities guaranteeing that the customer will honour his commitments imposed upon him under the law, failing which the bank will compensate to the extent of the amount guaranteed. These are usually given in the form of bonds and format of these guarantees are usually drawn by the courts or the concerned authority or are already prescribed by the statute as per which the guarantee is required.

6.10.8 Precautions for Issuing Letters of Guarantee

- *Appraisal of guarantee limit:* As issuance of guarantees involve financial commitment on the part of banks, guarantees should be issued only after careful appraisal of the capabilities of the borrower to perform and meet the commitments being guaranteed by the bank. Though the guarantee limits are classified as non-fund based facility, it becomes fund-based when guarantee is invoked and the banker is required to make payment on invocation. Under such circumstances it is necessary that proper assessment of the customer and his needs/capacity is made. Taking into account various factors. Guarantees should be issued only after strict compliance of terms and conditions of sanction.
- *Purpose of Guarantee:* Each guarantee must be for genuine trade or business transaction and for a definite object and enforceable on happening of a definite event.
- *Period:* Guarantee should be issued for a definite period depending upon the nature or guarantee and condition of sanction of facility. Normally the period should not exceed 10 years.
- *Amount:* Each guarantee must be for a specified amount commensurate with the customer's means and creditworthiness.
- *Limitation Clause:* The guarantees issued by the bank normally provide for a claim period in addition to the guarantee period. The beneficiary can invoke the guarantee before the expiry of the claim period for any default committed by the principal debtor during the guarantee period. The period up to which claim should be lodged with the bank should be clearly specified in the guarantee. The limitation clause reads as under:

- "Not withstanding anything contained herein, bank's liability under this Guarantee shall not exceed ₹ _________ (Rupees ________ only); this Guarantee shall be valid up to ________; and Bank is liable to pay the guaranteed amount or any part thereof under this guarantee only and only if a written claim or demand is served on or before __________ (date of expiry of claim period)."
- Guarantees in respect of disputed duties/taxes issued in favour of Govt. departments/ courts should be secured by 100% cash margin.
- *Onerous Clause:* The guarantee should be free from onerous clauses. Any clause on account of which the guaranteeing bank may be called upon to pay an amount beyond the amount agreed is termed as an onerous clause. Examples of onerous clauses are
  - — clause for payment of interest if claim amount is not remitted promptly;
  - — clause for payment of other charges/expenses incurred by the beneficiary to enforce settlement of claim, over and above the amount guaranteed.
- *Invocation of Guarantees by the beneficiary:* Where a 'guarantee is invoked, no attempt to delay the payment or facilitate the party to bring injunction restraining the payment should be made and payment should be made immediately on demand. However, banks should satisfy themselves that the guarantee has been invoked properly and as per the terms specified therein.

6.11 ESTABLISHMENT OF LETTER OF CREDIT

The major non-fund based facilities that are considered as a part of regular credit facilities are Letter of Credit (LC) and Letter of Guarantee (LG). As a part or their non-fund-based (fee-based) functions banks allow letters of credit and letters of guarantee facilities for their customers to meet their requirements. Banks charge commission for the services rendered by them and commitments undertaken by them by extending these facilities. As these facilities involve commitments on the part of the bank these are allowed after making out a very careful and detailed assessment of borrower's requirement and capacity. Only need-based facilities are extended after making a detailed appraisal of borrower's strengths and capabilities to honour the communicants as and when the same arise in respect of the facility.

❖ Letter of Credit Facility (LC)

❖ Need for the Facility

Buying and selling of goods is now not confined to a particular place or area. Because of the last communication and transport facilities entire world is the market. Since the seller does not know the buyer and his antecedents, he asks the buyer for a letter of credit from a bank in his favour to ensure that when the goods are dispatched and the documents of title to goods are sent along with bills of exchange, the payment would be forthcoming.

When a bank issues a letter of credit, it undertakes the responsibility to pay the beneficiary against documents drawn in accordance with the terms and conditions set out in the letter of credit. A letter of credit safeguards the interest of both the seller and the buyer. The bank will not make payment to the seller, unless the seller tenders documents drawn strictly in accordance with the terms and conditions specified by the buyer and mentioned in letter of credit. The seller is assured of payments, if he tenders documents to the bank as per terms of the letter of credit.

A letter of credit thus benefits both the seller and buyer and is a means to facilitate trade and commercial transactions. A letter of credit is a mechanism, which helps a trade transaction to be put through between a seller and a buyer.

6.11.1 What is a Letter of Credit?

A letter of credit is a written instrument issued by a bunker (opening bank) at the request or a buyer (applicant) in favour of seller (beneficiary), undertaking to honour drafts (bill of exchange) drawn by the seller in accordance with the terms and conditions specified in the letter of credit. A letter of credit opened by a bank at the request of the customer (buyer) in favour of the seller within the same country is known as inland letter of credit. If the buyer and seller are operating in different countries, the LC is known as foreign letter of credit. According to the terms of payment stipulated in letter of credit if the seller is required to tender documentary bills, i.e., bills accompanied with documents of title to goods, in addition to other documents, is known as documentary letter of credit.

Parties to a letter of credit: In a letter of credit transaction basically following five parties are involved.

(*i*) Applicant (Opener/Buyer)	The party (accountholder) on whose behalf the letter of credit is opened.
(*ii*) Opening Bank/Branch	The bank/branch which (issuing Bank/ Branch) establishes the letter of credit and undertakes to pay on behalf of the applicant.
(*iii*) Beneficiary (Seller)	The party in whose favour the letter of credit is opened.
(*iv*) Advising Bank/Branch	The bank/branch whose services are utilized for advising (transmitting) the letter of credit to the beneficiary.
(*v*) Negotiating Bank/Branch	The bank/branch which is designated in the letter of credit, to negotiate the documents and to make payment to the beneficiary.

❖ Obligations of Opening and Negotiating Banks

In a letter of credit transaction, the bank deals in documents and not in goods covered by documents. The LC opening bank and the negotiating bank are not bound by the terms of the contract of sale between the buyer and the seller, though the letter of credit is required to be established in conformity with the terms of the sale contract entered into by the buyer and seller. In so far as the LC opening bank is concerned, it is bound by the LC agreement (application) duly stamped and executed by the buyer and delivered to it. The negotiating bank is bound only by the terms of the letter of credit.

The opening bank assumes contingent liability while opening letter of credit, because it undertakes responsibility to pay bills drawn under letter of credit if tendered strictly in accordance with the terms and conditions of the letter of credit. When the bills are paid by the negotiating bank/branch the transaction becomes an advance extended by the negotiating bank against documents. Hence, banks should take due precautions while negotiating documents under letter of credit. While negotiating bills under a letter of credit it must be ensured that the documents are strictly in accordance with the terms and conditions of letter of credit.

6.11.2 Various types of Inland Letters of Credit

❖ Irrevocable (Without Recourse) Letter of Credit (LC)

All irrevocable letter of credit is one, which cannot be revoked, cancelled or amended without the consent of all the parties thereto. The LC opening bunk irrevocably commits itself to pay the beneficiary upon presentation of specified documents provided the terms and conditions of the letter of credit are complied with. The term 'without recourse' implies that no recourse can be had against the beneficiary of the credit in respect of the bills paid.

❖ Revocable (Without Recourse) Letter of Credit

A revocable letter of credit can be revoked, cancelled or amended at any time without prior notification to the beneficiary. There is no irrevocable commitment on the part of the LC opening bank to honour the bills' under the credit, as no consent of the beneficiary or other parties is necessary for revocation or amendment of the credit. The LC opening bank is, however, bound to reimburse the negotiating bank/branch for negotiations made prior to its receipt of the advice of amendment or revocation. The advice of amendment or revocation takes effect only if it is received by the negotiating bank/branch prior to the negotiation of bills under the credit.

❖ Fixed and Revolving Letter of Credit

A fixed LC is one where the total amount of bills to be negotiated is mentioned. For example, if a LC is for ₹ 20 lakh documents of the value not exceeding ₹ 20 lakh can be negotiated.

A revolving letter of credit is one which provides that the amount of drawings made under the credit may be reinstated and made available to the beneficiary again for further drawings during the currency of the credit, subject to certain conditions specified therein. Such a letter of credit may also provide the total extent of drawings. A revolving letter of credit obviates the need to establish a fresh credit each time the credit is fully utilized by negotiation, as the amount of drawings is reinstated subject to certain conditions.

Example:

A revolving LC is opened for ₹ 1 lakh and a bill for ₹ 1 lakh is negotiated under the LC. When the advice of payment of this bill by the drawee, is received from the LC opening branch, the amount of the bill, *viz.*, ₹ 1 lakh gets reinstated and further bills may be negotiated under the same LC to the extent of ₹ 1 lakh provided the period of the LC has not expired and the bill conforms to the terms of the LC.

There is another term back-to-back LC. This term is generally used in international trade. When a supplier receives a letter of credit for supply of certain goods, he may request the bank to issue LC in favour of the supplier of goods. Since the same goods are to be supplied to the opener of first LC, it is termed as back-to-back LC.

6.11.3 Precautions for Opening of Letter of Credit

Following precautions should be taken while opening LCs:

- LCs should be established in conformity with bank's internal guidelines, provisions of Uniform Customs and Practices for Documentary Credit (UCPDC 600).

- All other prevalent/applicable rules and regulations/practices, legal provisions/ RBI/ FEDAI guidelines should be complied with.
- If any limits are fixed for the opener or the LC the same should be strictly adhered to and prescribed terms and conditions/safeguards should be strictly complied with/followed.
- Properly stamped application form-cum-document for opening of LC should be obtained.

◆ ◆ ◆

7 RBI Control Supervision and SEBI Regulations

7.1 ROLE OF RESERVE BANK OF INDIA

This concept of dual responsibility is crucial to an understanding of the role of the Reserve Bank in the context of planned development. About the time India launched her First Five Year Plan in 1951, the Reserve Bank began to operate on a new concept of its promotional role, which implied the development of monetary and banking institutions in a planned manner. This new concept was very different from the accepted functions of a central bank. Further this role was frequently in conflict with its traditional restrictive role of controlling the inflation that was generated in the economy as a result of deficit financing which resulted on account of the fiscal policy. However, the Reserve Bank's promotional role was so essential that it had to be pursued with enthusiasm in the larger interest of the country. Simultaneously, with the acceptance by the Indian Government of the concept of development planning, the monetary authorities were obliged to keep inflationary pressures under effective control. Ostensibly, therefore, the success of the monetary measures depended not only upon the ingenuity with which the policy was formulated but also upon the development of financial institutions within the framework of which the authorities had to function. The conclusion, therefore, is inescapable that, beginning with the First Plan, it was essential for the Reserve Bank to deviate from the norm; and together with its normal central banking functions of credit regulation, the bank also devoted its energies to the development of credit institutions and modifying and normalising banking practices attune to development.

7.2 PROMOTIONAL AND REGULATION ROLES

A striking feature of the Reserve Bank of India Act was that it made agricultural credit the Bank's special responsibility. This reflected the realisation that the country's central bank should make special efforts to develop, under its direction and guidance, a system of institutional credit for a major sector of the economy, namely, agriculture, which then accounted for more than 50 per cent of the national income. However, major advances in agricultural finance materialised only after India's independence. Over the years, the Reserve Bank has helped to evolve a suitable institutional infrastructure for providing credit in rural areas.

Another important function of the Bank is the regulation of banking. All the scheduled banks are required to keep with the Reserve Bank a consolidated 3 per cent of their total deposits, and the Reserve Bank has power to increase this percentage up to 15. These banks must have capital and reserves of not less than ₹ 5 lakh. The accumulation of these balances with the Reserve Bank places it in position to use them freely in emergencies to support the scheduled banks themselves in times of need as the lender of last resort. To a certain extent, it is also possible for the Reserve Bank to influence the credit policy of scheduled banks by means of an open market operations policy, that is, by the purchase and sale of securities or bills in the market. The Reserve bank has another instrument or control in the form of the bank rate, which it publishes from time-to-time.

Further, the Bank has been given the following special powers to control banking companies under the Banking Companies Act, 1949:

(*a*) The power to issue licences to banks operating in India.

(*b*) The power to have supervision and inspection of banks.

(*c*) The power to control the opening of new branches.

(*d*) The power to examine and sanction schemes of arrangement and amalgamation.

(*e*) The power to recommend the liquidation of weak banking companies.

(f) The power to receive and scrutinise prescribed returns, and to call for any other information relating to the banking business.

(*g*) The power to caution or prohibit banking companies generally or any banking company in particular from entering into any particular transaction or transactions.

(*h*) The power to control the lending policy of, and advances by banking companies or any particular bank in the public interest and to give directions as to the purpose for which advances may or may not be made, the margins to be maintained in respect of secured advances and the interest to be charged on advances.

The various aspects of the supervisory/regulatory functions exercised by the Reserve Bank may be briefly mentioned as under:

1. Licensing of Banks: There is a statutory provision that a company starting banking business in India has first to obtain a licence from the Reserve Bank. If the Reserve Bank is dissatisfied on account of the defective features of the proposed company, it can refuse to grant the licence. The Bank is also empowered to cancel the license of a bank when it will cease to carry on banking business in India.

2. Approval of Capital, Reserves and Liquid Assets of Banks: The Reserve Bank examines whether the minimum requirements of capital reserve and liquid assets are fulfilled by the banks and approves them.

3. Branch Licensing Policy: The Reserve Bank exercises its control over expansion of branches by the banks through its branch licensing policy.

In September 1978, the RBI formulated a comprehensive branch licensing policy with a view to accelerate the pace of expansion of bank offices in the rural areas. This was meant to correct regional imbalances of the banking coverage in the country.

4. Inspection of Banks: The Reserve Bank is empowered to conduct inspection of banks. The inspection may relate to various aspects such as the banks' organisational structure, branch expansion, mobilisation of deposits, investments, credit portfolio management, credit appraisal, profit planning, manpower planning as well as assessment of the performance of banks in developmental areas such as deployment of credit to the priority sectors, etc. The Bank may conduct *ad hoc* investigation whenever there are complaints about major irregularities or frauds by certain banks.

The inspections are basically meant to improve the working of the banks and safeguard the interests of depositors and thereby develop a sound banking system in the country.

5. Control Over Management: The Reserve Bank also looks into the management side of the banks. The appointment, re-appointment or termination of appointment of the chairman and chief executive officer of private sector banks is to be approved by the Reserve Bank. The Bank's approval is also required for the remuneration, perquisites and post-retirement benefits given by a bank to its chairman and chief executive officer.

The Boards of the public sector banks are to be constituted by the Central Government in consultation with the Reserve Bank.

6. Control Over Methods: The Reserve bank exercises strict control over the methods of operation of the banks to ensure that no improper investment and injudicious advances are made by them.

7. Audit: Banks are required to get their Balance Sheets and Profit and Loss Accounts duly audited by the auditors approved by the Reserve Bank. In the case of the State Bank of India (SBI), the auditors are appointed by the Reserve Bank.

8. Credit Information Service: The Reserve Bank is empowered to collect information about credit facilities granted by individual banks and supply the relevant information in a consolidated manner to the banks and other financial institutions seeking such information.

9. Control Over Amalgamation and Liquidation: The banks have to obtain the sanction of the Reserve Bank for any voluntary amalgamation. The Reserve Bank in consultation with the Central Government can also suggest compulsory reconstruction or amalgamation of banks. It also supervises banks in liquidation. The liquidators have to submit to the Reserve Bank returns showing their positions. The Reserve Bank keeps a watch on the progress of liquidation proceedings and the expenses of liquidation.

10. Deposit Insurance: To protect the interest of depositors, banks are required to insure their deposits with the Deposit Insurance Corporation. The Reserve Bank of India has promoted such a Corporation in 1962, which has been renamed in 1978 as the Deposit Insurance and Credit Guarantee Corporation.

11. Training and Banking Education: The RBI has played an active role in making institutional arrangement for providing training and banking education to the bank personnel, with a view to improve their efficiency.

7.3 CONTROL OF CREDIT AND CURRENCY BY RESERVE BANK OF INDIA

It has been provided in the Preamble to the Reserve Bank of India Act that one of the functions of the Bank is to control currency and credit. The control that a Central Bank is able to exercise on the monetary system largely depends upon the control that it is able to exercise on the constituents of the purchasing power. In all countries, including India, token coins and currency notes form the bulk of the purchasing power, the latter being more important than the former. In countries where banking has developed, the deposit currency also plays an important role in the creation of credit and purchasing power.

Under Section 40 of the Reserve Bank of India Act, it is obligatory for the Bank to maintain the external value of the rupee.

The Reserve Bank of India is the custodian of the country's foreign exchange reserves. It has authority to enter into foreign exchange transactions both on its own and on behalf of the Government. It is obligatory for the Bank to sell and buy currencies of all the member countries of the International Monetary Fund to ensure smooth and orderly exchange arrangements and to promote a stable system of exchanged rates.

The Reserve Bank of India has resorted to the technique of exchange control to allocate its limited foreign exchange resources according to a scheme of priorities.

In India, exchange control was introduced under the Defence of India Rules in September, 1939. It was, however, statutorily laid down by the Foreign Exchange Management Act (FEMA) of 1999.

❖ Control of Currency

The Reserve Bank of India has been given the monopoly of note issue to enable it to exercise control over the volume of bank notes. Ordinarily, the expansion or contraction of currency is effected under Section 33 (*i*) by increasing or decreasing the assets of the Issue Department, which are kept in the form of rupee coins, including rupee notes, gold coin and bullion, rupee securities, including treasury bills and foreign securities. An expansion in currency can be effected by increasing any of these forms of assets and issuing notes of equal value from the Issue Department. A contraction in currency can be similarly effected by withdrawing notes from circulation and reducing any of the assets held by the Reserve Bank. Ordinarily, when it wants to expand currency, the bank increases the assets of the Issue Department by transferring rupee or foreign securities or both from the Banking Department to the Issue Department or by cancelling *ad hoc* treasury bills held in the Issue Department. Sometimes, currency is expanded or contracted as a result of a revaluation of securities held in the Issue Department.

The Reserve Bank is authorised to transact the following ordinary banking business:

(*a*) Acceptance of money on deposits without interest from the Central and State Governments, banks, local bodies and any other person.

(*b*) The purchase, sale and rediscount of bills of exchange and promissory notes drawn and payable in India and arising out of bonafide transactions, bearing two or more signatures, one of which must be that of a scheduled bank, and maturing within 90 days from the date of purchase or rediscount.

(*c*) The purchase, sale and rediscount of bills, drawn and payable in India for financing agricultural operations or marketing of crops, and maturing within 15 months from the date of purchase or rediscount.

(*d*) The purchase, sale and rediscount of bills issued or drawn for holding or trading in securities of the Central or State Governments and maturing within 90 days.

(*e*) The making of loans and advances to States, local bodies scheduled banks and State cooperative banks.

(*f*) The making of ways and means advances to Central and State Governments.

(*g*) The purchase and sale of securities of the Central and State Governments.

(*h*) The issue of demand drafts made payable at its own offices or agencies and making, issuing and circulating bank post bills.

(*i*) The borrowing of money from a scheduled bank in India of from central banks in other countries.

((*j*) The opening of an account, or making of an agency agreement, with central banks in other countries and acting as their agent and investing funds in their shares.

(*k*) The purchase and sale of gold and bullion.

(*l*) RBI also plays an important role in the maintenance of exchange value of the rupee and acts as an Agent of the Government in respect of India's membership of International Monetary Fund.

(*m*) All such functions as may be incidental to or consequential upon the exercise of its powers or the discharge of its duties under the Act.

❖ Money and Capital Markets

The Indian money market is less insulated from the money markets abroad due to the prevailing liberalisation in India and the absence of many controls on inflow and outflow of funds. The core of the Indian money market is the inter-bank call money market where the lenders and borrowers are mostly the banks. The UTI and the LIC also enter this market. The funds dealt with are the overnight money and funds up to seven days. There is no true secondary market for bills, either commercial or government, nor is there any acceptance business in India. Most of the bills are not genuine trade bills. Treasury bills are sold on tap by the RBI on behalf of the government and the main buyers are commercial banks.

In the long-term section of the organised sector, namely, the capital market, there are a number of institutions such as stock market where the old securities are dealt with, new issues market where new capital is raised, bullion exchange where gold and silver bullion are purchased and sold. The gilt-edged market has a special characteristic in that it includes both short-term and long-term. This market is also narrow and the main holders are commercial banks and other financial institutions. There are a number of specialised financial institutions in the capital market. Some of these institutions are Industrial Finance Corporation, Industrial Credit and Investment Corporation, Provident Funds, Pension Funds, State Financial Corporations, State Insurance Corporation, etc.

❖ RBI and Financial System

The Reserve Bank is the centre-piece of the financial system and the apex institution in the money market. It is concerned with the efficient and smooth functioning of the financial system. The Reserve Bank has to keep a watch on the developments both of daily, and seasonal nature, in the financial system. It provides liquidity with a view to facilitating the smooth functioning of the system and controlling it. The flow of liquidity is controlled through money supply change, reserve requirements of banks, open market purchases/sales of government securities, etc. The cost and availability of credit is also regulated by suitable monetary policy. The Reserve Bank can influence the operations in the financial system through not only the liquidity flow, but also through regulation of banking system, of bank loans, bank holdings of liquid assets, interest rates, public deposits with banks and non-bank, etc. In brief, the RBI has three types of functions in relation to the financial system — (*a*) Financial, (*b*) Regulatory, and (*c*) Developmental.

In India, the money market and the capital market are not properly developed. The link between these two segments as also between the organised and unorganised sectors, is poor. The RBI has in the past attempted to link unorganised and organised sectors in a systematic way, but even now the dichotomy between these two sectors persists. There is inadequate integration, cohesion and specialisation among the components in the financial system. The savings and banking habits are underdeveloped with the result that the operation of the monetary policy becomes less effective, throwing greater burden on the Reserve Bank.

❖ RBI as Leader

The preamble to the Reserve Bank of India Act says that the main function of the Bank is to regulate the issues of bank notes and keeping of reserves with a view to securing monetary stability in India and generally to operate the currency and credit system of the country to its advantage. Thus, it is not only a banker to the Government, but also a banker to the commercial banks, cooperative banks and other financial institutions, in which capacity the Reserve Bank grants accommodation and keeps the reserves of these institutions.

The Bank has also an important role to play statutorily on the maintenance of the external value of the rupee in view of the close inter-dependence of international trade and national economic well-being. The Bank has been entrusted with the custody of the country's international reserves and also represents the Government at the IMF and operates exchange control and other restrictions on foreign payments and receipts.

It would thus appear that the Reserve Bank's functions can be set out in terms of the various contact points it has with the economy: (*i*) Government finance, (*ii*) Finance to banking sector and thus to the private sector of the economy, (*iii*) Finance to foreign sector, and (*iv*) finance to non-banking financial sector. The Reserve Bank as the apex institution in the financial system is the source of all currency and credit in the economy by virtue of its being the creator of currency and also the custodian of the reserves of the commercial and cooperative banks.

The operations of the RBI influence the economy and are influenced by the economy in the sense that it is environment and the context which shape the policies of the Bank and the policies of the Bank have in turn their impact on the economy. The interactions between the RBI and the economy can be set out in terms of the changes in its assets and liabilities. The liabilities of the RBI give rise to changes in reserve money which produce a multiplier effect on the actual changes in money supply. The assets of the RBI explain the factors influencing the changes in liabilities and thus of reserve money.

Sectors of the Economy Influencing	*Liabilities Side*	*Assets Side*	*Sectors of the Economy Influencing*
Govt. Sector	Deposits of Government	Loans and advances to Government	Govt. sector
Private and business sector	Deposits of banks	Loans and advances to financial sector	Bank and non-bank financial sector
Private and foreign sector	Other deposits	Investments	Govt. sector
All sectors (Households in particular)	Other liabilities (notes in circulation)	(*a*) In Govt. securities (*b*) In private assets (*c*) In foreign assets Other assets	Private sector Foreign sector All sectors

The Reserve Bank's main activities in relation to these sectors can be classified under a finance function and a regulatory function. There is also a third function, *viz.*, a development function with reference to the financial system. As a regulator of the financial system, the Reserve Bank would need a well-developed and well-organised financial system in which its actions could percolate from one segment to the other easily and quickly with the result that its control could become effective. It would thus be in the interest of the Reserve Bank's control that it should help develop an integrated and cohesive functional system, mature in all respects, *viz.*, in respect of the institutional structure, the instruments traded and the interest rates in the economy. It should also ensure that credit gaps, both geographical and functional, are duly filled up. These credit gaps may be in the short-term or the long-term credit-end. The Reserve Bank has not only a stake in the short-term money market but also long-term money market; its actions percolate to the long-end in view of the various direct controls that it operates.

❖ RBI and Banks

As regards its regulatory role, the Reserve Bank controls and regulates the activities of the commercial banks in terms of the Banking Regulations Act, 1949. These regulatory provisions were extended to cooperative banks in 1966 in terms of the Banking Laws (application to Co-operative Societies) Act, 1965. To protect the interests of the depositors, the Bank had set up the Deposit Insurance Corporation in 1962 to insure are the deposits of the public and infuse confidence in the banking system. The bank had acquired powers to effect compulsory amalgamation of banks with a view to weed out the weak and sick units and to control the management and other aspects of operations of banks including loans, advances, investments, etc.

In respect of its promotional role, let us take the commercial and cooperative banks or short-term financial institutions, which are also part of the organised financial system. To bring about a wider diffusion of the benefits of banks, they were exhorted to open branches in rural and underdeveloped regions and to lend to neglected, weaker and underprivileged regions and to lend to neglected, weaker and underprivileged sections of the population. The scheme of social control of banks and the subsequent nationalisation of the 19 major banks were aimed at these promotional objectives. The lead bank scheme of allotting each of the districts to one or more of the banks for the purpose of development of these regions is yet another example of the promotional role of banks. Mention may also be made here of the promotional aspects of encouragement and concessional refinance from the RBI for priority sector lending by banks as well as the credit authorization scheme which requires prior sanction for lending to bigger industrial houses, which has since been withdrawn.

To sum up, central bank holds the deposits of banks and lends them in times of emergency and encouraging priority sector lending — two essential banking functions. Therefore, it is called the bankers' bank. This role has invested the central bank with the authority to regulate credit by banks and perform its supreme duty of maintaining the stability of the domestic currency.

The functions of central banks have changed overtime in their content and significance. While some have gained an importance, others have lost their historical eminence. Central Banks in developing countries performed more or less the same functions as the Central Banks in developed countries. However, in view of the economic environment in which they operate, they have to act more as catalysts of development than their counterparts in the developed countries. They have to play both a promotional and a regulatory role. Though at times there can be conflicts between these two roles, over the longer run, they are very much mutually compatible. Monetary policy in India has to be formulated and pursued in the context of a planned economy whose main objective is to accelerate the process of economic growth. The compulsion to expand development expenditures necessarily leads to an expansionary fiscal policy and monetary policy has to play the role of a countervailing force keeping monetary expansion under reasonable control in order to ensure an environment of reasonable price stability.

REDISCOUNT FACILITIES

Section of the Reserve Bank of India Act	*Nature of transaction*	*Documents eligible for purchase or rediscount*	*Maximum maturity period of documents (from the date of purchase or rediscount)*
1. 17(2) (a)	Financing bonafide commercial or trade transactions (Bills Rediscounting Scheme, 1970)	Bills of exchange and promissory notes, drawn on and payable in India, bearing two or more good signatures, one of which has to be that of a scheduled bank or a State cooperative bank.	180 days if the transaction relates to export of goods from India and 90 days in all other cases
2. 17(2) (b)	Financing agricultural operations or marketing of crops	Bills of exchange and promissory notes, drawn and payable in India and bearing two or more good signatures, one of which has to be that of a State Cooperative bank.	15 months
3. 17(2) (bb)	Financing the production or marketing activities of cottage and small-scale industries approved by the Bank	Bills of exchange and promissory notes, drawn and payable in India and bearing two or more good signatures, one of which has to be that of a State cooperative bank or a State Financial Corporation, and fully guaranteed State Government as to the payment of principal and interest.	12 months
4. 17(2) (c)	Holding or trading in securities of the Central Government or a State Government	Bills of exchange and promissory notes, drawn and payable in India and bearing the signature of a scheduled bank.	90 days
5. 17(3)(b)	International trade and other transactions (available only to a scheduled bank or a State cooperative bank)	Bills of exchange (including treasury bills) drawn in or on any place in any country outside India which is a member of the International Monetary Fund.	180 days if the transaction relates to export of goods from India and 90 days in all other cases.

Source: Reserve Bank of India: Functions of Working.

LOANS AND ADVANCES

Section of the Reserve Bank of India Act	*Purpose/nature of advance*	*Collateral Security*	*Duration of advance (i.e., repayable on)*
1. 17(3)(A) (since September 1962)	Financing of export trade — available to a scheduled bank or a state co-operative bank (Export Bills Credit Scheme and pre-shipment Credit Scheme)	Promissory notes of the borrowing bank supported by a declaration in writing of holding of bills of exchange of a value not less than the amount of such loan or advance, arising out of any transaction relating to the export of goods from India, and drawn in India and on any place in any country outside India which is a member of the IMF, or any other country notified by the Reserve Bank, and maturing not later than 180 days from the date of the loan or advance to an exporter or any other person in India towards the export of goods from India, the outstanding amount of which is not less than the loan or advance from the Reserve Bank (since February 1969).	On demand, or on the expiry of fixed periods not exceeding 180 days
2. 17(3B) (since December 1974)	Financing bonafide commercial or trade transactions, agricultural operations, marketing of crops or other agricultural purposes — available to a scheduled bank (including a Regional Rural Bank) or a State co-operative bank (Duty Draw-back Credit Scheme, 1976)	Promissory notes of the borrowing bank supported by a declaration in writing that it has made loans or advances for any of the stated purposes, the outstanding amount of which is not less than the loan or advance from the Reserve Bank.	On demand, or on the expiry of fixed periods not exceeding 180 days
3. 17(4*a*) to (*d*)	Loans and advances to a scheduled bank, state co-operative bank or State Financial Corporation Bill Market Scheme (1952-70)	(*a*) Stocks, funds and trustee securities (other than immovable property) or (*b*) Gold or silver or documents of title thereto or (*c*) Bills of exchange and promissory notes eligible for purchase or rediscount by the Bank, or fully guaranteed by a State Government as to repayment of principal and payment of interest or	On demand, or on the expiry of fixed periods not exceeding 90 days. Loans and advances made against the security of bills of exchange and promissory notes arising out of any transaction relating to the export of goods from India are repayable on demand, or on the expiry of fixed periods not exceeding 180 days.

		(*d*) Promissory notes of a scheduled bank or state cooperative bank supported by documents of title to goods, such documents having been transferred, assigned or pledged to such bank as security for a loan or advance made for bonafide commercial or trade transactions or for financing agricultural operations or the marketing of crops.	
4. 17(4)(1) (since July 1978)	Loans and advances, for the purchase of foreign exchange from the Bank for financing of the import of capital goods or for such other purposes as may be approved by the Central Government — available to scheduled banks. Industrial Development Bank of India. Industrial Finance Corporation, Export-Import Bank of India and other financial institutions approved by the Government.	Such security and on such other terms and conditions as may be approved by the Central Board of the Reserve Bank.	On demand or otherwise.
5. 17(12B) (since July 1978)	Loans and advances in foreign currencies for financing international trade or for the import of capital goods or for such other purposes as may be approved by the Central Government — available to scheduled banks, Industrial Development Bank of India, Industrial Finance Corporation, Export-Import Bank of India, any State Financial Corporation and other financial institutions approved by the Government.	Promissory notes of the borrowing bank or institution, supported by a declaration in writing that it has made loans and advances in foreign currencies for any of the stated purposes, the outstanding amount of which is not less than the loan or advance from the Reserve Bank	The terms and conditions will be as specified by the Central Board of the Reserve Bank.

Credit management to be effective must be comprehensive and must include both quantitative and qualitative credit measures. The problem of credit management cannot be tackled through a fragmented approach. An effective credit management requires a well-coordinated and comprehensive approach. The essence of the comprehensive approach lies not only in the integration of quantitative and selective credit management weapons but also hinges on an effective coordination and simultaneous and timely use of the three main techniques — monetary measures, fiscal measures, and measures of economic policy — for direct regulation, management and physical flow of funds to socially desirable and economically viable purposes or projects.

In addition, the Reserve Bank, like many other central banks in emerging market economies, has had to increasingly contend with maintaining financial stability. Besides, the Reserve Bank's role as manager of public debt also implies that the internal debt management function gets inextricably mixed with the monetary management function. In view of the limited number of instruments, the Reserve Bank has to prioritise its objectives given the circumstances. This constrains the degree of flexibility available to monetary policy in a complex macroeconomic environment.

7.4 MONETARY CONTROL

The Reserve Bank of India is mainly constituted as an apex authority for monetary management. Its primary function is to formulate and administer monetary policy. Monetary policy refers to "the use of instruments within the control of the central bank to influence the level of the aggregate demand for goods and services by regulation of the money supply and credit".

The Reserve Bank seeks to control and regulate the flow of credit in the economy such that it can sustain the tempo of development and promote the maintenance of internal price stability. It uses quantitative controlling weapons such as bank rate policy, open market operations and the reserve ratio requirement. Since 1956, it has increasingly relied on and resorted to selective credit controls for accelerating the rate of growth and for checking inflationary spurts.

In the post-independence era, with the enactment of the Banking Regulation Act, 1949, the Reserve Bank of India was invested with overriding powers to control the banking system and thus it emerged as a conscientious guardian and watchdog of the monetary structure of Indian economy. With the lapse of time, the scope of monetary policy in the country has been considerably widened to make adequate adjustments in the money credit structure in view of the changing needs of the developing economy envisaged under the Five Year Plans.

❖ Objectives of Economic Policies

Governments in the post-World War II era have proclaimed the objectives of their economic policies in wide humanitarian terms — the maintenance of full employment, well-rounded economic progress, and so on; and towards this end, they have also been easily adapting existing tools and fashioning new ones both in the national as well as the international sphere. These acts of the Government have resulted in setting up central banks which non-existed before nationalizing the existing ones, in placing additional responsibilities on them, in conferring, amending and extending it, and setting up several ancillary institutions to serve the ends of national and international economic policies in the monetary and banking spheres.

While the goals of a country's economic policy provide the general setting for the functioning of a central bank, the precise nature of its relationship with the banking system depends on the matrix of economic and environmental conditions in which it has to work and the type of responsibilities that are placed upon it. As regards the latter, while the exact wording differs as between the statute of one central bank and that of another, the maintenance of monetary stability through the regulation of the country's currency and credit system is the basic responsibility of all central banks. Some statutes spell out monetary stability into internal and external stability. But those that do not, imply this all the same. Again, in some statutes, the broad overall objectives of economic policy, such as sound economic development or the maintenance of full employment, are also specifically incorporated. However, even where this has not been done, central banks have to keep such objectives consciously before them all the time. This widening of the scope of the responsibility of central banks, whether explicit or implicit, has made their task much more difficult than it was in the past. The maintenance of monetary stability is now not an objective to be pursued for its own sake but only for the contribution that it can make to the attainment of the overall objectives. Too much of the former stifles the progress towards the latter, while a too rapid pursuit of the latter endangers the former and becomes the process of self-defeating, for it hinders the progress towards the attainment of these wider objectives. Central banks have, therefore, to strike a balance between the two and evolve a policy that ensures the maximum progress in an atmosphere of stability. In addition, many central banks are entrusted with mechanisms to cater to the needs of certain vital sectors of the economy of administering banking legislation with a view to protecting the interests of depositors and of administering exchange control.

❖ Central Bank and Banking System

The main relationship between the central bank and the banking system is the one that arises as a result of the former's basic responsibility. "The essence of central banking," Prof. Sayers observed, "is discretionary control of the monetary system". The discretion is to be exercised in the light of the objective the central bank happens to be pursuing. In the absence of a central bank, a country's monetary system suffers from certain rigidities. Discretionary control of the central bank, which means control adjusted to the needs of the situation, removes these. To enable them to make these adjustments, a central bank —

(*i*) Is given the monopoly of note issue;

(*ii*) Is required to hold the country's principal reserves of international liquidity;

(*iii*) Works as the bankers' bank;

(*iv*) Works as the Government's bank not only by handling the inflows and outflows of its funds but also by handling its debt operations; and

(*v*) Is armed with a host of 'weapons'. Thus, on the one hand, central banks are the ultimate source of liquidity in a country while, on the other, they possess a number of devices to control and direct its flow in the desired channels. Apart from the discharge of their basic function through the use of these powers, central banks are advisors to the governments on monetary and banking matters and maintain a liaison between governments and banking and financial institutions by appropriate solutions to them; and through these actions, they facilitate the attainment of their basic objective.

The Government of India, like many other growing nations, has been, and continues to be, anxious to embark on accelerated development plans in order to reach the stage of "drive to maturity" within the shortest possible time. As might be expected, the internal resources of the country have perpetually fallen short of the financial requirements of the Government-sponsored

Five Year Plans. Consequently, the Government has had to resort to the well-known method of deficit financing, through the creation of central bank credit. This method of financing is inflationary in character. Consequently, to keep the inflation within "safe limits", the Reserve Bank has been called upon to play the role of a "controller of inflation". Thus, with slight modifications, Senator 'Douglas' analogy has become applicable to the Reserve Bank. The task of trying to check inflation while extending credit, according to Douglas, "will be just as futile as when...(one fills) the glass of water and keep(s) pouring it in, and... (tries) to mop up the overflow water with a pocket handkerchief".

To analyse the issue, two fundamental factors that characterize the role of the Reserve Bank in the economic development of India may be mentioned. First, India has an economy of planned development, and the central banking policy has to fit itself within the framework of development plans. Second, the size and structure of the Five Year Plans are primarily decided upon not on the basis of the available financial resources but on the basis of the determination of the authorities to formulate plans of large dimensions. Once the size of a Five Year Plan (presently eleventh Five Year Plan) is determined, given limited financial resources, the Government has to resort to deficit financing for the reasons mentioned above. This is more than likely to create an inflationary situation, and the Bank has necessarily to function within the conditions created by the effort to implement the plan.

The primary responsibility of the monetary authorities of an underdeveloped country like India is to reduce the pressure of monetary demand without at the same time hampering production, so as to help maintain the predetermined pace of development. It has been reiterated on numerous occasions by the Reserve Bank that its aim is to "keep inflationary pressures at bay while the production forces are gathering momentum". It follows that an attempt to provide adequate finances for production on the one hand, and to control the inflation generated through deficit financing on the other, makes the task of the Bank all the more difficult. Nevertheless, the nature of the problem of the economic development of India, at least in the initial stages, was such that aiming at one of the above objectives at the cost of the other would only be self-defeating. Consequently, the monetary policy of necessity has to assume this dual responsibility.

7.5 DUAL RESPONSIBILITY OF RESERVE BANK OF INDIA

This concept of dual responsibility is crucial to our understanding of the role of the Reserve Bank. About the time India launched her First Five Year Plan, the Reserve Bank began to operate on a new concept of its promotional role, which implied the development of monetary and banking institutions in a planned economy. That concept was very different from the accepted functions of a central bank. Further, that role was frequently in conflict with its traditional restrictive role of controlling the conflict inflation that was generated in the economy as a result of deficit financing. However, the Reserve Bank's promotional role was so essential that it had to be pursued with enthusiasm. Simultaneously, with the acceptance by the Indian Government of the concept of development planning, the monetary authorities were obliged to keep inflationary pressures under effective control. Ostensibly, therefore, the success of the monetary measures depended not only upon the ingenuity with which the policy was formulated but also upon the development of financial institutions within the framework of which the authorities had to function. The conclusion therefore, is inescapable that, beginning with the First Plan, it was essential for the Reserve Bank to deviate from the norm; and together with its normal central banking functions of credit regulation, the Bank also devoted its energies to the development of credit institutions and practices.

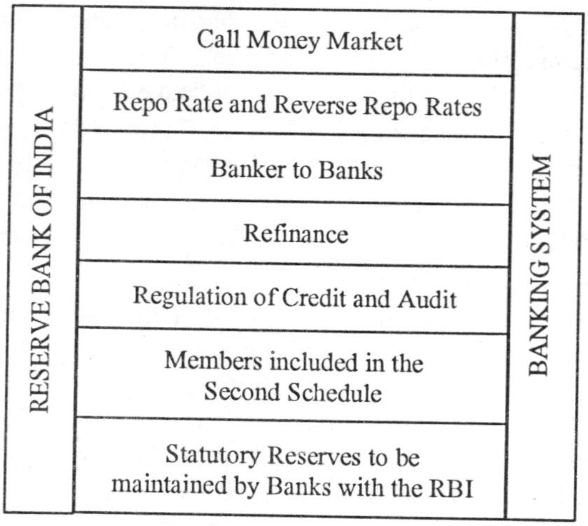

The Relation of the Reserve Bank with the Banking System

While the Reserve Bank's new concept of central banking was a happy one, as mentioned above, it often created a conflict between its promotional role and its restrictive role, which was often a thorny problem for it. The development of credit institutions and the advances by the Bank of productive credit through these institutions generated inflationary pressures in the economy. Such a situation only made the restrictive role of the Bank more imperative which was to control the inflation generated by accelerated deficit financing. This situation duly emphasized the conflict in the development phase of a developing nation which often arises between the short-run and long-run objectives of the monetary policy. The conflict could not be resolved by the sacrifice of one function in favour of the other. For, if through undue caution, the Bank withheld legitimate credit for agricultural and industrial production, these areas might never develop. In the ultimate analysis, therefore, the Bank could not help but endeavour to ensure a reconciliation between the two equally important aspects of its role: its promotional role of developing new institutions and helping certain sectors of the economy in acquiring the requisite credit, and its restrictive role as the controller of credit expansion in the economy.

A central bank necessarily functions within the limitations set by the current economic philosophy of a country. If the dominant problem in a country like India is one of planned development, and the efforts of the whole country are directed towards the mobilization of national resources with a view to optimising the rate of development, then there is a need for a new perspective on central bank objectives, namely, the necessity for augmenting credit facilities and giving a purposive direction to credit. The development of this new perspective is likely to compel the central bank to reformulate the monetary policy in a way which would encourage the flow of credit into desired directions without necessarily bringing about a contraction in the total quantum of credit.

In India, the monetary policy framework underwent a significant transformation to emerge as the chief instrument of macroeconomic stabilisation as well as a vehicle for the subsequent structural reforms in the financial system. The objective is to create a competitive environment in the financial sector while ensuring price stability and growth.

7.6 OBJECTIVES OF MONETARY POLICY

In a developing economy, the monetary policy has often got to be ambivalent. The objectives of the monetary policy may be stated as follows:

(*i*) To assist in the mobilization of savings in the community and promote capital formation;

(*ii*) To promote the spread of monetization and monetary integration in the country;

(*iii*) To provide the credit necessary for the fulfilment of the targets of production and trade;

(*iv*) To extend monetary support to the authorities in the central task of the allocation of resources by assisting them in the maintenance of an appropriate structure of relative prices;

(*v*) To maintain a general price stability and prevent inflationary tendencies from getting out of hand.

(*vi*) To maintain orderly conditions in the foreign exchange market;

(*vii*) To enhance the allocative efficiency of the financial markets; and

(*viii*) To sharpen the operating procedure of monetary policy — introducing transparency.

The importance of the monetary and banking systems in the generation of savings and in their mobilization is obvious. While inflationary financing at the initiative of the Government is an accepted method of development, it benefits directly only the public sector. The banking system of the country, has, however, a greater responsibility and freedom of operation in the field of financing development plans for the private sector. The monetary and credit policies of the central bank, therefore, will have to take account of the objectives of the monetary policy.

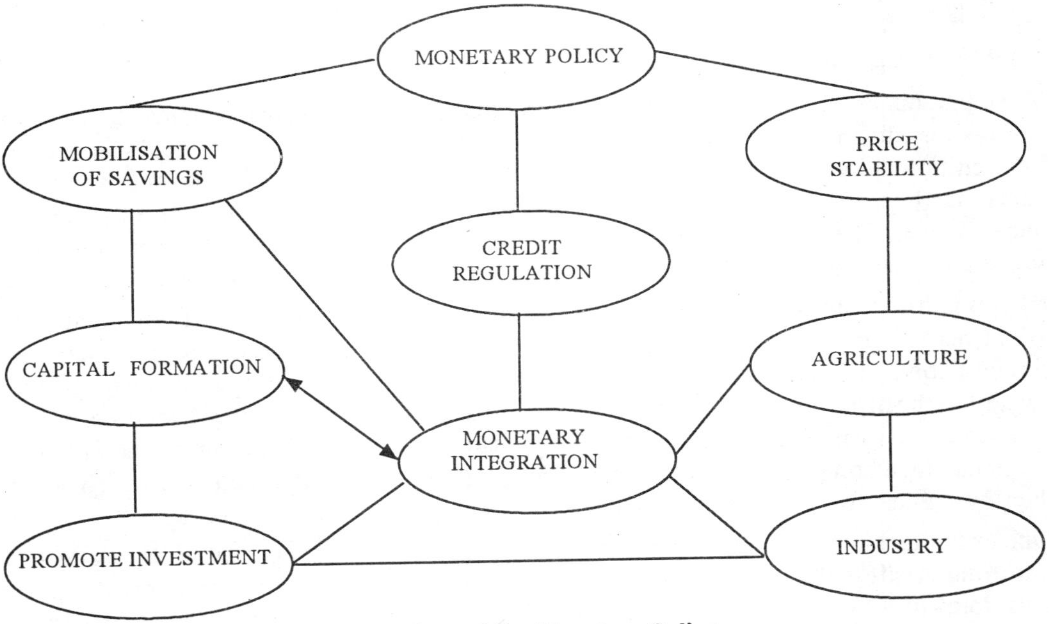

Objectives of the Monetary Policy

7.7 CREDIT CONTROL

In general, adjustment programmes are designed to achieve a certain growth target in some credit or monetary aggregate. In countries where financial innovations or a shift to a market orientation of the economy are taking place, the target for a particular monetary aggregate may become inappropriate and therefore may have to be revised.

In planned economies, for example, currency targets may be appropriate where use of deposits is strictly limited to plan transactions. Once the economy becomes more market-oriented, the monetary target may have to be changed and the programme modified. Market economies that use direct controls on interest rates and bank-specific credit ceilings to achieve monetary and credit targets may suffer from undesirable effects of such policies on resource allocation. These include low deposit rates and additional loan fees or service charges, disincentives to savings (once the credit targets are reached), and underdevelopment of interbank money markets. For these reasons, it is desirable to switch to indirect monetary control through reserve money management. The Fund, through its technical assistance, has assisted Costa Rica, Indonesia, and Mauritius in making this switch, which can take place with or without interest rate liberalization. Where liberalization of interest rates is contemplated, the switch to indirect controls is particularly important to enhance competition in the banking industry.

❖ Instruments of Monetary Policy

The tools available to the Reserve Bank for the attainment of its objectives are listed as follows:

(*i*) The Bank Rate and control over the lending rates of banks;

(*ii*) Open market operations;

(*iii*) Variable reserve requirements;

(*iv*) Selective controls; and

(*v*) Moral suasion.

The programmes of economic development have introduced a strong and continuous expansionary trend in bank credit in which two factors cause variations. For a variety of reasons, the use of the two traditional instruments of central bank control, *viz.*, the bank rate and open market operations, has been rather limited in India. Variable reserve requirements, too, have been used only once. On the other hand, selective credit controls and moral suasion have been used fairly widely during recent years.

(i) Bank Rate and the Banks' Lending Policy: Although the Bank Rate was intended to be used primarily as the rate for buying or rediscounting bills of exchange or other eligible commercial paper, in the absence of a genuine market in India for such credit instruments, the Bank Rate has been used mainly as the rate governing the Reserve Bank's lending policy. A consequence of this has been that the Bank Rate, instead of being the leader of short-term rates in the system, since bonds have generally been the predominant collateral against which advances are taken by banks from the Reserve Bank.

One of the factors which limits the use of frequent variations in the Bank Rate as a technique for controlling credit is the imperfection of the money market resulting in a rather wide spectrum of interest rates in the economy and the lack of cohesion amongst them. It has been the endeavour of monetary authorities to reduce the disparities in interest rates in different sectors of the market

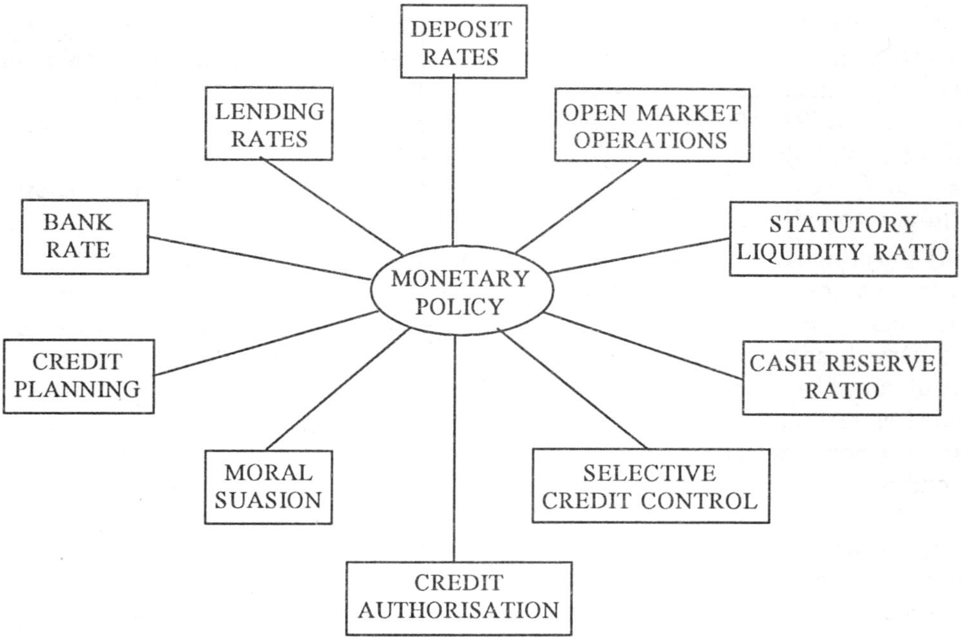

Instruments of Monetary Policy

for funds, more particularly with a view to lessening the high cost of credit to the weaker sectors of the economy. Hence, while the bank's lending rate to the organized money market has been stepped up in the manner described above, efforts have been made to reduce the cost for agriculture and small-scale industries by giving them finance at concessional rates.

In addition, for influencing the cost of bank credit, the Reserve Bank relies on direct control over the lending rates of banks. It derives its authority to regulate the interest rates of banks under Sections 21 and 35A of the Banking Regulation Act.

(ii) Open Market Operations: The use of this technique of controlling credit through its direct impact on the bank's liquidity position has been circumscribed by different factors at different periods in its history. In the early years of its existence, the scope for these operations was limited by the state of the economy. After the War, the cheap money policy coincided with the Government securities, to revert to a more normal pattern of distribution of their assessment through a liquidation of a part of these holdings. As mentioned earlier, late in 1951, the bank replaced the cheap money policy with that of discriminating support to the market. Thereafter, the growing needs of development, necessitating increasing efforts on the part of the authorities to sell more and more Government debt management have tended to become a one-way affair.

Amongst the factors which limit the scope for a greater use of open market operations in India may be cited the absence of a well-developed market for Treasury and commercial bills, and the predominance of certain types of institutional investors like banks, the Life Insurance Corporation, provident funds and trusts which are required by statute to hold a certain proportion of their assets in the form of Government securities. The first has meant that the Reserve Bank use its lending policy rather than open market operations at the short end of the market to control short-term fluctuations in credit. The Reserve Bank's open market operations have, therefore, to be in medium and long-term securities. Here, the latter factor necessitates a policy of gradualness in effecting changes in the long-term interest rate structure. Yet, open market operations are the best way to conduct monetary policy. For market stabilization, Market Stabilization Scheme (MSS) started by RBI from 23-2-2004. The ceiling on the bond issue by RBI was fixed for borrowings at ₹ 2,50,000 crore on 7-11-2007 with review for enhancement. Earlier the ceiling was fixed at ₹ 40,000 crore before 7-8-2007 and ₹ 1,50,000 crore thereafter. These bonds are issued to absorb call money rates.

(iii) Variable Reserve Requirements: Until October 1956, the Reserve Bank did not possess powers to vary the reserve requirements of banks, which were fixed at 5 per cent of demand liabilities and 2 per cent of time liabilities. The powers which it then acquired permitted the Bank to vary these up to 20 per cent of demand liabilities and 8 per cent of time liabilities. Also, it obtained powers to vary incremental reserve requirements, *i.e.,* the proportion to be maintained as reserves of increments after a certain date to deposits, up to 100 per cent of the increase in deposits to the overall maxima mentioned above. These powers were used in 1960 under conditions of a rapid rise in the liquidity of the banking system. In March 1960, scheduled banks were required to maintain with the Reserve Bank 25 per cent of the increase in their deposit liabilities over and above the minimum statutory reserves, *viz.,* 5 per cent of demand liabilities and 2 per cent of time liabilities. From 6 May, 1960, the requirement was raised to 50 per cent of the additions to deposit liabilities after that date. The measure was operative mainly over the slack season of 1960, towards the end of which came the fundamental change in the Bank's lending policy with the introduction of the three-tier system of lending rates. The measure was, therefore, withdrawn and the impounded deposits released in two instalments, one in November 1960 and the other in January 1961. It may be noted that banks were compensated by the Reserve Bank in respect of the interest lost by them following the impounding of additions to deposits. The compensation was initially equal to the average rate of interest paid by banks during the corresponding quarter, subject to a ceiling equal to the Bank Rate. Later, it was raised by 1/2 per cent with a corresponding increase in the ceiling.

In September 1962, the distinction maintained between demand and time liabilities for purposes of reserve requirements was abolished. The minimum requirements, with effect from 4th February, 1984 were 9 per cent of demand and time liabilities taken together, and they varied between 3 per cent and 15 per cent. This change was necessitated by the increasingly important role played by time deposits in the Indian money market. With the constantly increasing tempo of economic activity, there has been a very keen competition for funds, which has found expression in the growth of the volume, and a tendency towards the shortening of the maturity of time deposits. A sizable part of time deposits held by the banking system now partakes of the character of demand deposits. The CRR and SLR were 6% (from 24-4-2010) and 24% (from 18-12-2010) respectively, after hitting high (CRR 9% from 30-8-2008 and SLR 25% from 25-10-1997.

The Regional Rural Banks, had been allowed to maintain a lower level of cash reserve, *viz.,* 5.5 per cent from 17-1-2009, as in the case of scheduled State cooperative banks. This concession has been deemed necessary to increase their lending operations by not impairing their resources position. The exemption from the application of the provisions of Sub-section (1) of Section 42, in so far as they require a scheduled bank to maintain a cash reserve in excess of 3 per cent, is granted by notifications issued by the Bank from time-to-time under Sub-section (7) of that section which empowers it to exempt any scheduled bank with reference to the whole or any part of its reference to all or any of its offices or with reference to the whole or any part of its assets and liabilities.

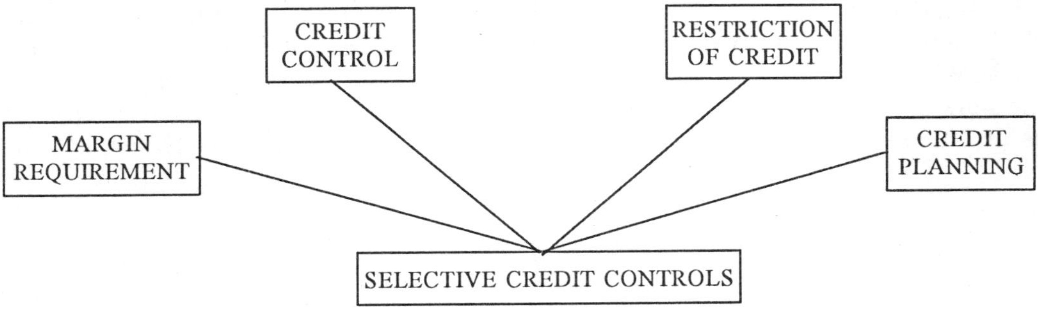

Forms of Selective Credit Controls

The cash reserve requirements for non-scheduled banks have been put down in Section 18 of the Banking Regulation Act. These banks have to maintain in cash with themselves or incurrent account with the Reserve Bank, the State Bank of India or any other notified in this behalf; or partly in cash and partly in such account, a minimum of 3 per cent of their total demand and time liabilities in India. The associate banks of the State Bank of India and all 20 nationalised banks have been notified by the Central Government for this purpose (as well as for the purpose of compliance with the liquid assets requirement under Section 24 (2A) of the Banking Regulation Act).

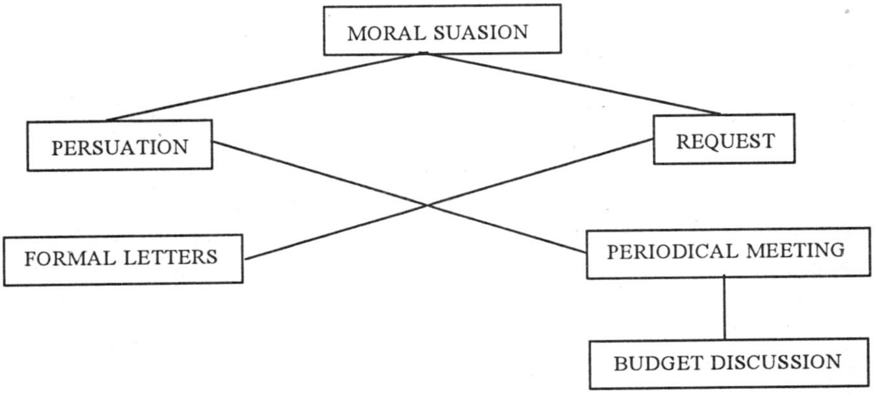

Indicates Ways and Means of Moral Suasion

(iv) Selective Credit Controls: Selective credit controls have been used by the bank mainly with a view to restraining excessive speculative stock-building of commodities in short supply either as a result of a crop shortage or as a result of a fall in the production of manufactured articles following raw materials shortages, etc. The commodities in respect of which these articles of consumption or items important for exports are foodgrains, oilseeds, jute, cotton textiles and sugar.

These controls have taken the form of objectives to increase the margin requirements, to regulate the size of credit limit per borrower with a view to ensure maintenance of an aggregate level of credit against a particular commodity at a certain level which may have reference to the level of credit maintained in the corresponding period in the past, etc. Adjustments to suit the needs of the economy in a particular region have also been incorporated in these controls. Besides exercising control on bank credit against the security of particular commodities in short supply, the Reserve Bank has also endeavoured to control excessive borrowing from the banking system by way of clean advances or against the security of other assets, such as shares and stocks. Initially, it took sometime for the banking system to get accustomed to these techniques. Extensive branch network and difficulties of communication as well as differences in the efficiency of the branches of different sizes and in different areas were some of the problems which had to be overcome.

The main instruments of selective controls in India are:

(*a*) Minimum margins (in a secured advance, the "margin" represents a portion of the value of the security charged to the bank, which is expected to have been paid for by the borrower out of his own resources) for lending against selected commodities;

(*b*) Ceilings on the levels of credit; and

(*c*) Charging minimum rate of interest on advances against specified commodities. While the two instruments control the quantum of credit, the third instrument works as a leverage on the cost of credit. On the whole, the banking system in India has shown a good appreciation of the needs of such controls and has cooperated quite well. As regards their overall efficiency, the experience in India has been the same as that of most other countries, namely, that their effectiveness in general is comparatively limited. Generally, they are successful if employed in combination with measures of general credit control.

(v) Moral Suasion: Moral suasion refers to the advice or indication given by the central bank, generally to banks and sometimes to other financial institutions also, in the matter of their lending and other operations with the objective that they might implement or follow it. Moral suasion may be quantitative in content, such as fixation of the aggregate amount of credit to be granted by banks during a period, or caution to be exercised in granting advances against commodities whose prices are subject to speculative tendencies. Periodically, letters are issued to banks urging them to exercise control over credit in general or advances against specified commodities or unsecured advances in particular. Discussions are also held from time-to-time with banks with the same objective. Wherever the use of moral suasion is possible, it makes it easier for the central bank to secure the willing and active cooperation of commercial banks in complying with the regulatory measures, both in letter and in spirit; it also enables the central bank to exert influence not only on the borrowing banks (which is possible by direct action) but also on the non-borrowing banks, and other credit and financial institutions, whose operations are significant enough to affect the credit policy of the central bank.

The Reserve Bank has found the technique of moral suasion, backed as it is by the Bank's vast powers of direct regulation, quite useful; and it has been able to build-up good informal relations with banks over the years. The use of this instrument is facilitated by the concentration of almost the entire banking business in the hands of the banks in the public sector.

One notable instance of moral suasion is the maintenance by banks of liquid assets (*i.e.*, the statutory liquidity ratio) at a level higher than that prescribed under Section 24 of the Banking Regulation Act. Although, statutorily, banks have to maintain liquid assets equal to 25 per cent of their demand and time liabilities, under instructions from the Bank, they actually maintain liquid assets at a much higher level. From time-to-time, the Bank has used moral suasion for various purposes, such as discouraging the use of bank credit for speculative purposes, achieving the desired degree of contraction in bank credit during the slack season, checking undue expansion of clean advances, helping Government's borrowing programme, etc. This has been done through both informal consultation and issuance of formal letters by the Governor of the Bank to scheduled banks. Even when using other instruments of control, the Bank has endeavoured to explain the problem to the banking system and enlist their cooperation in achieving its objective.

The task of the central bank becomes easier, however, if there is a proper understanding and respect between it and the banking system as to the responsibilities and capabilities of each. Above all, it must be realized that, in countries following a broad-based warfare policy, there is a fundamental community of interest between the central bank and the banking system. The latter is the essential medium through which a central bank's monetary policy can make itself effective. A well-organized banking system is, therefore, the first requirement of the success of a central bank. It need not then always use controlling instruments which force the banking system to act in the desired direction. It can achieve the same object through what is called "moral suasion", i.e., informing the banks what the central bank considers to be a desirable line of action and leave them to do the rest. For underdeveloped countries, the significance of this is that the central banks have to devote a considerable part of their energies to the provision of an efficient banking system. In some countries, this is done by the central bank itself undertaking either the whole business of commercial banking or at least such aspects of it as are immediately relevant in the interests of the development of the country. In others, it is attempted by offering various facilities to the banking system to enable it to expand and diversify its services, and if necessary, by subsidizing it up to ancillary money and capital market institutions.

A system of administered interest rates has also had an impact on the instruments on credit control. Since the interest rates offered on deposits and charged on lending are directly controlled by the monetary authorities, bank rate as an instrument of credit control has not much significance. Open market operations in Government securities have also become less relevant as instrument of credit control since the rates of interest offered on Government securities though reasonable are not truly competitive. It is in this context as mentioned earlier, the variable reserve ratio has emerged as an important instrument of credit control.

7.8 SECURITIES AND EXCHANGE BOARD OF INDIA (SEBI)

Under these circumstances, the government felt the need for setting up of an apex body to develop and regulate the stock market in India. Eventually, the Securities and Exchange Board of India (SEBI) was set up on April 12, 1988. To start with, SEBI was set up as a non-statutory body.

It took almost four years for the government to bring about a separate legislation in the name of Securities and Exchange Board of India Act, 1992 conferring statutory powers. The Act, charged to SEBI with comprehensive powers over practically all aspects of capital market operations.

❖ Objectives

According to the preamble of the SEBI Act, the primary objective of the SEBI is to promote healthy and orderly growth of the securities market and secure investor protection. For this purpose, the SEBI monitors the activities of not only stock exchanges but also merchant bankers, etc. The objectives of SEBI are as follows:

1. To protect the interest of investors so that there is a steady flow of savings into the capital market.
2. To regulate the securities market and ensure fair practices by the issuers of securities so that they can raise resources at minimum cost.
3. To promote efficient services by brokers, merchant bankers and other intermediaries so that they become competitive and professional.

❖ Functions

Section 11 of the SEBI Act specifies the functions as follows:

1. Regulatory Functions:

(*a*) Regulation of stock exchange and self-regulatory organisations.

(*b*) Registration and regulation of stock brokers, sub-brokers, registrar to all issues, merchant bankers, underwriters, portfolio managers and such other intermediaries who are associated with securities market.

(*c*) Registration and regulation of the working of collective investment schemes including mutual funds.

(*d*) Prohibition of fraudulent and unfair trade practices relating to securities market.

(*e*) Prohibition of insider trading in securities.

(*f*) Regulating substantial acquisitions of shares and takeover of companies.

2. Developmental Functions:

(*a*) Promoting investor's education.

(*b*) Training of intermediaries.

(*c*) Conducting research and published information useful to all market participants.

(*d*) Promotion of fair practices. Code of conduct for self-regulatory organisations.

(*e*) Promoting self-regulatory organisations.

❖ Powers

SEBI has been vested with the following powers:

1. Power to call periodical returns from recognised stock exchanges.
2. Power to call any information or explanation from recognised stock exchanges or their members.
3. Power to direct énquiries to be made in relation to affairs of stock exchanges or their members.
4. Power to grant approval to bye-laws of recognised stock exchanges.
5. Power to make or amend bye-laws of recognised stock exchanges.
6. Power to compel listing of securities by public companies.
7. Power to control and regulate stock exchanges.
8. Power to grant registration to market intermediaries.

9. Power to levy fees or other charges for carrying out the purpose of regulation.
10. Power to declare applicability of Section 17 of the Securities Contract (Regulation) Act is any state or area to grant licences to dealers in securities.

❖ Organisation

Chapter II of the SEBI Act deals with establishment, incorporation, administration and management of the Board of Directors, etc. The SEBI Act provides for the establishment of a statutory board consisting of six members. The chairman and two members are to be appointed by the Central Government, one member to be appointed by the Reserve Bank and two members having experience of securities market to be appointed by the Central Government. Section II deals with the powers of the Board.

SEBI has divided its activities into four operational departments namely primary market department, issue management and intermediaries department, secondary market department and institutional department, each headed by an Executive Director. Apart from these there are two other departments, *viz.*, Legal Department and Investigation Department, also headed by officials of the rank of Executive Directors.

Primary Market Department: Primary market department deals with all policy matters and regulatory issues relating to primary market, market intermediaries and matters pertaining to SRO's and redressal of investor grievances.

Issue Management and Intermediaries Department: This department is concerned with vetting of offer documents and other things like registration, regulation and monitoring of issue related to intermediaries.

Secondary Market Department: It looks after all the policy and regulatory issues for the secondary market; administration of the major stock exchanges and other matters related to it.

Institutional Investment Department: This department is concerned with framing policy for foreign institutional investors, mutual funds and other matters like publications, membership in international organisations, etc.

SEBI has two Advisory Committees, one each for primary and secondary markets. The committees are constituted from among the market players, recognised investor associations and eminent persons associated with the capital market. They provide advisory inputs in framing policies and regulations. These committees are non-statutory in nature and SEBI is not bound by the committees.

❖ SEBI and Central Government

The Central Government has the power to issue directions to the SEBI Board, to supersede the Board, if necessary and to call for returns and report, etc., as and when necessary. The Central Government has also powers to give any guidelines or to make regulations and rules for SEBI and its operations.

The activities of SEBI are financed by grants from the Government in addition to fees, charges, etc., collected by SEBI. The fund called the SEBI General Fund, is set up to which all grants, fees, charges, etc., are credited. The fund is used to meet the expenses of the Board and to pay salaries of staff and remuneration to officers, members of the Board, etc.

7.9 SEBI GUIDELINES

SEBI has brought out a number of guidelines separately, from time-to-time, for primary market, secondary market, mutual funds, merchant bankers, foreign institutional investors, investor protection, etc. The guidelines are described below:

1. Guidelines for Primary Market

New Company: A new company is one (*a*) which has not completed 12 months commercial production and does not have audited results, and (*b*) where the promoters do not have a track record.

These companies will have to issue shares only at par.

New Company set up by Existing Company: When a new company is being set up by existing companies with a five year track record of consistent profitability and a contribution of at least 50% in the equity of new company, it will be free to price its issue, i.e., it can issue its share at premium.

Private and Closely-held Companies: The private and closely-held companies having a track record of consistent profitability for at least three years, shall be permitted to price their issues freely. The issue price shall be determined only by the issues in consultation with lead managers to the issue.

Existing Listed Companies: The existing listed companies will be allowed to raise fresh capital by freely pricing expanded capital provided the promoter's contribution is 50% on first ₹ 100 crore of issue, 40% on next ₹ 200 crore, 30% on next ₹ 300 crore and 15% on balance issue amount.

❖ Reservation of Issues

Reservations under public subscription for various persons is made in the following manner:

1. Permanent employees	10%
2. Indian Mutual Funds	20%
3. Foreign Institutional Investors	15%
4. QIBs	20%
5. Shareholders	15%
6. Investor's contribution	20%

❖ Composite Issues

In the case of composite issue, i.e., right cum public issue by existing listed companies differential pricing shall be allowed. In other words, issue to the public can be priced differentially as compared to issue to right shareholders. However, justification for the price difference should be given in the offer document.

❖ Lock-in Period

Lock-in period is five years for promoter's contribution from the date of allotment or from the commencement of commercial production whichever is late. At present, the lock-in period has been reduced to one year.

❖ Guidelines for Public Issue

1. Abridged prospectus has to be attached with every application.
2. A company has to highlight the risk factors in the prospectus.
3. Objective of the issue and cost of project should be mentioned in the prospectus.
4. Company's management, past history and present business of the firm should be highlighted in the prospectus.
5. Particulars in regard to company and other listed companies under the same management which made any capital issues during the last three years are to be stated in the prospectus.
6. Justification for premium, in the case of premium is to be stated.
7. Subscription list for public issues should be kept open for a minimum of three days and a maximum of 7 working days.
8. The collection centres should be at least 30 which include all centres with stock exchanges.
9. Collection agents are not to collect application money in cash.
10. The quantum of issue, whether through a right or public issue, shall not exceed the amount specified in the prospectus. No retention of oversubscription is permissible under any circumstances.
11. A compliance report in the prescribed form should be submitted to SEBI within 21 days from the date of closure of issue.
12. The allotments have to be made in multiples of tradable lot shares of ₹ 10 each.
13. Issues by way of bonus, rights, etc., to be made in appropriate lots to minimise odd lots.
14. If minimum subscription of 90% has not been received, the entire amount is to be refunded to investors within 120 days.
15. The capital issue should be fully paid up within 120 days.
16. Underwriting has been made mandatory.
17. Limit of listing of companies issue in the stock exchange has been increased to ₹ 5 crore.
18. The gap between the closure dates of various issues, *viz.*, rights and public should not exceed 30 days.
19. Issues should make adequate disclosure regarding the terms and conditions of redemption, security conversion and other relevant features of the new instrument so that an investor can make reasonable determination of risks, returns, safety and liquidity of the instrument. The disclosure shall be vetted by SEBI in this regard.

❖ Secondary Market

Stock Exchange

1. Board of Directors of stock exchange has to be reconstituted so as to include non-members, public representatives, government representative to the extent of 50% of total number of members.

2. Capital adequacy norms have been laid down for members of various stock exchanges depending upon their turnover of trade and other factors.
3. Working hours for all stock exchanges have been fixed uniformly.
4. All the recognised stock exchanges will have to inform about the transaction within 24 hours.
5. Guidelines have been issued for introducing the system of market making in less liquid scrips in a phased manner in all stock exchanges.

Brokers

1. Registration of brokers and sub-brokers is made compulsory.
2. In order to ensure that brokers are professionally qualified and financially solvent, capital adequacy norms for registration of brokers have been evolved.
3. Compulsory audit of broker's book and filing of audit report with SEBI have been made mandatory.
4. To bring about greater transparency and accountability in the broker-client relationship, SEBI has made it mandatory for brokers to disclose transaction price and brokerage separately in the contract notes issued to client.
5. No broker is allowed to underwrite more than 5% of public issue.

❖ Foreign Institutional Investors (FIIs)

1. Foreign institutional investors have been allowed to invest in all securities traded in primary and secondary markets. Total registered FIIs were 1,482 at the end of May 2008.
2. There would be no restriction on the volume of investment for the purpose of entry of FIIs.
3. The holding of single FII in a company will not exceed the ceiling of 5% of the equity capital of a company. Disinvestment will be allowed only through stock exchanges in India. During January to June 2007, FII have invested ₹ 24,278 crore out of which ₹ 5,837 crore were invested in DLF issues.
4. FIIs have to pay a concessional tax rate of 10 per cent on large capital gain (more than one year) and 30 per cent on short-term capital gains. A tax rate of 20% on dividend and interest is prescribed.
5. From 1st October, 2010, all FIIs and their subaccounts must not have less than 20 investors excluding certain bodies like pension cells. And no FII investors can have more than 49% share in the total funds raised. During companies issuing IPOs have to list their shares within 7 days (as against 20 days earlier). Investment by FIIs raised to US 30 billion dollars in bonds in February 2011. FIIs had invested till November 2010 $ 28.91 bn. in equities.

❖ Bonus Issue

The guidelines relating to the issue of bonus shares have undergone several changes since 1969. The latest set of guidelines announced by SEBI were made effective from 2002. At present, there are in all 10 guidelines laid down for bonus shares.

1. There should be a provision in the Articles of Association of the Company for issue of bonus shares. If not, the company should pass a resolution at the General Body Meeting, making provision for capitalisation of profits. The proposal for bonus issues is recommended by the Board of Directors and then approved in the General Body Meeting.
2. The bonus is made out of free reserves built out of the genuine profits or share premiums collected in cash only.
3. Reserves created by revaluation of fixed assets are not permitted to be capitalised.
4. The declaration of bonus issue in lieu of dividend is not to be made.
5. Bonus issues are not permitted unless the partly paid shares existing are fully paid-up.
6. No bonus issue will be permitted if there is sufficient reasons to believe that the company has defaulted in respect of payment of statutory dues to the employees such as provident fund, gratuity, bonus, etc. Further, no bonus issue is permitted if the company defaults in payment of principal or interest on fixed deposits or on debentures.
7. No bonus issue can be made within 12 months of any public issue/rights issue.
8. A company which announces bonus issue after the approval of the Board of Directors must implement the proposals within a period of six months from the date of such proposal and shall not have the option of changing the decision.
9. Consequent to the issue of bonus shares, if the subscribed and paid-up capital exceed the authorised share capital, a resolution shall be passed by the company at its general body meeting for increasing the authorised capital.
10. Issue of bonus shares after any public/rights issue is subject to the condition that no bonus shall be made which will dilute the value or rights of a holder of debenture, convertible fully or partly.

The company shall forward a certificate duly signed by the issuer and duly countersigned by its statutory auditor or by a company secretary in practice to the effect that the terms and conditions for the issue of bonus shares as laid down in these guidelines have been complied with.

❖ Rights Issue

Section 81 of the Companies Act, 1956 specifies the conditions to be satisfied by a public company for issuing rights shares. SEBI has issued the following guidelines for the issue of rights shares.

1. Composite Issue: A public and rights issues can be made at different prices where these two kinds of issues are made as a composite issue by existing listed companies. There is no restriction in charging lower premium on rights issues than on public issues. The premium must be fixed by the Board of Directors in consultation with lead manager to the issue. Differential pricing in a composite issue is not permitted in the case of existing unlisted companies making public issue for the first time.

2. Appointment of Merchant Banker: Appointment of Merchant Banker is not mandatory, if the size of rights issue by a listed company does not exceed ₹ 50 lakh. For issues of listed companies exceeding ₹ 50 lakh, the issue is to be managed by an authorised merchant banker.

3. Minimum Subscription: If the company does not receive minimum subscription of 90 per cent of the issue amount including development of underwriters within 120 days from the date of opening of issue, the company has to refund the entire subscriptions within 130 days with interest 6% p.a. for delay beyond 78 days from the date of closure of the issue.

4. Preferential Allotment: No preferential allotment shall be made along with the rights issue. If a company wants to make preferential allotment it should be made independent of rights issue by complying the provisions of the Companies Act, 1956.

5. Underwriting: Underwriting of rights issue is not mandatory but as per SEBI (underwriter's) Rules and Regulations, 1993, rights issue can be underwritten.

6. Rights of FCD/PCD Holders: The proposed rights issue should not dilute the value or rights of fully or partly convertible debentureholders. If the conversion of FCDs/PCDs is due within a period of 12 months from the date of rights issue, reservation of shares out of rights issue is to be made for them in proportion to the convertible part of FCDs/PCDs.

7. Over Subscription not to be Retained: The quantum rights issue should not exceed as specified in the letter of offer. The companies are not allowed to retain oversubscription under any circumstances through rights issue.

8. Promoter's Contribution: If the promoter's shareholding in the equity at the time of the rights issue is more than 20 per cent of the issued capital, the promoters have to ensure that their equity holding do not fall below 20 per cent of the expanded capital.

If the promoter's holdings are less than 20 per cent of the issued capital, they shall take up the unsubscribed portion of the rights issue so that their holdings amount to 20 per cent of the expanded capital.

The lock-in period is two years for the shareholdings prior to the rights issue from the date of allotment in the rights issue.

9. Vetting of Letter of Offer by SEBI: The letter of offer pertaining to rights issue has to be vetted by SEBI and the concerned lead manager has to obtain SEBI clearance for the draft letter of offer before approaching stock exchange for fixing the record date for the proposed issue. A copy of letter of offer is forwarded to SEBI for information if the rights issue is less than ₹ 50 lakh. The responsibility of vetting the rights issue is passed on to Merchant Bankers in 1995. Rights issue not accompanied by public issue, if made three months prior to or three months after the public issue will not have to be vetted by SEBI.

10. Disclosure in the Letter of Offer: The letter of offer like the prospectus should conform to the disclosure prescribed in Form 2A under Section 56(3) of the Companies Act, 1956. Full justification and parameters used for issue price should clearly be mentioned in the letter of offer.

11. Advertisement in Newspaper: All listed companies making rights issue shall invariably issue an advertisement in at least two all India newspapers about the despatch of letters of offer, opening date, closing date, etc. Such advertisement should be at least one week before the date of opening of the subscription list.

12. Compliance Report: Within 45 days of closure of rights issue, a report in the prescribed form along with the compliance certificate from statutory auditor/practising charted accountant/ company secretary should be forwarded to SEBI by lead managers.

13. Applicability of SEBI Guidelines: The above guidelines with regard to rights issue apply only to rights issue made by existing listed companies.

14. Revised Disclosure Norms for Listed Companies: To enable the listed companies to raise funds easily from the primary market, the SEBI has amended its Disclosure and Investor Protection Guidelines in March, 2006. These guidelines are applicable to those listed companies that are regular in filing periodic returns with stock exchanges and have comprehensive investor grievances mechanism. The following are the important guidelines:

(*i*) Listed companies going in for a rights issue can now fix and disclose the issue price any time prior to fixing the record date in consultation with the designated stock exchange.

(*ii*) In the case of fixed price route, for public issues of such companies, the price can be fixed before filing of the prospectus with the Registrar of companies.

(*iii*) Further, companies making rights issues are now permitted to despatch an abridged letter of offer, containing disclosures as required in the abridged prospectus. However, such companies may provide the detailed letter of offer to any shareholder upon request.

(*iv*) Again, companies that have filed a draft offer document with full disclosures can now come out with further capital issues even before the shares pertaining to the document are listed on the bourses.

These guidelines do not apply to rights issue by existing private companies/closely held or other unlisted companies. They have to comply with the requirements as laid down in the Companies Act.

❖ Debentures

1. The amount of working capital debenture should not exceed 20% of the gross current assets.
2. The debt equity ratio should not exceed 2:1.
3. The rate of interest can be decided by the company.
4. Credit rating is compulsory for all debentures excepting debentures issued by public sector companies, private placement of Non-Convertible Debentures (NCD) with financial institutions and banks.
5. Debentures are to be redeemed after the expiry of seven years from the date of allotment. NCD is permitted to be redeemed at 5% premium.
6. Normally debentures above seven years cannot be issued.
7. Debentures issued to public have to be secured and registered.
8. A Debenture Redemption Reserve is to be set up out of profits of the company.
9. Debentures Trustee and Debenture Trust Deed are to be finalised within six months of the public offer.

Fully Convertible Debenture (FCD), Partly Convertible Debenture (PCD), Non-convertible Debentures (NCDs).

1. FCD/PCD/NCD issued for a period of more than 18 months are to be compulsorily credit rated.
2. The debentures converted within 18 months are treated as equity.

3. FCDs having conversion period more than 36 months will not be permitted.
4. The terms of issue should be predetermined and stated in the prospectus.
5. The interest rate can be determined by the issuer.
6. Conversion after 18 months from the date of allotment but before 36 months will be optional at the hands of the debentureholders.
7. Appointment of Debenture Trustees and Creation of Debenture Redemption Reserve are not necessary if the maturity period is 18 months or less.
8. The Debenture Trust Deed should be executed within six months of the closure of the issue.
9. The offer document should specify existing and future equity, long-term debt equity ratio, servicing of existing debentures, payment of interest on existing loans and debenture.
10. No objection for second or *pari passu* charge.
11. In the case of roll over of NCD portion of debentures, the following conditions are to be complied with:
    (*i*) Six months before the date of redemption, fresh credit rating should be obtained and it should be communicated to debentureholders.
    (*ii*) The company must have obtained the positive consent of debentureholders.
    (*iii*) SEBI should vet the role over and its terms and conditions.

❖ Guidelines for Protection

(i) Servicing of Debentures

A Debenture Redemption Reserve shall be created by companies issuing debentures on the following basis:

Existing companies need not create DRR up to the date of commercial production. DRR shall be created in equal instalments for the remaining period.

For new companies, creation of DRR will commence from the year the company earns profit and it should be created in equal or in one or more instalments for the remaining life of debentures.

In the case of PCDs, DRR should be created only for NCD portion.

DRR should be created up to 50% of the amount before redemption commences.

Withdrawal from DRR will be permitted only after 10 per cent of the liability is actually redeemed.

DRR will be treated as a part of general reserve for the purpose of bonus issue.

In the case of new companies, distribution of dividend shall require approval of trustees to the debenture issue and the lead institution, if any.

In the case of existing companies, prior permission of the lead institution for .declaring dividend exceeding 20 per cent or as per the loan covenants is necessary if the company does not comply with institutional conditions regarding interest and debt service coverage ratio.

(ii) Protection of Interest of Debentureholders

Trustees to the debenture issue shall be vested with the requisite powers for protecting the interest of debentureholders including a right to appoint a nominee director on the Board of the Company in consultation with institutional debentureholders.

Lead institution/investment institutions will monitor the progress in respect of debentures for project finance, modernisation, diversification, etc. The lead bank for the company will monitor debentures raised for working capital funds.

The company shall file with SEBI, a certificate from their bankers that the assets on which security is to be created are free from encumbrances and necessary permissions to mortgage the assets have been obtained or a no objection certificate from the financial institutions or banks for a second or *pari passu* charge in case where assets are encumbered.

The security should be created within six months from the date of issue of debentures. It can be created within 12 months provided 2% penal interest is paid to debentureholders.

If the security is not created even after 18 months, a meeting of the debentureholders shall be called within 21 days to explain the reasons thereof and the date by which the security would be created.

The trustees to the debentureholders will supervise the implementation of the conditions regarding creation of security for the debenture and debenture redemption reserve.

The trustees and institutional debentureholders should obtain a certificate from the company's auditors in respect of utilisation of funds during the implementation of period of projects and at the end of each accounting year in the case of debentures for working capital.

❖ Underwriters

1. No person can act as underwriter unless he holds certificate of registration granted by SEBI.
2. The certificate of registration is valid for a period of three years from the date of issue.
3. The total underwriting obligations should not exceed 20 times of his net worth.
4. In the case of development, the underwriter should subscribe to such securities within 30 days of the receipt of the intimation from the company.
5. The underwriter should furnish within a period of six months from the end of the financial year a copy of the balance sheet, profit and loss account, the statement of capital adequacy requirements and such other documents as required by SEBI.
6. The books of accounts should be maintained for a period of five years.

❖ Investor Protection

Investor protection is the major responsibility of the SEBI. SEBI has taken various measures to protect the interests of investors.

❖ Imposition of Penalties by SEBI

(*i*) Failure to enter into agreement with clients not to exceed ₹ 5 lakh for every failure.

(*ii*) Failure to redress investors' grievances — not to exceed ₹ 10,000 for each such failure.

(*iii*) Default in case of stock brokers —

- For failure to issue contract notes in the form and manner prescribed by the stock exchange — Not to exceed 5 times the amount for which the contract note was required to be issued.
- For *failure to deliver* any security/payment, the amount due to the investor in the manner and within the period specified in the regulations — Not to exceed ₹ 5,000 for each day of default.
- For changing brokerage in excess of that prescribed by the regulation not to exceed ₹ 5,000 or five times the excess charge, whichever is higher.

(*iv*) *Non-disclosure of acquisition of shares and takeovers:* Failure to disclose the aggregate of shareholding in a company, before acquiring any shares of that company, and also to make a public announcement for acquiring shares at a minimum price is liable to penalty not exceeding ₹ 5 lakh.

❖ New Issues

The issuing company should provide fair and correct information.

Allotment process should be transparent and not tainted by any bias.

The draft prospectus of the companies is scrutinised for full and fair disclosure.

No delay in refunds or despatch of share certificates.

Underwriting obligations is necessary to inspire confidence of investors.

Risk factors and highlights should be fairly stated without any bias in the prospectus.

Listing should be timely and transferability is ensured.

Both stock exchange and companies are responsible for investor protection in respect of free trading and transferability of shares.

The investor protection is to be ensured by not only the Director/Secretary of the company but by all the parties in the new issue process namely merchant bankers, registrars, collecting banks, stock exchange and SEBI.

Recently, SEBI has instituted the system of appointing its representatives to supervise the allotment process to ensure that no malpractices take place in allotment process.

7.10 PROHIBITION OF UNFAIR TRADE PRACTICES

❖ Regulation of Insider Trading (SEBI Amendment Bill 2002)

Insider trading takes place when insiders or any persons who by virtue of their position in office or otherwise, have access to unpublished price sensitive information relating to the affairs of the company and deal in the securities of such companies. SEBI regulates insider trading by imposing penalty from ₹ 5.00 lakh to ₹ 25 crore for those who indulge in insider trading and awarding of imprisonment to insider traders to be effective from July 2008.

❖ Investor Education

SEBI has issued a few investors guidance, advertisements and published a book on *'Investor Grievances — Rights and Remedies'*. SEBI has also registered certain active Investor's Association.

SEBI has issued an Advertisement Code for the issuers to ensure that the advertisements are fair and do not contain statements to mislead the investors or vitiate their informed judgement.

❖ Grievance Cell

An Investor Grievance Cell is set up to handle investor complaints.

7.11 BOOK-BUILDING

The normal method of offering shares at a price fixed by the issuers does not take into account the investors' demands. Hence, it is not considered as an efficient method. The book-building method, on the other hand, explicitly uses investors demand for shares at various prices as an important input to arrive at an offer price. The book-building is done in the following steps:

1. The company wishing to issue shares, approaches its merchant banker and informs him of the number of shares it wishes to issue and other material information on the company.
2. The merchant banker now invites his known investors to bid for the company's shares. The investors are generally institutional investors. These investors are asked to indicate the number of shares they would like to buy at different prices. Once the price is finalised, allocation is made on the basis of highest price bid.
3. If the company agrees with the offer price the issue goes through and the shares are allocated based on bids. The company has the option to cancel the issue if it feels that the price is too low.
4. The trading commences from the next day.

❖ Book-building in India

The book-building method of pricing securities is becoming popular in India. During 1997-98, various issuers like IPCL, HUDCO, HAL, IOC and Hindalco Industries have used book-building route to fix the coupon rate on their bond issues.

❖ Terms Associated with Book-building Process

Retail Investor

Retail investor refers to an investor who applies or bids for securities of a company for a value of not more than ₹ 1 lakh. If he bids for more than the value, he will be branded as non-institutional buyer.

Qualified Institutional Buyer (QIB)

Qualified Institutional Buyer means a public financial institution or a commercial bank or a mutual fund or FII or venture capitalist or an insurance company or any other such body corporate who applies or bids for securities.

Red Herring Prospectus (RHP)

It is nothing but a prospectus which does not have details of either price or number of shares being offered or the amount of issue. Generally, the price will not be disclosed, but the number of shares and price band will be disclosed. However, all details are made available to an investor on a day just prior to the date of issue open.

Offer Document

Offer document is nothing but a prospectus in the case of public issue or offer for sale and letter of offer in the case of rights issue. It has to be filed with the Registrar of Companies and Stock Exchanges.

Green Shoe Option

Green Shoe option means an option of allocating shares in excess of the shares floated in the public issue and operating a post-issue price stabilising mechanism for a period not exceeding 30 days. This permission has been granted to a company to be exercised with caution through a stabilising agent. As per this arrangement, an issue could be over allotted to the extent of a maximum of 15% of the issue size.

From an investors point of view, an issue with green shoe option provides more probability of getting shares allotted to him. It also ensures that the post-listing price will be more stable than the market price.

Syndicate Member

Syndicate member refers to a person whose work is to collect the entire bid forms in a book-built issue.

Floor Price/Cap Price/Cut off Price

In a book-building issue, the issuer is required to indicate either the price band or a floor price in the red herring prospectus. The lower end price is called the floor price and the higher end price is called cap price. The actual discovered price can be any price between the two and it is called cut off price.

❖ SEBI Guidelines on Book-building

SEBI issued guidelines for new issues through book-building so as to enable issuers to reap benefits arising out of price and demand discovery. The guidelines came into operational with effect from September 1997.

1. The option of 100% book-building shall be available only to those issuer companies which propose to make an issue of any size capital.
2. Book-building shall be for the portion other than the promoters contribution and allocation made to permanent employees of the issuer company and shareholders of the promoting companies in case of a new company and shareholders of group companies in case of existing companies.
3. The issuing company shall appoint category I Merchant Banker as book runner(s) and their names shall be mentioned in the draft prospectus submitted to SEBI. The lead merchant banker shall act as the Lead Book runner may appoint 'Syndicate Members' who shall be from those intermediaries who are registered with SEBI who are permitted to carry on activity as the 'underwriter'.
4. The draft prospectus shall be filed with SEBI by the Lead Merchant Bankers.
5. The issuer company, after receiving final observations, if any, on the offer document from SEBI make an advertisement in newspapers. The information in the advertisement shall contain:

(*i*) the date of opening and closing of the bidding.

(*ii*) the method and process of bidding.

(*iii*) the names and addresses of the syndicate members as well as bidding terminals for accepting bids.

6. The Book-runner's and the company shall determine the issue price based on the bids received through syndicate members. On determination of the price, the number of securities to be offered shall be determined.
7. Once the final price is determined all those bidders whose bids have found to be successful shall become entitled for allotment of securities.
8. On determination of the entitlement, the information regarding the same shall be intimated immediately to the investors.
9. The offer shall remain open for subscription from public for a period of at least three working days after completing all requirement of advertisement and despatch of issue material to Stock Exchanges. During the time when the offer is open, the investors who have received an intimation of entitlement of securities shall submit the application forms along with the application money.
10. Arrangement shall be made by the issuer for collection of the applications by appointing mandatory collection centres depending upon the size of the issue.
11. Allotment shall be made not later than 7 days from the closure of the issue failing which interest at the rate of 15% shall be paid to the investors. (New amendment from July 2008).
12. A final book of demand showing the results of allocation process shall be maintained by the book-runners.
13. SEBI shall have the right to carry out an inspection of the records, books and documents relating to the Book-building process.

With a view to benefitting small investors and to improving liquidity in the stock market, the SEBI has recently introduced some meaningful primary market reforms. Some of the important ones applicable to 'book-built' route are:

(*i*) A listed company should have a minimum public holding of 25 per cent of its shares on a continuous basis. This 'Free float' of 25 per cent refers to the non-promoter holdings.

(*ii*) The merchant bank's discretionary powers to allot shares to the Qualified Institutional Buyers (QIBs) have been done away with.

(*iii*) Among the QIBs' reservation of 50 per cent, mutual funds have been given a share of 5 per cent. However, they can apply for the remaining portion too.

(*iv*) The QIBs' have to bid with a margin money of 10 per cent of the application value.

These measures aim at bringing much benefits to retail investor by bringing needed liquidity in the market.

7.12 BUYBACK OF SHARES

Buyback of shares and securities is popular in countries like USA and UK. The government amended the Companies Act, 1956 in 2000 year to permit buyback of shares by promoters of companies. Accordingly, a company can buyback its own shares and other securities to the extent of 25 per cent of the paid-up capital and free reserves. The buyback can be transacted out of company's free reserve, securities premium account or proceeds of any earlier issues specially made for buyback purposes (Sec. 77A).

❖ What is Buyback?

Buyback is a method of cancellation of share capital. It leads to reduction in the share capital of a company as opposed to issue of shares which results in an increase in share capital.

❖ Why Buyback?

A company may go for buyback of its shares due to anyone or more of the following reasons:

1. To reduce equity base thereby injecting much needed flexibility.
2. To prevent takeover bids.
3. To return surplus cash to shareholders.
4. To increase the underlying share value.
5. To support the share price during periods of temporary weakness.
6. To maintain a target capital structure.

❖ Advantages

The major advantages of buyback of shares to investors, companies and the economy are the following:

❖ Investors

1. It is a viable proposition to investors to sell back the shares instead of going through the secondary market.
2. It will improve return on capital and net profitability, increase the earnings per share and provide higher price to investors.

❖ Companies

1. It offers flexibility to companies to reorganise their capital structure.
2. It helps to eliminate discontended shareholders, fractional shareholdings and odd lots and thereby render better service to remaining shareholders by way of sustained dividend and appreciation of share value in the long-run.
3. Buyback is an instrument to ward off hostile takeover bids,

❖ Economy

Buyback of shares helps to revive the capital market. The operation of demand and supply factors will boost prices of shares. It also offers liquidity to dormant shares.

During the year 2011, there are 8 companies which planned buyback of shares. Such companies are — Piramal Health Care/Lakshmi Machine Tools/India Infoline/FDC/Sasken Communication/ Hindustan Composites/ABG Infralogistics/Bhagyanagar India for ₹ 3,300 crore. But due to fall in prices of shares substantially during November and December 2010, the gain on shares has fallen 1.7% giving no incentive to sell the shares.

❖ SEBI Guidelines

The SEBI has been made as a regulatory authority of the licence to buyback shares by the Ordinance. The regulations of SEBI contains the following:

1. The companies are permitted to buyback the shares through six moves:

   (*i*) Tender offers

   (*ii*) Open offers

   (*iii*) Dutch auction

   (*iv*) Repurchase of odd lots

   (*v*) Reverse rights issue

   (*vi*) Employee stock option

   Tender offers will specify the exact price and will have only one price to offer.

   In the Dutch auction, shares offered at the lowest price would be given priority over others.

2. The companies are not permitted to buyback through negotiated deals, spot transactions and private placement.
3. Promoters have been debarred from participating if the company opts to buyback shares through stock exchange route.
4. Companies buying through stock exchanges must disclose purchase details daily.
5. The companies will have to specify the maximum price payable in the resolution seeking shareholders' approval.
6. The buyback should be done only in cash and an escrow account will have to be maintained by the merchant bankers.
7. No company is allowed to withdraw the buyback offer once it is announced.

Merchant bankers be associated in every offer for buyback wherein they would be required to give a due diligence certificate.

The Registrar of shares or transfer agents will have to certify that the company has adhered to all regulations.

◆ ◆ ◆

8 Stock Exchange Operations

8.1 INTRODUCTION AND CONCEPT

Stock exchanges contribute in a huge measure to the growth and expansion of natural business and to the ultimate benefit and well-being of the national economy and its people. They provide an ideal conduit through which enormous amounts of capital flows through the interconnected network of financial organisations to all corporate enterprises in the country. Thus, *Stock Exchanges* ensure liquidity and transferability of financial assets that are dealt with stock exchanges provide an organised marketplace for the investors to buy and sell securities freely. The market offers perfectly competitive conditions where a large number of sellers and buyers participate. Further, stock exchanges provide an auction market in which members of the exchange participate to ensure continuity of price and liquidity to investors. The efficient functioning of the stock exchange is responsible for creating a conducive climate for an active and growing primary market for new issues. Moreover, an active and a healthy secondary market in existing securities leads to a better psychology of expectations, considerably broadening the investment enquiries and thereby, rendering the task of *Raising Resources* by entrepreneurs easier. Good performance and outlook for equities in the stock exchanges imparts buoyancy to the new issue market. According to Section 2(3) of Securities Contract Regulations Act, 1956 — "*The Stock Exchange* has been defined as a body of individuals whether incorporated or not, constituted for the purpose of assisting, regulating or controlling the business of buying, selling or dealing in securities. The following securities can be traded at the stock exchange —

- Shares/scrips/stocks/bonds/debentures/debenture stocks or other marketable securities of a like nature in or of any incorporated company or other body corporate.
- Government securities, and
- Rights or interests in securities.

In India there are 24 stock exchange as below stated —

1. BSE Mumbai
2. NSE Mumbai
3. Ahmedabad
4. Kolkata —— They are only SEs
5. Madras
6. Delhi
7. Indore
8. Bangalore
9. Hyderabad
10. Cochin
11. U.P. Stock Exchange Kanpur
12. Pune
13. Ludhiana
14. Gauhati
20. Magadh Stock Exchange Patna
21. Jaipur
22. Bhubaneshwar
23. Over the Counter Exchange of India Ltd., (OTCEI)
24. Vadodara
25. Coimbatore
26. Interconnected Stock Exchange (Association of 15 stock exchanges). Three stock exchanges, *viz.*, Saurashtra (Rajkot), Mangalore, Meerut certificates were cancelled in April/July 2007 and Stock exchanges of Hyderabad/Magadh/Pune/Bhubaneshwar are in the form of companies limited by guarantees. Rest of the stock exchanges recognition is expiring in the year 2011.

❖ The Bombay Stock Exchange (BSE) Bombay Share Bazaar

Formerly, The Stock Exchange, Bombay is the oldest stock exchange in Asia and has the largest number of listed companies in the world, with 4,990 listed as of August 2010. It is located at Dalal Street, Mumbai, India. On August 2010, the equity market capitalization of the companies listed on the BSE was US$1.78 trillion making it the 4th largest stock exchange in Asia and the 11th largest in the world.

With over 4,996 Indian companies listed and over 7,700 scrips on the stock exchange, it has a significant trading volume. The BSE SENSEX (SENSitive indEX) also called the "BSE 30" is a widely used market index in India and Asia. Though many other exchanges exist, BSE and the National Stock Exchange of India account for most of the trading in shares in India. Its market capital is US$1.78 trillion was in October 2010.

The Bombay Stock Exchange is the oldest exchange in Asia. It traces its history to the 1850s, when four Gujarati and one Parsi stockbroker would gather under a banyan tree in front of Mumbai's Town Hall. The location of these meetings changed many times, as the number of brokers constantly increased. The group eventually moved to Dalal Street in 1874 and in 1875 became an official organisation known as 'The Native Share and Stock Brokers Association'. In 1956, the BSE became the first stock exchange to be recognised by the Indian Government under the Securities Contracts Regulation Act. The Bombay Stock Exchange developed the BSE Sensex in 1986, giving the BSE a means to measure overall performance of the exchange. In 2000 the BSE used this index to open its derivatives market, trading Sensex futures contracts. The development of Sensex options along with equity derivatives followed in 2001 and 2002, expanding the BSE's trading platform. Historically an open outcry floor trading exchange, the Bombay Stock Exchange switched to an electronic trading system in 1995. It took the exchange only fifty days to make this transition. This automated, screen-based trading platform called BSE On-line trading (BOLT) currently has a capacity of 8 million orders per day. The BSE has also introduced the world's first centralised exchange-based internet trading system, BSEWEBs is to enable investors anywhere in the world to trade on the BSE platform. The BSE is currently housed in Phiroze Jeejeebhoy Towers at Dalal Street, Fort area, Mumbai.

❖ National Stock Exchange of India (NSE) India

The National Stock Exchange (NSE) (Rashtriya Share Bazaar) is a stock exchange registered in Mumbai is one of the major Sensex exchanges in India with daily turnover and number of trades for both equities and derivative trading. NSE has a market capitalisation of around ₹ 72,62,507 crore (US$ 1,648.50 billion) (October 2010) and was expected to become the biggest stock exchange in India in terms of market capitalisation by 2009 end, although this has not yet occurred. Though a number of other exchanges exist, NSE and the Bombay Stock Exchange are the two most significant stock exchanges in India, and between them are responsible for the vast majority of share transactions. The NSE's key index is the SP CNX Nifty drawn as the NSE Nifty (Nariman Stock Exchange, Nifty) an index of fifty major stocks weighed by market capitalisation.

NSE is mutually-owned by a set of leading financial institutions, banks, insurance companies and other financial intermediaries in India but its ownership and management operate as separate entities. There are at least two foreign investors NYSE Euronext and Goldman Sachs who have taken a stake in the NSE. As of 2006, the NSE VSAT terminals, 2,799 in total, cover more than 1,500 cities across India. In October 2007, the equity market capitalisation of the companies listed on the NSE was US$ 1.46 trillion making it the second largest stock exchange in South Asia. NSE is the third largest stock exchange in the world in terms of the number of trades in equities. It is the second fastest growing stock exchange in the world with a recorded growth of 16.6%.

The National Stock Exchange of India was promoted by leading Financial Institutions at the behest of the Government of India and was incorporated in November 1992 as a tax-paying company. In April 1993, it was recognised as a stock exchange under the Securities Contracts (Regulation) Act, 1956. NSE commenced operations in the Wholesale Debt Market (WDM) segment in June 1991. The Capital Market (Equities) segment of the NSE commenced operations

8.2 STEPS IN STOCK TRADING

Following are the typical steps involved in trading on the stock exchange:

(1) Client Registration: The buyer approaches the broker and executes a client registration from wherein all details about the buyer are furnished. This forms the basis for trading in the exchange through the broker (registered are only) or sub-broker.

(2) Agreement: An agreement between the buyer and the broker as specified by the exchange concerned is entered into. This agreement is called the *Client Member Agreement.*

(3) Order Placing: Buyer places the order in writing with the broker for the purchase of certain number of scrips at a certain specified price.

(4) Order Confirmation: After collecting the order from the client, the broker places the order in his computer system, which is in turn transmitted to the computer system NSE/BSE at Mumbai. The order confirmation slip is obtained by the broker from the exchange.

(5) Trade Confirmation: A trade confirmation slip is generated as soon as the order is matched by the computer against the price generated by the matching algorithm (price-time priority). The trade confirmation slip gives details of the trade executed. The buyer makes payment of necessary margin money to the broker.

(6) Contract Note: The broker issues a contract note to the buyer in respect of all the orders that are executed during the day. Such a note spells out the obligations of the parties concerned, for the buyer to make payment and the broker to make delivery of scrips. Accordingly, the payment is made and the scrips are taken delivery by the buyer, which thus concludes the contract.

❖ Mechanism of Settlement

The process of fulfilment of the obligations of the trade by the parties to the transactions is known as *Settlement.* This implies payment of funds to the seller and delivery of securities to the buyer. Although in a traditional commodity market, a trade is negotiated and settled instaneously, i.e., payment is made and goods are taken delivery immediately settlement of trade is in a stock market, not instantaneous. For instance, payment for the purchase and delivery of shares takes a certain cycle.

Types of Settlement: There are two types of settlement of trade in vogue. They are *rolling settlement* and *Account period Settlement.*

Rolling Settlement: Under this system of settlement, the trades executed on a certain day have to be settled after a certain number of days depending on the nature of settlement cycle practised by the exchange concerned. Accordingly, where a settlement cycle specified is 7 + 3 it implies that trades executed on the first day (say a Monday) have to be settled on the fourth day (i.e., on Thursday) i.e., after the gap of 3 days. The Rolling settlement cycle is on the basis w.e.f. 1-4-2003.

Account Period System: Under this systems of settlement, trading is allowed to continue for a certain agreed period and it is possible for the investor to buy or sell for a certain number of days, and thereby accumulate a certain position during the period. At the end of this period, his obligation in terms of shares purchased or sold and the amount to be paid by him is worked out and communicated to him. The obligations of a broker are worked out after setting the trades. The working of the above system of settlement as practised in the NSE for its equity segment. Till 31st December, 2001, an Account Period Settlement was in vogue is discontinued since January 1st, 2002 pursuant to SEBI directives.

Settlement Guarantee Mechanism: The system which is devised to eliminate Counter Party Risks (default committed by either or both the parties to the transaction at the end of settlement period) is known as Settlement Guarantee Mechanism. According to this system. The NSE first introduced the system which is popular in the developed market. This is being adopted in other exchanges as well. According to the system, settlement of trade is undertaken by a separate legal agency called the *Clearing Corporation of India Ltd.,* established in April 2001 and started operation from 15-2-2002. The object of the institution is to help localize risk by preventing the contagion from spreading from a failed counterparty to others. The CCIL acts a counterparty in respect of every trade. It ensures and verifies that the deliveries of money and shares are made and passes them on to the respective brokers. If one of the brokers defaults, the CCIL ensures that the trade is carried out unhindered by making payment or making delivery of scrips on behalf of the defaulting broker who is thereafter dealt with by the CCIL separately. Such a function helps minimise the *Market Risk* and thus helps save the integrity and safety of the stock exchange.

8.3 MECHANICS OF OPERATIONS

This is an order-driven or a customer-driven trading system where customers' buy and sell orders are matched at a central point. The New York Stock Exchange (NYSE) is in *order-driven* auction market. This system allows the buyer and the seller to find a mutually agreeable price, with *No Intervention* from the broker dealers. The buy and sell orders are automatically matched and in case of any *Imbalances*, the specialists take up the job of filling in. The specialist is a single designated market maker who stands in the market at all times, adding effectiveness and efficiency into the trading mechanism, 90 per cent of the trading in NYSE is done this way.

In Indian markets, other than the BSE, the trading is mainly order-driven with the buyers and sellers transacting directly with one another. Although this does have the advantage of giving the investors a better price/growth of the markets has been hampered by a relatively high degree of volatility and liquidity.

Dealer Trading System: This is a quote-driven or dealer driven trading system where dealers compete to give the customers the best price. This type of trading takes place through an electronic media with the help of well networked computer system. The system runs the trading by trying to find the customer for the best price available. The National Association of Security Dealers Automated Quotation System (NASDAQ) is *Quote driven* as it is computerised network, which serves over the counter. The market makers quotes both *Bid and Ask* prices for the two sides of the markets, both buy and sell continuously. There are restrictions on the number of market makers in a given share. Competing market makers are obliged to quote the best and competitive prices through the system. Market makers offering the best price are assigned orders on rotating basis. *Bid price* is the price at which the dealer will buy a security and as *Ask Price* is that at which a dealer is willing to sell a security. The difference between bid and ask prices in any quotation is the *Spread.* The market makers are obliged to offer a continuous two-way market in all their registered securities. Transactions are reported within 90 seconds of execution.

Indonext: It is a common trading platform for interconnecting 18 regional stock exchanges. It has been set up as the Third National Stock Exchange on the lines of *Euronet,* for the stocks of small and medium capital companies. Indonext aims at offering exclusive trading in the case of companies with paid-up capital of ₹ 20 lakh. Trading on Indonext open to all members including NSE/BSE/ISEI/OTCEI and 18 regional stock exchanges.

❖ Stock Exchange Dealings

Type: The type and the nature of dealings on an Indian stock exchange are of 3 different categories. They are described as follows:

Spot Delivery: Wherein a contract the payment and delivery of securities take place on the spot, on the same day or on the next day, it is a case of *Spot Delivery*. The sale is said to be complete on the date of contract. These are essentially cash dealings and are primarily meant for investors. All listed securities are allowed trading in the spot market. All listed securities and allowed spot delivery.

Ready Delivery Market: Where settlement payment and delivery takes place within a fixed time period of not exceeding 7 days from the date of contract, it is a case of *Ready Delivery Contract.* There is usually hand delivery against full payment.

Forward Delivery Contract: Where the settlement — payment and delivery of securities take place once at the end of the month/quarter, it is a case of forward delivery contract. Such a contract has carry over facilities also. Every forward contract is due on the last Thursday of every month. Speculators are the main interested parties in their dealings.

Trading: The BSE, which had an open outcry trading system had switched over to a fully automated computerised mode of trading known as *Bolt* (BSE-On-line-Trading) system with effect from March 1995. Though the Bolt system the members can now enter orders from Trade Work Stations (TWSs) installed in their offices instead of assembling in the Trade Ring. The system is now order-driven facilities move efficient processing/automatic order matching and faster execution of orders in a transparent manner. Trading on Bolt is conducted from Monday to Friday between 9.00 a.m. and 3.30 p.m.

❖ Scrips Group

The scrips traded on the BSE have been classified into A/B_1/B_2/F and Z groups.

Group A shares represent large and well established companies having a broad investor-base. Companies with paid-up capital of ₹ 1,000 crore and above. These shares are actively traded. Naturally, these shares attract a lot of speculative multiples.

Group B shares are divided with B_1 and B_2 shares on the BSE. These shares have got equity base ₹ 500 crore to below ₹ 1,000 crore.

Group C shares only covers the odd lot securities in A/B_1/B_2 and Z groups and Right renunciations in all the groups of scrips in the equity segment. The facility not only offers an exit route to investors to dispose of their *odd lots*, but also provides them an opportunity to consolidate their securities into market lots.

Group F represents the debt market (fixed income securities), while the Z group was introduced by the BSE in July 1999 and even the companies which have *failed* to comply with listing requirements and/or failed to resolve *Investors Complaints* or have not made the required arrangements with both depositories, i.e., CDSL and NSDL for dematerilization of their securities by the specified date, i.e., 30-9-2001.

Closing Price: The closing prices of scrips are computed on the basis of weighted average price of all trades in the last 15 minutes of the Continuous Trading Session. However, if there is no trade during the last 15 minutes, then the last-traded price in the continuous trading session is taken as the official closing price.

TYPICAL SETTLEMENT CYCLE

Item	*Activity*	*Days*
Trading	Rolling Settlement Trading	T
Clearing	Custodial Confirmation	T + 1 working days
	Delivery generation	T + 1 working days
Settlement	Securities and Funds pay in	T + 2 working days
	Securities and funds - payout	T + 2 working days
Post-settlement	Valuation debit	T + 2 working days
	Auction	T + 3 working days
	Bad Delivery reporting	T + 4 working days
	Auction Settlement	T + 5 working days
	Close out	T + 5 working days
	Rectified bad Delivery pay-in, pay-out	T + 6 working days
	Re-bad delivery reporting and pick-up	T + 8 working days
	Close out of re-bad delivery	T + 9 working days

8.4 SURVEILLANCE BY EXCHANGE

One of the objectives of the Exchange is to promote and inculcate honourable and just practices of trade in securities and to discourage malpractices. The surveillance function at the exchange has assumed greater importance in recent times. The exchange has accordingly set up a separate surveillance department to keep a close watch on price movements of scrips, detect market manipulations like price triggering, etc., monitor abnormal prices and volumes which are not consistent with normal trading pattern. In May 2008, KGN share prices increased from ₹ 70 to ₹ 32,000 in a two hours period to which surveillance department of BSE came into action and stopped further trading. Next day the trading price was started with ₹ 5,000 to further surveillance in the matter.

Besides, the department also monitors the member-brokers' positions to ensure that defaults do not occur.

❖ Circuit Filters

The limit imposed by a stock exchange for the price of a security to move within a *prescribed board* is called circuit filters. The imposition of circuit filters on scrips ensures that the price of scrip cannot move upward or downward beyond the limit set for a day and a settlement. The objective is to prevent price manipulation. Under this dispensation, the large variation in the prices as well as the volumes of the scrips is scrutinised and appropriate actions taken. The scrips, which reach new high or new low, and companies which have high turnover, are *watched*. Similarly, the prices and volumes in the newly listed scrips are monitored. In case, certain abnormalities are noticed, then circuit filters are reduced to make it difficult for the price-manipulators to increase or push down the prices of scrips within a short period of time. The exchange imposes *special margin* on the scrips where it is suspected that there is an attempt to ramp up the prices by creating artificial volumes. In cases, where the abnormal movement continue despite the aforesaid measures trading in the scrip is suspended. As per the guidelines issued by SEBI, the stock exchanges are required to apply daily circuit filter of 8% on scrips quoting above ₹ 20. However, in respect of scrips quoting below ₹ 20, the exchanges are free to set their own circuit filters. The exchange has accordingly prescribed 8 circuit filters for scrips quoting above ₹ 10 but below ₹ 20 and for scrips quoting up to ₹ 10, daily and weekly circuit filters are 25% and 50% respectively. As directed by SEBI the circuit filter limit is 200 scrips, which are commonly traded and jointly identified by BSE and NSE scrips, which are under the compulsory rolling settlement, has been relaxed to 16% with effect from July 2000. In this connection, it has been decoded that if scrip touches 8% circuit filter band in *either direction,* the circuit filter would be relaxed by another 8% in that same direction. Detailed investigations are conducted in case where price manipulation is suspected and disciplinary action is taken against the member concerned, if warranted.

❖ Derivatives Trading

BSE launched the financial derivatives products in India, called the *Sensex futures.*

8.5 SENSEX INDEX

An index is an indicator of the broad market. For instance, tracking the changes in the *Sensex* enables one to effectively gauge stock market movements. The BSE-30 sensex first compiled in 1986, is a market capitalisation weighted index of 30 scrips. It represents 30 large well established and financially sound companies. The sensex also has the largest social recall attached with it. It was the first index to be launched by any stock exchange in India and has acquired a unique place in the collective memory of investors. The other index is BSE-500. This *Sensex* represents 14 major industries groups, which are large enough to be used for effective hedging. Presently, in 2011 there are total operative listed and traded shares are beyond 1,300.

❖ Trading in Sensex Futures

Given the lower cost structure and the overwhelming popularity of the sensex, sensex futures are expected to garner large volumes. The sensex futures are expected to become the most liquid contract in the country. This is because institutional investors in India and abroad, money managers and small investors use the sensex, when it comes to describing the mood of the Indian stock markets. Thus, it has been observed that the sensex is an effective proxy for the Indian stock markets. Higher liquidity in the product essentially translates to lower impact cost of trading in sensex futures. The arbitrage between the futures and the equity market is further expected to reduce impact cost. Trading in stock index futures is likely to be predominantly retail driven. Internationally, stock index futures are an institutional product with 60% of the volumes generated from hedging needs. Immense retail participation to the extent of 80-90% is expected in India based on the following factors —

- Stock index futures will require lower capital adequacy and margin requirements as compared to margins on carry forward of individual scrips.
- The brokerage costs on index futures will be much lower.
- Savings in cost is possible through reduced bid-ask spreads where stock are traded in packaged forms.
- The impact cost will be much lower in case of stock index futures as opposed to dealing in individual scrips.

The market is conditioned to think in terms of the index and therefore, would prefer to trade in stock index futures. Further, the chances of manipulation are much lesser. The stock index futures are expected to be extremely liquid given the speculative nature of our markets and the overwhelming retail participation expected to be fairly high. It is poised to become the most liquid contract in the world in terms of number of contracts traded, if not in terms of notional value. The advantage to the equity or cash market is in the fact that they would become less volatile as most of the speculative activity would shift to stock index futures. The stock index futures market should ideally have more depth, volumes and act as a stabilizing factor for the cash market. However, it is too early to base any conclusions on the volume or to form any firm trend.

❖ Operators in Derivative Market

Operators in a derivatives market include the following:

(1) **Hedgers:** Operators who want to transfer a risk component of their portfolio.

(2) **Speculators:** Operators, who intentionally take the risk from hedgers in pursuit of profit.

(3) **Arbitrageurs:** Operators who operate in the different markets simultaneously in pursuit of profit and eliminate mis-pricing.

On NSE derivatives that are dealt include —

— S and P CNX Nifty Futures

— S and P CNX Nifty Options

— Futures on individual securities

— Options on individual securities.

◆ ◆ ◆

9 Credit/Debit/Smart Cards and Housing Finance/ Bancassurance Services

9.1 PLASTIC CARDS CONCEPT

❖ Credit Cards

A Credit Card is an instrument of payment, which enables the cardholder to obtain either goods or services from merchants where arrangements have been made to reimburse the merchant. Cash card is also issued in addition to the credit card to enable the cardholder to use ATM and draw cash up to the specified limit. The outstanding amount is payable by the cardholder to the bank which carries a fixed amount of interest also.

A credit card is a source of revolving credit. A number of parties are involved in credit card transactions and there is a contract between the card issuer and cardholder whereby the cardholder is allowed to make use of the card at specified retail outlets, called Merchant Establishment (ME), to pay for the goods and services. There is also another separate agreement between the card organization and the Merchant Establishments. When a credit cardholder makes purchases from specified retail outlets the retail outlets make out bills to the account of the cardholder and obtain payment from the card organization, which in turn makes a monthly bill to the bank which issued the card. The bank makes payment to the debit of customer's account subsequently. The whole process takes about 30 to 40 days and during the period the cardholder enjoys credit. The credit card is a pay-later product as the holder is charged much after the purchase. Credit cards can also be issued as a co-branded card by a bank promoted jointly with another non-financial institution.

9.1.1 Credit Card System

Let us see how a credit card is issued and used. Generally, a bank enters into an agreement with its customer and issues the customer a credit card. A credit card is small plastic card around 8.5 cm by 5.5 cm. It has the name and the account number or tile holder embossed on it. In addition, the date up to which the card is valid will also be embossed and a specimen signature panel on the reverse. The card issuer should normally get the cardholder to sign on the specimen signature panel in his presence before parting with the credit card. A cardholder is also given the list or shops and establishments in each city where the card will be accepted in lieu or cash. The limit up to which the cardholder can make purchases in a month is also informed to the cardholder, this limit is called the card-limit. When a cardholder purchases or uses the service or a Merchant Establishment (ME), he or she gives the card to the shopkeeper at the time of payment. The ME verifies the card for validity date and then checks the booklet called "Hot list Bulletin". This "Hot list Bulletin" consists of all cards, which have OCCI lost, stolen, surrendered by customer or invalidated by the issuer. If the card is not hot listed, the ME will proceed to make a bill for purchases made. Each ME has a limit below which he can accept payment without seeking "Authorization". Such a limit is called ME's floor limit. The floor limit varies from ME to ME depending on their nature and location or the business. However, the cardholder need not know the floor limit, nor does the ME have to know the cardholder's limit. If the transaction exceeds the floor limit, the ME calls up the card issuer who may or may not authorize the transaction. If the card issuer refuses to authorize the transaction, the ME may advise the cardholder of the refusal of the issuer and may accept only cash instead of the card. The reasons for authorization refusal may be because of having intimation of the card having been stolen or lost, or the total value of transaction exceeding the card limit, arrears or default in payment by cardholder and so on.

Once authorization is received, along with the authorization code, or if the transaction value is below floor limit, the ME will prepare the credit card voucher called charge-slip, which is a detailed bill of the purchases made or services availed. This voucher, which is in triplicate, will have to be signed by the cardholder. When the signature is being taken on the vouchers. The ME will retain the card with him. This is to avoid forgery in case the card is stolen, since it is difficult even for a skilled forger to copy without a copy of the signature in front of him. After the credit card voucher is signed, the ME should verify whether the signature on the card panel matches with the signature on the voucher. The ME can refuse to part with the goods if the signature does not tally. After it is signed the ME will part with the goods along with a copy of the charge-slip. The ME uses what is known as an imprinter. Imprinted means that the image is transferred to the paper by applying to pressure and passing the roller over on the card with the paper below it. While the roller passes with pressure over the card, impression of the name and account number is transferred to the voucher. Although the charge slip is in triplicate, no carbon paper needs to be used as one side of the paper contains self-carbonizing chemicals. Imprinting selves two main purpose — one to avoid the mistakes in writing the names and account numbers (usually 12 or 16 digit long) and the second is to ensure that the voucher is indeed prepared using a card and is not a fictitious voucher. The credit cardholder should be vigilant and take care to note that the ME does not prepare multiple vouchers, which can be misused later. This is possible since the signature of the cardholder will be available on one or the vouchers, which can be used for forging signatures on the remaining vouchers.

The ME will collect all the charge-slip and present it to the issuing bank, which after verification, will credit the ME's account or pay cash, depending on the agreement between them. The issuing bank will retain the original copy of the credit card voucher signed by the customer. At the end of the month all the credit card vouchers are accumulated and arranged branch wise, customer wise, and their accounts debited with the total amount of their credit card vouchers. The customers are then informed of the debit and requested to deposit cash or credit their account in a specified time, generally 10 to 15 days. Generally, the task of collecting the credit card, vouchers and informing the respective branches of the extent of the use of the credit card is done at a centralized department This is because the credit cards will be used at MEs all over the country irrespective of which branch, the customer has an account and issued him/her the credit card. The other reason is that for authorizing transactions, above the floor limit, the authorising departments needs to have information at a central place so that it has the required information for taking an appropriate decision, as an incorrect refusal can lead to serious repercussions on customer service.

Many card issuers being banks also, allow withdrawal of cash for emergency purposes and levy a service fee for such withdrawals ranging from 24 p.a. to 36 p.a. Many banks also have credit cards which double up as ATM cards, thereby offering the credit cardholder the availability of cash 24 hours 365 days at a reasonable service charge, which can become very handy in case of emergency.

❖ Benefits of Credit Cards

- The credit cardholder has the flexibility and convenience to use, at home or abroad to meet his requirements. It is less time-consuming and carries better value than traveller's cheques. It provides automatic and instant credit to the cardholder. The customer need not carry cash and is empowered to spend wherever and whenever he wants with his credit card within the fixed limits prescribed by his bank.
- For the merchant establishment it is a guaranteed payment. It results in increased sales, immediate cash payment and greater security.
- For the banks, credit cards generate income from the card fees and interest charges from cardholders and services fees from retail outlets. It brings greater efficiency. It is a marketing tool as credit card users also use other banking products.

9.1.2 Debit Cards

A Debit Card is a payment card used to obtain cash, goods and services automatically debiting the payments to the cardholder's bank account immediately and, therefore, it is essentially a pay-now product. In a debit card when the holder makes a purchase, the merchant establishment swipes the card on an electronic data capture machine, which then debits the bank account of the cardholder. This means that the merchant establishment gets the credit immediately. A client needs to have bank account if he wants to have a debit card. In the debit card the limit of the cardholder will be the amount of funds which he has in his account. The debit cards are of two types, i.e., personal identification number (PIN) based on and signature based cards. A Switch Card is an electronic debit card, which enables holders to make payment at retail outlets. The payments are charged directly to the retailer's bank account from the cardholder's bank account and is thus, just an extension of the debit card.

To get a debit card, an individual opens an account with the issuing bank, which gives him a debit card along with a personal identification number. When he makes a purchase, he enters this number on the shop's PIN pad. When the card is swiped through the electronic terminal, it dials the issuing bank terminal and finds out from the bank whether to accept or decline the transaction. The customer can never overspend because the system will reject any transaction that exceeds the balance in his account and the bank will never face default because the amount spent is debited immediately from the customer's account.

❖ Benefits of Debit Cards

- There is no need to carry cash by the cardholder.
- It is quick and less complicated than using a cheque.
- It can also be used for withdrawal of cash.
- Its holders can have a record of the transactions in his bank statement which will enable him to plan and control the expenditure.
- It can be issued to any individual without assessing creditworthiness.

9.1.3 Smart Cards

A Smart Card, also known as *Stored Value Card,* is a pay-before product. Smart card is also known as a *Chip Card* which holds personal information about the cardholder and can be used with a personal identification number (PIN). It has a magnetic strip to read pre-recorded information in the card.

Smart card is a new generation portable computer. Embedded in the Smart Card is a microcomputer chip giving it intelligence and a memory capacity far beyond today's magnetic stripe cards, which can be used for many applications, and is small enough to be carried around at all times. Smart cards can be programmed to do any task within its processing power and memory capacity. Smart cards are prepaid cards giving entitlement to use of goods or services. Each time the card is used, the value of the goods or services received is reduced from the value on the card.

The Smart Card looks exactly like any other plastic card or an ATM card with an integrated circuit (IC Chip) installed. The IC contains memory, may contain a processor, and communicates with the external world through 4-5 contracts on the surface of the card. The size, position and utility of the contacts are specified by an international standard so that cards can interact with a variety of equipment.

There are two main types of smart cards: Intelligent Memory Chip and Microprocessor cards. Memory smart cards have been around for several years, being used in pay phones, identification, access control, voting, and other applications, These are used to store a value, which is counted down until the card is exhausted and then thrown away. Recharging the card for reuse is not usually allowed, as then the financial security of the system may be compromised. The main security risk is from counterfeiting.

Processor smart cards are the most advanced, and are ideally suited for banking and financial applications where reuse or the card is allowed. These cards have a built-in memory and the processor, along with an operating system perform the financial operations. As all the cards' intelligence is built-in, they can protect themselves against fraudulent operations. This protection is based on the Data Encryption Standard (DES) which is accepted by the International Standard Organization as safe enough for protecting electronic funds transfer (EFT) transactions.

A Smart card based system will have the following advantages:

- Since the smart card incorporates a secure identification system, it is possible to safely use these cards in an off-line mode. This means that the cost or telecommunication lines, the transaction processing hardware and software, and the secure power supplies are completely avoided.

- The system can have "manual ATMs": the technical performs the card processing and security functions, printing a slip, which authorizes the cashier to make the payment manually. These "manual ATMs" can be installed in bank branches, shops, railway stations, airports, shopping centres, etc. Since the operator is not responsible for the payment authorization, but only for the cash counting and handover the function can be provided by an outsider. In case the bank still wants automatic ATMs to be used, these are available with smart cards readers.
- The smart card can be used for cash deposit as well as withdrawal at "manual ATMs". This allows a person who has excess cash in hand (for example while travelling) to deposit it into the card and then withdraw it when required. This makes the smart card work like an instant traveller's cheque. This would really be useful for the people who travel between the metropolitan cities and the smaller towns buying and selling goods. Instead of carrying cash, they can carry the card, thereby safeguarding from theft or loss.
- Multinational Banks are issuing two different kinds of cards known as national and international cards. In national cards the payments can be made only in the currency of the cardholders country. In international cards payments can be made in foreign currency.
- **Security Advantages:** The smart card can store data and cannot be misused by any unauthorized person either physically or electronically. Unlike conventional magnetic strip card, which can be easily erased or copied, smart card has a protected and much larger memory. Smart cards also have confidential memory zones holding secret user information.

Smart cards are plastic cards just the size of a visiting card. It looks like any other credit card and only difference is that it carries a chip embedded in it on the reverse below the magnetic stripe. The aim of the smart card technology is to replace multiple number of cards with one or two smart cards with storable information.

❖ Smart Card Types

(i) Stored Value Cards: Stored value cards, also known as prepaid cards or value added cards. These cards either have a magnetic stripe or a computer chip in which the 'value is stored', which is available to the holder for access primarily at retail location. The consumer pays a bank or the provider of the card for the card loaded with the value. The consumer takes the card to the various locations and makes purchases. In payment he inserts the card into the POS terminal, and if necessary, enters the personal identification number (PIN). Funds are directly debited from the cards and transferred to the vendor's terminal. Merchant then can transfer the value accumulated to their bank account by remote login as frequently as they choose.

(ii) Magnetic Stripe Cards: The conventional ATM cards, credit cards, debit cards all contain magnetic stripe on the reverse, where the information is stored on 4 tracks. Smart card has the capacity to store lot more information than the magnetic stripe cards, as well as to perform calculations with the data.

(iii) Re-loadable and Disposable Cards: Re-loadable cards are those, in which once the stored value is depleted the value can be replenished by the consumer through a special terminal/

ATM either by paying cash or transferring amount from his account. Disposable cards generally come for specific value and once the value is exhausted the card has to be discarded.

(iv) Closed and Open Stored Value Cards: In a closed system, the value of the card can be used for goods and services only in specified locations like mass-transit system, for food, photocopying, books and vending items within a university campus. The most common example of closed system cards are phone cards, subway cards, etc. In open system, the cards of several issuers are mutually acceptable. During 1996 Olympics, three separate banks issued VISA cards, which were accepted by over 1500 merchants. Such an open system has made the cards to be known as 'Electronic Purse' or 'Electronic Wallet'.

❖ Contactless Smart Cards

This is similar to contact cards except for the type of powering used. This card does not have contact pad, inductive coupling, microwave coupling, optical coupling while surface acoustic coupling can be used to power the contactless card. However, inductive and capacitive couplings are most common. These cards are more reliable and have longer life than contact cards with surface contacts which are susceptible to damage and contamination. They are very soft and can withstand harsh environment. These cards can be kept in the wallet during travel and are more resistant to moisture, dust and dirt.

This can be used for a number of applications like paying for telephone bills or for bus ticketing. These cards are becoming more popular with transport companies. Under this system, the card is loaded with value and with each travel or usage the value is reduced. The costs of a Smart Card can vary from ₹ 150-250 depending upon the quality. Similarly, the cost of a credit card can vary from ₹ 50-150 depending upon the quality.

The cost of the card varies from one manufacture to another. The cards manufactured by Schlumberger, Gemplus, Bull CP8 range from less than $1 to $20. This includes the cost of silicon, the Micro-controller, and the plastic card itself. When we compare the cost of the credit card which range from 10 to 50 cents per piece, depending upon the quality of the card and includes the photo, hologram, embossing and so on.

❖ Advantages of Smart Card

- The cost of financial operation for the bank is much cheaper compared to magnetic stripe card.
- Since the stored value cards carry the monetary value with them, any transaction does not require the account to be used. As such these can be used by children, tourist and others, who do not have a bank account.

(vi) Kisan Credit Cards: The commercial banks have to provide credit to farmers to the extent of ₹ 22,000 crores which is impossible task for NABARD to provide refinance. Out of the 12.73 crore cultivators.

Kisan credit cards have been issued to only 46% upto March 2006. All farmers were to be provided with KCC by March 2007. Banks have also been directed to ensure that all farmers financed during the year be mandatory covered under KCC. During 2005-06 commercial banks issued 38.06 fresh KCC as against 47.27 lakh new farmers financed by them.

The Government is seriously considering the possibility of making loans upto ₹ 3 lakhs collateral free, (present limit is ₹ 50,000). The rate of interest is not the only cost incurred by the farmer for borrowing from institutional sources. The amount of credit is to be availed upto 20% of ₹ 3 lakh in cash, through credit cards and the rest in kind through purchases by March 2007 latest.

9.2 HOW TO MAKE PAYMENT OF CREDIT CARDS?

Credit cards bills can be paid by user by various system as —

(1) Drop Box: All ATM centres of banks have got drop boxes, which can be used for payment of bills. The cheque can be issued for amount depicting the 16 digit credit card number.

(2) Cash Payment: Cash can also be paid at the nearest branch of the bank. The deposit slip should have the credit card number specifically. Direct payment through your bank A/c can be made or auto payment system is available by standing instructions to bank.

(3) Payment through Phone-banking: If you have got phone banking facility then by instructions to bank payment can be made. Phone banking is availed through a PIN Number allotted by bank.

(4) Payment through Net Banking: If you have got 1 net banking facility then logging to the banks website, the payment can be made by transferring the amount to credit card account. For networking, password is issued to the customer.

(5) Payment through post: Some banks provide facility of payment of credit cards through cheque/draft sent through post/courier. Place of payment by post is printed on the monthly statement of the bank.

(vii) Co-Branding of Credit Cards (Plastic Money): In the present environment of making attractive the credit card issuing banks and companies have made arrangement or agreement to provide Value Added Service to their customers. Such arrangements with two brands or brand companies is called co-branding of plastic money. Such arrangements are made between issuing company such as bank and any retail outlet or service provider/goods provider credit cards issuers, airline companies, media/entertainment company, super market, hotel telecom companies, educational institutions charitable trusts, insurance companies. Such co-branded cards provide on purchases/services various kinds of discounts, reward-points, schemes, free trips/travel etc.

❖ Difference between Regular and Co-branded Cards

Almost all features of regular cards are available in co-branded credit cards except with additional facilities. But such facilities are available only when —

(*i*) such cards are used in co-branded outlets.

(*ii*) with charge slips bearing the co-branded issuer of cards such as in case of ICICI bank charge slips.

(*iii*) such cards are issued on higher annual fees which rank between ₹ 750 to ₹ 6,000 normally but maybe waived by certain companies in view of competition in the market. But get compensated by charging higher rate of interest say 28% p.a.

(*iv*) the reward points are higher in co-branded cards.

❖ Advantages:

Such cards are useful to persons who avail services frequently like petrol/diesel filling, mobile recharging, shopping from particular super market or mall or purchase of air-tickets etc.

- Attract new customers with tangible rewards.
- Build incremental sales through customers who, in the absence of a card may delay purchases or buy competitive products.
- Strengthen customers loyalty by offering value added incentives to buy the issuer's product or service.
- Increase brand awareness with value added benefits that encourage customers to use co-branded card more often.
- Enhance corporate image every time with card is used.
- By studying the buying behaviour of customers, new products and services targeted at cardholders through more effective sales promotions.
- Communicate with customers through monthly statements.
- Save money compared to issuing one's own credit card as one does not pay costs for processing payments and extending credit.
- Build valuable banking relationship with the financial institution that issues the co-branded card.

❖ Warnings

Before you go for co-branded credit cards, ascertain about the hidden charges the issuing company would be claiming in lieu of free offers, discounts and reward points.

(viii) Affinity card: With affinity card, a third party organisation — an alumini association or a charity or a museum, for example — receives a portio of each transaction made with the card. Some affinity card — partners, like professional sports teams or environmental protection foundations, may also offer perks like discounts at selected stores or a free gift with the first purchase made with the card. Affinity cards carry the name of a third party on the card, in addition to the name of the bank or financial institution that issue the card and the card brand.

❖ Precautions Required by the Banks and Users of Credit Cards

In the computer age, certain persons have very sharp brain and work better than any computer available. Hence there are certain precautions to be observed by the users of the credit cards:

(1) Blocking of Lost Credit Cards

When any credit card is lost the procedure is that the holder of credit card informs to the issuing bank, for blocking the credit cards, to save further losses due to misutilisation by the thief or miscreants. There is a case/incident happened in the year 2005 in Mumbai.

On 14-11-2005, Mr. Avinash Goel was looted in the Fort, Mumbai area, outside the J&K Bank Ltd., by serve thiefs at gun point and chopar. The thiefs looted ₹ one lakh and two credit cards of Shri Goel. One of the credit cards was in the name of his wife. Mr. Goel lodged police complaint and informed to the Standard Chartered Bank to get them blocked (in-operative). After some time Mr. Goel received two statements wherein it was showed that both the lost credit cards wee used to the extent of ₹ 3,60,000 inspite of blocking of both the accounts. On being investigated by police it was found that one Mahendra Jain issued forged receipt as purchases and earned 20% as commission from the user of credit cards. The user and thief of the credit card was Samir Mandani who purchased both the cards from Irfan Kutchi and another by amount of ₹ 50,000 and withdrew the amount of ₹ 3,60,000 through Standard Chartered Bank. Samir Mandani submitted two cheques for the minimum debit amount and withdrew from his account the entire balance excepting minimum balance. Resultantly the cheques were returned unpaid. No sooner the data of credit of cheque was entered in computer, the block got cleared and before the entry of bouncing cheque entered, the amount of ₹ 3,60,000 were withdrawn.

Comment: Blocking of credit account does not mean 100% safety to the owner of the credit card.

(2) Xerox Copy of Credit Cards of Both Sides

Xerox copy of any original should not be kept in open or uncared way.

In the year 2005 are Samir Sheikh of Mumbai (Thane) used to trace the security number of credit cards on the basis of xerox copy of the credit cards and used to pay the phone bills through online. On being caught by police, more than one thousand xerox copies of credit cards were seized by police from the house of Samir Sheikh.

Credit cards consist of number on its both sides but on the backside there is another 3 digit security code along with the main number.

Sheikh used to open security code and has/had been making online payments of phone bills. The matter came to light on the complaint lodged by an officer of a finance company, when he received message from his bank that his credit limit of ₹ 30,000 was full and exceeding.

On investigation the facts came to light.

Comments: Do not give xerox of credit cards to anyone or keep xerox unattended.

(3) Giving of Credit Card Number and PIN to Anyone

Sajid Sheikh B.Sc.(IT) graduate from Mumbai University was working in a call centre of Intelnet Global Service. He used to get credit card numbers alongwith personal identification number (PIN) from the clients at call centre are used to record their in his diary.

After one year service, he left the job and opened a website in the name of Make My Trip.com and used to book air tickets online for persons. On such booking he used to collect full cash payment in advance but used credit card numbers of those persons, whose details he had recorded in his diary while in call centre.

After sometime, on receipt of bank accounts on behalf of the card holders, the bank lodged complaint with the website. On enquiry it was traced that from one cyber cafe near Shital Cinema Kurla such operations were done. On trap laid Sheikh was caught and admitted that he had made money to the extent of ₹ 9,17,500 through booking of air tickets.

Comments: Do not give credit card number and PIN number to anyone, whether known or unknown to you.

❖ Credit Card Defaulters

The credit card default rate has gone up in 2005-06 to 7% due to consumers within the age group of 27 to 35 years. It is observed that this is due to the use of multiple credit cards and arbitrary distribution of cards by companies/banks without assessing repayment capacity. According to *Credit Card Management Consultancy,* the default rate which was about 6% in the 2004-05 has now increased to 7%. Card issuers have resorted to arbitrary distribution of cards without checking the repayment capacity of the consumers, *Who are Mostly Young.* Bank of Baroda which is following a "Catch Them Young" policy to expand its presence, however, said young consumers were more conscious of repaying the debts. But they are also more *Mobile* than others (due to change of jobs) which have led to this problem. Another reason is that most card issuers have been focussing on *distribution* of credit cards and not on the *Actually spends.*

❖ Online Credit Card Fraud: A Growing Reality in India

For safer online transactions:

- Use a secure web browser, look for an's' after the 'http' in the web page address
- Keep your password secret
- Never send payment information via email
- Reputable merchant sites use encryption technologies to protect private data from being accessed by others during a transaction.
- Monitor your monthly statements, especially after an overseas trip.
- Check transactions, even the small ones, because criminals test stolen accounts by buying inexpensive items
- Investigate suspicious activity to prevent fraud
- Notify your financial institution of suspicious email activity
- Only open and respond to emails that are from somebody you know

In India, credit card fraud is mostly limited to the physical space. Online con jobs make up just about 1% of the total numbers here, unlike 40% in the developed world. But, as consumers graduate to the shop-easy internet and pay with their cards, instances of fraud are bound to rise. As J. Y. Umranikar, additional DG, state cm, says: "(While) we don't have statistics, as access to the web increases, reported cases of card fraud will rise 20-30% every year. And this is only a surmise based on past experience." He insists that in online transactions, contracts are one-sided and the customer is always held responsible in case of fraud.

Phishing, where a consumer gets a fictitious email from a fake site or blog seeking sensitive card information, is a commonly used defrauding mechanism. To top it, "people are very careless in offering their card details," says Umranikar.

While consumer organisations TOI spoke to had little information about online fraud, card companies say it is increasing in e-ticketing, e-shopping and the service sectors, where no physical delivery of goods is involved. Shockingly, B Madhivanan, general manager at ICICI Bank, informs that 60% of online card fraud occurs only while buying an air ticket. He says that one way out is to insist on customer identity at the time of actually boarding a flight. Indian Airlines, for instance, asks for 'a' particular proof of identity; which a consumer has mentioned in the online form, such as a driving licence or a passport.

So till it becomes mandatory across all airlines, a consumer could as well be prepared to notice an inflated card statement despite going strictly by the rulebook.

In April this year, a 26-year-old Mumbai executive keyed in her credit card number and the three-digit security code on the e-booking site of an airline. She bought a ticket for Bangalore. In July; she was shocked to find a ₹ 20,000 additional credit drawn from her account. "Two tickets from the same airline were booked on two different days in June using my card," she says. The first was a Dwarka-Mumbai ticket for Rs 6,000, and the other, a Delhi-Dubai one for Rs 14,000. She did not get a response from her card company till August. "Then I approached the police to me an FIR. But they told me they did not know what a credit card was." Exasperated, she went to the cybercrime cell, which in turn asked her to first lodge an FIR with the police. She got a cybercrime officer to speak to the police and finally got her complaint registered.

On receiving a complaint, card companies say, a consumer is given a temporary credit that matches the disputed amount, and a case is resolved in a maximum of 60 days. The Mumbai executive, though, has been waiting for almost three months now.

For safer transactions, an advanced card such as Verified by Visa (VbV) and Master-card Secure Code comes in handy. Here, a consumer requires a password during a transaction to validate his identity.

CREDIT CARD USAGE CHARGES

	Citibank	*Corporation*	*HDFC Bank Classic*	*HSBC Silver*	*ICICI Bank*	*SBI Card*	*StanChart Classic*
Joining fee	Free	Free	Life time free	Free	Free	₹ 250	₹ 100
Annual fee	₹ 750	₹ 250	Life time free	₹ 700	Life time free	₹ 750	₹ 700, ₹ 750 from 2nd yr
Add on card	Free for the first year, additional card at ₹ 350	₹ 100	Life time free	Annual fee of ₹ 350	Life time free	Annual fee ₹ 250	No entrance, annual fee (₹ 400 annual charge from 2nd year
Minimum payment outstanding	5% of outstanding or ₹ 100*	5% of outstanding or ₹ 100*	5% of outstanding or ₹ 200*	5% of outstanding or ₹ 100*	5% of outstanding or ₹ 100*	5% of outstanding or ₹ 200*	5% of amount
Cash withdrawal fee	2% or ₹ 300*	2.5% or ₹ 100*	2.8% or ₹ 312*	2.8% or ₹ 262*	2.8% or ₹ 312*	2.8% or ₹ 162*	2.8% or ₹ 262*
Cash withdrawal interest	39.72% p.a	2% p.m	38% p.a	37.71% p.a	39.72% p.a	40.2%p.a	39.72% p.a
Min. and Max Int free period	17 days to 55 days	45 days	50 days	52 days	50 days	50 days	47 days
Rollover interest rate	3.5% p.m or 42% .p.a.	2%p.m 35.4% p .a	2.95% p.m or 41.75% p.a.	2.95%p.m	2.95% p.m or 41.75% p.a.	2.990/0 p.m or 41.75% p.a.	2.95% p.m or 41.75% p.a.#

Railway Ticket Booking and Cancellation Charges (counter booking) 2.5% of transaction value, Minimum ₹ 25.
*whichever is higher; **₹ 50 per transaction If money is withdrawn from Union Bank ATM/₹ 75 otherwise; # calculated on a per day basis. Rates are subject to change.
Source: websites of various banks

CREDIT CARD FRAUD

❖ Data used to Buy Air Tickets

The accused logged on to websites of leading private airlines and used the credit card details to book tickets. They would then hang around at restaurants and bars and offer the tickets at cheap rates and pocket the cash. *(Source:* TOI, 29-9-06.)

Over 100 people have approached the cyber crime investigation cell (CCIC) of the Mumbai police in the last 2006 and complained that someone had used their credit card numbers to book air tickets they had never sought or got.

A Dahisar Mumbai resident approached the cell saying he had received an intimation from his bank that ₹ 1.5 lakh had been used from his credit card to buy air tickets, Interestingly, the limit on the credit card was just ₹ 90,000.

"He had instructed the bank not to clear transactions of over ₹ 80,000 without his permission but the-bank-officials ignored his request and cleared an amount far more than his limit." said an officer.

Police said that in most of the cases the online tickets were booked with GoAir. Air Deccan and Kingfisher Airlines.

"The card details are mostly obtained from some restaurant, petrol pump or mall employees who swipe the card."

The D. N. Nagar police detected a case where a group of people booked air tickets on the internet using credit cards of card holders and later sold the tickets at a discount.

The accused, who had access to an individual's card number, its expiry date and most importantly the VCC Code (the additional three digits at the end of the card number printed on the signature strip on back of card), logged on to websites of leading private airlines and used the details to book tickets. The airlines issue a confirmation, the printout of which can be exchanged for a boarding pass at the airport The accused would then hang around at restaurants and bars and befriend frequent flyers. They would offer tickets at cheap rates and pocket the cash.

Though there are hundreds of such cases, the CCIC has been asked not to register the cases but send complainants to the concerned police stations. Sources said the cyber crime investigation cell officials have been asked "to just assist the police stations to solve a case".

The police have now directed the victims to report such cases to the police stations and take a acknowledgement copy from the police station and send it to the bank.

A few months ago in 2007, officials from the Bengaluru cyber crime cell had arrested two persons from Vashi and seized 20-25 credit cards from them. The duo used to book tickets paying for them by credit card and collected money from ticket buyers in cash.

❖ Credit Card with Keyboard

In order to control the on-line shopping by credit cards, American Global Payment Entrepreneur Cp. "VISA's European" has made such a credit card which is also having key-pad and a screen and the user can read the digital numbers. This card is named as *Visa Codesure*. It is having 12 buttoned keyboard, a screen and a battery and is usable up to three years. The user has to put password through keypad which will give a special password which would be having words and numbers. This would be essential for any website shopping. This card can only be used one who knows the PIN number. This card would give every time a new password which will allow internet shopping to do. (*Navbharat Times,* Newspaper dt. 19-7-2010)

9.3 HOUSING FINANCE

Housing is one of the basic necessities of human being and the capital requires, per house, is so large that few individuals can raise it from their own domestic savings. Finance for housing is provided in the form of mortgage loans (either equitable/registered mortgage). The suppliers of having finance in India are the following institutions —

(*a*) Housing and Urban Development (HUDCO)

(*b*) State Housing Boards

(*c*) Life Insurance Corporation of India

(*d*) Commercial banks

(*e*) General Insurance Companies

(*f*) National Housing Bank (NHB)

All commercial banks were required to finance for housing since November 1988 and for that 1.5% of their incremental deposits were set aside for housing finance. There are 22 housing finance subsidiaries of banks and other institutions at the end of 2005. Their names are stated below.

Total Housing Finance Companies registered under Section 29A(5) of National Housing Bank Act 1987 and with Tier-I capital of ₹ 10 crore or above (for the year ended 31st March, 2003 [Notification dt. 10-11-2003 by Department of Economic Affairs) to be treated as *Financial institution* as per SARFAESI Act, 2002).

1. HDFC Ltd., Mumbai
2. LIC Housing Finance Ltd., Mumbai
3. ICICI Home Finance Ltd., Mumbai
4. Canfin Homes Ltd., Bangalore
5. Birla Home Finance Ltd., New Delhi
6. Dewan Housing Finance Corp. Ltd., Mumbai
7. GIC Housing Finance Ltd., Mumbai
8. PNB Housing Finance Ltd., New Delhi
9. Sundaram Home Finance Ltd., Chennai
11. GRUH Finance Ltd., Ahmedabad
12. Tata Home Finance Ltd., New Delhi
13. CENT Bank Home Finance Ltd., Bhopal
14. Orissa Rural Housing and Development Corporation Ltd., Bhubaneshwar
15. Vysya Bank Housing Finance Ltd., Bangalore
16. Maharishi Housing Dev. Fin. Corporation Ltd., New Delhi
17. Corpbank Homes Ltd., Bangalore
18. Weizmann Homes Ltd., Mumbai
19. Vibank Housing Finance Ltd., Bangalore
20. National Trust Housing Finance Ltd., Manipal
21. Manipal Housing Finance Syndicate Ltd., Manipal.
22. REPCO Home Finance Ltd., Chennai
23. SICOM Housing Development Finance Ltd., Mumbai
24. All Commercial Banks/Foreign Banks

Commercial banks sanction loans to individuals/group of individuals and cooperative societies under their direct housing loan schemes for the following purposes —

- For construction/acquisition of new house or old house/flat (in multistoried buildings) which are not more than 10 years old.
- For *extension* of house/flat.
- For modification/upgradation/renovation/major repairs for owner occupied/tenant occupied or for purchase of second house/flat anywhere in India.
- Supplementary finance to meet the short-fall in funds required for purchase/construction of house against *pari passu* charge or *second charge* on the property.

Eligibility: Salaried persons/professionals/businessmen having sufficient disposable income to meet the repayment. The employment should be in State Government/Central Government/ public or private sectors/companies and establishments of repute: Non-resident Indians (NRIs) are also eligible for the housing loans.

Age Criteria: Minimum 21 years and maximum 55 years (extended up to 60 years in case of businessmen) and for service-class minimum residual service be 10 years (or lesser if loan is for 5 to 7 years only).

Ceiling of Loan: Maximum loan in rural/semi-urban areas ₹ 15 lakh.

In Metro/urban areas ₹ 100 lakh

For repairs/renovations (in all areas) ₹ 10 lakh

All above loans are covered under Priority Sector Advances (previous limit was up to ₹ 20 lakh advances now raised up to ₹ 30 lakh w.e.f. April 2008).

Minimum loan quantum is ₹ 5 lakh.

Margin: Minimum margin of 15% to 20% on total cost of home/flat (including property registration charges/society deposits + cost of home and other legal charges) loan amount depends on the repaying capacity of the borrowers.

Processing Fees: One time loan processing fee @ 0.25 to 0.50% (in some banks even no processing fee is charged) is required to be deposited in advance when the loan eligibility is worked out, by bank/financial institution.

Mortgage of House/Flat: Some of the banks require simple mortgage of house to be purchased while private/foreign banks provide loans against power of attorney document (on ₹ 200 stamp) in favour of the bank.

Interest Charging: Interest is charged on floating rate 10.60% to 11.50% (changes as per changes made in Base Rate by individual banks) or by fixed interest rate (fixed for minimum period of 3 years at a time). There is always a difference of 1.5% in floating and fixed rates. Fixed rates are always higher to floating interest rate.

Repayment of Loan: Repayment of loan is done by equated monthly instalments (EMIs). The maximum period of Housing Loan is 20 years (5 years for repairs loan) and minimum period is five years. In view of high interest rates and rising cost of flats/house the repayment period is allowed 15 years only to keep a safety margin for any future increases in interest rates. For every 3 years period advance monthly EMIs cheques are collected from the borrower.

Moratorium Period: If the house/flat is booked to be acquired after 2/3 years, which is a period of completion, then some banks starts FMI from the month after the advance date as such there is No Moratorium Period. While some banks starts deduction of EMI after the completion of the house/flat or 18 months from the first disbursement whichever is earlier but for the intermediary period banks charge only interest on the advance amount, monthly basis and for that they collect interest cheques, recoverable every month, till the completion of building is reported. Borrowers as such should not pay entire cost of house/flat to builders but should be paid according to the construction completed stage (i.e., for every slab of floor completed/plastering work/brick work/ sanitary fittings, etc.). Otherwise the borrower does not get the advantage of deduction for interest and principal under Income Tax Act, 1961. As such while finalising deal with builders and/or banks loan amount should be released as per work completion basis, otherwise there would be huge loss to the borrowers.

❖ Prepayment of Your Home Loan

Interest rates on home loans have gone up considerably in the recent past, resulting in a number of additional EMIs and inflating your total cost of borrowing. Under such circumstances, should you prepay your housing debt? Here's an answer...

The home loan partly seems to have finally come to an end because of higher interest rates and higher cost of houses/flats. The country's central bank stepped in to curb inflation and put a cap on excess liquidity in the banking system by hiking the Cash Reserve Ratio (CRR), 6% from 24-4-2010 and Repo Rate (8.00% from 26-7-2011) and Reverse Repo Rate (7.00% from 26-07-2011) amongst other directives. The direct impact of these moves was witnessed in the form of increased interest rates on all retail lending products of banks.

Since a housing loan is generally a larger sized loan with a fairly long tenure, the interest burden on such loans is also much higher than that on other loans. Therefore the recent spate of interest rate hikes on home loans has hit borrowers the most. "To prepay or not to prepay?" is the single most important question running through every home loan customer's mind today.

❖ Prepayment on your Home Loan

Prepayment is the lump sum principal repayment made on a loan, either partially or fully, prior to the maturity of the loan. By paying off your loan before the projected tenure, you can bring down the interest cost on your loan. However, before you retire your debt in this manner, there are a number of crucial factors you must consider.

❖ Prepayment Charges Levied

When you prepay the loan, your lender faces a loss of interest income. Due to this, a prepayment penalty is levied when you as make a bulk payment on your loan. Though prepayment fees vary, depending upon the outstanding loan amount, lender, etc., it generally ranges between 1 to 2 per cent of the amount being prepaid. If you make a substantial prepayment, you will land up paying a heavy prepayment fee. For instance, if your outstanding principal loan amount is ₹ 15 lakh at present and you wish to make a prepayment of ₹ 5 lakh, then, assuming that the penalty is 2 per cent, you will need to pay a prepayment charge of ₹ 10,000 (2 per cent of ₹ 5 lakh).

❖ Tax Rebate on Interest paid on Home Loans

Another key aspect to consider is the tax break that home loans offer. Under the Income Tax Act, you can get a deduction of up to ₹ 1.5 lakh against the interest payment on home loans for first house for self-use. Assuming that you fall into the highest tax slab of 33.66 per cent, the resultant savings in interest costs will amount to ₹ 50,490 (₹ 1.5 lakh × 33.66 per cent). Repaying a portion of your loan will bring down your interest cost but you will also have to forego the corresponding tax benefit on interest paid.

❖ Deploying the Funds into Investments

Before you prepay your loan, you must ascertain if the funds that you use for making prepayment can fetch you better returns if invested in other avenues, and if such returns are higher than the interest that you are paying on the loan. While it is mentally relieving to be debt free, you also need to think from the financial perspective.

❖ Prepay or Invest?

Let's incorporate the above mentioned factors into a hypothetical example in order to dilute the 'prepayment' dilemma. Assume that your principal loan outstanding currently stands at ₹ 5 lakh and your balance loan tenure is 6 years, i.e., 72 months. Assuming an EMI of ₹ 10,000 on your loan, the total EMI payable by you over the entire term will be ₹ 7.2 lakh (₹ 10,000 × 72) out of which interest cost will amount to ₹ 2.2 lakh (₹ 7.2 lakh minus ₹ 5 lakh). Let's further assume that your lender charges you a prepayment penalty of 2 per cent on your loan amount. Now, let's take a look at two scenarios — Prepaying your loan by ₹ 5 lakh and alternatively, investing this amount. The resultant outgo under each option will tell us whether you can take the 'prepayment' route.

❖ Option 1 — Prepayment of Home Loan

Under this scenario, your total cash outflow will comprise of the prepayment amount, plus the prepayment penalty. Keeping our earlier example in mind, you will pay ₹ 5 lakh (as prepayment) plus ₹ 10,000 as prepayment charges (2 per cent of ₹ 5 lakh loan outstanding). In addition, you will lose the tax benefit on interest payment on the loan as well as an 'opportunity loss' had you invested the money elsewhere.

❖ Option 2 — Invest the Money and Continue to Pay Regular EMIs on Loan

If you undertake this option, you will need to pay an interest of ₹ 2.2 lakh over the term of the loan. However, you will get a tax benefit of ₹ 66,000 (₹ 2.2 lakh × 30 per cent). Moreover, if you invest the amount of ₹ 5 lakh in a fixed deposit for 5 years with an annual return of 10 per cent, you will earn ₹ 2.5 lakh, which, after tax, will come to ₹ 1.75 lakh (assuming a tax rate of 30 per cent). In addition, you save on prepayment charges as well.

❖ Give a Thought to Other Finer Nuances as well

Before you make up your mind on whether to prepay your loan or not, you must also bear in mind the following, apart from the fundamental factors discussed above.

- Even with interest rates rising, a home loan is the cheapest loan that you can get. Moreover, it makes sense to keep servicing the loan if you expect a major expense coming your way in the near future.
- If you decide to prepay the loan, avoid doing so during the initial period of the loan since interest forms a major chunk of the EMI during the first few years of repayment. So, you will lose out a significant amount as tax rebate.

- Before retiring your home loan, settle your other 'consumption' debts such as credit card dues, personal loans and car loans if any.

❖ Is it Time to Prepay?

Not even market experts can accurately predict the movement of interest rates on home loans in the future. Use your discretion, analyse your set of financial needs, evaluate the financial benefits that you will derive under each option — prepaying and otherwise arid finally make a 'calculated' decision.

❖ Refinance Home Loan Offering Lower Interest Rates

Housing Development and Finance Corporation (HDFC) (Aug. 2007) cut the interest rate on its floating rate home loan to 10.5%.

All new disbursals now charged interest at 10.5% per annum. In addition, even those whose floating rate loan proposals had been cleared but not disbursed got the loan at 10.5% interest.

That is the simple part of it. The interest rate being offered by HDFC was extremely attractive and individuals who are currently paying floating rates of 11.5-12% with new generation private sector banks could well look to refinance their home loan.

Let us say you have a loan outstanding of ₹ 30 lakh; the remaining tenure of the loan is 15 years and you are currently paying an interest of 12% on your floating rate loan. The equated monthly instalment (EMI) for this works out to around ₹ 36,000 per month.

You can look to refinance your home loan from HDFC, which is currently charging 10.5% on its floating rate loans or from some public sector banks, which are also charging similar rates.

Refinancing essentially involves taking a new loan at a cheaper rate to repay the original loan.

Typically, a lender would levy a 2% prepayment charge when a home loan borrower decides to prepay his original loan by borrowing from another bank or housing finance company. On your loan outstanding of ₹ 30 lakh, this works out to ₹ 60,000.

So, is it worth getting a refinance in the first place?

Currently, the borrower needs to pay an EMI of ₹ 36,000 to repay his loan outstanding of ₹ 30 lakh over a period of 15 years. The rate of interest he is paying is 12%. After refinancing, the rate of interest comes down to 10.5%.

On this, if he were to continue paying his earlier EMI of ₹ 36,000, he would be able to repay the amount outstanding of ₹ 30 lakh in 150 months, i.e., 12.5 years - 2.5 years or 30 months less than the original period of 15 years. And what is the amount saved? A whopping ₹ 10.8 lakh (₹ 36,000 × 30 months)!

It sure makes sense to take refinance then, assuming, of course, that the floating interest rate will continue to stay at 10.5%.

Also, as the name suggests, floating rates can change. They are linked to what is known as the benchmark prime lending rate (BPLR) of the bank or housing finance company from which you take the home loan.

Hence, if the BPLR is 13.5% and floating rate home loans are at a discount of 1.5% to the BPLR, the floating rate works out to 12%. Therefore, whenever the BPLR is raised, the interest to be paid on the floating rate home loan goes up, or *vice versa*.

Given this, the interest rate on a floating rate home loan can vary. Let us say interest rates go up by 1%. Then, the floating rate loan charging 12% will go up to 13% and that charging 10.5% will go up to 11%. Even so, a difference of around 1.5% is likely to be maintained.

Thus, even if interest rates continue to go up, you are better of refinancing your home loan.

HOMEWORK

Say you have a home loan outstanding of ₹ 30 lakh over 15 years' tenure remaining and you are paying 12% interest on your floating rate loan at an EMI of ₹ 36,000 per month.

If you refinance the loan from HDFC, which charges 10.5% floating rate, you have to pay ₹ 60,000 to the original lender as prepayment charge at 2% of the loan outstanding.

But, at 10.5% interest post-refinance, the EMI of ₹ 36,000 would pay-off the loan in 12.5 years, or 30 months less than the original 15 years.

This means a saving of ₹ 10.8 lakh (₹ 36,000 × 30)

Subtract the prepayment amount of ₹ 60,000 from this and you still save over ₹ 10 lakh.

❖ Impact of Increase in CRR (by RBI) on Housing Loans

The Reserve Bank of India increased lending rates or pegged a higher Cash Reserve Ratio, home loan rates could head north again

Inflation has touched 9.24 per cent in India and every commodity has become costlier than before. The question being asked by home seekers, is whether home loans will meet the same fate? As it is, certain banks are said to have revised their original plans to reduce lending rates to this segment citing repercussions of the current rising inflation. Others have either withdrawn marginal reductions in home loan rates or discontinued 'festive' offers that would otherwise have been extended all through the summer vacation period.

What concerns prospective home buyers and existing home loan customers, is whether these are temporary blips on the home loan radar or an indication of housing finance lenders charging even higher rates than they are at present? Reserve Bank of India (RBI) has increased on 25-01-2011 lending rates or pegged a higher Repo Rate and Reverse Repo Rate to 8.0% and 7.0% respectively (from 26-7-2011) in the credit policy and in the process trigger off a northward movement of home loan rates once again?

When the RBI governor had hiked the CRR on 24-4-2010, it clearly signalled that money tightening would continue in the economy till the Consumer Price Index drops to comfortable levels. While the hike did pinch banks and led to many banks revising their deposit rates in order to maintain their spread, they somehow managed to avoid an interest rate rise where home loans were concerned.

Unfortunately, the then Finance Minister, P. Chidambaram had done precious little in this area apart from urging banks to reduce interest rates on home loans below ₹ 30 lakh to 8% in the year 2009. There was no extension of tax incentives for home loan customers and no direct facility to reduce the cost of funds for lending institutions.

Above all, there was absolutely no acknowledgement of the ground reality that a home loan of ₹ 30 lakh can hardly enable an aspiring family to buy a flat in extended suburbs line Vasai-Virar, Dombivali-Kalyan or the peripheral areas of Thane and Navi Mumbai. Although in October 2007, the RBI Governor had clearly given a direction that money supply would be choked as and when inflation rears its ugly face. The Indian economy has also become much more integrated with the global economy, so repercussions of any financial quandary faced by countries abroad cannot be avoided. In such circumstances, the slightest pressure from RBI could result in home loans becoming costlier, just like everything else in this inflation-hit country!

While the eagerly anticipated reduction in interest rates may no longer be feasible given the current economic scenario, just holding on to existing levels would at least ensure that there is no additional pressure on them at this stage. After all, *roti* and *kapda* have already become quite expensive, so it would help if the finance cost for the *makaan* at least remains constant!

❖ Interest Rate Options

Interest rates are the most dynamic aspect of a home loan and just about every applicant ponders about the advisability of going in for the fixed or floating rate option. This decision was relatively easy to take until a few years ago, when interest rates were headed south. However, since mid-2005 when the sustained reduction in rates stopped and a gradual rise began, floating rate customers had been concerned about the higher monthly repayments and/or increased tenures.

The thing to keep in mind is that experts have always suggested that it is better to go in of floating interest rates as they are comparatively cheaper than fixed loan component. For starters, there will always be an interest rate difference of one or two per cent between the fixed and floating home loan options. Secondly, since loan tenures are typically in the range of 7 to 15 years or so, interest rate cycles tend to even out over that period, so there is no need to panic and run for the fixed rate option unless if you are taking a short-term loan of just five years.

9.4 BANCASSURANCE

Bancassurance can be defined broadly as the sale of insurance products by banks and in concrete terms *Bancassurance* even known as all finance, constituting a package of financial services that can fulfil both *Insurance* and *Banking* needs at the same time. The motives behind bancassurance also vary. For banks, it is a means of product *Diversification* and a source of additional fee-income, while for instance, it is a tool of increasing their market penetration and premium turnover. For the customer, it is a bonanza, in terms of reduced price and high quality product and delivery at single point or doorstep. From the perspective of *Banks*, bancassurance is attractive because banks can —

(*i*) Secure an additional and more stable stream of income through diversification into insurance and reduce their reliance on interest spreads as the major source of income.

(*ii*) Leverage on their extensive customer base.

(*iii*) Sell a whole range of financial services to clients and insurance customer retention.

(*iv*) Reduce risk based capital requirement for the same level of revenue.

(*v*) Work towards the provision of integrated financial services tailored to the life cycle of customers.

(*vi*) Access funds that are otherwise kept with insurance companies who sometimes benefit from tax advantages.

(*vii*) Large number of bank branches (more than 74,000 in 2008) reaching even remote villages.

(*viii*) A growing middle income class due to availability of higher income.

(*ix*) Experienced in cross-selling and in customer segmentation.

(*x*) Regulatory changes under IRDA Act, 1999, have made bancassurance feasible and possible.

(*xi*) Large untapped growth potential.

(*xii*) Great deal of trusts in loans and advances require protection of the personal life of the borrowers.

(*xiii*) Reduction in operating expenses of bank due to increase in *fee income* from insurance.

❖ Success in Bancassurance

Success in bancassurance venture requires *change* in approach thinking and work culture on the part of everybody involved. Workforce of event level are so well entrenched in their classical way of working that there is a definite threat of resistance to any change that bancassurance may set in. Any reallocation to a new company or subsidiary or change from one work to a different kind of work will be resented with vehemence.

Another possible threat may come from *non-response* from the target customers. This kind of threat happened in USA in 1980. The investors in the banks' capital may turn their face off in case the *Rate of Return falls short* of existing rate of return on (or at least return of 20%) capital. Since banks and insurance companies, have major portion of their income coming from the investments, the return from bancassurance must at least match those returns. Also, if the reckless alliances are allowed to take place, thee will be *fierce competition* in the market resulting in lower prices and the bank assurance venture may *never reach break even*. But chances of such situation are very remote because the corporate agency to one bank has been given by one insurance company and not for the multi-corporate agencies to one bank.

❖ Buzzword in Selling Insurance

Global reinsurance major Swiss Re has forecast India and China to be hotbeds of bancassurance among the emerging economies. The business, where banks tie up with insurance forms for selling the latter's products, is expected to account for 13% and 5% of life and non-life insurance business respectively in the next five years, a Swiss Re report said. While almost every private and public sector bank in India is acting as a corporate agent of a life or a general insurance company, many have decided to be on their own and have floated insurance joint ventures. Industry analysts feel the dynamics of bancassurance in India will change when banks are allowed to be corporate agents for more than one insurance company.

The Insurance Regulatory, and Development Authority is said to have formed a committee to look into the issue. Most insurers feel the present rule of distribution is a little restrictive and will not help in increasing fee-based income significantly. Perhaps that is why most big banks find picking up strategic stakes in insurance ventures more lucrative. According to the Swiss Re report, bancassurance contributes to substantial new business growth in India, especially among private sector companies. Tie-ups with cooperative banks and regional rural banks are seen as a cost-effective vehicle for insurers to tap into rural communities and fulfil their rural sector obligations, it said. "In China, commercial banks have become a major distribution channel of insurance since the insurance law was revised in 2003. Banks are now not limited to being the agents for one insurance firm. In 2006, bank and postal agents collectively did CNY 113 billion of new life and health business, representing 53% of total new business", the report said. "Mature markets like Australia, Hong Kong and Singapore will continue to see banks taking a more aggressive stance to sell insurance in order to supplement their fee-based income. Surveys show consumers are more open to the idea of buying insurance from banks in most markets. Banks are finely segmenting their client base to push different insurance products", the Swiss Re report said.

However, banking and insurance operations in India and China are yet to converge as in continental Europe. "Banks in India and China sell insurance mainly on a contractual basis", Swiss Re observed. A trend noticed in the second half of 2006 in China is that insurance sold through banks experienced a negative growth largely due to a shifting in focus to fund business owing to the stock market rally. Industry sources said it would take sometime to see whether such a trend is seen in India. According to the report, while in bancassurance has been gaining popularity, it has also faced obstacles. Regulators are concerned that liberalisation will exacerbate market polarisation, for example, where large banks partner with only large insurers. At the same time, there are fears about upsetting existing channels, the time needed to train bank staff and mis-selling. The stakes are getting big in bancassurance. However, there are issues that need to be sorted by the regulator.

In the year 2008, banks ended up making profits of over 1,500 crore through the mundane job of selling life insurance. With commissions going over 35% of the first-year premium, perhaps no other business generates as high a margin as selling life insurance. Banks have come a long way since 2002 when they were first allowed to sell insurance products. Over the years, stakes have got very big in insurance distribution. With the law of diminishing returns kicking in as far as insurance agents are concerned, insurance companies are simultaneously looking at alternate channels — particularly bancassurance. Earlier, Aviva Life Insurance made an offer to HDFC Bank to get the second-largest private bank to sell its insurance policies. According to sources, Aviva promised HDFC Bank a better deal than what it is earning. The bank, however, turned down the offer as it expected to make similar money from selling insurance for its group company HDFC Standard Life. While no deal took place, the offer itself was seen by the industry as an indication of the kind of big money that is to be made out of selling life insurance.

In the game of distribution so far, there has been no relationship between the size of the distribution network and success in selling. State-owned banks, which account for over 90% of bank branches in the country, generate less than 10% of the bancassurance premium. The most successful distributors of insurance have been private and foreign banks that already have built an expertise in selling third-party products such as bonds and mutual funds. Most successful sellers of insurance are — ICICI Bank, HDFC Bank, Citibank. Standard Chartered, and ABN-Amro. Among state-owned banks, State Bank of India is gradually picking up sales of its insurance arm SBI Life. Union Bank too has had a focused approach to selling life insurance and is one of the largest insurance sellers among nationalised banks. But things will probably change with public sector banks as well. With most banks having routine banking jobs such as balancing the books to a core banking system (CBS), the front office has been freed for selling retail products including third-party products. Since margins in selling insurance are above 35% in the first year, banks will not mind if customers move money out of their savings or fixed deposits into insurance plans. Given the changes that are taking place in the banking and insurance industry, bancassurance throws up several new challenges for regulators and policymakers.

With so much money involved, there is a risk of predatory selling, considering that banks are able to exert undue influence. Although banks claim that it is the customer who makes the choice of product, there is anecdotal evidence to show that most policies sold by banks are those generating high commissions. In unit-linked insurance plans, it is almost impossible for a buyer to ascertain commissions or other charges applied in the first year. Given the negative impact high first-year commissions have on long-term yield, customers should be made aware of the level of insurance commission that is being paid out of the policy to ascertain whether the agent is pushing a high commission product.

Secondly, even in banks, it is only insurance-qualified employees who have passed that qualifying examination who are allowed to sell life insurance. But there is no way the prospect can ascertain whether the agent is indeed qualified. IRDA should provide a facility on its website to enable prospects check whether they are dealing with qualified salespersons.

Thirdly, the decision by banks to switch insurers or float their own companies have shown how fickle bancassurance relationships really are. Close to half a dozen state-owned banks have stopped selling products of life insurers after deciding to get into the business on their own.

In the private sector too there have been switches. Such switches tend to leave millions of 'orphaned' policies where there are no active agents to service existing clients. Since banks fall outside the purview of the insurance regulator, the onus has to be upon the insurance company to provide uninterrupted service to customers. The mutual fund experience has shown that a multi-party distribution experiment pushes up commissions. Yet a single party arrangement inhibits customer choice. The regulator could look at a middle path and certify products that are eligible for multi-bank distributions. For instance, single-premium investment plans and term-insurance plans where the pricing can be compared across a table should be introduced. Some of these issues have already been raised by the committee looking into the role of insurance intermediaries. The insurance regulator needs to take a decision on the report soon. Both insurers and banks have until now seen only the good times. Last year, the Sensex crossed the 16,000 level in mid-September and stayed there till March 7. All those who put money into equity ULIP schemes would have seen their principal amount shrink because of the crash in the market. If customers have not been explained the downside of unit-linked insurance plans, there could be a backlash and agents may find the onus upon them to explain that policies have not been mis-sold.

GROWING BIG

In India, bancassurance is expected to account for 13% and 5% of life and non-life insurance business respectively in five years (i.e., up to 2013).

The dynamics will change when banks are allowed to be corporate agents for more than one insurance company.

9.5 BILL DISCOUNTING

Bill discounting and bill purchasing are one of the modes of lending by banks. As compared to other modes of financing, bill discounting offers an easy mode of financing for a *short-term period* with early shiftable assets from the banker's point of view. Bill discounting has many advantages, *viz.,*

(*i*) The advance is self-liquidating in nature and gets adjusted automatically on payment of the bill. A three months usance bill discounted by bank will be adjusted on payment of bill (Hundi) on due date and as such will be adjusted automatically on payment.

(*ii*) Advances against documents is a *secured one.* The endorsement of the Hundi (bill) in favour of the bank, amounts to pledge of the goods to the bank. Further as a holder for value, the banker is in a position to proceed against the acceptor and the drawer of the bill, in case of dishonour.

(*iii*) Bill discounting is a short-term lending by banker. In cases of shortage of liquidity to bank, the bills could be rediscounted (in case of usance bills) with Discount and Finance House of India Ltd., (DFHI).

(*iv*) In finance against bills, the interest and commission is normally recovered in advances, at the time of discounting from the drawer of the bill, (in between 16 to 18% p.a. interest rate) hence it gives better yield as compared to other credits.

(*v*) It is easy to verify the end-use of credit which may be difficult in other forms of credit.

(*vi*) There is definite date of repayment.

(*vii*) Bills represent an easily shiftable assets.

(*viii*) The financing changes with the change of user of finance. If bill is drawn by corporate (of an industry) to wholeseller, it is an advance to that industry or are classified as industrial advances and if the same is drawn by wholeseller to retailer, it is an advance for trading purposes.

Categories of Bill Finance: Basically, a bank offers following categories of bill finance to a customer.

Bills Purchased: When the bank negotiates bills payable on demand whether *clean or documentary* (bill accompanied by documents of title are called documentary bills — while clean bills is when it is not accompanied by any document of title), the facility is known as *Bills Purchased.* The face value of the bill is immediately paid to the holder of the instrument/bill. The bank after purchasing the bill becomes the *holder in due course* of the bill and acquires all the rights of ownership over the instrument. Bills purchased facility is extended only in case of bills/instruments payable on demand.

Bills Discounting: This facility is extended by banker when the bills of exchange are payable after a particular period (usance) that is bills payable otherwise then on demand, or usance bill. In this facility a banker pays the face value of the bill *less discount* charges and becomes *holder in due course* and acquires all the rights under the bill.

❖ Various Negotiable Instruments

Promissory notes, bills of exchange and cheques are the most widely-used negotiable instruments. They are instruments in writing containing either an unconditional undertaking or order to pay a certain sum of money on demand or at a fixed future time to the order or a named person or to bearer.

- A *'promissory note'* is an instrument in writing (not being a bank note or a currency note) containing an unconditional undertaking, signed by the maker, to pay a certain sum or money only to, or to the order of a certain person, or to the bearer of the instrument.
- A *'bill of exchange'* is an instrument in writing containing an unconditional order, signed by the maker, directing a certain person to pay a certain sum of money only to, or to the order of, a certain person or to the bearer or the instrument.

- A *'cheque'* is a bill of exchange drawn on a specified banker and not expressed to be payable otherwise than on demand.

❖ Salient Features of Promissory Note, Bill of Exchange and Cheques

1. **Instruments in Writing:** Thus, promissory note as well as a bill of exchange should be in writing. It may be hand written, typed, printed or even engraved. There is no legal objection to the instrument being written in pencil but in practice it may be discouraged due to risk or alteration involved. It is necessary that the instrument should be signed by the maker. The maker or a bill of exchange or cheque is known as the drawer. It is not necessary that the entire instrument should be in the handwriting of the maker. It is enough if it bears his signature.

2. **Unconditional Promise/Order:** While a promissory note must contain an unconditional undertaking/promise by the maker to pay to his creditor, a Bill of Exchange must contain an unconditional order by the drawer (creditor) to pay to the drawee (debtor). The promise/order must be unconditional and the payment should not be made dependent upon the happening or occurrence of a particular event or on the fulfilment of any condition. But if the time for payment of the amount is expressed to be on the lapse of a certain period after the occurrence of a specified event, the promise or order to pay is not deemed 'conditional' provided the event is certain to happen according to ordinary expectation of mankind, although the time of happening may be uncertain.

The banker may refuse to honour a cheque having conditional order of the drawer. The drawer of the cheque may, however, cross the cheque and thereby instruct the banker the manner in which and the intermediary through which the payment is to be made. Such instructions do not make the order of the drawer a conditional one.

3. **Payment of Money:** The undertaking or order to pay should be to pay a certain sum of money and not anything else. The amount of the instrument must be certain. It should not be subject to any contingent or indefinite additions or deductions. The sum payable may be 'certain' although (*i*) it includes future interest, or (*ii*) it is payable at an indicated rate of exchange, or (*iii*) the instrument provides that on default of payment of an instalment, the balance unpaid shall become due.

4. **Time of Payment:** The time of payment of a promissory note or a Bill of Exchange must be certain. It should be payable on demand or at a fixed or determinable future time. It is payable on demand, i.e., immediately, if it is expressed to be payable on demand, or at sight, or on presentation, or if no time for payment is specified.

A bill or note payable after a specified period or on a future date is generally known as a "usance" bill or note. Such a bill or note attracts stamp duty depending upon its value, the usance and the purpose for which it is executed. If a bill is payable after a certain period it must be accepted by a drawee.

A cheque is always payable on demand, though words to this effect are not mentioned therein. If a cheque is a post-dated cheque, it does not constitute an order to the banker till the date specified therein approaches. Banks do not make payment of such cheques before the date given, in the cheque.

5. **The Payee:** The person to whom or to whose order money is undertaken or ordered to be paid in a promissory note or bill of exchange is called the payee. The payee must be a certain person. A promissory note or Bill of Exchange may be made payable to a named payee or to his

order, or to the bearer of the instrument. Where the instrument is not payable to the bearer, it should name or indicate a payee with reasonable certainty and he should be capable of being ascertained from the instrument itself.

A negotiable instrument may be made payable to two or more persons jointly or it may be made payable in the alternative to one of two or one of some of several payees. A promissory note or bill of exchange is payable to order if it is expressed to be so payable to a particular person and does not contain words prohibiting transfer or indicating an intention that it shall not be transferable. Such instruments can be transferred by endorsement and delivery.

An instrument is payable to the bearer if it is expressed to be so payable or if the only or the last endorsement is an endorsement in blank. Such instruments can be transferred by delivery of the instrument.

6. **Signature of the Drawer/Promisor:** A negotiable instrument is valid only if it bears the signatures of the drawer/promisor. In case of a cheque the signature of the drawer must tally with the specimen signature given to the banker at the time of opening of account.

7. **Delivery of the Instrument is Essential:** A negotiable instrument is deemed to have been drawn, when it is written by the person concerned and delivered to the other party to whom it is meant. The making, acceptance or endorsement of a negotiable instrument is completed by delivery. Delivery may be either actual or constructive.

8. Stamping of the instrument as per Stamp Act in force is also necessary as a note or bill without proper stamping cannot be admitted in evidence.

❖ Legal Relationship

The banker becomes a lawful holder of the bill, by taking a proper endorsement of bill in bank's favour. The bank becomes *payee* of the bill and is entitled to recover the amount represented by the bill. Let us see one important legal case reported in All India Reporter 1971 as under:

Shambumal Gangaram and another
vs.
State Bank of Mysore AIR, 1971 Mys. 156

This case was a legal action by bank for the recovery of the dues on the Local Bill Discounted account of a customer. The bank was providing bill discounting facilities by discounting the bills drawn on customer and endorsed by the customer is its favour. The amounts of bill were generally paid by the makers of the bills. However, several bills remained unpaid and bank filed a suit for recovery from the customer. The customer contended that bank should have filed suit against the makers of bill of exchange. The court rejected the argument of customer and directed him to pay the amount to bank holding that customer being endorsee, is liable to bank, who are holders in due course. Documentary bill being accompanied by a document of title to goods, *viz.*, Approved Transport Motor Receipt/railway receipt/warehouse receipt/bill of lading, etc.

❖ Guidelines for Finance Against Trade Bills

1. The bill must be signed by an authorised person of the firm/corporate/proprietor, enjoying the limit and should be drawn in favour of the start endorsed in favour of the bank.
2. The bill must comply with various terms of sanction and should invariably contain, the invoices. The amount in the bill and invoice should agree. Bill should accompany RR/

MTR/BL, etc., as per the terms, be drawn in favour of the bank. Documents should not be sent to consignees.

3. Before sanction of bills limit, credit report both on the customer (drawer) and the drawees on whom the bills are likely to be drawn should be taken and the financial creditworthiness of the parties should be ascertained.
4. The drawer and the drawees of this bills must be dealing in the same goods for which the bills are drawn.
5. Bills should be properly drawn and if it is an usance bill should be adequately and validly stamped.
6. Clean bills or document against acceptance bills should not be accepted under demand bills without prior sanction.
7. All bills should not be drawn on one centre and goods consigned to another centre.
8. If the bill is accepted by the drawee, it should be authenticated by the acceptor's bank or save documentary evidences should be there to confirm the signature.
9. Motor transport receipt should only be from the approved transporters' companies of IBA.
10. The bill should represent genuine transactions and movement of goods.
11. The goods should be covered by transit-insurance against fire/theft/civic commotions/ riots/floods and other risks.
12. When documents of title to goods is RR, the lien of the bank should be notified to railway station master of destination station, and proper follow-up has to be done to see that the goods are cleared within 7 days in non-notified centres as otherwise. Under Section 77(2) of Indian Railways Act, railways would not be responsible for the goods and these can be sold by public auction to recover their costs and penalties.
13. Bank should accept the *consignee copy* of the Motor Transport Receipt of title of goods of the latest date (not old date, i.e., order by 5 days or more).
14. Margin on bills may be maintained depending upon the bank's assessment of drawer and drawee of the bills and also on the basis of nature of the goods covered by the bill.
15. Bank should verify the correctness of sale price to confirm that there is *no-over-invoicing* of the amount of the bill with a view to draw excess credit from the banker.
16. The bank should also verify that the bill is not an *accommodation bill* (kite flying) whether thé drawee is not one of the raw material suppliers to the drawer.
17. The documents attached to the bill must be consistent with each other.
18. Due date register must be maintained and in case the bill remained *unpaid* on the due date, steps should be taken to recover the advance.
19. When the bill is not paid on due date, the bill should be recalled from the drawee end and the amount should be got reimbursed by debiting the drawer's account. If there is no sufficient balance/drawing power available either in the current account or the borrowal's cash credit overdraft account (as the case may be) the bill along with bank's charges/ overdue interest thereon, should be debited to a separate account under Bills Returns Unpaid Account. An advice regarding return of the bill and calling upon the drawer to

make goods the payment should be sent immediately by speed post/registered post and not by personal delivery by peon of the bank unless the authorised signatory is receiving the notice. In *no case*, the returned bill should be debited to an account where the balance is full to the limit/drawing power, as he bank would otherwise, lose lien/charge on the goods covered by the bill.

20. When the returned bill is a foreign bill, it is required to be noted and protested by a Notary Public (an advocate authorised by State Government to do such job) for its return either due to non-acceptance or *non-payment*. After getting the bill noted, it should be also got protested while in case of inland bills. Noting and protesting are not compulsory.

9.6 PRICING FINANCIAL SERVICES

Service costing and pricing is a host of comprehensive management tools that augment strategic planning to achieve the desired level of goal in any financial institution. These equip the management with the information they need about services costs and adopt suitable planning to deploy the available resources in an orderly way. **Pricing is a post costing phenomenon** where every financial institution's goal should be cost minimisation and price maximisation.

Pricing of services has a crucial rates. Preoccupied with quantum growth and overall returns, the pricing of services has not been consciously worked out in the Indian financial industry. The pricing has been done mainly based on what opponents decide and the *historical adhocism approach* oblivious of the cost considerations. In the present context of a perfect competitive environment pricing has become all the more important to protect and maximise profits. *Pricing is a powerful tool for enhancing competitionness, bench-marking and increase shareholders' value.*

9.6.1 Pricing Objectives/Common Misconceptions

Pricing of any service can be determined on the basis of —

(*a*) Full cost based pricing

(*b*) Contribution margin based pricing.

Pricing means exchange value of any service in terms of money. Pricing does include not only the cost of the product but also a portion of profit. The above two methods are for pricing any product/service. The full cost based pricing is also known as cost plus profit pricing. This pricing is based on the assumption that for the sustain growth of the production unit/service unit the recovery of cost and reasonable amount of profit is essential.

While the other method of contribution margin does away with the allocation of fixed cost (which is one of the contributions in the full cost method). The reasoning in this method is that the costs relevant to pricing are only those costs which would not have been incurred but for the output being priced. The cost being the incremental cost; it is rather complementary in nature. This pricing method is suitable in certain situations:

(*a*) Increasing profit by increasing volume of business.

(*b*) Sustaining competition in the market.

(*c*) Identifying the most profitable service out of various products/services.

(*d*) Improving sales-mix.

(*e*) For executing one-time orders

(*f*) To decide distress pricing.

Profit-caring is a function of setting any service. The cost volume profit relationship is a tool to show the relationship between cost permit, volume, sales mix, selling product, variable and fixed cost, in profit planning. This method is used in break even point. BEP means a point where the cost and selling price is equal, i.e., where there is no profit or loss. Below this point, there would be losses and if production is more than the BEP then there are chances of profits are there. BEP can also be defined as a point at which total revenues are exactly equal to total costs.

It is being expressed through an example:

Output in thousands	*5*	*10*	*15*	*20*	*25*
Fixed costs	₹ 2,000	₹ 2,000	₹ 2,000	₹ 2,000	₹ 2,000
Variable cost per unit/20 paise	₹ 1,000	₹ 2,000	₹ 3,000	₹ 4,000	₹ 5,000
Sales at 40 paise per unit	₹ 2,000	₹ 4,000	₹ 6000	₹ 8,000	₹ 10,000

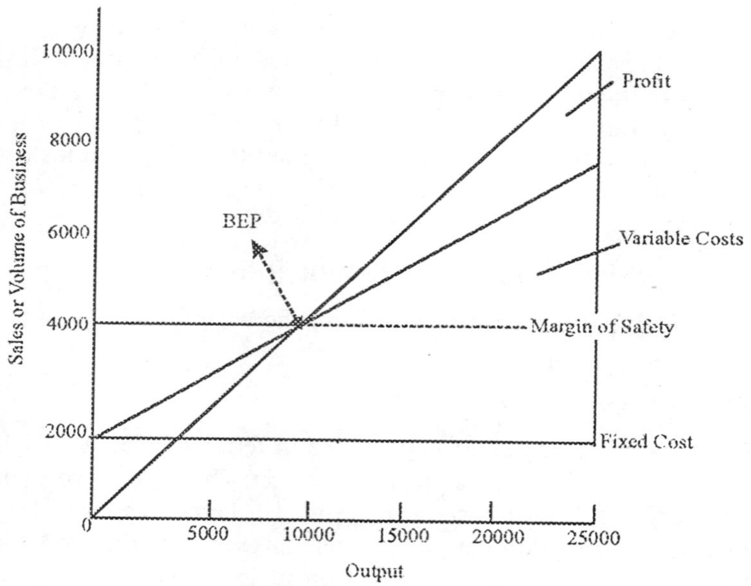

9.6.2 Break Even Point

In actual practice, the BFP chart is quite unlikely to look like straight-line graphs. One of the most frequent mistakes made with regard to break even charts is to suppose that as output rises, a proportional increase in sales revenue can be achieved and moreover, that this can be done with no changes per unit in variable costs or in total fixed costs. The BFP can be as under:

If the same is represented in algebraic way the calculation would be as IFCI Ltd., is incurring a loss of ₹ 40,000 in a month and necessary figures are as follows: Volume of business ₹ 1,20,000, variable cost ₹ 60,000, fixed cost ₹ 1,00,000. Discuss, what would be the sales value to BEP if

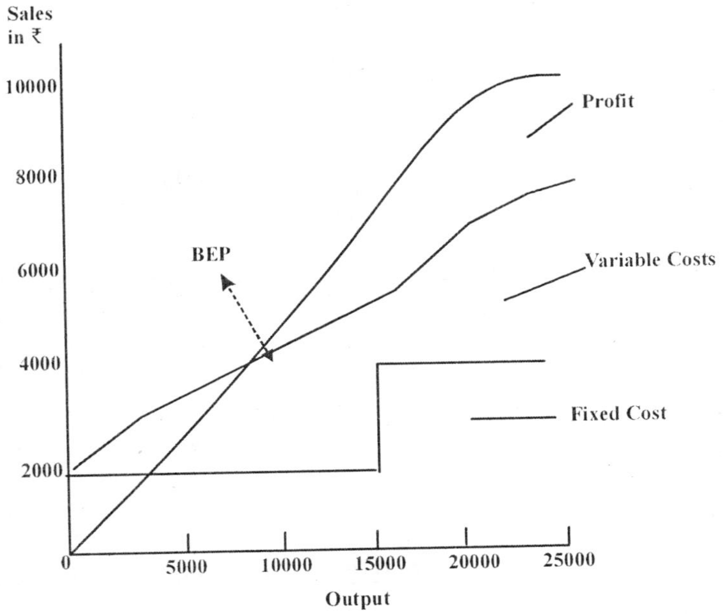

(*i*) the present sales level is maintained and selling price is increased.

(*ii*) the present selling price is maintained and the sales volume is increased.

Solution:

$$BFP = \frac{\text{Fixed Cost}}{\text{P / V ratio}} = \frac{\text{FC}}{\text{Variabe Cost / Sales}} = \frac{\text{FC}}{\text{(Selling Price — Variable Price)}}$$

$$= \frac{₹\,1,00,000 \times 1,20,000}{60,000}$$

$$= ₹\ 2,00,000$$

At sales volume of ₹ 2 lakh total fixed cost be recovered and there would be no loss, irrespective of whether sales price is increased or sales volume is increased.

Example 2:

	Actuals	*Projections*
Sales in units	10,000	20,000
Profit or loss	₹ 10,000 loss	₹ 10,000 Profit
Fixed costs	₹ 30,000	₹ 30,000
Variable cost per unit	₹ 8	₹ 8

Determine:

What increased sales volume is required at the present sale price, to yield zero profit, (to cover extra cost of packing ₹ 0.50 per cent).

Total sales revenue = Total costs – Loss

Total costs = FC + (VC × Sales per unit)

= 30,000 (8 × 10,000)

Total sales revenue = 1,10,000 – 10,000 = ₹ 1,00,000

Hence, selling price per unit $= \dfrac{\text{Sales Revenue}}{\text{Total Units Sales}} = \dfrac{1,00,000}{10,000} = ₹\ 10$

Zero Profit or BEP $= \dfrac{\text{FC}}{\text{SP} - \text{VC} - \text{Extra cost}} = \dfrac{30,000}{10 - 8 - 0.50} = \dfrac{30,000}{1.50} = 20,000 \text{ units}$

Example 3:

Calculate *BEP*

Fixed cost ₹ 1,80,000

Variable cost ₹ 2 per unit

Selling Price ₹ 20

If the company is earning a profit of ₹ 36,000 express the margin of safety.

Solution:

$$\text{BEP (Volume)} = \frac{\text{FC} \times \text{Selling Price}}{(\text{Selling Price} - \text{Variable Cost})} = \frac{1,80,000 \times 20}{(20-2)}$$

$$\text{P/V Ratio} = \frac{S - V}{S}$$

$$= \frac{1,80,000 \times 20}{18} = ₹\ 2,00,000$$

Ratio between fixed cost to selling price is 90%

Hence, to earn a profit of ₹ 36,000.

$$\frac{\text{FC} + \text{Profit}}{\text{Ratio of fixed cost to S.P.}} = \frac{1,80,000 + 36,000}{90\%} = ₹\ 2,40,000$$

Hence, Margin of safety is

₹ 2,40,000 – ₹ 2,00,000 = ₹ 40,000

being the additional amount over **fixed cost.**

Other Equations:

S – V = FC + Profit

$$S = \frac{\text{FC} + \text{Profit}}{\text{P/V}}$$

$$P/V = \frac{S-V}{S}$$

$$V = S - FC - Profit$$

Example 5:

Madhya Pradesh Financial Corporation Ltd., has been trying to decide what price to charge for a new service the corporation is introducing this year. The corporation with the help of market research conducted by the staff indicates the following price-volume relationship.

Price (Fee (₹)	*Processing Amount*
1,450	50,000
1,400	55,000
1,350	60,000
1,300	63,000
1,250	70,000

The variable cost is ₹ 600 and the total annual fixed costs are estimated at ₹ 2 lakh. The corporation believes that any product should be priced at 150% of the total cost. He decides to use ₹ 50,000 processing amount as the volume to determine the average unit cost and computes the cost at ₹ 1,000 per process (₹ 600 + 400 (₹ 2,00,000 ÷ 50,000). The corporation intends to set the price at ₹ 1,500. How far do you agree with the views of the corporation?

PRICING DECISION

Price	*Units*	*MC (S–V)*	*Total MC*	*Revenue (MC – FC)*
1,450	50,000	850	4,25,000	2,25,000
1,400	55,000	800	4,40,000	2,40,000
1,350	60,000	750	4,50,000	2,50,000
1,300	63,000	700	4,41,000	2,41,000
1,250	70,000	650	4,55,000	2,55,000

At price ₹ 1,250 the highest yield is there. Therefore, view of the corporation is setting the price at ₹ 1,500 is not agreeable. The corporation's mistake is to try to compute the average fixed cost per unit ₹ 1,000 is valid up to 50,000 amount volume and not beyond it. The corporation has not taken into consideration price volume relationship properly.

9.6.3 Pricing Factors

There are 4 pricing factors which are collectively called 4Cs of pricing.

Costs: Means variable and fixed costs associated with services. Variable costs tend to be relatively small compared to fixed cost in financial institutions. The higher the risk; higher the price needed to cover the costs. Due to staff competition in financial institutions are find it increasingly difficult to price their services on a *cost plus basis* as hitherto. In the present scenario, most of the customers do not mind paying a little extra, if they are getting services suiting to their preferences. In other words they prefer customised services.

Competition: Financial institutions use competitor's price as *benchmark*. Three options are available. Their price can be higher than their competitor's (premium pricing) lower than competitor (penetration pricing) or at par with the competitors (parity pricing). Highly differential services tend to be premium price. In markets, where customers are price-sensitive, financial institutions with lower cost structures may become successful with *participation pricing*. In others, where price competition is injurious, financial institutions are better off maintaining price parity and competing on other factors. Unless the pricing is competitive, it can make or break the success of the product. Customers' perception determines the price he/she is willing to pay for the services and *not actual value* that matters. Obviously, the financial institution benefits, if they are able to convince the customers that the value of their services is extremely high. Financial institutions can consider value pricing based on the value analysis of service offered by competitors.

Constraints of regulations and directives of RBI and Central Government due to which the pricing of services is beyond the control of individual banks. The financial institution has to take the price as given and work backwards to cut down its operating cost, in order to make profits. Financial institutions come to know the impact of *pricing* on a *service* only after a certain gestation period and understanding the elasticity of pricing. Fine tuning at the right time can serve the service to regain its balance and march towards success.

Service Cost: In simples accounting terms, service costing is the process of arriving at the total expenditure incurred for production of an output. The first step in measuring the relative services productivity is to break.

Each service to the smallest and most meaningful level. For example, mutual fund service needs to be broken down into several sub-segments. In the next step each service is strategised by its size. Although this process sounds tedious, many opportunities will be missed without such a detailed break down. The profitability of most services is heavily dependent on the turnover. In most of the financial institutions, the high turnover customers usually subsidize the low turnover customers. If the financial institutions fail to differentiate among its customers based on profitability or non-financial competitors and small institutions will continue to take its best customers.

Evaluating the relative profitability of each major services, is the first step in developing the right strategies to increase a financial institution's profitability and in enhancing its financial management process. There is significant difference between the general market financial services in terms of its visibility and marketability. So far, financial market is concerned, financial institutions are confined to a limited section in the society unlike other services which have a wider area. As financial services are much more complex, the costing approach in financial services is different. Financial institutions must evaluate their operating complexity, capacity considerations and the nature of competition before deciding which costing system to use. They should also make sure to adopt a system that reckon all useful information within their decision models. For example, in relation to operation complexity, a financial institution that produces one service would not need to use a complex cost system since all the overheads are incurred to support that one service, whereas when they produce multiple services they would have more complicated cost system decisions to make regarding the need for variable or *full cost* information and which costing system to use to determine this information. So far financial services are concerned, costing should include all cost objects, (e.g., process/service/customer, etc.), with the following targets:

(*a*) Providing a sound fundamental cost accounting framework.

(*b*) Improving the understanding of the organisational structure and behaviour by services/ business process and business activities.

(*c*) Highlighting opportunities to reduce/avoid costs.

(*d*) Improving cost planning and simulation capabilities.

(*e*) Supporting the cost management information needs of financial and non-financial functions including product design, engineering, purchasing and marketing, etc.

(*f*) Better utilization of administrative resources.

(*g*) Improving performance reporting.

(*h*) Increase the timeliness/efficiency/reliability and accessibility of financial information.

9.6.4 Steps Involved for Pricing

(*i*) Measure, how individual services and being used.

(*ii*) Measure, internal economies of each service.

(*iii*) Measure, costs of providing services and their profitability.

(*v*) Measure, the value of product and service portfolios.

(*vi*) Measure, value internally and to the market.

(*vii*) Measure, value of each customer *relationship*.

(*viii*) Calculate service taxes.

(*ix*) Segment of customer base, evaluation of customer dealings earlier.

(*x*) Formulate customer friendly services.

(*xi*) Ascertain service details of other financial control systems.

Pricing is a decision, market driven by a number of factors (both internal and external) in a financial institution. Asset-liability composition effects the pricing. Effective management of assets and liability management enables the financial institutions in deploying its funds in a productive way to avoid keeping funds idle.

Pricing Policy: The pricing policy of a financial institution is a written document that contains the pricing details of its services. The pricing policy is based on many variables that require experience and judgement to evaluate services effectively. A financial institution's pricing policy should cover the following key areas —

- Service fees which could be charged.
- Volume of turnover and their share in profits.
- Credit availability and compensating advance amounts available.
- Customer relationship pricing.
- Promotional pricing of new services.
- Other marketing elements such as service differentiation.

9.6.5 Deposit Pricing and Bank's Profitability

The pricing models in banks are of two types, *viz.*, Implicit and Explicit.

Implicitly Pricing — involves bundling together products and services and providing them at *lowers than market prices* as compensation for what cannot be provided explicitly. Examples of implicit pricing are:

- Below cost provisions of services (e.g., free checking).
- Added conveniences (opening branch offices/installing ATMs/extended business hours.
- Minimum balance requirements.
  (pensioners ₹ 20/other depositors in savings A/c ₹ 500 with cheque book facility ₹ 1,000 and so on).
- Restrictive (Limited cheque leaves issued as in case of savings A/c only 60 withdrawals in a year).

Explicit Pricing — relates to interest expenses where implicit pricing relates to non-interest expenses such as free checking and other services which are payments in kind. In deregulated economy banks are increasingly relying on explicit pricing and decreased use of implicit pricing. Examples of explicit pricing are:

- Interest payments
- Gifts like free mediclaim policy or accidental insurance of ₹ 5 lakh, etc.
- Service charges (cheque leaf charges)
- Fees (e.g., in overdrafts)

When the interest rates were at a *high* (as in the years, 2007, 2008 and 2011) banks emphasize explicit pricing over implicit pricing else they suffer disintermediation. When interest rates are *low* (as in the year 2003/2004/2005) the customers. were less sensitive (due to low opportunity costs) and as such cases implicit pricing becomes more important.

❖ Deposit Pricing Methods and Impact on Bank's Profitability

(a) Cost Revenue Analysis: The goal of bank management should be to *maximise* deposit revenues and *minimise* deposit costs so as to maximise bank's profitability. Cost revenue analysis is one way by which managers can better understand as to how deposit pricing decisions are affecting bank's profitability. The S-shape curve assumes economies of sale as deposits are expanded initially, which gradually reduce *cost per unit* deposits and causes the cost curve to increase at an increasing rate. Total bank costs equal to fixed costs and variable costs of deposits and other activities total bank revenues include deposit revenues, loan and security portfolio revenues and other revenues profit maximisation requires —

- Minimisation of total costs at each output level.
- Maximisation of total revenues at each output levels.
- Marginal total costs equal marginal total revenues.

(b) Marginal Costing Deposit Pricing: The added cost of bringing new funds is a better technique than the weighted average costs to help price deposits and other bank fund sources. The reason is that frequent changes in the interest rates will make average cost a *misleading* and unrealistic standard for pricing. For example, if the interest rates are *declining*, the marginal cost of raising new money may fall well below the average cost of all the funds raised by the bank. Some loans and investments that are unprofitable when compared to average cost will now look profitable when measured against the lower marginal interest cost, we must pay to day to make these new loans and investments. Conversely, if interest rates are *raising* (as in years 2007 and 2008), the marginal cost of today's new money may substantially exceed the bank's average cost of funds. And if the management grants new loans based on average cost, they may turnout to be highly unprofitable when measured against the higher marginal cost of raising new funds.

MC = Incremental cost = New deposits × Rate of interest + Rollover premium × Rate of interest.

Hence, MC is equal to 100 × incremental cost divided by incremental funds.

The following two general rules apply to marginal cost calculations in deposit accounts:

(*i*) When *raising rates,* the greater the proportion of non-rate sensitive money to new money, the higher the marginal cost of the new funds.

(*ii*) When dropping rates, the greater the percentage of funds that leave the lower marginal cost of the funds that left.

(c) Upscale Target Pricing: Upscale target pricing refers to the aggressive pricing of high balance and low activity deposits. Advertising programmes are organised to target established professionals/businessmen/managers and high income households with service fees that result in high profit margins. The upscale customers usually respond quickly to the deregulation is in progress and the prices would be falling with time.

(d) Promotional Pricing: This is used to introduce new products. The product is priced below its cost to attract customers. The potential reasons of promotional pricing are protecting market share/modifying existing products/developing brand recognition or overall bank image/ targeting particular market segments of the population.

(e) Relationship Pricing: The pricing is done according to the number of services used by the customers. Relationship banking is an expression that includes fulfilling long-term needs as opposed to immediate needs such as encashing a cheque. By deposit of substantial/selling multiple services, increases the dependence of the customer and makes it harder for him/her to switch over to other banks thereby making the relationship strong between the customer and the bank. It also promotes customer loyalty and makes the customer insensitive to the interest rates offered on deposits by competing financial institutions. The example is of Bank of Maharashtra's Mahabank Family Banking Card, which is issued to a depositor who has deposited a minimum of ₹ one lakh for 3 years in term deposits with the bank. The depositor gets following privileges —

- Free ATM card all adult family members having account with the bank.
- Bank's Master Credit Card to eligible members/add on card with *no charges.*
- Free remittance of funds from/to family members account by MT/DD.
- *No loan processing* charges for housing/consumer and educational loans.
- Concessions in rate of interest on housing/consumer and educational loan @ 1%.
- Special discounted rates for premiums of household insurance and Mediclaim policies from the Oriental Insurance Co. Ltd.
- Mahabank family overdraft facility of ₹ one lakh through card issuing branch to the nominated member.

◆ ◆ ◆

10 Treasury Management Services and Portfolio Management

10.1 CONCEPT

Traditionally, the role of the Treasury in Indian bank was limited to ensuring the maintenance of the RBI-stipulated norms for Cash Reserve Ratio (3% to 15%) presently it is 6% in 2011 which mandates that a minimum proportion of defined liabilities be kept as deposit with the Central Bank and Statutory Liquidity Ratio (SLR) (presently 24% and maximum 40% of the total demand and time liabilities). SLR obliges banks to invest a specified percentage of their liabilities in notified securities issued by the Government of India and State Governments or guaranteed by them. Activity in foreign exchange was confined to meeting merchants' and customers' requirements for *Imports, Exports* Remittances and deposits. Money Market hardly reflected the position of time liquidity in the system. RBI had initiated various measures to reform the money market and to develop the necessary institutional infrastructure and instruments needed to widen and deepen the money market. To start with Discount and Finance House of India (DFHI) was set up to provide to the market participants an institutional mechanism (in the form of a market-maker) to meet their liquidity requirements by dealing in *short-term money market instruments* like Treasury Bills/bills discounting/commercial paper/certificate of deposits, etc. To enable price discovery/cap on *Call Money* interest rate was removed in stages, and completely withdrawn in May 1989. NBFCs such as LIC/Mutual funds/financial institutions were over a period allowed to enter the call money market for *lending* only. While the reported misuse of Ready-Forward (Repos) transactions by some of the market participants had resulted in its partial ban for sometime, the instrument was subsequently *re*-introduced with necessary safeguards to prevent its misuse and an improved SGL transfer procedure facilitated its effective monitoring. The introduction of Delivery versus Payment (DVP) system for securities settlement at Public Debt Offices (PDO) substantially reduced the counterparty risk in security transfers and this also infused confidence in the introduction of *Repos* and expansion of the list of revocable securities. Repos is presently an important instrument in the money market. The present rate of Repo is 8.0% (w.e. from 26-07-2011).

Post-liberalisation/deregulation and financial market reforms, a vibrant *Bond market* has evolved in the country. This has enhanced the relative importance of investments and the investment portfolio in the balance sheets of banks. Investments are now viewed as an *alternative to credit*, the historical source of profits for banks. Further, being tradable assets, they offer both interest spread as well as capital appreciation. Just like equity prices and foreign exchange markets, interest rates (yields) on debt instruments are determined through the interplay of various economic/ financial (liquidity/inflation/government's/RBI's policies/growth/forex demand and supply/domestic interest rates *vis-a-vis* global, etc.), and political (local and international) factors and events. Given this, as in the case of equities and forex rates, bond yields can (and do) vary from moment-to-moment. The reflection of these changes in spot interest rates has seen the fluctuations in gilt-prices — as indeed those of all bonds, whether government or non-government.

Similarly, the rupees exchange rate with US dollar has become volatile. There is sufficient fluctuation both intra-day and inter-day prices enabling one to earn trading profits on buying and selling the currency. The forward market in India is another potential source of profits as, more often than not, it deviates from interest parity conditions. Cross-currency (US dollar/Yen, Pound Sterling/US dollar, US dollar/Indian rupees) trading opportunities are of course, older and have come to life in Indian banks after liberalisation. Downward and upward movements in *Gilt Yields* offer excellent scope and opportunities for the bank to trade in the underlying securities and earn profits such that trading in forex to take advantage of *currency* variations. An active treasury can *arbitrage* (earns profits without risk) by borrowing cheap (money market/forex market) and investing high in money in forex and bond markets. Bank treasuries deal with the customers enabling them to execute their transactions in financial markets. Apart from trade execution, in such situations, the bank is, in effect, lending its balance sheet so that counterparty-risk for both the customer and the deal counterparty is overcome.

Key and modern function of the treasury is Asset-liability management and hedging (i.e., insulating) the bank's balance sheet from interest and exchange rate fluctuations. This involves reordering the maturity and interest rate patterns of assets and liabilities either through direct portfolio actions or derivatives (e.g., *swaps* and *futures*) to minimise or eliminate the risks arising from mismatches between the two sides of the balance sheet.

❖ Sources of Profits of Treasury

The sources of profits of treasury are —

(*a*) *Investments:* where the bank earns a higher yield than its cost of funds. An example is buying a corporate bond yielding 8.37% and maturing in 3 years, financed by deposits costing only 7.5%.

(*b*) *Spreads* — between yields on money market assets and money market funding. The bank may, for instance, borrow short-term for 6% and deploy in commercial paper with returns of 7.5%.

(*c*) *Arbitrage:* is a buy/sell swap in the forex market, where the bank converts its rupee funds into a dollar deposit, earns *Libor* and gets back rupee on deposit maturity (*Libor* rate on 30-11-2007 was 5.34% current). This generates risk-free profit (arbitrage) if *Libor* plus the forward premium on dollar/rupee is more than the domestic interest rate.

(*d*) *Relative Value:* This is a form of arbitrage in which the bank exploits anomalies in market prices. The bank may have an AAA bond, which yields only 8% compared to another with the same rating and maturity, but of a different issuer which offers 8.5%. It is worthwhile to sell the first bond and invest in the second and improve the yield by 50 bps (basic points) without any incremental risk, as both bonds have the same credit quality.

(*e*) *Proprietary Trading:* The focus here is on short-term investments. The aim is to earn trading profits from movements in security and forex prices during a day or a few days of trading. These are mostly directional trades. Under this a dealer may buy 9.81% Government of India Securities 2013 at ₹ 116.56 at a yield of 8.40% in anticipation of the yield falling to 7.70% on fundamental or technical grounds. If this happens, the bond appreciates and the bank exists the position with a profit.

(*f*) *Customer Services:* Bank treasuries offer their products and services to customers/non-banking customers. The income of banks from these activities comprises fees for and/or margins on trade executions. Profits would be higher on structured (i.e., non-standard) transactions compared to plain vanilla (e.g., a straightforward buy/sell USD/INR) deals.

Treasuries are also involved in investment banking where their responsibility covers trade execution on behalf of the bank's clients in the cash or derivatives markets. (Institute of Chartered Accountants of India has framed the guidelines for Derivative Accounting, to be implemented by SEBI and RBI. It is called AS-30 and are recommendatory in nature from 1-4-2009 and compulsory from 1-4-2011. However, from 31st March, 2008, ICAI made it mandatory for corporates to provide for all *losses* in their forex derivatives to mark to market). These may generate good margins, depending on the complexity and skills required to design and put through customised structures in the market.

10.2 TREASURY ASSETS

Scope: Bank's balance sheet consists of treasury assets and liabilities on the one hand and non-treasury assets and liabilities on the other. There is a clear distinction between the two groups. Treasury assets are *marketable* or *tradable* subject to meeting legal obligations such as payment of stamp duty, etc. Another characteristics of treasury assets is that they can be *marked to market*. The only non-tradable treasury asset/liability is Inter-bank Participation certificate.

The various *treasury assets* are —

- Government Securities (Treasury Bills/State Govt. Securities)
- Commercial Paper
- Certificates of Deposits
- SLR Bonds
- Non-SLR Bonds
- Participation Certificates
- Equity Shares

While the treasury liabilities are —

- Call/notice/term money
- Certificates of Deposits
- Tier-II Capital Bonds (if issued by bank)

10.3 BANK'S TREASURY PRODUCTS

❖ Domestic Treasury Assets

1. Call/notice money lending.
2. Term money lending/inter-banks deposits
3. Certificates of Deposits - investments
4. Commercial Paper
5. Inter-bank participation certificates.
6. Derivative usance Promissory Notes/banks or corporates acceptances.
7. Reverse Repos/CBLO-backed lending through CCIL.
8. SLR Bonds — issued and guaranteed by Central/State Governments and notified by the RBI.
9. *Non-SLR Bonds:* Issued by financial institutions/banks/NBFCs (tier II capital) corporates/ State level enterprises/infrastructure projects.
10. Asset-backed securities (PTCS) of ARCIL
11. Private Placement
12. Floating Rate Bonds
13. Tax free bonds
14. Preference shares
15. Listed/Unlisted equity
16. Mutual funds
17. Treasury Bills/Bonds of State Government

❖ Liabilities Instruments

(*i*) Call/notice money borrowing
(*ii*) Term money borrowing
(*iii*) Certificates of Deposits issues
(*iv*) Inter-bank participation certificates
(*v*) Repos/CBLO-backed borrowing through CCIL
(*vi*) Refinance (RBI/SIDBI/NABARD/EXIM Bank/NHB)
(*vii*) Tier II bonds issued by banks.

❖ List of Foreign Treasury Products

(*a*) *Inter-bank:*

- Spot currencies
- Cash
- TOM

- Forward and Forward-Forward (Simultaneous purchase and sale of a currency for two different forward maturities)
- Foreign currency Placements/Investments and borrowings.

(*b*) *Merchant* (Initiated in branches):

- Pre-shipment foreign credit (PCFC)
- Foreign Currency Bills Purchased (FCBP)
- Foreign Currency Loans (FCLs)/FCNR (B) Loans
- Post-shipment Foreign Credit (PDFC)
- External Commercial borrowing (ECB)

(*c*) *Derivatives:*

- Interest Rate Swaps (IRSs)
- Forward Rate Agreements (FRAs)
- Interest Rate Futures
- Interest Rate Options
- Currency Options

(*d*) Corporates investments in subsidiaries and joint ventures are considered treasury assets. *Although* they are not traded and are permanent in nature.

10.4 FUNCTIONS OF TREASURY MANAGEMENT

Treasury operations of a commercial bank consist mainly of two vital functions, *viz.*,

(*a*) Ensuring strict compliance with the statutory requirements of maintaining the CRR and SLR, and

(*b*) Liquidity arrangement by: (*i*) ensuring the optimum utilisation of the residual resources through investments (*ii*) raising additional resources required for meeting credit demands at optimal cost, and (*iii*) managing market and liquidity risks in the transactions.

With financial market reforms, banks have been compelled to look for avenues for alternatives to credit (loans), the historical source of profits. It has been realised that credit function alone is not sufficient and banks should look to investments for earning market related returns on funds. Investments have thus gained importance as an equally important part of the banks' balance sheets. Therefore, over and above the SLR a substantial portion of banks resources are deployed in government/corporate bonds and other products as an alternative to credit or advances. The treasury operations also include providing of cover to the customers or the bank in respect of their foreign exchange exposure for their trade transactions like *export/imports/remittances,* etc. and extending products and services to its customers for hedging the interest rate risks. While doing so, the treasury also takes care of the associated functions like liquidity management and asset-liability management of the domestic as well as foreign exchange resources and deployment.

❖ Basic Treasury Functions

❖ Domestic Operations

- Maintenance of SLRs
- Managing Liquidity
- Profitability deployment of reserves
- Trading and arbitrage
- Hedging and cover operations
- Mid/back office functions

  (treasury functions are segregated as

  Front-office — Dealing — Risk-taking

  Mid-office — Risk management and MIS

  Back-office — Confirmations/Settlements/Accounting and reconciliation/statutory reports to RBI/management of *Nostro* funds/monitoring receipts of forex funds in inter-bank contracts)

❖ Forex Operations

- Extending cover to foreign exchange and trade transactions.
- Funding and managing forex assets and liabilities.
- Providing hedge to forex risks proprietary and for its constituents.
- Trading and arbitrage.
- Mid/back-office functions.

10.5 RESPONSIBILITIES OF TREASURY MANAGEMENT

Treasury management performs a myriad or functions such as balance sheet management/liquidity management/reserves management/funds management/investments/managing capital adequacy/transfer pricing/technology and operations/risks management/trading activities and offering hedge products. It has to work on arriving at an optimal size of the balance sheet/interface with various liability and asset groups internally, give correct pricing signals keeping in mind the liquidity profile of the bank. On the external front it has to provide active trading support to the market, make two-way prices, add to the liquidity and continuously strive to provide the customers with value-added solutions to their specific financial needs.

Balance Sheet Management: The ongoing reforms have provided the banks freedom to price most of their assets and liabilities by themselves although there exists a broad band specified by the RBI. The pricing of treasury assets and liabilities which form a critical mass of the balance sheet is therefore, very crucial to the balance sheet management. It is well-known that the balance sheet management is a dynamic and proactive process. It requires continuous monitoring, analysis of market changes and controls. Demand and supply forces will impact the optimal balance sheet size and its growth rate. An important aspect of balance sheet management is liquidity management. Liquidity essentially means the ability to meet all contractual obligations as and when they arise, as well as the ability to satisfy funds requirements to meet new business opportunities. Liquidity planning involves an analysis of all major cash flows that arise in the bank as a result of changes in the assets and liabilities and projecting these cash flows over the future. Ideally, balance sheet projections should be prepared for a 12-month period on a monthly basis. This would be in the nature of a monthly rolling forecast. This will enable the treasury manager to identify any potential liquidity problems that may arise in the future, such that corrective action can then be taken to maintain adequate liquidity. Liquidity analysis involves a study of the maturity profile of existing assets and liabilities over which is superimposed the impact of transactions that are planned for the future. Effective liquidity management requires careful attention to balance sheet structure and growth. A balance sheet that is growing rapidly needs careful scrutiny to determine whether the liquidity of the bank is being adversely affected. Very often banks put-up excessive assets in the form of cash credit loans or investments in securities without having matching source of funds of similar nature. A bank cannot afford to be driven just by volume goals which aim at a certain percentage growth in credit and deposits year-after-year. This is because balance sheet growth will call for additional capital in accordance with Basel-II guidelines, and capital is increasingly scarce. Therefore, the focus has now to shift on to the quality of assets, with return on assets being a key criterion for measuring the efficiency of deployment of funds.

❖ Transfer Pricing

The treasury not only provides the interface between the bank and the external market, it also provides an interface between the asset and liability groups of the bank. It helps to provide a balance between the two, so that optimum returns can be obtained on the assets without compromising liquidity. The funds of the bank are deployed in the most appropriate manner without sacrificing either yield or liquidity. This is done very effectively through the means of a *transfer pricing* mechanism administered by the treasury, which can provide correct signal to various business groups as to their future asset and liability strategies. Benchmarking of rates provides a ready reference for business groups about the correct business strategy to adopt given the balance sheet structure of the bank as well as the conditions prevailing in the money markets. Benchmarking is extremely important in today's market environment which allows free market pricing of assets and liabilities. Depending on the signals provided by the treasury in the form of *benchmark rates* for assets and liabilities, focus of the individual business groups can be shifted from asset growth to liability growth or *vice versa* as directed by the needs of the bank. Thus, a correct transfer pricing provides a versatile tool in the hands of the treasury manager in optimising the asset liability mix on the balance sheet and returns generated thereon.

❖ Reserve Management and Investments

In the Indian banking scenario a large asset base of a bank consists of investments on account of statutory reserves, management of these reserves is a very important factor in the overall profitability of the bank. It should ideally take into account both liquidity as well as yield considerations. Event though the longer maturities securities offer the highest yields, they are most susceptible to fall in price due to changes in the yield curve. On the other hand, short dated securities have low price risk but they also give lower returns. Therefore, the choice of an appropriate mix of maturity patterns in the SLR portfolio is a very important function of the treasury manager. Along with this, the market risk of the portfolio in terms of its price sensitivity to interest rate changes, needs to be quantified and periodically monitored by means of analytical tools such as duration analysis. Along with investment for SLRs the treasury also makes investments in various other kinds of instruments such as —

Certificates of Deposits

Commercial Papers

Public Sector Bonds

Units of Unit Trust of India

Corporate Debts, etc.

These investments decisions depend on factors such as bank's liquidity position, money market conditions/tenure of funding available/market liquidity in various instruments/yields and tax planning requirements.

❖ Trading and Distribution

Trading and distribution skills are keys to the success of any treasury. Tradability provides liquidity in various instruments and generates non-fund-based revenues. With increasing competition among banks spreads in traditional banking products are decreasing regularly. With the onset of reforms it is also seen that there is an increasing trend towards disintermediation in the financial markets. Fund-based exposures require balance sheet growth, and that in turn entails higher capital adequacy (in terms of Basel-II w.e.f. 31st March, 2009). In such a situation, non-fund-based revenue gains greater importance. It is here that the strength of the treasury lies. It can help to transform a borrower of funds into an issuer of debt. It can then distribute these debt instruments to investors who were till now only depositors. This will enable the bank to earn a free income without any balance sheet growth and without locking up funds of its own. Trading in instruments creates more liquidity and increases investor appetite.

❖ Customer Focus

In a competitive environment, treasury should never lose its customer focus. In addition to trading avenues, which are essentially volatile nature, treasury should also have non-volatile sources of revenue which are reflected in the diversified customer base of the bank. With the growing liberalisation and opening up of the economy to international financial markets and investors, the treasury departments of various banks would have to function in a multiproduct, multicurrency environment and cater to the multiple needs of its customers. Customers today, with the help of the Foreign Exchange Unit of the Treasury are able to raise foreign currency funds either through direct commercial borrowings or through use of export credit agency schemes and are also able to reduce the interest costs through embedded options or arrear swaps. While these products provide the client with the much desired interest saving, there are not without inherent risks. It is imperative for treasury to clearly define and explain these risks to their corporate clients and to help them effectively manage these risks keeping in mind the dynamic nature of the foreign exchange markets.

❖ Risk Management

Treasury risk management is a separate topic in its own right. The most important risks which treasury has to manage are liquidity risk and price risk in addition to counterparty risk and issuer risk. In order to manage various risks, there should be a well defined contingency liquidity plan, term structure for interest rate limits, maximum cumulative overflow limits, factor sensitivities, etc. These limits should be monitored by an independent risk manager and the reports highlighting these limits/their usage and excesses, if any, should be generated by an independent system/monitored and managed by technology and operations. The success of any treasury thus depends a great deal on strong risk management, independent back-office operations and first rate technology. These issues have become all the more important as profitability and commercial viability have become key criteria for assessing performance. And it is these very fundamentals that form the edifice of a successful treasury that can sustain efficient allocation of internal resources on the one hand and accelerate the globalisation of our financial markets on the other.

10.6 PORTFOLIO MANAGEMENT SERVICES

With a view to provide an opportunity to their clients to deploy their long-term investible funds in capital/debt market instruments, banks offer Portfolio Management Services (PMS). As the facility requires special skills, only those banks, which can render such services themselves, should undertake the activity. In India, the Portfolio Management Services are extended as per following guidelines:

(*i*) PMS should be in the nature of investment consultancy or management for a fee at customer's risk without guarantee as to return,

(*ii*) PMS should be for long-term investible funds (not less than one year) to build-up portfolio of securities.

(*iii*) Funds under PMS are not to be deployed in call money/bill market and lending to corporate bodies.

(*iv*) Client-wise account to be maintained, putting all debits, and credits through such accounts. Accountholder should be entitled to statement of account.

(*v*) Bank's own investment to be kept separate from PMS and transaction between the two should be at market rate. Banks can hold securities in their own name on behalf of the customer but appropriate indications should be given.

The concept of portfolio management can be understood through the following paragraph:

❖ What is Portfolio Management?

A portfolio is a basket of different type of securities belonging to an investor at a particular time with certain definite objectives. It may refer to any type of securities, *viz.*, Government securities, shares, debentures, bonds, etc., which are in the possession of an investor. Portfolio management relates to assisting investors, *viz.*, firms, trusts, funds and associations and individual residents and non-residents in managing their portfolio investment, by acting as agents, in acquiring securities, shares and debentures, planning a basket of scrips in their portfolio by judicious selection after evaluating current and future returns and after providing for elements of risk and uncertainty; reviewing the mix of portfolio continuously to maximize returns and minimize risks in consultations with and after approval by the principals.

Portfolio management is always a dynamic and flexible concept and needs constant review and proper planning for having optimum mix of different securities in different companies so as to minimize the risks and to ensure a reasonable return on the portfolio.

❖ Main Objectives of Portfolio Management

The objectives of portfolio management is to invest in securities in such a manner so as to maximize the returns and minimise the risks, in order to achieve the investment objectives. A good portfolio is one which has multiple objectives and which is able to attain a sound equilibrium between the competing objectives. The main objectives of portfolio management are:

- Safety of funds to be invested, i.e., safety of investments.
- Liquidity of investible funds, i.e., easy liquidity and marketability.
- Profitability/Reasonable Return on investment, i.e., capital appreciation and stable dividends.
- Taking minimum risk.
- Tax benefits.

These objectives can be achieved by following two fundamental principles of portfolio management, *viz.*,

- Careful and effective investment planning: and
- Constant/periodical review of investment strategy.

❖ Functions of a Portfolio Manager

Following are the important functions of portfolio managers.

- Advisory functions
- Carrying out market/economic surveys
- Financial analysis of data:
- Study of share/security market;
- Study of industry.

Portfolio management can be performed in the nature of investment consultancy/management for an agreed fee structure at customer's risk. The portfolio manager cannot guarantee or assure, either directly or indirectly, any return on account of such services.

10.7 PRINCIPLES OF PORTFOLIO MANAGEMENT

The emphasis of the portfolio management varies from investor-to-investor. Some investing companies may desire higher earnings, others may opt for capital gains and still others a combination of both. Despite these variations, there are several objectives which should be considered as basic to a well executed investment programmes. These might rightly be called as guiding principles in establishing an investment portfolio. These objectives are as under:

(a) Safety of Funds: Security of principal is the first consideration in selling investment objectives. Whatever securities are to be bought it must be ensured that the money invested will not be *lost*. Security investment is subject to *credit risk* which arises out of default of payment. *credit risk* in an investment would depend upon the debtor's ability and willingness to repay the funds on maturity. In respect of government securities, condition of the economy which supports the obligations, profitability performance of state units, and tax and borrowing powers of the government would determine the ability of the government issuing the securities. Willingness of the government is a product of attitude of public officials and the people towards debt repayment. The character of the people is very important in this respect because public officials derive their strength and mandate from them. Further, it is the people who dictate or express in the final analysis, the actions of public officials. The government of a prosperous country or region is considered to possess considerable ability to repay the debt. Tax structure and administrative tax machinery are essential for rating securities. Where tax rate is low, and coverage of tax is wider in scope, the government would be able to raise adequate amount of tax revenues to support its obligations provided the tax machinery is adequate and effective. Maximum tax rates limit a government in supporting its debt. From the view point of credit risk, bonds of the Central and State Governments are considered very safe because such bonds are backed up by the *tax paying capacity* of the whole nation and great borrowing powers of the Central Government. In case of foreign securities as well there is *credit risk* — not inconsiderable at times when foreign exchanges can be manipulated by governments through adverse fluctuations in the rates of exchange. Bonds of corporate industries are relatively more risky because repayment of the debt is tied to the earnings of the company which may be fluctuating.

(b) Stability of Price: Investors need a high degree of stability of principal money in their investment portfolios. Because of a thin equity cushion they cannot afford any loss or shrinkage in value of securities. The fluctuation in value of securities is of great significance to an investor. Each investor accepts the current yield of the market at the time he/she pays. If there is change in interest rates, the yield which the investor received when he bought may be above or below the current rate. In the event of sale of securities, the security holder would stand to lose or gain. In case of a rise in interest rate bonds carrying contractual interest rate will entail capital lose if these are disposed of before maturity. There would be no loss if they are *held till maturity.*

(c) Liquidity in Security: While choosing securities for an investor, liquidity principle should be adequately cared for. A liquid security is one which can be disposed of in substantial quantities at short notice with negligible capital *loss*. In case of securities, the term liquidity means high degree of marketability so that if at any time the company requires a large amount of cash to meet its *extraordinary demands* it can liquidate a portion of security investments unless they are such as can be placed quickly in the market and in fairly large blocks without any appropriate price disturbance, the company will not be able to realise funds at reasonable rates. Gilt-edged securities are disposed of easily against corporate shares *without suffering* material loss except listed securities in stock exchange under category 'A' class.

(d) Return on Portfolio: The portfolio should comprise such securities as may assure the investor a fair and stable return on the investments. While considering the income factor it would be pertinent to take into account rate of *interest* or *dividend* rate, which the securities carry, tax exemption benefit, loss or gain, if any, at the time of redemption.

(e) Capital Appreciation: Capital growth is necessary to improve the long range position of the investor to maintain purchasing power (as present rate of inflation is 8.75% on 31-5-2008) there should be appreciation more than this and offer flexibility of management capital growth focuses on yield and measure both risk and reward. The greater the prospects of capital growth, the *higher* the *yield* and *lower* the *risk*.

(f) Marketability: It refers to the ability to buy or sell a security easily and quickly and without involving material loss. It is the function of price and size of the market for given stock. Size of the market is conditioned by the size of the company/number of stockholders and the general public interest in the stock. Furthermore, high priced stocks are less marketable than *low priced*. The place where the stock is traded (i.e., stock exchange) also influences the marketability of a share/stock. For example, stocks traded in BSE or NSE markets have greater marketability than those traded in other stock exchanges which are not connected with BSE or NSE, Mumbai. Stocks of small-cap and Mid-cap companies are less marketable as compared to BSE sensex or Nifty companies. Quality of the management of the corporates also has bearing on the marketability of stocks.

(g) Assortment of Securities: Diversification is the venerable rule of the portfolio management. Through diversification of investments the management can reduce investment risks if it could not be avoided altogether. Risks of declining industries or industries suddenly adversely affected by new developments can be offset by diversification and competitive changes, where one company *advances* while another declines can also be offset in part. Diversification also attempts to *minimise* investment risks arising out of natural catastrophe which may affect a particular region of the country. Another important kind of assortment is *maturity assortment* in which investment portfolio is staggered over *different maturities* periods in such a way that a certain amount of securities mature at *Regular Intervals*.

(h) Taxability: Taxability of securities has gained considerable significance in the management of investment portfolio in the last 18 years. Many financial decisions, in today's society are governed by the *income tax factor*. The problem is how to retain as much of income and capital gains as possible. With progressive tax rates on ordinary income, it is difficult to save income. That is why while constructing investment portfolio the manager (or the investor) should include such securities as are exempted from levy of income and wealth taxes. As at present in 2008 year, the shares held for investment for one year and above, the dividend over such shares is fully exempted from income tax. However, they are covered under *capital gains*.

10.8 INGREDIENTS OF PORTFOLIO MANAGEMENT

Whenever endeavours are made to select securities for investment portfolio so as to satisfy investment needs of the organisation, it is said to be engaged in the portfolio management. Thus, the portfolio management includes planning/supervision/timing/rationalism and considervatism involved in the selection of securities to satisfy the organisation's investment objectives and such are discussed as under:

(a) Planning: It is the first ingredient of portfolio management. This implies that the management, while preparing a list of securities for a portfolio, will give due consideration into investment needs of the investor. As a matter of fact, the plan must reflect the investor's needs. If this is *not done*, the investment portfolio prepared by the manager might not meet the investors needs and at times land him/her in financial crises. If the investor desires higher income on its investment, he/she will select for the portfolio such securities from income type securities which promise greater income to the investor.

(b) Timing: Timing relevant to the portfolio is another ingredient of the portfolio management. While undertaking investment plan the portfolio investor should take into consideration *timing of investment*. When funds should be invested in securities and when it should be disposed of, so as to make maximum gains out of it must receive the attention. It is well-known that the share/stock prices move up and down very frequently even in a day due to Asian/European and American stock exchanges and also internal factors like change in inflation rate/CRR/SLR/repo and reverse repo rates. Political instability also affects the share market substantially.

(c) Conservatism and Rationalism: The investor should be *conservative* and act rationally while making decisions. The concept of conservation is extremely useful particularly in the area of investment where risk is inherent. It is prudent to accept reasonable gain for reasonable risk rather than to accept undue risk with a strong possibility of loss.

Investor should not assume that the decisions will be correct but they will be based on facts rather than on emotions. Every time a stock is to be purchased the investor should examine what place it has in the portfolio and what is expected of it.

(d) Regular Supervision of Securities: Effective portfolio management calls for regular supervision of securities in the portfolio. In the modern competitive market, where economic and business conditions change from time-to-time, it is expects of an investor that he/she should frequently analyse the company and the security to ensure that it fulfils the needs of the investor. If an analysis, it is found that the fundamental position of the security has undergone remarkable change, the security may be replaced. Such type of supervision precludes the investor from financial *loss* and therefore, should form inseparable part of the portfolio management.

(e) Performance Appraisal: Performance appraisal of the investment portfolio, to which we call recapitulation process in financial circles, is an important part of portfolio management in as much, as it ensures that the investors are meeting investment goals. If the specified goal has not been achieved, one must find out the underlying reason. Undoubtedly, there may be a myriad of factors responsible for the variation but the task should be undertaken. Regular performance appraisal tends to minimise the risk and improve yield.

10.9 INVESTMENT MANAGEMENT

Investors' have different motives for investing leaving aside a few, who have love the power and prestige of holding a major share or a *minor share* in a company, the majority of the investors have one of the following motives or a *combination* of them:

(*a*) Regular income either as dividend of interest.

(*b*) Capital gains or capital appreciation.

(*c*) Hedge against inflation, a positive real rate of return.

(*d*) Safety of funds and regularity of payment of interest and principal.

(*e*) Liquidity and marketability in the sense that investor can convert his/her investments into cash or liquidity and back again into investments when cash is not needed.

Investors generally desire to have the maximum return possible, as they like returns, but they dislike the risk, and the extent of risk aversion varies from investor-to-investor. But the return depends on the extent of risk that the investor takes. The return composes of a riskless return (normally paid on a Treasury Bills or a bank deposits) plus a risk premium depending on the risk taken by the investor.

Return is measured by taking the income plus the price change. Income is either dividend or *interest* and price change of the security is the capital gain or loss. The term yield is also used in respect of the *fixed income* securities. Thus, when we buy a 9.5% Central Government bond for ₹ 95. The coupon rate is 9.5% p.a. and face value is ₹ 100 but purchased for ₹ 95. The investor gets ₹ 9.50 by holding the bond for *one year* on an investment of ₹ 95. Then the yield works out to 9.5/95 = 10%. Thus, to generalise the return measurement as applicable to both variable dividend security and fixed income security we have —

$$\text{Total return} = \frac{\text{Income Received} + \text{Price Change}}{\text{Purchase price of asset}}$$

Where price change = Difference between price at end and price at beginning

❖ Investment Decision-making

Investment decision is vital for portfolio management. What to buy/sell are the first decisions to be made and at *what price*? The decision to buy or sell depends on the expectations or estimations of the fair intrinsic value of the shares, overvaluation/undervaluation of the shares and a number of other factors. The objectives of investors are income/capital appreciation/liquidity/marketability/safety and hedge against *inflation*. Alternative investment avenues with risk-return relationship are shown below:

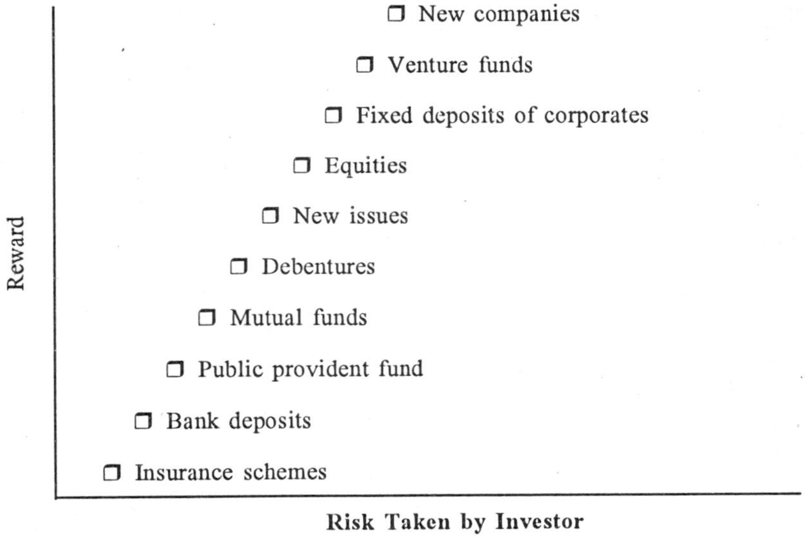

❖ Risk Measurement

Total risk of any investment is total variance or volatility of returns on that investment. This can be represented by spread or range of variations or fluctuations, creating uncertainty of the return and its amount. Range is the *spread or breath of variations*. The concepts of variance/standard deviation/covariance and beta coefficients, etc., are also used to explain the measure of risk. In the context of portfolio of assets or investment in any assets risk is inherent in all such dealings. This risk primarily arises first out of parting of your funds or loss of liquidity. Money lent or parted is always having an element of *risk*. This is the same as the concept of *total risk*.

Investments in public sector banks and private sector banks' deposits/postal deposits or certificates or postal insurance/public provident fund, etc., are *less risky*, but they are also not devoid of any risk. Risk may take the form of loss of time, cost involved in realisation of cash or theft of receipts/certificates, etc. These are very elementary forms of risk attached to any investment.

❖ Portfolio Risk

When two or more securities or assets are combined in a portfolio, their covariance or interactive risk is to be considered. Thus, if the returns on two assets move together their covariance is *positive* and the risk is more on such portfolio. If on the other hand, the returns move independently or in *opposite directions*, the covariance is *negative* and the risk in total will be lower. Mathematically, the *covariance* is defined as —

$$\text{Covxy} = \frac{1}{N}\sum^{N}\left(Rx - \bar{R}x\right)\left(Ry - \bar{R}y\right)$$

where Rx is return on security x, Ry return security y, and $\bar{R}x$ and $\bar{R}y$ are expected returns on them respectively and N is the number of observations.

The coefficient of correlation is another measure designed to indicate the similarity or dissimilarity in the behaviour of two variables. Coefficient of correlation of x and y can be defined as —

$$y\ x\ y = \frac{\text{Con } x\ y}{\sigma x\ \sigma y}$$ where y x y is coefficient of correlation of *x* and y.

Con x y is the covariance between *x* and y and σx is the standard deviation of *x* and σ y is the standard deviation of y.

Example:

	Return	Expected Return	Variance		
I	Stock x	7	9		− 2
	Stock y	13	9		+ 4
			Product		−2x + 4 = .8
II	Stock x	11	9		+2
	Stock y	5	9		− 4
			Product		− 8

where N = 2

The covariance equation is as follows —

$$\text{Cov} = \frac{1}{2}\ [(7-9)\ (13-9) + (11-9)\ (5-9)]$$

$$= \frac{1}{2}[(-8) + (-8)] = -8$$

The coefficient of correlation can be set out as follows:

$$yxy = \frac{-8}{(2)\times(4)} = \frac{-8}{8} = -1.0$$

When the coefficient of correlation between two securities is −1.0 (It is perfect negative correlation) while when it is + 1.0 (it is perfect positive correlation). If the coefficient is '0' then the returns are said to be independent.

◆ ◆ ◆

BIBLIOGRAPHY

1. Financial Markets and Services, Gordon-Natarajan (2006) Himalaya Publishing House Pvt. Ltd., Mumbai.
2. Indian Financial System, Vasant Desai (2005) Himalaya Publishing House Pvt. Ltd., Mumbai.
3. Financial Markets and Institutions, Dr. S. Gurusamy (2004), Vijay Nicole Imprints Pvt. Ltd., Chennai.
4. The Indian Banker, *Journal of Indian Banks' Association,* Sept. 2007.
5. Business and Corporate Laws, Institute of Chartered Accountants of India, New Delhi (2005).
6. Theory and Practice of Treasury and Risk Management in Banks (2006), Indian Institute of Banking and Finance, Mumbai.
7. Principles and Practice of Banking and Insurance, O.P. Agarwal (2006), Himalaya Publishing House Pvt. Ltd., Mumbai.
8. Banking and Insurance (2011) O.P. Agarwal, Himalaya Publishing House, Pvt. Ltd., Mumbai.
9. *DNA Money Daily,* Newspapers, Mumbai.
10. Fundamentals of the Indian Financial Systems — Vasant Desai (2005), Himalaya Publishing House Pvt. Ltd., Mumbai.
11. Basics of Banking and Finance (2011) Dr. K.M. Bhattacharya and O.P. Agarwal, Himalaya Publishing House Pvt. Ltd., Mumbai.
12. *Finsights Magazine,* Quarterly, ICFAI Business School, Mumbai.
13. Principles of Corporate Finance — Brealy Myers (2003), Tata McGraw-Hill Publishing Co. Ltd., New Delhi.
14. Merchant Banking — Principles and Practice — HR Machiraju (1998), New Age International (P) Ltd., New Delhi.
15. Securities Analysis and Portfolio Management — V.A. Avadhani (2008), Himalaya Publishing House Pvt. Ltd., Mumbai.

◆ ◆ ◆

